FINANCIAL
MANAGEMENT
and
POLICY

JAMES C. VAN HORNE

Stanford University

PRENTICE-HALL, INC.　　Englewood Cliffs, New Jersey 07632

FINANCIAL MANAGEMENT and POLICY

FOURTH EDITION

Library of Congress Cataloging in Publication Data

Van Horne, James C
  Financial management and policy.

  Includes bibliographies and index.
  1. Corporations—Finance. I. Title.
HG4011.V34 1977   658.1'5   76-20795
ISBN 0-13-315689-3

FINANCIAL MANAGEMENT AND POLICY
Fourth Edition
James C. Van Horne

10 9 8 7 6 5 4 3 2 1

PRENTICE-HALL INTERNATIONAL, INC., London
PRENTICE-HALL OF AUSTRALIA, PTY. LTD., Sydney
PRENTICE-HALL OF CANADA, LTD., Toronto
PRENTICE-HALL OF INDIA PRIVATE LIMITED, New Delhi
PRENTICE-HALL OF JAPAN, INC., Tokyo
PRENTICE-HALL OF SOUTHEAST ASIA PTE. LTD., Singapore
WHITEHALL BOOKS LIMITED, Wellington, New Zealand

to

MIMI
DREW
STUART
STEPHEN

CONTENTS

ix

PREFACE

Like previous editions of this book, *Financial Management and Policy* has as its purposes first, to develop an understanding of the rapidly evolving theory of finance so that the reader can evaluate the firm's investment, financing, and dividend decisions in keeping with an objective of maximizing shareholder wealth; second, to become familiar with the application of analytical techniques to a variety of problems in financial management; and third, to expose the reader to the institutional material necessary for a solid understanding of the environment in which financial decisions are made.

A number of changes have occurred in this edition. Perhaps the most important is a complete restructuring of the acceptance criterion for capital investments according to required rates of return for projects, for divisions of companies, for companies as a whole, and for acquisitions. Theoretical as well as practical problems involved in measuring these required rates of return and in determining their use are explored in depth. In this regard, Chapter 7, "Evaluation of Risky Investments—Required Rates of Return for Projects," and Chapter 8, "Required Rates of Return for Companies, Divisions and Acquisitions," are largely new. These chapters are tied closely to certain valuation concepts developed in Chapter 2, "Concepts in Valuation," and Chapter 3, "Valuations of the Firm," both substantially revised. Their revision will permit an easier and more thorough understanding of the valuation of securities under uncertainty.

Also new is Chapter 13, "Working-Capital Management and Efficient Market Considerations," where the components of working-capital management are linked to underlying valuation principles. The part dealing with the management of current assets has been moved up to follow Part III, "Financing and Dividend Policies." Also new are three appendixes on the effect of inflation on investment and financing decisions. These are appendixes to Chapters 4, 7, and 9.

Other chapters undergoing substantial revision include: Chapter 19, "Lease Financing," where the underlying valuation of the lease instrument is explored; and Chapter 22, "Financing with Options—the Convertible Security and Warrant," where new concepts with respect to option valuation are introduced. Major changes also occur in Chapter 9, "Theory of Capital Structure." More moderate but nonetheless significant changes occur in: Chapter 4, "Principles of Capital Investment"; Chapters 5 and 6, "Information Needed to Evaluate Risky Investments";

Chapter 11, "Dividends and Valuation"; Chapter 17, "Unsecured Short-Term Financing"; Chapter 18, "Secured Loans and Intermediate-Term Debt"; and Chapter 24, "Business Failure and Reorganization." Pertinent improvements are undertaken in the remaining chapters. For example, in Chapter 21 a section has been added on project financing; in Chapter 25 the section on the predictive power of financial ratios has been expanded.

The book assumes that the reader has a background in elementary algebra and statistics, including some probability concepts. Some knowledge of accounting and economics also is helpful. Most topics treated in the appendixes are somewhat more complex. Because these appendixes deal with special topics, however, the book's continuity is maintained even if this material is not covered. The order of chapters reflects my preferences for teaching the course, but the professor is free to approach them in whatever order seems appropriate. Tools of financial analysis and control purposely appear at the end of the book, as many students will have encountered them in courses in accounting. For those readers, Part VIII can serve as a review. If the reader has not previously had this background, the professor may wish to take up this material at the outset of the course.

A number of users of previous editions of *Financial Management and Policy* have offered comments which have been helpful to me in revising. In particular, I am grateful to Professors James L. Bicksler, Rutgers University; E. Eugene Carter, Massachusetts Institute of Technology; George W. Hettenhouse, Indiana University; Donald Lessard, Massachusetts Institute of Technology; Dennis Logue, Dartmouth College; Michael Rice, University of North Carolina; David Rush, University of Colorado; Richard White, University of North Florida; Jon Zach, Columbia University. Finally, I wish to express thanks to Ann Marie Ventura, who typed this revision.

Palo Alto, California   JAMES C. VAN HORNE

INTRODUCTION

GOALS and FUNCTIONS of FINANCE

The role of the financial manager in a modern company is ever-changing. His responsibilities are broadening and becoming more vital to the company's overall development. Once these responsibilities were confined mainly to keeping accurate financial records, preparing reports, managing the firm's cash position, and providing the means for the payment of bills. When liquidity was insufficient for the firm's prospective cash needs, the financial manager was responsible for procuring additional funds. However, this procurement often included only the mechanical aspects of raising funds externally on either a short-, an intermediate-, or a long-term basis.

In recent years, the influence of the financial manager has expanded far beyond these limited functions. Now his concern is with (1) the investment of funds in capital and other assets, and (2) obtaining the best mix of financing in relation to the overall valuation of the firm. The former determines the size of the firm, its profits from operations, its business risk, and its liquidity. The latter determines the firm's financial charges and its financial risk. As we shall see in this chapter, the financial manager needs a much broader outlook than he has ever needed before, for his influence reaches into almost all facets of the enterprise and into the external environment as well.

EVOLUTION OF FINANCE

In order to understand better the changing role of the financial manager and the evolution of his functions, it is useful to trace the changing character of finance as an academic discipline.[1] In the early part of this century, corporation finance emerged as a separate field of study, whereas before it was considered primarily as a part of economics. By and large, the field encompassed only the instruments, institutions, and procedural aspects of the capital markets. At that time, there were many consolidations, the largest of which was the colossal formation of U.S. Steel Corporation in 1900. These combinations involved the issuance of huge blocks of fixed-income and equity securities. Consequently, there was considerable interest in promotion, and in consolidations and mergers. Accounting data and financial records, as we know them today, were nonexistent. Only with the advent of regulations did disclosure of financial data become prevalent.

With the era of technological innovation and new industries in the 1920s, firms needed more funds. The result was a greater emphasis on liquidity and financing of the firm.[2] Considerable attention was directed to describing methods of external financing, and little to managing a firm

[1] See Ezra Solomon, "What Should We Teach in a Course in Business Finance?" *Journal of Finance*, 21 (May 1966), 411–15; and J. Fred Weston, *The Scope and Methodology of Finance* (Englewood Cliffs, N.J.: Prentice-Hall, 1966), Chapter 2.

[2] Weston, *Scope and Methodology of Finance*, p. 25.

internally. One of the landmark texts of this period was Arthur Stone Dewing's *Financial Policy of Corporations*, which, in a scholarly fashion, drew together existing thought, promulgated certain new ideas, and served to pattern the teaching of finance for many years to come.[3] During this period, there was widespread interest in securities, particularly in common stock. This interest became intense toward the end of the decade, and the role and function of the investment banker was particularly important in the study of corporate finance at this time.

The depression of the thirties necessarily focused the study of finance on the defensive aspects of survival. A great deal of attention was directed toward the preservation of liquidity and toward bankruptcy, liquidation, and reorganization. The principal concern in external financing was how a lender could protect himself. Conservatism, naturally, reigned supreme, with considerable emphasis on a company's maintaining a sound financial structure. The large number of abuses with debt—particularly those that occurred in connection with public utility holding companies—were brought into the limelight when many companies collapsed. These failures, together with the fraudulent maltreatment of numerous investors, brought cries for regulation. Regulation and increased controls on business by government were quick to follow. One result of these regulations was an increase in the amount of financial data disclosed by companies. This disclosure made financial analysis more encompassing, because the analyst was able to compare different companies as to their financial condition and performance.

Finance, during the forties through the early fifties, was dominated by a "traditional" approach. This approach, which had evolved during the twenties and thirties, was from the point of view of an outsider—such as a lender or investor—analyzing the firm and did not emphasize decision making within the firm. The study of external financing was still largely descriptive. During this period, however, a greater emphasis on analyzing the cash flows of the firm and on the planning and control of these flows from within did develop.

In the middle fifties, great interest developed in capital budgeting and allied considerations. This topic and the concurrent emphasis on present value served as a catalyst for the sweeping changes that subsequently occurred. With the development of new methods and techniques for selecting capital investment projects came a framework for the efficient allocation of capital within the firm. New fields of responsibility and influence for the financial manager included management of the total funds committed to assets and the allocation of capital to individual assets on the basis of an appropriate and objective acceptance criterion.

As a result of these developments, the financial manager had to

---

[3] Arthur S. Dewing, *The Financial Policy of Corporations* (New York: Ronald Press, 1920).

come squarely to grips with how investors and creditors valued the firm and how a particular decision affected their respective valuations. Valuation models were developed for use in financial decision making. Interestingly enough, many of the dividend valuation models developed during the fifties for the valuation of the firm were offshoots of the classic 1938 work of John Burr Williams.[4] Unfortunately, the impact of this work was not felt in finance for nearly twenty years. With the concern for valuation in the fifties, however, came a critical evaluation of the capital structure and the dividend policy of the firm in relation to its valuation as a whole. As a result of the widespread interest in capital budgeting, considerable strides have been made toward an integrated theory of finance.[5]

A major event in the 1960s was the development of portfolio theory and its eventual application to financial management. First exposited by Markowitz in 1952, the theory was later extended and considerably refined by Sharpe, Lintner, Mossin, Fama, and a number of others.[6] Basically, this theory tells us that the risk of an individual asset should not be judged on the basis of possible deviations from its expected return but rather in relation to its marginal contribution to the overall risk of a portfolio of assets. Depending on the degree of correlation of that asset with other assets in the portfolio, the asset will be more or less risky. Concurrent with this development was considerable theoretical and empirical work on the functioning of financial markets. The simple notion that the firm's debt and equity instruments are traded in markets that may be more or less efficient depending on the circumstances was really never fully understood until much of the work on portfolio theory and efficient markets had been done.

The further refinement of Sharpe's capital-asset pricing model for valuing financial assets brought with it the application of these ideas to financial management in the 1970s. The model suggested that some of the risk of the firm was not relevant to the investor in the firm's stock, as this risk could be diversified away in the portfolio of stocks he held. It also brought an increased focus on market imperfections when judging

---

[4] *The Theory of Investment Value* (Amsterdam: North Holland Publishing, 1964).

[5] In the early fifties, Friederich and Vera Lutz expounded a comprehensive theory of the firm in their famous book *The Theory of Investment of the Firm* (Princeton, N.J.: Princeton University Press, 1951). Much of the work on capital budgeting owes its origin to Joel Dean's renowned book *Capital Budgeting* (New York: Columbia University Press, 1951). These works served as building blocks for subsequent theoretical and managerial development in finance.

[6] See, for example, Harry M. Markowitz, *Portfolio Selection: Efficient Diversification of Investments* (New York: John Wiley, 1959); William F. Sharpe, *Portfolio Theory and Capital Markets* (New York: McGraw-Hill, 1970); John Lintner, "Security Prices, Risk and Maximal Gains from Diversification," *Journal of Finance*, 20 (December 1965), 587–616; Jan Mossin, *Theory of Financial Markets* (Englewood Cliffs, N.J.: Prentice-Hall, 1973); and Eugene F. Fama and Merton H. Miller, *The Theory of Finance* (New York: Holt, Rinehart & Winston, 1972).

decisions by the firm with respect to asset selection, financing, and dividends. In the ensuing chapters, we will devote considerable attention to the implications of these notions for financial management.

The use of the computer as an analytical tool added much to the development of finance during the fifties, sixties, and seventies. With its advent, complex information systems have been developed that provide the financial manager with the data needed to make sound decisions. In addition, great strides have been made in the application of analytical tools to financial problems. Increasingly, operations research and decision theory techniques are proving their worth. As better methods and applications are developed, more disciplined and fruitful financial analysis will be possible.

Overall, then, finance has changed from a primarily descriptive study to one that encompasses rigorous analysis and normative theory; from a field that was concerned primarily with the procurement of funds to one that includes the management of assets, the allocation of capital, and the valuation of the firm in the overall market; and from a field that emphasized external analysis of the firm to one that stresses decision making within the firm. Finance today is best characterized as everchanging, with new ideas and techniques. The role of the financial manager is considerably different from what it was fifteen years ago and from what it will no doubt be in another fifteen years. Academicians and financial managers must grow to accept the changing environment and master its challenge. In this regard, they must thoroughly understand the underlying objective of the firm.

OBJECTIVE OF THE FIRM

In this book, we assume that the objective of the firm is to maximize its value to its shareholders. Value is represented by the market price of the company's common stock, which, in turn, is a reflection of the firm's investment, financing, and dividend decisions.

PROFIT MAXIMIZATION VERSUS WEALTH MAXIMIZATION

Frequently, maximization of profits is regarded as the proper objective of the firm, but it is not as inclusive a goal as that of maximizing shareholder wealth. For one thing, total profits are not as important as earnings per share. A firm could always raise total profits by issuing stock and using the proceeds to invest in Treasury bills. Even maximization of earnings per share, however, is not a fully appropriate objective, partly because it does not specify the timing or duration of expected returns. Is the investment project that will produce a $100,000 return five years from now more valuable than the project that will produce annual returns of $15,000 in each of the next five years? An answer to this question depends upon the time value of money. Few existing stock-holders would think favorably of a project that promised its first return in one hundred years, no matter how large this return. We must take into account the time pattern of returns in our analysis.

Another shortcoming of the objective of maximizing earnings per share is that it does not consider the risk or uncertainty of the prospec-tive earnings stream. Some investment projects are far more risky than others. As a result, the prospective stream of earnings per share would be more uncertain if these projects were undertaken. In addition, a company will be more or less risky depending upon the amount of debt in relation to equity in its capital structure. This risk is known as financial risk; and it, too, contributes to the uncertainty of the firm to investors in the marketplace.

For the reasons given above, an objective of maximizing earnings per share may not be the same as maximizing market price per share. The market price of a firm's stock represents the focal judgment of all market participants as to what the value is of the particular firm. It takes into account present and prospective future earnings per share, the timing, duration, and risk of these earnings, and any other factors that bear upon the market price of the stock. The market price serves as a performance index or report card of the firm's progress; it indicates how well management is doing in behalf of its stockholders.

MANAGEMENT VERSUS STOCKHOLDERS

In certain situations, the objectives of management may differ from those of the firm's stockholders. In a large corporation whose stock is widely held, stockholders exert very little control or influence over the operations of the company. When the control of a company is separate from its ownership, management may not always act in the best interests of the stockholders.[7] Managements sometimes are said to be "satisficers" rather than "maximizers;"[8] they may be content to "play it safe" and seek an acceptable level of growth, being more concerned with perpet-uating their own existence than with maximizing the value of the firm to its shareholders. The most important goal to a management of this sort may be its own survival.[9] As a result, it may be unwilling to take reason-

---

[7] For a discussion of this question, see Gordon Donaldson, "Financial Goals: Management vs. Stockholders," *Harvard Business Review*, 41 (May–June 1963), 116–29.

[8] Herbert A. Simon, "Theories of Decision Making in Economics and Behavioral Science," *American Economic Review*, 49 (June 1959), 253–83. See also Weston, *Scope and Method-ology of Finance*, Chapter 2.

[9] In a study of owner-managed and nonowner-managed firms, J. W. Elliott, "Control, Size, Growth, and Financial Performance in the Firm," *Journal of Financial and Quantitative Analysis*, 7 (January 1972), 1309–20, found a higher propensity by the nonowner-managed firms for liquidity. This may be some indication of greater risk aversion on the part of these managers.

able risks for fear of making a mistake, thereby becoming conspicuous to outside suppliers of capital. In turn, these suppliers may pose a threat to management's survival.

It is true that in order to survive over the long run, management may have to behave in a manner that is reasonably consistent with maximizing shareholder wealth.[10] Nevertheless, the goals of the two parties do not necessarily have to be the same. Maximization of shareholder wealth, then, is an appropriate guide for how a firm *should* act. When management does not act in a manner consistent with this objective, we must recognize this as a constraint and determine the opportunity cost. This cost is measurable only if we determine what the outcome would have been had the firm attempted to maximize shareholder wealth.

A NORMATIVE GOAL

Because the principle of maximization of shareholder wealth provides a rational guide for running a business and for the efficient allocation of resources in society, we use it as our assumed objective in considering how financial decisions *should* be made. The purpose of capital markets is to efficiently allocate savings in an economy from ultimate savers to ultimate users of funds who invest in real assets. If savings are to be channeled to the most promising investment opportunities, a rational economic criterion must exist that governs their flow. By and large, the allocation of savings in an economy occurs on the basis of expected return and risk. The market value of a firm's stock embodies both of these factors. It therefore reflects the market's tradeoff between risk and return. If decisions are made in keeping with the likely effect upon the market value of its stock, a firm will attract capital only when its investment opportunities justify the use of that capital in the overall economy.

Put another way, the equilibration process by which savings are allocated in an economy occurs on the basis of expected return and risk. Holding risk constant, those economic units (business firms, households, financial institutions, or governments) willing to pay the highest yield are the ones entitled to the use of funds. If rationality prevails, the economic units bidding the highest yields will be the ones with the most promising investment opportunities. As a result, savings will tend to be allocated to the most efficient uses. Maximization of shareholder wealth then embodies the risk-return tradeoff of the market and is the focal point by which funds should be allocated within and among business firms. Any

---

[10]Robert Tempest Masson, "Executive Motivations, Earnings, and Consequent Equity Performance," *Journal of Political Economy*, 80 (November–December 1971), 1278–92, in a study of the post-World War II period found that firms with executives whose financial rewards were closely tied to the performance of the company's stock tended to out-perform other firms in stock return.

other objective is likely to result in the suboptimal allocation of funds and therefore lead to less than optimal capital formation and growth in the economy as well as a less than optimal level of economic want satisfaction.

This is not to say that management should ignore the question of social responsibility. As related to business firms, social responsibility concerns such things as protecting the consumer, paying fair wages to employees, maintaining fair hiring practices, supporting education, and becoming actively involved in environmental issues like clean air and water. Many people feel that a firm has no choice but to act in socially responsible ways; they argue that shareholder wealth and, perhaps, the corporation's very existence depend upon its being socially responsible. However, the criteria for social responsibility are not clearly defined, making formulation of a consistent objective function difficult.

Moreover, social responsibility creates certain problems for the firm. One is that it falls unevenly on different corporations. Another is that it sometimes conflicts with the objective of wealth maximization. Certain social actions, from a long-range point of view, unmistakably are in the best interests of stockholders, and there is little question that they should be undertaken. Other actions are less clear, and to engage in them may result in a decline in profits and in shareholder wealth in the long run. From the standpoint of society, this decline may produce a conflict. What is gained in having a socially desirable goal achieved may be offset in whole or in part by an accompanying less efficient allocation of resources in society. The latter will result in a less than optimal growth of the economy and a lower total level of economic want satisfaction. In an era of unfilled wants and scarcity, the allocation process is extremely important.

Many people feel that management should not be called upon to resolve the conflict posed above. Rather, society, with its broad general perspective, should make the decisions necessary in this area. Only society, acting through Congress and other representative governmental bodies, can judge the relative tradeoff between the achievement of a social goal and the sacrifice in the efficiency of apportioning resources that may accompany realization of the goal. With these decisions made, corporations can engage in wealth maximization and thereby efficiently allocate resources, subject, of course, to certain governmental constraints. Under such a system, corporations can be viewed as producing both private and social goods, and the maximization of shareholder wealth remains a viable corporate objective.

DEVELOPMENT OF THE BOOK

The functions of finance can be broken down into the three major decisions the firm must make: the investment decision, the financing decision, and the dividend decision. Each must be considered in relation to the objective of the firm; an optimal combination of the three decisions will maximize the value of the firm to its shareholders. Because the decisions are interrelated, we must consider their joint impact on the market price of the firm's stock. We now briefly examine each of them and their place in the subsequent chapters of this book.

INVESTMENT DECISION

The investment decision, perhaps, is the most important of the three decisions. Capital investment, a major aspect of this decision, is the allocation of capital to investment proposals whose benefits are to be realized in the future. Because the future benefits are not known with certainty, investment proposals necessarily involve risk. Consequently, they should be evaluated in relation to their expected return and risk, for these are the factors that affect the firm's valuation in the marketplace. Included also under the investment decision is the decision to reallocate capital when an asset no longer economically justifies the capital committed to it. The investment decision, then, determines the total amount of assets held by the firm, the composition of these assets, and the business-risk complexion of the firm as perceived by suppliers of capital. The theoretical portion of this decision is taken up in Part II. Fundamental to this decision is the appropriate acceptance criterion, or required rate of return, to employ. Because of the paramount and integrative importance of this issue, considerable attention is devoted to determining the appropriate required rate of return for an investment project, for a division of a company, for the company as a whole, and for a prospective acquisition.

In addition to selecting new investments, a firm must manage existing assets efficiently. The financial manager is charged with varying degrees of operating responsibility over existing assets. He is more concerned with the management of current assets than with fixed assets, and we consider the former topic in Part IV. Our concern in Part IV is with ways to manage current assets efficiently in order to maximize profitability relative to the amount of funds tied up in an asset. Determining a proper level of liquidity for the firm is very much a part of this management, and its determination should be in keeping with the firm's overall valuation. Although the financial manager has little or no operating responsibility for fixed assets and inventories, he is instrumental in allocating capital to these assets by virtue of his involvement in capital investment.

In Parts II and VII, we consider mergers and acquisitions from the standpoint of an investment decision. These external investment opportunities can be evaluated in the same general manner as an investment proposal that is generated internally. Also, in Part VII, we take up failures and reorganizations, which involve a decision to liquidate a company or to rehabilitate it, often by changing its capital structure. This decision should be based upon the same economic considerations that govern the investment decision.

FINANCING DECISION

The second major decision of the firm is the financing decision. Here the financial manager is concerned with determining the best financing mix or capital structure for his firm. If a company can change its total valuation by varying its capital structure, an optimal financing mix would exist in which market price per share could be maximized. In Chapters 9 and 10 of Part III, we take up the financing decision in relation to the overall valuation of the firm. Our concern is with exploring the implications of variation in capital structure on the valuation of the firm. In Parts V and VI, we examine the various methods by which a firm obtains short-, intermediate-, and long-term financing. The emphasis is not only on certain valuation underpinnings but also on the managerial aspects of financing as we analyze the features, concepts, and problems associated with alternative methods. In Part III, on the other hand, the focus is primarily theoretical.

DIVIDEND DECISION

The third important decision of the firm is its dividend policy, which is examined in Chapters 11 and 12 of Part III. The dividend decision includes the percentage of earnings paid to stockholders in cash dividends, the stability of absolute dividends over time, stock dividends, and the repurchase of stock. The dividend-payout ratio determines the amount of earnings retained in the firm and must be evaluated in the light of the objective of maximizing shareholder wealth. If investors at the margin are not indifferent between current dividends and capital gains, there will be an optimal dividend-payout ratio that maximizes shareholder wealth. The value of a dividend to investors must be balanced against the opportunity cost of the retained earnings lost as a means of equity financing. Thus, we see that the dividend decision must be analyzed in relation to the financing decision.

FINANCIAL MANAGEMENT

Financial management involves the solution of the three decisions of the firm discussed above. Together, they determine the value of the firm to its shareholders. Assuming that our objective is to maximize this value, the firm should strive for an optimal combination of the three decisions. Because these decisions are interrelated, they should be solved jointly. The decision to invest in a new capital project, for example, necessitates the financing of the investment. The financing decision, in turn, influences and is influenced by the dividend decision, for retained earnings used in internal financing represent dividends foregone by stockholders. With a proper conceptual framework, joint decisions can be reached that tend to be optimal. The important thing is that the financial managers relate each decision to its effect on the valuation of the firm.

Because of the importance of valuation concepts in understanding financial management, these concepts are investigated in depth in Chapters 2 and 3. Thus, the first three chapters serve as the foundation for the subsequent development of the book. Such key concepts as the time value of money, risk-return tradeoffs, market efficiency, portfolio theory, and the capital-asset pricing model are presented, because they transcend discussion in the remainder of the book.

In an endeavor to make optimal decisions, the financial manager makes use of certain analytical tools in the analysis, planning, and control activities of the firm. Financial analysis is a necessary condition, or prerequisite, for making sound financial decisions; we examine the tools of analysis in Part VIII. This material appears at the end of the book in order to set it apart from the book's sequence of development. Depending on the reader's background, it can be taken up early or used for reference purposes throughout.

PROBLEMS

1. Examine the functions of financial managers in several large U.S. corporations. Try to ascertain how the role of the financial manager has changed in these concerns over the past fifty years.

2. Inquire among several corporations in your area to find out if these firms have determined specific objectives. Is maximizing the value of the firm to its shareholders the major objective of most of these companies?

3. "A basic rationale for the objective of maximizing the wealth position of the stockholder as a primary business goal is that such an objective may reflect the most efficient use of society's economic resources and thus lead to a maximization of society's economic wealth." Briefly evaluate this observation.

4. Think of several socially responsible actions in which a corporation might engage. Evaluate these actions in relation to the allocation of resources in society under a wealth maximization objective.

SELECTED REFERENCES

Anderson, Leslie P., Vergil V. Miller, and Donald L. Thompson, *The Finance Function.* Scranton, Pa.: Intext, 1971.

Branch, Ben, "Corporate Objectives and Market Performance," *Financial Management,* 2 (Summer 1973), 24–29.

De Alessi, Louis, "Private Property and Dispersion of Ownership in Large Corporations," *Journal of Finance,* 28 (September 1973), 839–51.

Donaldson, Gordon, "Financial Goals: Management vs. Stockholders," *Harvard Business Review,* 41 (May–June 1963), 116–29.

Elliott, J. W., "Control, Size, Growth, and Financial Performance in the Firm," *Journal of Financial and Quantitative Analysis,* 7 (January 1972), 1309–20.

Findlay, M. Chapman, III, and G. A. Whitmore, "Beyond Shareholder Wealth Maximization," *Financial Management,* 3 (Winter 1974). 25–35.

Gaskill, William J., "What's Ahead for Corporations in Social Responsibility?" *Financial Executive,* 39 (July 1971), 10–18.

Grabowski, Henry G., and Dennis C. Mueller, "Managerial and Stockholder Welfare Models of Firm Expenditures," *Review of Economics and Statistics,* 54 (February 1972), 9–24.

"The Issues in Social Responsibility," *Financial Analysts Journal,* 27 (September–October 1971), 26–34.

Lewellen, Wilbur G., "Management and Ownership in the Large Firm," *Journal of Finance,* 24 (May 1969), 299–322.

Masson, Robert Tempest, "Executive Motivations, Earnings, and Consequent Equity Performance," *Journal of Political Economy,* 79 (November–December 1971), 1278–92.

Rentz, William F., and W. Morley Lemon, "Stock Incentive Plans for Decision Makers," Working Paper, Graduate School of Business, University of Texas, 1974.

Scanlon, John J., "Bell System Financial Policies," *Financial Management,* 1 (Summer 1972), 16–26.

Simkowitz, Michael A., and Charles P. Jones, "A Note on the Simultaneous Nature of Finance Methodology," *Journal of Finance,* 27 (March 1972), 103–8.

Solomon, Ezra, *The Theory of Financial Management,* Chapters 1 and 2. New York: Columbia University Press, 1963.

Weston, J. Fred, "New Themes in Finance," *Journal of Finance,* 29 (March 1974), 237–43.

——, *The Scope and Methodology of Finance.* Englewood Cliffs, N.J.: Prentice-Hall, 1966.

CONCEPTS
in
VALUATION

Given the objective discussed in Chapter 1, the firm should choose that combination of investment, financing, and dividend decisions that will maximize its value to its shareholders. These decisions affect the firm's value through their impact on its expected return-risk character. Because the return to stockholders is not known with certainty, risk necessarily is involved. It can be defined as the possibility that the actual return will deviate from that which was expected. Expectations are continually revised on the basis of new information about the investment, financing, and dividend decisions of the firm. In other words, on the basis of information about these three decisions, investors formulate expectations as to the return and risk involved in holding a common stock.

In this chapter and the next, we take up the valuation of financial market instruments, with particular emphasis upon common stocks. These chapters form the conceptual groundwork on which the subsequent analysis of the investment, financing, and dividend decisions of the firm is based.[1] Our concern will be with the expected return and risk associated with holding a security. Ultimately, we will be able to make some statements about the valuation of an individual firm under the assumption that investors are reasonably well diversified in their security holdings. Before we proceed, however, it is useful to consider the time value of money and how one calculates the present value and the internal rate of return from an investment. These principles are used not only in Chapters 2 and 3 but repeatedly throughout the book.

TIME VALUE OF MONEY

In any economy in which time preferences result in positive rates of interest, the time value of money is an important concept. For example, stockholders will place a higher value on an investment that promises returns over the next five years than on an investment that promises identical returns for years six through ten. Consequently, the timing of expected future cash flows is extremely important in the investment of funds. In essence, the methods proposed allow us to isolate differences in the timing of cash flows for various investments by discounting these cash flows to their present value.

---

[1] Because the investment decision involves not only investment in new projects but the management of existing assets as well, it embodies a host of decisions with respect to level of output, pricing, and the combination of factor inputs in the firm's production process. Because these policies involve considerations beyond the scope of this book, we do not consider them directly, but assume that they are embraced in the cash-flow information used in the evaluation of existing and new investment projects. For an excellent integration of production decisions into an overall valuation model of the firm, see Douglas Vickers, *The Theory of the Firm: Production, Capital, and Finance* (New York: McGraw-Hill, 1968); and Vickers, "Disequilibrium Structures and Financing Decisions in the Firm," *Journal of Business Finance & Accounting*, 1 (Autumn 1974), 375–87.

PRESENT VALUES

The present value of $1 received at the end of year n is

$$PV = \frac{1}{(1+k)^n} \qquad (2\text{-}1)$$

where PV is the present value and k the discount rate. To illustrate the construction of a present-value table, we make a few calculations using a discount rate of 10 percent. Suppose that we wish to know the present value of $1 received one year from today. The formula is

$$PV = \frac{1}{(1+0.10)} = 0.90909 \qquad (2\text{-}2)$$

Similarly, if we wish to know the present value of $1 received two years from today, the formula is

$$PV = \frac{1}{(1+0.10)^2} = \frac{1}{1.21} = 0.82645 \qquad (2\text{-}3)$$

Fortunately, a present-value table has been prepared that relieves us of making these calculations every time we have a problem to solve; it is shown in Table A-1 in Appendix A at the end of the book. We see in the table that for a 10 percent discount rate, the discount factors for one and two years in the future are 0.90909 and 0.82645, respectively—just as we calculated by hand.

If we had an uneven series of cash flows—$1 one year hence, $3 two years hence, and $2 three years from now—the present value of this series, using a 10 percent discount rate, would be

PV of $1 to be received at end of one year	$1(0.90909) =	0.90909
PV of $3 to be received at end of two years	$3(0.82645) =	2.47935
PV of $2 to be received at end of three years	$2(0.75131) =	1.50262
Present value of series		$4.89106

Given a present-value table, we are able to calculate the present value for any series of future cash flows in the above manner.

However, the procedure can be simplified for a series if the cash flows in each future period are the same. A series of this sort is known as an *annuity.* Suppose that in a series of future cash flows, $1 was to be received at the end of each of the next three years. The calculation of the present value of this stream, using the above procedure, would be

PV of $1 to be received in one year	= 0.90909
PV of $1 to be received in two years	= 0.82645
PV of $1 to be received in three years	= 0.75131
Present value of series	$2.48685

Handwritten margin notes:

What is the PV of $100 at $i=.10$ at end of 3 yrs?

To calculate on T.I.:

set mode CI

2nd ANCI

100 FV
10   %i
3   N 2nd PV

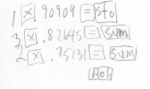

1 X .90909 = STO
3 X .82645 = SUM
2 X .75131 = SUM
        RCL

With an even series of future cash flows, it is unnecessary to go through these calculations. The discount factor, 2.48685, can be applied directly. We would simply multiply $1 by 2.48685 to obtain $2.48685. Present-value tables for even series of cash flows have been developed that allow us to look up the appropriate compound discount factor. An example is shown in Table A-2 in Appendix A at the end of the book. We note that the discount factor for an even series of cash flows for three years, using a 10 percent discount rate, is 2.4868—as we calculated. Thus, for an even series of cash flows, we simply multiply the appropriate discount factor times the cash flow. If we wish to know the present value, using an 8 percent discount rate, of a future stream of $5 cash flows to be received at the end of each year over a four-year period, the calculation would be

$$\$5(3.3121) = \$16.56 \tag{2-4}$$

Using the present-value tables shown in Tables A-1 and A-2 at the end of the book, we are able to calculate the present value of various future streams of cash flows.

INTERNAL RATE OF RETURN OR YIELD

The internal rate of return or yield for an investment is the discount rate that equates the present value of the expected cash outflows with the present value of the expected inflows. Mathematically, it is represented by that rate, r, such that

$$\sum_{t=0}^{n} \left[\frac{A_t}{(1 + r)^t} \right] = 0 \tag{2-5}$$

where A_t is the cash flow for period t, whether it be a net cash outflow or inflow, n is the last period in which a cash flow is expected, and the capital Greek sigma denotes the sum of discounted cash flows at the end of periods o through n. If the initial cash outlay or cost occurs at time o, Eq. (2-5) can be expressed as

$$A_0 = \frac{A_1}{(1 + r)} + \frac{A_2}{(1 + r)^2} + \cdots + \frac{A_n}{(1 + r)^n} \tag{2-6}$$

Thus, r is the rate that discounts the stream of future cash flows—A_1 through A_n—to equal the initial outlay at time o—A_0. To illustrate, suppose we have an investment opportunity that calls for a cash outlay at time o

of $18,000 and is expected to provide cash inflows of $5,600 at the end of each of the next five years. The problem can be expressed as

$$18,000 = \frac{5,600}{(1 + r)} + \frac{5,600}{(1 + r)^2} + \frac{5,600}{(1 + r)^3} + \frac{5,600}{(1 + r)^4} + \frac{5,600}{(1 + r)^5} \quad (2\text{-}7)$$

Solving for the internal rate of return, r, involves an iterative procedure using present values. Fortunately, there are computer programs for solving for the internal rate of return; and these programs eliminate the arduous computations involved. To illustrate a manual method, however, consider again our example. The cash-flow stream is represented by an even series of cash flows of $5,600, to be received at the end of each of the next five years. We want to determine the discount factor that, when multiplied by $5,600, equals the cash outlay of $18,000 at time 0. Suppose that we start with three discount rates—14 percent, 16 percent, and 18 percent—and calculate the present value of the cash-flow stream. Using the different discount rates, we find:

Discount Rate	Discount Factor	Cash Flow Each Year	Present Value of Stream
18%	3.1272	$5,600	$17,512.32
16	3.2743	5,600	18,336.08
14	3.4331	5,600	19,225.36

When we compare the present value of the stream with the initial outlay of $18,000, we see that the internal rate of return necessary to discount the stream to $18,000 falls between 16 and 18 percent, being closer to 16 than to 18 percent. To approximate the actual rate, we interpolate between 16 and 17 percent as follows:

	Discount Rate	Present Value
	16%	$18,336.08
	17	17,916.08
Difference	1%	$ 420.00
$\dfrac{336.08}{420.00} = 0.80$	16% + 0.80% = 16.8%	

Thus, the internal rate of return necessary to equate the present value of the cash inflows with the present value of the outflows is approximately 16.8 percent. It should be noted that interpolation gives only an approximation of the exact percent; the relationship between the two discount rates is not linear with respect to present value.

When, as above, the cash-flow stream is an even series, and the initial outlay occurs at time 0, there really is no need for trial and error. We simply divide the initial outlay by the cash flow and search for the nearest discount factor. Using our example, we divide $18,000 by $5,600, obtaining 3.214. The nearest discount factor on the five-year row in Table A-2 at the end of the book is 3.2743, and this figure corresponds to a discount rate of 16 percent. Inasmuch as 3.214 is less than 3.2743, we know that the actual rate lies between 16 and 17 percent and we interpolate accordingly. When the cash-flow stream is an uneven series, the task is more difficult; and here we must resort to trial and error. However, given practice, a person can come surprisingly close in selecting discount rates from which to start.

Actually, a present-value table is nothing more than a bond-yield table that takes account of compound interest. A more extensive discussion of the mathematics of compound interest and bond yields is found in the appendix to this chapter. Given the rudiments of the time value of money and discounting a cash-flow stream to its present value, we are able to proceed with our examination of the valuation of financial instruments.

EXPECTED RETURN FROM A STOCK INVESTMENT

When the individual investor purchases a common stock, he gives up current consumption in the hope of attaining increased future consumption. His expectation of higher future consumption is based on the dividends he expects to receive and, hopefully, the eventual sale of the stock at a price higher than his original purchase price. The individual must allocate his wealth at a given moment in keeping with his desired lifetime consumption pattern, which includes any bequest he wishes to make. If the future were certain and the time of death known, the individual could apportion his wealth so as to obtain the maximum possible satisfaction from present and future consumption. He would know the exact returns available from investment and the timing of these returns, as well as future income from noninvestment sources. Investment would be merely a means of balancing present against future consumption.[2]

RETURN ON INVESTMENT

Not knowing what lies in the future, the investor is unable to plan his lifetime consumption pattern with certainty. Because the returns from investment and the timing of those returns are uncertain, he

[2] See Irving Fisher, *The Theory of Interest* (New York: Augustus M. Kelley, 1965), Chapters 10–13.

compensates for the lack of certainty by requiring an expected return sufficiently high to offset it. But what constitutes the return on a common stock? For a one-year holding period, the benefits associated with ownership include the cash dividends paid during the year together with any appreciation in market price, or capital gain, realized at the end of the year. More formally, the one-period return is the sum of cash dividends received plus any capital gain or loss, all over the purchase price, minus one. Suppose that an individual were to purchase a share of DSS Corporation for $50 a share. The company was expected to pay a $2 dividend at the end of the year, and its market price after the payment of the dividend was expected to be $53 a share. The expected return would be

$$r = \frac{2.00 + 53.00}{50.00} - 1 = 0.10 \tag{2-8}$$

where r is the expected return. Another way to solve for r is

$$50.00 = \frac{2.00}{(1 + r)} + \frac{53.00}{(1 + r)} \tag{2-9}$$

When we solve for the rate of discount that equates the dividend and terminal value at the end of one year with the purchase price of the stock at time 0, we find it to be 10 percent. Thus, the investor expects a 10 percent return on his investment.

Now suppose that instead of holding the security one year, he intends to hold it two years and sell it at the end of that time. Moreover, suppose he expects the company to pay a $2.20 dividend at the end of year 2 and the market price of the stock to be $56.10 after the dividend is paid. His expected return can be found by solving the following equation for r:

$$50.00 = \frac{2.00}{(1 + r)} + \frac{2.20}{(1 + r)^2} + \frac{56.10}{(1 + r)^2} \tag{2-10}$$

When we solve for r by the method described earlier, we find it to be 10 percent also. For general purposes, the formula can be expressed as

$$P_0 = \sum_{t=1}^{2} \frac{D_t}{(1 + r)^t} + \frac{P_2}{(1 + r)^2} \tag{2-11}$$

where P_0 is the market price at time 0, D_t is the expected dividend at the end of period t, the capital Greek sigma denotes the sum of discounted dividends at the end of periods 1 and 2, and P_2 is the expected terminal value at the end of period 2.

If an investor's holding period were ten years, the expected rate of return would be determined by solving the following equation for r:

$$P_0 = \sum_{t=1}^{10} \frac{D_t}{(1 + r)^t} + \frac{P_{10}}{(1 + r)^{10}} \qquad (2\text{-}12)$$

Now, suppose that the investor were a perpetual trust fund and that the trustee expected to hold the stock forever. In this case, the expected return would consist entirely of cash dividends and perhaps a liquidating dividend. Thus, the expected rate of return would be determined by solving the following equation for r:

$$P_0 = \sum_{t=1}^{\infty} \frac{D_t}{(1 + r)^t} \qquad (2\text{-}13)$$

where ∞ is the sign for infinity.

It is clear that the intended holding period of different investors will vary greatly. Some will hold a stock only a few days, while others might expect to hold it forever. Investors with holding periods shorter than infinity expect to be able to sell the stock in the future at a price higher than they paid for it. This assumes, of course, that at that time there will be investors willing to buy it. In turn, these investors will base their judgments as to what the stock is worth on expectations of future dividends and future terminal value beyond that point. That terminal value, however, will depend upon other investors at that time being willing to buy the stock. The price they are willing to pay will depend upon their expectations of dividends and terminal value. And so the process goes through successive investors. Note that the total cash return to all successive investors in a stock is the sum of the dividends paid, including any liquidating dividend. Thus, cash dividends are all that stockholders as a whole receive from their investment; they are all the company pays out. Consequently, the foundation for the valuation of common stocks must be dividends.

The logical question to be raised is, Why do the stocks of companies that pay no dividends have positive, and often quite high, values? The answer is that investors expect to be able to sell the stock in the future at a price higher than they paid for it. Instead of dividend income plus terminal value, they rely only upon the terminal value. In turn, terminal value will depend upon the expectations of the marketplace at the end of the horizon period. The ultimate expectation is that the firm eventually will pay dividends, either regular or liquidating ones, and that future investors will receive a cash return on their investment. In the interim, however, investors are content with the expectation that they will be able to sell the stock at a subsequent time because there will be a market for it. In the meantime, the company is reinvesting earnings and, hopefully, enhancing its future earning power and ultimate dividends.

GROWTH MODELS

We saw in Eq. (2-13) that the return on investment is the rate of discount that equates the present value of the stream of expected future dividends with the current market price of the stock. If dividends of a company are expected to grow at a constant rate, g, in keeping, say, with a growth in earnings, Eq. (2-13) becomes

$$P_0 = \frac{D_0(1 + g)}{(1 + r)} + \frac{D_0(1 + g)^2}{(1 + r)^2} + \cdots + \frac{D_0(1 + g)^\infty}{(1 + r)^\infty} \qquad (2\text{-}14)$$

where D_0 is the dividend per share at time 0. Thus, the dividend expected in period n is equal to the most recent dividend times the compound growth factor, $(1 + g)^n$.

Assuming r is greater than g, Eq. (2-14) can be expressed as[3]

$$P_0 = \frac{D_1}{r - g} \qquad (2\text{-}15)$$

Rearranging, the expected return becomes

$$r = \frac{D_1}{P_0} + g \qquad (2\text{-}16)$$

The critical assumption in this valuation model is that dividends per share are expected to grow perpetually at a compound rate of g. For many companies, this assumption may be a fair approximation of reality. To illustrate the use of Eq. (2-16), suppose that A & G Company's

---

[3] If we multiply both sides of Eq. (2-14) by $(1 + r)/(1 + g)$ and subtract Eq. (2-14) from the product, we obtain

$$\frac{P_0(1 + r)}{(1 + g)} - P_0 = D_0 - \frac{D_0(1 + g)^\infty}{(1 + r)^\infty}$$

Because k_e is greater than g, the second term on the right side will be zero. Consequently,

$$P_0\left[\frac{1 + r}{1 + g} - 1\right] = D_0$$

$$P_0\left[\frac{(1 + r) - (1 + g)}{1 + g}\right] = D_0$$

$$P_0[r - g] = D_0(1 + g)$$

$$P_0 = \frac{D_1}{r - g}$$

If r were less than g, it is easy to determine that the market price of the stock would be infinite. See David Durand, "Growth Stocks and the Petersburg Paradox," *Journal of Finance*, 12 (September 1957), 348–63.

dividend per share at $t = 1$ was expected to be $3, to grow at a 4 percent rate forever, and that the current market price was $60 a share. The expected return would be

$$r = \frac{\$3}{\$60} + .04 = 9 \text{ percent} \qquad (2\text{-}17)$$

When the pattern of expected growth is such that a perpetual growth model is not appropriate, modifications of Eq. (2-14) can be used. A number of valuation models are based upon the premise that the growth rate will taper off eventually.[4] For example, the transition might be from a present above-normal growth rate to one that is considered normal. If dividends per share were expected to grow at an 8 percent compound rate for ten years and then grow at a 4 percent rate, Eq. (2-14) would become

$$P_0 = \sum_{t=1}^{10} \frac{D_0(1.08)^t}{(1 + r)^t} + \sum_{t=11}^{\infty} \frac{D_{10}(1.04)^{t-10}}{(1 + r)^t} \qquad (2\text{-}18)$$

The transition from an above-normal to a normal rate of growth could be specified as more gradual than the rate above. For example, we might expect dividends to grow at an 8 percent rate for five years, followed by a 6 percent rate for the next five years, and a 4 percent growth rate thereafter. The more growth segments that are added, the more closely the growth in dividends will approach a curvilinear function.

It seems clear that a company will not grow at an above-normal rate forever. Typically, companies tend to grow at a very high rate initially, after which their growth opportunities slow down to a rate that is normal for companies in general. If maturity is reached, the growth rate may stop altogether.[5] For any growth model, Eq. (2-14) can be modified so that it portrays the expected stream of future dividends.

HOLDING-PERIOD RISK

So far we have worked only with the expected return from holding a security. In a world of uncertainty, of course, this return may not be realized. Under such circumstances, the rate of return can be viewed as

[4] See W. Scott Bauman, "Investment Returns and Present Values," *Financial Analysts Journal*, 25 (November–December 1969), 107–18; Burton G. Malkiel, "Equity Yields, Growth, and the Structure of Share Prices," *American Economic Review*, 52 (December 1963), 1004–31; Charles C. Holt, "The Influence of Growth Duration on Share Prices," *Journal of Finance*, 17 (September 1962), 465–75; Eugene F. Brigham and James L. Pappas, "Duration of Growth, Changes in Growth Rates, and Corporate Share Prices," *Financial Analysts Journal*, 22 (May–June 1966), 157–62; Paul F. Wendt, "Current Growth Stock Valuation Methods," *Financial Analysts Journal*, 21 (March–April 1965), 3–15; and James M. Warren, "A Note on the Algebraic Equivalence of the Holt and Malkiel Models of Share Valuation," *Journal of Finance*, 29 (June 1974), 1007–10.

[5] See Holt, "Influence of Growth Duration on Share Prices," pp. 466–67.

**Table 2·1   Probability distribution of possible returns
for a one-year holding period**

Probability of occurrence	.05	.10	.20	.30	.20	.10	.05
Possible return	−.10	−.02	.04	.09	.14	.20	.28

a random variable subject to a probability distribution. Suppose, for example, that an investor believed that the possible one-year returns from investing in a particular common stock were those shown in Table 2-1. Rather than deal with the entire probability distribution, it is usually simpler to deal with only two parameters of the distribution. These parameters are the *expected value* and the *standard deviation*, the latter being a measure of dispersion.

The expected value of return is

$$\bar{R} = \sum_{i=1}^{n} R_i P_i \tag{2-19}$$

where R_i is the return for the ith possibility, P_i is the probability of occurrence of that return, and n is the total number of possibilities. The standard deviation is

$$\sigma = \sqrt{\sum_{i=1}^{n} (R_i - \bar{R})^2 P_i} \tag{2-20}$$

The square of the standard deviation, σ^2, is the variance of the distribution. To illustrate these measures, consider again the distribution of possible returns shown in Table 2-1. The expected value of return is

$$\bar{R} = -.10(0.05) - .02(0.10) + .04(0.20) + .09(0.30) + .14(0.20)$$
$$+ .20(0.10) + .28(0.05) = 9 \text{ percent} \tag{2-21}$$

The standard deviation is

$$\sigma = [(-.10 - .09)^2 0.05 + (-.02 - .09)^2 0.10 + (.04 - .09)^2 0.20$$
$$+ (.09 - .09)^2 0.30 + (.14 - .09)^2 0.20 + (.20 - .09)^2 0.10$$
$$+ (.28 - .09)^2 0.05]^{\frac{1}{2}} = [.00703]^{\frac{1}{2}} = 8.38 \text{ percent} \tag{2-22}$$

USE OF STANDARD DEVIATION INFORMATION

For the normal, bell-shaped probability distribution, approximately 0.68 of the distribution falls within one standard deviation of the expected value, 0.95 falls within two standard deviations, and 0.997 within three standard deviations. By expressing differences from the expected value in terms of standard deviations, we are able to determine the probability that the actual return will be greater or less than such and such an amount. To illustrate, suppose we wished to determine the probability that the actual return in our example would be less than zero. Standardizing the deviation from the expected value, we have 9 percent/8.38 percent = 1.07 standard deviations. Turning to the normal probability distribution table in Appendix B at the end of the book, we find that there is approximately a 14 percent probability that the actual return will be more than 1.07 standard deviations from the mean of the distribution. Therefore, there is a 14 percent likelihood that the actual return on investment will be zero or less.

Thus, the dispersion, or wideness, of the probability distribution of possible returns reflects the degree of investor uncertainty. A distribution with a small standard deviation relative to its expected value indicates little dispersion and a high degree of confidence in the outcome. A distribution with a large standard deviation relative to its expected value indicates a high degree of uncertainty about the possible return on investment. In the immediate discussion, we assume that probability distributions can be summarized in terms of two parameters—the expected value and the standard deviation. We now turn to the question of how investors view information about the possible returns associated with holding a security. That is, what are their utility preferences with respect to expected return and risk?

INVESTOR UTILITY PREFERENCES

In this section, we examine investor utility preferences as they specifically relate to security investments. The expected utility model presented is widely used in the literature on decision making under uncertainty. We employ it as a means for describing how individual investment decisions are made. In so doing, we hope to come to a better understanding of security risk and investor behavior with respect to such risk.

We assume that the objective of investors, as well as of other individuals, is to maximize their utility. In turn, utility is derived from present and prospective future consumption. We can think of the investor as deciding at various discrete intervals during his lifetime what portion of his wealth will be consumed and what portion invested. That portion invested is expected to increase future wealth, which, in turn, will be allocated between consumption and investment. Determination of an optimal consumption-investment sequence is complicated by the fact that we live in an uncertain world where future wealth levels associated with various investment decisions are not known with certainty.[6]

---

[6]See Eugene F. Fama and Merton H. Miller, *The Theory of Finance* (New York: Holt, Rinehart & Winston, 1972), Chapter 5.

Therefore, we assume that individuals maximize expected utility, which is a function of both expected return and uncertainty. The foundation for the expected utility theory is that individuals conform to certain axioms of rational and consistent choice.[7] It is useful to review these axioms prior to developing a utility function. Most will seem straightforward and logical, which is why they are said to describe rational behavior in the face of uncertainty.

AXIOMS OF RATIONAL BEHAVIOR

1. Individuals are able to order or rank alternatives and always prefer the larger outcome to the smaller, all other things the same.
2. Individuals' preferences are transitive. That is, if an individual prefers A to B and B to C, he must prefer A to C.
3. Various prospects are independent in the mind of the individual. Therefore, the relative ranking of two prospects is unaffected when the prospects are combined with a third prospect. For example, if an individual is indifferent between potatoes or rice (that is, he is equally disposed to eating one or the other), he will also be indifferent between meat *and* potatoes or meat *and* rice. This axiom implies that the expected utility of a combination of prospects is a linear combination of the utilities of those prospects.
4. For any prospect, there exists a certainty equivalent. For example, if an individual is presented with a fair coin toss where he receives $100 for heads and zero for tails, there is some amount of certain money that will result in his being indifferent between the toss of a coin and that amount. Moreover, the certain amount is intermediate between the largest and the smallest consequences—in our case, $100 and zero.

Assuming that individuals conform to these axioms of behavior, it is possible to derive a utility of wealth function for a particular individual. The index derived portrays the individual's preferences with respect to risky investments, which in turn are expressed as probability distributions of possible outcomes. In the subsequent section, we show how a utility of wealth function might be derived. This is followed by the application of the function to the problem of choosing among investment alternatives on the basis of the one that maximizes expected utility. Finally, we take up various utility functions in the context of our example. Hopefully, this discussion will give us a basic understanding of investor decision making under uncertainty.

[7]The utility approach considered in this section has its origin in the classic work of John von Neumann and Oskar Morgenstern, *Theory of Games and Economic Behavior*, rev. ed. (Princeton, N.J.: Princeton University Press, 1955). For an excellent discussion of the axioms as they pertain to investments, see Fama and Miller, *Theory of Finance*, pp. 192–96; J. Hirshleifer, *Investment, Interest, and Capital* (Englewood Cliffs, N.J.: Prentice-Hall, 1970), Chapter 8; and Harry M. Markowitz, *Portfolio Selection* (New York: John Wiley, 1959), Chapter 10.

To determine an individual's utility of wealth function, we might pose to him the opportunity to invest his initial wealth in a group of lotteries or gambles. By so doing, we are able to derive a utility index for money. We measure utility in units, which we call "utiles." Arbitrarily, we initially assign utile values of 0 and 1 to a pair of dollar amounts that represent extreme prospects—say zero dollars of wealth and $100,000 of wealth, respectively. It is important to stress that we measure only an ordinal utility index and not cardinal utility for the individual. We have assigned utility values arbitrarily to two amounts of money; consequently, our index, or scale, has no natural origin.[8]

Suppose now that we pose a risk situation to the individual by offering him an instantaneous lottery with a 0.5 chance of receiving no money, and a 0.5 chance of receiving $100,000. We then ask him how much he would be willing to pay for the lottery. If his answer is $33,000, we would attach a utile value of 0.5 to $33,000. Thus, we have determined the certainty equivalent at which the individual is indifferent between that sum and the lottery. Next, we have him consider a lottery providing a 0.4 probability of receiving $33,000 and a 0.6 probability of receiving $100,000. Suppose he were willing to buy this lottery for $63,000. The utile value of $63,000 is then

$$U(\$63,000) = 0.4U(\$33,000) + 0.6U(\$100,000)$$
$$= 0.4(0.5) + 0.6(1.0) = 0.80 \qquad (2\text{-}23)$$

We now offer him a lottery providing a 0.3 probability of receiving zero dollars and a 0.7 probability of receiving $33,000. Suppose he were willing to pay $21,000 for this lottery. The utile value of $21,000 can then be calculated as

$$U(\$21,000) = 0.3U(\$0) + 0.7U(\$33,000)$$
$$= 0.3(0) + 0.7(0.5) \qquad (2\text{-}24)$$
$$= 0.35$$

Similarly, we can pose other lotteries to him until we have enough observations to construct his utility of wealth function. This utility function can be graphed by drawing a line through the points. It may look like that shown in Figure 2-1; in the figure, dollars are plotted along the horizontal axis, while utile values are plotted on the vertical. Note that the individual's utility for wealth increases at a decreasing rate. This utility function is consistent with diminishing marginal utility and risk

[8] See Ralph O. Swalm, "Utility Theory—Insights into Risk Taking," *Harvard Business Review*, 44 (November–December 1966), 124–25.

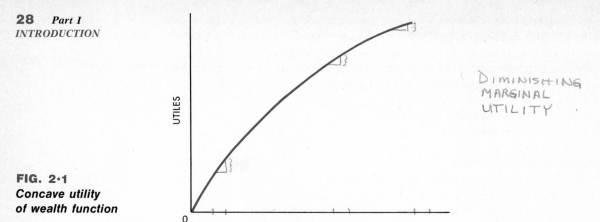

FIG. 2·1
Concave utility
of wealth function

aversion throughout. Each additional dollar gives the individual less utility or satisfaction than does the previous one. Thus, the individual is willing to take fair gambles only if the price is less than the expected value of these gambles. For example, the expected value of the first lottery is 0.5($0) + 0.5($100,000) = $50,000, yet he is willing to pay only $33,000 for it. Thus, the individual is averse to risk; in essence, he pays an insurance premium to avoid it.[9]

EXPECTED UTILITY OF AN INVESTMENT

Once an individual's utility function is specified, we are able to calculate the expected utility of an investment. This calculation involves multiplying the utile value of a particular outcome times the probability of its occurrence and adding together the products for all probabilities. To illustrate, consider two investments that provide the following probability distributions of instantaneous outcomes with respect to increments of wealth:

Investment A		Investment B	
Outcome	Probability	Outcome	Probability
$ 0	0.4	$33,000	0.4
33,000	0.1	63,000	0.6
100,000	0.5		

[9]For a much more extensive discussion of utility, see Von Neumann and Morgenstern, *Theory of Games and Economic Behavior;* Milton Friedman and Leonard J. Savage, "The Utility Analysis of Choices Involving Risk," *Journal of Political Economy,* 56 (August 1948), 279–304; R. Duncan Luce and Howard Raiffa, *Games and Decisions* (New York: John Wiley, 1957), Chapter 2; and Swalm, "Utility Theory," *Harvard Business Review,* 44 (November–December 1966), 123–36.

The expected monetary value of investment A is $0.4(0) + 0.1(\$33,000) + 0.5(\$100,000) = \$53,300$, while that for investment B is $0.4(\$33,000) + 0.6(\$63,000) = \$51,000$. Suppose that the individual's utility function is described by the risk aversion situation used in our illustration. The expected utility of investment A would be

$$U_A = 0.4U(\$0) + 0.1U(\$33,000) + 0.5U(\$100,000)$$
$$= 0.4(0) + 0.1(0.5) + 0.5(1.0) = 0.55 \qquad (2\text{-}25)$$

while that of investment B is

$$U_B = 0.4U(\$33,000) + 0.6U(\$63,000)$$
$$= 0.4(0.5) + 0.6(0.8) = 0.68 \qquad (2\text{-}26)$$

Thus, investment B provides the higher expected utility and is the preferred alternative from the standpoint of the individual examined. This preference occurs in spite of the higher expected monetary value of investment A. The possibility of a \$0 outcome detracts considerably from its utility value for the risk averter.

RISK AVERSION, PREFERENCE, AND NEUTRALITY

As stated earlier, Figure 2-1 portrays the utility function for a risk-averse investor. It is concave to the origin, which suggests that utility increases at a decreasing rate with successive increments in wealth. Therefore, the greater the variance, or standard deviation, of the probability distribution of possible returns for an investment, the less the expected utility of that investment. This was illustrated in the preceding section when we derived the expected utilities for two investment alternatives.

By way of another illustration, suppose an investor's utility of wealth function can be expressed by the following equation:[10]

$$U = 2X - 0.05X^2$$

where U is the number of utiles and X is the increments of wealth in units of \$1,000. Two investments are being considered: investment A has a 50 percent probability of providing a \$10,000 increment in wealth and a 50 percent probability of a \$20,000 increment, while investment B has a 50 percent probability of providing a zero increment in wealth and a 50 percent probability of a \$30,000 increment. We note that both invest-

---

[10] Eventually the quadratic equation shown will result in decreases in utility for subsequent increases in wealth. As is customary, we ignore this segment and define the relevant range as that where the first derivative is positive.

ments have the same expected monetary value, $15,000, but that investment B has the higher variance. The expected utilities of the two investments are

$$U_A = [2(10) - 0.05(10)^2]0.5 + [2(20) - 0.05(20)^2]0.5 = 17.5$$
$$U_B = [2(0) - 0.05(0)^2]0.5 + [2(30) - 0.05(30)^2]0.5 = 7.5$$

(2-27)

Thus, investment B, which has the greater variance of possible outcomes, has a much lower expected utility. For the risk averter, the certainty equivalent of a risky investment is always less than its expected monetary value. These illustrations show why the variance of a distribution is an appropriate measure of risk.

In addition to the concave utility function, there are two other types of functions. A convex utility function is shown in Figure 2-2a. This function implies that marginal utility is an increasing function of wealth. In this case, the individual prefers risk and is willing to pay more than the expected monetary value for a fair gamble. Stated differently, the certainty equivalent of a risky investment is more than its expected monetary value. The individual is a risk seeker and is unlikely to diversify his security holdings. Indeed such an individual frequently "plunges" by investing everything in a single investment opportunity.

Finally, Figure 2-2b describes a linear utility function in which marginal utility bears a constant relationship to wealth. The individual described by this function is said to be risk-indifferent or risk-neutral; he is willing to pay the expected value of a fair gamble. Although certain individuals may display combinations of risk aversion, risk preference, and risk neutrality at various levels of wealth, we assume that an individual's utility function is consistent throughout all levels of wealth. Moreover, we would expect most investors to be risk-averse. One can better appreciate this assertion if one considers a toss of a coin. While many of us would be willing to wager a few dollars on the toss of a coin at even odds, few people are willing to stake their entire wealth on such a toss. This behavior, of course, is consistent with a concave utility of wealth function. Accordingly, the major emphasis in this book will be on risk-averse investment behavior.

FIG. 2·2
Convex and linear utility of wealth functions

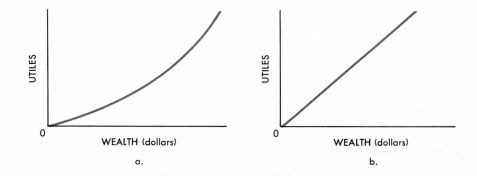

A MEAN-VARIANCE APPROACH
AND SOME LIMITATIONS

In the chapter that follows, we assume that investors select stocks according to the principle of maximizing expected utility. Expected utility is determined on the basis of the probability distribution of possible returns from an investment. In principle, the individual adjusts his asset holdings (both real and financial), his financial liabilities, and consumption so that the marginal utility derived from each asset and consumption is the same, as is the absolute magnitude of negative marginal utility associated with the issuance of financial liabilities. As one can imagine, the process is extremely complex and cumbersome.[11] To reduce the problem to manageable proportions, we assume that an individual is able to summarize his beliefs about the probability distribution of possible returns from an investment or portfolio of investments in terms of two parameters of the distribution.

These parameters are the expected value and the standard deviation; both measures were illustrated earlier. Thus, expected utility is expressed as a function of two parameters as opposed to the entire distribution of possible outcomes:[12]

$$E(U) = f(\overline{R}, \sigma) \qquad (2\text{-}28)$$

On the basis of expected return and standard deviation, then, investors determine the expected utility to be derived from an investment.

In a strict sense, the expected value and the standard deviation describe fully only a normal, symmetric, distribution. Two such distributions are shown in Figure 2-3. If the individual were risk-averse, he would prefer investment A, because it has less dispersion than investment B, but the same expected value of return. Now it is obvious that the risk of an investment to the individual is not dispersion per se but the possibility of downside deviations from the expected value of return. An investor would hardly consider upside deviations undesirable. For this

---

[11] For an analysis of the problem in this light, see James C. Van Horne, *Function and Analysis of Capital Market Rates* (Englewood Cliffs, N.J.: Prentice-Hall, 1970), Chapter 3.

[12] The approach described assumes that the standard deviation of the probability distribution is finite. Eugene F. Fama, "The Behavior of Stock-Market Prices," *Journal of Business*, 37 (January 1965), 34–105, building on an earlier investigation by Benoit Mandelbrot, showed that stock-market price changes conformed to a stable paretian distribution—a "fat-tailed" distribution—for which the variance and standard deviation do not exist. Other investigators have found similar results. Fama concludes, however, that the insights obtained from the mean-standard deviation model are valid as long as the distribution is a member of the stable family. See Fama, "Risk, Return and Equilibrium: Some Clarifying Comments," *Journal of Finance*, 23 (March 1968), 64. For discussion of the application of the two-parameter model to stable distributions with infinite variance, see Fama and Miller, *Theory of Finance*, pp. 261–74. The results are nearly the same, as we discuss later.

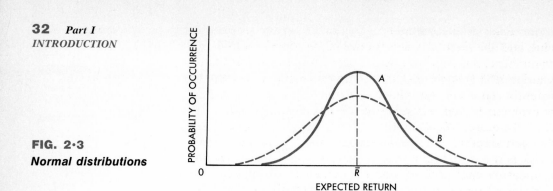

FIG. 2·3
Normal distributions

reason, the shape of the probability distribution may be important to him. To illustrate, the two distributions in Figure 2-4 have the same expected value and standard deviation. However, distribution *C* is skewed to the right, while distribution *D* is skewed to the left. To the extent that the investor prefers one distribution to the other, the standard deviation is not a sufficient measure of risk. Many investors would prefer the distribution skewed to the right, because it has a greater degree of downside protection and upside potential.

If the investor is concerned solely with the possibility of actual loss, he would be interested in only that portion of the probability distribution that represents a loss. The rest of the distribution would be ignored. Such an investor might simply establish a maximum tolerance or probability for loss and treat this percentage as a constraint in his selection process. Obviously, a measure of downside potential would be useful. Unfortunately, the mathematical calculation of a skewness measure is possible only for a simple problem; it is infeasible for a security with a large number of possible returns. Because of the difficulty of dealing mathematically with moments of the probability distribution higher than

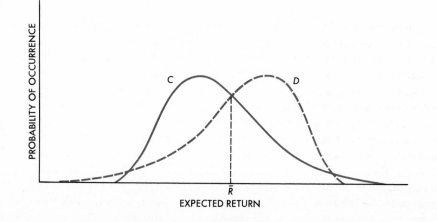

FIG. 2·4
Skewness

the second, our analysis is confined to the first two moments—the expected value and the standard deviation. For distributions that are reasonably symmetric, this approach may approximate closely investor attitudes toward risk. That is, the distribution with the greater dispersion would consistently represent the riskier security.

Another problem is that our measure of risk does not allow for different states of nature. Recall that it implies that risk is simply the possibility that actual returns will deviate from those that are expected. However, if risk is the deviation of actual returns from those that are desired, our measure may not be entirely satisfactory. Suppose an investor had different utilities for a given return, depending upon the state of nature in which it occurred. The state-preference approach to security valuation suggests that returns should be estimated across various states of nature. Investment selection, then, would depend upon the utility for money in the different states as well as upon the probability of occurrence of the various states. The security that maximized the investor's utility would be preferred. The state-preference approach implies that risk is the possibility that the desired, rather than the expected, return will not be achieved.[13] Although the state-preference approach has considerable theoretical merit, it poses operational difficulties in formulating returns and utilities for different states of nature. Consequently, we shall use the dispersion of the probability distribution of possible returns as a reasonable approximation of risk for the great body of investors.

[13] See Alexander A. Robichek, "Risk and the Value of Securities," *Journal of Financial and Quantitative Analysis*, 4 (December 1969), 513–38; Hirshleifer, *Investment, Interest, and Capital*, Chapters 9 and 10; Stewart C. Myers, "A Time-State Preference Model for Security Valuation," *Journal of Financial and Quantitative Analysis*, 3 (March 1968), 1–33; and William F. Sharpe, *Portfolio Theory and Capital Markets* (New York: McGraw-Hill, 1970), Chapter 10.

SUMMARY

In this book, we examine the impact of investment, financing, and dividend decisions on the value of the firm's common stock. A key concept underlying this valuation is the time value of money. Using present-value techniques, we are able to isolate differences in the timing of cash flows for various investments. In purchasing a common stock, the investor gives up present consumption with the expectation of increasing future consumption. The expected return is the rate of discount that equates the present market value of the stock with the present value of the stream of expected future dividends. Because cash dividends are all that investors as a whole receive from their investment, these dividends are the foundation for valuation. A dividend-valuation model is consistent with the fact that many investors expect to sell their stock in the future and realize a capital gain. Given the basic valuation model, we saw how it could be simplified to solve for different expectations as to future growth.

In investing, individuals attempt to maximize their expected utility, which is a function of expected return and risk, according to certain axioms of rational behavior. Depending on one's utility of wealth function, an investor will be risk-averse, risk-neutral, or risk-seeking. Once an individual's utility function is defined, it is possible to calculate the expected utility of an investment. In order to simplify the problem, however, we assume that individuals are able to summarize their beliefs about the probability distribution of possible returns from an investment in terms of two parameters of the distribution—the expected value and the standard deviation. Although one can argue that the standard deviation is not a fully appropriate measure of risk, more sophisticated measures are either too difficult mathematically or too abstract to be of practical value. Consequently, we assume that investors determine the expected utility to be derived from an investment on the basis of the expected value and standard deviation of the probability distribution of possible returns. In the subsequent chapter, we show how these concepts are applied to the selection of a portfolio of securities and the implications of such selection for the required rate of return and valuation of the individual firm.

APPENDIX

MATHEMATICS OF COMPOUND INTEREST, BOND YIELDS, AND PERPETUITIES

The present-value formulations in this chapter are analogous to compound interest on a bank deposit. If \$1 is deposited in a savings account at a bank that pays r percent a year compounded annually, the initial deposit at the end of one year increases to

$$TV_1 = \$1(1 + r) \tag{2A-1}$$

where TV_1 is the terminal value at the end of one year. At the end of two years, the terminal value is

$$TV_2 = \$1(1 + r)^2 \tag{2A-2}$$

Similarly, at the end of n years, the terminal value of the deposit is

$$TV_n = \$1(1 + r)^n \tag{2A-3}$$

If interest is paid more than once a year and compounded, Eq. (2A-3) must be modified. For example, suppose that the bank paid interest semiannually on a compound basis. The terminal value at the end of six months would be

$$TV_{1/2} = \$1\left(1 + \frac{r}{2}\right) \tag{2A-4}$$

and at the end of one year

$$TV_1 = \$1\left(1 + \frac{r}{2}\right)^2 \tag{2A-5}$$

If the interest rate paid were 4 percent compounded semiannually, the terminal value of a $1 deposit at the end of one year would be

$$TV_1 = \$1\left(1 + \frac{0.04}{2}\right)^2 = \$1(1.02)^2 = \$1.0404 \tag{2A-6}$$

The terminal value at the end of n years for a $1 deposit compounded m times a year is

$$TV_n = \$1\left(1 + \frac{r}{m}\right)^{mn} \tag{2A-7}$$

Thus, if interest were compounded daily on the basis of a 365-day year, the terminal value of a $1 deposit at the end of n years would be

$$TV_n = \$1\left(1 + \frac{r}{365}\right)^{365n} \tag{2A-8}$$

As m approaches infinity, the term $\left(1 + \frac{r}{m}\right)^{mn}$ can be expressed as e^{rn}, where e is approximately 2.71828 and is defined as

$$e = \lim_{m \to \infty}\left(1 + \frac{1}{m}\right)^m \tag{2A-9}$$

Thus, the terminal value at the end of n years where interest is compounded continuously is

$$TV_n = \$1e^{rn} \tag{2A-10}$$

Variations of this formula are seen frequently in the theoretical literature on growth stocks, whose earnings or dividends are expected to grow continuously at the rate g.

In the development of this chapter, we assumed that for purposes of calculating present values, interest was compounded annually. It will be recalled that the formula for the present value of a cash flow A_n received at the end of n years was

$$PV = \frac{A_n}{(1 + r)^n} \qquad (2A\text{-}11)$$

If interest is compounded continuously instead of annually, the formula for the present value of a cash flow received at the end of the nth year becomes

$$PV = \frac{A_n}{e^{rn}} = A_n e^{-rn} \qquad (2A\text{-}12)$$

The present value of a continuous stream of cash flows is

$$PV = \int_0^n A_t e^{-rt}\, dt \qquad (2A\text{-}13)$$

BOND YIELDS

The yield to maturity on a bond is the rate of discount that equates the present value of all future interest and principal payments with the market price of the bond. If interest payments are made at the end of each year, and the face value of the bond is $1,000, we solve the following equation for r, the yield to maturity:

$$P = \frac{I}{(1 + r)} + \frac{I}{(1 + r)^2} + \cdots + \frac{I}{(1 + r)^n} + \frac{1,000}{(1 + r)^n} \qquad (2A\text{-}14)$$

where P is the present market price, I is the annual interest payment as given by the coupon rate, and n is the number of years to final maturity. To illustrate, suppose that the 8% bonds of Bailey Corporation have ten years to final maturity and that the current market price is $950 a bond. Therefore

$$950 = \frac{80}{(1 + r)} + \frac{80}{(1 + r)^2} + \cdots + \frac{80}{(1 + r)^{10}} + \frac{1,000}{(1 + r)^{10}} \qquad (2A\text{-}15)$$

Solving for r in the manner described in the chapter, we find the yield to maturity to be 8.77 percent.

Suppose now that we reverse the example somewhat and that we wish to determine the market price necessary for an 8% ten-year bond to yield 7 percent to maturity. The equation becomes

$$P = \frac{80}{(1.07)} + \frac{80}{(1.07)^2} + \cdots + \frac{80}{(1.07)^{10}} + \frac{1,000}{(1.07)^{10}} \qquad \text{(2A-16)}$$

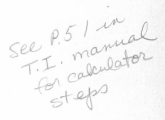

Referring to Table A-2 in Appendix A at the back of the book, the present value of $80 per year for ten years, discounted at 7 percent, is $561.89, and the present value of $1,000 received at the end of the tenth year is $508.35 (from Table A-1). The market price, P, is simply the sum of the present values of these two components, or $1,070.24.

If interest is paid more than once a year, Eq. (2A-14) needs to be modified somewhat. In keeping with the discussion in the preceding section, if interest is paid semiannually, the yield to maturity can be found by solving the following equation for r:

$$P = \frac{I/2}{\left(1 + \dfrac{r}{2}\right)} + \frac{I/2}{\left(1 + \dfrac{r}{2}\right)^2} + \frac{I/2}{\left(1 + \dfrac{r}{2}\right)^3} + \cdots + \frac{I/2}{\left(1 + \dfrac{r}{2}\right)^n} + \frac{1,000}{\left(1 + \dfrac{r}{2}\right)^n} \qquad \text{(2A-17)}$$

If the 7% bonds of IBK Corporation had ten years to final maturity, and the current market price were $1,040 per bond, Eq. (2A-17) becomes

$$1,040 = \frac{35}{\left(1 + \dfrac{r}{2}\right)} + \frac{35}{\left(1 + \dfrac{r}{2}\right)^2} + \frac{35}{\left(1 + \dfrac{r}{2}\right)^3} + \cdots + \frac{35}{\left(1 + \dfrac{r}{2}\right)^{20}} + \frac{1,000}{\left(1 + \dfrac{r}{2}\right)^{20}} \qquad \text{(2A-18)}$$

Solving the equation for r, we find the yield to maturity to be 6.64 percent. Similarly, the equation for calculating bond yields where interest is compounded m times a year is

$$P = \frac{I/m}{\left(1 + \dfrac{r}{m}\right)} + \frac{I/m}{\left(1 + \dfrac{r}{m}\right)^2} + \frac{I/m}{\left(1 + \dfrac{r}{m}\right)^3} + \cdots + \frac{I/m}{\left(1 + \dfrac{r}{m}\right)^{mn}} + \frac{1,000}{\left(1 + \dfrac{r}{m}\right)^{mn}} \qquad \text{(2A-19)}$$

Given any three of the four factors discussed above (coupon rate, final maturity, market price, and yield to maturity), we are able to solve for the fourth. Fortunately, elaborate bond value tables are available, so we need not go through the calculations. These tables are constructed in exactly the same manner as the present-value tables discussed previously. The only difference is that they take account of the coupon rate and of the fact that the face value of the bond will be paid at the final maturity date. An example of a bond-yield table for a 5 percent coupon rate, and semiannual interest payments, is shown in Figure 2-5. In the figure, the time to maturity is represented by the columns and the yield to maturity by the rows. The figures inside represent the prices, or

Mat. Yield	YEARS AND MONTHS 5%							
	18-9	18-10	18-11	19-0	19-1	19-2	19-3	19-4
3.95	113.81	113.85	113.90	113.94	113.98	114.02	114.06	114.10
4.00	113.10	113.14	113.18	113.22	113.26	113.29	113.33	113.37
4.05	112.39	112.43	112.47	112.51	112.54	112.57	112.61	112.65
4.10	111.69	111.72	111.76	111.80	111.83	111.86	111.90	111.93
4.15	110.99	111.03	111.06	111.10	111.13	111.16	111.19	111.22
4.20	110.30	110.33	110.37	110.40	110.43	110.45	110.48	110.51
4.25	109.62	109.65	109.68	109.71	109.73	109.76	109.79	109.81
4.30	108.94	108.97	109.00	109.03	109.05	109.07	109.10	109.12
4.35	108.27	108.29	108.32	108.35	108.37	108.39	108.41	108.43
4.40	107.60	107.62	107.65	107.67	107.69	107.71	107.73	107.75
4.45	106.94	106.96	106.98	107.00	107.02	107.04	107.06	107.08
4.50	106.28	106.30	106.32	106.34	106.35	106.37	106.39	106.40
4.55	105.63	105.65	105.66	105.68	105.70	105.71	105.72	105.74
4.60	104.98	105.00	105.01	105.03	105.04	105.05	105.07	105.08
4.65	104.34	104.35	104.37	104.38	104.39	104.40	104.41	104.43
4.70	103.70	103.72	103.73	103.74	103.75	103.76	103.77	103.78
4.75	103.07	103.08	103.09	103.11	103.11	103.12	103.12	103.13
4.80	102.45	102.45	102.46	102.47	102.48	102.48	102.49	102.49
4.85	101.83	101.83	101.84	101.84	101.85	101.85	101.86	101.86
4.90	101.21	101.21	101.22	101.23	101.23	101.23	101.23	101.23
4.95	100.60	100.60	100.61	100.61	100.61	100.61	100.61	100.61
5.00	99.99	99.99	100.00	100.00	100.00	99.99	99.99	99.99
5.05	99.39	99.39	99.39	99.39	99.39	99.38	99.38	99.38
5.10	98.79	98.79	98.79	98.79	98.78	98.78	98.78	98.77
5.15	98.20	98.20	98.20	98.20	98.19	98.18	98.17	98.17
5.20	97.61	97.61	97.61	97.60	97.59	97.58	97.58	97.57
5.25	97.03	97.03	97.02	97.02	97.00	96.99	96.99	96.98
5.30	96.45	96.45	96.44	96.43	96.42	96.41	96.40	96.39
5.35	95.88	95.87	95.86	95.86	95.84	95.83	95.82	95.81
5.40	95.31	95.30	95.29	95.28	95.27	95.25	95.24	95.23
5.45	94.75	94.73	94.72	94.72	94.70	94.68	94.67	94.66
5.50	94.19	94.17	94.16	94.15	94.13	94.11	94.10	94.09
5.60	93.08	93.06	93.05	93.04	93.02	93.00	92.98	92.96
5.70	91.99	91.97	91.96	91.94	91.92	91.89	91.87	91.85
5.75	91.45	91.43	91.42	91.40	91.37	91.35	91.33	91.31
5.80	90.92	90.90	90.88	90.86	90.83	90.81	90.79	90.77
5.90	89.86	89.84	89.82	89.80	89.77	89.74	89.72	89.69
6.00	88.83	88.80	88.78	88.75	88.72	88.69	88.67	88.64
6.10	87.80	87.77	87.75	87.72	87.69	87.66	87.63	87.60
6.20	86.80	86.77	86.74	86.71	86.68	86.64	86.61	86.58
6.25	86.30	86.27	86.24	86.21	86.17	86.14	86.11	86.08
6.30	85.80	85.77	85.74	85.72	85.68	85.64	85.61	85.58
6.40	84.83	84.79	84.76	84.73	84.69	84.66	84.62	84.59
6.50	83.87	83.83	83.80	83.77	83.73	83.69	83.65	83.61
6.60	82.92	82.88	82.85	82.82	82.77	82.73	82.69	82.66
6.70	81.99	81.95	81.92	81.88	81.84	81.79	81.75	81.71
6.75	81.53	81.49	81.45	81.42	81.37	81.33	81.29	81.25
7.00	79.28	79.24	79.20	79.16	79.11	79.06	79.02	78.97
7.25	77.12	77.07	77.03	76.99	76.93	76.88	76.83	76.79
7.50	75.04	74.99	74.94	74.90	74.84	74.78	74.73	74.69
8.00	71.10	71.05	71.00	70.95	70.89	70.83	70.77	70.72

1207

FIG. 2·5
Bond-yield table
Monthly Bond Values
(*Boston Financial
Publishing Company*, 1939)

present values, based upon a face value of $100. For example, the market price of a 5% bond with nineteen years to final maturity yielding 5.25 percent is $97.02. By consulting a bond-yield table, we are able to determine easily the yield to maturity of a bond—given its market price, coupon rate, and maturity date—or the market price for a particular yield—given the coupon rate and maturity date.

PERPETUITIES

It is conceivable that we might be confronted with an investment opportunity that, for all practical purposes, is a perpetuity. With a perpetuity, a fixed cash inflow is expected at equal intervals forever. A case in point is the British Consul, which is a bond with no maturity date; it carries the obligation of the British government to pay a fixed coupon perpetually. If the investment required an initial cash outflow at time 0 of A_0 and were expected to pay A^* at the end of each year forever, its yield is the discount rate, r, that equates the present value of all future cash inflows with the present value of the initial cash outflow

$$A_0 = \frac{A^*}{(1 + r)} + \frac{A^*}{(1 + r)^2} + \cdots + \frac{A^*}{(1 + r)^n} \qquad \text{(2A-20)}$$

In the case of a bond, A_0 is the market price of the bond and A^* the fixed annual interest payment. When we multiply both sides of Eq. (2A-20) by $(1 + r)$, we obtain

$$A_0(1 + r) = A^* + \frac{A^*}{(1 + r)} + \frac{A^*}{(1 + r)^2} + \cdots + \frac{A^*}{(1 + r)^{n-1}} \qquad \text{(2A-21)}$$

Subtracting Eq. (2A-20) from Eq. (2A-21)

$$A_0(1 + r) - A_0 = A^* - \frac{A^*}{(1 + r)^n} \qquad \text{(2A-22)}$$

As n approaches infinity, $A^*/(1 + r)^n$ approaches 0. Thus

$$A_0 r = A^* \qquad \text{(2A-23)}$$

and

$$r = \frac{A^*}{A_0} \qquad \text{(2A-24)}$$

Here r is the yield on a perpetual investment costing A_0 at time 0 and paying A^* at the end of each year forever. Suppose that we had the opportunity to buy for $1,000 a security that was expected to pay $70 a year forever. The yield, or internal rate of return, of the security would be

$$r = \frac{\$70}{\$1,000} = 7 \text{ percent} \qquad \text{(2A-25)}$$

PROBLEMS

1. Do the following exercises on present values.

   [A-1]

   (a) $100 at the end of three years is worth how much today?
   - (1) Assuming a discount rate of 10 percent $75.13
   - (2) Assuming a discount rate of 100 percent $12.50
   - (3) Assuming a discount rate of 0 percent $100.

   [A-2]

   (b) What is the aggregate present value of $500 received at the end of each of the next three years?
   - (1) Assuming a discount rate of 4 percent   1387.55
   - (2) Assuming a discount rate of 25 percent   976.

(c) $100 is received at the end of one year, $500 at the end of two years, and $1,000 at the end of three years. What is the aggregate present value of these receipts?
  (1) Assuming a discount rate of 4 percent
  (2) Assuming a discount rate of 25 percent

(d) $1,000 is to be received at the end of one year, $500 at the end of two years, and $100 at the end of three years. What is the aggregate present value of these receipts?
  (1) Assuming a discount rate of 4 percent
  (2) Assuming a discount rate of 25 percent

(e) Compare your solutions in 1(c) with those in 1(d) and explain the reason for the differences.

2. Do the following exercises on internal rates of return.

(a) An investment of $1,000 today will return $2,000 at the end of ten years. What is its *IRR*?

(b) An investment of $1,000 today will return $500 at the end of each of the next three years. What is its *IRR*?

(c) An investment of $1,000 today will return $1,000 at the end of one year, $500 at the end of two years, and $100 at the end of three years. What is its *IRR*?

(d) An investment of $1,000 will return $60 per year forever. What is its *IRR*?

3. Graph the present value of $1 per year for 5, 10, 15, 20, and 25 years at 0, 10, 20, 30, and 40 percent rates of discount. Explain the difference in the slopes of the curves.

4. The stock of the Health Corporation is currently selling for $20 and is expected to pay a $1 dividend at the end of the year. If an investor bought the stock now and sold it for $23 after receiving the dividend, what rate of return would he earn?

5. James Farnsworth Tuttle, founder and holder of the controlling interest in Tuttle, Inc., has vowed that his firm will never pay a dividend as long as he lives. His current life expectancy is twenty-five years. After that time it is estimated that Tuttle, Inc., could pay dividends of $50 per year per share forever. At present the firm could afford to pay $10 per share forever. The marginal Tuttle shareholder requires a 20 percent pretax return.

(a) What is the current value of Tuttle stock?

(b) What is the cost to each shareholder of James Farnsworth Tuttle's policies?

6. (a) The Pueblo Corporation paid a dividend of $1.50 per share last year; dividends of Pueblo are expected to grow at a rate of 10 percent indefinitely. The Pueblo stockholders are known to demand a 20 percent pretax return. At what price should Pueblo stock sell?

(b) Suppose that Pueblo dividends were expected to grow at 10 percent for only five more years, after which they would grow at 6 percent forever. At what price should Pueblo stock now sell?

7. Delphi Products Corporation currently pays a dividend of $2.00 per share and this dividend is expected to grow at a 15 percent annual rate for three years, then at a 10 percent rate for the next three years, after which it is expected to grow at a 5 percent rate forever.

   (a) What value would you place on the stock if a 9 percent rate of return were required?

   (b) Would your valuation change if you expected to hold the stock only three years?

8. You have been asked to graph Mr. Barclay's utility of wealth function. You feel that three observations are sufficient for this purpose and know that Mr. Barclay is quite wealthy. You begin by asking him what he would pay for a lottery with a .5 chance of receiving 0 and a .5 chance of receiving $1 million. He responds that he would pay $400,000. You then pose the following lotteries to him and his responses are:

Lottery	Price Mr. Barclay Will Pay
.5 chance to win $400,000 and .5 chance to win $1 million	$660,000
.6 chance to receive 0 and .4 chance to win $400,000	$120,000

   (a) Determine the utile values of these observations and plot Mr. Barclay's utility of wealth function.

   (b) What type of function is it? What does it tell you? What would a risk neutral utility function look like?

9. Suppose an investor's utility of wealth function can be expressed as

$$U = 1.5x - 0.1x^2$$

   where U is utility as denoted by utiles and x is increments of wealth, in units of $1,000. The investor is considering two possible investments which can be described by the following probability distributions:

Investment A		Investment B	
Prob.	x	Prob.	x
0.1	−4	0.3	1
0.3	0	0.4	2
0.4	4	0.3	3
0.2	8		

   (a) Compute the utile values associated with each of these investments. Which investment provides the greater utility?

   (b) Compute the expected value of wealth increment, x. Which investment provides the greater expected value of increment?

(c) If there is a difference between the preferred investment depending on the method employed, explain the reason for it.

10. Wally Whittier is considering investing in a security that has the following distribution of possible returns:

Probability	.10	.20	.30	.30	.10
Return	−.10	.00	.10	.20	.30

(a) What is the expected value of return and standard deviation associated with the investment?
(b) Is there much downside risk? How can you tell?

SELECTED REFERENCES

Bauman, W. Scott, "Investment Returns and Present Values," *Financial Analysts Journal,* 25 (November–December 1969), 107–18.

Blume, Marshall E., "On the Assessment of Risk," *Journal of Finance,* 26 (March 1971), 1–10.

Bower, Richard S., and Dorothy H. Bower, "Risk and the Valuation of Common Stock," *Journal of Political Economy,* 77 (May–June 1969), 349–62.

Brigham, Eugene F., and James L. Pappas. "Duration of Growth, Changes in Growth Rates, and Corporate Share Prices," *Financial Analysts Journal,* 22 (May–June 1966), 157–62.

Fama, Eugene F., "Components of Investment Performance," *Journal of Finance,* 27 (June 1972), 551–67.

———, "Multiperiod Consumption—Investment Decisions," *American Economic Review,* 60 (March 1970), 163–74.

Fama, Eugene F., and Merton H. Miller, *The Theory of Finance,* New York: Holt, Rinehart & Winston, 1972.

Gonedes, Nicholas J., "Information-Production and Capital Market Equilibrium," *Journal of Finance,* 30 (June 1975), 841–64.

Gordon, Myron, *The Investment, Financing, and Valuation of the Corporation.* Homewood, Ill.: Richard D. Irwin, 1962.

Haley, Charles W., and Lawrence D. Schall, *The Theory of Financial Decisions,* Chapter 5. New York: McGraw-Hill, 1973.

Hirshleifer, J., *Investment, Interest and Capital.* Englewood Cliffs, N.J.: Prentice-Hall, 1970.

Holt, Charles C., "The Influence of Growth Duration on Share Price," *Journal of Finance,* 17 (September 1962), 465–75.

Lerner, Eugene M., and Willard T. Carleton. *A Theory of Financial Analysis.* New York: Harcourt, Brace & Jovanovich, 1966.

Lorie, James H., and Mary T. Hamilton, *The Stock Market.* Homewood, Ill.: Richard D. Irwin, 1973.

Machol, Robert E., and Eugene M. Lerner, "Risk, Ruin, and Investment Analysis," *Journal of Financial and Quantitative Analysis,* 4 (December 1969), 473–92.

Malkiel, Burton G., "Equity Yields, Growth, and the Structure of Share Prices," *American Economic Review,* 53 (December 1963), 467–94.

Malkiel, Burton G., and John G. Cragg, "Expectations and the Structure of Share Prices," *American Economic Review,* 40 (September 1970), 601–17.

Mao, James C. T., "The Valuation of Growth Stocks: The Investment Opportunities Approach," *Journal of Finance,* 21 (March 1966), 95–102.

Modigliani, Franco, and Gerald A. Pogue, "An Introduction to Risk and Return," *Financial Analysts Journal,* 30 (March–April 1974), 68–80, and (May–June 1974), 69–86.

Mossin, Jan, *Theory of Financial Markets.* Englewood Cliffs, N.J.: Prentice-Hall, 1973.

Myers, Stewart C., "The Application of Finance Theory to Public Utility Rate Cases," *Bell Journal of Economics and Management Science,* 3 (Spring 1972), 58–97.

———, "A Time-State Preference Model of Security Valuation," *Journal of Financial and Quantitative Analysis,* 3 (March 1968), 1–34.

Ofer, Aharon R., "Investors' Expectations of Earnings Growth, Their Accuracy and Effects on the Structure of Realized Rates of Return," *Journal of Finance,* 30 (May 1975), 509–23.

Pogue, Gerald A., and Kishore Lall, "Corporate Finance: An Overview," *Sloan Management Review,* 15 (Spring 1974), 19–38.

Robichek, Alexander A., "Risk and the Value of Securities," *Journal of Financial and Quantitative Analysis,* 4 (December 1969), 513–38.

Robichek, Alexander A., and Stewart C. Myers, *Optimal Financing Decisions,* Chapters 4–6. Englewood Cliffs, N.J.: Prentice-Hall, 1965.

Sharpe, William F., *Portfolio Analysis and Capital Markets.* New York: McGraw-Hill, 1970.

Sloane, William R., and Arnold Reisman, "Stock Evaluation Theory: Classification, Reconciliation, and General Model," *Journal of Financial and Quantitative Analysis,* 3 (June 1968), 171–204.

Van Horne, James C., *The Function and Analysis of Capital Market Rates.* Englewood Cliffs, N.J.: Prentice-Hall, 1970.

Van Horne, James C., and William F. Glassmire, Jr., "The Impact of Unanticipated Changes in Inflation on the Value of Common Stocks," *Journal of Finance,* 27 (December 1972), 1081–92.

Van Horne, James C., and Raymond C. Helwig, *The Valuation of Small Bank Stocks.* East Lansing: Bureau of Business and Economic Research, Michigan State University, 1966.

Vickers, Douglas, *The Theory of the Firm: Production, Capital, and Finance.* New York: McGraw-Hill, 1968.

Warren, James M., "A Note on the Algebraic Equivalence of the Holt and Malkiel Models of Share Valuation," *Journal of Finance,* 29 (June 1974), 1007–10.

Wendt, Paul F., "Current Growth Stock Valuation Methods," *Financial Analysts Journal,* 33 (March–April 1965), 3–15.

VALUATION
of the FIRM

In this chapter, we continue our examination of valuation. Our ultimate goal is to come to an understanding of how a firm is valued in the market. Most investors are not concerned with a single investment opportunity, but rather with the possible returns from a portfolio of investments. We therefore concentrate on how investors select portfolios of securities. We then move on to consider how market equilibrium is achieved and how the individual firm is valued under the assumption that investors overall are efficiently diversified in the portfolios of common stocks they hold. The concepts advanced are basic to a good portion of the theoretical development of the book, so an understanding of them is essential. We begin with a discussion of market efficiency, the assumptions of which underlie the development of this chapter.

Basically efficient capital markets exist when security prices reflect all available public information about the economy, about financial markets, and about the specific company involved. Implied is that market prices of individual securities adjust very rapidly to new information. As a result, security prices are said to fluctuate randomly about their "intrinsic" values. To be sure, new information can result in a change in the "intrinsic" value of a stock, but subsequent stock price movements will follow what is known as a *random walk*.

EFFICIENT MARKET CONSIDERATIONS

THEORY OF EFFICIENT MARKETS

Eugene F. Fama has formalized this condition by the following expression:[1]

$$x_{j,t+1} = p_{j,t+1} - E(p_{j,t+1}|\phi_t) \tag{3-1}$$

where $x_{j,t+1}$ is the profit *in excess of* the equilibrium expected profit from investment in security j, $p_{j,t+1}$ is the actual market price of the security at time $t + 1$, and $E(p_{j,t+1}|\phi_t)$ is the expected market price of security j at time $t + 1$, given the information set ϕ_t at time t. According to the efficient markets notion,

$$E(x_{j,t+1}|\phi_t) = 0 \tag{3-2}$$

which merely states that expected excess profits from the use of the information set are zero.

---

[1]"Efficient Capital Markets: A Review of Theory and Empirical Work," *Journal of Finance*, 25 (May 1970), 384–87.

The efficient markets theory implies that past security-price movements cannot be used to predict future market prices in such a way as to earn excess profits from these predictions. If information about a change in the "intrinsic" value of a security were to diffuse slowly among market participants, there would develop a persistence in the series of security price changes beyond that expected if the series followed a random walk.[2] As a result, there would be opportunity for excess profits to be made based on some type of mechanical decision rule that was applied to past security-price movements. An example of such a decision rule is to buy a stock when its market price goes 5 percent above its 200-day moving average, and to sell it when it goes below the moving average by this percentage. One relevant comparison would be the profits realized from the application of such a rule with the profits realized from a simple buy-and-hold investment strategy. If the former exceeded the latter, there would be indication of the possibility of excess profits. The efficient markets theory implies that excess profits cannot last, because a sufficient number of market participants with sufficient resources will recognize the recurring pattern of price changes and will exploit the opportunity. In exploiting it, they will drive out the opportunity for further excess profits, causing the price series to approximate a random walk. Thus, competitive forces are said to result in an efficient market.

The sufficient conditions for such a market are that (1) there are no transaction costs; (2) information is available to all participants at no cost; and (3) all participants agree on the implications of available information for the current and future prices of each security.[3] Obviously, these conditions are not entirely met in practice. While security markets clearly would be efficient in the sense that security prices fully reflect all available information if they were met, in practice such markets may be efficient if these conditions are only "reasonably" met. To determine this, we must turn to the empirical evidence.

EMPIRICAL TESTS OF MARKET EFFICIENCY

Empirical tests have been conveniently categorized into three types:[4] weak-form, semistrong-form, and strong-form tests. We briefly consider each in turn.

Weak-form tests involve testing the dependence of successive security-price changes over time and whether or not mechanical trading rules using past price changes can earn excess profits. The first set of

---

[2] See Alan Seelenfreund, George G. C. Parker, and James C. Van Horne, "Stock Price Behavior and Trading," *Journal of Financial and Quantitative Analysis*, 3 (September 1968), 263–82.

[3] See Fama, "Efficient Capital Markets," pp. 387–88.

[4] Ibid., pp. 388–413.

tests have largely supported the idea that stock-price changes are independently distributed random variables. Moreover, empirical tests of mechanical trading rules, similar to those employed by a technical "chartist," also have tended to support the efficient markets theory.[5] As a result of these tests, the currently observed security price is said to be the best estimate of the "intrinsic" value of that security. Stated differently, a security-price series evidences random fluctuations about "intrinsic" value.

Semistrong tests of market efficiency are concerned with the speed of price adjustment to new information. Such studies have focused on changes in security prices relative to specific types of information, after isolating out systematic underlying market movements. The types of information examined include stock splits, annual and quarterly earnings announcements, differing forms of reported earnings, large secondary offerings of common stock (an underwritten sale of existing stock to institutions and individuals), new issues of stock, and new listings on a major stock exchange. Most of the semistrong tests have supported the efficient markets theory.[6] Stock prices appear to adjust quickly to public announcements concerning the company. If this is the case, a person could not expect to earn an excess profit by buying or selling a security upon the receipt of new publicly available information. As before, the collective action of a sufficient number of market participants buying or selling the stock causes a very rapid, if not virtually instantaneous, adjustment in price. It should be pointed out that not all of the semistrong tests are consistent with the efficient markets theory.[7] By and large, however, the theory is supported.

Finally, strong-form tests of efficient markets are concerned with whether all available information, both public and private, is reflected in the market price of the security. The question here is whether certain individuals have monopolistic ability to obtain information and whether they are able to show excess profits as a result.[8] Tests involving profes-

[5] These tests are well summarized in Fama, "Efficient Capital Markets"; Michael C. Jensen, *Studies in the Theory of Capital Markets* (New York: Praeger, 1972); and James H. Lorie and Mary T. Hamilton, *The Stock Market* (Homewood, Ill.: Richard D. Irwin, 1973), Chapter 4. See also Seelenfreund, Parker, and Van Horne, "Stock Price Behavior and Trading," for actual tests of various mechanical trading rules.

[6] For a discussion of these tests, see Fama, "Efficient Capital Markets"; Jensen, *Studies in the Theory of Capital Markets*; Lorie and Hamilton, *Stock Market*, Chapter 4; William H. Beaver, "The Behavior of Security Prices and Its Implications for Research Methods," *Supplement to the Accounting Review* (1972), 407–37; and Beaver, "The Implications of Security Price Research for Accounting," *Accounting Review*, 49 (July 1974), 563–71. See also James C. Van Horne, "New Listings and Their Price Behavior," *Journal of Finance*, 25 (September 1970), 783–94.

[7] For an examination of the limitations of existing tests as well as a presentation of contrary evidence, see David Downes and Thomas R. Dyckman, "A Critical Look at the Efficient Market Empirical Research Literature as It Relates to Accounting Information," *Accounting Review*, 48 (April 1973), 300–17.

[8] Again these tests are described in Fama, "Efficient Capital Markets"; and Lorie and Hamilton, *Stock Market*.

sional mutual fund managers suggest that such managers do not out-perform randomly selected portfolios. Few tests have been undertaken concerning other parties. Some tests involving specialists on a stock exchange and insiders (corporate officers and directors) suggest that such parties have monopolistic access to information and are able to use it to generate moderate excess profits. However, such testing is ex-tremely limited. *(highly regulated by S.E.C. today.)*

EFFICIENT MARKETS—A SUMMING UP

On balance, the evidence indicates that the market for stocks, particularly those listed on the New York Stock Exchange, is efficient. This is particularly true in the weak-form and semistrong-form tests. Security prices appear to reasonably reflect all available information, and market prices adjust quickly to new information. Market partici-pants seem to be ready to seize on any recurring price pattern so as to drive price changes about a security's "intrinsic" value to a random walk.

The concept of efficient markets underlies our discussion in the balance of this chapter. We assume that capital markets are efficient in allocating funds on the basis of expected return and risk. In turn, this enables us to make certain generalizations concerning market equilib-rium and the implications of such equilibrium for the valuation of the firm. We turn now to consideration of the relevant measure of portfolio risk, as opposed to the risk of an individual security.

MEASUREMENT OF PORTFOLIO RISK

Before proceeding to the question of portfolio selection by investors and the valuation of the firm, we must spend some time on the meas-urement of portfolio risk. The expected value of return for a portfolio causes us no problems in measurement. It is simply a weighted average of the expected rates of return of the securities comprising that portfolio and can be expressed as

$$\bar{R}_p = \sum_{j=1}^{m} A_j R_j \tag{3-3}$$

where A_j is the portion of funds invested in security j, R_j is the expected value of return for that security, and m is the total number of securities in the portfolio.

Unfortunately, the standard deviation of the portfolio is not so easily measured. It depends not only on the riskiness of the securities com-prising the portfolio but also on the relationships between these securities with respect to risk. Therefore, a simple weighted average of the individual standard deviations will not do. Instead, we have the following rather complicated formula for the standard deviation of a probability distribution of possible portfolio returns:

$$\sigma_p = \sqrt{\sum_{j=1}^{m} \sum_{k=1}^{m} A_j A_k r_{jk} \sigma_j \sigma_k} \qquad (3\text{-}4)$$

where m is the total number of securities in the portfolio, A_j is the proportion of the total funds invested in security j, A_k is the proportion invested in security k, r_{jk} is the expected correlation between returns for securities j and k, σ_j is the standard deviation about the expected value of return for security j, and σ_k is the standard deviation for security k. These standard deviations are calculated with Eq. (2-20) in the preceding chapter. Thus, the standard deviation of a portfolio depends upon (1) the correlation between expected returns of the various securities comprising the portfolio, (2) the standard deviation of each security, and (3) the proportion of funds invested in each security.

CORRELATION BETWEEN SECURITIES

The correlation between returns may be positive, negative, or zero, depending upon the nature of the association. A correlation coefficient of 1.00 indicates that variations in the return for one security are associated with proportional changes in the return for the other security; a correlation coefficient of -1.00 indicates that they vary inversely in the same proportions; and a zero coefficient indicates an absence of correlation. The correlation of returns between two securities can be expressed as

$$r_{jk} = \sum_{x=1}^{n} \left(\frac{R_{xj} - \bar{R}_j}{\sigma_j} \right) \left(\frac{R_{xk} - \bar{R}_k}{\sigma_k} \right) P_{xjk} \qquad (3\text{-}5)$$

where R_{xj} is the xth possible return for security j, $\bar{R}_j$ is the expected value of return for security j, R_{xk} is the xth possible return for security k, R_k is the expected value of return for security k, P_{xjk} is the joint probability that R_{xj} and R_{xk} will occur simultaneously, and n is the total number of joint possible returns. In other words, deviations from expected values of return for the two securities are normalized by dividing them by their respective standard deviations. When these normalized deviations are multiplied by each other, and their product is multiplied by the joint probability of occurrence and then summed, we obtain the correlation coefficient.

To illustrate the determination of the standard deviation for a portfolio using Eq. (3-4), consider an investor who holds a stock whose expected value of annual return is 10 percent, with a standard deviation of 15 percent. Suppose further that he is considering another stock with an expected value of annual return of 8 percent, a standard deviation of 12 percent, and that the expected correlation between the two stocks is 0.40. By investing equal portions in each of the stocks, the expected value of return for the portfolio would be

$$R_p = (0.5)0.10 + (0.5)0.08 = 9 \text{ percent} \tag{3-6}$$

This contrasts with a 10 percent return when the portfolio is comprised entirely of the first stock. However, the standard deviation for the probability distribution of possible returns for the new portfolio is

$$\sigma_p = [(0.5)^2(1.00)(0.15)^2 + (2)(0.5)(0.5)(0.4)(0.15)(0.12) \\ + (0.5)^2(1.00)(0.12)^2]^{1/2} = 11.3 \text{ percent} \tag{3-7}$$

From Eq. (3-4) we know that the covariance between the two stocks must be counted twice. Therefore, we multiply the covariance by two. When $j = 1$ and $k = 1$ for stock 1, the proportion invested (0.5) must be squared, as must the standard deviation (0.15). The correlation coefficient, of course, is 1.00. The same thing applies for stock 2 when $j = 2$ and $k = 2$. The important principle to grasp is that as long as the correlation coefficient between two securities is less than 1.00, the standard deviation of the portfolio will be less than the weighted average of the two individual standard deviations.

The example suggests that by diversifying one's holdings to include securities with less than perfect positive correlation among themselves, the risk-averse investor is able to reduce the dispersion of the probability distribution of possible returns relative to the expected value of return for that distribution. In so doing, he reduces the risk of holding securities. However, this diversification must be among the right type of securities. It is not enough for an investor simply to spread his investment among a number of securities; diversification must be among securities not possessing high degrees of positive correlation among themselves. It is evident from Eq. (3-4) that the dispersion of the probability distribution for a portfolio could be reduced to zero if securities with perfect negative correlation could be found. The objective of diversification, however, is not to reduce dispersion per se but to obtain the best combination of expected value of return and standard deviation. We will have considerably more to say about diversification later in the chapter; it is important now to present the rudiments of portfolio selection before getting into certain refinements.

The best combination of expected value of return and standard deviation depends upon the investor's utility function. This function is derived in the manner described in the preceding chapter. If an investor is risk-averse and associates risk with divergence from expected value of return, his utility function might be depicted graphically by Figure 3-1. The expected value of return is plotted on the vertical axis, while the standard deviation is along the horizontal. The curves are known as *indifference curves;* the investor is indifferent between any combination of expected value of return and standard deviation on a particular curve. In other words, a curve is defined by those combinations of expected return and standard deviation that result in a fixed level of expected utility.[9] From our discussion of expected utility theory in the preceding chapter, we know that all points on a specific indifference curve have the same certainty equivalent. The greater the slope of the indifference curves, the more averse the investor is to risk. As we move to the left in Figure 3-1, each successive curve represents a higher level of expected utility.

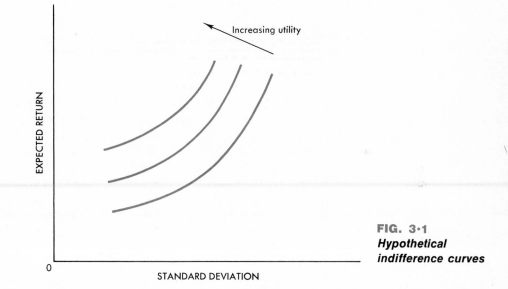

FIG. 3·1
Hypothetical indifference curves

The individual investor will want to hold that portfolio of securities that places him on the highest indifference curve, choosing it from the opportunity set of available portfolios. An example of an opportunity set, based upon the subjective probability beliefs of an individual investor, is shown in Figure 3-2. This opportunity set reflects all possible portfolios

[9] For further discussion and proof that indifference curves for a risk-averse investor are concave, see Eugene F. Fama and Merton H. Miller, *The Theory of Finance* (New York: Holt, Rinehart & Winston, 1972), pp. 226–28.

51

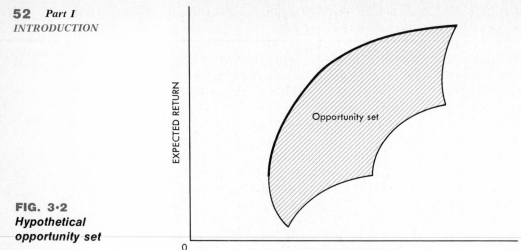

EXPECTED RETURN

Opportunity set

0

STANDARD DEVIATION

FIG. 3·2
Hypothetical
opportunity set

*efficient portfolio
gives highest return
at lowest std. dev'n
(risk)*

of securities as envisioned by the investor. The dark line at the top of the set is the line of efficient combinations, or the efficient frontier. It depicts the tradeoff between risk and expected value of return. According to the Markowitz mean-variance maxim, an investor should seek a portfolio of securities that lies on the efficient frontier.[10] A portfolio is not efficient if there is another portfolio with a higher expected value of return and a lower standard deviation, a higher expected value and the same standard deviation, or the same expected value but a lower standard deviation. If an investor's portfolio is not efficient, he can increase the expected value of return without increasing the risk, decrease the risk without decreasing the expected value of return, or obtain some combination of increased expected value and decreased risk by switching to a portfolio on the efficient frontier.[11]

As can be seen, the efficient frontier is determined on the basis of

[10] Markowitz, *Portfolio Selection: Efficient Diversification of Investments* (New York: John Wiley, 1959), Chapters 7 and 8.

[11] Baumol has proposed a modification of Markowitz's efficiency criterion for evaluating expected value and variance. This criterion involves the use of a lower confidence limit, represented by $E - K\sigma$, where E is the expected value, σ is the standard deviation from expected value, and K is a confidence coefficient. K is specified in terms of the number of standard deviations from expected value and represents the lowest plausible outcome from the standpoint of the investor. Given a lower confidence limit, an investor is able to determine how much risk he must assume in order to obtain a certain expected value. According to Baumol, only when $E - K\sigma$ decreases as portfolios with greater expected value are considered would there be a sacrifice of safety. Baumol's efficient-combination line is represented by the downward sloping portion of the $E - K\sigma$ curve and is a subset of Markowitz's line. As K increases, Baumol's efficient set approaches the Markowitz efficient set as a limit. See William J. Baumol, "An Expected Gain-Confidence Limit Criterion for Portfolio Selection," *Management Science*, 10 (October 1963), 174–82. It would be possible to incorporate Baumol's efficiency criterion into the above analysis.

dominance. Portfolios of securities tend to dominate individual securities because of the reduction in risk obtainable through diversification. As discussed before, this reduction is evident when one explores the implications of Eq. (3-4). The objective of the investor is to choose the best portfolio from those that lie on the efficient frontier. The portfolio with the maximum utility is the one at the point of tangency of the opportunity set with the highest indifference curve. This tangency is illustrated in Figure 3-3, and the portfolio represented by the point of tangency is the optimal one for an investor with those expectations and utility function.[12]

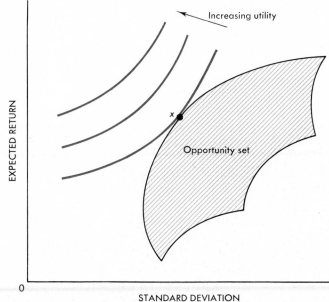

FIG. 3·3
Selection of
optimal portfolio

PRESENCE OF RISK-FREE SECURITY

If a risk-free security exists that yields a certain future return, the portfolio selection process described above must be modified. This security might be a U.S. Treasury security that is held to maturity. Although the yield is low relative to other securities, there is complete certainty as to return. Suppose for now that the investor is able not only to lend at the risk-free rate but to borrow at it as well. (We relax this assumption later on.) To determine the optimal portfolio under these

---

[12]For a more sophisticated and mathematical discussion of the point of tangency, see Fama and Miller, *Theory of Finance*, pp. 223–26 and 243–50. For ease of understanding, we purposely have kept the presentation graphical.

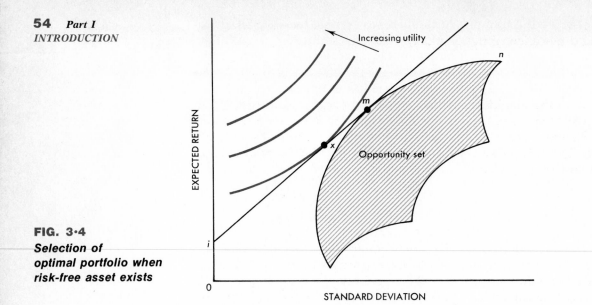

FIG. 3·4
*Selection of
optimal portfolio when
risk-free asset exists*

conditions, we first draw a line from the risk-free rate, *i*, through its point of tangency with the opportunity set of portfolio returns, as illustrated in Figure 3-4. This line then becomes the new efficient frontier. Note that only one portfolio of risky securities—namely, *m*—would be considered. In other words, this portfolio now dominates all others, including those on the efficient frontier of the opportunity set.

Any point on the straight line tells us the proportion of the risky portfolio, *m*, and the proportion of loans or borrowings at the risk-free rate. To the left of point *m*, the investor would hold both the risk-free security and portfolio *m*. To the right, he would hold only portfolio *m* and would borrow funds, in addition to his initial investment funds, in order to invest in it. The farther to the right in the figure, the greater borrowings will be. The optimal investment policy is determined by the point of tangency between the straight line in Figure 3-4 and the highest indifference curve. As shown in the figure, this point is portfolio *x* and it consists of an investment in both the risk-free security and the risky security portfolio, *m*. If borrowing were prohibited, the efficient frontier would no longer be a straight line throughout but would consist of line *i-m-n*. The optimal portfolio would be determined in the same manner as before—namely, the tangency of the efficient frontier with the highest indifference curve.

The expected return of a portfolio, where both borrowing and lending at the risk-free rate are possible, is

$$\bar{R}_p = wi + (1 - w)\bar{R}_m \qquad (3\text{-}8)$$

where *w* is the proportion of the risk-free security that is held and $\bar{R}_m$ is the expected return on the risky portfolio. If funds are loaned at the risk-free rate, w is positive; if funds are borrowed, w is negative. The standard deviation of the portfolio is

$$\sigma_p = (1 - w)\sigma_m \qquad (3\text{-}9)$$

where σ_m is the standard deviation for portfolio m. Because the risk-free security has no standard deviation, the standard deviation of the portfolio depends entirely upon the risk of portfolio m. The farther to the right in Figure 3-4, the more that is invested in portfolio m, and the more risky the overall portfolio.

CAPITAL MARKET LINE

Assuming both borrowing and lending at the risk-free rate, the straight line passing through the risk-free rate on the vertical axis and the expected return–standard deviation point for the market portfolio is known as the *capital market line*. It is shown in Figure 3-4, but we illustrate it separately in Figure 3-5. This line describes the tradeoff between expected return and risk for various holdings of the risk-free security and the market portfolio. The slope of the line represents the market price of risk. It tells us the amount of additional expected return that is required for an increment in standard deviation.

For example, if the slope is one-half, as shown in Figure 3-5, this means that for each increase in standard deviation of 2 percent, the expected return increases by 1 percent. We have assumed a risk-free rate of 5 percent in the figure. If a person were willing to accept a standard deviation of 14 percent for his portfolio, this would mean the expected return would be 5 percent + 0.5 (14 percent) = 12 percent. Mathe-

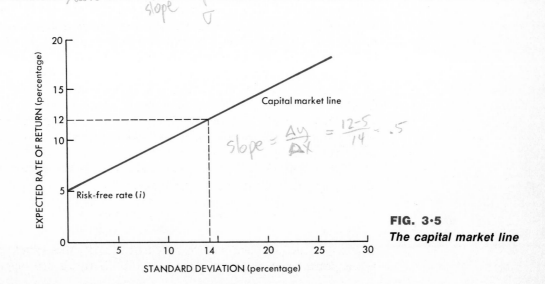

FIG. 3·5
The capital market line

matically, the relationship between expected return and standard deviation for a portfolio can be expressed as

$$\bar{R}_p = i + \left[\frac{\bar{R}_m - i}{\sigma_m}\right]\sigma_p \qquad (3\text{-}10)$$

where σ_p is determined with Equation (3-9). The term in brackets depicts the slope of the capital market line and, as we know, represents the market price of risk.

Separation Theorem

Note that in the construct of the capital market line, the utility preferences of the individual affect only the amount that is borrowed or loaned. They do not affect the optimal portfolio of risky assets. Turning to Figure 3-4, the investor would select portfolio m of risky assets no matter what the nature of his indifference curves. The reason is that when a risk-free security exists, and borrowing and lending are possible at that rate, the market portfolio dominates all others. Thus, the individual's utility preferences are independent or separate from the optimal portfolio of risky assets. This condition is known as the *separation theorem*.[13] Put another way, it states that the determination of an optimal portfolio of risky assets is independent of the individual's risk preferences. Such a determination depends only on the expected returns and standard deviations for the various possible portfolios of risky assets. In essence, the individual's approach to investing is two phased. First he determines an optimal portfolio of risky assets, and then he determines the most desirable combination of the risk-free security and this portfolio. Only the second phase depends on his utility preferences.

CAPITAL-ASSET PRICING MODEL

The selection process described in the preceding section requires one to compute a prohibitedly large number of correlation coefficients (one for each possible pairing of individual securities). For example, if five hundred securities were involved, it would require 124,750 computations.[14] To simplify the selection process, William F. Sharpe devised a method to make operational the portfolio model.[15] Instead of estimating the correlation between returns for a security and all other securities, one estimates the correlation between a particular security's return and that for some market index, such as Standard & Poor's 500-stock index.

---

[13] This theorem was originally stated by J. Tobin, "Liquidity Preference as Behavior towards Risk," *Review of Economic Studies,* 25 (February 1958), 65–86.

[14] The total number of correlation coefficients to be computed is $N(N - 1)/2$, where N is the number of securities.

[15] "A Simplified Model for Portfolio Analysis," *Management Science,* 9 (January 1963), 277–93.

This reduces substantially the number of correlation coefficient esti- mates to be made. From the work of Sharpe, and subsequent work by Lintner, there evolved what is known as the *capital-asset pricing model* for analyzing the market equilibrium tradeoff between expected return and risk. In this section, we examine how portfolio selection can be simplified and, more importantly, the implications of the capital-asset pricing model for the expected return of a specific security.

In addition to the assumptions already discussed, the capital-asset pricing model requires several more. We assume that investors have homogeneous expectations. That is, all investors view the opportunity set of individual securities in the same way with respect to expected return, standard deviation, and correlation among securities.[16] Though this condition is not necessary for deriving a model of market equilibrium,[17] it enables us to make generalizations not otherwise possible. In essence, we deal only with one efficient frontier as opposed to efficient frontiers for each investor and the interaction among investors. Because the value of any model is its predictive ability, we restrict the situation in this way in order to enhance the model's explanatory power. We assume also that perfect capital markets exist where all securities are infinitely divisible, where there are no transaction costs or taxes, and where information is available to all at no cost. Finally, we assume that investors have the same one-period time horizon, and that expectations are geared ac- cordingly.

While these rather restrictive assumptions are required if the model is to be developed in a rigorous manner, some can be relaxed and the model will still have general validity. In the last section, we explore certain relaxations and their effect on the generalizations possible about expected return and risk. For expository purposes now, however, we hold intact the above assumptions.

THE CHARACTERISTIC LINE

Our concern is with two types of investment opportunities: (1) a risk-free security as represented by, say, a Treasury bill; and (2) the market portfolio of all stocks as represented by some surrogate such as

---

[16] For a further discussion of these assumptions and of the capital-asset pricing model, see William F. Sharpe, "Capital Asset Prices: A Theory of Market Equilibrium under Condi- tions of Risk," *Journal of Finance*, 19 (September 1964), 425–42; Sharpe, *Portfolio Analysis and Capital Markets* (New York: McGraw-Hill, 1970), Chapters 5-6; John Lintner, "The Valuation of Risk Assets and the Selection of Risky Investments in Stock Portfolios and Capital Budgets," *Review of Economics and Statistics*, 47 (February 1965), 13–37; and Eugene F. Fama, "Risk, Return, and Equilibrium—Some Clarifying Comments," *Journal of Finance*, 23 (March 1968), 29–40.

[17] For the development of a model where expectations are not homogeneous, see James C. Van Horne, *The Function and Analysis of Capital Market Rates* (Englewood Cliffs, N.J.: Prentice-Hall, 1970), Chapter 3. As demonstrated, the model developed there has little predictive power.

the Standard & Poor's 500-stock index.[18] We wish to compare the expected return for an individual stock with the expected return for the market portfolio. In our comparison, we deal with returns in excess of the risk-free rate. The excess return is simply the expected return less the risk-free return.

If the expected relationship is based upon past experience, excess returns might be calculated using historical data. Suppose, for example, that we felt that monthly returns over the last five years were a good proxy for the future. For each of the last sixty months, we then would compute the following excess returns for the particular stock involved, call it YZ Company, and for the market portfolio, as represented by Standard & Poor's 500-stock index:

Month	YZ Company	S&P 500-Stock Index
1	$\dfrac{(V_{yz,1} - V_{yz,0} + D_{yz,1})}{V_{yz,0}} - i_1$	$\dfrac{(V_{sp,1} - V_{sp,0} + D_{sp,1})}{V_{sp,0}} - i_1$
2	$\dfrac{(V_{yz,2} - V_{yz,1} + D_{yz,2})}{V_{yz,1}} - i_2$	$\dfrac{(V_{sp,2} - V_{sp,1} + D_{sp,2})}{V_{sp,1}} - i_2$
$\vdots$		
60	$\dfrac{(V_{yz,60} - V_{yz,59} + D_{yz,60})}{V_{yz,59}} - i_{60}$	$\dfrac{(V_{sp,60} - V_{sp,59} + V_{sp,60})}{V_{sp,59}} - i_{60}$

where $V_{yz,t}$ and $V_{sp,t}$ are the market values of a share of YZ Company's stock and of the S&P 500-stock index at the end of month t, respectively; $D_{yz,t}$ and $D_{sp,t}$ are dividends per share for YZ Company and the S&P index for month t, respectively; and i_t is the yield to maturity of a one-month Treasury bill at the beginning of month t.

Having calculated historical excess returns for the stock in question and for the market portfolio, these returns can then be plotted. Figure 3-6 compares the expected excess returns for a stock with those for the market portfolio.[19] The dots represent the monthly plots of the excess returns, sixty in all. The dark line fitted to the dots describes the historical relationship between excess returns for the stock and excess returns for the market portfolio. This line is known as the *characteristic line,* and it is used as a proxy for the expected relationship between the two sets of excess returns.

One notes in the graph that the greater the expected excess return for the market, the greater the expected excess return for the stock.

[18] The immediate subsequent development draws on William F. Sharpe, "Efficient Capital Markets with Risk," Research Paper No. 71 (Stanford Graduate School of Business, 1972).

[19] For a more detailed, and actual, example, see Franco Modigliani and Gerald A. Pogue, "An Introduction to Risk and Return," *Financial Analysts Journal,* 30 (May–June 1974), 73–77.

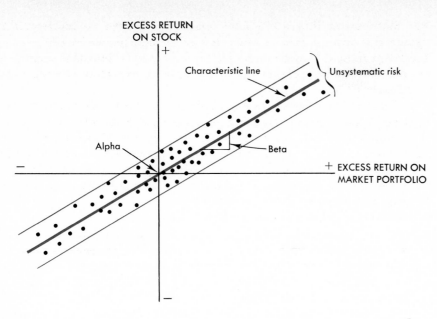

FIG. 3·6
*Relationship between
excess returns for stock
and excess returns
for market portfolio*

Three measures are important.[20] The first is known as the *alpha,* and it is simply the intercept of the characteristic line on the vertical axis. If the excess return for the market portfolio were expected to be zero, the alpha would be the expected excess return for the stock. In theory, the alpha for an individual stock should be zero.[21] Using past data to approximate the characteristic line, however, alphas that differ from zero might be observed if the market were in disequilibrium or if there were market imperfections. We assume for now, however, that the alpha for a particular stock is zero.

THE SYSTEMATIC RISK AS MEASURED BY BETA

The second measure with which we are concerned, and the most important, is the *beta.* The beta is simply the slope of the characteristic line. If the slope is one, it means that excess returns for the stock vary proportionally with excess returns for the market portfolio. In other words, the stock has the same unavoidable risk as the market as a whole. A slope steeper than one means that the stock's excess return varies more than proportionally with the excess return of the market portfolio.

[20] Sharpe, "Efficient Capital Markets with Risk."

[21] The alpha for the market portfolio is simply a weighted average of the alphas for the individual stocks making up the portfolio. As efficient markets and the resulting arbitrage will assure that no alpha for an individual stock will be negative, every alpha must be zero for the weighted average to be zero. See Sharpe, "Efficient Capital Markets with Risk." It should be pointed out that some empirical tests have shown positive alphas for low beta stocks and negative alphas for high beta stocks. Various reasons have been advanced for this occurrence.

Put another way, it has more unavoidable risk than the market as a whole. This type of stock is often called an "aggressive" investment. A slope less than one means that the stock has less unavoidable or systematic risk than the market as a whole. This type of stock is often called a "defensive" investment.

The greater the slope of the characteristic line for a stock, as depicted by its beta, the greater its systematic risk. This means that for both upward and downward movements in market excess returns, movements in excess returns for the individual stock are greater or less depending on its beta. For example, if the beta for a particular stock were 1.70 and the market excess return for a specific month were −2.00 percent, this would imply an expected excess return for the stock of −3.40 percent. Thus, the beta represents the systematic risk of a stock due to underlying movements in security prices. This risk cannot be diversified away by investing in more stocks, as it depends on such things as changes in the economy and in the political atmosphere which affect all stocks.

Empirical work on the stability of historical beta information over time suggests that past betas are useful in predicting future betas. However, the ability to predict seems to vary with the size of the portfolio. The larger the number of securities in a portfolio, the greater the stability of the beta for that portfolio over time.[22] However, even for the individual stock, past beta information has been found to have reasonable predictive value. Put another way, measured betas show significant stability over time even at the individual security level. In addition to portfolio size, betas tend to show greater stability over time the longer the time intervals being studied.

(Avoidable)

UNSYSTEMATIC RISK AND DIVERSIFICATION

The last of the three measures with which we are concerned is the dispersion of estimates around the characteristic line. In a regression analysis, this is depicted by the standard error of estimate. The greater

[22] For such tests, see Marshall E. Blume, "On the Assessment of Risk," *Journal of Finance,* 26 (March 1971), 1–10; Robert A. Levy, "On the Short Term Stationarity of Beta Coefficients," *Financial Analysts Journal,* 27 (November–December 1971), 55–62; Jerome B. Baesel, "On the Assessment of Risk: Some Further Considerations," *Journal of Finance,* 29 (December 1974), 1491–94; Robert C. Klemkosky and John D. Martin, "The Adjustment of Beta Forecasts," *Journal of Finance,* 30 (September 1975), 1123–28; and William F. Sharpe and Guy M. Cooper, "Risk-Return Classes of New York Stock Exchange Common Stocks," *Financial Analysts Journal,* 28 (March–April 1972), 46–54. There appears to be some tendency for the measured betas of individual securities to revert over time toward the beta of the market portfolio, or toward one. See also R. Richardson Pettit and Randolph Westerfield, "Using the Capital Asset Pricing Model and the Market Model to Predict Security Returns," *Journal of Financial and Quantitative Analysis,* 9 (September 1974), 579–607, who used the capital-asset pricing model to predict actual returns on securities. They found such predictions to be nonstationary and biased, thereby casting doubt on the model's ability to explain actual security returns.

[handwritten annotations: Systematic = due to overall mkt risk. Unsystematic = due to specific risk factors of the particular company (can be diversified away)]

the uncertainty in predicting a stock's characteristic line, the greater the unsystematic risk is said to be. The equation for fitting the characteristic line to the observations for security j is

$$R_j - i = a_j + \beta_j(R_m - i) + e_j \qquad (3\text{-}11)$$

where a_j is the constant term, β_j is the regression coefficient or beta, R_m is the return on the market index, i is the risk-free rate, and e_j is the error term.

The amount of unsystematic risk is described by the dispersion of the error term for the various observations (see Figure 3-6). The expected value of the distribution of error terms is zero, and the error terms for different securities are assumed to be uncorrelated.[23] All of this follows if capital markets are efficient in the sense that security prices fully reflect all available information. As discussed in the early part of the chapter, empirical tests suggest that capital markets are reasonably efficient and that fluctuations of market prices around "intrinsic" values are essentially random. As a result, the assumptions that the error terms have an expected value of zero and are uncorrelated among securities seem reasonable.

Thus, the total risk involved in holding a stock is comprised of two parts: the systematic component and the unsystematic component. The first is due to overall market risk and it cannot be diversified away. The second risk component, however, is unique to the particular company, being independent of economic, political, and other factors that affect securities in a systematic manner. By diversification, this risk can be reduced and even eliminated if diversification is efficient. Therefore, not all of the risk involved in holding a stock is relevant; part of it can be diversified away.

To explore the concept of diversification in more depth, consider the responsiveness of a portfolio's returns to changes in returns for the market portfolio as depicted by the index. This responsiveness can be represented as

$$\beta_p = \sum_{j=1}^{k} A_j\beta_j \qquad (3\text{-}12)$$

[handwritten annotation: Beta = Excess Returns on stk / Excess Ret. on mkt Portfolio]

where k is the total number of securities comprising the portfolio, and A_j is the proportion of the total portfolio value represented by security j. In

---

[23] It is assumed also that the error term is uncorrelated with the index. For a discussion of the empirical difficulty involved in testing this model, see Michael C. Jensen, "Capital Markets: Theory and Evidence," *Bell Journal of Economics and Management Science*, 3 (Autumn 1972), 363–91.

words, the responsiveness of the overall portfolio to the index, β_p, is simply a weighted average of the individual β_j's of securities that comprise that portfolio. Each security is weighted by the ratio of its total market value to the value of all securities in the portfolio. If the rates of return on various securities are correlated with each other only through the index, the standard deviation of the distribution of possible returns for the portfolio is

$$\sigma_p = \sqrt{\beta_p^2 \sigma_I^2 + \sum_{j=1}^{n} A_j^2 e_j^2} \tag{3-13}$$

where σ_I^2 is the variance of the index. The first term on the right represents the risk associated with the index, while the second represents the unique risk attributable to the individual securities making up the portfolio.

The greater the diversification of a portfolio, the less the unique, or unsystematic, risk of that portfolio. It has been shown that unsystematic risk is reduced at a decreasing rate toward zero as more randomly selected securities are added to the portfolio. Various studies suggest that fifteen to twenty stocks selected randomly are sufficient to eliminate most of the unsystematic risk of a portfolio.[24] Thus, a substantial reduction in unsystematic risk can be achieved with a relatively moderate amount of diversification. Conceptually, diversification can be viewed in the manner portrayed in Figure 3-7.[25] As the number of randomly selected securities held in the portfolio is increased, the total risk of the portfolio is reduced in keeping with the reduction in unsystematic risk. However, such a reduction is at a decreasing rate. Efficient diversification reduces the total risk of the portfolio to the point where only systematic risk remains.

For the well-diversified portfolio, then, the second term on the right in Equation (3-13) approaches zero, and the important risk of a security is the responsiveness of its return to changes in the return on the market

---

[24] For a discussion of this issue and various tests, see Jack Evans and Stephen H. Archer, "Diversification and the Reduction of Dispersion: An Empirical Analysis," *Journal of Finance*, 23 (December 1968), 761–67; Wayne H. Wagner and Shiela Lau, "The Effect of Diversification on Risk," *Financial Analysts Journal*, 26 (November–December 1971), 48–53; Robert C. Klemkosky and John D. Martin, "The Effect of Market Risk on Portfolio Diversification," *Journal of Finance*, 30 (March 1975), 147–54; John G. McDonald, "Investment Objectives: Diversification, Risk and Exposure to Surprise," *Financial Analysts Journal*, 32 (March–April 1975), 42–49; M. J. Brennan, "The Optimal Number of Securities in a Risky Asset Portfolio When There Are Fixed Costs of Transacting: Theory and Some Empirical Results," *Journal of Financial and Quantitative Analysis*, 10 (September 1975), 483–95; and K. H. Johnson and D. S. Shannon, "A Note on Diversification and the Reduction of Dispersion," *Journal of Financial Economics*, 1 (December 1974), 365–72.

[25] This example comes from Modigliani and Pogue, "An Introduction to Risk and Return," *Financial Analysts Journal*, 30 (March–April 1974), 74–75.

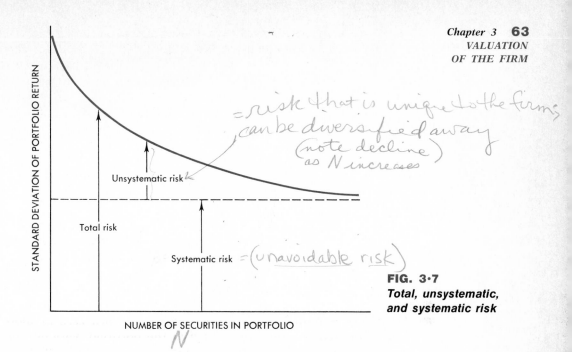

(handwritten annotations:)
= risk that is unique to the firm;
can be diversified away
(note decline
as N increases)

Systematic risk = (unavoidable risk)

FIG. 3·7
*Total, unsystematic,
and systematic risk*

(axis labels:) STANDARD DEVIATION OF PORTFOLIO RETURN
Unsystematic risk
Total risk
NUMBER OF SECURITIES IN PORTFOLIO
N

portfolio, as denoted by its beta. Implied then in the capital-asset pricing model is that all risk other than systematic risk has been diversified away. Stated differently, if capital markets are efficient and investors at the margin are well diversified, the important risk of a stock becomes its unavoidable or systematic risk.

EXPECTED RETURN FOR INDIVIDUAL SECURITY

For the individual security, then, the relevant risk is not the standard deviation of the security itself (total risk), but the marginal effect the security has on the standard deviation of an efficiently diversified portfolio (systematic risk). As a result, a security's expected return should be related to its degree of systematic risk, not to its degree of total risk. The former is the risk that matters to an investor holding a well-diversified portfolio. In market equilibrium, the relationship between an individual security's expected rate of return and its systematic risk, as measured by beta, will be linear. The relationship is known as the *security market line,* and it is illustrated in Figure 3-8.

Under the assumptions of the capital-asset pricing model, all securities lie along this line. The figure shows that the expected return on a risky security is a combination of the risk-free rate plus a premium for risk. For example, if the systematic risk of a particular security were represented by y on the horizontal axis in the figure, its expected return would be x, consisting of the risk-free rate, i, plus a risk premium, $x - i$.

(handwritten margin note:)
for ind'l sec'y
– look at systematic risk, (since the unsys. risk can be diversified away – and is therefore irrelevant)

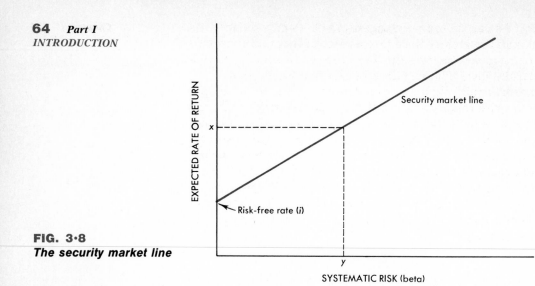

FIG. 3·8
The security market line

If a particular security's returns were uncorrelated with returns on the market portfolio, by definition it would be risk-free even though it might have a significant amount of total risk. In other words, the security has very desirable diversification properties when combined in a large portfolio of securities. In such a portfolio, its unsystematic risk could be reduced to zero. As its systematic risk is zero, the required return on the security would be the risk-free rate. However, virtually all stocks have positive systematic risk in the sense that they vary in some measure with the market.[26] Therefore, this topic is of more theoretical than practical interest.

We see in Figure 3-8 that the greater the systematic risk of a security, the greater the return that is required by the market. The relationship between the expected return for security j and its systematic risk can be expressed mathematically as

$$\bar{R}_j = i + (\bar{R}_m - i)\beta_j \tag{3-14}$$

where again i is the risk-free rate, $\bar{R}_m$ is the expected value of return for the market portfolio, and β_j is the beta coefficient for security j as

---

[26] On occasions in the past, gold-mining stocks have had negative betas. In recent years, however, their betas have been positive, although very low. In the context of the capital-asset pricing model, a stock with a negative beta would require an expected return that was even less than the risk-free rate. Such a security would lower the risk of the portfolio.

defined earlier.[27] As can be seen, the greater the beta of a security, the greater the risk and the greater the expected return that is required. By the same token, the lower the beta, the lower the risk, the more valuable it becomes, and the lower the expected return that is required.

Thus, in market equilibrium the capital-asset pricing model implies an expected return-risk relationship for all individual securities. The risk an investor associates with realizing a stream of expected future dividends depends upon the correlation of that stream with expected dividend streams available from other securities in the market. The risk of an individual security to him is the marginal effect it has on the dispersion of the distribution of possible portfolio returns. Although the model is framed in terms of certain simplifying assumptions, this basic conclusion and the concept of market equilibrium hold when such assumptions are relaxed.

IMPLICATIONS FOR THE VALUATION OF THE FIRM

Our purpose in this chapter has been to explore some of the foundations of valuation in a market context. No claim is made that the treatment is complete. However, the concepts discussed give us the background necessary to explore more fully the valuation implications of decisions by the individual firm. As we have seen, value depends not only upon the security, or firm, itself but upon other securities available for investment. By analyzing decisions in relation to their likely effect on expected return and systematic risk, one is able to judge their effect on valuation. According to the presentation so far, unsystematic or risk unique to the firm is not important because it can be diversified away.

In keeping with the capital-asset pricing model and the separation theorem which follows, we are able to make certain generalizations about the valuation of a firm without having to determine directly the risk preferences of investors. If we assume that management wishes to act in the best interests of the owners of the firm, it will attempt to maximize the market value of the stock. Recall from Chapter 2 that the market value per share could be expressed as the present value of the stream of expected future dividends:

$$P_0 = \sum_{t=1}^{\infty} \frac{D_t}{(1 + k)^t} \tag{3-15}$$

[27] The expected return can also be expressed as $\bar{R}_j = i + \left(\dfrac{\bar{R}_m - i}{\sigma_m^2}\right)(r_{jm}\sigma_j\sigma_m)$ where σ_m^2 is the variance of the probability distribution of possible returns for the market portfolio, and $(r_{jm}\sigma_j\sigma_m)$ is the covariance of returns for security j with those of the market portfolio. We see then that $\beta_j = (r_{jm}\sigma_j\sigma_m)/\sigma_m^2 = (r_{jm}\sigma_j)/\sigma_m$, where r_{jm} is the correlation coefficient between excess returns for security j and those of the market, and σ_j is the standard deviation of the probability distribution of possible returns for security j.

where P_0 is the market price per share at time 0, D_t is the expected dividend at the end of period t, and k is the required rate of return. The capital-asset pricing model approach allows us to determine the appropriate discount rate to employ in discounting expected dividends to their present value. The rate used will be the risk-free rate plus a premium sufficient to compensate for the systematic risk associated with the expected dividend stream.[28] The greater the systematic risk, of course, the greater the risk premium and the return required, and the lower the value of the stock, all other things the same. Thus, the discussion in this chapter has been pointed toward determining required rates of return for individual securities.

Seemingly, all decisions of the firm should be judged in a market context using the capital-asset pricing model. Recall, however, that the model presented has a number of simplifying assumptions. Some of these do not hold in the real world. To the extent that they do not, unique or unsystematic risk may become a factor affecting valuation. Indeed, a good portion of our discussion in Parts II and III is devoted to exploring market imperfections that make unique risk a factor of importance.

Nonetheless, the capital-asset pricing model serves as a useful framework for evaluating financial decisions. The basic tenets of the model hold even when assumptions are relaxed to reflect real-world conditions. Given that investors tend to be risk-averse, a positive tradeoff exists between risk and expected return for efficient portfolios. Moreover, expected returns for individual securities should bear a positive relationship to their marginal contributions of risk to the market portfolio (i.e., systematic risk).[29] In the ensuing chapters, we will make frequent references to the capital-asset pricing model. Let us turn now to modifying some of the assumptions, which also shall occupy our attention in later chapters.

RELAXING ASSUMPTIONS IN THE MODEL

In this section, we examine briefly the effect of relaxing some of the earlier assumptions of the capital-asset pricing model. The first is that the investor can both borrow and lend at the risk-free rate. Obviously, the investor can lend at this rate. If the borrowing rate is higher, however, an imperfection is introduced, and the capital market line is no longer linear throughout. As shown in Figure 3-9, it is straight through market portfolio M_l. This segment represents combinations of the risk-free asset and the market portfolio M_l. Because the borrowing rate is higher, another tangency point is introduced, namely M_b. The

[28] See Gerald A. Pogue and Kishore Lall, "Corporate Finance: An Overview," *Sloan Management Review*, 15 (Spring 1974), 26.
[29] See Fama and Miller, *Theory of Finance*, p. 295.

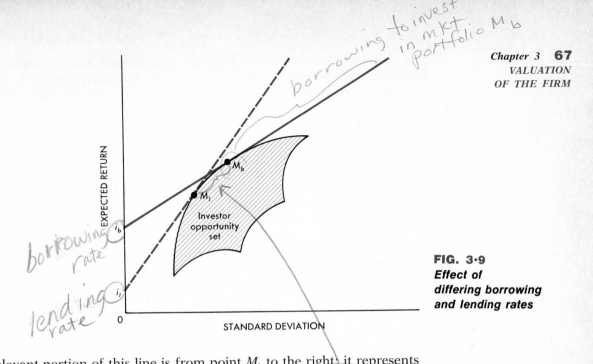

borrowing to invest in mkt. portfolio M_b

borrowing rate

lending rate

FIG. 3·9
Effect of differing borrowing and lending rates

relevant portion of this line is from point M_b to the right; it represents borrowing to invest in the market portfolio M_b. The segment of the capital market line between M_l and M_b is curved and is simply a portion of the efficient frontier of the opportunity set of risky securities. As is evident from the figure, the greater the spread between the borrowing and the lending rates, the greater the curved segment in the capital market line. Different borrowing rates for different investors complicates the picture even more because the equilibration process involves an interaction among investors.

Relaxation of another major assumption, homogeneous expectations, complicates the problem in a different way. With heterogeneous expectations, a complex blending of expectations, wealth, and utility preferences across individual investors emerges in the equilibrating process. In essence, each investor has his own capital market line. This complex equilibrating process has been examined by the author elsewhere and will not be presented here.[30] The principal implication is that precise generalizations are not possible; the overall capital market line becomes fuzzy. With only moderate heterogeneity in expectations, however, the basic tenets of the capital-asset pricing model still hold and rough estimates of the expected return-risk tradeoffs for portfolios and individual securities are possible. Still, the lack of precise description must be recognized.[31]

[30] Van Horne, *Function and Analysis of Capital Market Rates,* Chapter 3.

[31] Another assumption is that the probability distributions of possible returns on all portfolios are normal. As long as the distributions are close to symmetric, however, this condition is met in a practical sense.

Transaction costs also affect market equilibrium. The greater these costs, the less investors will undertake transactions to make their portfolios truly efficient. Rather than all portfolios being on the efficient frontier or capital market line, some may be on one side or the other because transaction costs more than offset the advantages of being right on the line. In other words, there may be bands on either side of the capital market line within which portfolios would lie. The greater the transaction costs, the wider the bands might be. Similarly, when securities are not infinitely divisible, as is the case in the real world, investors are able to achieve an efficient portfolio only up to the nearest share of stock or the nearest bond.

Another capital market imperfection is the differential tax on dividends and capital gains. This imperfection makes dividend-paying stocks less attractive than "capital gains" stocks, which pay little or no dividends, all other things the same. We will have much more to say about this imperfection in Chapter 11 when we discuss dividend policy. The last imperfection we consider is imperfections in information to investors. Recall that an assumption of perfect capital markets is that all information about a firm is instantaneously available to all investors without cost. To the extent that there are delays in and costs to information, there will be differing expectations among investors for this reason alone. The effect here is the same as that for heterogeneous expectations, which we discussed earlier.

In summary, the introduction of capital market imperfections and the relaxation of other assumptions complicates the generalizations possible with the capital-asset pricing model.[32] A number of authors have expanded the model by relaxing the major assumptions and have found the theory to be fairly robust even with such relaxation.[33] However, while the basic relationship between expected return and risk for individual securities holds, this relationship is not as clear or as exact as described previously. In general, the greater the imperfections, the more important the unique, or unsystematic, risk of the firm. Recall that the capital-asset pricing model assumes that this risk can be diversified away. If it cannot, certain implications of the model do not entirely hold. In the chapters that follow, we will analyze further these imperfections and how they affect the valuation of the firm as well as influence the decisions of the financial manager.

[32] For further discussion of the effects of relaxing these assumptions, see Archer and Francis, *Portfolio Analysis*, pp. 126–32; Jensen, "Capital Markets: Theory and Evidence," 373–91; and James C. T. Mao, "Security Pricing in an Imperfect Capital Market," *Journal of Financial and Quantitative Analysis*, 6 (September 1971), 1105–16.

[33] For a review of these studies, see Jensen, "Capital Markets: Theory and Evidence," 371–91. For empirical support of the major propositions of the capital-asset pricing model, see Eugene F. Fama and James D. MacBeth, "Risk, Return, and Equilibrium: Empirical Tests," *Journal of Political Economy*, 81 (May–June 1973), 607–36.

SUMMARY

Capital markets are said to be efficient when security prices fully reflect all available information. In such a market, security prices adjust very rapidly to new information. As a result, fluctuations in market prices around "intrinsic" values are essentially random. Empirical tests of market efficiency suggest that the market for stocks listed on the New York Stock Exchange is highly efficient. This assumption was the taproot from which other assumptions grew in the theoretical development of the chapter.

The risk of a portfolio of securities depends importantly upon the correlation of possible returns between securities in that portfolio. By diversifying one's holdings to include securities that are not perfectly correlated with each other, an investor can reduce risk relative to expected return. The investor will wish to hold that portfolio that results in the greatest utility. It is determined by the point of tangency between the opportunity set of portfolios of securities and the highest indifference curve. If a risk-free security exists, portfolio selection involves not only a portfolio of risky securities but also the risk-free asset.

The capital-asset pricing model allows us to draw certain implications about the expected return and risk of a specific security and about the valuation of the firm. The key assumptions in the model are that perfect capital markets exist and that investors have homogeneous expectations. In this context, the relevant risk of a security is the marginal effect it has on the risk of the market portfolio. In market equilibrium, the expected return of an individual security is the risk-free rate plus a linear function of the covariance of the security's return with that of the market. The greater the covariance, the greater the risk of the security and the greater the return that is required. The total risk of a security can be broken down into systematic and unsystematic components. Systematic risk is that risk that cannot be diversified away, for it affects all securities in the market. Unsystematic risk is unique to the particular security and can be eliminated in an efficiently diversified portfolio.

This notion was illustrated using an index model in which security returns are related to returns for a market index. For the well-diversified portfolio, the marginal risk of a security is the responsiveness of its return to changes in the market index. The capital-asset pricing model has a number of implications for the cost of capital of the firm and for the firm's investment in assets. We shall explore these implications in subsequent chapters as well as relax some of the assumptions of the model in order to evaluate the implications under real-world conditions.

$$(slope)$$
$$\bar{R}_j = i + \beta_j(\bar{R}_m - i)$$

1. Securities x and y are expected to provide the following returns under three different states of nature. Compute the correlation coefficient for the correlation between their returns.

State of Nature	Expected Return Security x	Expected Return Security y	Probability of State Occurring
Recession	−.05	.05	.2
Normal	.10	.07	.6
Boom	.21	.11	.2

2. Securities D, E, and F have the following characteristics with respect to expected return, standard deviation, and correlation between them:

			Correlation Coefficients		
	R	σ	D-E	D-F	E-F
Company D	.08	.02	.4	.6	
Company E	.15	.16	.4		.8
Company F	.12	.08		.6	.8

What is the expected value of return and standard deviation of a portfolio comprised of equal investments in each?

3. The securities of Companies A and B have the expected return and standard deviations given below; the expected correlation between the two stocks is 0.20.

	R	σ
Company A	.20	.20
Company B	.10	.03

(a) Compute the risk and return for the following portfolios:
    (1) 100 percent A
    (2) 100 percent B
    (3) 80 percent A—20 percent B
    (4) 80 percent B—20 percent A
    (5) 60 percent A—40 percent B
    (6) 60 percent B—40 percent A
    (7) 50 percent A—50 percent B

(b) Graph your results.

(c) Which of these portfolios is optimal? Why?

(d) Suppose that the investor could borrow or lend at 6 percent. How would this affect your graph?

4. The following portfolios are available in the market:

Portfolio	A	B	C	D	E
Expected return	.13	.05	.11	.15	.09
Standard deviation	.11	.02	.08	.15	.05

(a) Assume that you can invest in only one of these portfolios; that is, it is not possible to mix portfolios. Plot the risk-return tradeoff. Which portfolio do you prefer?

(b) Assume now that you are able to borrow and lend at a risk-free rate of 4 percent. Which portfolio is preferred? Would you borrow or lend at the risk-free rate to achieve a desired position? What is the effect of borrowing and lending on the expected value of return and upon the standard deviation?

5. In the context of the capital-asset pricing model, what is the expected return of security j if it has the following characteristics and if the following information holds for the market portfolio?

Standard deviation, security j	.20
Standard deviation, market portfolio	.15
Expected return, market portfolio	.10
Correlation between possible returns for security j and the market portfolio	.80
Risk-free rate	.04

(a) What would happen to the required return if the standard deviation of security j were higher?

(b) What would happen if the correlation coefficient were less?

(c) What is the functional relationship between the required return for a security and market risk?

6. The portfolio of Sal Sanchez consists of 30 percent of security x, 40 percent of y, and 30 percent of z. When the returns of these securities are compared historically with Standard & Poor's 500-stock index, it is found that the betas are $\beta_x = 1.43$, $\beta_y = 0.78$, and $\beta_z = 1.10$. Moreover, the standard deviations of the error terms for the three securities are $e_x = 0.22$, $e_y = 0.10$, and $e_z = 0.16$. The standard deviation of returns for the Standard & Poor's 500-stock index is 0.15. Determine the responsiveness of Mr. Sanchez's overall portfolio to the Standard & Poor's index and also compute the standard deviation of returns for the portfolio.

7. What are the critical assumptions in the capital-asset pricing model? What are the implications of relaxing these assumptions?

SELECTED REFERENCES

Baesel, Jerome B., "On the Assessment of Risk: Some Further Considerations," *Journal of Finance,* 29 (December 1974), 1491–94.

Beaver, William H., "The Behavior of Security Prices and Its Implications for Research Methods," *Supplement to the Accounting Review* (1972), pp. 407–37.

Ben-Zion, Uri, and Sol S. Shalit, "Size Leverage, and Dividend Record as Determinants of Equity Risk," *Journal of Finance,* 30 (September 1975), 1015–26.

Blume, Marshall E., "Betas and Their Regression Tendencies," *Journal of Finance,* 30 (June 1975), 785–96.

———, "On the Assessment of Risk," *Journal of Finance,* 26 (March 1971), 1–10.

Blume, Marshall, and Irwin Friend. "A New Look at the Capital-Asset Pricing Model," *Journal of Finance,* 28 (March 1973), 19–34.

Brennan, M. J., "The Optimal Number of Securities in a Risky Asset Portfolio When There Are Fixed Costs of Transacting: Theory and Some Empirical Results," *Journal of Financial and Quantitative Analysis,"* 10 (September 1975), 483–96.

Downes, David, and Thomas Dyckman, "A Critical Look at the Efficient Market Empirical Research Literature as It Relates to Accounting," *Accounting Review,* 48 (April 1973), 300–17.

Elton, Edwin, and Martin J. Gruber, "Estimating the Dependence Structure of Share Prices—Implications for Portfolio Selection," *Journal of Finance,* 28 (December 1973), 1203–32.

———, *Finance as a Dynamic Process,* Chapter 5. Englewood Cliffs, N.J.: Prentice-Hall, 1975.

Evans, Jack, and Stephen H. Archer, "Diversification and the Reduction of Dispersion: An Empirical Analysis," *Journal of Finance,* 23 (December 1968), 761–67.

Fama, Eugene F., "Components of Investment Performance," *Journal of Finance,* 27 (June 1972), 551–67.

———, "Efficient Capital Markets: A Review of Theory and Empirical Work," *Journal of Finance,* 25 (May 1970), 383–417.

———, "Efficient Capital Markets: Restatement of the Theory," *Journal of Finance,* forthcoming.

———, "Multiperiod Consumption—Investment Decisions," *American Economic Review,* 60 (March 1970), 163–74.

———, "Risk, Return, and Equilibrium," *Journal of Political Economy,* 79 (January–February 1971), 30–55.

———, "Risk, Return, and Equilibrium: Some Clarifying Comments," *Journal of Finance,* 23 (March 1968), 29–40.

Fama, Eugene F., and James D. MacBeth, "Risk, Return, and Equilibrium: Empirical Tests," *Journal of Political Economy,* 81 (May–June 1973), 607–36.

Fama, Eugene F., and Merton H. Miller, *The Theory of Finance,* New York: Holt, Rinehart & Winston, 1972.

Francis, Jack Clark, "Intertemporal Differences in Systematic Stock Price Movements," *Journal of Financial and Quantitative Analysis,* 10 (June 1975), 205–20.

Hakansson, Nils H., "Capital Growth and the Mean-Variance Approach to Portfolio Selection," *Journal of Financial and Quantitative Analysis,* 6 (January 1971), 517–58.

Haley, Charles W., and Lawrence D. Schall, *The Theory of Financial Decisions,* Chapters 5–7. New York: McGraw-Hill, 1973.

Hamada, Robert S., "Portfolio Analysis, Market Equilibrium and Corporation Finance," *Journal of Finance,* 24 (March 1969), 13–32.

Hirshleifer, Jack, "Investment Decisions under Uncertainty: Applications of the State-Preference Approach," *Quarterly Journal of Economics,* 80 (May 1966), 252–77.

———, *Investment, Interest and Capital.* Englewood Cliffs, N.J.: Prentice-Hall, 1970.

Jensen, Michael C., "Capital Markets: Theory and Practice," *Bell Journal of Economics and Management Science,* 3 (Autumn 1972), 357–98.

———, "Risk, the Pricing of Capital Assets, and the Evaluation of Investment Portfolios," *Journal of Business,* 42 (April 1969), 167–247.

———, *Studies in the Theory of Capital Markets.* New York: Praeger, 1972.

Johnson, K. H. and D. S. Shannon, "A Note on Diversification and the Reduction of Dispersion," *Journal of Financial Economics,* 1 (December 1974), 365–72.

Klemkosky, Robert C., and John D. Martin, "The Adjustment of Beta Forecasts," *Journal of Finance,* 30 (September 1975), 1123–28.

Lev, Baruch, *Financial Statement Analysis.* Engelwood Cliffs, N.J.: Prentice-Hall, 1974.

Levy, Robert A., "On the Short Term Stationarity of Beta Coefficients," *Financial Analysts Journal,* 27 (November–December 1971), 55–62.

Lintner, John, "Security Prices, Risk and Maximal Gains from Diversification," *Journal of Finance,* 20 (December 1965), 587–616.

———, "The Aggregation of Investors' Judgments and Preferences in Purely Competitive Security Markets," *Journal of Financial and Quantitative Analysis,* 4 (December 1969), 347–400.

———, "The Market Price of Risk, Size of Market and

Investor's Risk-Aversion," *Review of Economics and Statistics,* 52 (February 1970), 87–99.

Litzenberger, Robert H., and Alan P. Budd, "Corporate Investment Criteria and the Valuation of Risk Assets," *Journal of Financial and Quantitative Analysis,* 5 (December 1970), 395–420.

Lorie, James H., and Mary T. Hamilton, *The Stock Market.* Homewood, Ill.: Richard D. Irwin, 1973.

McDonald, John C., "Investment Objectives, Diversification, Risk and Exposure to Surprise," *Financial Analysts Journal,* 32 (March–April 1975), 42–49.

Mayers, David, "Nonmarketable Assets and the Determination of Capital Asset Prices in the Absence of a Riskless Asset," *Journal of Business,* 46 (April 1973), 258–67.

Mao, James C. T., "Security Pricing in an Imperfect Capital Market," *Journal of Financial and Quantitative Analysis,* 6 (September 1971), 1105–16.

Merton, Robert C., "Theory of Finance from the Perspective of Continuous Time," *Journal of Financial and Quantitative Analysis,* 10 (November 1975), 659–74.

Modigliani, Franco, and Gerald A. Pogue, "An Introduction to Risk and Return," *Financial Analysts Journal,* 30 (March–April 1974), 68–80, and (May–June 1974), 69–86.

Mossin, Jan., *Theory of Financial Markets.* Englewood Cliffs, N.J.: Prentice-Hall, 1973.

Myers, Stewart C., "A Time-State Preference Model of Security Valuation," *Journal of Financial and Quantitative Analysis,* 3 (March 1968), 1–34.

———, "The Application of Finance Theory to Public Utility Rate Cases," *Bell Journal of Economics and Management Science,* 3 (Spring 1972), 58–97.

Pettit, R. Richardson, and Randolph Westerfield, "Using the Capital Asset Pricing Model and the Market Model to Predict Security Returns," *Journal of Financial and Quantitative Analysis,* 9 (September 1974), 579–606.

Pogue, G. A., "An Extension of the Markowitz Portfolio Selection Model to Include Variable Transactions Costs, Short Sales, Leverage Policies and Taxes," *Journal of Finance,* 25 (December 1970), 1005–27.

Pogue, Gerald A., and Kishore Lall, "Corporate Finance: An Overview," *Sloan Management Review,* 15 (Spring 1974), 19–38.

Rubinstein, Mark, "Securities Market Efficiency in an Arrow-Debreu Economy," *American Economic Review,* 65 (December 1975), 812–24.

Seelenfreund, Alan, George G. C. Parker and James C. Van Horne, "Stock Price Behavior and Trading," *Journal of Financial and Quantitative Analysis,* 3 (September 1968), 263–82.

Sharpe, William F., "A Simplified Model for Portfolio Analysis," *Management Science,* 10 (January 1963), 277–93.

———, "Capital Asset Prices: A Theory of Market Equilibrium under Conditions of Risk," *Journal of Finance,* 19 (September 1964), 425–42.

———, "Efficient Capital Markets with Risk," Research Paper No. 71, Stanford Graduate School of Business, 1972.

———, *Portfolio Analysis and Capital Markets.* New York: McGraw-Hill, 1970.

Sharpe, William F., and Guy M. Cooper, "Risk-Return Classes of New York Stock Exchange Common Stocks," *Financial Analysts Journal,* 28 (March–April 1972), 46–54.

Tobin, James, "Liquidity Preference as Behavior Towards Risk," *Review of Economic Studies,* 25 (February 1958), 65–86.

Van Horne, James C., *The Function and Analysis of Capital Market Rates.* Englewood Cliffs, N.J.: Prentice-Hall, 1970.

INVESTMENT in ASSETS and REQUIRED RETURNS

PRINCIPLES
of
CAPITAL
INVESTMENT

Capital investment involves a current cash outlay in the anticipation of benefits to be realized in the future. In keeping with our discussion in Chapters 2 and 3, an investment proposal should be judged in relation to whether it provides a return equal to or greater than that required by investors. Thus, the required return is the link by which we relate the effect of an investment decision to share price. Much of our analysis of how investment projects affect share price draws heavily upon the valuation concepts presented in Chapters 2 and 3. Although our objective in the subsequent five chapters is to come to grips with this issue, we first must take up certain fundamental concepts and that is the purpose of this chapter. To simplify the presentation of these basics, we assume for now that the required rate of return on investment projects is given and is the same for all projects. This assumption necessitates our holding constant the financing and dividend decisions of the firm. Moreover, it implies that the selection of any investment project or combination of projects does not alter the business-risk complexion of the firm as perceived by suppliers of capital.

In the next two chapters, we relax this assumption and allow for the fact that different projects have different degrees of business risk. Consequently, the selection of an investment project may affect the business-risk complexion of the firm, which, in turn, may affect the required rate of return of investors and share price. In the same chapters, we consider ways to take account of risk for individual projects and external acquisitions. In addition, we take up the question of the divestiture of a portion of the enterprise within a capital-budgeting framework. In Chapters 7 and 8, we focus on the required rate of return for a project, for a division of a company, for the company as a whole, and for an acquisition. In these latter chapters, we go "full circle" in tying together the valuation concepts discussed earlier with the capital investment cash-flow information discussed in this and the next two chapters. In the end, we hope to arrive at a complete understanding of the information needed to evaluate capital investments and the appropriate acceptance criterion. It is important to stress, then, that certain facilitating assumptions imposed in this chapter subsequently will be relaxed once we have an understanding of the rudiments of capital budgeting.

RELEVANT INFORMATION

Capital budgeting involves the generation of investment proposals; the estimate of cash flows for the proposals; the evaluation of cash flows; the selection of projects based upon an acceptance criterion; and, finally, the continual reevaluation of investment projects after their acceptance. The first four are examined in this chapter, although the fourth is analyzed in much greater depth in Chapters 7 and 8. The last aspect, the continual reevaluation of existing projects, is taken up in Chapter 6 when we consider the question of divestiture.

Depending upon the firm involved, investment proposals can emanate from a variety of sources. For purposes of analysis, projects may be classified into one of five categories:

1. New products or expansion of existing products
2. Replacement of equipment or buildings
3. Research and development
4. Exploration
5. Others

The last category comprises miscellaneous items such as the expenditure of funds to comply with certain health standards or the acquisition of a pollution-control device. In the case of a new product, the proposal usually originates in the marketing department. On the other hand, a proposal to replace a piece of equipment with a more sophisticated model usually emanates from the production area of the firm. In each case, it is important to have efficient administrative procedures for channeling investment requests.

Most firms screen proposals at multiple levels of authority. For a proposal originating in the production area, the hierarchy of authority might run from section chiefs to (1) plant managers to (2) the vice-president for operations to (3) a capital-expenditures committee under the financial manager to (4) the president to (5) the board of directors. How high a proposal must go before it is finally approved usually depends upon its size. The greater the capital outlay, the greater the number of screens usually required. Plant managers, for example, may be able to approve moderate-sized projects on their own; but final approval for larger projects is received only at higher levels of authority. Because the administrative procedures for screening investment proposals vary greatly from firm to firm, it is not possible to generalize. The best procedure will depend upon the circumstances. Where projects are approved at multiple levels, it is very important that the same acceptance criterion be applied objectively and consistently throughout the organization.[1] Otherwise, capital is likely to be misallocated in the sense that one division might accept a project that another would reject.

[1] For surveys of the administrative practices of companies with respect to capital budgeting as well as of the evaluation techniques being used, see J. William Petty, David F. Scott, Jr., and Monroe M. Bird, "The Capital Expenditure Decision-Making Process of Large Corporations," *Engineering Economist*, 20 (Spring 1975), 159–72; and Thomas Klammer, "Empirical Evidence of the Adoption of Sophisticated Capital Budgeting Techniques," *Journal of Business*, 45 (July 1972), 387–97. See also James B. Weaver, "Organizing and Maintaining a Capital Expenditure Program," *Engineering Economist*, 20 (Fall 1974), 1–36, for a discussion of administrative procedures. Finally, for a discussion of the importance of a postcompletion audit as well as of its form, see James S. Schnell and Roy S. Nicolosi, "Capital Expenditure Feedback: Project Reappraisal," *Engineering Economist*, 19 (Summer 1974), 253–61.

ESTIMATING CASH FLOWS

*cash,
not
income!*

One of the most important tasks in capital budgeting is estimating future cash flows for a project. The final results we obtain are really only as good as the accuracy of our estimates. The reason we express the benefits expected to be derived from a project in terms of cash flows rather than in terms of income is that cash is what is central to all decisions of the firm. The firm invests cash now in the hope of receiving cash returns in a greater amount in the future. Only cash receipts can be reinvested in the firm or paid to stockholders in the form of dividends.[2] Thus, cash, not income, is what is important in capital budgeting.

For each investment proposal, we need to provide information on expected future cash flows on an after-tax basis. In addition, the information must be provided on an incremental basis so that we analyze only the difference between the cash flows of the firm with and without the project. For example, if a firm contemplates a new product that is likely to compete with existing products, it is not appropriate to express cash flows in terms of the estimated sales of the new product. We must take into account that there probably will be some "cannibalization" of existing products and make our cash-flow estimates on the basis of incremental sales.

To illustrate the information needed for a capital-budgeting decision, consider the following situation. Suppose a firm is considering the introduction of a new product. In order to launch the product, it will need to spend $150,000 for special equipment and the initial advertising campaign. The marketing department envisions the product life to be six years and expects incremental sales revenue to be:

cash inflows:

Year 1	Year 2	Year 3	Year 4	Year 5	Year 6
$60,000	$120,000	$160,000	$180,000	$110,000	$50,000

Cash outflows include labor and maintenance costs, material costs, and various other expenses associated with the product. As with sales, these costs must be estimated on an incremental basis. In addition to these outflows, the firm will need to pay higher taxes if the new product generates higher profits; and this incremental outlay must be included. Suppose that on the basis of these considerations the firm estimates total incremental cash outflows to be:

[2] See D. E. Peterson, *A Quantitative Framework for Financial Management* (Homewood, Ill.: Richard D. Irwin, 1969), p. 335.

Cash outflows:

Year 1	Year 2	Year 3	Year 4	Year 5	Year 6
$40,000	$70,000	$100,000	$100,000	$70,000	$40,000

Because depreciation is a noncash expense, it is not included in these outflows. The expected net cash flows from the project are:

	Initial Cost	Year 1	Year 2	Year 3	Year 4	Year 5	Year 6
Cash inflows		$60,000	$120,000	$160,000	$180,000	$110,000	$50,000
Cash outflows	$150,000	40,000	70,000	100,000	100,000	70,000	40,000
Net cash flows	−$150,000	$20,000	$ 50,000	$ 60,000	$ 80,000	$ 40,000	$10,000

Thus, for an initial cash outflow of $150,000, the firm expects to generate net cash flows of $20,000, $50,000, $60,000, $80,000, $40,000, and $10,000 over the next six years. These cash flows represent the relevant information we need in order to judge the attractiveness of the project.

To go to a somewhat more complicated replacement-decision example, suppose that we are considering the purchase of a turret lathe to replace an old lathe and that we need to obtain cash-flow information in order to evaluate the attractiveness of this project. The purchase price of the new machine is $18,500; and it will require an additional $1,500 to install, bringing the total cost to $20,000. The old machine can be sold for its depreciated book value of $2,000. The initial net cash outflow for the investment project, therefore, is $18,000. The new machine is expected to cut labor and maintenance costs and effect other cash savings totaling $7,600 a year before taxes for the next five years, after which it is not expected to provide any savings, nor is it expected to have a salvage value. These savings represent the net savings to the firm if it replaces the old machine with the new. In other words, we are concerned with the difference between the cash flows resulting from the two alternatives—continuing with the old machine or replacing it with a new one.

Because machines of this sort have useful lives in excess of one year, their cost cannot be charged against income for tax purposes but must be depreciated over the depreciable life of the asset. Depreciation then is deducted from income in order to compute taxable income. If the firm employs straight-line depreciation, the annual depreciation charge is 20 percent of the total depreciable cost of $20,000, or $4,000 a year. Assume additionally that the corporate federal income tax rate is 50 percent. Moreover, assume that the old machine has a remaining depreciable life of five years, that there is no expected salvage value at the end of this time, and that the machine also is subject to straight-line depreciation. Thus, the annual depreciation charge on the old machine is 20 percent of its depreciated book value of $2,000, or $400 a year. Because we are interested in the incremental impact of the project, we must subtract depreciation charges on the old machine from depreciation charges on the new one to obtain the incremental depreciation charges associated with the project. Given the information cited, we now are able to calculate the expected net cash flow (after taxes) resulting from the acceptance of the project.

$\frac{2000}{5} = \$400$ depn

	Book Account	Cash-Flow Account
Annual cash savings	$7,600	$7,600
Depreciation on new machine	4,000	
Less depreciation on old machine	– 400	
Additional depreciation charge	$3,600	
Additional income before taxes	4,000	
Income tax (50%)	2,000	2,000
Additional income after taxes	$2,000	
Annual net cash flow		$5,600

In figuring the net cash flow, we simply deduct the additional cash outlay for federal income taxes from the annual cash savings. The expected annual net cash inflow for this replacement proposal is $5,600 for each of the next five years; this figure compares with additional income after taxes of $2,000 a year. The cash flow and net profit figures differ by the amount of additional depreciation. As our concern is not with income, as such, but with cash flows, we are interested in the right-hand column. For an initial cash outlay of $18,000, then, we are able to replace an old lathe with a new one that is expected to result in net cash savings of $5,600 a year over the next five years. As in the previous example, the relevant cash-flow information for capital-budgeting purposes is expressed on an incremental, after-tax basis.

Efficient procedures must be set up to collect the information necessary for the capital-budgeting decision. This information must be standardized as much as possible for all investment proposals; otherwise, proposals cannot be compared objectively. We recognize the difficulty in quantifying expected cash flows for certain investment proposals. The returns on all investments, other than the U.S. Treasury securities held to maturity, are subject to varying degrees of uncertainty. In addition, projects proposed for safety or environmental reasons are difficult to quantify, often representing a constraint of what *must* be done as opposed to what *might* be done. Despite these problems, in most cases management must make some estimate of the probable outcome if it is to consider an investment proposal. These estimates can be subject to probability distributions; indeed, using probability distributions is desirable, as we shall see in Chapters 5 and 6. In this chapter, however, we work with the expected values of these estimates.

Once we have collected the necessary information, we are able to evaluate the attractiveness of the various investment proposals under consideration. Because our purpose in this chapter is to examine the basic concepts of capital budgeting, we assume that the risk or quality of all investment proposals under consideration does not differ from the risk of existing investment projects of the firm and that the acceptance of any proposal or group of investment proposals does not change the relative business risk of the firm. The investment decision will be either to accept or to reject the proposal. In this section, we evaluate four approaches to capital budgeting: the average-rate-of-return method; the payback method; the internal-rate-of-return method; and the net-present-value method. The first two represent approximate methods for assessing the economic worth of a project. For simplicity, we assume throughout that the expected cash flows are realized at the end of each year.

METHODS FOR EVALUATING EXPECTED PROFITABILITY

AVERAGE RATE OF RETURN

The average rate of return is an accounting method and represents the ratio of the average annual profits after taxes to the average investment in the project. In our first example, the average annual book earnings for the five-year period are $2,000; and the average net investment in the project, assuming straight-line depreciation, is $18,000/2, or $9,000. Therefore

$$\text{Average rate of return} = \frac{\$2,000}{\$9,000} = 22.22 \text{ percent} \qquad (4\text{-}1)$$

The average-rate-of-return method is sometimes based upon the original investment rather than upon the average investment. In the above example, the average rate of return would be $2,000/$18,000 = 11.11 percent under this version of the average-rate-of-return method.

The principal virtue of the average rate of return is its simplicity; it makes use of readily available accounting information. Once the average rate of return for a proposal has been calculated, it may be compared with a required, or cutoff, rate of return to determine if a particular proposal should be accepted or rejected. The principal shortcomings of

faults {

the method are that it is based upon accounting income rather than upon cash flows and that it fails to take account of the timing of cash inflows and outflows. The time value of money is ignored; benefits in the last year are valued the same as benefits in the first year.

Suppose that we have three investment proposals, each costing $9,000 and each having an economic and depreciable life of three years. Assume that these proposals are expected to provide the following book profits and cash flows over the next three years:

Period	Project A		Project B		Project C	
	Book Profit	Net Cash Flow	Book Profit	Net Cash Flow	Book Profit	Net Cash Flow
1	$3,000	$6,000	$2,000	$5,000	$1,000	$4,000
2	2,000	5,000	2,000	5,000	2,000	5,000
3	1,000	4,000	2,000	5,000	3,000	6,000

If straight-line depreciation is employed, each proposal will have the same average rate of return—$2,000/4,500, or 44.44 percent. However, few, if any, firms would regard the three projects as equally favorable. Most would prefer Project A, which provides a larger portion of total cash benefits in the first year. For this reason, the average rate of return leaves much to be desired as a method for project selection.

PAYBACK METHOD

The payback period of an investment project tells us the number of years required to recover our initial cash investment. It is the ratio of the initial fixed investment over the annual cash inflows for the recovery period. For our example,

$$\text{Payback period} = \frac{\$18,000}{\$5,600} = 3.2 \text{ years} \tag{4-2}$$

If the annual cash inflows are not equal, the job of calculation is somewhat more difficult. Suppose that annual cash inflows are $4,000 in the first year, $6,000 in the second and third years, and $4,000 in the fourth and fifth years. In the first three years, $16,000 of the original investment will be recovered, followed by $4,000 in the fourth year. With an initial cash investment of $18,000, the payback period is: 3 years + ($2,000/$4,000), or $3\frac{1}{2}$ years.

If the payback period calculated is less than some maximum acceptable payback period, the proposal is accepted; if not, it is rejected.

For example, if the required payback period is four years, the project in our example would be accepted. The major shortcoming of the payback method is that it fails to consider cash flows after the payback period; consequently, it cannot be regarded as a measure of profitability. Two proposals costing $10,000 each would have the same payback period if they both had annual net cash inflows of $5,000 in the first two years. However, one project might be expected to provide no cash flows after two years, while the other might be expected to provide cash flows of $5,000 in each of the next three years. Thus, the payback method can be very deceptive as a yardstick of profitability. In addition to this shortcoming, the method does not take account of the magnitude or timing of cash flows during the payback period; it considers only the recovery period as a whole.

Nevertheless, the payback method continues in use, frequently as a supplement to other, more sophisticated, methods. It does afford management limited insight into the risk and liquidity of a project. The shorter the payback period, supposedly, the less risky the project, and the greater its liquidity. The company that is cash poor may find the method to be very useful in gauging the early recovery of funds invested. There is some merit to its use in this regard, but the method does not take into account the dispersion of possible outcomes—only the magnitude and timing of the expected value of these outcomes relative to the original investment. Therefore, it cannot be considered an adequate indicator of risk. When the payback method is used, it is more appropriately treated as a constraint to be satisfied than as a profitability measure to be maximized.[3]

INTERNAL-RATE-OF-RETURN METHOD

Because of the various shortcomings in the average-rate-of-return and payback methods described above, it generally is felt that discounted cash-flow methods provide a more objective basis for evaluating and selecting investment projects. These methods take account of both the magnitude and the timing of expected cash flows in each period of a project's life. The two discounted cash-flow methods are the internal-rate-of-return and the present-value methods; the mechanics of these methods were described in Chapter 2. Recall that the internal rate of return for an investment proposal is the discount rate that equates the

---

[3] See H. Martin Weingartner, "Some New Views on the Payback Period and Capital Budgeting Decisions," *Management Science*, 15 (August 1969), 594–607. For a detailed analysis of the payback method and the accounting-rate-of-return method as approximations of the internal rate of return, see Marshall Sarnat and Haim Levy, "The Relationship of Rules of Thumb to the Internal Rate of Return: A Restatement and Generalization," *Journal of Finance*, 24 (June 1969), 479–89.

for every streams

IRR: initial outlay
discount annual cash flows
factor then look up % in Table A-2

present value of the expected cash outflows with the present value of the expected inflows. It is represented by that rate, r, such that

$$IRR: \quad \sum_{t=0}^{n} \left[\frac{A_t}{(1 + r)^t} \right] = 0 \qquad (4\text{-}3)$$

where A_t is the cash flow for period t, whether it be a net cash outflow or inflow, and n is the last period in which a cash flow is expected. If the initial cash outlay or cost occurs at time 0, Eq. (4-3) can be expressed as

$$A_0 = \frac{A_1}{(1 + r)} + \frac{A_2}{(1 + r)^2} + \cdots + \frac{A_n}{(1 + r)^n} \qquad (4\text{-}4)$$

IRR

Thus, r is the rate that discounts the stream of future cash flows—A_1 through A_n—to equal the initial outlay at time 0—A_0. For our example, the problem can be expressed as

$$18{,}000 = \frac{5{,}600}{(1 + r)} + \frac{5{,}600}{(1 + r)^2} + \frac{5{,}600}{(1 + r)^3} + \frac{5{,}600}{(1 + r)^4} + \frac{5{,}600}{(1 + r)^5} \qquad (4\text{-}5)$$

Solving for r either by means of a computer or by the manual method described in Chapter 2, we find the internal rate of return for the project to be 16.8 percent. When solving for r, it is important to recognize the possibility that there may be more than one internal rate of return that equates the present value of cash inflows with the present value of cash outflows. This can occur when there are net cash outflows in more than one period and the outflows are separated by one or more periods of net cash inflows. We examine the problem in Appendix A at the end of this chapter but should point out at this time that the existence of multiple internal rates of return is unusual. For the typical capital budgeting project a unique internal rate of return exists.

Acceptance criterion

The acceptance criterion generally employed with the internal-rate-of-return method is to compare the internal rate of return with a required rate of return, known also as the cutoff, or hurdle, rate. If the internal rate of return exceeds the required rate, the project is accepted; if not, it is rejected. For example, if the required rate of return were 10 percent and this criterion is used, the investment proposal considered above would be accepted. If the required rate of return is the return investors expect the firm to earn on the project, accepting a project with an internal rate of return in excess of the required rate of return should result in an increase in the market price of the stock, because the firm accepts a project with a return greater than that required to maintain the present market price per share. Much more will be said in Chapters 7 and 8 about relating the investment decision to the objective of the firm. We assume for now that the required rate of return is given.

PRESENT-VALUE METHOD

Like the internal-rate-of-return method, the present-value method is a discounted cash-flow approach to capital budgeting. With the present-value method, all cash flows are discounted to present value using the required rate of return. The net-present value of an investment proposal is

$$NPV = \sum_{t=0}^{n} \frac{A_t}{(1 + k)^t} \qquad (4\text{-}6)$$

where k is the required rate of return. If the sum of these discounted cash flows is equal to, or greater than, 0, the proposal is accepted; if not, it is rejected. Another way to express the acceptance criterion is to say that the project will be accepted if the present value of cash inflows exceeds the present value of cash outflows. The rationale behind the acceptance criterion is the same as that behind the internal-rate-of-return method. If the required rate of return is the return investors expect the firm to earn on the investment proposal, and the firm accepts a proposal with a net-present value greater than zero, the market price of the stock should rise. Again, the firm is taking on a project with a return greater than that necessary to leave the market price of the stock unchanged.

If we assume a required rate of return of 10 percent after taxes, the net-present value of our example problem is

$$NPV = -18{,}000 + \frac{5{,}600}{(1.10)} + \frac{5{,}600}{(1.10)^2} + \frac{5{,}600}{(1.10)^3} + \frac{5{,}600}{(1.10)^4} + \frac{5{,}600}{(1.10)^5}$$

$$= -18{,}000 + 21{,}228.48 = \$3{,}228.48 \qquad (4\text{-}7)$$

An easier way to solve this problem, of course, is by direct reference to Table A-2 in Appendix A at the end of the book, where we find the appropriate discount factor—3.7908—and multiply $5,600 by it to obtain $21,228.48. Subtracting the initial outlay of $18,000, we obtain $3,228.48. Inasmuch as the net-present value of this proposal is greater than 0, the proposal should be accepted, using the present-value method.

With the internal-rate-of-return method, we are given the cash flows and solve for the rate of discount that equates the present value of the cash inflows with the present value of the outflows. The internal rate of return is then compared with the required rate of return to determine whether the proposal should be accepted. With the present-value method, we are given the cash flows and the required rate of return and solve for the net-present value. The acceptability of the proposal is determined by whether the net-present value is equal to, or greater than, 0.

It is obvious that different net-present values will be given for different required rates of return. With a 10 percent required rate, the following cash-flow streams have equivalent net-present values—namely, $3,228:

	Cash Flows					
Years	**0**	**1**	**2**	**3**	**4**	**5**
Proposal 1	−$18,000	$5,600	$5,600	$5,600	$5,600	$5,600
Proposal 2	−18,797	4,000	5,000	6,000	7,000	8,000
Proposal 3	−16,446	7,000	6,000	5,000	4,000	3,000

However, with different required rates of return, the net-present values of the proposals are:

	Net-Present Value						
Discount Rate	**0%**	**4%**	**8%**	**10%**	**12%**	**16%**	**20%**
Proposal 1	$10,000	$6,930	$4,359	$3,228	$2,187	$336	−$1,253
Proposal 2	11,203	7,565	4,546	3,228	2,019	−114	−1,928
Proposal 3	8,554	6,162	4,131	3,228	2,390	888	−418

We see that the relative desirability of the proposals changes with changes in the discount rate. The higher the discount rate, the more valued is the proposal with early cash inflows, proposal 3. The lower the discount rate, the less important the timing of the cash flows and the more valued is the proposal with the greatest absolute amount of cash inflows, proposal 2. The example serves to illustrate the importance of the discount rate used in the calculations. Different answers will be given, depending upon the discount rate employed.

MUTUAL EXCLUSION
AND DEPENDENCY

In evaluating a group of investment proposals, it is important to determine whether the proposals are independent of each other. A proposal is said to be mutually exclusive if the acceptance of it precludes the acceptance of one or more other proposals. For example, if the firm is considering investment in one of two temperature-control systems, acceptance of one system will rule out acceptance of the other. Two mutually exclusive proposals cannot both be accepted.

A *contingent* or *dependent* proposal is one whose acceptance depends upon the acceptance of one or more other proposals. An example of a contingent proposal might be an investment in a large machine, which depends upon the construction of an addition to a plant. A combination of investment proposals containing a contingent proposal must contain the proposal(s) upon which it is dependent. When an investment proposal is not independent of all other proposals, this occurrence must be recognized and investment decisions made accordingly.

PROFITABILITY INDEX

The profitability index, or benefit-cost ratio, of a project is the present value of future net cash flows over the initial cash outlay. It can be expressed as

$$PI = \frac{\sum_{t=1}^{n} \dfrac{A_t}{(1 + k)^t}}{A_0} \tag{4-8}$$

For our example,

$$PI = \frac{\$21,228.48}{\$18,000.00} = 1.18 \tag{4-9}$$

[handwritten annotation: PV of future cash flows]

[handwritten annotation: initial cash investment]

As long as the profitability index is equal to or greater than 1.00, the investment proposal is acceptable. In calculating the profitability index, we compute the net rather than the aggregate index. The aggregate index is simply the present value of cash inflows over the present value of cash outflows. The reason we use the net index is that we wish to differentiate the initial cash outlay from subsequent cash outlays. The initial outlay is discretionary in the sense that the firm can choose to either commit funds to the project or to employ them elsewhere. Subsequent cash outflows are not discretionary in this sense; they are embodied in the system. The aggregate index does not differentiate between the cash outlay the firm has to put up initially and subsequent cash outlays.[4] For

[4] See Bernhard Schwab and Peter Lusztig, "A Comparative Analysis of the Net Present Value and the Benefit-Cost Ratio as Measures of the Economic Desirability of Investments," *Journal of Finance*, 24 (June 1969), 507–11.

this reason, the net profitability index is a more rational measure of profitability than is the aggregate index.

For any given project, the net-present-value method and the profitability index give the same accept-reject signals. If we must choose between mutually exclusive projects, however, the net-present-value measure is preferred because it expresses in absolute terms the expected economic contribution of the project. In contrast, the profitability index expresses only the relative profitability. To illustrate, consider the following mutually exclusive projects:

	Project A	*Project B*
Present value of net cash flows	$20,000	$8,000
Initial cash outlay	$15,000	$5,000
Net-present value	$ 5,000	$3,000
Profitability index	1.33	1.60

According to the net-present-value method, Project *A* would be preferred; whereas according to the profitability indexes, Project *B* would be preferred. Because the net-present value represents the expected economic contribution of a project, we should prefer *A* to *B*. Thus, the net-present-value method is the better of the two methods when we must choose between mutually exclusive projects that involve different initial cash outlays.

PRESENT-VALUE METHOD VERSUS INTERNAL-RATE-OF-RETURN METHOD

In general, the present-value and internal-rate-of-return methods lead to the same acceptance or rejection decision. In Figure 4-1, we illustrate graphically the two methods applied to a typical investment project. The figure shows the relationship between the net-present value of a project and the discount rate employed. When the discount rate is 0, net-present value is, simply, the total cash inflows less the total cash outflows of the project. Assuming that total inflows exceed total outflows and that outflows are followed by inflows, the typical project will have the highest net-present value when the discount rate is 0. As the discount rate increases, the present value of future cash inflows decreases relative to the present value of cash outflows.[5]

If the required rate of return is less than the internal rate of return, we would accept the project using either method. Suppose that the

---

[5] Again, we must recognize the possibility of multiple internal rates of return. See Appendix A at the end of this chapter.

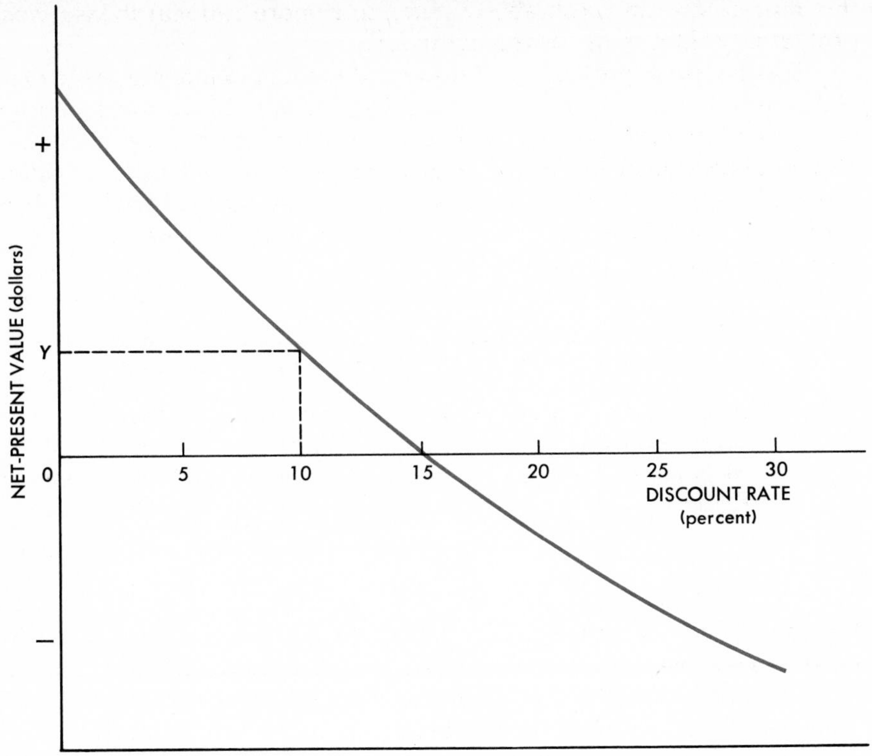

FIG. 4·1
Relation between
discount rate
and net-present value

required rate were 10 percent. As seen in Figure 4-1, the net-present value of the project then would be Y. Inasmuch as Y is greater than 0, we would accept the project using the present-value method. Similarly, we would accept the project using the internal-rate-of-return method because the internal rate exceeds the required rate. For required rates greater than the internal rate of return, we would reject the project under either method. Thus, we see that the internal-rate-of-return and present-value methods give us identical answers with respect to the acceptance or rejection of an investment project.

DIFFERENCES BETWEEN METHODS

However, important differences exist between the methods, and they must be recognized. When two investment proposals are mutually exclusive, so that we can select only one, the two methods may give contradictory results. To illustrate the nature of the problem, suppose a firm had two mutually exclusive investment proposals that were expected to generate the following cash flows:

Year	Cash Flows				
	0	1	2	3	4
Proposal A	−$23,616	$10,000	$10,000	$10,000	$10,000
Proposal B	−23,616	0	5,000	10,000	32,675

Internal rates of return for proposals A and B are 25 percent and 22 percent, respectively. If the required rate of return is 10 percent, however, and we use this figure as our discount rate, the net-present values of proposals A and B are $8,083 and $10,347, respectively. Thus, proposal A is preferred if we use the internal-rate-of-return method, whereas proposal B is preferred if we use the present-value method. If we can choose but one of these proposals, we obviously have a conflict:

Compounding rate The conflict between these two methods is due to differences in the implicit compounding of interest. The IRR method implies that funds are compounded at the internal rate of return. For proposal A, the assumption is that $23,616 invested at 25 percent will compound in such a way as to release $10,000 at the end of each of the next four years. The present-value method implies compounding at the required rate of return used as the discount rate. For proposal A, the assumption is that $8,083 plus $23,616 or $31,699 invested at 10 percent will compound in such a way as to release $10,000 at the end of each of the next four years. Since the proposal cost $23,616, its worth or present value is $31,699 minus this amount, or $8,083.

To illustrate further the nature of the problem, consider two additional mutually exclusive proposals with the following cash flows:

Time	Cash Flows			
	0	1	2	3
Proposal C	−$155.22	100.00	0	100.00
Proposal D	−155.22	0	0	221.00

The net-present value of each of these proposals is $10.82 if we assume a required rate of return of 10 percent. However, we would be indifferent

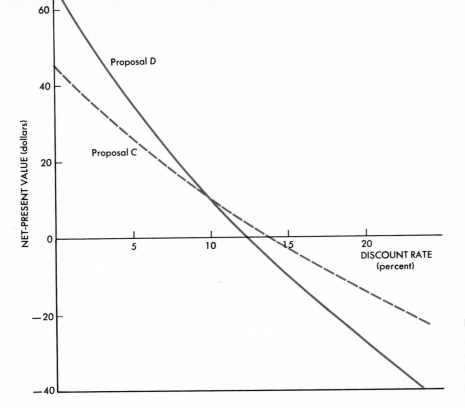

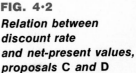

FIG. 4·2
*Relation between
discount rate
and net-present values,
proposals C and D*

between the two proposals only if the firm had opportunities for re-investment at a rate of 10 percent. More specifically, it must be able to realize a reinvestment rate of 10 percent through time 3 on the $100 cash inflow for proposal C at time 1. This concept is illustrated in Figure 4-2, where the functional relationship between net-present value and the discount rate is graphed for the two proposals. The intercepts on the 0 horizontal line represent the internal rates of return of the two proposals that equate their net-present values to 0. For proposal *C*, the internal rate of return is 14 percent; for proposal *D*, it is 12.5 percent. The intercepts on the vertical axis represent total cash inflows less total cash outflows for the two proposals, because the discount rate is 0. We see that proposal *D* ranks higher than proposal *C* if the required rate of return is below 10 percent and lower if it is above 10 percent. At the point of intersection, 10 percent, the proposals have identical net-present values. Given a marginal reinvestment rate of 10 percent, then, the two pro-posals would have equal ranking. For reinvestment rates other than this percentage, we would prefer one proposal to the other. In a similar manner, other mutually exclusive investment proposals can be evaluated according to the intersections.[6]

WHICH METHOD PROVIDES BETTER RESULTS?

The question to be answered is, Which method—the internal-rate-of-return method or the present-value method—is better for purposes of evaluating investment proposals? Actually, the question hinges upon what is the appropriate rate of reinvestment for the intermediate cash flows. The internal-rate-of-return method implies a reinvestment rate equal to the internal rate of return, whereas the present-value method implies a reinvestment rate equal to the required rate of return used as the discount factor. Perhaps the ideal solution would be to take the expected rate of reinvestment for each period and calculate a terminal value. However, this procedure involves additional computational steps that many do not feel to be worthwhile.

If a choice must be made, the present-value method generally is considered to be superior theoretically.[7] With the internal-rate-of-return method, the implied reinvestment rate will differ depending upon the cash-flow stream for each investment proposal under consideration. For proposals with a high internal rate of return, a high reinvestment rate is assumed; for proposals with a low internal rate of return, a low reinvestment rate is assumed. Only rarely will the internal rate of return calculated represent the relevant rate for reinvestment of intermediate cash flows. With the present-value method, however, the implied reinvestment rate—namely, the required rate of return—is the same for each proposal. In essence, this reinvestment rate represents the minimum return on opportunities available to the firm, given our assumptions. To the extent that we can regard the required rate of return, k, as an approximate measure of the opportunity rate for reinvestment, the present-value method is preferred over the internal-rate-of-return method.

However, the internal-rate-of-return method can be modified so that it involves an incremental type of analysis. When one is faced with two mutually exclusive investment proposals, both of whose internal rates of return exceed the required rate of return, the following additional steps could be undertaken:[8]

[6] Under certain circumstances, it is possible to have multiple intersections. Because these circumstances tend to be unusual, we will not go into an analysis of them. For further discussion, see J. Hirshleifer, "On the Theory of Optimal Investment Decision," *Journal of Political Economy*, 66 (August 1958), 95–103.

[7] Hirshleifer, "On the Theory of Optimal Investment Decision," pp. 95–103; and James H. Lorie and Leonard J. Savage, "Three Problems in Rationing Capital," *Journal of Business*, 28 (October 1955), 229–39.

[8] I am grateful to R. E. Kameros for suggesting this approach. See H. Martin Weingartner, "The Excess Present Value Index—A Theoretical Basis and Critique," *Journal of Accounting Research*, 1 (Autumn 1963), 213–24.

1. Calculate the differential cash flows between the two proposals.
2. If the internal rate of return on the differential cash flows exceeds the required rate of return, the project with the greater nondiscounted net cash flows should be selected.

To illustrate, consider again proposals *A* and *B* and the differential cash flows:

	Cash Flows				
Year	0	1	2	3	4
Proposal A	−$23,616	$10,000	$10,000	$10,000	$10,000
Proposal B	−23,616	0	5,000	10,000	32,675
B less A	0	−$10,000	−5,000	0	22,675

The internal rate of return that equates outflows of $10,000 and $5,000 at the end of years 1 and 2, respectively, with an inflow of $22,675 at the end of year 4 is 16.65 percent. Because this rate exceeds the required rate of return of 10 percent, proposal *B* should be selected, despite the fact that its internal rate of return is 22 percent compared with 25 percent for proposal *A*.

Thus, the internal-rate-of-return method can be modified to deal with the special case of mutually exclusive investment proposals. Given such a modification, it provides a decision identical to that given by the net-present-value method. Many financial managers feel that the internal rate of return is easier to visualize and to interpret than is the net-present-value measure. In addition, one does not have to specify a required rate of return in the calculations. To the extent that the required rate of return is but a rough estimate, the use of the internal-rate-of-return method may permit a more realistic comparison of projects. The principal shortcoming of the method is the possibility of multiple internal rates of return, a subject that we discuss in Appendix A at the end of this chapter.

CASH-FLOW INFORMATION REVISITED

In our replacement example, we assumed straight-line depreciation and no salvage value. For continuity, we then investigated the various methods for evaluating investment proposals, using this example as our illustration throughout. We need now to digress for a while in order to examine the effect of accelerated depreciation and of salvage value upon the cash flows. Recall that the replacement of the old machine with a new one was expected to result in annual cash savings of $7,600 a year over the next five years. Straight-line depreciation charges on the new

7600
- 3600
4000

machine were $4,000 a year; and when we subtracted $400 annual depreciation charges on the old machine, we obtained incremental depreciation charges of $3,600 a year. Thus, the additional income before taxes was $4,000, resulting in additional taxes of $2,000 a year, assuming a 50 percent tax rate. When this $2,000 outlay was subtracted from the $7,600 cash savings, the net cash inflow became $5,600 a year. Consider now the modification of the example occasioned by accelerated depreciation and salvage value.

ACCELERATED DEPRECIATION

Accelerated depreciation can be either the double-declining-balance method or the sum-of-the-years'-digits method. The formula for the double-declining-balance method is $2(1/n)$, or 2 divided by one over the depreciable life of the asset. In the case of a five-year depreciable life, the annual depreciation charge would be $2(1/5)$, or 40 percent of the depreciated book value balance at the beginning of the year. If the depreciable value were $10,000 initially, depreciation charges would be $4,000 in the first year, $2,400 in the second (40 percent of $10,000 − 4,000), and so on. A second method of accelerated depreciation is the sum-of-the-years'-digits method. Here, we add up each year of the depreciable life of the asset to obtain the denominator. In our case, the denominator is $1 + 2 + 3 + 4 + 5 = 15$. The numerator is the depreciable life for the first year, the depreciable life minus 1 for the second year, and so on. Thus, the first-year depreciation charge on an asset having a five-year depreciable life would be 5/15, followed by 4/15, 3/15, 2/15, and 1/15 for the remaining years. Given a depreciable value of $20,000 in our example and a five-year depreciable life, the annual depreciation charges for these accelerated methods are:

Year	Double-Declining Balance (40%)	Sum of the Years' Digits
1	$ 8,000.00	$ 6,666.67
2	4,800.00	5,333.33
3	2,880.00	4,000.00
4	1,728.00	2,666.67
5	2,592.00	1,333.33
	$20,000.00	$20,000.00

Note that for the first method, the firm is able to claim the full remaining depreciable value of the asset in the last year, rather than only 40 percent of it.

If the old machine were still depreciated on a straight-line basis of

$400 a year, the additional depreciation charge and annual net cash flow
for these two methods over the five-year period would be:

Chapter 4   **95**
*PRINCIPLES
OF CAPITAL
INVESTMENT*

Year	Double-Declining Balance (40%)		Sum of the Years' Digits	
	Additional Depreciation	Net Cash Flow	Additional Depreciation	Net Cash Flow
1	$7,600.00	$7,600.00	$6,266.67	$6,933.33
2	4,400.00	6,000.00	4,933.33	6,266.67
3	2,480.00	5,040.00	3,600.00	5,600.00
4	1,328.00	4,464.00	2,266.67	4,933.33
5	2,192.00	4,896.00	933.33	4,266.67

We see that the use of accelerated depreciation increases the depreciation charge in the early years of the project's life over what it would be
if straight-line depreciation were used, resulting in lower taxes and
higher cash flows in these years. The use of accelerated depreciation
changes the timing of cash flows from what they would be if straight-line
depreciation were used. If money does have a time value, accelerated
depreciation is advantageous to the firm. For example, the internal rate
of return using the double-declining-balance method is 18.7 percent,
compared with 16.8 percent when the straight-line method of depreciation is employed. The net-present value, assuming a required rate of
return of 10 percent, is $3,743.33 under the double-declining-balance
method, compared with $3,228.48 under the straight-line method. For the
sum-of-the-years'-digit method, the internal rate of return is 18.5 percent
and the net-present value, $3,708.30. Thus, the method of depreciation
affects the timing of cash flows and the resulting attractiveness of the
investment project. The total amount of taxes is not reduced with
accelerated depreciation; taxes simply are paid at a date later than
would be the case with straight-line depreciation.

SALVAGE VALUE AND TAXES

The cash-flow pattern also will differ from that shown in the example if the new machine is expected to have a salvage, or scrap, value at
the end of the five-year period. When there is a salvage value, it may
affect depreciation charges as well as the cash flow in the last year
Assume that the salvage value of the new machine is expected to be
$2,000 at the end of the fifth year. The total depreciable value becomes
$18,000 instead of $20,000; and, assuming straight-line depreciation,
annual depreciation charges for the new machine become $3,600 instead

of $4,000. If we follow through with the previous calculations, we find that the annual net cash flow for years 1 through 4 is $5,400 instead of $5,600. The net cash flow in the fifth year is $5,400, plus the salvage value of $2,000, or $7,400.

In addition to the salvage value, there are other tax considerations. If the machine can be sold for more than its depreciated book value, the difference is subject to income taxes if the sales price is less than the machine's original cost. For example, if the machine could be sold for $4,000 instead of $2,000, there would be a gain of $2,000. If the corporate tax rate were 50 percent, the total cash proceeds realized from the sale would be $3,000. As long as the gain is less than the total depreciation claimed, it is reported as fully taxable income. In our example, the machine cost $20,000 and $18,000 in depreciation is claimed through year 5. As the $2,000 gain is less than the total depreciation claimed, it is taxed at the ordinary corporate tax rate of 50 percent. If the machine could be sold for $23,000, however, $18,000 of the total gain of $21,000 would be reported as fully taxable income, while $3,000 would be subject to the capital gains tax treatment, which usually is more favorable.[9] There are many other variations that we could illustrate, but these examples are enough to show that tax considerations are very important in calculating the cash flow.

CAPITAL RATIONING

Capital rationing occurs anytime there is a budget ceiling, or constraint, on the amount of funds that can be invested during a specific period of time, such as a year. Such constraints are prevalent in a number of firms, particularly in those that have a policy of financing all capital expenditures internally. Another example of capital rationing is when a division of a large company is allowed to make capital expenditures only up to a specified budget ceiling, over which the division usually has no control. With a capital-rationing constraint, the firm attempts to select the combination of investment proposals that will provide the greatest profitability.

To illustrate, suppose a firm had the following investment opportunities, ranked in descending order of profitability indexes (the ratio of the present value of future net cash flows over the initial cash outlay):

Proposal	4	7	2	3	6	5	1
Profitability index	1.25	1.19	1.16	1.14	1.09	1.05	0.97
Initial outlay	$400,000	$100,000	$175,000	$125,000	$200,000	$100,000	$150,000

[9] See *Federal Tax Course* (Englewood Cliffs, N.J.: Prentice-Hall, 1975), Chapters 6 and 22.

If the budget ceiling for initial outlays during the present period were $1 million, and the proposals were independent of each other, we would select proposals in descending order of profitability until the budget was exhausted. With capital rationing, we would accept the first five proposals, totaling $1 million in initial outlays. In other words, we do not necessarily invest in all proposals that increase the net-present value of the firm; we invest in an acceptable proposal only if the budget constraint allows such an investment. In the above example, we do not invest in proposal 5, even though the profitability index in excess of 1 would suggest its acceptance. The critical aspect of the capital-rationing constraint illustrated is that capital expenditures during a period are strictly limited by the budget ceiling, regardless of the number of attractive investment opportunities.

SIZE OF INITIAL OUTLAY AND MULTIPERIOD PROBLEMS

Under capital rationing, the objective is to select the combination of investment proposals that provides the highest net-present value, subject to the budget constraint for the period. If this constraint is strictly enforced, it may be better to accept several smaller, less profitable proposals that allow full utilization of the budget than to accept one large proposal that results in part of the budget's being unused. Suppose that we had the following investment opportunities:

Proposal	3	1	2	4
Profitability index	1.15	1.13	1.11	1.08
Initial outlay	$200,000	$125,000	$175,000	$150,000

If the budget constraint were $300,000 for the period, we should accept proposals 1 and 2 rather than proposal 3, despite the fact that the profitability indexes are lower for the first two proposals. The total net-present value of proposals 1 and 2 is

$$\begin{aligned}
\text{Proposal 1} \quad &\$125,000(1.13 - 1) = \$16,250 \\
\text{Proposal 2} \quad &\$175,000(1.11 - 1) = \underline{\$19,250} \\
&\qquad\qquad\qquad\qquad\quad \$35,500
\end{aligned}$$

whereas the net-present value of proposal 3 is

$$\text{Proposal 3} \quad \$200,000(1.15 - 1) = \$30,000$$

The total net-present value of proposals 1 and 2 is higher than that of proposal 3 because we are able to use more of the available budget.

Thus, the "lumpiness" of the initial outlays makes full utilization of the budget an important consideration for the firm that rations capital. Implied in the evaluation above is that uninvested capital has a net-present value of 0; that is, it corresponds to an investment yielding the required rate of return. If the net-present value of uninvested capital is less, the full utilization of the budget becomes a more important consideration.

A fixed one-period constraint is highly artificial. Seldom will a budget be set so rigidly that it does not provide for some flexibility. In addition, the cost of certain investment projects may be spread over several years. Consequently, we must consider more than just a one-period constraint. With a multiperiod analysis, the postponement of investment proposals is possible. If there is an abundance of acceptable investment proposals this year, the least profitable may be postponed until a subsequent period when the budget will permit investment.

Moreover, a one-period analysis does not take account of intermediate cash flows generated by a project. Some projects provide relatively high net cash flows in the early years; these cash flows serve to reduce the budget constraints in the early years because they may be used to finance other investment projects. A project with net cash flows expected to occur entirely in the first several years may be more valuable to the firm than a project with an identical initial outlay and profitability index, but which is expected to produce net cash flows over a longer span of time. For the reason discussed above, we should consider more than one period in the allocation of limited capital to investment projects.

OPPORTUNITY COSTS AND OBJECTIONS TO CAPITAL RATIONING

The cost to the firm of a budget ceiling might be regarded as the opportunity foregone on the next most profitable investment after the cutoff. In our first example, the opportunity foregone by the $1 million budget ceiling is proposal 5, which has a profitability index of 1.05. Though all cash flows are discounted at the required rate of return, we do not necessarily accept proposals that provide positive net-present values. Acceptance is determined by the budget constraint, which tells us which proposals can be accepted before the budget is exhausted. To be sure, the required rate of return sets a lower limit; we would not accept proposals yielding less than this required rate even if the budget were not exhausted.[10] However, we may reject projects that provide

---

[10] The exception is contingent projects, as illustrated earlier.

positive net-present values, as was shown with proposal 5. Under capital rationing, the required rate of return is not the acceptance criterion. Should it then be used as the discount rate in present-value calculations, or should the opportunity cost be used? The implied discount rate in any budget period is the yield foregone on the most profitable investment opportunity rejected, or the required rate of return, whichever is the higher.[11]

Capital rationing usually results in an investment policy that is less than optimal. In some periods, the firm accepts projects down to its required rate of return; in others, it may reject projects that would provide returns substantially in excess of the required rate. If the required rate of return corresponds to the project's cost of capital, and the firm actually can raise capital at that approximate real cost, should it not invest in all projects yielding more than the required rate of return? If it rations capital and does not invest in all projects yielding more than the required rate, is it not foregoing opportunities that would enhance the market price of its stock?

In the final analysis, the firm should accept all proposals yielding more than their costs of capital. By so doing, it should increase the market price per share because projects are accepted that will provide a return higher than that necessary to maintain the present market price per share. Certainly, there are circumstances that complicate the use of this rule. However, in general, this policy should tend to maximize the market price of the stock over the long run. If capital is rationed, and projects are rejected that would yield more than their real cost of capital, the firm's investment policy, by definition, is less than optimal. Management could increase the value of the firm to the shareholders by accepting these projects.

---

[11] In a mathematical programming approach, the opportunity rate for investment corresponds to the dual variable. Thus, the discount rate depends upon the optimal solution, which in turn depends upon the discount rate employed. For an analysis of this problem of mutual dependence and various proposals for its resolution or lack of resolution, see William J. Baumol and Richard E. Quandt, "Investment and Discount Rates under Capital Rationing—A Programming Approach," *Economic Journal,* 75 (June 1965), 317–29; H. Martin Weingartner, "Criteria for Programming Investment Project Selection," *Journal of Industrial Economics,* 15 (November 1966), 65–76; Peter Lustzig and Bernhard Schwab, "A Note on the Application of Linear Programming to Capital Budgeting," *Journal of Financial and Quantitative Analysis,* 3 (December 1968), 427–31; and Willard T. Carleton, "Linear Programming and Capital Budgeting Models: A New Interpretation," *Journal of Finance,* 24 (December 1969), 825–33. See also Edwin J. Elton, "Capital Rationing and External Discount Rates," *Journal of Finance,* 25 (June 1970), 573–84; Stewart C. Myers, "A Note on Linear Programming and Capital Budgeting," *Journal of Finance,* 27 (March 1972), 89–92; Charles W. Haley and Lawrence D. Schall, "A Note on Investment Policy with Imperfect Capital Markets," *Journal of Finance,* 27 (March 1972), 93–96; and R. M. Burton and W. W. Damon, "On the Existence of a Cost of Capital under Pure Capital Rationing," *Journal of Finance,* 29 (September 1974), 1165–73.

Mathematical programming can be used to allocate capital under conditions of capital rationing.[12] The most comprehensive treatment of the problem has been by Weingartner.[13] His basic model, which uses the Lorie-Savage problem as a point of departure, may be expressed as

Maximize
$$\sum_{j=1}^{n} b_j x_j$$

Subject to
$$\sum_{j=1}^{n} c_{tj} x_j \leq C_t \qquad \text{(4-10)}$$

$$0 \leq x_j \leq 1$$

where b_j is net-present value of investment proposal j, x_j is an amount between 0 and 1, c_{tj} is the net cash outlay required for proposal j in period t, and C_t is the budget constant in period t. In words, the model maximizes the net-present value from currently available investment proposals, given the budget constraint in each period.

To illustrate, consider the Lorie-Savage example, which involves budget constraints for two periods.[14] This example was employed by Weingartner, and it is shown in Table 4-1. The present values of the two budget constraints are $50 in period 1 and $20 in period 2. If the projects under consideration are independent, Eq. (4-10) can be expressed as

Maximize
$$14x_1 + 17x_2 + 17x_3 + 15x_4 + 40x_5 + 12x_6 + 14x_7 + 10x_8 + 12x_9 \quad \text{(4-11)}$$
Subject to
$$12x_1 + 54x_2 + 6x_3 + 6x_4 + 30x_5 + 6x_6 + 48x_7 + 36x_8 + 18x_9 \leq 50$$
$$3x_1 + 7x_2 + 6x_3 + 2x_4 + 35x_5 + 6x_6 + 4x_7 + 3x_8 + 3x_9 \leq 20$$
$$0 \leq x_j \leq 1, \ (x_j = 1, \dots, 9)$$

The solution of this problem is shown in Table 4-2.[15] From the table we see that, under the direct-problem variables, we should invest to the extent of 100 percent in projects 1, 3, 4, and 9; 97 percent in project 6; and 4.5 percent in project 7. Substituting these values into the objective function of Eq. (4-11), the increase in present value from this optimal solution is found to be $70.27.

Weingartner analyzes the dual variables as the opportunity costs, or

[12] This section supposes a familiarity with mathematical programming. It should be omitted if the reader does not have such familiarity.

[13] H. Martin Weingartner, *Mathematical Programming and the Analysis of Capital Budgeting Problems.* Copyright © H. Martin Weingartner, 1963.

[14] Lorie and Savage, "Three Problems in Rationing Capital," pp. 229–39.

[15] Weingartner, *Mathematical Programming*, p. 18.

Table 4·1   Investment proposals available

Investment Project	Present Value of Outlay, Period 1	Present Value of Outlay, Period 2	Present Value of Investment
1	$12	$ 3	$14
2	54	7	17
3	6	6	17
4	6	2	15
5	30	35	40
6	6	6	12
7	48	4	14
8	36	3	10
9	18	3	12

Source: Lorie and Savage, "Three Problems in Rationing Capital."

"shadow prices," of the budget constraints for the various future periods. These variables tell us the present value that can be gained if a budget constraint is relaxed by $1.[16] For example, the dual variable of 0.136 for period 1 indicates that present value can be increased by $0.136 if the budget in period 1 is increased from $50 to $51; while the dual variable of 1.864 for period 2 indicates that present value can be increased by $1.864 if the budget is increased from $20 to $21. Dual variables are valuable in deciding whether to shift funds from one period to another and in evaluating the desirability and timing of external financing.

Table 4·2   Optimal values for example problem

Direct	$X_1 = 1.0$	$X_2 = 0$	$X_3 = 1.0$	$X_4 = 1.0$	$X_5 = 0$	$X_6 = 0.97$	$X_7 = 0.045$	$X_8 = 0$	$X_9 = 1.0$
Dual*	$W_1 = 0.136$	$W_2 = 1.864$							

* W_1 and W_2 are the dual variables for the budget constraints in periods 1 and 2. The dual variables for the constraints, $0 \leq x_j \leq 1$, are not shown.

EXTENSIONS AND MODIFICATIONS

We note in this example problem that the investment projects are divisible in the sense that a partial undertaking of an investment proposal is possible. In the optimal program, both projects 6 and 7 were fractional. However, most investment projects are not divisible; they are either accepted, whereupon an absolute amount is invested, or rejected, in which case investment is 0. To deal with this problem, Weingartner develops an integer programming model by requiring the x_j to be an integer of either 0 or 1. Thus, fractional investment in a proposal is

[16] For a more detailed analysis of dual variables, see the appendix to Chapter 18.

precluded by virtue of the fact that the x_j is an "either/or" variable. For the example problem, the optimal solution using integer programming calls for accepting projects 1, 3, 4, 6, and 9. When compared with Table 4-2, we see that the solutions are quite similar.

The model can also be modified to take account of mutually exclusive and contingent projects. If investment projects 1, 4, and 5 were mutually exclusive, for example, we could simply add the constraint, $x_1 + x_4 + x_5 \leq 1$. With integer programming and this constraint, we are assured that only one of these projects will appear in the final solution. If project 2 is contingent upon the acceptance of project 3, the constraint, $x_2 \leq x_3$, would assure that this contingency was recognized in the solution.

In addition, the model can be extended to handle manpower and other constraints of this type.[17] For a labor constraint

$$\sum_{j=1}^{n} d_{jt}x_j \leq L_t \qquad (4\text{-}12)$$

where d_{jt} is the number of man-hours of a certain type labor input required for project j in period t; and L_t is the number of such hours available in that period. Restrictions for other scarce resources also can be formulated in this manner. Moreover, the model can be expanded to allow for liquidity requirements in various periods and for the reinvestment of intermediate cash flows from one investment project into other projects. The model also can be adapted to situations of borrowing funds in the external market, subject to certain constraints. For the deterministic case, then, the integer programming technique can be realistically adapted to many "real-world" constraints.

LIMITATIONS

The principal difficulty of mathematical programming approaches to capital budgeting, however, is that they are based upon the assumption that all future investment opportunities are known. In reality, the generation of investment opportunities is an unfolding process. Consequently, the budget constraints for other than the earliest years are not likely to be binding. There simply are not enough known investment opportunities. Only as new investment proposals are generated are these budgets likely to be fully utilized. Therefore, the selection process must

---

[17] See Weingartner, *Mathematical Programming*, Chapters 7–9. For an additional illustration, see G. David Quirin, *The Capital Expenditure Decision* (Homewood, Ill.: Richard D. Irwin, 1967), pp. 185–97.

be revised continually. As new proposals are generated, they should be evaluated on a consistent basis.

Most programming approaches for capital budgeting do not allow for uncertainty in the cash-flow estimates. Attempts have been made to introduce probabilistic concepts through chance constraint programming. With chance constraints, lower levels of cash flows must be satisfied with some minimum probability. It is possible also to specify chance constraints for the net-present value of a combination of investment projects.[18] Overall, the treatment of uncertainty in this manner has not been particularly satisfactory, primarily because of the lack of realism.[19] More encompassing results with respect to the full range of possible outcomes can be achieved with simulation. Another problem is the assumption of capital rationing and the resulting issue of investment decisions that are less than optimal. This issue was discussed earlier in the chapter. Despite these limitations, however, mathematical programming provides a systematic and comprehensive means for screening investment projects.

[18] See Peterson, *Quantitative Framework for Financial Management*, pp. 459–77.

[19] For an extensive review of such issues, see Richard H. Bernhard, "Mathematical Programming Models for Capital Budgeting—A Survey, Generalization, and Critique," *Journal of Financial and Quantitative Analysis*, 4 (June 1969), 111–58. See also H. Russell Fogler, "Ranking Techniques and Capital Budgeting," *Accounting Review*, 47 (January 1972), 134–43.

SUMMARY

In this chapter, we have examined various methods of capital budgeting, concentrating in particular on the internal-rate-of-return and present-value methods. An important topic taken up initially was the collection of the cash-flow information essential for the evaluation of investment proposals. Capital-budgeting methods, including the average-rate-of-return and payback methods, were evaluated under the assumption that the acceptance of any investment proposal does not change the business-risk complexion of the firm as perceived by suppliers of capital. It was shown that the two discounted cash-flow methods—internal rate of return and net-present value—were the only appropriate means by which to judge the economic contribution of an investment proposal.

The important distinction between the internal-rate-of-return method and the present-value method is the implied compounding rate. Depending upon the situation, contrary answers can be given with respect to the acceptance of mutually exclusive investment proposals. On theoretical grounds, a case can be made for the superiority of the present-value method. The problem of capital rationing was examined, and we concluded that such a policy is likely to result in investment decisions that are less than optimal. With capital rationing, however, one can use mathematical programming for purposes of selecting the optimal set of investment proposals. The technique was illustrated and its shortcomings examined.

Although the capital-budgeting methods discussed in this chapter appear to be very exact, it should be pointed out that we are able only to approximate the true value of an investment proposal to the firm. The meaningfulness of the values we calculate is only as good as our cash-flow estimates and the required rate of return employed. In the next two chapters, we consider the cash-flow estimates in greater detail; in Chapters 7 and 8, we evaluate the required rate of return. Together, these chapters provide the basis for making sound investment decisions in keeping with the objective of maximizing the market price of the company's stock. In subsequent chapters, the link between investment in capital projects and the objective of the firm will become clearer.

APPENDIX A   MULTIPLE INTERNAL RATES OF RETURN

In a well-known article, Lorie and Savage pointed out that certain streams of cash flows may have more than one internal rate of return.[20] To illustrate the problem, suppose that we had the following stream of cash flows corresponding to the "pump" proposal of Lorie and Savage:

Year	0	1	2
Cash flow	−$1,600	$10,000	−$10,000

In this example, a new, more effective pump is substituted for an existing pump. On an incremental basis, there is an initial outlay followed by net cash inflows resulting from the increased efficiency of the new pump. If the quantity of oil, for example, is fixed, the new pump will exhaust this supply more quickly than the old pump would. Beyond this point of exhaustion, the new pump alternative would result in an incremental outflow, because the old pump would still be productive.

When we solve for the internal rate of return for the above cash-flow stream, we find that it is not one rate, but two: 25 percent and 400

---

[20] See Lorie and Savage, "Three Problems in Rationing Capital," pp. 235–38.

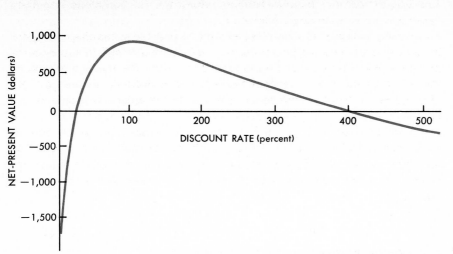

FIG. 4·3
Dual rates of return

percent. This unusual situation is illustrated in Figure 4-3, where the discount rate is plotted along the horizontal axis and net-present value along the vertical axis. At a 0 rate of discount, the net-present value of the project, −$1,600, is negative, due to the fact that the total non-discounted cash outflows exceed total nondiscounted inflows. As the discount rate increases, the present value of the second-year outflow diminishes with respect to the first-year inflow; and the present value of the proposal becomes positive when the discount rate exceeds 25 per-cent. As the discount rate increases beyond 100 percent, the present value of all future cash flows (years 1 and 2) diminishes relative to the initial outflow of −$1,600. At 400 percent, the present value of all cash flows again becomes 0.

This type of proposal differs from the usual case, shown in Figure 4-1 in this chapter, in which net-present value is a decreasing function of the discount rate, and in which there is but one internal rate of return that equates the present value of all inflows with the present value of all outflows. An investment proposal may have any number of internal rates of return, depending upon the cash-flow pattern. Consider the following series of cash flows:

Year	0	1	2	3
Cash flow	−$1,000	$6,000	−$11,000	$6,000

In this example, discount rates of 0, 100 percent, and 200 percent result in the net-present value of all cash flows equaling 0.

The number of internal rates of return is limited to the number of reversals of sign in the cash-flow stream. In the above example, we have three reversals and three internal rates of return. Although a multiple reversal in signs is a necessary condition for multiple internal rates of return, it is not sufficient for such an occurrence. The occurrence of multiple internal rates of return also depends upon the magnitude of cash flows. For the following series of cash flows, there is but one internal rate of return (32.5 percent), despite two reversals of sign:

Year	0	1	2
Cash flow	−$1,000	$1,400	−$100

We note that the equation for solving for the internal rate of return, Eq. (4-3), is an nth degree polynomial. For most investment projects, there is but one internal rate of return, and all but one of the n roots are imaginary. For dual rates of return, $n − 2$ roots are imaginary, and so on.

When confronted with a proposal having multiple rates of return, how does one decide which is the correct rate? In our dual-rate example, is the correct rate 25 percent or 400 percent? Actually, neither rate is correct, because neither is a measure of investment worth.[21] In essence, the firm has "borrowed" $10,000 from the project at the end of year 1 and will pay it back at the end of year 2. The relevant question is, What is it worth to the firm now to have the use of $10,000 for one year beginning at the end of year 1? This question, in turn, depends upon the investment opportunities available to the firm for that period of time. If the firm could earn $2,000 on the use of these funds and realize these earnings at the end of the period, the value of this opportunity would be $2,000, to be received at the end of year 2. This amount would then be compared with the initial outlay of $1,600 to determine whether the project is worthwhile. Similarly, other proposals can be evaluated in this manner to determine whether they are worthwhile.[22]

APPENDIX B

INFLATION AND CASH-FLOW ESTIMATES

In estimating cash flows, it is important that anticipated inflation be taken into account. Often there is a tendency to assume that price levels remain unchanged throughout the life of the project. Frequently, this

[21] Ezra Solomon, "The Arithmetic of Capital-Budgeting Decisions," *Journal of Business*, 29 (April 1956), 124–29.

[22] For a rigorous analysis of the problem of multiple rates of return, see Daniel Teichroew, Alexander A. Robichek, and Michael Montalbano, "An Analysis of Criteria for Investment and Financing Decisions under Certainty," *Management Science*, 12 (November 1965), 151–79.

assumption is imposed unknowingly; future cash flows simply are estimated on the basis of existing prices. However, a bias arises in the selection process in that the required rate of return for the project is usually based on current capital costs, which in turn embody a premium for anticipated inflation. The purpose of this appendix is to illustrate this bias.[23]

Assume a situation where the hurdle rate for a project is its required rate of return as perceived by investors and creditors. (The ways by which it is measured are taken up in Chapter 7.) There is general agreement that security prices depend on anticipated changes in prices. In fact, over eighty years ago Irving Fisher expressed the nominal rate of interest on a financial instrument as the sum of the real rate and the rate of price change expected over the life of the instrument.[24] This observed phenomenon has come to be known as the *Fisher effect*.[25] Implied is that the required rate of return for a project is

$$R_j = R_j^* + \rho \qquad (4\text{B-1})$$

where R_j is the required rate of return in nominal terms, R_j^* is the required rate in real terms, and ρ is the weighted average anticipated rate of inflation over the life of the project.[26]

If anticipated inflation is embodied in the acceptance criterion, it is important that it be reflected in the estimated cash flows for the project as well. The expected cash flows of a project are affected by anticipated inflation in several ways. If cash inflows ultimately arise from the sale of a product, these inflows are affected by expected future prices. As for cash outflows, inflation affects both expected future wages and material costs. Note that future inflation does not affect depreciation charges on existing assets. Once the asset is acquired, these charges are known with certainty. The effect of anticipated inflation on cash inflows and cash outflows will vary with the nature of the project. In some cases, cash inflows, through price increases, will rise faster than cash outflows; while in other cases the opposite will hold. No matter what the relationship, it is important that it be embodied in the cash-flow estimates. Otherwise, a bias of the type described before arises.

To illustrate this bias, assume that a project that cost $100,000 at time 0 was under consideration and was expected to provide cash-flow

---

[23] Appendix B is based on James C. Van Horne, "A Note on Biases in Capital Budgeting Introduced by Inflation," *Journal of Financial and Quantitative Analysis*, 6 (January 1971), 653–58.

[24] *Appreciation and Interest* (New York: Macmillan, 1896).

[25] In the appendix to Chapter 9, we explore the Fisher effect in more detail. Our purpose now is just to point out the biases possible from lack of consideration of inflation in the cash-flow estimates.

[26] In the appendix to Chapter 7, we investigate the impact of uncertain inflation on the required rate of return. For now, we work with the expected value of inflation.

benefits over the next five years. Assume further straight-line depreciation of $20,000 a year and a corporate tax rate of 50 percent. Suppose
that cash flows were estimated on the basis of price levels at time 0, with
no consideration to the effect of future inflation upon them, and that
these estimates were:

	Period				
	1	**2**	**3**	**4**	**5**
Expected cash inflow, I_t	$30,000	$40,000	$50,000	$50,000	$30,000
Expected cash outflow, O_t	10,000	10,000	10,000	10,000	10,000
	$20,000	$30,000	$40,000	$40,000	$20,000
Times (1 − tax rate)	.50	.50	.50	.50	.50
	$10,000	$15,000	$20,000	$20,000	$10,000
Depreciation times tax rate	10,000	10,000	10,000	10,000	10,000
Net cash flow	$20,000	$25,000	$30,000	$30,000	$20,000

If the project's required rate of return were 12 percent, the net-present
value of the project would be −$3,192. As this figure is negative, the
project would be rejected.

However, the results are biased in the sense that the discount rate
embodies an element attributable to anticipated future inflation,
whereas the cash-flow estimates do not. Suppose that the existing rate of
inflation, as measured by changes in the price-level index, were 5 percent, and that this rate was expected to prevail over the next five years. If
both cash inflows and cash outflows were expected to increase at this
rate, the net-present value of the project would be

$$NPV_o = \sum_{t=1}^{5} \frac{[I_t(1.05)^t - O_t(1.05)^t][.5] + 20,000_t[.5]}{(1.12)^t} - 100,000$$

$$= \$5,450 \qquad\qquad\qquad\qquad (4\text{B-}2)$$

where I_t is the cash inflow in year t, O_t is the cash outflow in year t, and
$20,000 is the annual depreciation in year t which is multiplied by the tax
rate to give the tax-shield cash savings. Because the net-present value is
positive, the project would be acceptable now, whereas before it was
not. To reject it under the previous method of estimating cash flows
would result in an opportunity loss to stockholders, for the project
provides a return in excess of that required by investors.

The example serves to illustrate the importance of taking anticipated
inflation into account explicitly when estimating future cash flows. Too
often, there is a tendency not to consider its effect in these estimates.

Because anticipated inflation is embodied in the required rate of return, not to take account of it in the cash-flow estimates will result in a biased appraisal of the project and, in turn, the possibility of a less than optimal allocation of capital.

PROBLEMS

1. The Symington Corporation is considering investing in one of two mutually exclusive projects. Each requires an immediate cash outlay of $1,000. Project A has a life of four years; project B, five years. Both projects will be depreciated on a straight-line basis (no salvage). The firm's tax rate is 50 percent, and its required return is 10 percent. Net cash flows generated by each investment have been projected as follows:

Net cash flows:

Years	1	2	3	4	5
A	$300	$300	$400	$400	0
B	$300	$300	$200	$200	$200

(a) Compute the payback for each investment.

(b) Compute the average rate of return for each investment. ← *avg. annual after-tax profit / avg. investment*

(c) Compute the profitability index for each investment.

(d) Which alternative would you select? Why?

2. What criticisms may be offered against the average-rate-of-return method as a capital-budgeting technique? What criticisms may be offered against the payback method?

300 - 250 dep / 50 +   300 - 250 / 50 +   400 - 250 / 150 +   400 - 250 / 150

400/4 = 100

3. A company can make either of two investments at period p_0. Assuming a required rate of return of 10 percent, determine for each project: (a) the payback period, (b) the profitability index, (c) the internal rate of return. You may assume straight-line depreciation.

1000/2 = 500

100/500 = 20%

	A	B
Investment	$20,000	$28,000
Expected life (no salvage)	5 yrs.	5 yrs.
Projected net income (after interest and taxes):		
Year 1	$ 5,000	$ 8,000
Year 2	5,000	8,000
Year 3	6,000	8,000
Year 4	6,000	8,000
Year 5	6,000	8,000

for Payback add back deprec.

7000 = 4000 +
9000 = 4000 +

Against Pay Back:

a) disregards post pay-back cash flows (which may be significant)

b) disregards timing of cash flows during payback period

Against Avg RR:

a) uses book value not actual cash flow

b) time value of $ is ignored

4. Two mutually exclusive projects have projected cash flows as follows:

Period	0	1	2	3	4
A	−$10,000	$5,000	$5,000	$5,000	$5,000
B	−$10,000	0	0	0	$30,000

(a) Determine the internal rate of return for each project.

(b) Assuming a required rate of return of 10 percent, determine the present value for each project.

(c) Which project would you select? Why? What assumptions are inherent in your decision?

5. The Homes Corporation is faced with two mutually exclusive investment proposals. One would cost $100,000 and provide net cash benefits of $30,000 per year for five years. The other would cost $50,000 and provide net cash benefits of $16,000 for five years. Homes has a 10 percent after-tax opportunity cost of funds. Compute the net-present value and profitability index of each project. Which should be accepted?

6. Rework problem 5, assuming a 17 percent opportunity cost of funds. How would this change your answer?

7. One of the largest and most profitable companies in the country is faced with the prospect of having to replace a large stamping machine. Two machines currently being marketed will do the job satisfactorily. The Superior Stamping machine costs $50,000 and will require cash running expenses of $20,000 per year. The Peerless machine costs $75,000, but running expenses are only expected to be $15,000 per year. Both machines have a ten-year useful life with no salvage value and would be depreciated on a straight-line basis.

(a) If the company pays a 50 percent tax rate and has a 10 percent after-tax required rate of return, which machine should it purchase?

(b) Would your answer be different if the required return were 8 percent?

8. Rework problem 7, assuming that the Peerless machine has a $10,000 salvage value and the Superior machine has a $5,000 salvage value.

9. The Burdick Company plans its capital budget on a two-year basis. For the next two years, a maximum $1,750,000 has been allocated; this money is currently on hand. Some proposals could be undertaken immediately, while others will not be ready until next year. The profitability index of each proposal is figured from the point of initial investment. None of the proposals will generate a cash inflow during the two-year period under consideration. The company pays taxes at a 50 percent rate and requires an after-tax rate of return of 12 percent.

Treasury bills are yielding 6 percent. Determine which of the following investments should be undertaken:

	Available This Year			Available Next Year	
Project	Amount	Profitability Index	Project	Amount	Profitability Index
1	$500,000	1.05	7	$500,000	1.30
2	100,000	1.31	8	300,000	1.20
3	250,000	1.17	9	400,000	1.12
4	350,000	0.97	10	100,000	1.05
5	300,000	1.22			
6	400,000	1.10			

10. The Simplex Company has $1,000,000 allocated for capital-budgeting purposes. The following proposals and associated profitability indexes have been determined:

Project	Amount	Profitability Index
1	$500,000	1.22
2	150,000	.95
3	350,000	1.20
4	450,000	1.18
5	200,000	1.20
6	400,000	1.05

(a) Which of the above investments should be undertaken?

(b) Would the firm be maximizing the price of the common stock by turning down projects having an index larger than one?

11. The Primal-Dual Corporation is considering the following investment proposals:

Project	Initial Outlay Required	Outlay Required in Period 1	Net-Present Value
1	$100	$50	$20
2	40	10	5
3	120	80	40
4	80	25	14
5	20	15	10
6	60	30	18

The projects are independent and divisible. The company has budget constraints of $220 at time 0 and $110 at the end of period 1.

Set up the selection process as a mathematical programming problem where you wish to maximize net-present value available from investment subject to the two budget constraints.

12. An investment has an outlay of $800 today, an inflow of $5,000 at the end of one year, and an outflow of $5,000 at the end of two years. What is its internal rate of return? If the initial outlay were $1,250, what would be its *IRR*? (*Hint:* This case is an exception rather than the rule.)

13. An investment has an inflow of $200 today, an outflow of $300 at the end of one year, and an inflow of $400 at the end of two years. What is its internal rate of return?

SELECTED REFERENCES

Baumol, William J., and Richard E. Quandt, "Investment and Discount Rates Under Capital Rationing—A Programming Approach," *The Economic Journal,* 75 (June 1965), 317–29.

Bernhard, Richard H., "Mathematical Programming Models for Capital Budgeting—A Survey, Generalization, and Critique," *Journal of Financial and Quantitative Analysis,* 4 (June 1969), 111–58.

Bierman, Harold, Jr., and Seymour Smidt, *The Capital Budgeting Decision,* 3rd ed. New York: Macmillan, 1971.

Burton, R. M., and W. W. Damon, "On the Existence of a Cost of Capital under Pure Capital Rationing," *Journal of Finance,* 29 (September 1974), 1165–74.

Elton, Edwin J., "Capital Rationing and External Discount Rates," *Journal of Finance,* 25 (June 1970), 573–84.

Elton, Edwin J., and Martin J. Gruber, *Finance as a Dynamic Process,* Chapters 7 and 8. Englewood Cliffs, N.J.: Prentice-Hall, 1975.

Fama, Eugene E., and Merton H. Miller. *The Theory of Finance,* Chapter 3. New York: Holt, Rinehart & Winston, 1972.

Fogler, H. Russell, "Ranking Techniques and Capital Rationing," *Accounting Review,* 47 (January 1972), 134–43.

Haley, Charles W., "Taxes, the Cost of Capital and the Firm's Investment Decisions," *Journal of Finance,* 26 (September 1971), 901–18.

Haley, Charles W., and Lawrence D. Schall, "A Note on Investment Policy with Imperfect Capital Markets," *Journal of Finance,* 27 (March 1972), 93–96.

Hastie, K. Larry, "One Businessman's View of Capital Budgeting," *Financial Management,* 3 (Winter 1974), 36–44.

Johnson, Robert W., *Capital Budgeting.* Belmont, Calif.: Wadsworth, 1970.

Klammer, Thomas, "Empirical Evidence of the Adoption of Sophisticated Capital Budgeting Techniques," *Journal of Business,* 45 (July 1972), 387–97.

Lorie, James H., and Leonard J. Savage, "Three Problems in Rationing Capital," *Journal of Business,* 28 (October 1955), 227–39.

Mao, James C. T., "The Internal Rate of Return as a Ranking Criterion," *Engineering Economist,* 11 (Winter 1966), 1–13.

Merrett, A. J., and Allen Sykes, *Capital Budgeting and Company Finance.* London: Longmans, Green, 1966.

Murdick, Robert G., and Donald D. Deming, *The Management of Corporate Expenditures.* New York: McGraw-Hill, 1968.

Myers, Stewart C., "Interactions of Corporate Financing and Investment Decisions—Implications for Capital Budgeting," *Journal of Finance,* 29 (March 1974), 1–26.

———, "A Note on Linear Programming and Capital Budgeting," *Journal of Finance,* 27 (March 1972), 89–92.

Oakford, Robert V., *Capital Budgeting.* New York: Ronald Press Co., 1970.

Petty, J. William, David F. Scott, Jr., and Monroe M. Bird, "The Capital Expenditure Decision-Making Process of Large Corporations," *Engineering Economist,* 20 (Spring 1975), 159–72.

Quirin, G. David, *The Capital Expenditure Decision.* Homewood, Ill.: Richard D. Irwin, 1967.

Sarnat, Marshall, and Haim Levy, "The Relationship of Rules of Thumb to the Internal Rate of Return: A Restatement and Generalization," *Journal of Finance,* 24 (June 1969), 479–89.

Schnell, James S., and Roy S. Nicolosi, "Capital Expenditure Feedback: Project Reappraisal," *Engineering Economist,* 19 (Summer 1974), 253–61.

Schwab, Bernhard, and Peter Lusztig, "A Comparative Analysis of the Net Present Value and the Benefit-Cost Ratios as Measures of the Economic Desirability of Investments," *Journal of Finance,* 24 (June 1969), 507–16.

Solomon, Ezra, "The Arithmetic of Capital-Budgeting Decisions," *Journal of Business,* 29 (April 1956), 124–29.

———, *The Management of Corporate Capital.* New York: Free Press, 1959.

———, *The Theory of Financial Management.* New York: Columbia University Press, 1963.

Teichroew, Daniel, Alexander A. Robichek, and Michael Montalbano, "An Analysis of Criteria for Investment and Financing Decisions under Certainty," *Management Science,* 12 (November 1965), 151–79.

———, "Mathematical Analysis of Rates of Return under Certainty," *Management Science,* 11 (January 1965), 395–403.

Van Horne, James C., "Capital Budgeting under Conditions of Uncertainty as to Project Life," *Engineering Economist,* 17 (Spring 1972), 189–99.

———, "A Note on Biases in Capital Budgeting Introduced by Inflation," *Journal of Financial and Quantitative Analysis,* 6 (March 1971).

Vickers, Douglas, *The Theory of the Firm: Production, Capital and Finance.* New York: McGraw-Hill, 1968.

Weaver, James B., "Organizing and Maintaining a Capital Expenditure Program," *Engineering Economist,* 20 (Fall 1974), 1–36.

Weingartner, H. Martin, "Capital Budgeting of Interrelated Projects: Survey and Synthesis," *Management Science,* 12 (March 1966), 485–516.

———, "The Excess Present Value Index—A Theoretical Basis and Critique," *Journal of Accounting Research,* 1 (Autumn 1963), 213–24.

———, "The Generalized Rate of Return," *Journal of Financial and Quantitative Analysis,* 1 (September 1966), 1–29.

———, *Mathematical Programming and the Analysis of Capital Budgeting Problems.* Copyright © H. Martin Weingartner, 1963.

———, "Some New Views on the Payback Period and Capital Budgeting Decisions," *Management Science,* 15 (August 1969), 594–607.

Whisler, William D., "Sensitivity Analysis of Rates of Return," *Journal of Finance,* 31 (March 1976), 63–70.

INFORMATION NEEDED to EVALUATE RISKY INVESTMENTS 1

In the preceding chapter, we assumed that acceptance of any investment proposal or group of proposals did not alter the business-risk complexion of the firm as perceived by suppliers of capital. These assumptions allowed us to work with the expected values of projected cash flows, thereby facilitating greatly the introduction of capital budgeting. We know, however, that different investment proposals have different degrees of risk. If the acceptance of an investment proposal or group of proposals alters the business-risk complexion of the firm, investors and creditors are likely to view the company differently before and after the acceptance of the proposal(s).[1] Consequently, the total valuation of the company may change. In evaluating investment proposals, a firm should take into account the effect that their acceptance will have on its perceived risk, as envisioned by investors and creditors.

In this chapter and the next, we take up the kinds of information necessary to evaluate risky investments. In so doing, we hope to provide insight into how risk may be quantified by the firm. We begin in this chapter with the measurement of risk for individual projects under a variety of assumptions. Chapter 6 focuses on the measurement of risk when sequential decisions are involved, when the possibility of abandonment exists, and, finally, when a portfolio of assets is being investigated. In Chapters 7 and 8, we discuss the use of the information developed in these two chapters in reaching capital investment decisions. It involves us in the various ways management can assess the likely impact of an investment decision on share price. Thus, Chapters 5 through 8 must be viewed as a package. First we need information about the risk involved in a particular investment proposal or proposals, and then we must reach a decision with respect to its (their) desirability.

The riskiness of an investment proposal is defined in this book as the variability of its possible returns. Decision situations may be broken down into three types: certainty, risk, and uncertainty. The distinction between risk and uncertainty is that risk involves situations in which the probabilities of a particular event occurring are known; whereas with uncertainty, these probabilities are not known.[2] The problems we ana-

INTRODUCTION

---

[1] For surveys of the way large companies view the risk of a project and of the methods of risk evaluation employed, see J. William Petty, David F. Scott, Jr., and Monroe M. Bird, "The Capital Expenditure Decision-Making Process of Large Corporations," *Engineering Economist*, 20 (Spring 1975), 166–68; Thomas Klammer, "Empirical Evidence of the Adoptions of Sophisticated Capital Budgeting Techniques," *Journal of Business*, 45 (July 1972), 391; and Eugene F. Brigham and Richard H. Pettway, "Capital Budgeting by Utilities," *Financial Management*, 2 (Autumn 1973), 11–22. For a survey of the attitudes of large firms toward risk and the derivation of implied utility functions, see Willis R. Greer, Jr., "Theory versus Practice in Risk Analysis: An Empirical Study," *Accounting Review*, 49 (July 1974), 496–505.

[2] See R. Duncan Luce and Howard Raiffa, *Games and Decisions* (New York: John Wiley, 1957), p. 13.

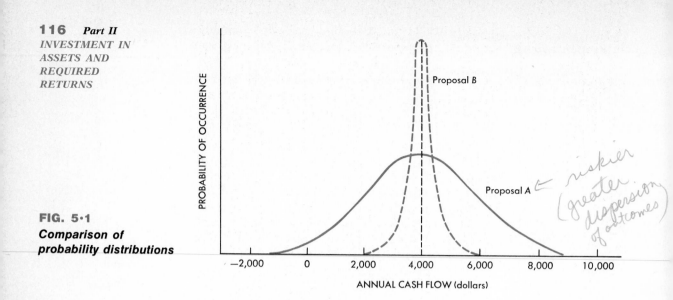

FIG. 5·1

Comparison of
probability distributions

lyze in this chapter involve risk situations, although frequently the terms *risk* and *uncertainty* are used interchangeably. A wide range of factors gives rise to risk in capital investments. The economy in general, economic factors peculiar to investment, competition, technological development, consumer preferences, and labor conditions, as well as other factors, make it impossible to foretell the future. Consequently, the revenues, costs, and economic life of a particular investment are less than certain.

With the introduction of risk, a firm no longer may be indifferent between two investment proposals having the same net-present values or internal rates of return as was the case in Chapter 4. These measures of profitability are based only upon the expected values of the possible cash flows in various future periods. Suppose that we had two investment proposals, each costing $8,000 at time 0 and having expected cash inflows of $4,000 in each of the next three years, after which no cash flows or salvage values were expected. According to the discussion in previous chapters, the firm would rank these two proposals equally. However, suppose the probability distributions of the annual cash flows were those shown in Figure 5-1.

Can we conclude that the value of each of these investment opportunities is the same when the dispersion of the probability distribution of possible cash flows for proposal *A* is greater than that for proposal *B*? If risk is associated with the deviation of actual outcome from that which was expected, proposal *A* is the riskier investment. It is clear that risk is important and must be incorporated into our analysis.

STANDARD DEVIATION AND EXPECTED VALUE

Chapter 5 **117**
*INFORMATION
NEEDED TO
EVALUATE RISKY
INVESTMENTS I*

What is needed is a measure of risk that gives information about the dispersion or tightness of the probability distribution. We know from Chapter 2 that the conventional measure of dispersion is the standard deviation, which, for a single period's possible outcome, is

$$\sigma = \sqrt{\sum_{x=1}^{n} (A_{xt} - \bar{A}_t)^2 P_{xt}} \tag{5-1}$$

where A_{xt} is a cash flow for the xth possibility in period t, P_{xt} is the probability of occurrence of that cash flow, and $\bar{A}_t$ is the expected value of cash flows in period t. The square of the standard deviation, σ^2, is the variance. The expected value is calculated by

$$\bar{A}_t = \sum_{x=1}^{n} A_{xt} P_{xt} \tag{5-2}$$

To illustrate these concepts, suppose two investment proposals had the following discrete probability distribution of expected cash flows in each of the next three years:

Proposal C		Proposal D	
Probability	Cash Flow	Probability	Cash Flow
0.10	$3,000	0.10	$2,000
0.20	3,500	0.25	3,000
0.40	4,000	0.30	4,000
0.20	4,500	0.25	5,000
0.10	5,000	0.10	6,000

The expected value of cash flows in each of the next three years for proposal C is

$$\bar{A} = 0.10(3,000) + 0.20(3,500) + 0.40(4,000) + 0.20(4,500)$$
$$+ 0.10(5,000) = \$4,000$$

which is the same as that for proposal D:

$$\bar{A} = 0.10(2,000) + 0.25(3,000) + 0.30(4,000) + 0.25(5,000)$$
$$+ 0.10(6,000) = \$4,000$$

However, the standard deviation for proposal C is

$$\sigma = [0.10(3{,}000 - 4{,}000)^2 + 0.20(3{,}500 - 4{,}000)^2 + 0.40(4{,}000 \\ - 4{,}000)^2 + 0.20(4{,}500 - 4{,}000)^2 + 0.10(5{,}000 - 4{,}000)^2]^{1/2} \\ = [300{,}000]^{1/2} = \$548$$

while that for proposal D is

$$\sigma = [0.10(2{,}000 - 4{,}000)^2 + 0.25(3{,}000 - 4{,}000)^2 + 0.30(4{,}000 \\ - 4{,}000)^2 + 0.25(5{,}000 - 4{,}000)^2 + 0.10(6{,}000 - 4{,}000)^2]^{1/2} \\ = [1{,}300{,}000]^{1/2} = \$1{,}140$$

Thus, proposal D has a significantly higher standard deviation, indicating a greater dispersion of possible outcomes.

A measure of relative dispersion is the coefficient of variation, which simply is the standard deviation of the probability distribution over its expected value. This coefficient serves as a relative measure of the degree of business risk. Because the coefficient of variation for proposal D, 0.29, is greater than that for proposal C, 0.14, we would say that proposal D had the greater degree of risk. Resort to a relative measure of risk is necessary if a comparison between projects involves considerably different absolute magnitudes of expected value and standard deviation. Frequent reference will be made to these concepts in the remainder of this chapter.

We assume that management evaluates investment proposals on the basis of information about the expected value and dispersion of the probability distributions of possible future cash flows. As discussed in Chapter 2, management may also be concerned with the shape of a distribution as depicted by its skewness. Although it would be possible to incorporate a skewness measure into our analysis of risk, for simplicity we shall deal only with the expected value and the dispersion of the probability distribution.

MEASURING RISK: INDEPENDENCE OF CASH FLOWS OVER TIME

The preceding discussion points to the importance of risk in capital budgeting. In the remainder of this chapter, we consider ways to measure it under varying assumptions as to cash-flow behavior. The idea is to develop pertinent information about the expected value and dispersion of the probability distribution of possible returns. We begin by considering a single project where the cash flows are independent from period to period. Once we have illustrated the basic method of analysis, we will move on to consider varying degrees of correlation of cash flows over time in the remainder of the chapter.

EXPECTED VALUE AND STANDARD DEVIATION

Chapter 5 **119**
INFORMATION
NEEDED TO
EVALUATE RISKY
INVESTMENTS I

Suppose that we are evaluating an investment proposal in which the probability distributions of cash flows for various future periods are independent of one another. In other words, the outcome in period t does not depend upon what happened in period $t - 1$. Stated differently, there is no causative relationship between cash flows from period to period. The causative events in one period are assumed to be independent of causative events in other periods; therefore, the period-to-period cash flows are independent of one another.[3] In subsequent sections, we will explore cash-flow streams that are perfectly correlated over time and those that are partially correlated. For now, however, our example is framed in terms of independent cash flows over time.

The expected value of the probability distribution of possible net-present values for the proposal is

$$NPV = \sum_{t=0}^{n} \frac{\overline{A}_t}{(1 + i)^t} \qquad (5\text{-}3)$$

where $\overline{A}_t$ is the expected value of net cash flow in period t, i is the risk-free rate, and n is the number of periods over which cash flows are expected.

The risk-free rate is used at this time as the discount rate because we attempt to isolate the time value of money. To include a premium for risk in the discount rate would result in double counting with respect to our analysis. The required rate of return for a project embodies a premium for risk. If this rate is used as the discount rate, we would be adjusting for risk in the discounting process itself. (The greater the discount rate, the greater the risk adjustment, assuming a constant risk-free rate.) We then would use the probability distribution of net-present values to judge the risk of the proposal. However, the probability distribution is obtained using a risk-adjusted discount rate. In essence, we would adjust for risk a second time in our analysis of the dispersion of the probability distribution of possible net-present values. Because of the problems inherent in double counting for risk, we take account only of the time value of money in the discounting process.[4]

Given the assumption of serial independence of cash flows for

---

[3] For a discussion of this assumption as well as those for perfect correlation and partial dependency, see Lynn E. Bussey and G. T. Stevens, Jr., "Formulating Correlated Cash Flow Streams," *Engineering Economist*, 18 (Fall 1972), 10–14.

[4] This is not to say that for purposes of reaching an accept or reject decision the expected values of cash flows should be discounted at the risk-free rate. Indeed, in Chapter 7, we show that the appropriate discount rate is the required rate of return, which embodies a premium for the project's risk. For discounting the dispersion of the distribution, however, we use the risk-free rate for the above-mentioned reasons.

WITH INDEPENDENCE :

various future periods, the standard deviation of the probability distribution of net-present values is

$$\sigma = \sqrt{\sum_{t=0}^{n} \frac{\sigma_t^2}{(1 + i)^{2t}}} \qquad (5\text{-}4)$$

where σ_t is the standard deviation of the probability distribution of possible net cash flows in period t. To illustrate the calculations involved with Eq. (5-3) and Eq. (5-4), suppose that we had an investment proposal costing $10,000 at time 0 that was expected to generate net cash flows during the first three periods with the probabilities shown in Table 5-1. The expected values of net cash flows for periods 1, 2, and 3 are $5,000, $4,000, and $3,000, respectively. The standard deviation of possible cash flows for period t, σ_t, is computed by

$$\sigma_t = \sqrt{\sum_{x=1}^{5} (A_{xt} - \bar{A}_t)^2 P_{xt}} \qquad (5\text{-}5)$$

where A_{xt} is the xth possible net cash flow, $\bar{A}_t$ is the expected value of net cash flow for period t, and P_{xt} is the probability of occurrence of A_{xt}.

Table 5·1   Expected cash flows for example problem

Period 1		Period 2		Period 3	
Probability	Net Cash Flow	Probability	Net Cash Flow	Probability	Net Cash Flow
0.10	$3,000	0.10	$2,000	0.10	$1,000
0.25	4,000	0.25	3,000	0.25	2,000
0.30	5,000	0.30	4,000	0.30	3,000
0.25	6,000	0.25	5,000	0.25	4,000
0.10	7,000	0.10	6,000	0.10	5,000

In the above example, the standard deviation of possible net cash flows for period 1 is

$$\begin{aligned} \sigma_1 = [&0.10(3,000 - 5,000)^2 + 0.25(4,000 - 5,000)^2 \\ &+ 0.30(5,000 - 5,000)^2 + 0.25(6,000 - 5,000)^2 \\ &+ 0.10(7,000 - 5,000)^2]^{1/2} = \$1,140 \end{aligned} \qquad (5\text{-}6)$$

Because the probability distributions for periods 2 and 3 have the same dispersion about their expected values as that for period 1, σ_2 and σ_3 are $1,140 also. Given this information, we are able to calculate the expected value of net-present value for the proposal as well as the standard deviation about this expected value. If we assume a risk-free rate of 4 percent, the expected value of net-present value for the proposal is

$$NPV = -10{,}000 + \frac{5{,}000}{(1.04)} + \frac{4{,}000}{(1.04)^2} + \frac{3{,}000}{(1.04)^3} = \$1{,}173 \qquad (5\text{-}7)$$

Using Eq. (5-4), under the assumption of mutual independence of cash flows over time, the standard deviation about the expected value is

$$\sigma = \sqrt{\frac{1{,}140^2}{(1.04)^2} + \frac{1{,}140^2}{(1.04)^4} + \frac{1{,}140^2}{(1.04)^6}} = \$1{,}827 \qquad (5\text{-}8)$$

see Appendix B-1 (P. 746)

STANDARDIZING THE DISPERSION

The expected value and the standard deviation of the probability distribution of possible net-present values give us a considerable amount of information by which to evaluate the risk of the investment proposal. If the probability distribution is approximately normal, we are able to calculate the probability of the proposal's providing a net-present value of less or more than a specified amount. For example, suppose that we wish to determine the probability that the net-present value of the project will be zero or less. To determine this probability, we first calculate the difference between zero and the expected value of net-present value for the project. In our example, this difference is $-\$1,173$. We then standardize this difference by dividing it by the standard deviation of possible net-present values. The formula is

"Z-score"

$$S = \frac{X - NPV}{\sigma} \qquad (5\text{-}9)$$

where X is the outcome in which we are interested, NPV is the expected value, and σ the standard deviation of the probability distribution. In our case,

$$S = \frac{0 - 1{,}173}{1{,}827} = -0.642$$

This figure tells us that a net-present value of 0 lies 0.642 standard deviations to the left of the expected value of the probability distribution of possible net-present values.

To determine the probability that the net-present value of the project will be zero or less, we consult a normal probability distribution table found in Appendix B at the back of this book. (More detailed tables are found in most statistics texts.) With respect to the problem at hand, we find that there is a 0.26 probability that an observation will be less

FIG. 5·2
*Probability
density function,
example problem*

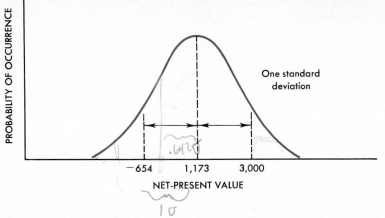

than −0.642 standard deviations from the expected value of that distribution. Thus, there is a 0.26 probability that the net-present value of the proposal will be zero or less. Put another way, there is a 0.26 probability that the internal rate of return of the project will be less than the risk-free rate. If we assume a continuous distribution, the probability density function of our example problem can be shown in Figure 5-2.

The mean of the probability distribution of possible net-present values is $1,173. One standard deviation on either side of the mean gives us net-present values of −$654 and $3,000. With a normal distribution, 0.683 of the distribution or area under the curve falls within one standard deviation on either side of the mean or expected value. Thus, we know that there is approximately a two-thirds probability that the net-present value of the proposal examined will be between −$654 and $3,000. We know also that there is a 0.26 probability that the net-present value will be less than 0 and a 0.74 probability that it will be greater than 0. By expressing differences from the expected value in terms of standard deviations, we are able to determine the probability that the net-present value for an investment proposal will be greater or less than a particular amount. Often it is useful to express the area under the curve and to the right of a particular amount as a cumulative probability distribution. For our example problem, this distribution is shown in Figure 5-3. It tells us the probability that the actual net-present value will be at least as great as the amounts shown on the horizontal axis.

Knowledge of these probabilities is fundamental for a realistic assessment of risk. For example, suppose that the firm is considering another investment project, proposal Y. The probability density function for this proposal is shown in Figure 5-4, as is that for our example problem, proposal X. We see that the expected value of net-present value for proposal Y, $2,200, is higher than that for proposal X, $1,173; but there is also greater dispersion of the probability distribution about the expected value. If risk is directly related to dispersion, proposal Y has both a higher expected profitability and a greater risk than does proposal X.

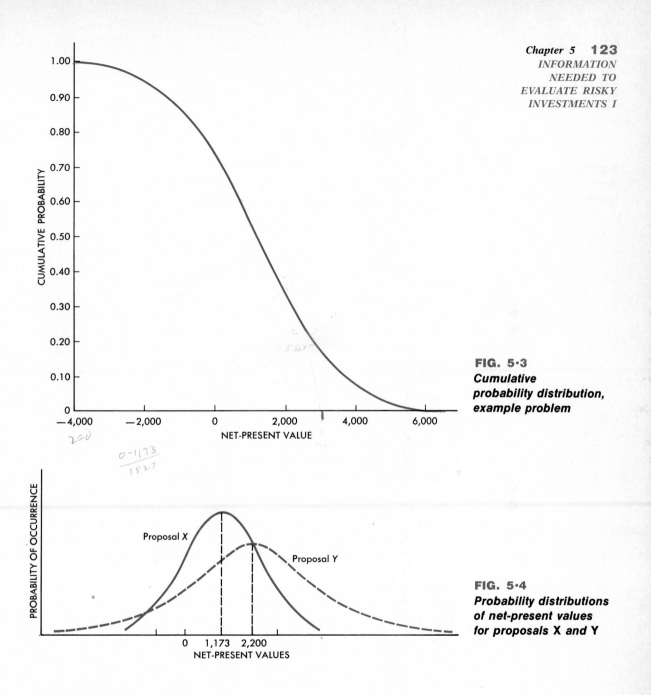

FIG. 5·3
*Cumulative
probability distribution,
example problem*

FIG. 5·4
*Probability distributions
of net-present values
for proposals X and Y*

INFORMATION GENERATED

The approach outlined above can be adapted to internal rates of return. What is involved is expression of the distribution in terms of possible internal rates of return as opposed to net-present values. By varying the discount rate, i, in Eq. (5-4), one obtains standard deviations for different discount rates. For each standard deviation, the probability that net-present value will be zero or less can be computed. These probabilities then are plotted with the discount rate along the horizontal axis in ascending order and with the corresponding probabilities on the vertical axis. A probability distribution of possible internal rates of return emerges from which the expected value and standard deviation can be computed. Using the standard deviation together with the expected value of possible internal rates of return, one is able to perform the same type of analysis as before. Whether net-present values or internal rates of return are used, the approach provides management with important information from which it is able to judge the risk of a project. This information was missing in the conventional evaluation of capital-budgeting projects in Chapter 4, where only the expected values of future cash flows were used.

In the above examples, we have assumed normal probability distributions. Although this property is very desirable for purposes of calculation, it is not a necessary condition for the use of the above approach. Even when the distribution is not normal, we usually are able to make reasonably strong probability statements by using Tchebycheff's inequality. This approach is based upon the fact that regardless of the form of the distribution, there is a close relationship between the magnitude of deviations from the expected value of the distribution and probability.[5] Again, we are interested in the area under the curve, or probability density function, that is to the left or right of a particular net-present value or internal rate of return. By computing this area, we are able to determine the probability that the index will be greater or less than a particular amount and judge the risk of the project accordingly.

ESTIMATING FUTURE CASH FLOWS

Instead of expressing estimates of future cash flows in terms of a discrete probability distribution, we might specify them only in terms of the expected value and standard deviation of the probability distribution. For example, we might ask management for estimates of the most likely cash flow and the maximum possible deviation on either side. This type of estimating procedure corresponds to the PERT method, whereby, most likely, optimistic and pessimistic estimates are made. If we assume a normal distribution of net cash flows for various future periods, we are able to use the maximum possible deviation to determine the standard deviation.

With a normal distribution, we know that the probabilities that the

---

[5] For an extensive discussion and application of this technique, see Stephen L. Buzby, "Extending the Applicability of Probabilistic Management and Control Models," *Accounting Review*, 49 (January 1974), 42–49.

actual value will fall within 1, 2, or 3 standard deviations on either side of the most likely value are 0.683, 0.954, and 0.997, respectively. If management felt that there were a 5 percent probability that the maximum possible deviation would be positive and an equal probability that it would be negative, we would consult a normal probability distribution table and find that this probability corresponds to approximately 1.65 standard deviations on either side of the most likely value. In other words, 90 percent of a normal probability distribution falls within 1.65 standard deviations on either side of the most likely value—the mean. By dividing the maximum deviation by 1.65, we obtain the standard deviation for the probability distribution. Thus, if the most likely value of net cash flow for period t were $5,000 and the minimum and maximum cash flows were $3,000 and $7,000, respectively, the standard deviation would be $2,000/1.65 = $1,212.

This relatively simple approach enables us to obtain the probability information necessary to determine the expected value of net-present value for an investment proposal and the standard deviation about this expected value.[6] The approach differs somewhat in mechanics but not in concept from the discrete probability-distribution approach described earlier. To use the approach, however, it is important that the probability estimates be approximately normal.

DEPENDENCE OF CASH FLOWS OVER TIME

In the preceding section, we assumed serial independence of cash flows from one future period to another. For most investment proposals, however, the cash flow in one future period depends in part upon the cash flows in previous periods. If an investment proposal turns bad in the early years, the probability is high that cash flows in later years also will be lower than originally expected. To assume that an extremely unfavorable or favorable outcome in the early life of an investment proposal does not affect the later outcome is unrealistic in most investment situations. The consequence of cash flows being correlated over time is that the standard deviation of the probability distribution of possible net-present values or possible internal rates of return is larger than it would be if we assumed independence. The greater the degree of correlation, the greater the dispersion of the probability distribution. The expected value of net-present value, however, is the same, regardless of the degree of correlation over time. In this section, we explore varying degrees of dependence of cash flows over time.

---

[6] See Frederick S. Hillier, "A Basic Approach to the Evaluation of Interrelated Investments," in R. F. Byrne, W. W. Cooper, A. Charnes, O. A. Davis, and D. A. Bradford, *Studies in Budgeting* (Amsterdam: North Holland Publishing, 1971). For a further discussion of how probabilistic estimates can be made, see Bussey and Stevens, "Formulating Correlated Cash Flow Streams," pp. 5–9.

PERFECT CORRELATION

Cash flows are perfectly correlated over time if the deviation of an actual cash flow for a period from the mean of the probability distribution of expected cash flows for that period implies that cash flows in all other periods deviate in exactly the same relative manner. In other words, the cash flow in period t depends entirely upon what happened in previous periods. If the actual cash flow in period t is X standard deviations to the right of the expected value of the probability distribution of possible cash flows for that period, actual cash flows in all other periods will be X standard deviations to the right of the expected values of their respective probability distributions. Stated differently, the cash flow in any period is a linear function of the cash flows in all other periods. The formula for the standard deviation of a perfectly correlated stream of cash flows over time is[7]

$$\sigma = \sum_{t=0}^{\infty} \frac{\sigma_t}{(1 + i)^t} \tag{5-10}$$

To illustrate its use, consider the same example as before. The standard deviation about the expected value of net-present value for the proposal, using Eq. 5-10, is

$$\sigma = \frac{1,140}{(1.04)} + \frac{1,140}{(1.04)^2} + \frac{1,140}{(1.04)^3} = \$3,164$$

This compares with a standard deviation of \$1,827 when we used Eq. (5-4) under the assumption of serial independence over time. Thus, the standard deviation for a perfectly correlated stream of cash flows is significantly higher than the standard deviation for the same stream under the assumption of mutual independence. The standard deviation for a less than perfectly correlated stream of cash flows will be somewhere between these two values. The probabilistic analysis of a project with a perfectly correlated stream of cash flows over time is the same as that illustrated previously for a project with an uncorrelated stream.

---

[7] The standard deviation of the probability distribution of possible internal rates of return can be determined in the same manner as described before. The discount rate is varied in Eq. (5-10) to obtain different standard deviations, the probability of net-present value being less than zero is determined for each discount rate, these probabilities are arranged to form a probability distribution of IRRs, and the standard deviation of the distribution is calculated.

HILLIER'S MODEL

Hillier combines the assumption of mutual independence and perfect correlation in developing a model to deal with mixed situations.[8] The model enables the analysis of investment proposals in which some of the expected cash flows over time are related closely, and others are fairly independent. To illustrate the model, suppose that a firm is considering the introduction of a new product with returns expected over the next five years. Because the product's market reception is uncertain, management feels that if initial reception exceeds expectations, reception in later years also will exceed expectations in about the same proportion. For simplicity, it is believed that the net marketing cash flows (sales minus marketing and advertising expenses) can be treated as perfectly correlated over time.

On the other hand, estimates of the initial investment in the project and of production costs are reasonably reliable, so that any deviation from expectations is assumed to be attributable to random fluctuations. Consequently, initial investment and net production cash flows are regarded as being mutually independent over time. The probability information for the introduction of the new product is shown in Table 5-2. Assume that each of the probability distributions involved can be

Table 5·2   Expected cash flows for new product

Year	Source	Expected Value of Net Cash Flow (in thousands)	Standard Deviation (in thousands)
0	Initial investment	−$600	$ 50
1	Production cash outflow	− 250	20
2	Production cash outflow	− 200	10
3	Production cash outflow	− 200	10
4	Production cash outflow	− 200	10
5	Production outflow—salvage value	− 100	15
1	Marketing	300	50
2	Marketing	600	100
3	Marketing	500	100
4	Marketing	400	100
5	Marketing	300	100

Source: Hillier, "Derivation of Probabilistic Information," p. 454.

[8] Frederick S. Hillier, "The Derivation of Probabilistic Information for the Evaluation of Risky Investments," *Management Science*, 9 (April 1963), 443–57. The model has been expanded by B. Wagle, "A Statistical Analysis of Risk in Capital Investment Projects," *Operational Research Quarterly*, 18 (March 1967), 13–33.

regarded as normal. If 4 percent is used as the risk-free rate, the expected value of net-present value for the proposal is

$$
NPV = \sum_{t=0}^{5} \frac{A_t}{(1.04)^t}
$$

$$
= -600 + \frac{300 - 250}{(1.04)} + \frac{600 - 200}{(1.04)^2} + \frac{500 - 200}{(1.04)^3}
$$

$$
+ \frac{400 - 200}{(1.04)^4} + \frac{300 - 100}{(1.04)^5} = \$420 \tag{5-11}
$$

Calculating the standard deviation of the probability distribution about the expected value is considerably more complex, for we take into account both a perfectly correlated stream and an independent stream of cash flows. The formula for the standard deviation is

↙ indep.   ↙ correl.

$$
\sigma = \sqrt{\sum_{t=0}^{n} \frac{\sigma^2 y_t}{(1+i)^{2t}} + \sum_{k=1}^{m} \left(\sum_{t=0}^{n} \left[\frac{\sigma z_t^{(k)}}{(1+i)^t} \right] \right)^2} \tag{5-12}
$$

where $\sigma^2 y_t$ is the variance for an independent net cash flow in period t, and $\sigma z_t^{(k)}$ is the standard deviation for stream k of a perfectly correlated net cash flow in period t. For our problem, there is but one perfectly correlated stream of cash flows, so that $m = 1$ in the equation. However, Eq. (5-12) can treat any number of perfectly correlated streams. The standard deviation for the example problem is

$$
\sigma = \sqrt{\sum_{t=0}^{5} \frac{\sigma^2 y_t}{(1.04)^{2t}} + \left(\sum_{t=0}^{5} \left[\frac{\sigma z_t}{(1.04)^t} \right] \right)^2}
$$

$$
= \sqrt{50^2 + \frac{20^2}{(1.04)^2} + \cdots + \frac{15^2}{(1.04)^{10}} + \left(\frac{50}{(1.04)} + \cdots + \frac{100}{(1.04)^5} \right)^2}
$$

$$
= \$398 \tag{5-13}
$$

Thus, the expected value of net-present value of the proposal is \$420,000, and the standard deviation of the probability distribution is \$398,000. In the same manner as in our earlier example, we can determine the probability that the net-present value of the project will be less than zero and the probability that it will be greater or less than other specified amounts. These probabilities give management a great deal of insight into the risk of the project.

MODERATE CORRELATION

Chapter 5 **129**
INFORMATION
NEEDED TO
EVALUATE RISKY
INVESTMENTS I

Although Hillier's approach goes a long way toward coping with the correlation of cash flows over time, one obvious problem is that cash flows must be classified as either independent or perfectly correlated over time. For many investment proposals, cash flows fall into neither of these categories but show less than perfect correlation over time. Whereas it would be possible to classify a cash-flow stream into the nearest category without serious distortion if the correlation were high or low, such a classification is not appropriate if the correlation is moderate. One method for handling the problem of moderate correlation is with a series of conditional probability distributions.

To illustrate, suppose that the investment in a project costing $10,000 at time 0 were expected to generate net cash flows in periods 1, 2, and 3 with the probabilities in Table 5-3, p. 130. As seen in the table, there are 27 possible cash-flow series. The last column depicts the joint probability of occurrence of a particular cash-flow series. For series 1, the joint probability of a −$6,000 cash flow in period 1 being followed by cash flows of −$2,000 and $5,000 in periods 2 and 3, respectively, is .25 × .30 × .25 = .01875. Similarly, joint probabilities for the other cash-flow series can be determined in this manner.[9]

The use of conditional probability distributions enables us to take account of the correlation of cash flows over time. In the above example, the cash flow in period 3 depends upon what happened in periods 1 and 2. However, the correlation of cash flows over time is not perfect. Given a cash flow in period 1, the cash flow in period 2 can vary within a range. Similarly, the cash flow in period 3 can vary within a range, given the outcomes in periods 1 and 2.

The calculation of the expected value of net-present value using this approach is the same as before (Eq. (5-3)). The standard deviation may be determined mathematically for the simple case by

$$\sigma = \sqrt{\sum_{x=1}^{l} (NPV_x - \overline{NPV})^2 P_x} \qquad (5\text{-}14)$$

where NPV_x is the net-present value for series x of net cash flows, covering all periods, $\overline{NVP}$ is the expected value of net-present value of the proposal, and P_x is the probability of occurrence of that series. For the above example, there are 27 possible series of cash flows, so that $l = 27$. The first series is represented by a net cash flow of −$10,000 at

---

[9] For another illustration of this type, using various scenarios of events to determine the dependence of cash flows over time, see Charles P. Bonini, "Comment on Formulating Correlated Cash Flow Streams," *Engineering Economist*, 20 (Spring 1975), 210–14.

Table 5·3 Illustration of conditional probability distribution approach

| Period 1 | | Period 2 | | Period 3 | | | |
Initial Probability P(1)	Net Cash Flow	Conditional Probability P(2|1)	Net Cash Flow	Conditional Probability P(3|2,1)	Net Cash Flow	Cash Flow Series	Joint Probability P(1,2,3)
				.25	$5,000	1	.01875
		.30	−$2,000	.50	7,000	2	.03750
				.25	9,000	3	.01875
				.25	7,000	4	.02500
.25	−$6,000	.40	1,000	.50	9,000	5	.05000
				.25	11,000	6	.02500
				.25	9,000	7	.01875
		.30	4,000	.50	11,000	8	.03750
				.25	13,000	9	.01875
				.30	10,000	10	.03750
		.25	3,000	.40	12,000	11	.05000
				.30	14,000	12	.03750
				.30	12,000	13	.07500
.50	−4,000	.50	6,000	.40	14,000	14	.10000
				.30	16,000	15	.07500
				.30	14,000	16	.03750
		.25	9,000	.40	16,000	17	.05000
				.30	18,000	18	.03750
				.25	15,000	19	.01875
		.30	8,000	.50	17,000	20	.03750
				.25	19,000	21	.01875
				.25	17,000	22	.02500
.25	−2,000	.40	11,000	.50	19,000	23	.05000
				.25	21,000	24	.02500
				.25	19,000	25	.01875
		.30	14,000	.50	21,000	26	.03750
				.25	23,000	27	.01875

time 0, −$6,000 at time 1, −$2,000 at time 2, and $5,000 at time 3. The probability of occurrence of that series is .01875. For the internal-rate-of-return approach, the standard deviation is

$$\sigma = \sqrt{\sum_{x=1}^{l} (IRR_x - \overline{IRR})^2 P_x} \qquad (5\text{-}15)$$

where IRR_x is the internal rate of return for series x of net cash flows, and $\overline{IRR}$ is the expected value of internal rate of return.

Unfortunately, for complex situations, the mathematical calculation of the standard deviation is unfeasible. For these situations, we can *approximate* the standard deviation by means of simulation. With simulation, the net-present values or internal rates of return for randomly selected series of cash flows are calculated. These net-present values or internal rates of return then are ordered according to their probability of occurrence, and a probability distribution of possible net-present values or internal rates of return is formed. The expected value and standard deviation of the probability distribution can then be calculated and this information analyzed in the same manner as before.[10]

We have seen that our assumption as to the degree of correlation of cash flows over time is an important one. The risk of a project will be considerably greater if the cash flows are highly correlated over time than if they are mutually independent, all other things being the same. Although independence often is assumed for ease of calculation, this assumption greatly underestimates project risk if in fact the cash flows are highly correlated over time. Thus, it is important that careful consideration be given to the likely degree of dependence of cash flows over time. Otherwise, the assessment of risk may well be distorted. Of the approaches for dealing with the problem, the use of conditional probabilities is the most accurate, although the most difficult to implement.

In an important contribution to evaluating risky investments, David B. Hertz proposed the use of a simulation model to obtain the expected return and dispersion about this expected return for an investment proposal.[11] Hertz considers the following factors in evaluating an investment proposal:

**A SIMULATION
APPROACH**

Market Analysis
1. Market size
2. Selling price

---

[10] It should be noted that the distribution of simulated internal rates of return for a project generally will not have the same "profile" as the distribution of net-present values. Simulated internal rates of return for cash flows above the mean of the distribution of cash flows are closer to the mean of the distribution of simulated internal rates of return than are simulated internal rates of return for cash flows below the mean of the distribution of cash flows. As a result, there is a bias toward skewness to the left in the distribution of simulated internal rates of return. Therefore, the mean of the distribution of simulated internal rates of return generally will be less than the mean of the distribution of internal rates of return. Elaboration on this point is contained in Alexander A. Robichek, "Two Errors in Interpreting the Results of Risk Analysis" (unpublished research paper, Stanford Graduate School of Business).

[11] David B. Hertz, "Risk Analysis in Capital Investment," *Harvard Business Review*, 42 (January–February 1964), 95–106; and Hertz, "Investment Policies That Pay Off," *Harvard Business Review*, 46 (January–February 1968), 96–108.

3. Market growth rate

4. Share of market (which results in physical sales volume)

Investment Cost Analysis

5. Investment required

6. Residual value of investment

Operating and Fixed Costs

7. Operating costs

8. Fixed costs

9. Useful life of facilities

Probability distributions are assigned to each of these factors, based upon management's assessment of the probable outcomes. Thus, the possible outcomes are charted for each factor according to their probability of occurrence.

Once the probability distributions are determined, the next step is to determine the average rate of return that will result from a random combination of the nine factors listed above. To illustrate the simulation process, assume that the market-size factor had the following probability distribution:

Market size (in thousand units)	450	500	550	600	650	700	750
Probability	.05	.10	.20	.30	.20	.10	.05

Now suppose that we have a roulette wheel with 100 numbers, on which numbers 1 to 5 represent a market size of 450,000 units, 6 to 15 represent a market size of 500,000, 16 to 35 a market size of 550,000 units, and so on through 100. As in roulette, we spin the wheel, and the ball falls in one of the 100 slots—number 26. For this trial, then, we simulate a market size of 550,000 units. Fortunately, we do not have to have a roulette wheel to undertake a simulation; the same type of operation can be carried out on a computer in a much more efficient manner.

Simulation trials are undertaken for each of the other eight factors. The first four factors (market analysis) give us the annual sales per year, while factors 7 and 8 give us the operating costs and fixed costs per year. Together, these six factors enable us to calculate the annual earnings per year. When trial values for these six factors are combined with trial values for the required investment, the useful life, and the residual value of the project, we have sufficient information to calculate the return on investment for that trial run. Thus, the computer simulates trial values for each of the nine factors and then calculates the return on investment based upon the values simulated. The process is repeated a number of times; each time we obtain a combination of values for the nine factors and the return on investment for that combination. When the trial is repeated often enough, the rates of return obtained can be plotted in a frequency distribution.

From this frequency distribution, we are able to evaluate the expected return and the dispersion about this expected return, or risk, in the same manner as before—in other words, we can determine the probability that an investment will provide a return greater or less than a certain amount. By comparing the probability distribution of rates of return for one proposal with the probability distribution of rates of return for another, management is able to evaluate the respective merits of different risky investments. Hertz's simulation method has been used widely and applied to a wide variety of investment projects. In one interesting application, Lawrence Kryzanowski, Peter Lusztig, and Bernhard Schwab present an algorithm for implementing the technique in the case of an actual proposed plant expansion by a major natural resource firm.[12] The interested reader should review their article.

Before closing, two points should be made about the simulation method. Although the simulation model computes the average rate of return on investment, the method could easily be modified to calculate the internal rate of return, the net-present value, or the profitability index.[13] In addition, although Hertz allows for dependency among the nine factors,[14] the model presented treats the factors as though they were independent. To the extent that dependency exists among factors, it must be taken into account in determining the probability distributions. For example, there is likely to be significant correlation between the market size and the selling price. These interrelationships add considerable complexity to the estimating procedure. Notwithstanding the added complexity of estimating and specifying the relationships between factors, it must be done if the model is to provide realistic results. These estimates may be based upon empirical testing when such testing is feasible. Once the relationships are incorporated in the model, those factors that are correlated would be simulated jointly. Rates of return for the simulated trials would be calculated and a frequency distribution of simulated trials formed in the same manner as before.

[12]"Monte Carlo Simulation and Capital Expenditure Decisions—A Case Study," *Engineering Economist*, 18 (Fall 1972), 31–48.

[13]Again there is the problem discussed in footnote 10 in working with simulated internal rates of return.

[14]Hertz, "Risk Analysis in Capital Investment," p. 101.

SUMMARY

In this chapter, we recognize that investment proposals have differing degrees of business risk. In addition to the expected profitability of a proposal, we must analyze possible deviations in profitability from that which is expected. Risk is expressed in terms of the dispersion of the probability distribution of possible net-present values or possible internal rates of return and is measured by the standard deviation. The focus of this chapter was on measuring the standard deviation under a variety of assumptions and to use it in relation to the expected value of the distribution in order to determine the probability of certain events occurring.

We first explored the measurement of risk under the assumption of serial independence of cash flows over time. We then considered its measurement when cash flows from one period to the next are dependent over time. Here we looked at perfect correlation, at situations where some components of the cash-flow stream are perfectly correlated over time while other components are independent, and at the use of conditional probability distributions for dealing with situations of moderate correlation of cash flows over time. We saw also that simulation techniques show promise for the analysis of risk. In the next chapter, we continue our discussion of the measurement of expected return and standard deviation for risky investments and, in Chapters 7 and 8, the evaluation of this information.

PROBLEMS

1. The Rettig Company can invest in one of the two mutually exclusive projects. The two proposals have the following discrete probability distributions of net cash flows for period p:

A		B	
Probability	Cash Flow	Probability	Cash Flow
.20	$1,000	.10	$1,000
.30	2,000	.40	2,000
.30	3,000	.40	3,000
.20	4,000	.10	4,000

(a) Without calculating a mean and a coefficient of variation, can you select the better proposal, assuming a risk-averse management?

(b) Verify your intuitive determination.

2. The probability distribution of possible net-present values for project x has an expected value of $20,000 and a standard deviation of $10,000. Assuming a normal distribution, calculate the probability that the net-present value will be zero or less; that it will be greater than $30,000; and that it will be less than $5,000.

3. The Dewitt Corporation has determined the following discrete probability distributions for net cash flows generated by a contemplated project:

Period 1		Period 2		Period 3	
Prob.	Cash Flow	Prob.	Cash Flow	Prob.	Cash Flow
.10	$1,000	.20	$1,000	.30	$1,000
.20	2,000	.30	2,000	.40	2,000
.30	3,000	.40	3,000	.20	3,000
.40	4,000	.10	4,000	.10	4,000

(a) Assume the probability distributions of cash flows for future periods are independent. Also, assume that the after-tax risk-free rate is 4 percent. If the proposal will require an initial outlay of $5,000, determine the expected value of the net-present value.

(b) Determine the standard deviation about the expected value.

(c) If the total distribution is approximately normal and assumed continuous, what is the probability of the net-present value being zero or less?

(d) What is the probability that the net-present value will be greater than zero?

(e) What is the probability that the profitability index will be 1.00 or less?

(f) What is the probability that the profitability index will be greater than 2?

4. Gomez Drug Products Company is considering investing in a new drug project with an estimated life of three years. If demand for the new drug in the first period is favorable, it is almost certain that it will be favorable in periods 2 and 3. By the same token, if demand is low in the first period, it will be low in the two subsequent periods as well. Owing to this likely demand relationship, the company feels that an assumption of perfect correlation of cash flows over time is appropriate. The cost of the project is $1 million, and possible cash flows for the three periods are:

Period 1		Period 2		Period 3	
Prob.	Cash Flow	Prob.	Cash Flow	Prob.	Cash Flow
.10	$ 0	.15	$ 100,000	.15	$ 0
.20	200,000	.20	400,000	.20	150,000
.40	400,000	.30	700,000	.30	300,000
.20	600,000	.20	1,000,000	.20	450,000
.10	800,000	.15	1,300,000	.15	600,000

Assuming the risk-free rate is 4 percent and it is used as the discount rate, calculate the expected value and standard deviation of the probability distribution of possible net-present values. Assuming a normal distribution, what is the probability of the project providing a net-present value of zero or less, of $300,000 or more, of $1,000,000 or more? Is the standard deviation calculated larger or smaller than it would be under an assumption of independence of cash flows over time?

5. The Dewitt Corporation (problem 3) has determined that its cash-flow distributions are not independent. Further, the company has estimated that the period 1 results will affect the period 2 flows as follows:

If P_1 = $1,000, the distribution for P_2 is:

.50	$1,000
.40	2,000
.10	3,000

If P_1 = $2,000, the distribution for P_2 is:

.20	$1,000
.50	2,000
.30	3,000

If P_1 = $3,000, the distribution for P_2 is:

.10	$1,000
.20	2,000
.50	3,000
.20	4,000

If P_1 = $4,000, the distribution for P_2 is:

.10	$2,000
.30	3,000
.50	4,000
.10	5,000

(a) What is the most probable cash flow for P_2? What is the probability that this flow will occur?

(b) What is the probability that the cash flow for P_2 will be $5,000?

(c) What is the probability that the cash flow for P_2 will be $6,000?

(d) If P_1 = $3,000, what is the probability P_2 = $3,000?

(e) What is the probability that P_1 = $1,000 and P_2 = $1,000?

(f) What is the probability that P_2 will be greater than $3,000?

(g) If P_1 = $5,000, what is the probability that P_2 = $3,000?

(h) What is the probability that P_2 will be greater than $3,000, given the fact that P_1 is greater than $3,000?

(i) If P_2 = $3,000, what is the probability that P_1 = $3,000?

6. The Hume Corporation is faced with several possible investment projects. For each, the total cash outflow required will occur in the initial period. The cash outflows, expected net-present values, and standard deviations are as follows. (All projects have been discounted at the risk-free rate of 4 percent, and it is assumed that the distributions of their possible net-present values are normal.)

Project	Cost	Net-present Value	σ
A	$100,000	$10,000	$20,000
B	50,000	10,000	30,000
C	200,000	25,000	10,000
D	10,000	5,000	10,000
E	500,000	75,000	75,000

(a) Construct a risk profile for each of these projects in terms of the profitability index.

(b) Ignoring size problems, are there some projects that are clearly dominated by others?

(c) May size problems be ignored?

(d) What is the probability that each of the projects will have a net-present value ≥ 0?

(e) What decision rule would you suggest for adoption of projects within this context? Which (if any) of the above projects would be adopted under your rule?

7. The Bertz Company uses a simulation approach to judge investment projects. Three factors are employed: market demand, in units; price per unit minus cost per unit; and investment required at time *0*. These factors are felt to be independent of one another. In analyzing a new consumer product, Bertz estimates the following probability distributions:

Annual Demand		Price Minus Cost per Unit		Investment Required	
Prob.	Units	Prob.	Dollars	Prob.	Dollars
.05	10,000	.10	$3.00	.30	$1,800,000
.10	20,000	.20	4.50	.40	2,000,000
.20	30,000	.40	6.00	.30	2,300,000
.30	45,000	.20	7.00		
.20	60,000	.10	8.00		
.10	75,000				
.05	90,000				

(a) Using a random number table or some other random process, simulate twenty or more trials for these three factors and compute the return on investment for each trial. (Note: return = profit/ investment.)

(b) Approximately what is the most likely return? How risky is the project?

SELECTED REFERENCES (*see chap. 6*)

INFORMATION NEEDED to EVALUATE RISKY INVESTMENTS II

In this chapter, we continue our discussion of developing the information necessary for the evaluation of risky investments. First, we explore the use of decision trees to deal with investments involving sequential decisions over time. We next consider the effect that the possibility of abandoning has upon a project's expected return and risk. Additionally, we take up the measurement of risk when a portfolio of assets is involved. While our concern here is with the incremental risk a project contributes to the overall portfolio, it should be stressed at this time that an evaluation based on such a measure is valid only under certain circumstances. These circumstances are identified and analyzed in Chapter 7; as in the preceding chapter, our focus in this chapter is on measuring risk. Finally, we explore the information necessary to evaluate a prospective acquisition. All of this information is used in the next two chapters when we consider the evaluation of risky investments in firm-risk and market-risk contexts.

In capital budgeting, some investment opportunities involve a sequence of decisions over time. Heretofore, we have considered only a single accept-reject decision at the outset of the project. An analytical technique used in sequential decisions is the decision tree, where various decision points are studied in relation to subsequent chance events. This technique enables one to choose among alternatives in an objective and consistent manner.

DECISION-TREE APPROACH FOR SEQUENTIAL DECISIONS

To illustrate the method, let us suppose that a firm is considering the introduction of a new product. Initially, it must decide whether to distribute the product in the Midwest or nationally. Regional distribution will require an expenditure of $1 million for a new plant and for the initial marketing effort. Depending upon demand during the first two years, the firm then would decide whether or not to expand to national distribution. If it goes from regional to national distribution, it will need to spend an additional $3 million for expansion of the existing plant and to make an additional marketing effort. Of course, the firm can distribute nationally from the very outset. If it does, it will cost $3 million to construct a plant and to launch the marketing of the product. Thus, we see that there are economies associated with distributing nationally at the outset. For one thing, building a large plant is less expensive than building a small one and having to enlarge it later. Moreover, there are economies in marketing.

The decision process is illustrated graphically by the decision tree shown in Figure 6-1. The squares represent decision points. For example, the first decision is whether to distribute regionally or nationally.The circles represent chance event nodes. If the firm decides to distribute nationally at the outset, there is 0.4 probability that demand will prove to be high, 0.4 that demand will turn out to be medium, and 0.2 that it will

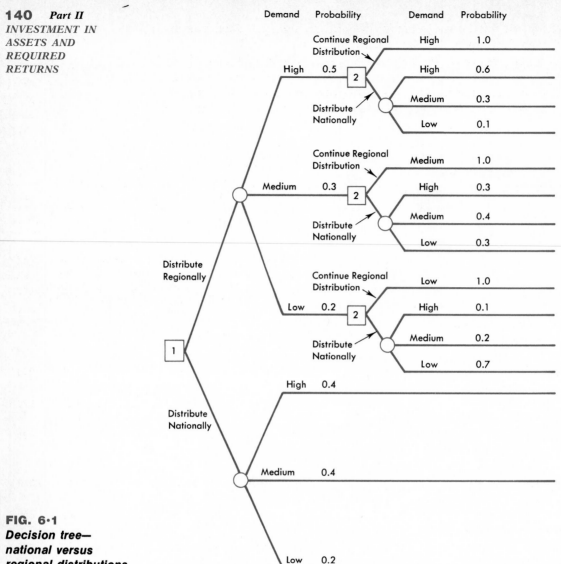

FIG. 6·1
Decision tree—
national versus
regional distributions

be low. On the other hand, if the firm distributes regionally, there is 0.5 probability that demand will be high, 0.3 probability that it will be medium, and 0.2 probability that it will be low. At the end of year 2, the firm must decide whether to continue to distribute regionally, in which case demand will continue to be high, low, or medium, or whether it should distribute nationally, in which case the national demand is shown by the subsequent chance event in the figure.

In all cases, the product is expected to have a life of eight years. Moreover, we assume for simplicity's sake that at the end of the eighth year, the plant has no more useful life and no salvage value. The expected cash flows over the eight years are shown in Table 6-1 for the various outcomes. We note in the table that if the firm switches from regional to national distribution at the end of year 2, there is a cash expenditure of $3 million at the end of the year. When this expenditure is combined with the cash flow generated from regional demand for the

Table 6·1 Expected cash flows for various branches of decision tree (000 omitted)

	Time									NPV
	0	1	2	3	4	5	6	7	8	
Regional distribution throughout										
High demand	−$1,000	$100	$ 300	$ 400	$ 500	$ 400	$ 300	$ 200	$100	$ 947.4
Medium demand	−1,000	0	150	250	350	250	200	100	50	136.2
Low demand	−1,000	−100	0	100	200	100	100	50	0	−637.1
Regional distribution followed by national distribution:										
High regional—high national demand	−1,000	100	−2,700	1,200	1,800	2,400	1,800	1,200	800	4,096.9
High regional—medium national demand	−1,000	100	−2,700	700	1,200	1,800	1,200	700	500	1,573.1
High regional—low national demand	−1,000	100	−2,700	200	700	1,300	700	200	200	−704.1
Medium regional—high national demand	−1,000	0	−2,850	1,100	1,700	2,300	1,700	1,100	700	3,377.4
Medium regional—medium national demand	−1,000	0	−2,850	600	1,100	1,700	1,200	600	400	932.6
Medium regional—low national demand	−1,000	0	−2,850	100	600	1,100	700	100	100	−1,426.8
Low regional—high national demand	−1,000	−100	−3,000	1,000	1,500	2,100	1,500	1,000	600	2,411.2
Low regional—medium national demand	−1,000	−100	−3,000	500	1,000	1,500	1,000	500	300	51.9
Low regional—low national demand	−1,000	−100	−3,000	0	500	900	500	0	0	−2,307.5
National distribution throughout:										
High demand	−3,000	300	1,000	1,500	2,000	1,500	1,000	700	300	4,030.5
Medium demand	−3,000	0	500	1,000	1,500	1,000	500	100	100	1,151.6
Low demand	−3,000	−300	0	500	1,000	500	0	−100	−100	−1,727.3

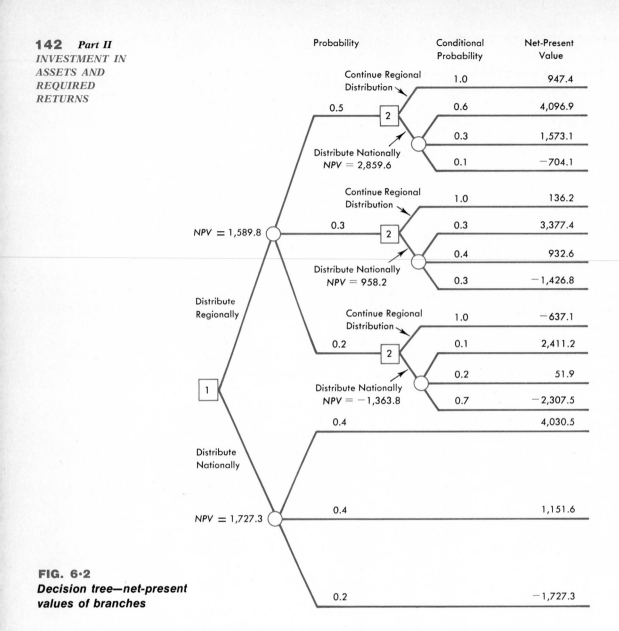

Probability		Conditional Probability	Net-Present Value

Continue Regional Distribution — 1.0 — 947.4

0.5 — [2]

0.6 — 4,096.9

0.3 — 1,573.1

Distribute Nationally NPV = 2,859.6 — 0.1 — −704.1

Continue Regional Distribution — 1.0 — 136.2

0.3 — [2]

0.3 — 3,377.4

0.4 — 932.6

Distribute Nationally NPV = 958.2 — 0.3 — −1,426.8

NPV = 1,589.8

Distribute Regionally

Continue Regional Distribution — 1.0 — −637.1

0.2 — [2]

0.1 — 2,411.2

0.2 — 51.9

Distribute Nationally NPV = −1,363.8 — 0.7 — −2,307.5

[1]

0.4 — 4,030.5

Distribute Nationally

NPV = 1,727.3

0.4 — 1,151.6

0.2 — −1,727.3

FIG. 6·2
*Decision tree—net-present
values of branches*

year, we obtain the net cash flow for year 2. In general, the lower the combination of regional and national demand, the lower the cash-flow sequence. Assuming a risk-free rate of 4 percent after taxes, the net-present values of the various combinations are shown in the last column of the table. We need now to incorporate these net-present values into our decision tree. In Figure 6-2, they are shown at the branch tips, indicating the expected net-present values associated with the sequence of decisions and chance events comprising the branch.

OPTIMAL SET OF DECISIONS

Chapter 6 **143**
*INFORMATION
NEEDED TO
EVALUATE RISKY
INVESTMENTS II*

The optimal sequence of decisions is determined by "rolling back" the tree from the right-hand side. In other words, we appraise first the most distant decision—namely, the choice of whether or not to switch from national to regional distribution. To do so we must determine the expected value of net-present value for national distribution, given that demand for the regional distribution proves to be high, medium, or low. The expected value of net-present value is simply the net-present values at the branch tips times the probabilities of occurrence. For high regional demand, the expected value of net-present value for subsequent national distribution is

$$NPV = 0.6(4,096.9) + 0.3(1,573.1) + 0.1(-704.1)$$
$$= \$2,859.6 \tag{6-1}$$

This amount appears at the chance event node for national distribution, given high regional demand.

In a similar fashion, the expected values of net-present value for national distribution, given medium and low regional demands, are computed and shown at the appropriate chance event nodes. We note that the expected value of net-present value for national distribution, given low regional demand, is −\$1,363,800. This figure compares with an expected net-present value of −\$637,100 if the firm continues with regional distribution. Thus, if regional demand is low, the firm should not distribute nationally but should continue to distribute regionally. On the other hand, if regional demand turns out to be either high or medium, the firm should go to national distribution, for the expected value of net-present value is higher than it is if the firm continues with regional distribution. By backward induction, then, we are able to determine the optimal decision at the most distant decision point.

The next step is to determine the optimal decision at the first decision point—that is, to decide whether to distribute nationally or regionally at the outset. The expected value of net-present value for regional distribution, given optimal decisions at decision point 2, is

$$NPV = 0.5(2,859.6) + 0.3(958.2) + 0.2(-637.1) = \$1,589.8 \tag{6-2}$$

Note that if regional demand is high or medium, we use the expected value of net-present value associated with subsequent national distribution. If regional demand is low, we use the expected net-present value associated with continuing regional distribution. The expected value of net-present value for initial national distribution is

$$NPV = 0.4(4,030.5) + 0.4(1,151.6) + 0.2(-1,727.3)$$
$$= \$1,727.3 \tag{6-3}$$

Thus, the expected value of net-present value for initial national distribution exceeds that for initial regional distribution. Moreover, when we compute the standard deviation of the probability distribution of possible net-present values, we find it to be $2,123,400 for initial national distribution compared with $2,145,500 for initial regional distribution. Therefore, initial national distribution dominates initial regional distribution with respect to both expected return and dispersion. The economies associated with building the plant and initiating the marketing effort all at once as opposed to piecemeal more than offset the flexibility associated with regional distribution initially with the later possibility of national distribution. Thus, initial national distribution is the preferred alternative. Whether management will want to undertake the project, however, will depend upon its risk preferences. Given the expected value and standard deviation of the probability distribution of possible net-present values for initial national distribution, it must decide whether the project is worthwhile. This decision will be based upon considerations discussed in the next two chapters.

We have seen that a decision-tree approach allows us to handle sequential investment decisions. By backward induction, we are able to determine optimal decisions at various decision points. Alternative branches are eliminated on the basis of dominance.[1] The approach will be used in the next section when we consider abandonment.

MEASURING RISK WHEN THE POSSIBILITY OF ABANDONMENT EXISTS

At times it may be desirable to abandon a project, even though its economic life is not over. Recognition of this possibility may enhance the project's expected return as well as lower its risk over what would be the case if abandonment value were ignored. The economic rationale for abandonment is the same as that for capital budgeting. Funds should be removed from a project, or disinvested, whenever the project does not economically justify use of these funds.

For ease of understanding, we assume initially that disinvestment does not alter the business-risk complexion of the firm as a whole or the covariance of its stock with other stocks in the market. Under such circumstances, the opportunity cost of funds tied up in a project is the firm's cost of capital. In general, an investment project should be abandoned when its abandonment value exceeds the present value of the project's subsequent expected future cash flows, discounted at the cost-of-capital rate. In certain cases, this rule must be modified so that

[1] For additional discussion of the decision-tree approach to capital investment, see John F. Magee, "Decision Trees for Decision Making," *Harvard Business Review*, 42 (July–August 1964), 126–38; Magee, "How to Use Decision Trees in Capital Investment," *Harvard Business Review*, 42 (September–October 1964), 79–96; and Richard F. Hespos and Paul A. Strassmann, "Stochastic Decision Trees for the Analysis of Investment Decisions," *Management Science*, 9 (August 1966), 244–59.

abandoning the project at a later time can be considered. The abandonment value of a project is assumed to represent its disposal value, which would become available to the firm either in cash or cash savings.[2] An asset does not actually have to be sold to be abandoned; it may simply be employed in another area of the enterprise. In either case, an abandonment value can be estimated.

The abandonment rule posed above can be expressed more formally as[3]

1. Compute the present value of the sum of cash flows expected to be generated from the project and the expected abandonment value at the end of the holding period. If there were n years remaining in the life of the project, there would be n possible holding periods, and n present values to compute. Thus,

$$PV_{\tau \cdot a} = \sum_{t=\tau+1}^{a} \frac{A_t}{(1 + k)^{(t-\tau)}} + \frac{AV_a}{(1 + k)^{(a-\tau)}} \qquad (6\text{-}4)$$

where
$PV_{\tau \cdot a}$ = present value at time τ of expected future net cash flows through period a, plus the present value of the expected abandonment value at the end of period a
a = period in which the project is abandoned
A_t = expected net cash flow of the project in period t
k = cost-of-capital rate
AV_a = expected abandonment value at the end of period a

Present values are computed under the assumption of abandonment in every period $\tau + 1 \leq a \leq n$, where n is the remaining life of the project.

2. Having calculated n present values, we then compare the largest such value, Max. $PV_{\tau \cdot a}$, with the current abandonment value, AV_τ. If Max. $PV_{\tau \cdot a}$ is greater than AV_τ, we continue to hold the project and evaluate it again at time $\tau + 1$, based upon our expectations at that time.

3. If Max. $PV_{\tau \cdot a}$ is equal to or less than AV_τ, we compare $PV_{\tau \cdot a}$ for $a = n - 1$ with AV_τ. If $PV_{\tau \cdot n-1} > AV_\tau$, we would hold the project and evaluate it again at time $\tau + 1$, the same as in step 2. If $PV_{\tau \cdot n-1} \leq AV_\tau$, we then compare $PV_{\tau \cdot n-2}$ with AV_τ. This procedure is continued until either the decision to hold is reached or $a = \tau + 1$.

4. If $PV_{\tau \cdot a} \leq AV_\tau$ for all $\tau + 1 \leq a \leq n$, then we would abandon the project at time τ.

In other words, these steps would have us abandon a project only if the present value of possible future benefits is less than the current

---

[2] For an excellent discussion of measuring cash flows and abandonment value, see Gordon Shillinglaw's two articles, "Profit Analysis for Abandonment Decision," and "Residual Values in Investment Analysis," both reprinted in Ezra Solomon, ed., *The Management of Corporate Capital* (New York: Free Press, 1959), pp. 269–81 and 259–68, respectively.

[3] See Alexander A. Robichek and James C. Van Horne, "Abandonment Value and Capital Budgeting," *Journal of Finance*, 22 (December 1967), 577–89; Edward A. Dyl and Hugh W. Long, "Comment," *Journal of Finance*, 24 (March 1969), 88–95; and Robichek and Van-Horne, "Reply," ibid, 96–97.

abandonment value and if it does not appear that abandoning the project in the future would be more favorable than doing so currently. To continue with a project that the above rules suggest should be given up means that capital is being less than optimally employed. From an economic standpoint, the project simply is not earning its keep; therefore, it should be abandoned. In the discussion that follows, we assume that projects are abandoned according to the rules given above.

EFFECT UPON PROJECT SELECTION

The recognition of abandonment value may have a significant effect upon project selection. Implied in most capital-budgeting decisions is the notion that funds will be committed to an investment proposal over its entire estimated life.[4] Proposals are evaluated as though all outlays were sunk. However, many projects have significant abandonment values. Too often, this value is ignored, despite the fact that it can affect a project's expected profitability and risk. In this section, we propose another decision-tree approach for incorporating abandonment value into the analysis for capital budgeting. As some readers will appreciate, an abandonment problem can be formulated in a dynamic programming context.[5] For complex problems involving a number of branches and periods, this approach should be used. For purposes of illustration, however, we do not do so.

Consider an investment proposal that costs $3,000 at time zero and is expected to generate net cash flows over the next two years. These cash flows and their probabilities of occurrence are shown as a series of conditional probabilities in Table 6-2. For simplicity of illustration, we assume that after the second year, the proposal is not expected to provide any cash flow or residual value. We also assume an expected abandonment value of $1,500 at the end of the first period. There are nine possible series of cash flows over the two-year period, the first series representing a cash flow of $1,000 in period 1, followed by a cash flow of 0 in period 2. The joint probability of each series of cash flows is shown in the last column of the table; for the first series, it is 0.25 × 0.25 = 0.0625.

If we assume a required rate of return of 10 percent and use this rate as our discount factor, we are able to determine the expected value of net-present value of the proposal without abandonment by (1) computing the net-present value for each cash-flow series; (2) obtaining the expected net-present value for each series by multiplying the computed net-present value by the probability of occurrence of that series; and (3)

---

[4] This section is adapted from Robichek and Van Horne, "Abandonment Value and Capital Budgeting."

[5] Charles P. Bonini, "Evaluation of Project Risk in Capital Investments with Abandonment Options," Research Paper No. 224 (Stanford Graduate School of Business, September 1974).

Table 6·2   Conditional probability distribution series for abandonment example

Period 1		Period 2		
Cash Flow	Initial Probability P(1)	Cash Flow	Conditional Probability P(2|1)	Joint Probability P(1, 2)
		$ 0	0.25	0.0625
$1,000	0.25	1,000	0.50	0.1250
		2,000	0.25	0.0625
		1,000	0.25	0.1250
2,000	0.50	2,000	0.50	0.2500
		3,000	0.25	0.1250
		2,000	0.25	0.0625
3,000	0.25	3,000	0.50	0.1250
		3,500	0.25	0.0625
		$0		

Abandonment value $1,500

adding the expected net-present values of all sequences. The standard deviation about the expected value of net-present value can be found using Eq. (5-14) in the preceding chapter. When we carry out these computations, we find the expected value of net-present value and the standard deviation to be $444 and $1,313, respectively, under the assumption of no abandonment.

When we allow for the possibility of abandonment, however, the results change dramatically. Following the decision rules specified earlier, we would divest ourselves of the project if its abandonment value at the end of period 1 exceeds the expected cash flows for the subsequent period, discounted at 10 percent.[6] Because cash flows are only expected for two periods, the possibility of abandoning the project beyond period 1 does not exist. Consequently, a number of the computational steps involved in the abandonment decision rules discussed are not applicable in this case. Referring again to Table 6-2, we find that we should abandon the project at the end of the first period if the cash flow in that period turns out to be $1,000. The reason is that the expected value of present value of possible cash flows in period 2, discounted to period 1, $909, is less than the abandonment value at the end of the period, $1,500. If the cash flow in period 1 turns out to be either $2,000 or $3,000, however, abandonment would not be worthwhile because the

[6] For purposes of illustration, we assume that the abandonment value is known with certainty. The approach could be modified to include a probability distribution of abandonment values.

Table 6·3   Conditional probability distribution series for revised case

Period 1		Period 2		
Cash Flow	Initial Probability P(1)	Cash Flow	Conditional Probability P(2|1)	Joint Probability P(1, 2)
$2,500	0.25	$ 0		0.2500
		1,000	0.25	0.1250
2,000	0.50	2,000	0.50	0.2500
		3,000	0.25	0.1250
		2,000	0.25	0.0625
3,000	0.25	3,000	0.50	0.1250
		3,500	0.25	0.0625

expected value of present value of period 2 cash flows discounted to period 1 exceeds $1,500.

When we allow for abandonment, the expected cash flows in Table 6-2 must be revised; these revisions are shown in Table 6-3. For the first branch in Table 6-2, the cash flow for period 1 becomes $2,500, the sum of the $1,000 cash flow during the period plus the abandonment value of $1,500. Because the proposal is abandoned at the end of period 1, there is no cash flow for this branch in period 2. Recalculating the expected value of net-present value deviation for the proposal based upon the information, we find them to be $578 and $1,110, respectively. Note the significant improvement in net-present value and the lower risk when the possibility of abandonment is considered.[7] A portion of the downside

---

[7] The consideration of abandonment value also affects the shape of the probability distribution as denoted by its skewness. A measure of relative skewness is $V/2SV$, where V is the variance of the distribution, and SV is the semivariance. Semivariance is the variance of the probability distribution to the left of the expected value of net-present value and may be thought to represent a measure of downside risk. Mathematically, it can be expressed as

$$SV(X) = \sum_{i=1}^{E(X)} [X_i - E(X)]^2 P(X_i)$$

where X_i is the net-present value observation, $E(X)$ is the expected value of net-present value, and the net-present value observations are ordered from low to high. For symmetrical probability distributions, $V/2SV$ equals one; for distributions skewed to the right, it is greater than one; for distributions skewed to the left, it is less than one. Using the cash-flow information in Tables 6-2, and 6-3, we find $V/2SV$ to be 0.962 and 1.145, respectively.

Thus, the consideration of abandonment changes the probability distribution for the proposal from one that is skewed slightly to the left to one that is skewed to the right. To the extent that management prefers distributions skewed to the right, the change is desirable; for it indicates that some of the downside risk has been eliminated. If management has a preference with respect to the shape of probability distribution (presumably it would favor a distribution skewed to the right), allowance for abandonment will affect these preferences.

risk for the proposal is eliminated if it is abandoned when events turn unfavorable. For example, with abandonment, there is no probability that net-present value will be less than $228; without abandonment, there is an 18.75 percent probability that net-present value will be less than that amount.

IMPLICATIONS

Although our example has purposely been kept simple, it does illustrate the importance of considering abandonment value when evaluating investment proposals.[8] Not to do so will result in an incomplete appraisal of the economic worth of an investment opportunity. The funds committed to certain proposals are relatively flexible; whereas those committed to others are not. For example, an investment in a multipurpose plant in a large city differs considerably from an investment in a special-purpose metal extraction complex in the wilderness of Canada. The former is reasonably marketable and may have a fairly high abandonment value; the latter represents a sunk cost that may never be recovered.[9] If the two projects had the same expected values of net-present values and standard deviations about these expected values, we would much prefer the former investment. A conventional analysis in capital budgeting, however, would not consider the important difference in abandonment values. If capital is to be allocated optimally, we must take into account possible differences in the future mobility of funds when evaluating investment proposals.

Heretofore, our concern has been with measuring risk for a single investment project. When multiple investment projects are involved, the measurement of risk may differ from that for a single project owing to the properties of diversification. Diversification of securities was illustrated in Chapter 3, and this concept applies also to capital assets. However, it is important to recognize that investment in capital assets differs somewhat from that in securities. For one thing, capital assets typically are not divisible, whereas securities are. Moreover, it usually is much more costly, and sometimes impossible, to divest oneself of a capital asset, whereas selling a marketable security is relatively easy. Finally, there is the problem of mutual exclusion and contingency that

**MEASURING RISK:
MULTIPLE
INVESTMENT
PROJECTS**

---

[8] In Robichek and Van Horne, "Abandonment Value and Capital Budgeting," a simulation method is developed to serve as a "practical" substitute for the conditional probability approach illustrated in Tables 6-2 and 6-3. The latter approach is unfeasible when the possible number of cash-flow series is large.

[9] As mentioned before, an investment project does not have to be sold externally to have abandonment value. Abandonment value can be depicted by the economic use of the asset in fields of endeavor within the firm other than those in which it is currently being used.

does not occur with securities.[10] All of these factors make diversification with respect to capital assets more "lumpy" than diversification with securities. Whether diversification of capital assets is a thing of value for the firm is a subject of considerable controversy, and this controversy will be analyzed in the next two chapters. Our purpose here is only to show how to measure risk for combinations of risky investments, given the fact that such a measure is desired.

As was true earlier, the two pieces of information we seek are the expected value and standard deviation of the probability distribution of possible net-present values for the combination of projects being analyzed. The expected value usually is simply a weighted average of the expected values of the projects making up the combination. Under certain circumstances, this rule may be inappropriate. If two projects are complementary, such that they share costs and/or reinforce each other in generating income, the expected value of net-present value for the two projects combined is greater than the sum of the parts. On the other hand, two competing investments might be less attractive in combination than individually.[11] In both cases, allowance must be made for the fact that the expected value of a combination is different from the sum of the parts.

From Chapter 3, we know that the total variance, or risk, of a combination of risky investments depends to a large extent upon the degree of correlation between the investments.[12] The standard deviation of the probability distribution of possible net-present values for a portfolio of capital investments can be expressed as

$$\sigma = \sqrt{\sum_{j=1}^{m} \sum_{k=1}^{m} r_{jk}\sigma_j\sigma_k} \tag{6-5}$$

where m is the total number of assets in the portfolio, r_{jk} is the expected correlation between the net-present values for investments j and k, σ_j is the standard deviation about the expected value of net-present value for investment j, and σ_k is the standard deviation for investment k.

Equation (6-5) indicates that the standard deviation, or risk, of a portfolio of projects depends upon (1) the degree of correlation between various projects and (2) the standard deviation of possible net-present values for each project. We note that the higher the degree of positive correlation, the greater the standard deviation of the portfolio of

---

[10] See Haim Levy and Marshall Sarnat, "The Portfolio Analysis of Multiperiod Capital Investments under Conditions of Risk," *Engineering Economist*, 16 (Fall 1970), p. 8.

[11] See Frederick S. Hillier, "A Basic Model for Capital Budgeting of Risky Interrelated Projects," *Engineering Economist*, 17 (Fall 1971), 10–11.

[12] The development of this section assumes that the reader has covered portfolio selection in Chapter 3.

projects, all other things remaining constant. Moreover, the greater the standard deviations of the individual projects, the greater the standard deviation of the portfolio, if the correlation is positive. The standard deviations of the individual investment projects, necessary for the calculation of Eq. (6-5), are obtained through the methods presented in the preceding chapter.

CORRELATION BETWEEN PROJECTS

As was the case with a portfolio of securities discussed in Chapter 3, the correlation between expected net-present values of two projects may be positive, negative, or zero, depending upon the nature of the association. A correlation coefficient of 1.00 indicates that the net-present values of two investment proposals vary directly in the same proportional manner; a correlation coefficient of −1.00 indicates that they vary inversely in the same proportional manner; and a zero correlation coefficient usually indicates that they are independent.

For most pairs of investment projects, the correlation coefficient lies between 0 and 1.00. The lack of negatively correlated projects is due to most investments being correlated positively with the economy. Still it is possible to find projects having low or moderate degrees of correlation. For example, management might have reason to expect only slight correlation between an investment project involving an electronics product and one involving a new consumer product. It might, however, expect high positive correlation between investments in a milling machine and a turret lathe if both machines are to be used in the production of industrial lift trucks. Projects in the same general line of business tend to be highly correlated with each other, while projects in essentially unrelated lines of business tend to have low degrees of correlation.

Estimates of correlation coefficients must be carefully made if the standard deviation obtained in Eq. (6-5) is to be realistic. When investment projects are like projects with which the firm has had experience, it may be feasible to compute the correlation coefficients using historical data. For other investments, however, estimates of correlation coefficients must be based solely on an assessment of the future. Instead of estimating the correlation between pairs of investment projects directly, it may be better to employ an index model and estimate the correlation between an investment and some index, such as the Gross National Product or an industry production index. From these estimates, the standard deviation for a portfolio of investment projects can be approximated. The use of an index model was described in Chapter 3. As discussed there, using such a model reduces greatly the number of correlation coefficient estimates.

It is not unreasonable to suppose that management is able to make fairly accurate estimates of the correlation between investment projects or the correlation between an investment project and some index. To the extent that actual correlation differs from that expected, future correlation estimates on existing projects should be revised in keeping with the learning process. The learning process also applies to future estimates of correlation between investments similar to existing investments.

Instead of the approach discussed above, one may resort to methods that have been developed to simulate joint returns for a portfolio of investment projects. Cohen and Elton propose that the firm should specify the functional relationships between cash flows for a project and various factors giving rise to these cash flows.[13] The joint probability distribution of the various underlying factors must then be specified. Once these relationships are described, cash flows in each period for each investment can be simulated. For each simulation run, the net-present values of the individual investment projects are calculated. When these are summed, one obtains the net-present value of the portfolio. By simulating a number of times, a distribution of possible portfolio net-present values is formed, from which the expected value and standard deviation can be computed.

A somewhat similar approach, but one that uses simulation and stochastic linear programming, has been proposed by Salazar and Sen (SS).[14] They explore two types of uncertainty. The first involves possible changes in GNP and competitive factors likely to affect cash flows. The probabilities of occurrence of various outcomes for each of these factors are expressed as a probability tree, and their joint probability determined. The second type of uncertainty has to do with uncertainty once GNP and competitive factors are known. Given a particular branch of the probability tree involving GNP and competitive factors, possible cash flows are expressed as normal probability distributions. With this probabilistic information, SS simulate various outcomes, using the Weingartner mathematical programming model (described in Chapter 4). The branch tree and random components are simulated for each investment proposal under consideration and for portfolios of projects. In the end, one obtains a probability distribution of terminal worths for each portfolio, and the expected value and standard deviation of the distribution can be computed. The approach is similar to that used in an index model. The end product is information about the expected return and risk for various portfolios of projects.

The final output of simulation approaches—namely, the expected value and standard deviation of the probability distribution of possible portfolio net-present values—is the same as that generated through the

---

[13] Kalman J. Cohen and Edwin J. Elton, "Inter-Temporal Portfolio Analysis Based upon Simulation of Joint Returns," *Management Science,* 14 (September 1967), 5–11.

[14] Rudolfo C. Salazar and Subrata K. Sen, "A Simulation Model of Capital Budgeting under Uncertainty," *Management Science,* 15 (December 1968), 161–79. For a similar approach, see R. K. Harvey and A. V. Cabot, "A Decision Theory Approach to Capital Budgeting under Risk," *Engineering Economist,* 20 (Fall 1974), 37–49.

correlation coefficient approach described earlier. Actually, the two approaches are quite similar. In the simulation approach, we specify the functional relationship between project cash flows; in the correlation coefficient approach, we specify the relationship between the net-present values for various projects. In both cases, the accuracy of the final results hinges on the accuracy of these specifications. If accurate, the two approaches will give similar results. Because using correlation coefficients is less involved, we shall assume the use of this approach in the subsequent discussion.

FEASIBLE COMBINATIONS AND DOMINANCE

We now have a procedure for determining the total expected value and the standard deviation of the probability distribution of possible net-present values for a combination of investments. A combination includes all existing investment projects and one or more proposals under consideration. We assume that a firm has existing investment projects generating expected future cash flows and that disinvestment with respect to these projects is not possible. Existing projects comprise a subset that is included in all combinations. Proposals under consideration are assumed to represent all future proposals on the investment horizon.

The next step involves evaluating all feasible combinations of existing projects and proposals under consideration according to their expected values of net-present value and standard deviations to see which combinations dominate. Figure 6-3 is an example of a scatter diagram; here the expected value of net-present value is along the horizontal axis, and the standard deviation is on the vertical axis. Each dot represents a feasible combination of proposals under consideration and existing investment projects for the firm.

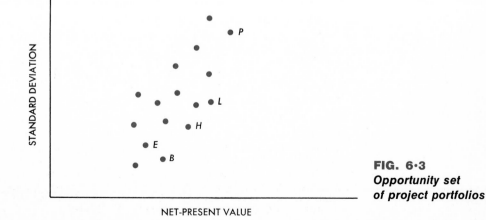

FIG. 6·3
Opportunity set
of project portfolios

Collectively, the dots represent the total set of feasible combinations of investment opportunities available to the firm. This set corresponds to the opportunity set of security portfolios discussed in Chapter 3, the major difference being that combinations of investment projects are not as divisible as portfolios of securities. Certain dots in Figure 6-3 dominate others in the sense that they represent a higher expected value of net-present value and the same standard deviation, a lower standard deviation and the same expected value of net-present value, or both a higher expected value and a lower standard deviation. The dots that dominate others are those that are farthest to the right in Figure 6-3, and they correspond to the efficient frontier for an opportunity set of security portfolios. If *E* represents the existing portfolio of investment projects, we see that it is dominated by combinations *H, L,* and *P* with respect to expected value of net-present value and by combination *B* with respect to both expected value of net-present value and standard deviation. Other dots dominate *E,* but these are not on the frontier. With the type of information in Figure 6-3, most combinations of investment proposals can be eliminated simply because they are dominated by other combinations. The efficient frontier represented by these dots also can be generated using integer programming.[15] In Chapter 8, we take up the evaluation of this information and the acceptance criterion.

It is important to recognize that the combination of projects ultimately chosen determines the new investment proposal or proposals that will be accepted. An exception occurs only when the portfolio selected is comprised of existing projects. In this situation, no investment proposals under consideration would be accepted. In our case, the portfolio of existing projects is represented by dot *E* in Figure 6-3. Therefore, the selection of any of the four outlying portfolios would imply the acceptance of one or more new investment proposals. Those investment proposals under consideration that were not in the portfolio finally selected would be rejected, of course. The incremental expected value of net-present value and standard deviation can be determined by measuring on the horizontal and vertical axes the distance from dot *E* to the dot representing the combination finally selected. Instead of working with net-present values, the framework described can be expressed in terms of internal rates of return. The reader should easily be able to visualize this change, for the principles are the same.

ACQUISITION OF ANOTHER COMPANY

Investment proposals under consideration are not necessarily confined to proposals generated internally. A proposal can consist of the acquisition of a company, or a portion thereof. The topic of acquisitions

[15] See D. E. Peterson and D. J. Laughhunn, "Capital Expenditure Programming and Some Alternative Approaches to Risk," *Management Science,* 17 (January 1971), 320–36.

is treated in Chapter 23; in the present chapter, we consider the capital-budgeting aspects of the problem. In principle, the prospective acquisition is much the same as any investment proposal; there is an initial outlay of cash or stock, followed by expected future benefits. The major difference is that with acquisitions, the initial cost may not be established; indeed, it frequently is subject to bargaining. The framework for analyzing the expected return and risk involved with an acquisition is similar to that discussed above. The critical thing is the accurate measurement of incremental cash flows, a topic to which we now turn.

MEASURING CASH FLOWS

In order to consider an acquisition in a capital-budgeting framework, expected future cash flows must be expressed on a basis consistent with those for investment proposals generated internally. In evaluating the prospective acquisition, the buying company should first estimate the future cash income the acquisition is expected to add.[16] Because we are interested in the marginal impact of the acquisition, these estimates should embody any expected economies, known as synergism, which are involved in the merger. In Chapter 23, it is established that certain mergers produce very important synergistic effects; as a result, the combination of the two companies is more valuable than the sum of the parts.

In an acquisition, there are the usual problems with respect to estimating future cash flows. However, the process may be somewhat easier than for a capital-budgeting proposal, because the company being acquired is a going concern. The acquiring company buys more than assets; it buys experience, an organization, and proven performance. The estimates of sales and costs are based upon past results; consequently, they are likely to be more accurate than the estimates for a new investment proposal.

In making the various estimates, it is important to isolate from consideration the capital structure that results from the merger. The reason is that once the merger is consummated, the buying company can modify the capital structure that results from the merger. Therefore, prospective incremental cash income from the acquisition should be estimated before interest charges. In other words, we attempt to measure the expected incremental earning power of the acquisition, apart from considerations of financing.

---

[16] See Samuel Schwartz, "Merger Analysis as a Capital Budgeting Problem," in William W. Alberts and Joel E. Segall, eds., *The Corporate Merger* (Chicago: University of Chicago Press, 1966), pp. 139–50.

Table 6·4 Illustration of incremental cash flows from an acquisition

	Average for Years (in thousands)				
	1–5	*6–10*	*11–15*	*16–20*	*21–∞*
Expected cash income from acquisition before taxes	$1,500	$2,000	$2,500	$3,000	$3,200
Taxes	500	700	1,000	1,200	1,300
Expected cash income after taxes	$1,000	$1,300	$1,500	$1,800	$1,900
Investment required	800	900	800	700	600
Net cash flow	$ 200	$ 400	$ 700	$1,100	$1,300

Expected incremental cash income should be adjusted for taxes. As was the case in Chapter 4, we deduct expected depreciation charges from cash income and compute the amount of taxes to be paid on the residual. By subtracting expected taxes from expected incremental cash income, we obtain cash income after taxes for each future period. From this expected cash income after taxes, we must subtract any new investments the acquiring firm believes it will have to make in order to generate the expected stream of earnings. The residual represents the expected cash flow after taxes for the period. It is extremely important that we take account of these investments; otherwise, incremental cash-flow estimates will be biased upward. An error frequently made is to treat as cash flows expected future earnings after taxes of the firm being considered for acquisition. The problem is that an earnings estimate for a future period usually is predicated upon reinvesting a portion of earnings from previous periods.[17] To use expected earnings in evaluating an acquisition results in double counting, as does the use of expected future earnings per share in a dividend valuation model.[18] In summation, the appropriate measure of incremental cash flow is expected earnings after taxes plus depreciation in each future period, less any investment required in that period.

To illustrate the information needed, suppose the incremental cash flows shown in Table 6-4 were expected from an acquisition. In the same manner, the firm should specify other possible net cash-flow series, with a probability attached to each. In other words, it needs to obtain a probability tree of possible net cash flows. The method for obtaining this probability tree was illustrated in Chapter 5; therefore, we do not discuss it here.

---

[17] It is also assumed that funds generated through depreciation allowances are reinvested to maintain the company's existing level of earnings.

[18] I am grateful to H. E. Borgstrom, Jr., for pointing this out.

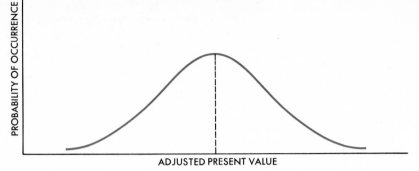

FIG. 6·4
Probability distribution
of possible
present values for a
prospective acquisition

If the acquisition were to be analyzed in isolation of other companies or stocks in the market, we would need to develop information on the dispersion of possible outcomes. (An example of such a situation might be an acquiring company whose stock was privately held and which wished to satisfy only the utility preferences of its owner(s)). Given the various net cash-flow series, each should be discounted to its present value using the risk-free rate. The result is a probability distribution of possible present values for the acquisition. An example of such a distribution is shown in Figure 6-4, and the expected value of present value and standard deviation can be easily determined.

If the acquisition is evaluated with respect to its marginal impact on the risk of the firm as a whole, however, we need additional information. More specifically, we need to estimate correlation coefficients for the relationships between the acquisition's present value and the present values for existing projects as well as investment proposals under consideration. (If an index model is used, we would estimate the correlation between the prospective acquisition and the index.) The acquisition then becomes one more investment proposal in a portfolio of projects to be considered. Note, however, that we have calculated only the present value of the acquisition. If the price to be paid is known, it should be subtracted from the expected value of present value to obtain the expected value of *net*-present value. With this information, one is able to evaluate the acquisition as part of a portfolio of projects in the same manner as described earlier. In most cases, however, the price to be paid is not set and must be negotiated.

In Chapter 8, we will investigate the question of whether an acquisition should be evaluated in isolation or as one of many companies whose stocks are publicly traded. Our concern in this chapter has been only with the information needed for the various types of evaluation possible. We leave to later the valuation principles inherent in the problem.

In this chapter, we explored the use of decision trees to deal with risky investments that involve sequential decisions over time. Also considered was the effect that abandonment value has on the expected return and risk of a project. A project should be abandoned whenever the incremental return on its abandonment value is less than the minimum acceptable standard and it does not appear that abandonment in the future would be more favorable than current abandonment. Consideration of abandonment value may increase the expected return and lower the risk over what would be the case if such value is ignored.

A portfolio approach was presented for measuring the marginal risk of a project in relation to existing investment projects and proposals under consideration. As indicated, this approach has merit only under certain circumstances. Finally, we considered the types of information necessary to evaluate an acquisition. In general, an acquisition can be evaluated in much the same manner as an investment proposal generated internally. Of crucial importance, however, is the expression of expected cash flows in a manner consistent with internal projects; a specific method was presented for accomplishing such expression.

In the next two chapters, we consider the evaluation of investments given information about risk and expected return developed in this and the preceding chapter. We will investigate the acceptance or rejection of risky investments in relation to the objective of maximizing share price. Our discussion will involve us in the valuation of the firm and in the considerable theoretical controversy that surrounds the question of risky investments and acquisitions. Again, we point out that Chapters 5 through 8 must be treated as a package; the measurement of risk in this and the preceding chapter is valuable only in relation to the ultimate evaluation of the proposal(s).

PROBLEMS

1. The Kazin Corporation is considering introducing a new product, which it can distribute initially either in the state of Georgia or in the entire Southeast. If it distributes in Georgia alone, plant and marketing will cost $5 million, and Kazin can reevaluate the project at the end of three years to decide whether to go regional. To go regional at the end of three years would cost another $10 million. To distribute regionally from the outset would cost $12 million. The risk-free after-tax cost of funds to the firm is 4 percent. In either case, the product will have a life of six years, after which the plant will be worthless. Given the following data, what policy should Kazin adopt?

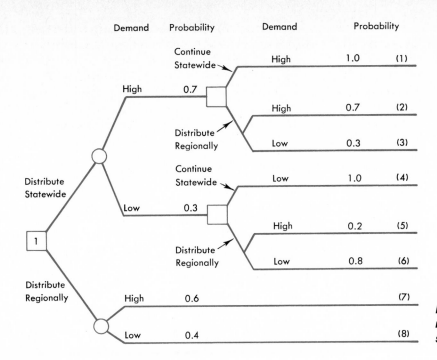

Demand	Probability	Demand	Probability

*Decision tree—
regional versus
statewide distribution*

Expected cash flows (in thousands)

				Years			
Branch	0	1	2	3	4	5	6
1	−$ 5,000	$1,000	$ 3,000	$ 5,000	$ 7,000	$ 4,000	$2,000
2	— 5,000	1,000	3,000	— 7,000	10,000	20,000	8,000
3	— 5,000	1,000	3,000	— 7,000	8,000	6,000	4,000
4	— 5,000	200	400	1,000	2,000	1,000	200
5	— 5,000	200	400	— 11,000	8,000	15,000	5,000
6	— 5,000	200	400	— 11,000	3,000	4,000	4,000
7	— 12,000	3,000	10,000	15,000	20,000	12,000	5,000
8	— 12,000	1,000	2,000	3,000	4,000	3,000	1,000

2. The Sniffle Corporation has determined the following distribution of net cash flows for a contemplated project:

Year 1	Year 2	Year 3
$ 5,000 (.5)	$ 3,000 (.6)	$ 1,000 (.7)
		$ 2,000 (.3)
	$ 6,000 (.4)	$ 8,000 (.5)
		$10,000 (.5)
$10,000 (.5)	$10,000 (.5)	$ 6,000 (.8)
		$ 8,000 (.2)
	$15,000 (.5)	$20,000 (.5)
		$25,000 (.5)

The firm has a required after-tax rate of return of 10 percent. The abandonment value of the project is as follows:

After Year 1		After Year 2	
Prob.	*Amount*	*Prob.*	*Amount*
.5	$8,000	.5	$2,000
.3	5,000	.3	1,500
.2	4,000	.2	1,000

(a) At the end of year 1, the project generated cash flows of $5,000. Should it be abandoned?

(b) At the end of year 2, the project generated a cash flow of $3,000. Should it be abandoned?

3. ABC Corporation is considering investing in a special-purpose piece of machinery costing $9,000 with a life of two years, after which there is no expected salvage value. The possible incremental net cash flows are:

Year 1		Year 2	
Cash Flow	*Probability*	*Cash Flow*	*Conditional Probability*
$6,000	.3	$2,000	.3
		3,000	.5
		4,000	.2
7,000	.4	4,000	.3
		5,000	.4
		6,000	.3
8,000	.3	6,000	.2
		7,000	.5
		8,000	.3

The company's cost of capital is 8 percent.

(a) Calculate the expected value and standard deviation of the probability distribution of possible net-present values.

(b) Suppose now that the possibility of abandonment exists and that the abandonment value of the project at the end of year 1 is $4,500. Calculate the new expected value and standard deviation assuming the company abandons the project if it is worthwhile to do so. Compare your calculations with those in 3(a). What are the implications?

4. The Cenno Company has a required rate of return of 10 percent after taxes and pays a tax rate of 50 percent. It currently owns a G & H Drill Press, which it bought last year for $10,000. This drill press has a ten-year, straight-line depreciation schedule, with no salvage value assumed. Because of a great demand for drill presses, it would be possible to sell the press for a net price to the company (after costs of removal, etc.) of the net book value of the press. The G & H Drill Press is expected to make a contribution to profit before depreciation and taxes of $2,000 per year for the remainder of its useful life.

At this point, the Ft. John Machinery Company offers to accept the G & H Drill Press plus $7,000 in exchange for its new Super Drill Press. The Super Press has an expected useful life of fifteen years, at which time it would have a salvage value of $1,000; this machine would also be depreciated on a straight-line basis. The Super Press would be expected to make a $3,000 yearly contribution to profit before depreciation and taxes.

As financial VP of the Cenno Company, you have adequate cash available for any of these alternatives and also other investment opportunities. What should you do?

5. The Windrop Company is considering investment in two of three possible proposals, the cash flows of which are normally distributed. The expected net-present value (discounted at the risk-free rate of 4 percent) and the standard deviation for each proposal are given as follows:

	1	2	3
Expected net-present value	$10,000	$8,000	$6,000
Standard deviation	4,000	3,000	4,000

Assuming the following correlation coefficients for each possible combination, which two proposals dominate?

Proposals	1	2	3	1 and 2	1 and 3	2 and 3
Correlation coefficients	1.00	1.00	1.00	.60	.40	.70

6. Zello Ice Cream Company is considering investing in a new product line—puddings. The expected value and standard deviation of the probability distribution of possible net-present values for the product line are $12,000 and $9,000, respectively. The company's existing lines are ice cream, cottage cheese, and yogurts. The expected values of

net-present value and standard deviation for these product lines are:

	Net-Present Value	σ
Ice cream	$16,000	$8,000
Cottage cheese	20,000	7,000
Yogurts	10,000	4,000

The correlation coefficients between products are:

	Ice Cream	Cottage Cheese	Yogurts	Puddings
Ice cream	1.00			
Cottage cheese	.90	1.00		
Yogurts	.80	.84	1.00	
Puddings	.40	.20	.30	1.00

(a) Compute the expected value and the standard deviation of the probability distribution of possible net-present values for a combination consisting of existing products.

(b) Compute the expected value and standard deviation for a combination consisting of existing products plus puddings. Compare your results in (a) and (b). What can you say about the pudding line?

7. The Plaza Corporation is confronted with several combinations of risky investments:

Old Portfolios:	Net-present Value	σ
A	$100,000	$200,000
B	20,000	80,000
C	75,000	100,000
D	60,000	150,000
E	50,000	20,000
F	40,000	60,000

New Portfolios:	Net-present Value	σ
G	$120,000	$170,000
H	90,000	70,000
I	50,000	100,000
J	75,000	30,000

(a) Plot the above portfolios.

(b) Which portfolios dominate?

8. The R. Z. Frank Company is considering the acquisition of Aziz Car Leasing Company. Frank estimates that Aziz will provide incremental net income after taxes of $2 million in the first year, $3 million the second, $4 million the third, $5 million in each of the years 4 through 6, and $6 million annually thereafter. Due to the need to replenish the fleet, heavier than usual investments are required in the first two years. Capital investments and depreciation charges are expected to be:

Year	1	2	3	4	5	6	7 on
Capital investment (in millions)	$5	$5	$4	$4	$4	$4	$4
Depreciation (in millions)	$3	$4	$4	$4	$4	$4	$4

The risk-free rate is 4 percent and Aziz has $40 million in debt. Compute the adjusted present value of the acquisition based on these expectations. If you had a range of possible outcomes, how would you obtain the information necessary to analyze the acquisition?

SELECTED REFERENCES

Bierman, Harold Jr., and Warren H. Hausman, "The Resolution of Investment Uncertainty through Time," *Management Science,* 18 (August 1972), 654–62.

Bierman, Harold, Jr., and Seymour Smidt, *The Capital Budgeting Decision,* Part III. New York: Macmillan, 1971.

Bonini, Charles P., "Comment on Formulating Correlated Cash Flow Streams," *Engineering Economist,* 20 (Spring 1975), 209–14.

————"Evaluation of Project Risk in Capital Investments with Abandonment Options," Research Paper No. 224, Stanford Graduate School of Business, 1974.

Boudreaux, Kenneth J., "Divestiture and Share Price," *Journal of Financial and Quantitative Analysis,* 10 (November 1975), 619–26.

Brigham, Eugene F., and Richard H. Pettway, "Capital Budgeting by Utilities," *Financial Management,* 2 (Autumn 1973), 11–22.

Brumelle, Shelby L., and Bernhard Schwab, "Capital Budgeting with Uncertain Future Opportunities: A Markovian Approach," *Journal of Financial and Quantitative Analysis,* 7 (January 1973), 111–22.

Bussey, Lynn E., and G. T. Stevens, Jr., "Formulating Correlated Cash Flow Streams," *Engineering Economist,* 18 (Fall 1972), 1–30.

Buzby, Stephen L., "Extending the Applicability of Probabilistic Management Planning and Control Models," *Accounting Review,* 49 (January 1974), 42–49.

Byrne, R., A. Charnes, A. Cooper, and K. Kortanek, "Some New Approaches to Risk," *Accounting Review,* 63 (January 1968), 18–37.

Carter, E. Eugene, *Portfolio Aspects of Corporate Capital Budgeting.* Lexington, Mass.: D.C. Heath, 1974.

Cohen, Kalman J., and Edwin J. Elton, "Inter-Temporal Portfolio Analysis Based upon Simulation of Joint Returns," *Management Science,* 14 (September 1967), 5–18.

Edelman, Franz, and Joel S. Greenberg, "Venture Analysis: The Assessment of Uncertainty and Risk," *Financial Executive,* 37 (August 1969), 56–62.

Greer, Willis R., Jr., "Capital Budgeting Analysis with the Timing of Events Uncertain," *Accounting Review,* 45 (January 1970), 103–14.

———, "Theory versus Practice in Risk Analysis: An Empirical Study," *Accounting Review,* 49 (July 1974), 496–505.

Harvey, R. K., and A. V. Cabot, "A Decision Theory Approach to Capital Budgeting under Risk," *Engineering Economist,* 20 (Fall 1974), 37–49.

Hayes, Robert H., "Incorporationg Risk Aversion into Risk Analysis," *Engineering Economist,* 20 (Winter 1975), 99–121.

Hertz, David B., "Investment Polices That Pay Off," *Harvard Business Review,* 46 (January–February 1968), 96–108.

———, "Risk Analysis in Capital Investment," *Harvard Business Review,* 42 (January–February 1964), 95–106.

Hespos, Richard F., and Paul A. Strassmann, "Stochastic Decision Trees for the Analysis of Investment Decisions," *Management Science,* 11 (August 1965), 244–59.

Hillier, Frederick S., "The Derivation of Probabilistic Information for the Evaluation of Risky Investments," *Management Science,* 9 (April 1963), 443–57.

———, "A Basic Model for Capital Budgeting of Risky Interrelated Projects," *Engineering Economist,* 20 (Fall 1974), 37–49.

Jarrett, Jeffrey E., "An Abandonment Decision Model," *Engineering Economist,* 19 (Fall 1973), 35–46.

Keeley, Robert, and Randolph Westerfield, "A Problem in Probability Distribution Techniques for Capital Budgeting," *Journal of Finance,* 27 (June 1972), 703–9.

Kryzanowski, Lawrence, Peter Lusztig, and Bernhard Schwab, "Monte Carlo Simulation and Capital Expenditure Decisions—A Case Study," *Engineering Economist,* 18 (Fall 1972), 31–48.

Levy, Haim, and Marshall Sarnat, "The Portfolio Analysis of Multiperiod Capital Investment under Conditions of Risk," *Engineering Economist,* 16 (Fall 1970), 1–19.

Lewellen, Wilbur G. and Michael S. Long, "Simulation versus Single-Value Estimates in Capital Expenditure Analysis," *Decision Sciences* 3 (1973), 19–33.

Lockett, A. Geoffrey, and Anthony E. Gear, "Multistage Capital Budgeting under Uncertainty," *Journal of Financial and Quantitative Analysis,* 10 (March 1975), 21–36.

Magee, J. F., "How to Use Decision Trees in Capital Investment," *Harvard Business Review,* 42 (September–October 1964), 79–96.

Peterson, D. E., and D. J. Laughhunn, "Capital Expenditure Programming and Some Alternative Approaches to Risk," *Management Science,* 17 (January 1971), 320–36.

Petty, J. William, David F. Scott, Jr., and Monroe M. Bird, "The Capital Expenditure Decision-Making Process of Large Corporations," *Engineering Economist,* 20 (Spring 1975), 159–72.

Porter, R. Burr, Roger P. Bey, and David C. Lewis, "The Development of a Mean-Semivariance Approach to Capital Investment," *Journal of Financial and Quantitative Analysis,* 10 (November 1975), 639–49.

Robichek, Alexander A., "Interpreting the Results of Risk Analysis," *Journal of Finance,* 30 (December 1975), 1384–86.

Robichek, Alexander A., and Stewart C. Myers, "Conceptual Problems in the Use of Risk-Adjusted Discount Rates," *Journal of Finance,* 21 (December 1966), 727–30.

———, *Optimal Financing Decisions,* Chapter 5, Englewood Cliffs, N.J.: Prentice-Hall, 1965.

Robichek, Alexander A., and James C. Van Horne, "Abandonment Value and Capital Budgeting," *Journal of Finance,* 22 (December 1967), 577–89; Edward A. Dyl and Hugh W. Long, "Comment," *Journal of Finance,* 24 (March 1969), 88–95; and Robichek and Van Horne, "Reply," ibid., 96–97.

Salazar, Rudolfo C., and Subrata K. Sen, "A Simulation Model of Capital Budgeting under Uncertainty," *Management Science,* 15 (December 1968), 161–79.

Sundem, Gary L., "Evaluating Capital Budgeting Models in Simulated Environments," *Journal of Finance,* 30 (September 1975), 977–92.

Van Horne, James C., "The Analysis of Uncertainty Resolution in Capital Budgeting for New Products," *Management Science,* 15 (April 1969), 376–86.

———, "Capital-Budgeting Decisions Involving Combinations of Risky Investments," *Management Science,* 13 (October 1966), 84–92.

———, "Capital Budgeting under Conditions of Uncertainty as to Project Life," *Engineering Economist,* 17 (Spring 1972), 189–99.

Wilson, Robert B., "Investment Analysis under Uncertainty," *Management Science,* 15 (August 1969), 650–64.

EVALUATION of RISKY INVESTMENTS: REQUIRED RATES of RETURN for PROJECTS

A BRIEF CHARTING OF OUR COURSE

Having examined the measurement of risk for the individual investment proposal and combinations of proposals in Chapters 5 and 6, we turn now to the way this information might be evaluated in order to reach investment decisions consistent with a goal of maximizing the value of the firm to its stockholders. Both this chapter and the next are devoted to this endeavor. In this chapter, we take up the evaluation of individual investment projects. In Chapter 8, we consider the acceptance criterion for the company as a whole and for a division thereof under restricted assumptions as to the homogeneity of project risk, and we explore the evaluation of acquisitions.

The first part of this chapter discusses the implications the capital-asset pricing model has for decisions involving risky investments. This model was presented in Chapter 3 and involved such assumptions as efficient and perfect capital markets, well-diversified investors, and homogeneous expectations on their part. Given these assumptions, we will see that the required rate of return for a project depends only on that project's *systematic risk*. Recall that this is the risk associated with underlying movements in security prices and cannot be diversified away. The implication of this approach is that diversification of assets by the firm is not a thing of value. Accordingly, management should ignore the impact the project has on the firm's total variability of returns. The only thing that is important is the project's systematic risk, and this risk is completely divorced from the present risk complexion of the firm. On the surface, this may seem rather implausible. However, it will be shown that this implication follows from the assumptions implicit in the capital-asset pricing model. As a result, the diversification attributes of a project should not be considered in the investment decision.

If some of the underlying assumptions do not hold, however, the effect of a project on the overall risk of the firm may be a factor of importance. Bankruptcy costs, in particular, may affect things in this way. In the second part of this chapter, we explore the evaluation of risky investments when the impact of their acceptance on the total risk of the firm is a factor of importance. Under such circumstances, a project's diversification properties with respect to the total risk of the firm are a relevant consideration. Consequently, the firm would want to consider the "portfolio" effect of the project on its existing asset portfolio.

Having covered market-risk and firm-risk approaches to evaluating risky investments, we then attempt to reconcile the two approaches. Whether a person supplements the capital-asset pricing model approach with an analysis of the project's impact on the overall risk of the firm depends on the strength of one's convictions regarding the assumptions underlying the former approach. Bankruptcy costs and other underlying assumptions are examined. In the end, it will be seen that we advocate a combined approach to the problem. It is important to recognize that the topic of risky capital investments has undergone a considerable change in thinking in recent years. We hope to capture some of the controversy involved, but in the process the reader may become frustrated with the unsettled nature of the issue.

This leads us to the last part of the chapter. While conceptually a case can be made for a combined approach, using the capital-asset pricing model and a total variability analysis, we recognize that in practice many companies do not evaluate risky investments in this manner. Decision making is more subjective in nature. Even here, however, the expected return and risk of a project can be quantified and such information provided to management. Management, in turn, is able to make informed investment decisions based on this information. In the last section, we explore this approach. As we shall see, the critical factor is how accurately management is able to link risk-return information for an investment project with share price. The linkage tends to be subjective, thus detracting from the merit of this approach.

Having briefly charted the somewhat murky and unsettled waters that lie ahead, we are ready to begin. It is important that the reader keep this overview in mind as he sorts out some of the conflicting approaches to the problem. Depending on one's judgment of the importance of certain capital market imperfections, one approach or the other will seem more important.

We turn now to the evaluation of investment proposals in a market equilibrium context.[1] Essentially, we will study the risk-return impact of a proposal on investors' portfolios of stocks rather than on the firm's portfolio of assets. In this regard, our concern is with systematic rather than with total risk. Assume initially that the firm has an all-equity capital structure. This facilitating assumption will be relaxed later in the section. Recall from Chapter 3 that according to the capital-asset pricing model, the expected rate of return on security j is

EVALUATING PROJECTS IN A CAPITAL-ASSET PRICING MODEL CONTEXT

$$R_j = i + \frac{\bar{R}_m - i}{\sigma_m^2}(r_{jm}\sigma_j\sigma_m) \qquad (7\text{-}1)$$

where i = risk-free rate

$\bar{R}_m$ = expected rate of return on the market portfolio of risky assets

σ_j = standard deviation of the probability distribution of possible returns for security j

σ_m = standard deviation of the probability distribution of possible returns for the market portfolio

r_{jm} = correlation between rates of return for security j and the market portfolio

[1] This section assumes the reader has covered Chapters 2 and 3.

The term $(r_{jm}\sigma_j\sigma_m)$ is the covariance of returns for security j with those of the market portfolio. For the diversified investor, $r_{jm}\sigma_j$ represents the portion of the total standard deviation of security j that is undiversifiable. In other words, the investor cannot avoid this risk through diversification, because it arises from general movements in the market. The difference between total risk for security j, as measured by its standard deviation σ_j, and systematic risk is the risk that can be eliminated through efficient diversification. The term $(\bar{R}_m - i)/\sigma_m^2$ represents the market equilibrium relationship between risk and returns in excess of the risk-free rate. From Chapter 3, we know that it represents a measure of market-risk aversion and, when depicted graphically, the relationship is known as the security market line. (See Figure 3-8 in Chapter 3.) Implied is that in market equilibrium, security prices will be such that there is a linear tradeoff between the required rate of return and risk. The slope of the line indicates the degree of systematic risk for security j.

APPLICATION TO CAPITAL BUDGETING

This framework has been applied to capital-budgeting projects.[2] It implies that projects should be judged in relation to their systematic risk. Thus, the appropriate discount rate for project k is

$$R_k = i + \frac{\bar{R}_m - i}{\sigma_m^2}(r_{km}\sigma_k\sigma_m) \tag{7-2}$$

where R_k = required rate of return for capital-budgeting proposal k

$\quad\quad \sigma_k$ = standard deviation of the probability distribution of possible returns for proposal k

$\quad\quad r_{km}$ = correlation between rates of return for proposal k and the market portfolio

---

[2] See Donald L. Tuttle and Robert H. Litzenberger, "Leverage, Diversification and Capital Market Effects on a Risk-Adjusted Capital Budgeting Framework," *Journal of Finance*, 23 (June 1968), 427–43; John Lintner, "The Valuation of Risk Assets and the Selection of Risky Investments in Stock Portfolios and Capital Budgets," *Review of Economics and Statistics*, 47 (February 1965), 13–27; Jan Mossin, "Equilibrium in a Capital Asset Model," *Econometrica*, 34 (October 1966), 768–75; Robert S. Hamada, "Portfolio Analysis, Market Equilibrium and Corporation Finance," *Journal of Finance*, 24 (March 1969), 13–31; Robert H. Litzenberger and Alan P. Budd, "Corporate Investment Criteria and the Valuation of Risk Assets," *Journal of Financial and Quantitative Analysis*, 5 (December 1970), 395–420; Mark E. Rubinstein, "A Mean-Variance Synthesis of Corporate Financial Theory," *Journal of Finance*, 28 (March 1973), 167–82; Lawrence D. Schall, "Asset Valuation, Firm Investment, and Firm Diversification," *Journal of Business*, 45 (January 1972), 11–28; and Harold Bierman, Jr., and Jerome E. Hass, "Capital Budgeting under Uncertainty: A Reformulation," *Journal of Finance*, 28 (March 1973), 119–29.

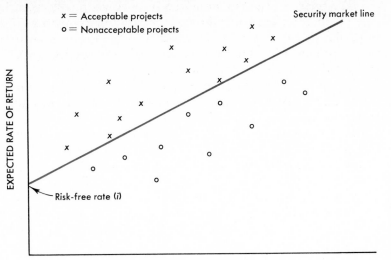

FIG. 7·1

*Relationship between
expected return
and covariance*

We know from Chapter 3 that the beta of an asset is $\beta_k = (r_{km}\sigma_k\sigma_m)/\sigma_m^2$, so Eq. (7-2) can be expressed in terms of the more familiar

$$R_k = i + (\bar{R}_m - i)\beta_k \qquad (7\text{-}3)$$

where β_k is the slope of the characteristic line which describes the relationship between expected excess market rates of return for the project and expected excess returns for the market portfolio.[3] Later in this section we will show how the beta for a project can be determined and discuss the problems inherent in its determination. Now, however, we want to continue to concentrate on the general implications of the capital-asset pricing model approach to evaluating risky investments.

The acceptance criterion using this approach is to invest in a project if its expected return exceeds the required return, R_k, as determined with Eq. (7-3). The process can be viewed graphically in Figure 7-1. The line in the figure represents the security market line, and, as we know, it describes the market-determined relationship between systematic risk and required rate of return. All projects with expected internal rates of return lying on or above the line should be accepted, for they provide excess returns. These projects are depicted by the x's. All projects lying below the line, shown by the o's, would be rejected. The acceptance of

---

[3] The capital-asset pricing model is single period in time frame. For the extension of its application to capital-budgeting decisions involving multiperiod investments, see Richard Roll and Marcus C. Bogue, "Capital Budgeting of Risky Projects with Imperfect Markets for Physical Capital," *Journal of Finance*, 29 (May 1974), 606–12.

projects lying above the line should result in an increase in share price, for investors will bid up the price of the stock until in equilibrium the expected returns for all projects of the firm are on the security market line.[4]

The goal of the firm in this context is to search for investment opportunities lying above the line. If product markets were perfect, one could not expect to find such opportunities. Investment opportunities would lie along or below the line, and the firm could expect to earn no more than the required rate of return. Thus, the combination of perfect product markets along with perfect capital markets would rule out the ability of firms to earn excess returns for their stockholders. Put another way, firms could expect to earn no more on a project than the return required by the market on the basis of the systematic risk involved.

If product markets are less than perfect owing to such things as lags in adjustment, constraints on resource allocation, monopolistic powers, barriers to entry, etc., it is possible to find projects with expected returns above the security market line. While competition among firms will tend to drive expected returns toward the line, there may be sufficient lags so as to allow excess returns to be temporarily earned. The mark of a successful company is one that is able to continually identify and exploit such opportunities. In what follows, we assume that product markets are less than perfect.

IMPLICATIONS AND SUPPORT
OF POSITION

One implication of the capital-asset pricing model approach to evaluating risky investments is that the required rate of return for the project does not depend on the company undertaking the investment. Given the project's systematic risk, the market expects a single return. Therefore, the required rate of return on the project is the same for any firm that might invest in it. Stated differently, the systematic risk of a project is the same for all firms; therefore, the project's required return is the same. This is not to say that the project is equally valuable to all firms. Some firms will be able to derive greater incremental cash flows from it than others. Because of differences in expertise, management efficiency, synergism, and so forth, the expected return can vary among firms. Consequently, the project will be more valuable to some firms than to others. However, the acceptance standard will be the same for all firms considering the project.

Because the capital-asset pricing model assumes that all risk other

---

[4] For proof that if a project's expected return exceeds the required rate under the assumptions above, market value share will rise, see Bierman and Hass, "Capital Budgeting under Uncertainty: A Reformulation," pp. 122–25.

than systematic risk is diversified away by investors in their portfolios of stocks, diversification by the firm in its portfolio of capital assets is not a thing of value. In other words, the model implies that the firm is unable to do something for investors that they cannot do for themselves.[5] Given the assumptions of the model, investors are able to achieve the same diversification as the firm is able to do for them. One could argue that while investors are able to diversify across companies whose stocks are publicly traded, they cannot diversify across capital assets held by these companies. In other words, they purchase shares in the income stream of the company as a whole, not in the income streams of the individual assets of the company.

However, investors do not need to acquire direct claims on capital assets in order to accomplish such diversification. As long as there is information available about the actual returns on individual assets, investors are able to effectively diversify across capital assets of individual companies. In essence, an investor can replicate the return stream of the individual capital asset held by a firm.[6] For example, suppose a firm holds three productive assets—A, B, and C—and that complete information exists about the actual ex-post returns on these assets. In order to "invest" in asset A, but not in assets B and C, the investor could buy x percent of the stock of the company. He then would sell claims against himself based on promises to pay x percent of the future income streams associated with assets B and C. That is, in a particular year if asset B were to provide a $100 return and asset C a $200 return, he would pay $100x$ and $200x$ to the holders of the claims. In this way, the investor is able to effectively replicate the income stream of a single capital asset of a firm, that of asset A in our example.

It is in this sense that investors are able to diversify effectively across capital assets of individual firms. As a result, the firm is said not to be able to do something for investors through diversification of capital assets that they cannot do for themselves. Therefore, investment projects should be evaluated only on the basis of their systematic risk, not on the basis of their total risk or the incremental risk they contribute to the firm as a whole.

We have tried to present the implications of the capital-asset pricing model for capital investment in their purest form. From Chapter 3, we know that there are many assumptions implicit in the model. When these assumptions are relaxed, certain implications arising from the use of the model must be modified. Later in this chapter we explore such

[5] For an evaluation of this concept in a state-preference mold, see Stewart C. Myers, "Procedures for Capital Budgeting under Uncertainty," *Industrial Management Review*, 9 (Spring 1968), 1–15.

[6] See Schall, "Asset Valuation, Firm Investment, and Firm Diversification," pp. 13–21, for amplification on this point as well as proof of the irrelevancy of diversification decisions by the firm.

modifications. First, however, we need to show how the required rate of return for a project can be measured, using the capital-asset pricing model approach.

MEASURING THE REQUIRED RETURN

To measure the required rate of return for an investment proposal using the capital-asset pricing model approach, one needs to estimate the relationship between its cash flows and the returns available on the market portfolio. Using the index model method described in Chapter 3, the required rate of return on project k can be expressed as

$$R_k = i + \beta_k[R_m - i] \tag{7-4}$$

where β_k is a measure of the responsiveness of the excess return for the project (over the risk-free rate, i) to the excess return on the market portfolio, $R_m - i$. Though this expression of a project's required rate of return is simple enough in concept, its measurement is complicated by the fact that the usual measures of return for a stock and for a project are not directly comparable. As pointed out in Chapters 2 and 3, the return for a stock or for a portfolio of stocks is expressed as the return on investment for a month, a quarter, or a year, depending on the time frame used. Thus, the return on investment is

$$R = \frac{P_t - P_{t-1} + D_t}{P_{t-1}} \tag{7-5}$$

where P_t = price of stock or market index at time t

D_t = dividend paid during period t

Using historical data, the excess return for the stock is regressed against the excess return for the market index to obtain the beta, or regression coefficient. This coefficient indicates the responsiveness of excess returns for a stock to excess returns for the market index. Because one-period returns are measured in the same way for both series, the procedure is appropriate.

With investment projects, however, profitability usually is expressed in terms of the internal rate of return or the net-present value. Both involve multiperiod as opposed to single-period time frames. Therefore, the return for the market index, a single-period measure, and the return for a capital investment project, a multiperiod measure, are not directly comparable.[7] Moreover, there is a problem in the way the two measures

---

[7] For further discussion of this problem, see Donald R. Lessard and Richard S. Bower, "An Operational Approach to Risk Screening," *Journal of Finance*, 28 (May 1973), 321–38.

are calculated. The return on investment for the market index involves the change in its capitalized value from the start of a period to the end. The cash-flow measures of profitability for an investment project do not take account of changes in capitalized value from period to period. Thus, there is a basic problem of incompatibility between the two measures of return.

SURROGATE MARKET INFORMATION

One way to come to grips with the problem is to try to express the profitability of an investment project in terms of its cash flow during the period and its change in value from the beginning of the period to the end. In this way, the two return measures would be compatible. The one-period return for an investment project would be

$$R_t = \frac{V_t + A_t - V_{t-1}}{V_{t-1}} \tag{7-6}$$

where V_t = the market value of the project at the end of period t

A_t = net cash flow received at the end of period t

The difficulty, of course, is in estimating the value of the project at the end of a period. One approach is to use externally determined market values for the asset. In the case of certain investment projects, the market value is fairly well established. For machine tools, for example, a secondary market of sorts exists where prices are established for used machines of various ages. Other assets have similar markets where prices can be determined. Later in this section, we will illustrate the derivation of the required rate of return using this method. First, however, we wish to explore other surrogates.

In many cases, the project is sufficiently similar to a company whose stock is publicly held so that one is able to use that company's beta in deriving the required rate of return for the project. In the case of large projects, such as new products, one frequently can identify publicly traded stocks that are engaged entirely, or almost entirely, in this type of operation. The important thing is to identify a company or companies with systematic risk characteristics similar to the project in question.

Suppose, for example, that a steel company was considering the formation of a real estate subsidiary. As there are a number of real estate companies with publicly traded stocks, one simply could determine the beta for one of those companies or a group of them and use it in Eq. (7-4) to derive the required rate of return for the project. Note that the relevant required rate of return is not that for the steel company, but that for other real estate firms. Stated differently, the real estate venture of the steel company is viewed by the market in the same way as are other firms engaged solely in real estate. By concentrating on companies in the same line of business as that which the firm desires to enter, surrogates of this sort often can be found which approximate the systematic risk of the project. While an exact duplication of the project's risk is unlikely, reasonable approximations are possible.[8]

To illustrate, suppose that the average beta for a sample of real estate companies whose stocks were publicly traded and whose basic businesses were similar to the venture contemplated by the steel company were 1.6. We then could use this beta as a surrogate for the beta of the project. If we expected the average return on the market portfolio of stocks to be 10 percent and the risk-free rate to be 5 percent, the required rate of return for the project would be $R_k = .05 + (.10 - .05)1.6 = 13$ percent. Therefore, 13 percent would be used as the required rate of return for the project. If the real estate venture were expected to provide an internal rate of return in excess of, or equal to, this rate, the project would be accepted. If not, it would be rejected.

For publicly held stocks, one does not have to calculate the betas oneself. Instead, a number of services provide historical beta information on stocks. These betas are computed on the basis of weekly, monthly, or quarterly data for three to ten years in the past. Services

---

[8]Another approach to the problem is to develop betas for a company, or part thereof, based on accounting data. Here an accounting measure of return for a company or division, such as the return on assets, is related to an economy-wide index of returns, such as the average return on assets for nonfinancial corporations. Regressing the former on the latter, a beta or regression coefficient is determined which is said to depict the systematic risk of returns for the company or division. The procedure for determining and evaluating accounting betas is analogous to that used for market betas previously illustrated. The appeal of this approach is that it does not require data on market returns for the project. Such data often are difficult, if not impossible, to obtain. In contrast, data on accounting returns are readily available.

Recognizing the advantages of data availability, then, the question becomes whether accounting betas are good surrogates for market betas. While various empirical studies show a significant statistical association between accounting and market betas for companies, the explanatory power is only moderate. For the individual company, the ability to predict market betas on the basis of accounting betas is too low to make the approach anything but a crude approximation. Therefore, we concentrate on developing market return information. For a development of the accounting–market beta issue as well as empirical tests in this regard, see William Beaver, Paul Kettler, and Myron Scholes, "The Association between Market Determined and Accounting Determined Risk Measures," *Accounting Review,* 45 (October 1970), 654–82; William Beaver and James Manegold, "The Association between Market-Determined and Accounting-Determined Measures of Systematic Risk: Some Further Evidence," *Journal of Financial and Quantitative Analysis,* 10 (June 1975) 231–84; H. Richardson Pettit and Randolph Westerfield, "A Model of Capital Asset Risk," *Journal of Financial and Quantitative Analysis,* 7 (March 1972), 1649–68; Myron J. Gordon and Paul J. Halpern, "Cost of Capital for a Division of a Firm," *Journal of Finance,* 29 (September 1974), 1153–63; Nicholas J. Gonedes, "A Note on Accounting-Based and Market-Based Estimates of Systematic Risk," *Journal of Financial and Quantitative Analysis,* 10 (June 1975), 355–65; and John S. Bildersee, "The Association between a Market-Determined Measure of Risk and Alternative Measures of Risk," *Accounting Review,* 50 (January 1975), 81–98.

providing beta information include Merrill Lynch, Pierce, Fenner and Smith and the Value Line Investment Survey. These services allow one to obtain betas for a particular company with relative ease. Thus, when a prospective investment project is similar to a company whose stock is publicly traded, one should definitely use such beta information.

ILLUSTRATION OF DERIVATION OF REQUIRED RATE OF RETURN

In this section, we illustrate the derivation of the required rate of return for a project when the beta surrogate of a publicly traded company is not available. The example has been simplified to work with annual as opposed to quarterly, monthly, or weekly data. Also for the sake of simplicity we assume an all-equity company. A careful study of this example will show how beta information can be derived in practice and how such information can be used to approximate the required rate of return for a project.

Suppose Albar Dairy Products Company is considering investing in a multiple-purpose machine costing $100,000 to use in the production of cottage cheese. The company has had experience with similar machines in the past and feels it is appropriate to use past behavior as a proxy for the future. Suppose that the history of a comparable machine was that shown in Table 7-1. In this table, the external market price of the asset is an estimate of the price prevailing in the market for used machines. This value is set by the forces of supply and demand. The return computed in

Table 7·1 History of machine used by Albar Dairy Products Company

Year-End	(1) Purchase Price	(2) External Market Value	(3) Actual Net Cash Flow (after tax)	(4) Annual Return $\dfrac{(2)_t + (3)_t - (2)_{t-1}}{(2)_{t-1}}$
19—0	$100,000	$100,000	$ 0	
19—1		84,000	27,000	.110
19—2		64,000	22,000	.024
19—3		53,000	26,000	.234
19—4		40,000	20,000	.132
19—5		33,000	18,000	.275
19—6		24,000	13,000	.121
19—7		19,000	12,000	.292
19—8		13,000	8,000	.105
19—9	(Salvage value)	9,000	5,000	.077

column (4) is simply the external value at the end of the year less the beginning value plus the net cash flow that occurred, all over the beginning value.

Now that the project cash flows are expressed in terms of market-based annual returns, we are able to use Eq. (7-4) to compute the beta. To illustrate, suppose the Standard and Poor's 500-stock index showed the one-year returns reported in column (1) of Table 7-2. These returns are computed with Eq. (7-5) and comprise capital gains or losses, together with dividends received. The risk-free rate, shown in column (2), might simply be the yield available on relative short-term government securities. The average risk-free rate for the total period is shown at the bottom of the column. In the third column, we subtract the risk-free rate from the R_{mt} to obtain the excess market return. The arithmetic mean of these returns is shown at the bottom of the column.

In the next column, we compute the deviations from the arithmetic mean. In column (5), these deviations are squared. The variance of the excess market returns is shown at the bottom of column (5), and it is simply the arithmetic average of the squared deviations. In column (6) the returns for the project are presented (see column (4) of Table 7-1; for simplicity, we round to the nearest percentage). The next column represents the one-year excess returns for the project (actual return less the risk-free rate), with the arithmetic mean shown at the bottom. In column (8), we show the deviation in return from the mean. In column (9) we multiply deviations for excess market returns, column (4), times deviations for excess project returns, column (8). The arithmetic mean represents the covariance between the two sets of excess returns, and it is shown at the bottom of the column.

Table 7·2   Actual return for market index and computation of variance and covariance

Year	(1) R_{mt}	(2) i_t	(3) $R_{mt} - i_t$	(4) $(R_{mt} - i_t)$ $- .049$	(5) $[(R_{mt} - i_t)$ $- .049]^2$	(6) R_{kt}	(7) $R_{kt} - i_t$	(8) $(R_{kt} - i_t)$ $- .108$	(9) (4) × (8)
19—1	.26	.03	.23	.181	.0328	.110	.080	(.028)	(.0051)
19—2	(.09)	.03	(.12)	(.169)	.0286	.024	(.006)	(.114)	.0193
19—3	.22	.03	.19	.141	.0199	.234	.204	.096	.0135
19—4	.16	.04	.12	.071	.0050	.132	.092	(.016)	(.0011)
19—5	.12	.04	.08	.031	.0010	.275	.235	.127	.0039
19—6	(.10)	.05	(.15)	(.199)	.0396	.121	.071	(.037)	.0074
19—7	.24	.05	.19	.141	.0199	.292	.242	.134	.0189
19—8	.11	.06	.05	.001	.0000	.105	.045	(.063)	(.0001)
19—9	(.08)	.07	(.15)	(.199)	.0396	.077	.007	(.101)	.0201
Average return	.093	.044	.049	Var $(R_{mt} - i_t) = .0207$		.152		.108 Cov. $(R_{mt} - i_t, R_{kt} - i_t) = .0085$	

Given this covariance term as well as the variance of excess market returns (bottom of Column (5)), we are able to compute the beta or responsive coefficient in Eq. (7-4). It is simply[9]

$$\beta_k = \frac{\text{Cov.}(R_m - i, R_k - i)}{\text{Var. } R_m - i} = \frac{.0085}{.0207} = 0.41 \qquad (7\text{-}7)$$

This beta suggests that the project has only moderate systematic risk. Recall from Chapter 3 that any beta less than 1.00 is said to characterize a defensive investment. Given the beta, we have the most important piece of information necessary to calculate the project's required rate of return.

However, there are two additional pieces of information necessary before we can make such a computation—the expected risk-free rate and the market rate of return. As with the beta, one is interested in likely *future* outcomes. If the past seems like a reasonable proxy for the future, however, one might use average historical rates of return. For example, suppose one felt that the arithmetic means of the risk-free rates and market returns that prevailed over the nine-year period in our example were reasonable proxies for the future. From Table 7-2, these averages are seen to be 4.4 percent and 9.3 percent, respectively. With this additional information, we now are able to estimate the required rate of return for the project. Using Eq. (7-3), it is

$$R_k = \overline{i} + (\overline{R}_m - \overline{i})\beta_k = .044 + (.093 - .044) .41 = .064 \qquad (7\text{-}8)$$

where $\overline{i}$ and $\overline{R}_m$ are the arithmetic means of risk-free rates and actual S & P 500-stock index returns respectively. Thus, the required rate of return, or cost of capital, for the project is 6.4 percent. The reason the required return is less than the average return for the market index, 9.3 percent, is that the project has a relatively low covariance with the market index.

The critical assumption is that past experience is a good proxy for the future. That is, the association between project returns and market returns is likely to be the same in the future as it has been in the past. If this assumption holds, R_k can be used as an approximation of the project's required rate of return. Expected net cash flows for the new, but similar, project would be discounted at this rate. If the net-present value were positive, the project would be accepted; if not, it would be rejected. To illustrate the acceptance criterion, suppose the expected net

[9] In the context of Eq. (7-2), we see that $\beta_k = (r_{km}\sigma_k\sigma_m)/\sigma_m^2$.

cash flows for the project were:

Time	0	1	2	3	4	5	6	7	8	9
Expected net cash flow after tax (in thousands)	($100)	$28	$25	$22	$19	$16	$14	$12	$10	$8

When we discount this cash-flow stream at the proposed required rate of return of 6.4 percent, we find the net-present value to be $21,308. Because this figure is positive, the proposal should be accepted according to the method employed.

QUALIFICATIONS AS TO MEASURING VALUATION CHANGES

As can be visualized, the procedure is crude in that we use the past as a proxy for the future. Nevertheless, all cost-of-capital calculations are similarly plagued. The real problem is when the project being evaluated is unlike past projects with which the firm or outside specialists have had experience. Here estimates of the responsiveness of project returns to market returns must be estimated subjectively, and they are subject to considerable error.

If the project is relatively self-contained, such as a new division, it should be compared with another firm or subsidiary of a firm. If the firm or subsidiary has publicly traded stock, it is an easy matter to use such returns to compute the beta and the required rate of return for the project. As suggested earlier in our example of a steel company investing in a real estate venture, this proxy is likely to be quite accurate. Whenever possible, then, comparisons of a project with publicly held companies should be used. Obviously, if the project involved is an acquisition of a publicly held company, one does not have to use a proxy at all, but can use the actual returns to investors of the company being considered for acquisition to determine the beta.

The important thing is that the project return estimates be rooted in market data either directly or indirectly. Estimates of beta will vary in quality with the comparability of the project with assets whose capitalized value can be determined from period to period. For many investment projects, reasonable market-based estimates are possible. Once the beta is specified, the other data are readily available and the required rate of return for the project can be determined.

However, certain projects are sufficiently unique to make the estimation of beta nothing more than a guess. This operational shortcoming of the capital-asset pricing model approach must be recognized. We will again discuss this problem as well as others when we attempt to reconcile market and nonmarket approaches to capital budgeting for risky investments.

EVALUATION OF PROJECTS SOLELY IN TERMS OF THE TOTAL RISK OF THE FIRM

We stated in the introduction to this chapter that if some of the assumptions of the capital-asset pricing model do not hold, the effect of a project on the total risk of the firm may be important. Leaving aside for the moment whether or not these assumptions hold, we want to explore here the evaluation of risky investments if they do not. That is, we assume that the *only* thing that is important is the risk and return of the individual firm, and that projects are evaluated with respect to their marginal impact on these two factors. In the subsequent section, we examine the critical assumptions of the capital-asset pricing model and attempt to reconcile the capital-asset pricing model approach with the total variability approach presented in this section. Our attention now, however, is directed to the evaluation of risky investments solely in relation to their impact on the total risk and return of the firm.

EVALUATION OF COMBINATIONS OF RISKY INVESTMENTS

From Chapter 5, we know that the marginal risk of an individual proposal to the firm as a whole depends upon its correlation with existing projects as well as its correlation with proposals under consideration that might be accepted. We suggested that the appropriate information was the standard deviation and expected value of the probability distribution of possible net-present values for all feasible combinations of existing projects and investment proposals under consideration. We consider now the selection of the most desirable combination, deferring until later in the chapter the fundamental question of whether a portfolio approach should be used at all. We assume that management is interested only in the marginal impact of an investment proposal on the risk complexion of the firm as a whole.

The selection of the most desirable combination of investments will depend upon its utility preferences with respect to net-present value and variance, or standard deviation. If management is averse to risk and associates risk with the variance of net-present value, its utility function may be similar to that shown in Figure 7-2.[10] As discussed in Chapter 3, the curves in the figure are indifference curves; management is indifferent to any combination of expected value of net-present value and

---

[10] See Chapter 2 for a discussion of one way to map a decision maker's utility preferences.

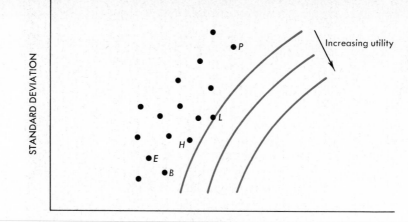

FIG. 7·2
*Selection of the
best project portfolio*

standard deviation on a particular curve. Thus, a specific curve portrays the tradeoff between the two parameters for a particular company. The indifference curves in Figure 7-2 suggest that management's utility function is a monotonic increasing concave one, indicating decreasing marginal rates of substitution between standard deviation and net-present value. As the dispersion of possible net-present values of the firm increases, it takes increasing amounts of net-present value for management to accept additional increments of risk.

As we move to the right in Figure 7-2, each successive curve represents a higher level of utility. Thus, management would choose the combination of investments that lies on the highest indifference curve, the one farthest to the right, because this curve represents the greatest utility. This combination is determined by the intersection of a dot in the figure—point *L*—with the highest indifference curve. Point *L* represents the portfolio of existing projects and proposals under consideration that possesses the most desirable combination of expected value of net-present value and risk. One should recognize that the presentation above is mainly conceptual in that it assumes a utility function for management can be graphed. In fact, a group utility function can be derived only under very restricted conditions.[11]

PROJECT COMBINATION DOMINANCE

However, the framework for evaluating combinations of risky investments developed above is quite useful even if management's utility function is not defined. For example, we might present management

[11] See Robert Wilson, "The Theory of Syndicates," *Econometrica*, 36 (January 1968), 119–32.

with the information shown by the dots in Figure 7-2. With this, management can eliminate most combinations simply because they are dominated by other combinations. Unless management is quite averse to risk, it probably would consider only four portfolios of risky investments, *B, H, L,* and *P.* From these management would choose the one that it felt offered the best combination of expected return and risk.

This selection determines the new investment proposal or proposals that will be accepted. An exception would occur only when the portfolio selected was comprised of existing projects. In this situation, no investment proposals under consideration would be accepted. If the portfolio of existing projects were represented by portfolio *E* in Figure 7-2, however, the selection of any of the four portfolios would imply the acceptance of one or more new investment proposals. Those investment proposals under consideration that were not in the portfolio finally selected would be rejected, of course.

If management's indifference curves were approximately linear, the evaluation procedure described above would be reduced to a simple comparison of reward-to-variability ratios with and without the investment proposal(s) under consideration. In the case of only one proposal being considered, it should be accepted if

$$\frac{\overline{NPV}_{k+e}}{\sigma_{k+e}} > \frac{\overline{NPV}_e}{\sigma_e} \tag{7-9}$$

where $\overline{NPV}_{k+e}$ = expected value of the probability distribution of possible net-present values for all existing assets, *e*, and the proposal under consideration, *k*

σ_{k+e} = standard deviation of this probability distribution

$\overline{NPV}_e$ = expected value of the probability distribution of possible net-present values for all existing assets

σ_e = standard deviation of this probability distribution

The approach can be expanded to include multiple investment proposals under consideration in obvious ways.

In summary, management is able to determine which investment proposals under consideration offer the best marginal contribution of expected value of net-present value and standard deviation to the firm as a whole. In determining the standard deviation for a portfolio, consideration is given to the correlation of an investment proposal with existing investment projects, as well as with other new investment proposals. Implied in this evaluation is that the total risk of the firm is what is important; therefore, investment decisions should be made in light of their marginal impact on total risk. The evaluation is firm-risk oriented in the sense that management does not consider explicitly the impact of the project on investors' portfolios, only upon the portfolio of assets of the firm.

We have examined two ways to evaluate risky investments. One involves evaluating a project in relation to its systematic risk; the other involves analyzing the incremental impact of the project on the business-risk complexion of the firm as a whole. The obvious question is, Which is correct? Perhaps the best insight into this question can be gained if we examine in more detail the assumptions of the capital-asset pricing model. Recall that the risk or total variability of an individual stock is comprised of nondiversifiable, or systematic, risk as well as residual risk. The assumptions of the capital-asset pricing model imply that the latter risk can be diversified away by efficient investors and, consequently, is not a factor affecting value. If the assumptions of the capital-asset pricing model do not entirely hold under real-world conditions, residual risk may be a factor that, in some measure, affects the value of the firm. In this case, the impact of a project on the firm's total variability of returns would be of some importance.

CRITICAL ASSUMPTIONS
IN THE CAPITAL-ASSET PRICING MODEL

One assumption in the capital-asset pricing model is particularly crucial, and that is that the cost of insolvency or bankruptcy is zero. If a firm fails, assets presumably can be sold for their economic values without selling or legal costs. After creditors have been paid, the residual proceeds are distributed to stockholders. As long as assets can be sold at their economic values in a frictionless world, investors are able to diversify effectively their risk. Under real-world conditions, however, assets often have to be sold in bankruptcy at distress prices. Moreover, there are selling costs, legal fees, and other out-of-pocket costs involved. Finally, there are a number of delays involved in a creditor takeover, due to the cumbersome legal process. During this time, asset values can deteriorate and there is the opportunity cost of the delays as well. All of these factors represent a "drain on the system" to suppliers of capital and work either directly or indirectly to the detriment of stockholders, the residual owners of the firm.

It is important to recognize that the probability of a firm's becoming insolvent depends on its *total* risk, not just its *systematic* risk. Therefore, a case can be made for choosing projects in light of their effect on both the systematic and the total (systematic plus residual) risk of the firm. Put another way, when insolvency and/or bankruptcy costs are significant, investors may well be served by the firm's paying attention to the total risk of the firm in capital budgeting for risky investments and not just its systematic risk. If management exercises a degree of risk aversion greater than that which would maximize shareholder wealth, it will place an even greater emphasis upon residual risk.

Other market imperfections also make residual risk important.

Recall that the capital-asset pricing model assumes borrowing and lending by investors is possible at the same rate, that there are no transaction costs, and that information is available without cost to all market participants. In the real world, the borrowing rate typically exceeds the lending rate, there are transactions costs, and investors incur costs in obtaining information. All of these factors limit the effectiveness with which investors are able to diversify away unsystematic, or residual, risk. As a result, residual risk becomes a factor of at least some importance in valuation. Although these imperfections probably are not as important as the cost of insolvency and/or bankruptcy, nonetheless they contribute to the importance of residual risk.

A DUAL APPROACH

Where does this leave us? It suggests that one should consider the impact of a project on both the systematic risk and the total risk of the firm.[12] If both the capital-asset pricing model approach and the total variability approach for evaluating a project give clear accept or reject signals, those signals should be followed. The obvious problem is when one approach gives an accept signal and the other a reject one. When this occurs, management needs to assess which approach is more applicable. If the stock of the company involved is publicly held, if the possibility of insolvency is remote, and if the firm is able to realistically express expected project returns in terms of changes in market-based capitalized values on a one-period basis, a strong case can be made for using the signal given by the capital-asset pricing model. However, if the stock is traded in a market with high transaction and information costs, if the possibility of insolvency and/or bankruptcy is significant, and if the expression of project returns in terms of market-based returns is crude, greater reliance should be placed on the total variability approach. Even here, however, one should recognize that a portion of the residual risk can be diversified away.

It should be obvious that the methods proposed are not operationally perfect. Still, they represent a means for judging risky investments. In the years to come, we can expect the state of the art to be improved. It is clear that the impact of a project on risk is important and must be considered if the firm is to make investment decisions that maximize shareholder wealth. It also is clear that management must consider the effect of a project not only upon the risk complexion of the firm but upon the systematic risk of investors. The latter is a relatively new consideration that is only beginning to have operational feasibility. Although the approach has many difficulties, we can expect to see

[12]This posture is taken also by Lessard and Bower, "Operational Approach to Risk Screening," pp. 321–38.

improvements in the future. The idea that the market for common stocks is relatively efficient forces a firm in this direction if its objective is truly one of maximizing shareholder wealth.

EVALUATION OF A SINGLE PROJECT IN A FIRM-RISK CONTEXT

Although we have advocated the combined approach described above for evaluating risky investments, we must recognize that other approaches are used. In fact, most firms use neither of the two approaches examined in their evaluation of risky investments. The risk and return of individual projects often is quantified, and management makes a decision whether to accept or reject the project on the basis of this information. In so doing, it assesses neither the systematic risk of the project nor its likely effect on the variability of cash flows and earnings of the firm as a whole.

We have purposely postponed consideration of this approach until last. It is not that we do not recognize the practical reasons for its use, but we wanted to present the sounder conceptual approach first. Lest one feel that this was for nought, it should be remembered that actual practices with respect to the evaluation of risky investments have changed dramatically over time. Whereas a short time back risk was seldom quantified and investment projects were evaluated on the basis of their expected accounting rates of return, many companies now quantify risk in a sophisticated manner and most use discounted cash-flow types of analyses. It is not unreasonable to expect that the approach suggested earlier in this chapter will find increasing acceptance. Indeed, certain corporations are already using variations of it. With this in mind, let us consider the evaluation of individual projects in a firm-risk context.

EXPECTED VALUE–STANDARD DEVIATION JUDGMENTS

From Chapter 5, we saw that information about the expected return and risk of the probability distribution of possible returns can be determined for the individual investment proposal. Given this information, the question becomes whether the project should be accepted or rejected. For purposes of illustration, we will work only with the expected value and standard deviation of the probability distribution of possible net-present values. Because the concepts presented are applicable for the internal-rate-of-return method, it is not necessary to illustrate them twice. Recall from Chapter 5 that the information generated for an investment proposal was the probability distribution of possible net-present values using the risk-free rate as the discount factor. From this distribution, one is able to derive the probability that the net-present value of the project will be zero or less. This probability corresponds to the probability that the project's internal rate of return will be less than the risk-free rate.

In the evaluation of a single proposal, it is unlikely that management would accept an investment proposal having an expected value of net-present value of zero unless the probability distribution had no dispersion. In this special case, the proposal, by definition, would be riskless. For risky investments, the net-present value would have to exceed zero. How much it would have to exceed zero before acceptance were warranted depends upon the amount of dispersion of the probability distribution and the utility preferences of management with respect to risk.

USE OF RISK PROFILES

In order to facilitate project selection as well as to make it consistent over time, management may wish to formulate maximum risk profiles. To express the probability distributions in relative instead of absolute terms, we can convert the net-present value probability distribution into a distribution of possible profitability indexes. For proposal X, our example problem in Chapter 5, the initial cash outflow was $10,000 and the expected value of the probability distribution of net-present values was $1,173. Thus, the profitability index is ($1,173 + $10,000)/$10,000 = 1.12. The profitability index for zero net-present value is (0 + $10,000)/$10,000 = 1.00. Similarly, we can convert the entire probability distribution to a probability distribution of possible profitability indexes. The converted probability distribution for the example problem is seen in Figure 7-3.

If management has specified maximum risk profiles for various expected values of profitability indexes, one would simply compare proposal X with the maximum risk profile for an expected value of

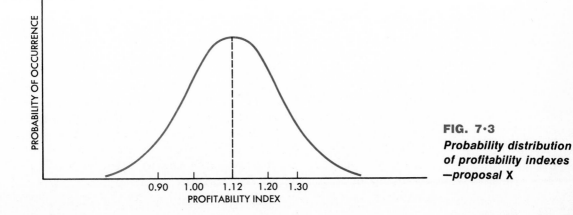

FIG. 7·3
Probability distribution of profitability indexes —proposal X

profitability index of 1.12. If the dispersion of the proposal is less than that for the risk profile, the proposal would be accepted. If not, it would be rejected. The maximum level of dispersion permitted, as depicted by the risk profile, will increase with the expected value of profitability index. For a profitability index of 1.02, the dispersion of the maximum risk profile will be narrower than that for a profitability index of 1.10. An illustration of some hypothetical risk profiles is shown in Figure 7-4. We

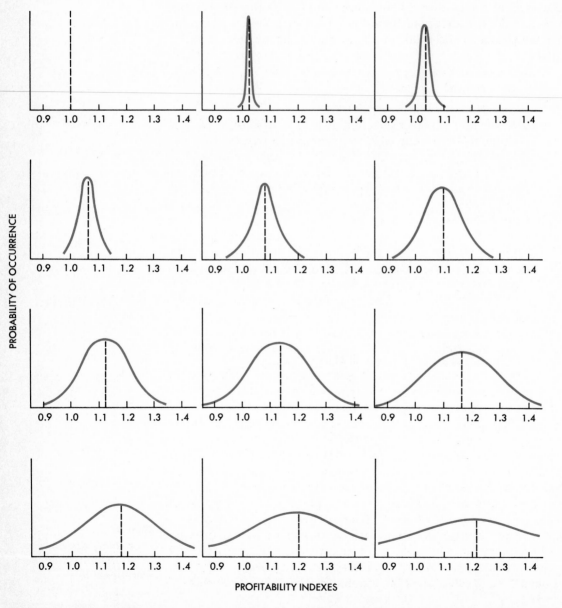

FIG. 7·4 *Risk profiles*

note that the greater the expected value of profitability index, the greater the dispersion that is tolerable to management.

Once maximum risk profiles are specified, project selection becomes automatic. For a given expected value of profitability index, the dispersion of the probability distribution for the proposal must be less than or equal to that for the maximum risk profile in order for the proposal to be accepted. Management's specification of these risk profiles will depend upon its tolerances. While one would expect the allowable dispersion to increase with increases in the expected value of profitability index, as shown in Figure 7-4, there is still the question of whether the profiles overall are too conservative or too liberal.

The real problem, of course, is that the link to share price is not direct. Management is presented with information about the expected return and risk of a project and on the basis of this information reaches a decision. However, there is no direct link to the likely reaction of well-diversified investors. This link depends entirely upon the perceptiveness of management in judging investors' tradeoff between profitability and risk. Moreover, there is no analysis of the impact of the project on the total risk of the firm; as we know, this factor becomes important if capital markets are less than perfect. In essence, the project is evaluated in isolation of investors and of existing investment projects. For these reasons, the approach leaves much to be desired. Still, we must recognize that in practice most investment decisions are made by management in this way. By providing management with information about the dispersion of possible outcomes, more informed decisions are possible than in the conventional capital-budgeting analysis where only the expected values of cash flows are considered.

SUMMARY

In this chapter, we considered the evaluation of risky investments, given information developed in the preceding chapter about the expected value and the standard deviation of the probability distribution of possible returns. The first approach was the application of the capital-asset pricing model to capital investments. This approach relates the acceptance of a project to the undiversifiable risk of investors. Thus, projects are evaluated in a market context, and the cost of capital, or required rate of return, is computed for each project. The method was illustrated with an example. We saw that there is a problem of incompatibility between the usual measures of return for stocks and for capital investment projects. This problem can be resolved by expressing project returns on a one-period basis and in terms of changes in capitalized value. The principal implication of the approach is that investors are able to diversify away all residual risk on their own. Therefore, diversification by the firm of capital investment projects and, particularly, of acquisitions is not a thing of value. Investors are able to accomplish the same thing on their own.

The second approach examined was the evaluation of projects with respect to their incremental impact on the total return and risk of the firm. Here one is concerned with various combinations of existing investment projects and investment proposals under consideration. A portfolio framework was presented for analyzing the tradeoff between risk and expected value of net-present value for different combinations of investments. Management can then choose the best combination of risk and return for the firm as a whole. This approach has particular value in the case of a privately held company. It also has merit if the assumptions of the capital-asset pricing model do not entirely hold in practice.

In the next section, we attempted to reconcile the two approaches under real-world conditions. We saw that the capital-asset pricing model depends on several assumptions, one of which is perfect markets. When we allow for the cost of bankruptcy as well as other market imperfections, residual risk becomes a factor of importance. In such cases, a dual system for evaluating risky investments can be used where both the capital-asset pricing model and the total variability approaches are employed.

Finally, we presented the evaluation of single investment projects without reference to either systematic risk considerations or considerations of the impact of the project on the total risk of the firm. Here management makes a decision to accept or reject a project on the basis of the expected value and standard deviation of the distribution of possible returns. Because of the reasons cited, the link to share price is far from direct and the approach accordingly suffers. Still, it is widely used and represents a step toward increasing sophistication in the evaluation of risky investments. In the next chapter, "Required Rates of Return for Companies, for Divisions, and for Acquisitions," we continue our investigation of the evaluation of risky investments.

APPENDIX

EFFECT OF UNCERTAIN INFLATION ON REQUIRED RETURNS

In the development of the required rate of return for a project in this chapter, we have not taken explicit account of the impact of inflation. Recall from Appendix B to Chapter 4 the need to recognize inflation in the cash-flow estimates for a project. Otherwise, the capital-budgeting process is biased, owing to the measured required rate of return containing in it an inflation premium. We suggested that unless the cash-flow estimates take account of inflation, the selection process may err in the direction of rejection. That is, a harsher acceptance criterion is imposed than is justified. Throughout that appendix, our discussion was framed in terms of the expected level of inflation. In this appendix, we wish to explore the effect of inflation variance. More specifically, we investigate the effect of uncertain inflation on the systematic risk of the firm and on the required rate of return for a project.

A. H. Chen and A. J. Boness have formulated the following expression for the expected rate of return for a stock when there is uncertain inflation:[13]

$$R_j = i + \theta[S \text{ Cov.}(\widetilde{R}_j, \widetilde{R}_m) - W \text{ Cov.}(\widetilde{R}_j, \widetilde{R}_a)] \qquad \text{(7A-1)}$$

where $\widetilde{R}_j$ = the nominal rate of return on security j, which is a random variable

$\widetilde{R}_m$ = the nominal rate of return on the market portfolio

i = the nominal risk-free rate, which is known with certainty

θ = the market-risk aversion factor, or market price of risk, to be discussed later

S = the aggregate market value of all stocks

$\text{Cov.}(\widetilde{R}_j, \widetilde{R}_m)$ = the covariance between returns on stock j and those for the market portfolio

W = the aggregate investable wealth of all investors

$\text{Cov.}(\widetilde{R}_j, \widetilde{R}_a)$ = the covariance between returns on stock j and the rate of inflation

The term in the brackets represents the beta, or measure of systematic risk of the stock. It is comprised of two parts: (1) the covariance between the stock's rate of return and that of the market portfolio, and (2) the covariance between the stock's rate of return and the inflation rate.

If the latter covariance term is positive, the stock tends to show a higher nominal return the higher the rate of inflation. This, of course, is a desirable property in an era of inflation, because part or all of the loss in real return is offset. As a result, stocks with positive return-inflation covariances require lower returns in the market than would otherwise be the case.[14] On the other hand, if the return-inflation covariance term is negative, the stock's return would tend to be lower the higher the rate of inflation. In a period of inflation this feature is undesirable, and the stock would require a higher return than would otherwise be the case. In essence, Chen and Boness superimpose the consideration of inflation on the capital-asset pricing model to take explicit account of its impact on the covariance of real returns of a stock with those of the market

---

[13]"Effects of Uncertain Inflation on the Investment and Financing Decisions of a Firm," *Journal of Finance*, 30 (May 1975), 469–84. For an extended theoretical treatment of the topic, see Nestor Gonzalez Gaviria, "Inflation and Capital Asset Market Prices: Theory and Tests." (unpublished Ph.D. dissertation, Stanford University, 1973).

[14]The opposite would occur in a period of deflation. Here a positive return-inflation covariance term would be undesirable, and such a stock would require a higher return than would otherwise be the case.

portfolio. Underlying all of this is that the equilibrating process occurs in terms of real rather than nominal returns.

Given our previous discussion in this chapter, the implication of this for capital investment decisions is fairly obvious. If one is concerned only with the expected return and systematic risk of the project in real terms (residual risk is unimportant), one can apply a variation of Eq. (7A-1) to the project. Instead of stock j, we would deal with project k. According to Chen and Boness, its required rate of return would be

$$R_k = i + \lambda^*[\text{Cov.}(\widetilde{R}_k, \widetilde{R}_m) - (W/S)\text{Cov.}(\widetilde{R}_k, \widetilde{R}_a)] \qquad (7A\text{-}2)$$

where λ^* is the market price of risk when uncertain inflation exists. If one is concerned only with the expected return and systematic risk of the project, it would be accepted if its expected return exceeded or equaled R_k, and rejected if it were less. The same types of generalizations as were made for the stock would hold here, so we need not repeat them. If residual risk is deemed to be a factor of importance, it would be analyzed in the manner taken up in the chapter.

Having presented the important implications of the Chen and Boness approach for taking explicit account of uncertain inflation, we focus now on how Eq. (7A-1) was derived. Assuming the market for stocks equilibrates in terms of real returns, an individual investor's ending wealth would be

$$\widetilde{Y}_i = W_i(i - \widetilde{R}_a) + \sum_j S_{ij}(\widetilde{R}_j - i) \qquad (7A\text{-}3)$$

where $\widetilde{Y}_i$ = the ending real wealth of investor i, which is a random variable

W_i = investor i's investable wealth

S_{ij} = the market value of investor i's holdings of stock j

If investors have quadratic utility functions, the expected utility of investor i with respect to ending real wealth would be

$$EU_i(\widetilde{Y}_i) = E_i(\widetilde{Y}_i) - C_i[V_i(\widetilde{Y}_i) + E_i(\widetilde{Y}_i)^2] \qquad (7A\text{-}4)$$

where $E_i(\widetilde{Y}_i)$ is the expected value of ending real wealth, $V_i(\widetilde{Y}_i)$ is its variance, and C_i is a coefficient of risk aversion for investor i. The expected value of ending real wealth for investor i is

$$E_i(\widetilde{Y}_i) = W_i[i - E(\widetilde{R}_a)] + \sum_j S_{ij}[E(\widetilde{R}_j) - i] \qquad (7A\text{-}5)$$

while the variance is

$$V_i(\widetilde{Y}_i) = W_i^2 \text{Var.}(\widetilde{R}_a) + \left(\sum_j S_{ij}\right)\text{Cov.}(\widetilde{R}_j, \widetilde{R}_m) - 2W_i \sum_j S_{ij} \text{Cov.}(\widetilde{R}_j, \widetilde{R}_a)$$

$$(7A\text{-}6)$$

Given this development, Chen and Boness derive the following demand function for investor i for stock j:

$$[E(\tilde{R}_j) - i]\left[\frac{1}{2C_i} - E_i(\tilde{Y}_i)\right] = \left(\sum_j S_{ij}\right)\text{Cov.}(\tilde{R}_j, \tilde{R}_m) - W_i\,\text{Cov.}(\tilde{R}_j, \tilde{R}_a) \quad \text{(7A-7)}$$

For all investors, i, we have the following demand function for the stock j:

$$[E(\tilde{R}_j) - i]\left[\frac{1}{\sum_i 2C_i} - \sum_i E_i(\tilde{Y}_i)\right]$$
$$= S\,\text{Cov.}(\tilde{R}_j, \tilde{R}_m) - W\,\text{Cov.}(\tilde{R}_j, \tilde{R}_a) \quad \text{(7A 8)}$$

Therefore, the equilibrium return for stock j is

$$E(\tilde{R}_j) = i + \frac{S\,\text{Cov.}(\tilde{R}_j, \tilde{R}_m) - W\,\text{Cov.}(\tilde{R}_j, \tilde{R}_a)}{\dfrac{1}{\sum_i 2C_i} - \sum_i E_i(\tilde{Y}_i)} \quad \text{(7A-9)}$$

which simplifies to

$$E(\tilde{R}_j) = i + \theta[S\,\text{Cov.}(\tilde{R}_j, \tilde{R}_m) - W\,\text{Cov.}(\tilde{R}_j, \tilde{R}_a)] \quad \text{(7A-10)}$$

where
$$\theta = \frac{1}{\dfrac{1}{\sum_i 2C_i} - \sum_i E_i(\tilde{Y}_i)}$$

This equation of course is the same as Eq. (7A-1). Having gone full circle, we can now conclude this appendix.

PROBLEMS

1. The capital-asset pricing model suggests that the required rate of return on a project is

$$R_k = i + \frac{\bar{R}_m - i}{\sigma_m^2}(r_{km}\sigma_k\sigma_m),$$

where the symbols are identified under Eq. (7-2). If an index model is used, how is the beta, the responsiveness coefficient, defined in terms of the above equation? Substituting beta into the above equation, what does it become?

2. The North Bend Bait Company is contemplating an investment to get it into the production and sale of spinning rods and reels. Heretofore, it

has produced only artificial baits. The financial manager of the company, Mr. Bruno Litzenberger, feels that the only way to analyze the merit of the project is with a capital-asset pricing model approach. Fortunately, there is a publicly held company that is in the business of producing only spinning fishing equipment—Super Splash Spinning Corporation. Mr. Litzenberger feels it appropriate to use this company as a benchmark for measuring risk.

The actual returns to investors in Super Splash Spinning Corp. over the last ten years were those shown in the following table. Also shown are one-year returns for Standard & Poor's 500-stock index and the risk-free rate.

Year-End	Annual Return Super Splash Spinning Corporation	Annual Return Market Index	Risk-Free Rate
19–1	.15	.26	.02
19–2	(.03)	(.09)	.02
19–3	.17	.22	.02
19–4	.12	.16	.02
19–5	.08	.12	.03
19–6	.02	(.10)	.03
19–7	.16	.24	.03
19–8	.14	.11	.03
19–9	(.05)	(.08)	.04
19–0	.12	.14	.04

(a) Compute the beta for Super Splash Spinning Corporation.

(b) What is the cost of capital for the project? What assumptions are critical?

3. The spinning rod and reel project in problem 2 costs $700,000 and is expected to provide the following incremental net cash flows:

Year	1	2	3	4	5	6	7	8	9	10
Net cash flow (in thousands)	$50	$100	$125	$125	$150	$150	$150	$100	$75	$50

No cash flows are predicted beyond ten years, as North Bend Bait Company has found that the product life for profitable operations is about ten years. North Bend has an all-equity capital structure. Should the company undertake the spinning equipment project?

4. Labill Heavy Duty Truck Company is considering the purchase of a very sophisticated piece of machinery to be used in putting together truck frames. During the last ten years it has used a less-sophisticated piece of equipment. A viable secondary market existed for this equipment, and the external market value as well as the actual incremental net cash flows generated as a result of having the equipment are as follows:

	Purchase Price	External Market Value	Actual Net Cash Flow
Start	$400,000	$400,000	$ —
19–1	—	360,000	120,000
19–2	—	300,000	50,000
19–3	—	250,000	125,000
19–4	—	220,000	80,000
19–5	—	180,000	70,000
19–6	—	150,000	30,000
19–7	—	120,000	76,000
19–8	—	80,000	70,000
19–9	—	50,000	20,000
19–0	—	40,000	17,000

(a) Compute the annual returns, using external market values as the base.

(b) If the information on annual returns for the market index and for the risk-free rate is the same as that shown in problem 2, compute the cost of capital for the project, assuming past relationships are a reasonable proxy for the future.

(c) Suppose the new machine cost $700,000 and the expected cash flows are exactly the same as in problem 3 for the spinning equipment project. Should the new machine be purchased? If your answer differs from that in problem 3, explain the reason why.

5. The Empire Mining Company's existing portfolio of assets has an expected value of net-present value of $30 million and a standard deviation of $20 million. The company is considering four new explorations. The sixteen possible portfolios have the following characteristics:

Possible Portfolio	Expected Net-Present Value (in millions)	Standard Deviation (in millions)
1. Existing assets (EA) only	$30	$20
2. EA plus #1	33	23
3. EA plus #2	32	21
4. EA plus #3	35	24
5. EA plus #4	34	25
6. EA plus 1 and 2	35	23
7. EA plus 1 and 3	38	25
8. EA plus 1 and 4	37	26
9. EA plus 2 and 3	37	24
10. EA plus 2 and 4	36	25
11. EA plus 3 and 4	39	28
12. EA plus 1, 2, and 3	40	26
13. EA plus 1, 2, and 4	39	27
14. EA plus 1, 3, and 4	42	30
15. EA plus 2, 3, and 4	41	28
16. EA plus 1, 2, 3, and 4	44	31

(a) Plot these various portfolio possibilities on graph paper.

(b) With a firm-risk approach to evaluating risky investment, which portfolio do you prefer?

(c) If you had a risk-neutral utility function, which portfolio would you choose?

6. Two investment proposals are under consideration that are mutually exclusive. The following information is relevant:

	Expected Value of Net-Present Value	*Standard Deviation*
Proposal *A*	$10,000	$ 5,000
Proposal *B*	12,000	10,000

What is the probability that the actual net-present value will be zero or less? Which proposal would you accept?

SELECTED REFERENCES

Beaver, William, Paul Kettler, and Myron Scholes, "The Association between Market Determined and Accounting Determined Risk Measures," *Accounting Review,* 45 (October 1970), 654–82.

Beaver, William, and James Manegold, "The Association between Market Determined and Accounting Determined Measures of Systematic Risk: Some Further Evidence," *Journal of Financial and Quantitative Analysis,* 10 (June 1975).

Bierman, Harold, Jr., and Jerome E. Hass, "Capital Budgeting under Uncertainty: A Reformulation," *Journal of Finance,* 28 (March 1973), 119–30.

Bildersee, John S., "The Association between a Market-Determined Measure of Risk and Alternative Measures of Risk," *Accounting Review,* 50 (January 1975), 81–98.

Chen, A. H., and A. J. Boness, "Effects of Uncertain Inflation on the Investment and Financing Decisions of a Firm," *Journal of Finance,* 30 (May 1975), 469–84.

Fama, Eugene F., and Merton H. Miller, *The Theory of Finance,* Chapter 7 New York: Holt, Rinehart & Winston, 1972.

Gonedes, Nicholas J., "A Note on Accounting-Based and Market-Based Estimates of Systematic Risk," *Journal of Financial and Quantitative Analysis,* 10 (June 1975), 355–65.

Gonzalez-Gariria, Nestor, "Inflation and Capital Asset Market Prices: Theory and Tests," Ph.D. dissertation, Stanford University, 1973.

Haley, Charles W., "The Valuation of Risk Assets and the Selection of Risky Investments in Stock Portfolios and Capital Budgets: A Comment," *Review of Economics and Statistics,* 61 (May 1969), pp. 220–21; and Lintner, "A Reply," ibid., 222–24.

Hamada, Robert S., "Investment Decision with a General Equilibrium Mean-Variance Approach," *Quarterly Journal of Economics,* 85 (November 1971), 667–83.

———, "Portfolio Analysis, Market Equilibrium and Corporation Finance," *Journal of Finance,* 24 (March 1969), 13–31.

Hayes, Robert H., "Incorporating Risk Aversion into Risk Analysis," *Engineering Economist,* 20 (Winter 1975), 99–121.

Hillier, Frederick S., "A Basic Model for Capital Budgeting of Risky Interrelated Projects," *Engineering Economist,* 17 (Fall 1971), 1–30.

Jaffee, Jeffrey F., and Gershon Mandelker, "Test of the Fisher Effect for Risky Assets," *Journal of Finance,* 31 (May 1976).

Keeley, Robert H., and Randolph Westerfield, "A Problem in Probability Distribution Techniques for Capital Budgeting," *Journal of Finance,* 27 (June 1972), 703–709.

Lessard, Donald R., and Richard S. Bower, "An Operational Approach to Risk Screening," *Journal of Finance,* 28 (May 1973), 321–38.

Lintner, John, "The Evaluation of Risk Assets and the Selection of Risky Investments in Stock Portfolios and Capital Budgets," *Review of Economics and Statistics,* 47 (February 1965), 13–37.

Litzenberger, Robert H., and Alan P. Budd, "Corporate Investment Criteria and the Valuation of Risk Assets," *Journal of Financial and Quantitative Analysis,* 4 (December 1970), 395–419.

Mossin, Jan, *Theory of Financial Markets,* Chapters 7–8 Englewood Cliffs, N.J.: Prentice-Hall, 1973.

Myers, Stewart C., "Procedures for Capital Budgeting under Uncertainty," *Industrial Management Review,* 9 (Spring 1968), 1–15.

Pettit, H. Richardson, and Randolph Westerfield, "A Model of Capital Asset Risk," *Journal of Financial and Quantitative Analysis,* 7 (March 1972), 1649–68.

Roll, Richard, and Marcus C. Bogue, "Capital Budgeting of Risky Projects with Imperfect Markets for Physical Capital," *Journal of Finance,* 29 (May 1974), 606–12.

Rubinstein, Mark E., "A Mean-Variance Synthesis of Corporate Financial Theory," *Journal of Finance,* 28 (March 1973), 167–82.

Salazar, Rudolfo C., and Subrata K. Sen, "A Simulation Model of Capital Budgeting under Uncertainty," *Management Science,* 15 (December 1968), 161–79.

Schall, Lawrence D., "Asset Valuation, Firm Investment, and Firm Diversification," *Journal of Business,* 45 (January 1972), 11–28.

————, "Firm Financial Structure and Investment," *Journal of Financial and Quantitative Analysis,* 6 (June 1971), 925–42.

Stanley, David T., and Marjorie Girth, *Bankruptcy: Problem, Process, Reform.* Washington, D.C.: Brookings Institution, 1971.

Stapleton, Richard C., "Portfolio Analysis, Stock Valuation and Capital Budgeting Rules for Risky Projects," *Journal of Finance,* 26 (March 1971), 95–118.

Sundem, Gary L., "Evaluating Simplified Capital Budgeting Models Using a Time-State Preference Metric," *Accounting Review,* 49 (April 1974), 306–20.

Tuttle, Donald L., and Robert H. Litzenberger, "Leverage, Diversification and Capital Market Effects on a Risk-Adjusted Capital Budgeting Framework," *Journal of Finance,* 23 (June 1968), 427–43.

Van Horne, James C., "The Analysis of Uncertainty Resolution in Capital Budgeting for New Products," *Management Science,* 15 (April 1969), 376–86.

————, "Capital-Budgeting Decisions Involving Combinations of Risky Investments," *Management Science,* 13 (October 1966), 84–92.

————, "Optimal Initiation of Bankruptcy Proceedings by Debt Holders," *Journal of Finance,* 31 (June 1976).

Weston, J. Fred, "Investment Decisions Using the Capital Asset Pricing Model," *Financial Management,* 2 (Spring 1973), 25–33.

REQUIRED RATES of RETURN for COMPANIES, DIVISIONS, and ACQUISITIONS

In this chapter, we extend our evaluation of risky investments to the company as a whole, to divisions of a company, and to prospective acquisitions. Our focus is on determining the required rate of return for each. In the case of a company or sub unit thereof, there is an aggregation of assets. As we shall see, the use of an aggregate required rate of return is appropriate only when those assets are homogeneous with respect to risk, and investment proposals under consideration are of the same character. If investment projects are widely variant with respect to risk, an aggregate required rate of return is not appropriate as an acceptance criterion.

The advantage to using an aggregate required rate is, of course, its simplicity. Once it is computed, projects can be evaluated using a single rate which does not change unless underlying conditions change. This avoids the problems involved in computing individual required rates of return for each investment proposal, as was taken up in the last chapter. However, it is important that if an aggregate required rate of return is used, projects correspond to the above conditions.

The development of this chapter will parallel to some extent that of Chapter 7. First we consider the required rate of return under the assumptions of the capital-asset pricing model and then move on to consider other means for measuring it. The degree to which the former approach needs modification depends on the strength of one's convictions regarding the assumptions inherent in the model. We begin with the cost of capital of a company and then consider the required rate of return for a division. Most of the concepts applicable to the company apply also to the division. Therefore, in discussing the latter, we concentrate on the distinguishing features as well as the implications involved in the use of a divisional cost of capital. Finally, we consider the evaluation of a potential acquisition and the appropriate acceptance criterion for that decision.

COST OF CAPITAL OF THE FIRM

The overall cost of capital of a firm is comprised of the costs of the various components of financing. The most difficult of these costs to measure is the cost of equity capital, and this topic will occupy most of our attention. However, we also consider the costs of debt and preferred stock. To the extent that the historical cost of a source of funds parallels closely the present cost, historical costs may give us some insight. However, our concern is with the *marginal* cost of a specific source of financing. Only if the past is a good surrogate for the future are historical costs of use to us. After covering the various individual costs, we will show how they can be combined into an overall cost of capital for the company.

COST OF EQUITY CAPITAL
IN A MARKET CONTEXT

In theory, *cost of equity capital* can be defined as the minimum rate of return that a company must earn on the equity-financed portion of its investments in order to leave unchanged the market price of its stock. From the preceding chapter and Chapter 3, we know that the capital-asset pricing model implies that the required return on a stock is

$$R_j = i + \left(\frac{R_m - i}{\sigma_m^2}\right)(r_{jm}\sigma_j\sigma_m) \qquad (8\text{-}1)$$

where i = the risk-free rate

R_m = the expected value of return for the market portfolio

σ_m = standard deviation of the probability distribution of possible market returns

σ_j = standard deviation of the probability distribution of possible returns for security j

r_{jm} = correlation coefficient between returns for security j and the market portfolio

The last term, $(r_{jm}\sigma_j\sigma_m)$, represents the covariance of returns for security j with those of the market. We know that the greater the covariance, the greater the return that will be required for security j. The key consideration is that investors cannot diversify away this risk. Therefore, the greater the covariance, the greater the systematic risk and the greater the required return. This required return represents the cost of equity capital of the firm in a market context.

Measuring the cost of equity capital

If the historical relationship between security returns and those for the market portfolio is believed to be a reasonable proxy for the future, one can use past returns to generate the information necessary to compute the required rates of return. Recall from Chapters 3 and 7 that Eq. (8-1) can be expressed as

$$R_j = i + (R_m - i)\beta_j \qquad (8\text{-}2)$$

where beta is the measure of the responsiveness of the excess return for the security to the excess return for the market portfolio. If a broad-based market index, such as Standard & Poor's 500-stock index, is used as a surrogate for the market portfolio, the actual return on security j, less the risk-free rate, in each period would be regressed against the return for the market index, less the risk-free rate. The return for a particular period is simply the ending price less the beginning price plus dividends received during the period, all over the beginning price.

The regression equation is

$$R_{jt} - i_t = \beta_j(R_{mt} - i_t) \tag{8-3}$$

where R_{jt} is the return for security j in period t, i_t is the risk-free rate in period t, β_j is the regression coefficient, and R_{mt} is the return for the market index in period t. Using a reasonable number of past observations, a regression study is run and the regression coefficient, β_j, generated. As in the preceding chapter, the estimated required rate of return can be approximated by

$$R_j = \overline{i} + (\overline{R}_m - \overline{i})\beta_j, \tag{8-4}$$

where $\overline{i}$ is the arithmetic mean of the i_t which prevailed over the sample period and $\overline{R}_m$ is the mean of the R_{mt} realized over this period.[1] In the context of Eq. (8-1), β_j is simply $r_{jm}\sigma_j\sigma_m/\sigma_m^2$.

It is important to recognize that $\overline{R}_m$ and $\overline{i}$ are used as surrogates for the expected return for the market index and the expected risk-free rate. When the past is not believed to be a good proxy for the future, it may be better to estimate these returns directly. One then would use the regression coefficient, β_j, which is based on the past relationship between the security's return and the market return, together with direct estimates of $\overline{i}$ and $\overline{R}_m$, to solve for company j's cost of equity capital in Eq. (8-4).

As mentioned in the preceding chapter, several services provide beta information on stocks that are actively traded. These betas are computed on the basis of weekly, monthly, and quarterly data for anywhere from three to ten years in the past. Among the larger "beta providers" are Merrill Lynch, Pierce, Fenner and Smith and the Value Line Investment Survey. Through these services one can readily obtain the beta for a company, thereby facilitating the calculation of the cost of equity capital for that company.

An example   To illustrate the calculation of beta and the cost of equity capital by hand, however, we turn to a simple example. Instead of using monthly or quarterly data, on which most beta calculations are based, we use annual data for ease of understanding. Suppose that during the last ten years, the one-year returns for the Standard & Poor's 500-stock index were those shown in column (1) of Table 8-1, and that returns for security j were those shown in column (2). The arithmetic means of the returns are shown at the bottom of the two columns. In the third column, the risk-free rate as depicted by the yield on short-term government securities is shown, with the arithmetic mean computed at the bottom.

---

[1] For further discussion along these lines, see J. Fred Weston, "Investment Decisions Involving the Capital Asset Pricing Model," *Financial Management* 2 (Spring 1973), 25–33.

Table 8·1   Computation of covariance between R_m and R_j for 19—0 to 19—9.

Year	(1) R_{mt}	(2) R_{jt}	(3) i_t	(4) $R_{mt} - i_t$	(5) $R_{jt} - i_t$	(6) $(R_{mt} - i_t)$ $-.040$
19—0	.00	.05	.04	(.04)	.01	(.00)
19—1	.26	.31	.03	.23	.28	.19
19—2	(.09)	(.14)	.03	(.12)	(.17)	(.16)
19—3	.22	.18	.03	.19	.15	.15
19—4	.16	.21	.04	.12	.17	.08
19—5	.12	.17	.04	.08	.13	.04
19—6	(.10)	(.07)	.05	(.15)	(.12)	(.19)
19—7	.24	.22	.05	.19	.17	.15
19—8	.11	.16	.06	.05	.10	.01
19—9	(.08)	(.14)	.07	(.15)	(.21)	(.19)
Average return	.084	.095	.044	.040	.051	

The fourth and fifth columns reflect excess market and security j returns. (We simply subtract the risk-free rate from actual returns.) Again, the mean values are shown at the bottom. In column (6), we compute the deviations of actual excess market returns from the mean value of such returns, .04. In the next column, these deviations are squared and the mean, which represents the variance of the excess returns, is shown at the bottom of the column. In column (8), deviations of security j excess returns from the mean value of such returns are shown. Finally, in the last column, we multiply the deviations for market excess returns, column (6), times deviations for security j excess returns, column (8). The arithmetic average here represents the covariance between the two sets of excess returns, and it is shown at the bottom of column (9).

Given the covariance, together with the variance for excess market returns, the beta, β_j, is simply

$$\beta_j = \frac{\text{Cov.}(R_{mt} - i, R_{jt} - i)}{\text{Var.}(R_{mt} - i)} = \frac{.0207}{.0187} = 1.107 \qquad (8\text{-}5)$$

This result suggests that returns for security j behave in much the same way as the market, although there is somewhat more risk. (A beta of 1.00 would indicate exact correspondence.) If we assume that the appropriate risk-free rate is an average of risk-free rates that prevailed over the period, .044, the required rate of return for security j is (see Eq. 8-4):

$$R_j = .044 + (.084 - .044)1.107 = .0883$$

Thus, the required rate of return or cost of equity capital is approximately 8.83 percent for security j. In a manner similar to our example, we

(7)	(8) $(R_{jt} - i_t)$ $-.051$	(9)
Col. (6)^2		Col. (6) $\times$ Col. (8)
.0000	(.041)	.0000
.0361	.229	.0435
.0256	(.221)	.0354
.0225	.099	.0149
.0064	.119	.0095
.0016	.079	.0032
.0361	(.171)	.0325
.0225	.119	.0179
.0001	.049	.0005
.0361	(.261)	.0496
Var. $(R_{mt} - i_t)$ = .0187	**Cov. $(R_{mt} - i_t, R_{jt} - i_t)$ = .0207**	

can approximate the cost of equity capital for other securities using the capital-asset pricing model approach. The critical assumption is that the past relationship between a security's return and the market return will hold in the future.

Once the required rate of return for security j has been determined, it is used as the cost of equity capital. In essence, we are saying that this is the rate that investors expect the firm to earn on its equity. This cost then is employed in a weighted-average cost of capital for the firm. Determination of the latter will be taken up shortly, once we have explored further the cost of equity capital as well as the costs of other sources of financing.

SOME QUALIFICATIONS

As discussed in the preceding chapter, the capital-asset pricing model assumes the presence of perfect capital markets. Under this as well as other assumptions, the required rate of return on equity is determined by the company's systematic risk. When these assumptions are relaxed to take account of real-world conditions, the residual risk of a stock may take on a degree of importance. Recall that the total risk of a security is comprised of its systematic risk as well as its residual risk. The assumption of the capital-asset pricing model is that the latter can be completely diversified away, which leaves us only with the former risk.

However, we showed in Chapter 7 that the costs of bankruptcy work to the detriment of stockholders. In essence, these costs represent external drains on the system. As they cannot be diversified away by investors, the total risk of the firm becomes a factor of concern. Stated differently, the probability of a firm going bankrupt depends on the total variability of its cash flows. If there were no costs associated with a creditor takeover, investors would concern themselves only with the systematic risk of a security. As long as the assets of the bankrupt firm could be sold or traded at their economic values, no penalty would be involved. The fact that an individual firm might go bankrupt would be embraced in the overall systematic risk the investor was willing to tolerate in his portfolio.

With bankruptcy costs, however, there is a penalty to the investor. The greater the cost of bankruptcy and the greater the probability of its occurrence, the more concerned the investor will be with the total risk of the firm. Thus, the greater the residual risk of a company, the greater the expected bankruptcy costs to be incurred, holding systematic risk constant. As a result, investors will demand a higher required return for the company than that dictated by its systematic risk alone. Therefore, the required rate of return given by the capital-asset pricing model needs to be adjusted upward if this factor is to be taken into account. Stipulating the exact adjustment is difficult in practice, though in theory it can be rigorously specified.[2] However, we know that the greater the probability of bankruptcy occurring, the greater the upward adjustment necessary. Fragmentary evidence suggests that administrative expenses in a business bankruptcy are approximately 20 percent of the value of the estate.[3] By multiplying the probability of occurrence of bankruptcy times the asset value of the firm under distress conditions times 20 percent, one obtains a very crude picture of the expected bankruptcy costs that might be involved. The required rate of return would be adjusted upward accordingly.

In addition to bankruptcy costs, other relaxations in the assumptions of the capital-asset pricing model will result in residual risk being a factor of importance. In effect, imperfections in the capital markets impede investment behavior consistent with efficient diversification. Therefore, the greater the imperfections, the greater the allowance that must be made for residual risk, and the greater the upward adjustment necessary in the required rate of return.

Flotation costs Another direct qualification is that for the flotation costs involved in the sale of common stock. The capital-asset pricing model tells us the return investors require on a stock under the assumptions stated earlier. If a company sells a new issue of common stock, however, the proceeds of the sale are usually less

---

[2] For a state-preference approach to the measurement of bankruptcy costs, see James C. Van Horne, "Optimal Initiation of Bankruptcy Proceedings by Debt Holders," *Journal of Finance*, 31 (June 1976).

[3] See David T. Stanley and Marjorie Girth, *Bankruptcy: Problem, Process, Reform* (Washington, D.C.: Brookings Institution, 1971).

than the current market price per share. In general, a new issue must be priced below the current market price; in addition, there are out-of-pocket flotation costs.[4] As a result of these factors, the net proceeds from the sale of the stock are less than the current market price per share times the number of shares issued. Accordingly, the cost of equity capital calculations should be modified to take this into account.

For example, suppose the cost of equity capital for a company was found to be 12 percent. Suppose further that of the equity capital employed over time, one-fourth comes from the sale of new stock, with the balance coming from retained earnings. Finally, suppose that for a new issue, flotation costs and underpricing result in the company's receiving only 90 percent of the current market price of the stock. Making these adjustments, the cost of equity capital would be

$$\text{Adjusted } R_j = (.12/.90).25 + (.12).75 = .1233$$

Thus, for every $4 in equity capital, $1 must come from new issues of common stock. When one takes account of the flotation costs involved, it raises the cost of equity capital from 12 percent to 12.33 percent.

Flotation costs represent a capital market imperfection which make new issues of common stock a more "expensive" form of financing than retained earnings. While the type of adjustment illustrated above is approximate, it is necessary if the firm raises significant amounts of equity capital via the new-issue route. Our example assumes the issue is sold to new investors. If the issue is a rights offering to existing stockholders, in theory the amount of underpricing does not matter. Therefore, the adjustment would involve only out-of-pocket flotation costs. (We will discuss the question of a rights offering versus a public offering in depth in Chapter 20.)

ANOTHER WAY TO MEASURE THE COST OF EQUITY CAPITAL

In measuring the cost of equity capital, one is concerned with approximating the rate of return required by investors. The capital-asset pricing model approach, with appropriate adjustments, is one means by which this can be done. In the context of the dividend capitalization model presented in Chapters 2 and 3, we attempt to determine the appropriate rate of discount that equates the present value of all expected future dividends per share, as perceived by investors at the margin, with the current market price per share. Another way we might approach the problem of determining the required rate of return is to estimate the stream of expected future dividends and then solve for the

[4] See Chapter 20 for a discussion of these costs.

rate of discount that equates this stream with the current market price of the stock.[5]

Briefly reviewing from Chapter 2, the value of a share of stock to investors can be viewed as the present value of the expected future stream of income paid to them. Because dividends are all that stockholders as a whole receive from their investment, this stream of income is the cash dividends paid in future periods and, perhaps, a final liquidating dividend. At time 0, the value of a share of stock is

$$P_0 = \frac{D_1}{(1 + k_e)} + \frac{D_2}{(1 + k_e)^2} + \cdots + \frac{D_\infty}{(1 + k_e)^\infty}$$

(8-6)

$$P_0 = \sum_{t=1}^{\infty} \frac{D_t}{(1 + k_e)^t}$$

$P_0 X = D$

$X = \frac{D}{P_0}$

where P_0 is the value of a share of stock at time 0. D_t is the dividend per share expected to be paid in period t, and k_e is the appropriate rate of discount.

We suggested in Chapter 2 that investors formulate subjective probability distributions of dividends per share expected to be paid in various future periods. For the individual investor, the D_t in Eq. (8-6) are the expected values, or means, of these probability distributions. For the market as a whole, the D_t represent the expected values for investors at the margin, and k_e is the market discount factor appropriate for the risk involved. The *cost of equity capital* is defined as the market rate of discount, k_e, that equates the present value of all expected future dividends per share with the current market price of the stock. This cost is found by solving Eq. (8-6) for k_e.

If dividends per share are expected to grow at a constant rate, g, and k_e is greater than g, we discovered in Chapter 2 that

$$P_0 = \frac{D_1}{k_e - g}$$

(8-7)

where D_1 is the dividend per share expected to be paid at the end of period 1. Thus, the cost of equity capital would be

$$k_e = \frac{D_1}{P_0} + g$$

(8-8)

The critical assumption, of course, is that dividends per share are expected to grow at a compound rate of g forever. In certain situations, this assumption may be a fair approximation of investor expectations.

---

[5] This rate would then be adjusted upward for flotation costs and underpricing if stock is sold externally.

For example, if ABC Company's expected dividend per share at the end of period 1 is $2, the current market price is $40, and earnings and dividends per share are expected to grow about 4 percent per annum in keeping with growth in the economy, the company's cost of equity capital is

$$k_e = \frac{2}{40} + .04 = 9 \text{ percent}$$

For the k_e to be realistic, expectations in the marketplace must be such that dividends per share are believed to grow in fact at a rate of g. The important factor, then, is measuring the growth in dividends per share as perceived by investors at the margin.

To the extent that the past trend in earnings per share is felt to be meaningful for predicting this expected future growth, it may be used as the growth variable. For example, suppose a company had the following history of earnings per share:

	Earnings per Share		Earnings per Share
1968	$1.50	1973	$2.19
1969	1.68	1974	2.38
1970	1.78	1975	2.49
1971	1.92	1976	2.45
1972	2.07	1977	2.70

If one averaged the figures for the first three years and the last three years, he would find that the compound annual growth rate between these two averages is 6.4 percent. If it is felt that this growth rate is the best approximation of expected future growth perceived by investors at the margin and that a perpetual-growth model is an appropriate valuation model, Eq. (8-8) might be used in determining the cost of equity capital.

When the expected growth in dividends per share is other than perpetual, a modification of Eq. (8-6) can be used. As brought out in Chapter 2, a number of valuation models assume that the growth rate will eventually taper off. Frequently, the transition is from an above-normal growth rate to one that is considered normal. For example, if dividends were expected to grow at a 15 percent compound rate for five years, at a 10 percent rate for the next five years, and then grow at a 5 percent rate, we would have

$$P_0 = \sum_{t=1}^{5} \frac{D_0(1.15)^t}{(1 + k_e)^t} + \sum_{t=6}^{10} \frac{D_5(1.10)^{t-5}}{(1 + k_e)^t} + \sum_{t=11}^{\infty} \frac{D_{10}(1.05)^{t-10}}{(1 + k_e)^t} \qquad (8\text{-}9)$$

We see that the current dividend, D_0, is the base on which the expected growth in future dividends is built. By solving for k_e, we obtain the cost of equity capital as defined. For example, if the current dividend, D_0, were \$2 a share and market price per share, P_0, were \$75, k_e in Eq. (8-9) would be 9.5 percent. For other patterns of expected future growth, the equation can be easily modified to deal with the situation. The more growth segments we specify, of course, the more the growth pattern will approximate a curvilinear relationship.

For all growth situations, the important thing is to solve for the k_e that equates the expected future dividends perceived by investors at the margin with the current market price of the stock. Because expected growth in dividends is not directly observable, it must be estimated. Herein lies the major difficulty involved in estimating the cost of equity capital. For reasonably stable patterns of past growth, one might project this trend into the future.[6] However, we must temper the projection to take account of current market sentiment. Insight into such sentiment can come from reviewing various analyses of the industry and company by investment advisers as well as from articles about the company in financial newspapers and magazines.

On the basis of the long-range plans of the company, the financial manager can make internal estimates of expected future growth in earnings per share and dividends per share. These estimates should take account of economic and other factors that bear on the firm's future operating performance. Because the financial manager has access to a great deal of relevant information, his estimates of future earnings may be the most accurate of all. However, it is important that investors also expect these earnings. There is an obvious bias if the financial manager uses his estimate of growth to solve for k_e and his estimate differs significantly from that of the market. The important question to ask is, What growth in dividends do investors at the margin expect that leads them to pay x dollars for a share of stock? Every effort should be made to get as accurate a handle as possible on this expected growth pattern. Once it is obtained, it is an easy matter to solve for the cost of equity capital as defined.

If measurement were exact and certain assumptions held, the discount rate determined by this method would be the same as the required rate of return determined by the capital-asset pricing model approach. When the assumptions underlying the capital-asset pricing model do not seem appropriate to the situation involved, the second approach serves as a useful benchmark for adjusting the required rate of

[6] For an analysis of the accuracy of earnings-per-share forecasts produced by various mechanical forecasting techniques using past data, see Edwin J. Elton and Martin J. Gruber, "Earnings Estimates and the Accuracy of Expectational Data," *Management Science*, 18 (April 1972), 409–24. The article also serves as a presentation of these techniques. For yet another method for estimating expected growth, see Aharon R. Ofer, "Investors' Expectations of Earnings Growth, Their Accuracy and Effects on the Structure of Realized Rates of Return," *Journal of Finance*, 30 (May 1975), 509–23.

return. By now it should be apparent that measuring the cost of equity capital of a company is an inexact science. We can only hope to approximate it as accurately as possible.

We believe that the methods suggested above enable such an approximation. However, we will be more or less accurate depending on the situation. Usually we are able to place far more confidence in estimates for a large company whose stock is actively traded on the New York Stock Exchange and whose systematic risk is close to that of the market as a whole than we are in estimates for a moderate-sized machine tool company whose stock is inactively traded in the over-the-counter market and whose systematic risk is very large. We must live with the inexactness involved in the measurement process and try to do as good a job as possible. We turn now to measuring the costs of other types of financing. These types pose far fewer problems than the cost of equity capital, as the brevity of their treatment will attest.

COST OF DEBT

The explicit cost of debt can be derived by solving for that discount rate, k, that equates the net proceeds of the debt issue with the present value of interest plus principal payments, and then adjusting the explicit cost obtained for the tax effect. If we denote the after-tax cost of debt by k_i, it can be approximated by

$$k_i = k(1 - t) \qquad (8\text{-}10)$$

where k is the internal rate of return or yield, and t is the marginal tax rate. Because interest charges are tax deductible, the after-tax cost of debt is substantially less than the before-tax cost. If a company were able to sell a new issue of twenty-year bonds with an 8 percent coupon rate and realize net proceeds (after underwriting expenses) of $1,000 for each $1,000 face value bond, k would be 8 percent.[7] If the federal income tax rate were 50 percent,

---

[7] When the price paid for a bond differs from its face value, the premium or discount is amortized for federal income tax purposes. If the premium or discount is significant, the after-tax cost of debt should take it into account. The approximate cost of a bond sold at a discount or a premium is

$$k_i = \frac{(1 - t)\left[C_t + \frac{1}{n}(P - I_0)\right]}{\frac{1}{2}(P + I_0)}$$

where P is the face value of the bond (usually $1,000), I_0 is the price at which the bond is sold, n is the number of years to maturity, and C_t is the fixed interest cost in all periods. $1/n(P - I_0)$ represents the amortization of the discount or premium over the life of the bond, and the denominator represents the average amount outstanding. If sinking-fund payments are made, the formula must be revised. The formula above is but an approximation of the explicit cost because it does not take account of annual compounding. See G. David Quirin, *The Capital Expenditure Decision* (Homewood, Ill.: Richard D. Irwin, 1967), pp. 100–101.

$$k_i = 8.00(1 - 0.50) = 4.00 \text{ percent}$$

We note that the 4 percent after-tax cost in our example represents the marginal, or incremental, cost of additional debt. It does not represent the cost of debt already employed.

The explicit cost of debt is considerably cheaper than the cost of another source of financing having the same k but where the financial charges are not deductible for tax purposes. Implied in the calculation of an after-tax cost of debt is the fact that the firm is profitable. Otherwise, it does not gain the tax benefit associated with interest payments. The explicit cost of debt for an unprofitable firm is the before-tax cost, k.

If a firm has the policy of maintaining a given proportion of debt in its capital structure, debt is never really paid. Individual debt instruments are paid, of course, but they are replaced by new debt. Thus, debt can be regarded as a permanent part of the financing mix. Under these circumstances, the appropriate formula for calculating the explicit cost of debt is the formula for a perpetuity:

$$k_i = \frac{C_t}{I_0}(1 - t) \tag{8-11}$$

where C_t is the fixed interest cost in all periods, and I_0 is the net proceeds of the issue.[8]

COST OF PREFERRED STOCK

The cost of preferred stock is a function of its stated dividend. As we discuss in Chapter 21, this dividend is not a contractual obligation on the part of the firm but is payable at the discretion of the board of directors. Consequently, unlike debt, there is no risk of legal bankruptcy. However, from the standpoint of common stockholders, preferred stock represents a security senior to their interests. Because most corporations that issue preferred stock intend to pay the stated dividend, the dividend on the preferred stock represents a prior claim on income.[9] As preferred stock has no maturity date, its cost may be represented as

$$k_p = \frac{D}{I_0} \tag{8-12}$$

where D is the stated annual dividend and I_0 represents the net proceeds of the preferred stock issue. If a company were able to sell a $7\frac{1}{2}$ percent

---

[8] For the mathematics of perpetuities, see the appendix to Chapter 2.

[9] The consequences of not paying the dividend are examined in Chapter 21.

preferred stock issue ($100 par value) and realize net proceeds of $98½ a share, the cost of the preferred stock would be $7½/98½ = 7.61$ percent. Note that this cost is not adjusted for taxes, because the preferred stock dividend is paid after taxes. Thus, the explicit cost of preferred stock is substantially greater than that for debt.

OTHER TYPES OF FINANCING

Although equity, debt, and preferred stock are the major sources, there are other types of financing. These include leasing, convertible securities, warrants, and other options. Because determining the costs of these types of financing involves some special and rather complex valuation issues, we postpone their treatment until Chapters 19 and 22. For our purposes in this chapter, knowing the costs of equity, debt, and preferred stock financing is sufficient for illustrating the overall cost of capital of a firm. When costs are later determined for other types of financing, they can be inserted in the weighting scheme to be discussed now.

WEIGHTED-AVERAGE COST OF CAPITAL

Once the costs of the individual components of the capital structure have been computed, these costs may be weighted according to some standard and a weighted-average cost of capital calculated. As an illustration of *only the mechanics* of the calculations, suppose that a firm had the following capital structure at the latest statement date:

	Amount	Proportion
Debt	$ 30 million	30%
Preferred stock	10 million	10
Common stock	20 million	20
Retained earnings	40 million	40
	$100 million	100%

Suppose further that the firm computed the following after-tax costs for these component methods of financing:

	Cost
Debt	4.0%
Preferred stock	8.0
Common stock (new)	11.0
Retained earnings	10.0

The cost of common stock is based on the external sale of a new issue to the public, whereas the cost of retained earnings is taken to be the required rate of return on equity. The slight difference in these two costs is attributable to flotation costs and underpricing associated with the sale of a new issue. If the present weights are used, the weighted-average cost of capital for this example problem is:

(1) *Method of Financing*	(2) *Proportion*	(3) *Cost*	(4) *Weighted Cost (2 × 3)*
Debt	30%	4.0%	1.20%
Preferred stock	10	8.0	0.80
Common stock	20	11.0	2.20
Retained earnings	40	10.0	4.00
Weighted-average cost of capital			8.20%

Given the assumptions of this example, we find the measured weighted-average cost of capital to be 8.2 percent.

With the calculation of a weighted-average cost of capital, the critical question is whether the figure represents the firm's real cost of capital. The answer to this question depends upon how accurately we have measured the individual marginal costs, upon the weighting system, and upon certain other assumptions. Assume for now that we are able to measure accurately the marginal costs of the individual sources of financing; let us examine the importance of the weighting system.[10]

Marginal weights

The critical assumption in any weighting system is that the firm will in fact raise capital in the proportions specified. Because the firm raises capital *marginally* to make a *marginal* investment in new projects, we need to work with the marginal cost of capital to the firm as a whole. This rate depends upon the package of funds employed to finance investment projects.[11] In other words, our concern is with new or incremental capital, not with capital raised in the past. In order for the weighted-average cost of capital to represent a marginal cost, the weights employed must be marginal; that is, the weights must correspond to the proportions of financing inputs the firm intends to employ. If they do

[10] For additional analysis of the weighting system, see Michael J. Brennan, "A New Look at the Weighted Average Cost of Capital," *Journal of Business Finance*, 5, No. 1 (1973), 24–30; and Timothy J. Nantell and C. Robert Carlson, "The Cost of Capital as a Weighted Average," *Journal of Finance*, 30 (December 1975), 1343–55.

[11] See Wilbur G. Lewellen, *The Cost of Capital* (Belmont, Calif.: Wadsworth, Inc., 1969), p. 87.

not, capital is raised on a marginal basis in proportions other than those used to calculate this cost. As a result, the real weighted-average cost of capital will differ from that calculated and used for capital-investment decisions. An obvious bias results. If the real cost is greater than that which is measured, certain investment projects will be accepted that will leave investors worse off than before. On the other hand, if the real cost is less than the measured cost, projects will be rejected that could increase shareholder wealth. Therefore, the 8.2 percent weighted-average cost of capital computed in our example is realistic only if the firm intends to finance in the future in the same proportions as its existing capital structure.

It is recognized that the raising of capital is "lumpy," and strict proportions cannot be maintained. For example, a firm would have difficulty in financing each project undertaken with 35 percent debt, 10 percent preferred stock, and 55 percent retained earnings. In practice, it may finance with debt in one instance and with preferred stock or retained earnings in another. Over time, most firms are able to finance in roughly a proportional manner. It is in this sense that we try to measure the marginal cost of capital for the package of financing employed. Another problem is that retained earnings, an important source of funds for most firms, are constrained by the absolute amount of earnings. If a firm's investment opportunities warrant expansion at a rate faster than the growth in earnings, financing by means of retained earnings must diminish relative to other means. Where the expansion is expected to be continuous for a number of years, the financing mix of the firm is subject to a constraint with respect to the ability of the firm to retain earnings. This constraint must be recognized. Frequently, however, expansion is concentrated in a few years so that over the long run a firm is able to finance with a roughly constant proportion of retained earnings.

Change in capital structure

A problem occurs whenever the firm wishes to change its capital structure. The costs of the component methods of financing usually are based upon the existing capital structure, and these costs may differ from those that rule once the firm has achieved its desired capital structure. Because the firm cannot measure its costs directly at the desired capital structure, these costs must be estimated. During the period of transition from the present capital structure to one that is desired, the firm usually will rely upon one type of financing. For example, it might finance with debt until the desired capital structure is achieved. Although there may be some discrepancy, it is best to use the estimated weighted-average cost of capital based upon the financing mix to be employed once the desired capital structure is reached. There would be no transitional problem if the firm undertook an immediate change in its capital structure by issuing debt and repurchasing stock. However, most firms are reluctant to do this; consequently, the transition period usually will be gradual and will involve some problems.

RATIONALE FOR WEIGHTED-AVERAGE COST

The rationale behind the use of a weighted-average cost of capital is that by financing in the proportions specified and accepting projects yielding more than the weighted-average cost, the firm is able to increase the market price of its stock. This increase occurs because investment projects accepted are expected to yield more on their equity-financed portions than the cost of equity capital, k_e. Once these expectations are apparent to the marketplace, the market price of the stock should rise, all other things remaining the same. The firm has accepted projects that are expected to provide a return greater than that required by investors at the margin, based on the risk involved.

Using Eq. (8-6) as our valuation model and holding constant the dividend policy of the firm, we see that the acceptance of the projects raises expected future dividends per share, D_t, in the numerator of the equation. If the equity-financed portion of the new investment projects consists of a common-stock offering, market price per share will rise with an upward shift in expectations of future dividends per share. Embodied in these expectations is the dilution that necessarily will occur with the common-stock offering. In other words, the rise in expected future earnings must be sufficient to raise expected future *dividends per share*, not just expected future dividends.

If the equity-financed portion of the new investment projects consists of retained earnings, no dilution will occur. Here the rise in expected future dividends per share must be sufficient so that when the incremental increases are discounted by the market discount rate, k_e, their present value exceeds the equity capital employed in the projects. One can visualize the process as the firms employing investors' capital at time 0 to invest in a project whose cash-flow benefits are expected to give rise to higher future dividends. In order for the project to be worthwhile, the present value of the incremental dividends must equal or exceed the equity capital employed in it. If the present value exceeds the equity capital employed in the project, the market price of the stock, P_0, will rise. If the present value is just equal to the amount of equity capital employed, P_0 will remain unchanged.[12]

The use of a weighted-average cost of capital figure must be quali-

---

[12] As an aside, market price per share will rise over time if the firm invests in projects whose return on the equity-financed portion just equals the cost of equity capital. This type of situation is known as expansion. In essence, dividends per share would rise over time

fied for the points raised earlier. It assumes that the investment proposals being considered do not differ in systematic risk from that of the firm and that the residual risk of the proposals does not provide any diversification benefits to the firm, if indeed residual risk is a factor of importance. Only under these circumstances is the cost of capital figure obtained appropriate as an acceptance criterion. These assumptions are extremely binding. They imply that the projects of a firm are completely homogeneous with respect to risk and that only projects of exactly the same risk will be considered.

In practice, of course, the issue is one of degree. If the conditions above are approximately met, the company's weighted-average cost of capital may be used as the acceptance criterion. For example, if a firm produced only one product and all proposals considered were in conjunction with the marketing and production of that product, the use of the firm's overall cost of capital as the acceptance criterion might be appropriate. (Even here, however, there may be significant enough differences in risk among investment proposals to warrant separate consideration.) For a multiproduct firm with investment proposals of varying risk, the use of an overall required rate of return is inappropriate. Here the required rate of return for the specific proposal should be used, as determined with the methods proposed in the preceding chapter. The key, then, is the homogeneity of existing investment projects and investment proposals under consideration with respect to risk. While this condition may be met for certain companies, we would expect it to be met more often for sub units of companies, such as divisions.

DIVISIONAL COSTS OF CAPITAL

Where the use of a company-wide cost of capital is inappropriate as an acceptance criterion, the use of a divisional cost of capital may be valid. By *division*, we mean some sub unit of a company that carries on a set of activities that can be differentiated from the other activities of the

---

because of the increase in earnings occasioned by the reinvestment of retained earnings. As a result, the present value of expected future dividends also would rise over time. For example, if a perpetual-growth model were applicable,

$$P_0 = \frac{D_1}{k_e - g}$$

If expectations and the market rate of discount remained unchanged, the market price at time 1 would be

$$P_1 = \frac{D_2}{k_e - g}$$

Because D_2 is greater than D_1, P_1 would be greater than P_0. Similarly, it can be shown that $P_t > P_{t-1}$ for all t under our assumptions.

firm. Usually these activities are differentiated along product or service lines as well as along management lines. Henceforth, we will refer to these sub units as divisions, whether they be called subsidiaries, divisions, units, or whatever.

Each division employs in it assets which must be financed. The question is, What is an appropriate acceptance criterion? Again the key is the homogeneity of activities. If the products or services involved are homogeneous with respect to risk, and new investment proposals are of the same sort, a case can be made for a divisional cost of capital as the acceptance criterion. It represents the transfer price of capital from the company to the division. Stated differently, it is the rate of return the company expects the division to earn on its capital investments. The question is, What is the proper rate of return for a division, assuming the activities of that division are homogeneous with respect to risk?

DETERMINING A DIVISION'S REQUIRED RATE OF RETURN

The concepts taken up in the preceding chapter and earlier in this one can be applied here. As we have gone through the mechanics of measurement several times before, we assume the reader is able to undertake the necessary calculations. Therefore, our presentation will be mainly verbal, with an emphasis on implications.

As with individual investment projects and the company as a whole, the capital-asset pricing model can be used to determine a required rate of return on equity for a division. What one would do is try to identify companies with publicly traded stocks which were engaged solely in the line of business of the division. This would involve a careful comparison of the products and/or services involved. For an electrical products division, for example, one would concentrate on companies engaged solely in the manufacture and sale of electrical products. Sometimes the matching can only be approximate. The important thing is to try to find a publicly traded company or companies that have nearly the same degree of systematic risk as the division.

Once the company is identified, its beta can be computed and the required rate of return on equity determined according to the procedures illustrated in our previous examples. Having determined the required rate of return on equity for the company, it is used as a proxy for the required rate of return on equity for the division. In other words, the beta information for a company whose stock is publicly traded is substituted for that of the division. The implication is that the systematic risk of the company is the same as that for the division.

In situations where it is difficult to identify companies that closely parallel the division in question, one can resort to the methods taken up in the last chapter where we measured the beta for a project based on the market value of the specific asset. However, the much preferred and more accurate way is to find a company whose stock is publicly traded. Usually, this is much easier for a division than it is for an individual investment project. There usually exist companies that carry on activities similar to those of the division. The principal exception would be an industry comprised entirely of multidivision companies.

Once the cost of equity capital for the division is determined, it is combined with the cost of debt and other sources of financing to obtain a weighted-average cost of capital for the division. The amount of nonequity financing that is assigned to the division is an important consideration. It should be approximately the same relative amount as that used by the proxy company on which determination of the division's required return on equity is based. The problem is that the overall nonequity financing of the firm must be allocated to its individual divisions. If the external companies on which beta information is based collectively use proportionally more or less nonequity financing than the firm, either too much or too little nonequity financing is allocated. If the differences are not large, the problem may not be important. We must stress, however, that the proportion of nonequity financing allocated to a division cannot be significantly out of line with that of the external company being used. Otherwise, one will not get a reasonable proxy for the systematic risk involved in that division.

The weighting process and the calculation of the weighted-average cost of capital is the same as in the previous section. What we end up with is a required rate of return for investment proposals undertaken by that division. This is the return demanded by investors for projects having the same proportional systematic risk as the division now possesses.

IMPLICATIONS FOR PROJECT SELECTION

Once divisional costs of capital are computed for each division, capital is allocated, or transferred, throughout the firm on a risk-adjusted return basis. The higher the systematic risk of a division, the higher the required rate of return. This approach provides a consistent framework for allocating capital among divisions with greatly different risks. Too often in a multidivision firm, a single cutoff rate is used for project selection. An edict comes from above stating that "no project shall be undertaken unless it provides a return of 15 percent"! The problem is that certain "safe" projects with little systematic risk are rejected because they do not provide a return above the company's stated goal. However, some of these projects may provide expected returns greater than the "true" cost of capital for the division. In contrast, divisions characterized by large systematic risk may accept projects with expected returns higher than the company-wide norm, but lower than they should earn given the systematic risk involved.

This problem is illustrated in Figure 8-1. The horizontal dashed line is the company's overall cost of capital, and the bars represent the costs of capital for the various divisions of the company, based on their systematic risk. The *x*'s and *o*'s represent investment projects of the type described: namely, those with expected returns below the company's overall cost of capital, but above the division's cost of capital; and those with expected returns above the company's cost of capital, but below the division's cost of capital. The rejection of the former projects and acceptance of the latter is suboptimal. The former provide expected returns in excess of that return required by the market for the systematic risk involved, while the latter provide expected returns lower than that required. While the problem may seem obvious, this very thing happens either directly or indirectly in many a multidivision company.

The incentives in such a company are such that divisions with low systematic risk often are too conservative in project generation and selection, while divisions with large systematic risk are too aggressive. Too often there is a tendency for a company to put its money in those divisions providing the greatest growth opportunities, and to ration capital to other divisions so that they will accept only projects consistent with the overall growth objectives. Frequently, the high-growth divisions have a "license" to do most anything they want, as long as the expected returns on the projects selected are above the company's overall required return. However, some of the projects selected provide too low an expected return for the systematic risk involved. As a result, the company may become riskier over time without commensurate increases in expected return.

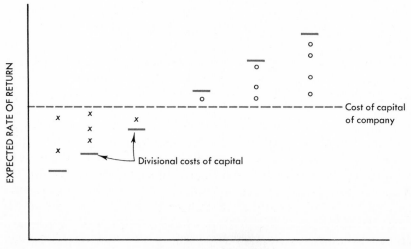

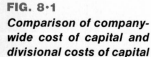

FIG. 8·1

Comparison of company-wide cost of capital and divisional costs of capital

The incentive scheme is skewed in the direction of growth and the acceptance of risky projects. "Safe" divisions may be starved for capital, even though they are able to generate investment proposals that are expected to provide returns in excess of those required for the systematic risk involved. The problem is a mistaken belief that growth is the panacea for all problems. The value of a firm rests on two foundations—expected return and risk. Growth in the former is good, but growth in the latter is bad. Whether the overall result is good or bad depends on the combined effect of these two factors.

What is needed is a system for allocating capital to divisions on a risk-adjusted return basis. The approach presented provides such a means. As long as investment proposals emanating from the division are homogeneous with respect to systematic risk, the approach will result in consistent investment decisions being made among the divisions of a company. When investment proposals are not homogeneous, they should be evaluated on a proposal-by-proposal basis, using the methods taken up in the preceding chapter.

RESIDUAL RISK CONSIDERATIONS

In our discussion of the required rate of return for a division, we have considered only the systematic risk of that division. Implied is that the market evaluates the parts of a company, in our case its divisions, separately according to their systematic risk. (The reasoning behind this assumption was taken up in the preceding chapter, so we will not repeat it here.) As in all of our previous discussions, the question becomes, What happens if residual risk is important? As we know from before, the greater the imperfections in the capital markets, generally the greater the importance of residual risk. However, it is not the residual risk of the division that is important, but the residual risk of the firm as a whole. Take the imperfection of bankruptcy costs, for example. A particular division might experience difficulties and go into bankruptcy on its own, but the company as a whole would not because of the offsetting performance of other divisions which are not experiencing such adversities. It is only if the firm as a whole goes bankrupt that bankruptcy costs are incurred.

Following the methods outlined in the preceding chapter, one can determine the impact of a division on the total risk of the firm (that is, its systematic and residual risk). In that chapter, a dual approach for evaluating risky investments was presented. Recall that this consisted of evaluating investment proposals according to the capital-asset pricing model and then according to their incremental impact on the total risk of the firm. Accept or reject decisions are reached for both approaches. Where these decisions are the same, there is no problem. When conflicting decisions are reached, however, the final decision depends on the perceived importance of imperfections in the capital markets. On the basis of this, one would favor one approach or the other and would make a decision.

The same dual approach can be applied to the evaluation of the divisions of a company. Such an approach results in one's using the capital-asset pricing model to determine the "underlying" required rate of return for the division commensurate with the systematic risk involved. Analysis of the impact of the various divisions on the total risk of the firm allows consideration of the diversification properties of those divisions. This consideration is important only if imperfections exist in the capital markets which make the residual risk of a firm a significant factor to investors. Thus, we are able to take account of residual risk in the same manner as we did for individual investment projects.

EVALUATING ACQUISITIONS

The last topic in this chapter is the evaluation of acquisitions. We saw in Chapter 6 that an acquisition can be analyzed according to its expected return and risk in the same manner as any capital investment. In what should by now be a familiar procedure, we examine the issue under the assumptions of the capital-asset pricing model and then under conditions where residual risk might be a factor of at least some importance.

EVALUATION UNDER THE ASSUMPTIONS OF THE CAPITAL-ASSET PRICING MODEL

Given the assumptions of the model, it is clear that investors are able to achieve the same diversification as the firm is able to do for them. This point is particularly apparent in the case of the acquisition of a company whose stock is publicly held. In fact, the investor has an advantage in that he is able to diversify by buying only a few shares of stock, whereas the acquisition for the buying company is much more "lumpy." Thus, the acquiring firm is unable to do something for investors that they are not able to do for themselves at least as efficiently. Therefore, pure diversification by the firm through acquisitions is not a thing of value.[13] The whole will simply equal the sum of the parts.

This is not to say that an acquisition will not enhance the value of

---

[13] For further discussion of this point, see Stewart C. Myers, "Procedures for Capital Budgeting under Uncertainty," *Industrial Management Review*, 9 (Spring 1968), 1–15; Jan Mossin, "Equilibrium in a Capital Asset Model," *Econometrica*, 34 (October, 1966), 768–75; Haim Levy and Marshall Sarnat, "Diversification, Portfolio Analysis, and the Uneasy Case for Conglomerate Mergers," *Journal of Finance*, 25 (September 1970), 795–802; and Michael Gort, "An Economic Disturbance Theory of Mergers," *Quarterly Journal of Economics*, 83 (November 1969), 624–42.

the firm to its shareholders. Indeed, economies may be involved that benefit the acquiring firm and its stockholders. The prospect of synergism may make a prospective acquisition more attractive to one company than to another. However, diversification itself would not be beneficial.[14] In particular, conglomerate mergers where the sole purpose is diversification would be suspect: they would not enhance shareholder wealth. If an acquisition is to be worthwhile, there must be the prospect of synergism. In other words, the acquiring company must be able to effect operating economies, distribution economies, or other things of this sort if the acquisition is to be a thing of value.

It is an easy matter to measure the required rate of return for the acquisition of a company whose stock is publicly traded. Direct beta information is available, so one simply calculates the required rate using the procedures illustrated earlier. No proxy is necessary. The expected incremental cash flows arising from the acquisition[15] are then discounted at the required rate of return. If the present value of these cash flows exceeds the purchase price, the acquisition is worthwhile; if not, it should be rejected.

The important thing to remember is that under the assumptions of the capital-asset pricing model, the present value of cash flows will exceed the purchase price *only* if there is synergism. Stated differently, in the absence of synergism, the expected return arising from the acquisition will be no more than the required return. This suggests that the analysis of a prospective acquisition should focus on the likelihood of synergism. For the acquiring company, this usually means doing those things that it does well. Acquiring a company in an unrelated line of business where management has no expertise is unlikely to produce synergism. There are too many cases of this having been done under the mistaken belief that it is the only way to achieve growth. Too often the result is that inefficiencies develop, and the acquiring company earns an incremental return less than that required by the market for the systematic risk involved. As a result, the market price of the stock suffers relative to what would have occurred if the acquisition had not been made.

If the stock of the prospective acquisition is priced efficiently in the market, the acquiring company will pay at least what the company is worth as an independent entity. If a premium is paid, and it usually must be paid, then the acquiring company pays more than the acquisition is worth as an independent operation. Only if synergism is possible can the premium be offset and the acquisition provide an incremental expected return equal to or greater than that required by the market, given the

---

[14] See William W. Alberts, "The Profitability of Growth by Merger," in William W. Alberts and Joel E. Segall, eds., *The Corporate Merger* (Chicago: University of Chicago Press, 1966), p. 272.
[15] The development of this information was taken up in Chapter 6.

systematic risk involved. In evaluating an acquisition, then, one should concentrate on the prospect of synergism. Only this will make the acquisition a thing of value, given our assumptions.

THE DIVERSIFICATION EFFECT

If residual risk is felt to be important or if management is concerned only with the impact of an acquisition on the expected risk and return of the firm as a whole, the evaluation process needs to be altered. One can evaluate an acquisition from the standpoint of the "portfolio" effect on the firm. This was illustrated for investment proposals in Chapter 7, and the procedures are the same for an acquisition. To briefly reiterate them in this context, however, recall from Chapter 6 our discussion of how to derive the probability distribution of possible incremental present values arising from an acquisition. If the price to be paid has been established, it should be subtracted from the expected value of present value to obtain the expected value of *net*-present value. The next step is to estimate the correlation coefficients for the relationship between the net-present value for the prospective acquisition and the net-present values for existing projects and investment proposals under consideration.

The acquisition then becomes one more investment proposal in a portfolio of projects to be considered. The methods of analysis and selection are the same as those employed in the preceding chapter. Management chooses the best combination of expected value of net-present value and risk. If the portfolio of projects represented by this combination includes the prospective acquisition, the firm should acquire the company involved. In this way, an acquisition is evaluated in the same manner as any internally generated investment proposal. A decision is made in keeping with the marginal impact of the acquisition on the total risk of the firm.

Whether the capital-asset pricing model approach is altered depends upon the importance of the diversification effect. In turn, its importance depends upon imperfections in the capital market. If significant imperfections exist, such as bankruptcy costs, a case can be made for the diversification properties of an investment being important.[16] As with individual assets or divisions, the acquisition then would be evaluated according to the systematic risk involved as well as according to its incremental impact on the total risk of the firm.

Even in the absence of bankruptcy costs, Wilbur G. Lewellen argues

[16] For an analysis of the conditions under which an acquisition benefits stockholders, see Robert C. Higgins and Lawrence D. Schall, "Corporate Bankruptcy and Conglomerate Merger," *Journal of Finance*, 30 (March 1975), 106–111. In this article, Higgins and Schall consider the covariance of bankruptcy costs with the market return, a consideration that we do not explore. The greater the covariance, the less important bankruptcy costs become, and vice versa.

that mergers result in "financial synergism," beneficial to investors.[17] By merging, he contends that the debt capacity of the combined entity will be greater than the sum of the individual debt capacities of the two companies involved. If, in a world of taxes, debt funds are "cheaper" than equity funds,[18] borrowing more will increase the value of the equity. The reason debt capacity supposedly increases is that the variance about the mean of two streams of cash flows can be reduced by combining them.[19] By reducing the dispersion of the probability distribution of possible cash flows relative to the mean of the distribution, the probability that principal and interest payments on the debt will not be met is reduced. As a result, lenders are willing to lend more to the combined entity than they are willing to lend to the two companies separately. (The reduction in relative dispersion of cash flows affords them a greater degree of protection.) One might be tempted to argue that a lender can achieve this diversification on his own. Though it is true that a lender can diversify loans, he is unable to reduce the probability that independent companies will default because he cannot merge their cash flows. Only through an actual merger are these cash flows fused and *relative* dispersion reduced. For reasons of "financial synergism" then, Lewellen argues that mergers, and particularly conglomerate mergers, enhance shareholder wealth.

Higgins and Schall take issue with this conclusion.[20] They agree that a merger between two firms reduces the bankruptcy risk to creditors by providing a form of coinsurance in the sense that the premerger cash flows of the two firms are fused. However, they argue that under perfect capital market assumptions, this benefits only the debtholders. The market price of the debt instruments rises and, because the total value of the company remains the same under the assumption of perfect capital markets, equity values fall.[21] Thus, Higgins and Schall suggest that equity values usually decrease with mergers, even though creditors benefit. They state that this can be prevented only if the premerger debt is retired at its premerger market value. In this case, equityholders do not suffer, as debt can later be reissued at higher postmerger values. While the argument above is an interesting one, it depends on a degree of segmentation between debt and equity markets. If such segmentation does not exist and there are common investors in both markets, one party would not tend to gain at the expense of the other.

When we leave the "zero-sum" game posed above and allow for taxes and bankruptcy costs, it is possible for equityholders to gain

---

[17] "A Pure Financial Rationale for the Conglomerate Merger," *Journal of Finance*, 26 (May 1971), 521–37.

[18] This issue is analyzed in Chapter 9.

[19] This statement assumes that less than perfect correlation exists between the two streams.

[20] Higgins and Schall, "Corporate Bankruptcy and Conglomerate Merger," pp. 93–106.

[21] With taxes, increased leverage in keeping with the increased debt capacity occasioned by the merger works to the advantage of equityholders. This advantage must be balanced against the disadvantage mentioned above, according to Higgins and Schall.

through merging, apart from any synergistic effects. This gain depends on the diversification effects of a merger resulting in the greater use of "cheaper" debt funds (owing to taxes) and/or a reduction in expected bankruptcy costs. Both of these factors (taxes and bankruptcy costs) are defined as market imperfections. While we would not imagine these imperfections to have a large impact on the value of the acquiring firm, they nonetheless may be important enough to make the diversification effect of a merger a significant factor. In most cases, however, the really important thing to evaluate in a prospective acquisition is the prospect for synergism. This is particularly true if a premium in stock value must be offered in order to acquire the company.

SUMMARY

The use of the cost of capital for a company or division as an acceptance criterion is predicated on its activities being homogeneous with respect to risk, and investment proposals under consideration being of the same sort. A company has available to it an assortment of financing methods, each with a cost. By far the most difficult to measure is the cost of equity capital. One way to measure it is with a capital-asset pricing model approach. With this approach, we are able to determine the return investors require the company to earn on equity, given the systematic risk involved. To the extent that imperfections exist in the capital markets and they are felt to be important, this required rate of return may have to be adjusted upward to reflect the significance of residual risk. Another way to measure the cost of equity capital is to solve for the rate of discount that equates the stream of expected future dividends, as perceived by investors at the margin, with the current market price of the stock.

Once the costs of the individual methods of financing are determined, a weighted-average cost of capital for the firm can be computed. The weights employed should correspond to the proportions with which the firm intends to finance. Once computed, the weighted-average cost is used as the basis for accepting or rejecting investment projects. The rationale for its use was explored in some detail. Again, a key condition is the homogeneity of existing investment projects and investment proposals under consideration with respect to risk. When this condition does not hold, the overall company cost of capital should not be used as an acceptance criterion.

Often the condition above is met for divisions of a company but is not met for the company as a whole. Again using the capital-asset pricing model approach, one can determine the required return on equity for that division. The important thing is to identify a publicly traded company whose line of business and systematic risk closely parallels that of the division. This company then is used as a proxy for developing beta information. Once the cost of equity is determined, it is combined with other costs in a weighted-average cost of capital for the division. The implications of its use in project selection were discussed, and it was concluded that the approach has considerable merit for allocating capital among the divisions of a company on a consistent risk-adjusted return basis. We then extended our discussion to allow for residual risk being a factor of importance and analyzed it along the lines proposed in the preceding chapter. Where the condition of homogeneity of projects with respect to risk is not met, investment proposals emanating from a division should be evaluated using the required rate of return for the project and not that for the division.

In the final section, we took up the evaluation of acquisitions. If most of the assumptions of the capital-asset pricing model hold, it is clear that investors are able to achieve the same diversification on their own as the acquiring company is able to do for them. Therefore, diversification by the firm in acquisitions would not be a thing of value. This argues that a company should focus its analysis on the likelihood of synergism when studying prospective acquisitions. Only synergism will result in incremental value being gained. We then examined the conditions under which the diversification effect in mergers might be a factor of importance. These were found to be the presence of bankruptcy costs and taxes.

PROBLEMS

1. On March 10, International Copy Machines (ICOM), one of the "favorites" of the stock market, was priced at $300 per share. This price was based on an expected annual growth rate of at least 20 percent for quite some time in the future. In July, economic indicators turned down, and investors revised downward to 15 percent their estimate for future growth of ICOM. What should happen to the price of the stock? Assume the following:

   (a) A perpetual-growth valuation model is a reasonable representation of the way the market values ICOM.

   (b) The measured cost of equity capital to the firm is the true cost.

   (c) The firm does not change its dividend, the risk complexion of its assets, or its degree of financial leverage.

   (d) The firm pays a current dividend of $3 per share.

2. K-Far Stores has launched an expansion program that should result in the saturation of the Bay Area marketing region of California in six years. As a result, the company is predicting a growth in earnings of 12 percent for three years, 6 percent for years four through six, after which it expects constant earnings for the foreseeable future. The company expects to increase its dividend per share, now $1, in keeping with this growth pattern. Currently, the market price of the stock is $25 per share. Estimate the company's cost of equity capital.

3. During the last six years, excess returns above the risk-free rate were the following for the market index and for the common stock of Rayfil Manufacturing Company:

Year	1	2	3	4	5	6
Excess return market	.08	(.02)	.14	.18	(.06)	.04
Excess return Rayfil	.02	.06	.22	.17	(.02)	(.03)

Over this same period, the risk-free rate averaged 4 percent. On the basis of this limited information, compute the cost of equity capital of the firm in the context of the capital-asset pricing model.

4. Over the same period of time as in problem 3, Kay Wyman Stores, Inc., had the following excess returns:

Year	1	2	3	4	5	6
Excess return Kay Wyman Stores	.12	(.07)	.26	.28	(.12)	.06

What is the cost of equity capital? Why does it differ from that of Rayfil Manufacturing Company in problem 3?

5. Assuming the firm has a tax rate of 50 percent, compute the after-tax cost of the following:

   (a) A bond, sold at par, with a $9\frac{1}{4}$ percent coupon.

   (b) A twenty-year, $8\frac{1}{2}$ percent, $1,000 par bond sold at $900 less a 5 percent underwriting commission. (Use an approximation method.)

   (c) A preferred stock sold at $100 with a 7 percent coupon and a call price of $110 if the company plans to call the issue in five years. (Use an approximation method.)

   (d) A common stock selling at $20 and paying a $2 dividend, which is expected to be continued indefinitely.

   (e) The same common stock if dividends are expected to grow at the rate of 5 percent per year.

   (f) A common stock, selling at $30 per share, of a company that engages in no external financing. The stock earns $5 per share, of which one-half is paid in dividends. The shareholders expect the company to earn a constant after-tax rate of 10 percent on investments.

   (g) (1) A common stock selling for $21 whose dividends are expected to be $1 per year for the next five years and $2 per year forever thereafter. (2) If expectations hold true and the discount rate is the same, what should be the price of the stock at the beginning of the year 6?

6. The Kalog Precision Tool Company was recently formed to manufacture a new product. The company has the following capital structure:

10% debentures of 1999	$6,000,000
8% preferred stock	2,000,000
Common stock (320,000 shares)	8,000,000
	$16,000,000

6/16 = .375 × 5
2/16 = .125 × 8
8/16 = .500 × 14

The common stock sells for $25 a share and the company has a marginal tax rate of 50 percent. A study of publicly held companies in this line of business suggests that the required return on equity is about 14 percent for a company of this sort. (A capital-asset pricing model approach was used to determine the required rate of return.)

(a) Compute the firm's present weighted-average cost of capital.

(b) Is the figure computed an appropriate acceptance criterion for evaluating investment proposals? *if co. will maintain this cap'l struct. if invest. proposals have the same risk.*

(c) Would it be appropriate for a division of the company?

7. The Williams Warbler Company is contemplating acquiring the Acme Brass Company. Incremental cash flows arising from the acquisition are expected to be the following:

	Average of Years (in thousands)		
	1–5	6–10	11–∞
Cash flow after taxes	$100	$150	$200
Investment required	50	60	70
Net cash flow	$ 50	$ 90	$130

$$R_j = i + \beta_j(\bar{R}_m - i)$$
$$= .05 + 1.6(.10 - .05)$$
$$\bar{R}_j = .13$$

Acme has an all-equity capital structure. Its beta is 1.60, based on the past sixty months of data relating its excess return to that of the market. The expected risk-free rate is 5 percent, and the expected return on the market portfolio is 10 percent.

(a) What is the maximum price that Williams Warbler Company might pay for Acme?

(b) On what assumptions does a price that high depend?

SELECTED REFERENCES

Alberts, W. W., and S. H. Archer, "Some Evidence on the Effect of Company Size on the Cost of Equity Capital," *Journal of Financial and Quantitative Analysis,* 8 (March 1973), 229–45.

Archer, Stephen H., and Leroy G. Faerber, "Firm Size and the Cost of Equity Capital," *Journal of Finance,* 21 (March 1966), 69–84.

Arditti, Fred D., "The Weighted Average Cost of Capital: Some Questions on its Definition, Interpretation and Use," *Journal of Finance,* 28 (September 1973), 1001–8.

———, "Risk and the Required Return on Equity," *Journal of Finance,* 22 (March 1967), 19–36.

Beranek, William, "The Cost of Capital, Capital Budgeting, and the Maximization of Shareholder Wealth," *Journal of Financial and Quantitative Analysis,* 10 (March 1975), 1–21.

Boness, A. James, "A Pedagogic Note on the Cost of Capital," *Journal of Finance,* 19 (March 1964), 99–106.

Bower, Richard S., and Jeffrey M. Jenks, "Divisional Screening Rates," *Financial Management,* 4 (Autumn 1975), 42–49.

Brennan, Michael J., "A New Look at the Weighted Average Cost of Capital," *Journal of Business Finance,* 5, No. 1 (1973), 24–30.

Elton, Edwin J., and Martin J. Gruber, "Asset Selection with Changing Capital Structure," *Journal of Financial and Quantitative Analysis,* 8 (June 1973), 459–74.

———, "The Cost of Retained Earnings—Implications of Share Repurchase," *Industrial Management Review,* 9 (Spring 1968), 87–104.

————, "Earnings Estimates and the Accuracy of Expectational Data," *Management Science,* 18 (April 1972), 409–24.

————, "Valuation and Asset Selection under Alternative Investment Opportunities," *Journal of Finance,* 31 (May 1976).

Fama, Eugene F., and Merton H. Miller, *The Theory of Finance,* Chapter 7, New York: Holt, Rinehart & Winston, 1972.

Gordon, Myron J., and Paul J. Halpern, "Cost of Capital for a Division of a Firm," *Journal of Finance,* 29 (September 1974), 1153–63.

Haley, Charles W., "A Note on the Cost of Debt," *Journal of Financial and Quantitative Analysis,* 1 (December 1966), 72–93.

————, "Taxes, the Cost of Capital, and the Firm's Investment Decisions," *Journal of Finance,* 26 (September 1971), 901–17.

Hamada, Robert S., "Investment Decision with a General Equilibrium Mean-Variance Approach," *Quarterly Journal of Economics,* 85 (November 1971), 667–83.

————, "Portfolio Analysis, Market Equilibrium and Corporation Finance," *Journal of Finance,* 24 (March 1969), 13–31.

Haugen, Robert A., and Prem Kumar, "The Traditional Approach to Valuing Levered-Growth Stocks," *Journal of Financial and Quantitative Analysis,* 9 (December 1974), 1031–44.

Haugen, Robert A., and Terence C. Langetieg, "An Empirical Test for Synergism in Merger," *Journal of Finance,* 30 (September 1975), 1003–14.

Higgins, Robert C., and Lawrence D. Schall, "Corporate Bankruptcy and Conglomerate Merger," *Journal of Finance,* 30 (March 1975), 93–114.

Joehnk, Michael D., and James F. Nielsen, "The Effects of Conglomerate Merger Activity on Systematic Risk," *Journal of Financial and Quantitative Analysis,* 9 (March 1974), 215–26.

Levy, Haim, and Marshall Sarnat, "Diversification, Portfolio Analysis and the Uneasy Case for Conglomerate Mergers," *Journal of Finance,* 25 (September 1970), 795–802.

Lewellen, Wilbur G., *The Cost of Capital,* Belmont, Calif.: Wadsworth, 1969.

————, "A Pure Financial Rationale for the Conglomerate Merger," *Journal of Finance,* 26 (May 1971), 521–37.

Linke, Charles M., and Moon K. Kim, "More on the Weighted Average Cost of Capital: A Comment and Analysis," *Journal of Financial and Quantitative Analysis,* 9 (December 1974), 1069–81.

Litzenberger, Robert H., and Alan P. Budd, "Corporate Investment Criteria and the Valuation of Risk Assets," *Journal of Financial and Quantitative Analysis,* 4 (December 1970), 395–419.

Litzenberger, Robert H., and O. Maurice Joy, "Decentralized Capital Budgeting Decisions and Shareholder Wealth Maximization," *Journal of Finance,* 30 (September 1975), 993–1002.

Litzenberger, Robert H., and C. U. Rao, "Estimates of the Marginal Rate of Time Preference and Average Risk Aversion of Investors in Electric Utility Shares," *Bell Journal of Economics and Management Sciences,* 2 (Spring 1971), 333–91.

————, "Portfolio Theory and Industry Cost-of-Capital Estimates," *Journal of Financial and Quantitative Analysis,* 7 (March 1972), 1443–62.

Mandelker, Gershon, "Risk and Return: The Case of Merging Firms," *Journal of Financial Economics,* 1 (December 1974), 303–35.

Mossin, Jan, *Theory of Financial Markets,* Chapters 7–8, Englewood Cliffs, N.J.: Prentice-Hall, 1973.

Myers, Stewart C., "The Application of Finance Theory to Public Utility Rate Cases," *Bell Journal of Economics and Management Science,* 3 (Spring 1972), 58–97.

Nantell, Timothy J., and C. Robert Carlson, "The Cost of Capital as a Weighted Average," *Journal of Finance,* 30 (December, 1975), 1343–55.

Ofer, Aharon R., "Investors' Expectations of Earnings Growth, Their Accuracy and Effects on the Structure of Realized Rates of Return," *Journal of Finance,* 30 (May 1975), 509–23.

Reilly, Raymond R., and William E. Wecker, "On the Weighted Average Cost of Capital," *Journal of Financial and Quantitative Analysis,* 8 (January 1973), 123–26.

Rubinstein, Mark E., "Corporate Financial Policy in Segmented Securities Markets," *Journal of Financial and Quantitative Analysis,* 8 (December 1973), 749–62.

————, "A Mean-Variance Synthesis of Corporate Financial Theory," *Journal of Finance,* 28 (March 1972), 167–82.

Schall, Lawrence D., "Asset Valuation, Firm Investment, and Firm Diversification," *Journal of Business,* 45 (January 1972), 11–28.

————, "Firm Financial Structure and Investment," *Journal of Financial and Quantitative Analysis,* 6 (June 1971), 925–42.

Stapleton, Richard C., "Portfolio Analysis, Stock Valuation and Capital Budgeting Rules for Risky Projects," *Journal of Finance,* 26 (March 1971), 95–118.

Tuttle, Donald L., and Robert H. Litzenberger, "Leverage, Diversification and Capital Market Effects on a Risk-Adjusted Capital Budgeting Framework," *Journal of Finance,* 23 (June 1968), 427–43.

Van Horne, James C., *The Function and Analysis of Capital Market Rates.* Englewood Cliffs, N.J.: Prentice-Hall, 1970.

————, "Optimal Initiation of Bankruptcy Proceedings by Debt Holders," *Journal of Finance,* 31 (June 1976).

FINANCING and DIVIDEND POLICIES

THEORY of
CAPITAL
STRUCTURE

In Part II, we were concerned with how capital might be allocated to investment proposals, given a certain financing mix. In this chapter and the next, we are concerned with whether the way in which investment proposals are financed matters; and, if it does matter, what is the optimal capital structure? If we finance with one mix of securities rather than another, is the market price of the stock affected? If the firm can affect the market price of its stock by its financing decision, it will want to undertake a financing policy that will maximize market price. For simplicity, we examine the question of capital structure in terms of the proportion of debt to equity. However, the principles taken up in this chapter can be easily expanded to include consideration of the specific type of security being issued.

First we explore the theory with respect to the valuation of the firm. From previous discussion of the capital-asset pricing model, one's intuition should be that if the assumptions of the model hold, variations in the proportion of debt in the capital structure will not affect the firm's total valuation. That is, in the absence of taxes, bankruptcy costs, and other imperfections of this sort, the value of the firm is independent of its capital structure. If firms are valued only according to their systematic risk in a no-tax world, the degree of leverage should not matter. Unlike the development of the last two chapters, however, we do not begin with an analysis of the issue in the context of the capital-asset pricing model. While the subject could be developed in this manner, for ease of understanding we take a different tack.

Our examination involves a partial equilibrium analysis where we hold constant the investment and dividend decisions of the firm and try to determine the effect of a change in financing mix on share price. In this regard, we focus on the arbitrage process as the means by which equilibrium is achieved. Upon completion of this presentation, we then examine the problem in terms of the capital-asset pricing model. As we will see, the former development leads into the latter. Hopefully, this treatment will provide not only an easier understanding of the problem but also a much richer insight. Following this, we relax the initial assumptions and study the impact of various capital-market imperfections on the way capital structure decisions affect the valuation of the firm. In the end, we hope to make some generalization about the implications of the theory presented for financing decisions. In the subsequent chapter, we consider how a firm in practice can determine a capital structure suitable for its particular situation.

INTRODUCTION TO THE THEORY

Even a casual review of the literature brings one quickly to the key question of whether or not capital structure matters. Can the firm affect its total valuation and its cost of capital by changing its financing mix? In this section, our attention is directed to the question of what happens to the total valuation of the firm and to its cost of capital when the ratio of debt to equity, or degree of leverage, is varied. In this regard, we use a capital market equilibrium approach. The advantage of this approach is that it allows us to abstract from factors other than leverage which affect valuation.

ASSUMPTIONS AND DEFINITIONS

So that the analysis that follows can be presented as simply as possible, we make the following facilitating assumptions:

1. We assume that there are no income taxes. This assumption is removed later.

2. The ratio of debt to equity for a firm is changed by issuing debt to repurchase stock or issuing stock to pay off debt. In other words, a change in capital structure is effected immediately. In this regard, we assume no transaction costs.

3. The firm has a policy of paying 100 percent of its earnings in dividends. Thus, we abstract from the dividend decision.

4. The expected values of the subjective probability distributions of expected future operating earnings for each company are the same for all investors in the market.

5. The operating earnings of the firm are not expected to grow. The expected values of the probability distributions of expected operating earnings for all future periods are the same as present operating earnings.

Using Solomon's symbols and some of his examples, we are concerned with the following three rates[1]

Cost of debt:
$$k_i = \frac{F}{B} = \frac{\text{Annual interest charges}}{\text{Market value of debt outstanding}} \qquad (9\text{-}1)$$

In this equation, k_i is the yield on the company's debt, assuming this debt to be perpetual.

req'd rate of return
(cost of equity):
$$k_e = \frac{E}{S} = \frac{\text{Earnings available to common stockholders}}{\text{Market value of stock outstanding}} \qquad (9\text{-}2)$$

The required rate of return for investors in a firm whose earnings are not expected to grow and that has a 100 percent dividend-payout ratio is the

---

[1] Ezra Solomon, *The Theory of Financial Management* (New York: Columbia University Press, 1963), Chapters 7–9. For an analysis of the use of these rates in calculating a weighted average cost, see Timothy J. Nantell and C. Robert Carlson, "The Cost of Capital as a Weighted Average," *Journal of Finance*, 30 (December 1975), 1343–55.

earnings/price ratio. Given our restrictive assumptions, then, the earnings/price ratio represents the market rate of discount that equates the present value of the stream of expected future dividends with the current market price of the stock. This is not to say that it should be used as a general rule to depict the cost of equity capital (see Chapter 8). We use it only because of its simplicity in illustrating the theory of capital structure. The final rate we consider is

(weighted avg cost of cap)

overall
capitalization
$$k_o = \frac{O}{V} = \frac{\text{Net operating earnings}}{\text{Total market value of the firm}} \quad (9\text{-}3)$$
(value of debt & equity).

where $V = B + S$. Here, k_o is an overall capitalization rate for the firm. It is defined as the weighted-average cost of capital and may also be expressed as

$$k_o = k_i \left(\frac{B}{B + S} \right) + k_e \left(\frac{S}{B + S} \right) \quad (9\text{-}4)$$

Our concern will be with what happens to k_i, k_e, and k_o when the degree of leverage, as denoted by the ratio B/S, increases.

$$LEVERAGE = \frac{B}{S} = \frac{debt}{equity}$$

NET INCOME APPROACH

Durand has proposed two approaches to the valuation of the earnings of a company: the net income approach (NI) and the net operating income approach (NOI).[2] These approaches represent the extremes in valuing the firm with respect to the degree of leverage. Because they give us a basis for additional discussion, we consider them in turn. To illustrate the net income approach, assume that a firm has $3,000 in debt at 5 percent interest, that the expected value of annual net operating earnings is $1,000, and that the equity-capitalization rate, k_e, is 10 percent. Given this information, the value of the firm may be calculated as

O	Net operating earnings	$ 1,000
F	Interest	150
E	Earnings available to common stockholders	$ 850
k_e	Equity-capitalization rate	0.10
S	Market value of stock	$ 8,500
B	Market value of debt	3,000
V	Total value of firm	$11,500

[2] David Durand, "The Cost of Debt and Equity Funds for Business," in Ezra Solomon, ed., *The Management of Corporate Capital* (New York: Free Press, 1959), pp. 91–116.

With the net income approach, earnings available to common stock-holders are capitalized at a constant rate, k_e. The implied overall capitalization rate in the above example is

$$K_o = \frac{O}{V} = \frac{\$1,000}{\$11,500} = \underline{8.7 \text{ percent}}$$

Assume now that the firm increases its debt from \$3,000 to \$6,000 and uses the proceeds of the debt issue to repurchase stock. Also, suppose that the interest rate on debt remains unchanged at 5 percent. The value of the firm then is

Increasing debt lowers K_o

O	Net operating earnings	\$ 1,000
F	Interest	300
E	Earnings available to common stockholders	\$ 700
k_e	Equity-capitalization rate	0.10
S	Market value of stock	\$ 7,000
B	Market value of debt	6,000
V	Total value of firm	\$13,000

The implied overall capitalization rate now is

weighted avg cost of capital

$$k_o = \frac{O}{V} = \frac{\$1,000}{\$13,000} = \underline{7.7 \text{ percent}}$$

According to the net income approach, the firm is able to increase its total valuation, V, and lower its cost of capital, k_o, as it increases the degree of leverage. As a result, the market price per share increases. To illustrate, assume in our example that the firm with \$3,000 in debt has 850 shares of common stock outstanding. Thus, the market price per share is \$10 a share (\$8,500/850). The firm issues \$3,000 in additional debt and, at the same time, repurchases \$3,000 of stock at \$10 a share, or 300 shares in total. It then has 550 shares outstanding. We saw in the example that the total market value of the firm's stock after the change in capital structure is \$7,000. Therefore, the market price per share is \$7,000/550 = \$12.73, where before it was \$10.

Graphically, the approach is illustrated in Figure 9-1. The degree of leverage, B/S, is plotted along the horizontal axis, while the percentage rate for k_i, k_e, and k_o is on the vertical axis. This graph can be constructed based upon the hypothetical examples we have shown. As can be seen, the critical assumptions of the net income approach are that k_i and, more particularly, k_e remain unchanged as the degree of leverage increases. As the proportion of cheaper debt funds in the capital structure is increased, the weighted-average cost of capital, k_o, decreases and

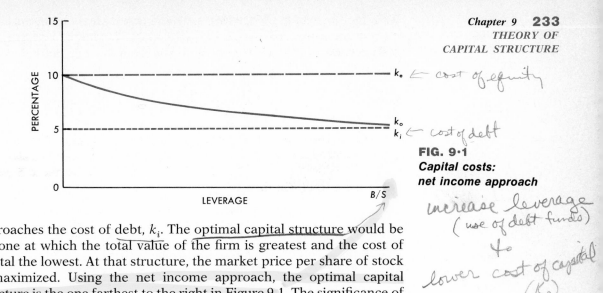

k_e ← cost of equity

k_o ← cost of debt
k_i ←

FIG. 9·1
Capital costs:
net income approach

increase leverage
(use of debt funds)
to
lower cost of capital
(K_o)

approaches the cost of debt, k_i. The optimal capital structure would be the one at which the total value of the firm is greatest and the cost of capital the lowest. At that structure, the market price per share of stock is maximized. Using the net income approach, the optimal capital structure is the one farthest to the right in Figure 9-1. The significance of this approach is that a firm can lower its cost of capital continually and increase its total valuation by the use of debt funds. Again, the critical assumption is that the firm does not become increasingly more risky in the minds of investors and creditors as the degree of leverage is increased.

NET OPERATING INCOME APPROACH

We turn now to the net operating income approach. The assumption here is that the overall capitalization rate of the firm, k_o, is constant for all degrees of leverage. Assume the same example as before but with k_o equal to 10 percent. For $3,000 in debt, we have

O	Net operating income	$ 1,000
k_o	Overall capitalization rate	0.10
V	Total value of firm	$10,000
B	Market value of debt	3,000
S	Market value of stock	$ 7,000

The implied equity-capitalization rate in this case is[3]

$$k_e = \frac{E}{S} = \frac{\$850}{\$7,000} = 12.1 \text{ percent}$$

[3]k_e also can be calculated as

$$k_e = k_o + (k_o - k_i)\frac{B}{S}$$

With this approach, net operating income is capitalized at an overall capitalization rate to obtain the total market value of the firm. The market value of the debt then is deducted from the total market value to obtain the market value of the stock.

Suppose, as before, that the firm increases the amount of debt from $3,000 to $6,000 and uses the proceeds of the debt issue to repurchase stock. The valuation of the firm then is

O	Net operating income	$ 1,000
k_o	Overall capitalization rate	0.10
V	Total value of firm	$10,000
B	Market value of debt	6,000
S	Market value of stock	$ 4,000

The implied equity-capitalization rate is

$$k_e = \frac{E}{S} = \frac{\$700}{\$4,000} = 17.5 \text{ percent}$$

We see that the equity-capitalization rate, k_e, rises with the degree of leverage. This approach implies that the total valuation of the firm is unaffected by its capital structure. Graphically, the approach is shown in Figure 9-2.

The critical assumption with this approach is that k_o is constant regardless of the degree of leverage. The market capitalizes the value of the firm as a whole; as a result, the breakdown between debt and equity

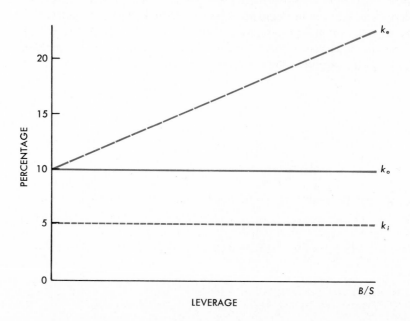

FIG. 9·2
Capital costs: net operating income approach

is unimportant. An increase in the use of supposedly "cheaper" debt funds is offset exactly by the increase in the equity-capitalization rate, k_e. Thus, the weighted average of k_e and k_i remains unchanged for all degrees of leverage. As the firm increases its degree of leverage, it becomes increasingly more risky; and investors penalize the stock by raising the equity-capitalization rate (lowering the P/E ratio) directly in keeping with the increase in the debt-to-equity ratio. As long as k_i remains constant, k_e is a constant linear function of the debt-to-equity ratio.

According to the net operating income approach, the real cost of debt and the real cost of equity are the same—namely, k_o. The cost of debt has two parts: the explicit cost represented by the rate of interest, and the implicit cost, or "hidden" cost, which is represented by the increase in the equity-capitalization rate that accompanies an increase in the proportion of debt to equity. Because the cost of capital of the firm cannot be altered through leverage, this approach implies that there is no one optimal capital structure. All capital structures are optimal, for market price per share does not change with leverage. To illustrate, assume again that our example firm with $3,000 in debt has 850 shares of common stock outstanding. The market price per share in this case is $7,000/850 = $8.23. With the $3,000 in additional debt, the firm repurchases $3,000 of stock at $8.23 a share, or 364 shares in total. Therefore, the market price per share after the change in capital structure is $4,000/(850 − 364) = $8.23, the same as before. Thus, capital structure would be a matter of indifference to the investor.

So far, our discussion of the net operating income approach has been purely definitional; it lacks behavioral significance. However, Modigliani and Miller, in their famous 1958 article, offered behavioral support for the independence of the total valuation and the cost of capital of the firm from its capital structure.[4] Before taking up the implications of their position, however, we examine the traditional approach to valuation.

TRADITIONAL APPROACH

The traditional approach to valuation and leverage assumes that there is an optimal capital structure and that the firm can increase the total value of the firm through the judicious use of leverage. Actually, this approach encompasses all the ground between the net income approach and the net operating income approach. To illustrate one variation of the approach, assume that our hypothetical firm has $3,000

[4] Franco Modigliani and Merton H. Miller, "The Cost of Capital, Corporation Finance and the Theory of Investment," *American Economic Review*, 48 (June 1958), 261–77.

in debt at 5 percent interest. Assume, however, that the equity-capitalization rate is 11 percent, rather than the 10 percent or 12.1 percent assumed with the net income or net operating income approaches illustrated previously. The valuation of the firm then is

O	Net operating income	$ 1,000
F	Interest on debt	150
E	Earnings available to common stockholders	$ 850
k_e	Equity-capitalization rate	0.11
S	Market value of stock	$ 7,727
B	Market value of debt	3,000
V	Total value of firm	$10,727

$\frac{E}{S} \rightarrow k_e$

The implied overall capitalization rate is

Weighted avg cost of cap:

$$k_o = \frac{O}{V} = \frac{\$1,000}{\$10,727} = 9.3 \text{ percent}$$

This example suggests that the firm can lower its cost of capital and increase the total value of the firm and share price by leverage. With no leverage, $B/S = 0$; and the overall capitalization rate, k_o, is 10 percent. Although investors raise the equity-capitalization rate, k_e, as the firm becomes more financially risky with leverage, the increase in k_e does not offset entirely the benefit of using cheaper debt funds. As a result, total valuation and share price increase, and the cost of capital decreases. With $3,000 in debt and 850 shares outstanding, the market price per share is $7,727/850 = $9.09. This contrasts with $8.23 under the assumption of a net operating income approach to valuation.

The traditional approach implies that beyond some point, k_e rises at an increasing rate with leverage. Moreover, k_i also may rise beyond some point. To illustrate, suppose now that the firm increases its debt from $3,000 to $6,000 and uses the proceeds of the debt issue to repurchase stock. Assume also that the average rate of interest on all debt rises to 6 percent and that the equity-capitalization rate, k_e, at that degree of leverage is 14 percent. The valuation of the firm then is

O	Net operating income	$ 1,000
F	Interest on debt	360
E	Earnings available to common stockholders	$ 640
k_e	Equity-capitalization rate	0.14
S	Market value of stock	$ 4,571
B	Market value of debt	6,000
V	Total value of firm	$10,571

$\frac{640}{.14}$

The implied overall capitalization rate is

$$k_o = \frac{O}{V} = \frac{\$1,000}{\$10,571} = 9.5 \text{ percent}$$

equity-capitalization rate

Thus, the total valuation of the firm is lower and its cost of capital slightly higher than when the amount of debt was \$3,000. This result is due to the increase in k_e and, to a lesser extent, the increase in k_i. From these two observations, we know that the optimal capital structure in this example occurs before a debt-to-equity ratio of 6,000/4,571, or 1.31.

Graphically, one variation of the traditional approach is shown in Figure 9-3. As can be seen in the figure, k_e is assumed to rise at an increasing rate with leverage, whereas k_i is assumed to rise only after significant leverage has occurred. At first, the weighted-average cost of capital declines with leverage because the rise in k_e does not offset entirely the use of cheaper debt funds. As a result, the weighted-average cost of capital, k_o, declines with moderate use of leverage. After a point, however, the increase in k_e more than offsets the use of cheaper debt funds in the capital structure, and k_o begins to rise. The rise in k_o is supported further once k_i begins to rise. The optimal capital structure is the point at which k_o bottoms out; in the figure, this optimal capital structure is point X.

Thus, the traditional position implies that the cost of capital is not independent of the capital structure of the firm and that there is an optimal capital structure. At that optimal structure, the marginal real cost of debt (explicit and implicit) is the same as the marginal real cost of

*at optimal structure
marginal cost
of debt = marginal
cost of equity*

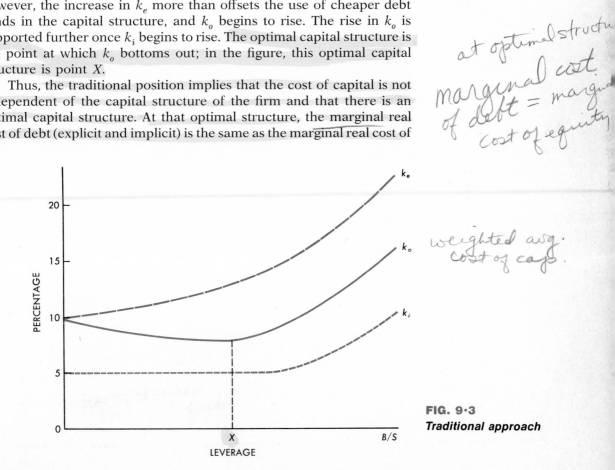

*weighted avg.
cost of cap.*

FIG. 9·3
Traditional approach

equity in equilibrium. For degrees of leverage before that point, the marginal real cost of debt is less than that of equity; beyond that point, the marginal real cost of debt exceeds that of equity.

Variations of approach

There are wide variations in the traditional approach. As we mentioned earlier, the approach falls somewhere between the extremes, the net income and the net operating income approaches. Some members of the traditional school would contend that k_e does not actually rise until after some critical point. Only after this point is reached do investors recognize the increasing financial risk of the company and penalize the market price of the stock accordingly. This variation of the traditional position implies that a company is able to lower its cost of capital significantly with the initial use of leverage. This variation is shown in Figure 9-4.

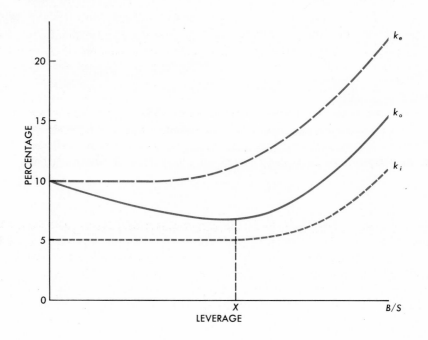

FIG. 9·4
Traditional approach:
k *constant at first*

Others view the cost-of-capital curve, k_o, as being saucer-shaped with a horizontal middle range.[5] This variation is shown in Figure 9-5. It suggests that there is a range of optimal capital structures in which the cost of capital is minimized and the total value of the firm maximized. In this range, changes in leverage have a negligible effect upon the total value of the firm. Thus, the traditional position allows for considerable

[5] Solomon, *Theory of Financial Management*, pp. 93–98.

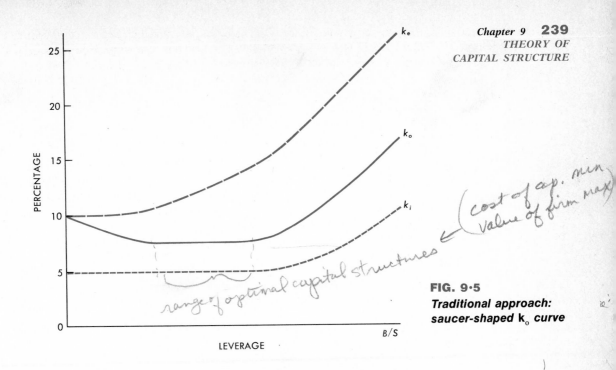

FIG. 9·5
*Traditional approach:
saucer-shaped* k$_o$ *curve*

variation in the optimal capital structure for different firms. Having taken up the net income, net operating income, and traditional approaches to valuation, we now are able to consider in more detail the question of whether capital structure matters.

MODIGLIANI-MILLER POSITION

As mentioned previously, Modigliani and Miller (MM) advocate that the relationship between leverage and the cost of capital is explained by the net operating income approach. They make a formidable attack on the traditional position by offering behavioral justification for having the cost of capital, k_o, remain constant throughout all degrees of leverage. As their assumptions are extremely important, it is necessary to spell them out.

1. Capital markets are perfect. Information is costless and readily available to all investors; there are no transaction costs; and all securities are infinitely divisible. Investors are assumed to be rational, and to behave accordingly.

2. The average expected future operating earnings of a firm are represented by a subjective random variable. It is assumed that the expected values of the probability distributions of all investors are the same. Implied in the MM illustration is that the expected values of the probability distributions of expected operating earnings for all future periods are the same as present operating earnings.

3. Firms can be categorized into "equivalent return" classes. All firms within a class have the same degree of business risk. As we shall see later, this assumption is not essential for their proof.

4. The absence of corporate income taxes is assumed. MM remove this assumption later.

In taking the net operating income approach, MM draw essentially the same conclusions as described when we discussed that approach. Their three basic propositions are[6]

1. The total market value of the firm and its cost of capital are independent of its capital structure. The total market value of a firm is given by capitalizing the expected stream of operating earnings at a discount rate appropriate for its risk class.

2. The expected yield of a share of stock, k_e, is equal to the capitalization rate of a pure equity stream, plus a premium for financial risk equal to the difference between the pure equity-capitalization rate and k_i, times the ratio B/S. In other words, k_e increases in a manner to offset exactly the use of cheaper debt funds.

3. The cutoff rate for investment purposes is completely independent of the way in which an investment is financed. This proposition along with the first implies a complete separation of the investment and financing decisions of the firm.

ARBITRAGE SUPPORT OF PROPOSITIONS

MM argue that the total risk for all security holders of a firm is not altered by changes in its capital structure. Therefore, the total value of the firm must be the same regardless of its financing mix. The crucial support for this hypothesis is the presence of arbitrage in the capital markets. Arbitrage precludes perfect substitutes from selling at different prices in the same market. In their case, the perfect substitutes are two or more firms in the same homogeneous risk class that differ only with respect to capital structure. MM contend that the total value of these firms has to be the same; otherwise, arbitragers will enter and drive the values of the two firms together. The essence of their argument is that arbitragers are able to substitute personal leverage for corporate leverage.[7]

Consider two firms that comprise a single risk class. These firms are identical in every respect except that Company *A* is not levered and Company *B* has $30,000 of 5% bonds outstanding. According to the traditional position, Company *B* may have a higher total value and lower

---

[6] Modigliani and Miller, "Cost of Capital, Corporation Finance and the Theory of Investment."

[7] Ibid., pp. 270–72.

average cost of capital than Company *A*. The valuation of the two firms is assumed to be the following:

		Company A	Company B
O	Net operating income	$ 10,000	$ 10,000
F	Interest on debt		1,500
E	Earnings available to common stockholders	$ 10,000	$ 8,500
k_e	Equity-capitalization rate	0.10	0.11
S	Market value of stock	$100,000	$ 77,272
B	Market value of debt		30,000
V	Total value of firm	$100,000	$107,272
k_o	Implied overall capitalization rate	10%	9.3%
B/S	Debt-to-equity ratio	0	38.8%

[handwritten margin notes: levered firm 5% Bonds O/S $30,000; higher stk price; higher total value ← lower avg cost of cap. Leverage]

MM maintain that this situation cannot continue, for arbitrage will drive the total values of the two firms together. Company *B* cannot command a higher total value simply because it has a different financing mix than Company *A*. MM argue that investors in Company *B* are able to obtain the same dollar return with no increase in financial risk by investing in Company *A*. Moreover, they are able to do so with a smaller investment outlay.[8] Because investors would be better off with the investment requiring the lesser outlay, they would sell their shares in Company *B* and buy shares in Company *A*. These arbitrage transactions would continue until Company *B*'s shares declined in price and Company *A*'s shares increased in price enough so that the total value of the two firms was identical.

To illustrate, suppose that a rational investor owned 1 percent of Company *B*, the levered firm, worth $772.72 (market value). Given this situation, he should

1. Sell his stock in Company *B* for $772.72.
2. Borrow $300 at 5 percent interest. This personal debt is equal to 1 percent of the debt of Company *B*—his previous proportional ownership of the company.
3. Buy 1 percent of the shares of Company *A*, the unlevered firm, for $1,000.

Prior to this series of transactions, the investor's expected return on investment in Company *B* was 11 percent on a $772.72 investment, or

[8]This arbitrage proof appears in Franco Modigliani and Merton H. Miller, "Reply to Heins and Sprenkle," *American Economic Review*, 59 (September 1969), 592–95.

$85. His expected return on investment in Company *A* is 10 percent, or
$100 on an investment of $1,000. From this return, he must deduct the
interest charges on his personal borrowings. Thus, his net dollar return is

Return on investment in Company *A*	$100
Less interest (300 × 0.05)	15
Net return	$ 85

We see then that his net dollar return, $85, is the same as it was for his
investment in Company *B*. However, his cash outlay of $700 ($1,000 less
personal borrowings of $300) is less than the $772.72 investment in
Company *B*, the levered firm. Because of the lower investment, the
investor would prefer to invest in Company *A* under the conditions
described. In essence, the investor is able to "lever" the stock of the
unlevered firm by taking on personal debt.

The action of a number of rational investors undertaking similar
arbitrage transactions will tend to drive up the price of Company *A*
shares, and lower its k_e, and drive down the price of Company *B*,
increasing its k_e. This arbitrage process will continue until there is no
further opportunity for reducing one's investment outlay and achieving
the same dollar return. At this equilibrium, the total value of the two
firms must be the same. As a result, their average costs of capital, k_o, also
must be the same.

If for some reason the value of the unlevered firm, Company *A*, were
to exceed that of the levered firm, Company *B*, arbitrage would work in
the opposite direction. Suppose that Company *A* in our example had an
equity capitalization rate of 8 percent, giving it a total market value of
$125,000. Here, the investor owning 1 percent of Company *A*'s shares
would sell his holdings for $1,250. He then would buy 1 percent of the
stock of Company *B* for $772.72 as well as buy 1 percent of the debt of
that company for $300. His total expected dollar return in Company *B*
would be

Return on investment in Company *B* stock	$ 85
Return on investment in Company *B* debt	15
Net return	$100

This return is the same as his expected return in Company *A*'s stock.
Thus, his total return is the same as before; and he needs to invest only
$1,072.72, compared with $1,250.00 previously. As a result, he would
prefer investing in Company *B*. Again, the action of a number of investors behaving in this manner will tend to drive the total values of the two
firms together. The principle involved is simply that investors are able to
reconstitute their former positions by offsetting changes in corporate
leverage with changes in personal leverage. As a result, the investment
opportunities available to them are not altered by changes in the capital
structure of the firm.

**Extreme
leverage**

In making their stand, MM not only deny that a judicious amount of leverage may lower the weighted-average cost of capital, but that extreme leverage will raise it. According to their hypothesis, the weighted-average cost-of-capital line, k_o, is horizontal throughout all degrees of leverage. However, we know that the cost of borrowing can rise with excessive leverage. Beyond a certain point of leverage, we would expect the firm to pay increasingly higher interest rates on borrowings. The greater the leverage, the lower the coverage of fixed charges and the more risky the loan.

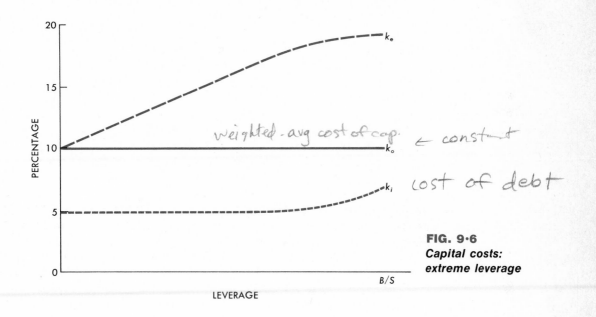

FIG. 9·6
*Capital costs:
extreme leverage*

Even with a rise in k_i, however, MM still maintain that the weighted-average cost-of-capital line, k_o, is horizontal. They argue that when k_i increases, k_e will increase at a decreasing rate.[9] This notion is illustrated in Figure 9-6. Given the assumptions of perfect capital markets, k_o must remain constant. Again, any denial of the cost of capital of a firm being independent of its capital structure must be based upon the belief that the assumption of perfect capital markets and completely rational investors is unrealistic. In particular, a number of authors have found the contention that investors become relatively less risk-averse with extreme leverage to be quite objectionable. It is clear that MM are on weaker ground in defending their thesis for the extreme leverage case

[9] Modigliani and Miller, "Cost of Capital, Corporation Finance and the Theory of Investment."

than for leverage at the other end of the scale. To dispute their stand, however, one must look to imperfections in the capital markets, the analysis of which we take up shortly.

SITUATION IN THE CONTEXT OF THE CAPITAL-ASSET PRICING MODEL

It is important to realize that proof of the proposition that leverage does not matter does not depend on two firms' belonging to the same risk class. This assumption was invoked in order that we might more easily illustrate the arbitrage process. However, equilibrium occurs across securities of different companies on the basis of expected return and risk. If the assumptions of the capital-asset pricing model discussed in Chapters 3, 7, and 8 hold, only the systematic risk of a stock is important. It follows, then, that leverage does not matter in the context of the capital-asset pricing model.

From our earlier discussion of the model, we know that the equilibrium expected return for a stock can be expressed as

$$k_e = i + \frac{R_m - i}{\sigma_m^2}(r_{em}\sigma_e\sigma_m) \tag{9-5}$$

where i = the risk-free rate

R_m = expected return on the market portfolio

r_{em} = the correlation coefficient between k_e and R_m

σ_e = standard deviation of the probability distribution of possible k_e's

σ_m = standard deviation of the probability distribution of possible R_m's

The term in parentheses is the expected covariance between returns on the stock and returns on the market portfolio. Thus, the expected return on a stock is determined by its correlation with the market portfolio and its standard deviation, a measure of risk. Similarly, the expected return on the company's debt can be expressed as follows, assuming it is priced according to the capital-asset pricing model:

$$k_{\text{debt}} = i + \frac{R_m - i}{\sigma_m^2}(r_{\text{debt},m}\sigma_{\text{debt}}\sigma_m) \tag{9-6}$$

where $r_{\text{debt},m}$ is the correlation coefficient between returns on the company's debt and returns on the market portfolio, which is comprised of both debt and equity instruments, and σ_{debt} is the standard deviation of the probability distribution of possible returns for the company's debt.

The covariance between returns on the stock of a levered company and returns on the market portfolio can be expressed as[10]

$$r_{em}\sigma_e\sigma_m = \left(\frac{B+S}{S}\right)(r_{em}\sigma_e\sigma_m)^* + \left(1 - \frac{B+S}{S}\right)(r_{debt,m}\sigma_{debt}\sigma_m) \qquad (9\text{-}7)$$

where $(r_{em}\sigma_e\sigma_m)^*$ is the expected covariance between returns on the stock *in the absence of leverage* and returns on the market portfolio, and B and S are the market values of the company's debt and equity, respectively. In other words, the starred term is the expected covariance if the company had an all-equity capital structure. Substituting Eq. (9-7) into Eq. (9-5) and rearranging, we obtain

$$k_e = i + \left[\frac{R_m - i}{\sigma_m^2}\right]\left[\frac{B+S}{S}(r_{em}\sigma_e\sigma_m)^* - \frac{B}{S}(r_{debt,m}\sigma_{debt}\sigma_m)\right]$$

$$= i + \left[\frac{R_m - i}{\sigma_m}\right]\left[\frac{B+S}{S}(r_{em}\sigma_e)^* - \frac{B}{S}(r_{debt,m}\sigma_{debt})\right] \qquad (9\text{-}8)$$

As $(B+S)/S$ is the same as $1 + B/S$, we can express Eq. (9-8) as

$$k_e = i + \left(\frac{R_m - i}{\sigma_m}\right)(r_{em}\sigma_e)^* + \frac{B}{S}\left[\left(\frac{R_m - i}{\sigma_m}\right)(r_{em}\sigma_e)^*\right.$$

$$\left. - \left(\frac{R_m - i}{\sigma_m}\right)(r_{debt,m}\sigma_{debt})\right] \qquad (9\text{-}9)$$

Finally, this becomes

$$k_e = k_e^* + \frac{B}{S}(k_e^* - k_{debt}) \qquad (9\text{-}10)$$

where k_e is the expected or required rate of return on a levered stock, k_e^* is the required return if the company were not levered, and k_{debt} is the required return on the company's debt.

Thus, the required rate of return on equity is a linear function of the firm's debt-to-equity ratio in the context of the capital-asset pricing model. This of course is the same as proposition II of MM, which states

[10] This development is based on Robert A. Haugen and James L. Pappas, "Equilibrium in the Pricing of Capital Assets, Risk-Bearing Debt Instruments and the Question of Optimal Capital Structure," *Journal of Financial and Quantitative Analysis*, 6 (June 1971), 943–54. See also Yutaki Imai and Mark E. Rubinstein, "Comment," and Haugen and Pappas, "Reply," *Journal of Financial and Quantitative Analysis*, 7 (September 1972), 1995–2004. Essentially the same point was made earlier by Robert S. Hamada, "Portfolio Analysis, Market Equilibrium and Corporation Finance," *Journal of Finance*, 24 (March 1969), 13–19. The reader is referred to the Haugen and Pappas article and reply for the derivation of Eq. (9-7).

that k_e is a linear function of leverage. Therefore, the arbitrage proof of MM is not dependent upon the existence of homogeneous risk classes.[11] In fact, there need not be any two firms in the market with exactly the same risk characteristics. The risk-class notion was introduced by MM merely to simplify the illustration of the equilibrium process; none of their basic propositions depend upon it. All propositions can be illustrated in the context of the capital-asset pricing model, though with more difficulty. The essential point is that given the assumptions listed before, a firm cannot change its total value or its weighted-average cost of capital by leverage. Consequently, the financing decision does not matter from the standpoint of an objective of maximizing market price per share.

RELAXING THE ASSUMPTIONS, AND THE IMPLICATIONS OF SUCH

Given the assumption inherent in perfect capital markets, the market equilibrating process assures the validity of MM's thesis that the cost of capital and total valuation of a firm are independent of its capital structure. To dispute this stand, one needs to look for capital market imperfections that impede the equilibration of security prices according to their expected returns and systematic risk. Under these circumstances, leverage may have an effect on the value of the firm and its cost of capital. However, the imperfections not only must be material, but they must be one-directional. For example, we know that transaction costs restrict the arbitrage process described earlier. That is, arbitrage will take place only up to the limits imposed by transaction costs. However, the net effect of this imperfection is not predictable as to direction if in fact there is a net effect at all.[12]

In what follows, we examine certain imperfections that may have a predictable effect on the question of whether capital structure decisions matter. We defer until last the most important imperfection, corporate income taxes, because there is agreement on its impact. After we have

[11] For extended treatment of this issue in addition to the Haugen and Pappas and the Hamada references cited in footnote 10, see Mark E. Rubinstein, "A Mean-Variance Synthesis of Corporate Financing Theory," *Journal of Finance*, 28 (March 1973), 167–82; Joseph E. Stiglitz, "A Reexamination of the Modigliani-Miller Theorem," *American Economic Review*, 59 (December 1969), 784–93; Stiglitz, "On the Irrelevance of Corporate Financial Policy," *American Economic Review*, 64 (December 1974), 851–66; Jan Mossin, "Security Pricing and Investment Criteria in Competitive Markets," *American Economic Review*, 59 (December 1969), 749–56; Irwin Tepper, "Revealed Preference Methods and the Pure Theory of the Cost of Capital," *Journal of Finance*, 28 (March 1973), 35–48; and Peter R. Lloyd-Davies, "Optimal Financial Policies in Imperfect Markets," *Journal of Financial and Quantitative Analysis*, 10 (September 1975), 457–66.

[12] The presence of transaction costs may result in incomplete markets in that distinct marketable securities do not correspond to every contingency in the world. Under these circumstances, it may be possible for a company to tailor a security issue to a particular class of investors to take advantage of the situation. However, the effect here is not systematic as to direction. See J. Hirshleifer, *Investment, Interest, and Capital* (Englewood Cliffs, N.J.: Prentice-Hall, 1970), pp. 264–75.

presented the various imperfections, we will attempt to reconcile the more important of them with respect to the question of determining an optimal capital structure.

BANKRUPTCY COSTS

If there is a possibility of bankruptcy, and if administrative and other costs associated with bankruptcy are significant, the levered firm may be less attractive to investors than the unlevered one. With perfect capital markets, zero bankruptcy costs are assumed. If the firm goes bankrupt, assets presumably can be sold at their economic values with no liquidating or legal costs involved. Proceeds from the sale are distributed according to the claim on assets described in Chapter 24. If capital markets are less than perfect, however, there may be bankruptcy costs, and assets may have to be liquidated at less than their economic values. These costs and the "shortfall" in liquidating value from economic value represent a drain in the system from the standpoint of debt and equity holders.

In the event of bankruptcy, security holders as a whole receive less than they would in the absence of bankruptcy costs. To the extent that the levered firm has a greater possibility of bankruptcy than the unlevered one,[13] it would be a less attractive investment, all other things the same.[14] The possibility of bankruptcy usually is not a linear function of the debt/equity ratio, but it increases at an increasing rate beyond some threshold.[15] As a result, the expected cost of bankruptcy increases in this manner and would be expected to have a corresponding negative effect upon the value of the firm and upon its cost of capital.[16] As this imper-

---

[13] It is possible, of course, that neither firm has a possibility of bankruptcy.

[14] For further discussion of this point, see Nevins D. Baxter, "Leverage, Risk of Ruin and the Cost of Capital," *Journal of Finance*, 22 (September 1967), 395–403; and P. A. Tinsley, "Capital Structure, Precautionary Balances, and Valuation of the Firm: The Problem of Financial Risk," *Journal of Financial and Quantitative Analysis*, 5 (March 1970), 33–62.

[15] Joseph E. Stiglitz, "Some Aspects of the Pure Theory of Corporate Finance: Bankruptcies and Takeovers," *Bell Journal of Economics and Management Science*, 3 (Autumn 1972), 458–82, suggests that bankruptcy affects the cost of capital even in the absence of bankruptcy costs. He contends that because of a divergence in expectations as to the chance of bankruptcy between the lender and the borrower, the interest rate is an increasing function of the debt/equity ratio. With bankruptcy penalties, the scale of the firm becomes important and the firm's investment and financing decisions are no longer independent.

[16] Using a state-preference approach in a world of taxes and bankruptcy penalties, Alan Kraus and Robert H. Litzenberger, in "A State-Preference Model of Optimal Financial Leverage," *Journal of Finance*, 28 (September 1973), 911–22, show that with discrete states of nature the relationship between the value of the firm and the amount of debt is jagged. Value is increased with leverage up to the point where a further debt increase causes a change in state from a state in which the firm would be solvent to one in which it would be insolvent. At that point the market value drops due to bankruptcy penalties. It increases with subsequent leverage (because of the tax advantage of debt) only to fall when another change in state occurs.

fection has been considered at length in previous chapters, we do not discuss it further. However, the brevity of treatment is not meant to convey any lack of importance to the leverage question. In fact, it probably is one of the two most important imperfections, particularly when it comes to extreme leverage.

CORPORATE AND HOMEMADE LEVERAGE NOT BEING PERFECT SUBSTITUTES

The perceived risks of personal leverage and corporate leverage may differ. Implied in the MM analysis is that personal and corporate leverage are perfect substitutes. If the investor borrows personally and pledges his stock as collateral, he is subject to possible margin calls. Many investors view this possibility with considerable alarm. Moreover, personal leverage involves a certain amount of inconvenience on the part of the investor, which he does not experience with corporate leverage. For these reasons, personal leverage may not be a perfect substitute for corporate leverage in the minds of many investors.

However, arbitrage need not occur in terms of the individual actually borrowing in the market. The same thing may be accomplished by his changing his holdings of bonds. Moreover, the arbitrage process is not confined to individuals. If opportunities for profit exist, financial intermediaries may enter the scene and replicate the financial claims of either the levered or the unlevered company and buy the stock of the other. The free entry of financial intermediaries without cost will assure the efficient functioning of the arbitrage process, which in turn will result in the irrelevance of corporate leverage.[17] Therefore, we are inclined to discount the importance of this argument.

Another consideration under this heading is the impact of margin requirements. The Federal Reserve regulates the percentage of advance under a margin loan. This precludes a person from borrowing the full value of the stock pledged as collateral. Thus, the requirement restricts the ability of arbitragers to substitute "homemade" leverage for corporate leverage. One means for circumventing this requirement is to purchase the stock of a company with debt as opposed to purchasing the stock of a company without debt and then attempting to replicate such debt with homemade leverage. The margin requirement then is said to encourage the use of debt financing by companies.[18]

[17] See Stiglitz, "Reexamination of the Modigliani-Miller Theorem," pp. 786–88 and Stiglitz, "On the Irrelevance of Corporate Financial Policy," pp. 864–65.
[18] Lloyd-Davies, "Optimal Financial Policy in Imperfect Markets," 467–69.

Due to capital market imperfections, the effective cost of borrowing may be higher for the individual than for the corporation. The corporation is larger and is likely to be able to borrow at a lower rate of interest than that available on a personal loan. If so, the levered company could have a somewhat greater total value than the unlevered firm for this reason alone.[19] Again it should be pointed out that the individual can engage in arbitrage by varying his holdings of bonds.

INSTITUTIONAL RESTRICTIONS

Restrictions on investment behavior may retard the arbitrage process. Many institutional investors, such as pension funds and life insurance companies, are not allowed to engage in the "homemade" leverage that was described. In addition, stock and bond investments often are restricted by regulatory bodies to a list of companies meeting certain quality standards. One of these standards is that the company involved have only a "safe" amount of leverage. If a company breaches that amount, it may be removed from the acceptable list, thereby precluding certain institutions from investing in it. This reduction in investor demand can have an adverse effect on the market value of the company's financial instruments.

David W. Glenn argues that the combination of restrictions on the investment behavior of financial institutions, together with restrictions on short sales, results in there being an optimal capital structure for the firm.[20] By way of definition, a *short sale* is the borrowing of a security and selling it with the obligation to deliver the borrowed security back to the lender some time in the future. One hopes to buy the security back at a lower price than that at which it was sold, thereby realizing a profit from the two transactions. The presence of restrictions on the investment behavior of institutions will result in those securities approved for investment selling at higher prices than otherwise would be the case. If unrestricted investors (those investors who are not legally restricted in their investment behavior) could freely engage in short selling, they would eliminate the higher relative prices for these securities. Unrestricted investors would sell short the approved securities and use the proceeds of the short sale to buy other securities that were more favor-

---

[19]For further discussion of this point, see David P. Baron, "Default Risk, Homemade Leverage, and the Modigliani-Miller Theorem," *American Economic Review*, 64 (March 1974), 176–82.

[20]"Super Premium Security Prices and Optimal Corporate Financing Decisions," *Journal of Finance*, 31 (May 1976).

ably priced in the market, given their expected return and systematic risk.

The action of a number of unrestricted investors behaving in this manner would drive down the prices of approved securities and up the prices of other securities until equilibrium was achieved. However, this process depends on there being no restrictions on short sales. In practice, the proceeds of a short sale are not available to the party selling the security short, but rather are held in escrow. Moreover, there is a margin requirement. These impediments to short selling result in unrestricted investors' not being able to eliminate the premiums in prices for securities that are approved investments for restricted institutional investors. Under these circumstances, an optimal capital structure exists, according to Glenn. For most firms, it would involve issuing the maximum amount of debt consistent with obtaining a preferential investment grade rating suitable for institutional investors.

CORPORATE INCOME TAXES

When we allow for corporate income taxes, we must reexamine the earlier arguments for irrelevance. Because the payment of interest is deductible for tax purposes, leverage lowers the weighted-average after-tax cost of capital found with the MM position. To illustrate, suppose that the expected value of annual net operating income for two firms is $2,000 before taxes, the corporate income tax rate is 50 percent, the after-tax capitalization rate is 8 percent for both companies, and that Company *A* has no debt, whereas Company *B* has $8,000 in 5% bonds. According to the MM position, the total values of the two companies would be:

	Company A	Company B
1. Net operating income	$ 2,000	$ 2,000
2. Taxes	1,000	1,000
3. Profit before interest, but after taxes	$ 1,000	$ 1,000
4. After-tax capitalization rate for debt-free company	.08	.08
5. Capitalized value of (3)	$12,500	$12,500
6. Interest on debt	0	400
7. (1 − Tax rate) (6)	0	200
8. Tax savings on interest	0	$ 200
9. Interest rate		.05
10. Capitalized value of (8)	0	4,000
11. Total value of firm (5) + (10)	$12,500	$16,500

$K_0 = .160 \qquad .123$

The higher total value of Company B is due to the deductibility of interest payments. Because of the tax benefit described, the firm can increase its total value with leverage under the MM position.

With taxes, the value of the firm, according to MM, is[21]

$$V = \frac{O(1 - t)}{\rho_k} + tB \tag{9-11}$$

where t = the corporate tax rate, ρ_k is the after-tax capitalization rate for a company with no debt in a given risk class, and O and B, as before, are expected net operating income and the market value of debt, respectively. As before, a 100 percent dividend-payout ratio is assumed. Equation (9-11) suggests that the government subsidizes debt capital so that the greater the amount of debt, the greater the value of the firm and the lower the cost of capital. The cost of capital on a tax-adjusted basis where L is the "target" proportion of debt is[22]

$$k_o = \rho_k(1 - tL) \tag{9-12}$$

Thus, MM recognize that with the introduction of corporate income taxes, the cost of capital can be lowered with leverage.[23] We note, however, that their position implies that a firm can lower its cost of capital continually with increased leverage. The greater the leverage, the higher the total value of the firm and the lower its cost of capital. In order to achieve an optimal capital structure, the firm should strive for the maximum amount of leverage. Proponents of the traditional position would argue that the cost of capital must rise with extreme leverage owing to increased financial risk. Consequently, the optimal capital structure is not the one that calls for the maximum use of debt. Again, the MM thesis is on the weakest ground when leverage is extreme. In defense, MM suggest that the firm should adopt a "target debt ratio" so as not to violate limits on leverage imposed by creditors. The implication is that debt funds simply are refused beyond some point. The introduction of debt limits, however, implies that the cost of capital rises beyond a point and that there is an optimal capital structure.

IMPLICATIONS OF TAXES AND MARKET IMPERFECTIONS

Where does this leave us with respect to the proportion of debt to employ? It should be apparent from the controversy presented that no universally accepted answer exists. It depends upon one's views of the

[21] Merton H. Miller and Franco Modigliani, "Some Estimates of the Cost of Capital to the Electric Utility Industry," *American Economic Review*, 56 (June 1966), 339–40.

[22] Ibid., p. 342.

[23] See Modigliani and Miller, "Corporate Income Taxes and the Cost of Capital: A Correction," *American Economic Review*, 53 (June 1963), 433–42.

strengths of the various arguments presented. If one believes that capital markets are perfect, that investors are rational, and that there are a sufficient number of arbitragers with funds to drive out any advantage between stocks differing only in the degree of leverage, then one must basically accept the MM position. In a world of taxes, this implies that an optimal capital structure will have in it a very high proportion of debt.

If one allows for bankruptcy costs, and if the probability of bankruptcy increases at an increasing rate with the degree of leverage, extreme leverage is likely to be penalized by investors. (As discussed earlier, bankruptcy costs represent a drain in the system to security holders.) In a world of both taxes and bankruptcy costs, there would likely be an optimal capital structure even if all of the other behavioral tenets of the MM position held. The cost of capital of a firm would decline as leverage was first employed because of the tax advantage of debt. Gradually, however, the prospect of bankruptcy would become increasingly important, causing the cost of capital to decrease at a decreasing rate as leverage increased. As leverage became extreme, the bankruptcy effect might more than offset the tax effect, causing the cost of capital of the firm to rise. By definition, this would be the point at which the capital structure of the firm was optimal. The joint effect of taxes and bankruptcy is illustrated in Figure 9-7 for a hypothetical firm.

If one feels other imperfections and/or behavioral factors dilute the MM position further, the point at which the cost-of-capital line turns up would be earlier than that depicted in the figure. Recall that these imperfections include higher costs of borrowing for individuals than for corporations as a rule, institutional restrictions, and imperfections in information. The greater the importance one attaches to these factors, the less effective the arbitrage process becomes, and the greater the case that can be made for an optimal capital structure. In conclusion, there are a number of reasons for believing that an optimal capital structure exists in theory. Depending upon one's views as to the strengths of the

FIG. 9·7

*Cost of capital
with taxes
and bankruptcy costs*

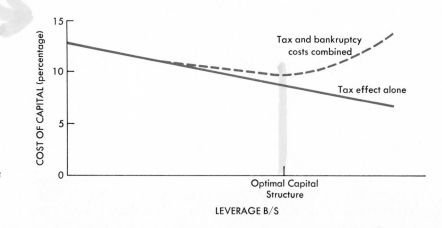

various capital market and behavioral imperfections, the expected optimal capital structure may occur earlier or later along the scale of possible leverage.

Chapter 9 **253**
THEORY OF
CAPITAL STRUCTURE

SUMMARY

A great deal of controversy has developed over whether the capital structure of a firm, as determined by its financing decision, affects its cost of capital. Traditionalists argue that the firm can lower its cost of capital and increase market value per share by the judicious use of leverage. However, as the company levers itself and becomes increasingly risky financially, lenders begin to charge higher interest rates on loans. Moreover, investors penalize the price/earnings ratio increasingly, all other things being the same. Beyond a point, the cost of capital begins to rise. According to the traditional position, that point denotes the optimal capital structure. Modigliani and Miller, on the other hand, argue that in the absence of corporate income taxes, the cost of capital is independent of the capital structure of the firm. They contend that the cost of capital and the total market value of the firm are the same for all degrees of leverage.

We saw that the behavioral support for their position was based upon the arbitrage process. Arguments for the relevance of capital structure decisions must be rooted in capital markets being less than perfect. In this regard, we examined several imperfections, including bankruptcy costs, differences between corporate and "homemade" leverage, institutional restrictions on investors, and corporate taxes. With the introduction of corporate income taxes, debt has a tax advantage and serves to lower the cost of capital, even in the MM case. The traditional position implies, however, that the cost of capital will rise eventually with additional leverage, whereas the MM position implies a continually decreasing cost of capital with leverage. Unfortunately, empirical testing has been little more than suggestive with respect to the true relationship between leverage and the cost of capital. We know, however, that the combination of corporate income taxes and bankruptcy costs may result in an optimal capital structure. In the next chapter, we examine ways by which a firm can analyze which capital structure is appropriate.

EFFECT OF INFLATION ON DEBT FINANCING

APPENDIX

It is generally agreed that the nominal rate of interest on a bond embodies a premium for inflation. As discussed in Appendix B to Chapter 4, the impact of inflation on nominal yields has come to be known as the *Fisher effect*. Many years ago Irving Fisher expressed the nominal rate of interest on a bond as the sum of the real rate and the rate of price change expected to occur over the life of the instrument.[24] Fisher obtained an estimate of the latter by regressing the nominal rate on a geometrical declining weighted average of past rates of price change. The distributed lag technique for estimating future inflation has been used by a number of subsequent investigators. These studies have shown that prior to the mid-1960s there were long lags in the formation of price expectations. That is, bond yields adjusted very slowly to past changes in prices, taking a number of years before a change in inflation was fully reflected.[25]

Studies using the distributed lag type of analysis with data obtained since the mid-1960s have shown a marked acceleration in the formulation of price expectations.[26] With the sharp increase in the rate of inflation since that time, bond yields have been found to adjust relatively quickly to these changes in prices. Price expectations, as reflected in bond yields, appear to adjust more rapidly to large observed changes in prices, such as those that have occurred since the mid- to late-1960s, than they do to small changes. Rather than use a distributed lag model of past price changes, other investigators have used inflation forecasts by a group of business economists. They have found these estimates to be relatively accurate in depicting the inflation premium embodied in nominal yields.[27] All in all, then, the evidence, particularly in recent years, supports the notion of a Fisher effect, where nominal rates of interest embody an element attributable to expected future inflation. While the relationship usually is not found to be one-for-one, it is nonetheless quite important.

Given the fact that bond yields embody expectations of future inflation, what are the implications for the firm? One important implication is the redistributional effects of inflation on debtors and creditors.

[24] *Appreciation and Interest* (New York: Macmillan, 1896). Actually, Fisher expressed the nominal rate as $R + \rho + R\rho$, where R is the real rate, ρ is the expected rate of inflation, and $R\rho$ is the product of the two. Like others, we ignore the product term, as it has not been found to be important.

[25] See, for example, William E. Gibson, "Price Expectations Effects on Interest Rates," *Journal of Finance*, 25 (March 1970), 19–34; Roman L. Weil, "Realized Interest Rates and Bondholders' Returns," *American Economic Review*, 60 (June 1970), 502–11; and Martin Feldstein and Otto Eckstein, "The Fundamental Determinants of the Interest Rate," *Review of Economics & Statistics*, 52 (November 1970), 363–75.

[26] See Patric H. Hendershott and James C. Van Horne, "Expected Inflation Implied by Capital Market Rates," *Journal of Finance*, 28 (May 1973), 301–14; William P. Yohe and Dennis P. Karnosky, "Interest Rates and Price Level Changes, 1952–69," *Review of the Federal Reserve Bank of St. Louis*, 52 (December 1969), 18–38; and Thomas F. Cargill and Robert A. Meyer, "Interest Rates and Prices Since 1950," *International Economic Review*, 15 (June 1974), 458–71.

[27] See William F. Gibson, "Interest Rates and Inflationary Expectations: New Evidence," *American Economic Review*, 62 (December 1972), 854–65; and David H. Pyle, "Observed Price Expectations and Interest Rates," *Review of Economics and Statistics*, 54 (August 1972), 275–80. The survey consists of one by Joseph A. Livingston of the *Philadelphia Bulletin* of between forty and sixty well-known business economists on a semiannual basis.

Simply phrased, the question here is whether debtors or creditors gain during periods of inflation. This in turn depends on whether the inflation is anticipated. If anticipated, it will be incorporated in the rate of interest and firms will repay debt obligations in keeping with anticipated inflation.[28] In other words, the terms of the loan will reflect anticipated inflation. If inflation occurs over the life of the debt instrument in exactly the manner that was anticipated at the time the terms were set, the borrower will neither gain nor lose with respect to the inflation that actually occurs.

It is only if there is an *unanticipated increase* in inflation that the borrower tends to gain. This gain occurs in an opportunity sense because the borrower previously has "locked in" financing at a lower cost than currently prevails. Put another way, the firm is able to pay off the obligation with "cheaper" money than was originally believed. The opposite occurs for the financial assets of a firm. With an unanticipated increase in inflation, a creditor suffers in that his real rate of return is less than that anticipated at the time the contract was made.

In the case of an unanticipated decrease in inflation, a debtor tends to suffer and a creditor gain. This occurs because the real rate of return is higher than that originally anticipated. Thus, the important thing is not inflation *per se*, but the unanticipated change in inflation. This can be either positive or negative. Unfortunately, many of the earlier studies on debtor-creditor gains or losses with inflation considered only the rate of inflation over time, and not whether it was anticipated or unanticipated.

Unanticipated increases in inflation result in a transfer of real wealth from net creditors to net debtors, whereas the opposite occurs with unanticipated decreases. A *net creditor* is defined as one whose financial assets exceed his financial liabilities, whereas for the *net debtor* the opposite holds. Whether a given company gains or loses with respect to inflation depends on whether there is an unanticipated increase or decrease in inflation and whether the firm is a net debtor or a net creditor. In the aggregate, nonfinancial corporations have been consistent net debtors while households have been consistent net creditors. However, individual companies can be net debtors or net creditors, and this can vary over time.[29] Over the post-World War II period, substantial inflation has occurred. G. L. Bach and James B. Stephenson estimate that the total dollar value of creditors' claims in the United States which

---

[28] For a theoretical analysis of this point, see James C. Van Horne and William F. Glassmire, Jr., "The Impact of Unanticipated Inflation on the Value of Common Stocks," *Journal of Finance*, 27 (December 1972), 1081–92. See also Donald A. Nichols, "A Note on Inflation and Common Stock Values," *Journal of Finance*, 23 (September 1968), 655–57; and Brian Motley, "Inflation and Stock Values: Comment," *Journal of Finance*, 24 (June 1969), 530–35.

[29] For a discussion of this question, see Louis De Alessi, "Do Business Firms Gain from Inflation? Reprise," *Journal of Business*, 48 (April 1975), 264–66. A major earlier work on the subject which involved empirical tests was by Reuben A. Kessel, "Inflation-Caused Wealth Redistribution: A Test of a Hypothesis," *American Economic Review*, 46 (March 1956), 43–66.

were wiped out by inflation over the 1946–71 period amounted to $1.2 trillion.[30] This figure does not allow for the fact that part of the inflation was anticipated and, therefore, offset by increased interest payments to creditors. However, if inflation was partially unanticipated over the period, and most believe that it was significantly unanticipated, the redistribution effects of real wealth transfer from net creditors to net debtors were enormous. Therefore, it is not unreasonable to believe that nonfinancial corporations in the aggregate gained by virtue of being net debtors on average over this period of time.[31]

The critical question for the individual firm is whether it is better to be a net debtor or a net creditor. While most would agree that a sizable portion of the inflation that occurred from 1946 to 1971 was unanticipated, it is not clear at the current high levels of inflation that further unanticipated increases will consistently occur. With an unanticipated decrease in inflation, of course, the net debtor firm and its stockholders lose. Only if an individual firm can correctly forecast unanticipated changes in inflation and adjust its position accordingly is it likely to show gains in the future.

At the present high levels of inflation, there is little reason to believe that future unanticipated changes in inflation will all be positive. Whether a firm can predict inflation better than can the market for debt instruments is problematical. If it cannot, it should simply accept the rate of inflation embodied in interest rates as the best estimate of future inflation. Thus, it is extremely important to differentiate anticipated from unanticipated inflation, and to concentrate on the latter in judging whether it is better to move in the direction of being a net creditor or a net debtor.

PROBLEMS

1. The Malock Company has net operating earnings of $10 million and $20 million of debt with a 7 percent interest charge. In all cases, assume no taxes.

    (a) Using Durand's net income method and an equity-capitalization rate of $12\frac{1}{2}$ percent, compute the total value of the firm and the implied overall capitalization rate.

    (b) Next, assume that the firm issues an additional $10 million in debt and uses the proceeds to retire stock; the interest rate and equity-capitalization rate remain the same. Compute the new total value of the firm and overall capitalization rate.

[30] "Inflation and the Redistribution of Wealth," *Review of Economics and Statistics*, 56 (February 1974), 1–13.

[31] Bach and Stephenson, in "Inflation and the Redistribution of Wealth," show that while nonfinancial corporations in the aggregate have been consistent net debtors since the 1930s, only during the 1960s were they heavy net debtors.

(c) Using Durand's net operating income concept and an overall capitalization rate of 11 percent, compute the total market value, the stock-market value, and the implied equity-capitalization rate for the Malock Company prior to the sale of additional debt.

(d) Determine the answers to (c) if the company were to sell the additional $10 million in debt.

2. Reconsider the Malock Company, with its $10 million in net operating income, $20 million of 7 percent debt, and $12\frac{1}{2}$ percent equity-capitalization rate.

(a) Compute 1(a) above if you have not already done so.

(b) Assume that the Malock Company now issues an additional $10 million of debt at an interest rate of 8 percent without altering the equity-capitalization rate. Compute the new total value of the firm and the implied overall capitalization rate.

(c) Recompute (b) under the assumption that the sale of additional debt would have caused the equity capitalization to rise to 15 percent.

(d) Recompute all of the above under the assumption that the company pays taxes at a 50 percent rate. Use a net income approach with a $12\frac{1}{2}$ percent after-tax equity-capitalization rate. In (c) above, however, continue to use the 15 percent equity-capitalization rate.

3. The Blalock Corporation has a $1 million capital structure and will always maintain this book value amount. Blalock currently earns $250,000 per year before taxes of 50 percent, has an all-equity capital structure of 100,000 shares, and pays all earnings in dividends. The company is considering issuing some debt in order to retire some stock. The cost of the debt and the price of the stock at various levels of debt are given below. It is assumed that the new capital structure would be reached all at once by purchasing stock at the current price. In other words, the following table is a schedule at a point in time.

Amount of Debt	Average Cost of Debt	Price of Stock
—	—	$10.00 *current price*
$100,000	6.0%	10.50
200,000	6.0	10.80
300,000	6.5	11.00
400,000	7.0	11.15
500,000	8.0	10.50
600,000	10.0	9.50

(a) By observation, what do you think is the optimal capital structure?

(b) Construct a graph in terms of k_e, k_i, and k_o based upon the above data.

(c) Are your conclusions in (a) confirmed?

4. The Veblen Company and the Knight Company comprise a single risk class. These firms are identical in every respect except that the Veblen Company is not levered, while the Knight Company has $1 million in 6% bonds outstanding. The valuation of the two firms is assumed to be the following:

		Veblen	*Knight*
O	Net operating income	$ 300,000	$ 300,000
F	Interest on debt	—	60,000
E	Earnings to common	$ 300,000	$ 240,000
k_e	Equity-capitalization rate	.125	.140
S	Market value of stock	$2,400,000	$1,714,000
B	Market value of debt	—	1,000,000
V	Total value of firm	$2,400,000	$2,714,000
k_o	Implied overall capitalization rate	12.5%	11.0%
B/S	Debt/equity ratio	0	58.4%

(a) An investor owns $10,000 worth of Knight stock. Show the process and the amount by which he could reduce his outlay through the use of arbitrage.

(b) According to Modigliani and Miller, when will this arbitrage process cease?

(c) What arguments can be raised against this hypothesis?

5. Sam Peltz is planning to form a corporation. He has determined that $10 million will be required as an initial capital investment. Several financial backers have indicated that they would be willing to buy the bonds of the new corporation or personally lend Sam the capital he needs. Sam has delineated these alternative financing plans:

(1) Form the corporation with 1 million shares of $10 par stock, borrowing the entire $10 million from his associates on a personal basis (paying 6 percent interest on his note).

(2) Form the corporation with 500,000 shares of $10 par stock, borrowing the $5 million from his associates on a personal basis (6 percent note). Sell $5 million worth of 6% bonds to his associates.

(3) Form the corporation with 250,000 shares of $10 par stock, borrowing $2.5 million from his associates on a personal basis (6 percent note). Sell $7.5 million worth of 6 percent bonds to his associates.

(a) Assuming no corporate or personal taxes, which of the three alternatives should Sam select if the firm is expected to earn $1 million per year before the payment of interest? Assume that all of net earnings are paid out in dividends.

(b) Assuming a 50 percent corporate income tax and a personal income tax rate for Sam of 40 percent, which of the three alternatives should Sam select if the firm were expected to earn the same amount as in (a)? Assume all earnings are paid out in dividends.

6. Bakor Baking Company has an all-equity capital structure, net operating income before taxes of $400,000, and an after-tax capitalization rate of 10 percent. The corporate tax rate is 50 percent.

   (a) Assuming perfect capital markets, graph the cost of capital of the firm for various levels of debt. (Assume that the firm issues debt to repurchase stock, thereby effecting an immediate change in its capital structure.) What happens to the cost of capital with leverage?

   (b) Assume now that bankruptcy costs exist. What happens to the cost of capital in the above example as leverage increases?

SELECTED REFERENCES

Arditti, Fred D., "The Weighted Average Cost of Capital: Some Questions on Its Definition, Interpretation and Use," *Journal of Finance*, 28 (September 1973), 1001–9.

Bach, G. L., and James B. Stephenson, "Inflation and the Redistribution of Wealth," *Review of Economics and Statistics*, 56 (February 1974), 1–13.

Baron, David P., "Default Risk and the Modigliani-Miller Theorem: A Synthesis," *American Economic Review*, 66 (March 1976), 204–12.

——, "Firm Valuation, Corporate Taxes, and Default Risk," *Journal of Finance*, 30 (December 1975), 1251–64.

Baumol, William, and Burton G. Malkiel, "The Firm's Optimal Debt-Equity Combination and the Cost of Capital," *Quarterly Journal of Economics*, 81 (November 1967), 547–78.

Baxter, Nevins D., "Leverage, Risk of Ruin, and the Cost of Capital," *Journal of Finance*, 22 (September 1967), 395–404.

Body, Zvi, "Common Stocks as a Hedge against Inflation," *Journal of Finance*, 31 (May 1976).

Boness, A. James, Andrew H. Chen, and Som Jatusipitak, "On Relations among Stock Price Behavior and Changes in the Capital Structure of the Firm," *Journal of Financial and Quantitative Analysis*, 7 (September 1972), 1967–82.

Boot, John C. G., and George M. Frankfurter, "The Dynamics of Corporate Debt Management, Decision Rules, and Some Empirical Estimates," *Journal of Financial and Quantitative Analysis*, 7 (September 1972), 1956–66.

Bower, Richard S., and Dorothy H. Bower, "Risk and the Valuation of Common Stock," *Journal of Political Economy*, 77 (May–June 1969), 349–62.

Brigham, Eugene F., and Myron J. Gordon, "Leverage, Dividend Policy, and the Cost of Capital," *Journal of Finance*, 23 (March 1968), 85–104.

Davenport, Michael, "Leverage and the Cost of Capital: Some Tests Using British Data," *Economica*, May 1971, pp. 136–62.

Durand, David, "Costs of Debt and Equity Funds for Business: Trends and Problems of Measurement," reprinted in *The Management of Corporate Capital*, ed. Ezra Solomon, pp. 91–116. New York: Free Press, 1959.

Elton, Edwin J., and Martin J. Gruber, "Valuation and the Cost of Capital for Regulated Industries," *Journal of Finance*, 26 (June 1971), 661–70.

Fama, Eugene F., and Merton H. Miller, *The Theory of Finance*, Chapter 4. New York: Holt, Rinehart & Winston, 1972.

Gibson, William E., "Price Expectations Effects on Interest Rates," *Journal of Finance*, 25 (March 1970), 19–34.

Glenn, David W., "Institutional Portfolio Restrictions, Capital Market Equilibrium, and Pareto Efficiency," Working Paper, University of Utah, October 1975.

——, "Super Premium Security Prices and Optimal Corporate Financing Decisions," *Journal of Finance*, 31 (May 1976).

Gonzalez, Nestor, Robert Litzenberger, and Jacques Rolfo, "On Mean Variance Models of Capital Structure and the Absurdity of Their Predictions," Research Paper, Stanford Graduate School of Business, 1975.

Haley, Charles W., and Lawrence D. Schall, *The Theory of Financial Decisions*, Chapters 10 and 11. New York: McGraw-Hill, 1973.

Hamada, Robert S., "The Effect of the Firm's Capital Structure on the Systematic Risk of Common Stocks," *Journal of Finance*, 27 (May 1972), 435–52.

——, "Portfolio Analysis, Market Equilibrium, and Corporation Finance," *Journal of Finance*, 24 (March 1969), 13–31.

Haugen, Robert A., and James L. Pappas, "Equilibrium in the Pricing of Capital Assets, Risk-Bearing Debt Instruments, and the Question of Optimal Capital Structure," *Journal of Financial and Quantitative Analysis*, 6 (June 1971), 943–53. See also Yutaka Imai and Mark Rubinstein, "Comment," *Journal of Financial and Quantitative Analysis*,

7 (September 1972), 2001–3; and Haugen and Pappas, "Reply," ibid., 2005–8.

Haugen, Robert A., and Dean W. Wichern, "The Intricate Relationship Between Financial Leverage and the Stability of Stock Prices," *Journal of Finance,* 30 (December 1975), 1283–92.

Heins, A. James, and Case M. Sprenkle, "A Comment on the Modigliani-Miller Cost of Capital Thesis," *American Economic Review,* 59 (September 1969), 590–92.

Hendershott, Patric H., and James C. Van Horne, "Expected Inflation Implied by Capital Market Rates," *Journal of Finance,* 28 (May 1973), 301–14.

Jaffee, Jeffrey F., and Gershon Mandelker, "Test of the Fisher Effect for Risky Assets," *Journal of Finance,* 31 (May 1976).

Keane, Simon M., "Some Aspects of the Cost of Debt," *Accounting and Business Research* (Autumn 1975), 298–304.

Krainer, Robert E., "A Reexamination of the Theory of Monopsonistic Discrimination in the Capital Market," *Journal of Business,* 47 (July 1974), 429–39.

Kraus, Alan, and Robert H. Litzenberger, "A State-Preference Model of Optimal Financial Leverage," *Journal of Finance,* 28 (September 1973), 911–22.

Krouse, Clement G., "Optimal Financing and Capital Structure Programs for the Firm," *Journal of Finance,* 27 (December 1972), 1057–72.

Kumar, Prem, "Growth Stocks and Corporate Capital Structure Theory," *Journal of Finance,* 30 (May 1975), 533–47.

———, "Market Equilibrium and Corporation Finance: Some Issues," *Journal of Finance,* 29 (September 1974), 1175–88.

Lewellen, Wilbur G., *The Cost of Capital,* Chapters 3–4. Belmont, Calif: Wadsworth, 1969.

Lintner, John, "The Cost of Capital and Optimal Financing of Corporate Growth," *Journal of Finance,* 18 (May 1963), 292–310.

———, "Dividends, Earnings, Leverage, Stock Prices and the Supply of Capital to Corporations," *Review of Economics and Statistics,* 44 (August 1962), 243–69.

Lloyd-Davies, Peter R., "Optimal Financial Policy in Imperfect Markets," *Journal of Financial and Quantitative Analysis,* 10 (September 1975), 457–82.

Malkiel, Burton G., *The Debt-Equity Combination of the Firm and the Cost of Capital: An Introductory Analysis.* New York: General Learning Press, 1971.

Merton, Robert C., "On the Pricing of Corporate Debt: The Risk Structure of Interest Rates," *Journal of Finance,* 29 (May 1974), 449–70.

Miller, M. H., and Franco Modigliani, "Cost of Capital to Electric Utility Industry," *American Economic Review,* 56 (June 1966), 333–91.

Modigliani, Franco, and M. H. Miller, "The Cost of Capital, Corporation Finance and the Theory of Investment," *American Economic Review,* 48 (June 1958), 261–97.

———, "The Cost of Capital, Corporation Finance and the Theory of Investment: Reply," *American Economic Review,* 48 (September 1958), 655–69; "Taxes and the Cost of Capital: A Correction," ibid., 53 (June 1963), 433–43; "Reply," ibid., 55 (June 1965), 524–27; "Reply to Heins and Sprenkle," ibid., 59 (September 1969), 592–95.

Mossin, Jan, "Security Pricing and Investment Criteria in Competitive Markets," *American Economic Review,* 59 (December 1969), 749–56.

Nantell, Timothy J., and C. Robert Carlson, "The Cost of Capital as a Weighted Average," *Journal of Finance,* 30 (December 1975), 1343–55.

Nelson, Charles, "Inflation and the Rate of Return on Common Stocks," *Journal of Finance,* 31 (May 1976).

Robichek, Alexander A., and Stewart C. Myers, *Optimal Financing Decisions.* Englewood Cliffs, N.J.: Prentice-Hall, 1965.

Robichek, Alexander A., Robert C. Higgins, and Michael D. Kinsman. "The Effect of Leverage on the Cost of Equity Capital of Electric Utility Firms," *Journal of Finance,* 28 (May 1973), 353–67.

Rubinstein, Mark E., "Corporate Financial Policy in Segmented Securities Markets," *Journal of Financial and Quantitative Analysis,* 8 (December 1973), 749–62.

———, "A Mean-Variance Synthesis of Corporate Financial Theory," *Journal of Finance,* 28 (March 1973), 167–82.

Schall, Lawrence D., "Firm Financial Structure and Investment," *Journal of Financial and Quantitative Analysis,* 6 (June 1971), 925–42.

Scott, J. H., Jr., "A Theory of Optimal Capital Structure," *Bell Journal of Economics,* 7 (Spring 1976), 33–54.

Smith, Vernon L., "Default Risk, Scale, and the Homemade Leverage Theorem," *American Economic Review,* 62 (March 1972), 66–76.

Solomon, Ezra, "Leverage and the Cost of Capital," *Journal of Finance,* 18 (May 1963), 273–79.

———, "Measuring a Company's Cost of Capital," *Journal of Business,* 28 (October 1955), 240–52.

———, *The Theory of Financial Management.* New York: Columbia University Press, 1963.

Stiglitz, Joseph E., "On the Irrelevance of Corporate Financial Policy," *American Economic Review,* 64 (December 1974), 851–66.

———, "A Reexamination of the Modigliani-Miller Theorem," *American Economic Review,* 59 (December 1969), 784–93.

———, "Some Aspects of the Pure Theory of Corporate Finance: Bankruptcies and Take-overs," *Bell Journal of Economics and Management Science,* 3 (Autumn 1972), 458–82.

———, "Theory of Finance," *Bell Journal of Economics and Management Science,* 3 (Autumn 1972), 458–82.

Tepper, Irwin, "Revealed Preference Methods and the Pure Theory of the Cost of Capital," *Journal of Finance,* 28 (March 1973), 35–48.

Tinsley, P. A., "Capital Structure, Precautionary Balances, and Valuation of the Firm: The Problem of Financial Risk," *Journal of Financial and Quantitative Analysis,* 5 (March 1970), 33–62.

Van Horne, James C., and William F. Glassmire, Jr., "The Impact of Unanticipated Inflation on the Value of Common Stocks," *Journal of Finance,* 27 (December 1972), 1081–92.

Vickers, Douglas, "The Cost of Capital and the Structure of the Firm," *Journal of Finance,* 25 (March 1970), 35–46.

Weil, Roman L., "Realized Interest Rates and Bondholders' Returns," *American Economic Review,* 60 (June 1970), 502–11.

Williams, Edward E., "Cost of Capital Functions and the Firm's Optimal Level of Gearing," *Journal of Business Finance,* 4 (No. 2), 78–83.

Wippern, Ronald F., "Financial Structure and the Value of the Firm," *Journal of Finance,* 21 (December 1966), 615–34.

CAPITAL STRUCTURE DECISION of the FIRM

In theory, the optimal capital structure is one in which the marginal real cost of each available method of financing is the same. By *real cost*, we mean the sum of both the explicit and the implicit costs. Up to now, our discussion has been theoretical. We now wish to consider how the financial manager might determine in practice an appropriate capital structure for his particular firm. The real difficulty, of course, is in estimating the implicit costs of nonequity financing.

Our concern in this chapter, then, is with ways of coming to grips with the formidable problem of determining an appropriate capital structure. In this regard, we examine various methods of analysis that can be used in practice. None of the methods considered is completely satisfactory in itself. Taken collectively, however, they provide the financial manager with sufficient information for making a rational decision. One should hold no illusions that the financial manager will be able to identify the precise percentage of debt that will maximize share price. Rather, he should try to determine the approximate proportion of debt to employ in keeping with an objective of maximizing share price. In the last part of the chapter, we explore briefly the questions of timing and flexibility of a single security issue.

One widely used means of examining the effect of leverage is to analyze the relationship between earnings before interest and taxes (EBIT) and earnings per share (EPS). Essentially, the method involves the comparison of alternative methods of financing under various assumptions as to EBIT.[1] To illustrate, suppose that a firm wished to compare the impact on earnings per share of financing a $10 million expansion program either with common stock at $50 a share or with 8% bonds. The tax rate is 50 percent, and the firm currently has an all-equity capital structure consisting of 800,000 shares of common stock. At $50 a share, the firm will need to sell 200,000 additional shares in order to raise $10 million. If we choose a hypothetical EBIT level of $8 million, earnings per share for the two alternatives would be:

EBIT–EPS ANALYSIS

	Common-Stock Financing	Debt Financing
EBIT	$8,000,000	$8,000,000
Interest	$ 0	$ 800,000
Earnings before taxes	$8,000,000	$7,200,000
Taxes	$4,000,000	$3,600,000
Earnings after taxes	$4,000,000	$3,600,000
Shares outstanding	1,000,000	800,000
Earnings per share	$4.00	$4.50

[1] For detailed discussion of the calculations involved in this type of analysis, see Chapter 27. Our concern in the present chapter is with how the method might be used.

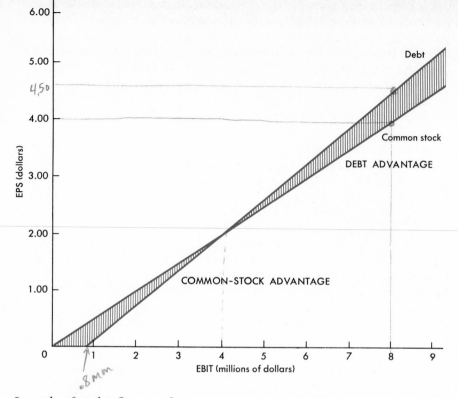

FIG. 10·1
EBIT-EPS chart

In order for the firm to show zero earnings per share under the debt alternative, it is clear that it will need to have EBIT of $800,000.

With this information, we are able to construct an EBIT–EPS chart, and it is shown in Figure 10-1. The incercepts on the horizontal axis represent the amount of before-tax charges. For equity, the intercept is zero; for debt, it is $800,000. We then plot earnings per share for both alternatives under the assumption of an EBIT of $8 million. When we connect the intercepts with the appropriate EPS points at an EBIT level of $8 million, we obtain the straight lines shown. They tell us the earnings per share for the two financing alternatives that will occur under varying levels of EBIT.

ANALYSIS OF INTERSECTION

Because the debt line has a steeper slope, it intersects the common-stock line at an EBIT level of $4 million. At all levels of EBIT above $4 million, there is an earnings-per-share advantage to the use of debt. At levels of EBIT below $4 million, the advantage is in favor of common-stock financing.

Constructing an EBIT–EPS chart gives the financial manager information about the differential impact on earnings per share of alternative methods of financing. We note that as long as the firm is able to earn more than 8 percent before taxes on its investment, debt financing will show an EPS advantage. But the method does not consider directly the implicit costs associated with debt. In an analysis of financial risk, however, an EBIT–EPS chart can be useful to the financial manager. He can compare the point of intersection with the most likely level of EBIT; he can also determine the probability that EBIT will fall below that point.

For example, suppose that actual EBIT in our example presently is $7 million and that the company is considering the debt alternative. Given the business risk of the company and the possible fluctuations in EBIT, the financial manager should assess the probability of EBIT's falling below $4 million. If the probability is negligible, the use of the debt alternative would be supported. On the other hand, if EBIT presently is only slightly above the indifference point and the probability of EBIT's falling below this point is high, the financial manager may conclude that the debt alternative is too risky. In summary, the greater the level of EBIT and the lower the probability of downside fluctuation, the stronger the case that can be made for the use of debt.

To further illustrate this concept, suppose the firm were considering financing the $10 million expansion program not only with all common stock or all debt but also with half common stock at $50 a share and half debt at 8 percent. Suppose further that if the economy is normal, EBIT is expected to be $6 million. If a recession occurs, however, EBIT is expected to be $2 million; whereas if boom conditions occur, it is expected to be $10 million. The effect of these conditions on earning per share under the various financing alternatives is shown in Table 10-1. We see that in the case of a recession, all common-stock financing has the most favorable impact on earnings per share, while under normal and

Table 10·1   Effect of economic conditions on earnings per share under the various financing alternatives (in millions of dollars)

	Common-Stock Financing			Common-Stock and Debt Financing			Debt Financing		
	Recession	Normal	Boom	Recession	Normal	Boom	Recession	Normal	Boom
EBIT	$2.0	$6.0	$10.0	$2.0	$6.0	$10.0	$2.0	$6.0	$10.0
Interest	$0	$0	$ 0	$0.4	$0.4	$ 0.4	$0.8	$0.8	$ 0.8
Earnings before taxes	$2.0	$6.0	$10.0	$1.6	$5.6	$ 9.6	$1.2	$5.2	$ 9.2
Taxes	$1.0	$3.0	$5.0	$0.8	$2.8	$ 4.8	$0.6	$2.6	$ 4.6
Earnings after taxes	$1.0	$3.0	$ 5.0	$0.8	$2.8	$ 4.0	$0.6	$2.6	$ 4.6
Shares outstanding	1.0	1.0	1.0	0.9	0.9	0.9	0.8	0.8	0.8
Earnings per share	$1.00	$3.00	$ 5.00	$0.89	$3.11	$ 5.33	$0.75	$3.25	$ 5.75

boom economic conditions, all debt financing is the most favorable alternative. The table gives further insight into how leverage accelerates the impact of changes in EBIT on earnings per share.

Although an EBIT–EPS chart does not focus on the implicit costs of senior securities, the financial manager is able to obtain insight into these implicit costs through proper analysis. Although crude, the method is a useful supplement to other methods of analysis.

CASH-FLOW ANALYSIS

When considering the appropriate capital structure, it is extremely important to analyze the cash-flow ability of the firm to service fixed charges. The greater the dollar amount of senior securities the firm issues and the shorter their maturity, the greater the fixed charges of the firm. These charges include principal and interest payments on debt, lease payments, and preferred stock dividends. Before assuming additional fixed charges, the firm should analyze its expected future cash flows, for fixed charges must be met with cash. The inability to meet these charges, with the exception of preferred stock dividends, may result in financial insolvency. The greater and more stable the expected future cash flows of the firm, the greater the debt capacity of the company. Debt capacity is used in a broad sense to mean all senior securities. From an internal standpoint, the financial risk associated with leverage should be analyzed on the basis of the firm's ability to service fixed charges. This analysis should include the preparation of cash budgets to determine whether the expected cash flows are sufficient to cover the fixed obligations.[2]

PROBABILITY OF CASH INSOLVENCY

Necessarily, however, the analysis must consider the probability distribution of cash flows, for we are concerned with possible deviations in actual cash flows from those that are expected. As we discuss in Chapter 26, cash budgets can be prepared for a range of possible outcomes, with a probability attached to each. This information is extremely valuable to the financial manager in evaluating the ability of the firm to meet fixed obligations. Given the probabilities of particular cash-flow sequences, he is able to determine the amount of fixed charges and debt the company can undertake while still remaining within the insolvency limits tolerable to management.

Suppose management feels that a 5 percent probability of being out of cash is the maximum that can be tolerated, and that this probability corresponds to a cash budget prepared under pessimistic assumptions.

[2]The preparation of cash budgets is discussed in Chapter 26.

In this case, debt might be undertaken up to the point where the cash balance under the pessimistic cash budget is just sufficient to cover the fixed charges associated with the debt. In other words, debt would be increased to the point at which the additional cash drain would cause the probability of cash insolvency to equal the risk tolerance specified by management. It is not necessary that debt be increased to this point, of course. Note that the method of analysis simply provides a means for assessing the effect of increases in debt on the risk of cash insolvency. On the basis of this information, management would determine the most appropriate level of debt.

Donaldson has proposed a similar type of analysis.[3] He suggests that the ultimate concern of a company is whether cash balances during some future period will be involuntarily reduced below zero. Therefore, he advocates examining the cash flows of the company under the most adverse circumstances—that is, in his definition, under recession conditions. These conditions may or may not be the most adverse; however, in keeping with the spirit of his proposal, the firm should evaluate its cash flows under adverse circumstances. Donaldson defines the net cash balance in a recession as

$$CB_r = CB_o + NCF_r \qquad (10\text{-}1)$$

where CB_o = cash balance at start of recession

$\qquad NCF_r$ = net cash flows during recession

Donaldson then analyzes the cash-flow behavior of a firm during a recession by calculating a probability distribution of expected net cash flows.[4] By combining the beginning cash balances, CB_o, with the probability distribution of recession cash flows, NCF_r, he prepares a probability distribution of cash balances in the recession—CB_r.

To ascertain its debt capacity, a firm first would calculate the fixed charges associated with additional increments of debt. For each addition, the firm then would determine the probability of being out of cash, based upon the probability distribution of cash balances during the recession. As before, management could set tolerance limits on the probability of being out of cash. For example, suppose the firm were considering issuing \$20 million in additional debt and that the annual fixed charges were \$3 million. By subtracting \$3 million from the expected cash balances shown for the probability distribution of CB_r, we

[3]Gordon Donaldson, *Corporate Debt Capacity* (Boston: Division of Research, Harvard Business School, 1961). See also Donaldson, "Strategy for Financial Emergencies," *Harvard Business Review,* 47 (November–December 1969), 67–79.

[4]The determinants of net cash flows with which he works are sales collections, other cash receipts, payroll expenditures, raw-material expenditures, and nondiscretionary cash expenditures. By analyzing each of these determinants, he determines the range and probability of recession net cash flows.

obtain the probability distribution of CB_r with the addition of $20 million in debt. If the probability of being out of cash with this increment of debt is negligible, Donaldson would contend that the company has unused debt capacity. Therefore, it would be possible to increase the amount of debt until the probability of being out of cash equaled the risk tolerance of management.

Donaldson extends his analysis to calculate the probability of *cash inadequacy.* Our discussion before was in terms of *cash insolvency,* which is defined as lack of cash after all nonessential expenditures have been cut. Cash inadequacy is said to occur if the firm is out of cash after making certain desired expenditures such as dividends, R & D expenditures, and capital expenditures. Thus, cash insolvency is the extreme

Table 10·2   Inventory of resources to meet possible cash drains

Resources	Available for Use Within: One Quarter	One Year	Three Years
I. Uncommitted reserves			
Instant reserves			
Surplus cash	$		
Unused line of credit	$		
Negotiable reserves			
Additional bank loans			
Unsecured	$		
Secured	$		
Additional long-term debt		$	
Issue of new equity		$	
II. Reduction of planned outflows			
Volume-related			
Change in production schedule	$		
Scale-related			
Marketing program		$	
R & D budget		$	
Administrative overhead		$	
Capital expenditures		$	
Value-related			
Dividend payments		$	
III. Liquidation of assets			
Shutdown		$	
Sale of unit			$
	$	$	
		$	$
Total resources			$

Source: Donaldson, "Strategy for Financial Emergencies," p. 72.

form of cash inadequacy. In all cases, the firm should take stock of the

Chapter 10 **269**
CAPITAL STRUCTURE
DECISION OF THE FIRM

resources it has at its disposal to meet an unexpected cash drain.[5] Typically, a number of alternatives are available, ranging from the use of surplus cash to the sale of fixed assets at distress prices. Donaldson categorizes these resources into uncommitted reserves, the reduction of outflows, and the liquidation of assets. These categories and their various subsets are shown in Table 10-2. Once an inventory of resources has been compiled, the adequacy of these resources should be judged in relation to potential cash drains. Embodied in this analysis should be the fixed charges associated with various levels of debt. Thus, the liquidity of the firm should be analyzed in relation to its debt capacity.

CASH-FLOW ANALYSIS AND DEBT-TO-EQUITY RATIOS

A probabilistic approach to analyzing the ability of a firm to service fixed charges is extremely useful. In this regard, simulation can be employed to determine the outcome under changing conditions. The analysis of the cash-flow ability of the firm to service fixed charges is perhaps the best way to analyze financial risk, but there is some question as to whether the external market analyzes a company in this manner. Sophisticated lenders and institutional investors certainly analyze the amount of fixed charges and evaluate financial risk in keeping with the ability of the firm to service these charges. However, individual investors may look more to the book value proportions of debt to equity in judging financial risk.

There may or may not be a reasonable correspondence between the ratio of debt to equity and the amount of fixed charges relative to the firm's cash-flow ability to service these charges. Some firms may have relatively high ratios of debt to equity but substantial cash-flow ability to service debt. Consequently, the analysis of debt-to-equity ratios alone can be deceiving, and an analysis of the magnitude and stability of cash flows relative to fixed charges is extremely important in determining the appropriate capital structure for the firm. To the extent that creditors and investors analyze a firm's cash-flow ability to service debt, and management's risk preferences correspond to those of investors, capital structure decisions made on this basis should tend to maximize share price.

COMPARISON OF CAPITAL STRUCTURE RATIOS

OTHER METHODS OF ANALYSIS

Another method of analyzing the appropriate capital structure for a company is to evaluate the capital structure of other companies having similar business risk. Companies used in this comparison may be those

---

[5] Donaldson, "Strategy for Financial Emergencies."

in the same industry. If the firm is contemplating a capital structure significantly out of line with that of similar companies, it is conspicuous to the marketplace. This is not to say, however, that the firm is wrong; other companies in the industry may be too conservative with respect to the use of debt. The optimal capital structure for all companies in the industry might call for a higher proportion of debt to equity than the industry average. As a result, the firm may well be able to justify more debt than the industry average. Because investment analysts and creditors tend to evaluate companies by industry, however, the firm should be able to justify its position if its capital structure is noticeably out of line in either direction.

REGRESSION STUDIES AND SIMULATION

A number of companies are undertaking regression studies in an effort to determine the effect of capital structure on stock valuation. Most of the empirical testing has involved regression studies in which either the "measured" average cost of capital or the earnings/price ratio is used as the dependent variable and either leverage or leverage plus additional explanatory variables are used as the independent variable(s). When independent variables additional to leverage are employed, the analysis is known as a multiple-regression study. The purpose of a multiple-regression study is to hold constant statistically other factors that affect valuation in order to obtain an unbiased estimate of the effect of leverage on valuation. By and large, the regression studies undertaken have been based upon cross-sectional samples of firms in a particular industry.

In general, the results of empirical testing of the relationship between leverage and cost of capital have been tenuous. The major difficulty is in holding constant all other factors that affect valuation. In particular, future growth, as perceived by investors at the margin, is extremely hard to measure. Most regression studies have used the past growth in earnings per share or the past growth in total assets as a proxy for expected future growth as perceived by investors at the margin. To the extent that these past growth measures do not account fully for growth as perceived by investors at the margin, other variables, including leverage, may be a proxy for growth.

In addition to the biases described above, there are several others that plague empirical testing. Frequently, the range of leverage for a sample of companies in the same industry is narrow. Without extreme values of leverage, a regression study is unlikely to denote a very strong relationship between leverage and the cost of capital or leverage and the earnings/price ratio. If all firms in a sample are at an optimal capital structure, an unbiased regression study would fail to show any relationship between leverage and valuation. In summary, there are a number of

and the cost of capital. Consequently, evidence of this relationship is only suggestive. Nevertheless, regression studies based upon a sample of similar companies may give the firm some insight into the impact of leverage on the market price of its stock.

In addition to regression analysis, simulation is being employed increasingly as a means of providing management with valuation information about the expected consequences of a particular investment, financing, or dividend decision. For example, management might be considering a large increase in the proportion of debt to equity because the firm needs to buy out certain minority interests. Before actually making the decision, management may wish to simulate the expected effect of this action on the market price of the stock. By observing the range of simulated outcomes, management has better information on which to base its decision. Most simulation problems in finance are stochastic and involve the use of probabilistic models. These models make use of the Monte Carlo technique described in Chapter 5. If the probability distributions are accurate and the interrelationship of variables properly specified, simulation can be an extremely valuable aid in formulating financial decisions.

However, the results achieved are no better than the probability information used and the realism of the interrelationship of variables specified. Probabilistic information usually is based upon empirical testing of valuation models, the results of which have been far from precise or consistent. An equally thorny problem is the specification of the relationship between variables. Again, empirical studies have been less than satisfactory in sorting out the interrelationships in a consistent manner. We do not wish to undervalue the importance of regression analysis and simulation techniques in providing valuation information to the financial manager, but it is important to point out the practical limitations of the models. The state of the art is not sufficiently advanced for a financing decision to be based solely upon share-price models. However, we can expect to see increasing efforts to lessen the difficulties that have hampered their acceptance by financial managers.

SURVEY OF ANALYSTS AND INVESTORS

The firm may profit also by talking with investment analysts, institutional investors, and investment houses to obtain their views on the appropriate amount of leverage. These analysts examine many companies and are in the business of recommending stocks. Therefore, they have an influence upon the market, and their judgments with respect to how the market evaluates leverage may be very worthwhile. Similarly, a firm may wish to interview lenders to see how much debt it can undertake before the cost of borrowing is likely to rise. Finally, the management of a company may develop a "feel" for what has happened in the past to the market price of the stock when they have issued debt. As suggested in Chapter 8, the financial manager must think the way investors think if he is to evaluate the impact of a financial decision on share price.

The methods described above for analyzing the appropriate amount of leverage do not give an exact answer. Nevertheless, by undertaking a variety of analyses, the financial manager should be able to determine, within some range, the appropriate capital structure for his firm. By necessity, the final decision has to be somewhat subjective. However, it can be based upon the best information available. In this way, the firm is able to obtain the capital structure most appropriate for its situation—the one hopefully that will tend to maximize the market price of the stock, all other factors held constant.

TIMING AND FLEXIBILITY

Once a firm has determined an appropriate capital structure, it still has the problem of timing security issues. When external financing is required, a company is often faced with the question of how to time an issue appropriately and whether to use debt or common stock. Because financing is "lumpy," it is difficult for a firm to maintain strict proportions in its capital structure. Frequently, it must decide whether to finance now with a stock issue and later with a debt issue, or vice versa. Consequently, it is forced to evaluate the alternative methods of financing in light of general market conditions and expectations for the company itself. If interest rates are high and expected to fall, management may wish to postpone the debt issue and go with common-stock financing now. On the other hand, if the market for the company's stock is depressed but is expected to improve as better earnings are realized, management may prefer to postpone the equity issue until a later date and issue debt now.

If it chooses this alternative, however, it may sacrifice a certain amount of flexibility. If the debt issue is substantial and things take a turn for the worse, the firm may be forced to issue stock on unfavorable terms in the future. In order to preserve its flexibility in tapping the capital markets, it may be better for a firm to issue stock now so as to have unused debt capacity for future needs. The preservation of unused debt capacity can be an important consideration for the company whose funds requirements are sudden and unpredictable. It gives the company financial maneuverability by virtue of leaving the options open. This flexibility, of course, could also be achieved simply by maintaining excess liquidity. However, there is an opportunity cost that might be avoided by maintaining flexibility in the raising of funds.

For a growth company, however, preservation of financial maneuverability has a drawback. By issuing stock now so as to have unused debt capacity, the company will probably have to issue more shares than it would if it postponed the stock issue. Consequently, there is more dilution to existing shareholders over time. The tradeoff is between preserving financial flexibility and dilution in earnings per share. If the price of the stock is high, however, and expected to fall, the firm can achieve both flexibility and minimum dilution by issuing stock now.

Although the benefits of good timing usually are limited for debt financing, they can be substantial for equity financing. Depending upon the stock market in general and expectations for the firm in particular, the price of the stock can vary significantly. Management has an implied responsibility to existing stockholders to try to sell a stock issue at as favorable a price as possible. By the same token, it has a responsibility to try to place debt at as favorable an interest rate as possible. While the timing of a stock issue is probably the more important of the two, they both have a significant influence upon earnings per share. In Part VI, we examine in depth specific methods of long-term financing. Included in this analysis is a discussion of the timing of a specific security issue and the flexibility afforded by the instrument.

SUMMARY

In deciding upon an appropriate capital structure, the financial manager should consider a number of factors. He can obtain considerable insight from an analysis of the cash-flow ability of the firm to service fixed charges associated with senior securities and leasing. By evaluating the probability of cash insolvency, he is able to determine the debt capacity of the firm. Another method is to analyze the relationship between earnings before interest and taxes (EBIT) and earnings per share for alternative methods of financing. When this analysis is expanded to consider likely fluctuations in EBIT, light is shed on the question of financial risk.

In addition, the financial manager can learn much from a comparison of capital structure ratios for similar companies, through regression studies and simulations, and through discussions with investment analysts, investment bankers, and lenders. Collectively, the methods of analysis taken up in this chapter should provide sufficient information on which to base a capital structure decision. Once an appropriate capital structure has been determined, the firm should finance investment proposals in roughly those proportions.

Finally, we examined the problem of timing a debt or equity issue. Where sequential financing is involved, the choice of debt or equity has an important influence on the future financial flexibility of the firm.

1. Hi Grade Regulator Company currently has 100,000 shares of common stock outstanding with a market price of $60 per share. It also has $2 million in 6 percent bonds. The company is considering a $3 million expansion program that it can finance with either (1) all common stock at $60 a share; (2) straight bonds at 8 percent interest; (3) preferred stock at 7 percent; (4) half common stock at $60 per share and half 8 percent bonds.

   (a) For a hypothetical EBIT level of $1 million, calculate the earnings per share for each of the alternative methods of financing. Assume a corporate tax rate of 50 percent.

   (b) Construct an EBIT–EPS chart. What are the indifference points between alternatives? What is your interpretation of them?

2. Hi Grade Regulator Company (see problem 1) expects the EBIT level after the expansion program to be $1 million, with a two-thirds probability that it will be between $600,000 and $1,400,000.

   (a) Which financing alternative do you prefer? Why?

   (b) Suppose that the expected EBIT level were $1.5 million and that there were a two-thirds probability that it would be between $1.3 million and $1.7 million. Which financing alternative do you prefer now? Why?

3. The Power Corporation currently has 2 million shares outstanding at a price of $20 each and needs to raise an additional $5 million. These funds could be raised with stock or 10 percent debentures. Expected EBIT after the new funds are raised will be normally distributed with a mean of $4 million per year forever and a standard deviation of $2 million. Power Corporation has a 50 percent tax rate. What is the probability that the debt alternative is superior with respect to earnings per share?

4. Gamma Tube Company plans to undertake a $12 million capital improvement program and is considering how much debt to use. It feels that it could obtain debt financing at the following interest rates (assume that this debt is perpetual):

Amounts	First $4 million	Next $3 million	Next $3 million	Next $2 million
Interest cost	7 percent	8 percent	9 percent	10 percent

   The company has made projections of its net cash flows (exclusive of new financing) during a period of adversity such as a recession. In a recession, it expects a net-cash flow of $3 million with a standard deviation of $2 million (assume a normal distribution). Its beginning cash balance is $500,000. If the company is willing to tolerate only a 5 percent probability of running out of cash during a recession, what is the maximum proportion of the $12 million capital improvement program that can be financed with debt?

5. The Great Northwest Oil Corporation has decided that it must raise $100 million within the next six months to finance an expansion program. The firm believes it now has an optimal capital structure. Never-

theless, GNOC realizes that this "ideal" structure may be temporarily sacrificed unless the needed funds are secured on a proportionate basis to the current structure. It has been determined that the "normalized" price of the firm's common stock is $100 per share, though the current price is only $80 because of a general stock-market decline. Further, high interest rates have reduced the price of the firm's AAA– rated bonds to yield 8 percent to maturity. The prime rate available to the firm for a one-year bank loan is $8\frac{1}{2}$ percent. What alternative financing (and timing) plans are open to the firm? Outline the separate assumptions that must be made in order to justify each alternative.

GNOC Capital Structure

Bonds	$250,000,000
Common stock	200,000,000
Retained earnings	300,000,000
	$750,000,000

6. *Research Project* Compile a list of business firms operating in your area. On the basis of information available to you, group these firms into roughly equivalent risk classes.

   Next, obtain a recent balance sheet for each firm. Does each firm in a given risk class have a similar capital structure? Could any divergence reflect the risk preferences of management?

   Finally, compute the average capital structure of the firms in a given risk class. Place these averages on a continuum running from the average of the class of least risk to that of the greatest. Can a trend be noted? Are there significant deviations from this trend?

SELECTED REFERENCES

Bierman, Harold, Jr., "Risk and the Addition of Debt to the Capital Structure," *Journal of Financial and Quantitative Analysis,* 3 (December 1968), 415–23.

Donaldson, Gordon, *Corporate Debt Capacity.* Boston: Division of Research, Harvard Business School, 1961.

———, "New Framework for Corporate Debt Capacity," *Harvard Business Review,* 40 (March–April 1962), 117–31.

———, "Strategy for Financial Emergencies," *Harvard Business Review,* 47 (November–December 1969), 67–79.

Elton, Edwin J., and Martin J. Gruber, "Valuation and the Cost of Capital for Regulated Industries," *Journal of Finance,* 26 (June 1971), 661–70.

Handorf, William C., "Flexible Debt Financing," *Financial Management,* 3 (Summer 1974), 17–23.

Litzenberger, Robert H., and C. U. Rao, "Portfolio Theory and Industry Cost of Capital Estimates," *Journal of Financial and Quantitative Analysis,* 7 (March 1972), 1443–62.

Melnyk, Z. Lew, "Cost of Capital as a Function of Financial Leverage," *Decision Sciences,* 1 (July–October 1970), 372–86.

Morris, James R., "On Corporate Debt Maturity Strategies," *Journal of Finance,* forthcoming.

Robichek, Alexander A., Robert C. Higgins, and Michael D. Kinsman, "The Effect of Leverage on the Cost of Equity Capital of Electric Utility Firms," *Journal of Finance,* 28 (May 1973), 353–67.

Robichek, Alexander A., and Stewart C. Myers, *Optimal Financing Decisions,* Chapter 8. Englewood Cliffs, N.J.: Prentice-Hall, 1965.

Schwartz, Eli, and J. Richard Aronson, "Some Surrogate Evidence in Support of the Concept of Optimal Capital Structure," *Journal of Finance,* 22 (March 1967), 10–18.

Scott, David F., Jr., and John D. Martin, "Industry Influence on Financial Structure," *Financial Management,* 4 (Spring 1975), 67–73.

DIVIDENDS
and
VALUATION

The third major decision of the firm is its dividend policy. In this chapter, we investigate only one aspect of dividend policy—the percentage of earnings paid to stockholders in cash. In the next chapter, we take up other aspects of dividend policy. The dividend-payout ratio, of course, determines the amount of earnings retained in the firm and affects the total amount of internal financing. Consequently, it must be analyzed in relation to the overall financing decision. In this chapter, we evaluate dividend policy in light of the objective of the firm—namely, to maximize the value of the firm to its shareholders. Shareholder wealth includes not only the market price of the stock but also current dividends. Again, we assume that business risk is held constant; that is, the acceptance of any investment proposal does not affect the business-risk complexion of the firm as perceived by suppliers of capital.

MEASUREMENT OF EARNINGS

The dividend-payout ratio of a firm obviously depends upon the way earnings are measured. For ease of theoretical exposition, we use accounting net earnings but assume that these earnings conform to the true economic earnings of the firm. In practice, net earnings may not so conform; as a result, they may not be an appropriate measure of the ability of the firm to pay dividends. Certain writers argue that cash flow, the sum of earnings and depreciation, is a better measure of the capacity of a firm to pay dividends. John A. Brittain, for example, suggests that the liberalization of depreciation allowances in the post-World War II period renders net earnings an invalid measure of the ability of corporations to pay dividends.[1] On the basis of an empirical study of the 1920–60 period, he found that cash flow did a significantly better job of explaining corporate dividends than did net earnings. He takes this finding as support for the idea that corporations recognize the illusory nature of reported earnings and instead base dividends upon cash flow. Although the argument that cash flow best approximates the "true" earnings of a firm is persuasive, we shall continue to use net earnings in the theoretical development that follows.

In order to evaluate properly the question of whether dividend policy affects shareholder wealth, it is necessary to examine first the firm's policy solely as a financing decision involving the retention of earnings. Consider the situation in which the use of funds from earnings, and the dividend policy that results, is strictly a financing decision. As

DIVIDEND POLICY AS A RESIDUAL DECISION

[1]John A. Brittain, *Corporate Dividend Policy* (Washington, D.C.: Brookings Institution, 1966), Chapter 3.

long as the firm has investment projects whose returns exceed those that are required, it will use retained earnings, and the amount of senior securities the increase in equity base will support, to finance these projects. If the firm has retained earnings left over after financing all acceptable investment opportunities, these earnings would then be distributed to stockholders in the form of cash dividends. If not, there would be no dividends. If the number of acceptable investment opportunities involved a total dollar amount that exceeded the amount of retained earnings plus the senior securities these retained earnings will support, the firm would finance the excess with a combination of a new equity issue and senior securities.

When we treat dividend policy as strictly a financing decision, the payment of cash dividends is a passive residual.[2] The amount of dividend payout will fluctuate from period to period in keeping with fluctuations in the amount of acceptable investment opportunities available to the firm. If these opportunities abound, the percentage of dividend payout is likely to be zero. On the other hand, if the firm is unable to find profitable investment opportunities, dividend payout will be 100 percent. For situations between these two extremes, the payout will be a fraction between 0 and 1.

DIVIDENDS AS A PASSIVE RESIDUAL

The treatment of dividend policy as a passive residual determined strictly by the availability of acceptable investment proposals implies that dividends are irrelevant; the investor is indifferent between dividends and capital gains. If investment opportunities promise a return greater than their required return, the investor is happy to have the company retain earnings. Contrarily, if the return is less than the required return, he prefers dividends. Supposedly, if the firm can earn more on projects than the required return, then investors are perfectly happy to let the firm retain as much in earnings as it needs to finance the investments.

A residual theory of dividend policy does not necessarily mean that dividends need fluctuate from period to period in keeping with fluctuations in investment opportunities. A firm may smooth out actual payments by saving some funds in surplus years in anticipation of deficit ones.[3] If forecasting is relatively accurate, the firm can establish its dividend payment at a level at which the cumulative distribution over time corresponds to cumulative residual funds over the same period.

---

[2] Ezra Solomon, *The Theory of Financial Management* (New York: Columbia University Press, 1963), pp. 139–40.

[3] See Robert C. Higgins, "The Corporate Dividend-Saving Decision," *Journal of Financial and Quantitative Analysis*, 7 (March 1972), 1531–38, who finds some empirical support for the notion that single-period dividends are a function of a longer-term trend.

The fact that dividends do not correspond to residual funds period by period does not negate the residual theory of dividends.

Chapter 11 **279**
DIVIDENDS AND
VALUATION

The critical question is whether dividends are more than just a means of distributing unused funds. Should dividend policy be an active decision variable as opposed to a passive one? To answer these questions, we must examine more thoroughly the argument that dividends are irrelevant so that changes in the payout ratio (holding investment opportunities constant) do not affect shareholder wealth.

The most comprehensive argument for the irrelevance of dividends is found in Modigliani and Miller's 1961 article.[4] They assert that, given the investment decision of the firm, the dividend-payout ratio is a mere detail. It does not affect the wealth of shareholders. MM argue that the value of the firm is determined solely by the earning power on the firm's assets or its investment policy and that the manner in which the earnings stream is split between dividends and retained earnings does not affect this value. The critical assumptions of MM are[5]

IRRELEVANCE OF DIVIDENDS

1. Perfect capital markets in which all investors are rational. Information is available to all at no cost; transactions are instantaneous and without cost; securities are infinitely divisible; and no investor is large enough to affect the market price of a security.
2. An absence of flotation costs on securities issued by the firm.
3. A world of no taxes.
4. A given investment policy for the firm, not subject to change.
5. Perfect certainty by every investor as to future investments and profits of the firm. MM drop this assumption later.

DIVIDENDS VERSUS TERMINAL VALUE

The crux of MM's position is that the effect of dividend payments on shareholder wealth is offset exactly by other means of financing. Consider first selling additional stock in lieu of retaining earnings. When the firm has made its investment decision, it must decide whether to retain earnings or to pay dividends and sell new stock in the amount of these dividends in order to finance the investments. MM suggest that the sum of the discounted value per share after financing and dividends paid is equal to the market value per share before the payment of dividends. In other words, the stock's decline in market price because of external

[4] Merton H. Miller and Franco Modigliani, "Dividend Policy, Growth, and the Valuation of Shares," *Journal of Business*, 34 (October 1961), 411–33.
[5] See also John Lintner, "Dividends, Earnings, Leverage, Stock Prices and the Supply of Capital to Corporations," *Review of Economics and Statistics*, 44 (August 1962), 243–69.

financing offsets exactly the payment of the dividend. Thus, the stockholder is said to be indifferent between dividends and the retention of earnings.

The market price of a share of stock at the beginning of a period is defined as equal to the present value of the dividend paid at the end of the period plus the market price at the end of the period.[6] Thus

$$P_0 = \frac{1}{1 + \rho}(D_1 + P_1) \tag{11-1}$$

where P_0 = market price per share at time 0

ρ = capitalization rate for firm in that risk class (this rate is assumed to be constant throughout time)

D_1 = dividend per share at time 1

P_1 = market price per share at time 1

Assume that n is the number of shares of record at time 0 *(all shares outstanding)* and that m is the number of new shares sold at time 1 at a price of P_1. Eq. (11-1) then can be rewritten as

$$nP_0 = \frac{1}{(1 + \rho)}[nD_1 + (n + m)P_1 - mP_1] \tag{11-2}$$

In words, the total value of all shares outstanding at time 0 is the present value of total dividends paid at time 1 on those shares plus the total value of all stock outstanding at time 1, less the total value of the new stock issued. The total amount of new stock issued is

$$mP_1 = I - (X - nD_1) \tag{11-3}$$

where I = total new investments during period 1

X = total net profit of firm for the period

The total amount of financing by the sale of new stock is determined by the amount of investments in period 1 not financed by retained earnings. By substituting Eq. (11-3) into Eq. (11-2), MM find that the nD_1 term cancels out and

$$nP_0 = \frac{1}{(1 + \rho)}[(n + m)P_1 - I + X] \tag{11-4}$$

Because D_1 does not appear directly in the expression and because X, I, $(n + m)P_1$, and ρ are assumed to be independent of D_1, MM conclude that the current value of the firm is independent of its current dividend

---

[6] Miller and Modigliani, "Dividend Policy, Growth, and the Valuation of Shares" See also Myron J. Gordon, "Optimal Investment and Financing Policy," *Journal of Finance*, 18 (May 1963), 264–72.

decision.[7] What is gained by the stockholder in increased dividends is offset exactly by the decline in the terminal value of his stock. MM go on to show that nP_0 is unaffected not only by current dividend decisions but by future dividend decisions as well. Under the assumption of perfect certainty by all investors, the price of the stock at time 1, time 2, and time n is determined solely by Eq. (11-4). Thus, stockholders are indifferent between retention and the payment of dividends (and concurrent stock financing) in all future periods. As a result, shareholder wealth is unaffected by current and future dividend decisions; it depends entirely upon the expected future earnings stream of the firm.

Given MM's assumptions of perfect certainty as well as their other assumptions, the irrelevance of dividends follows. As with our example for corporate leverage, arbitrage assures that the sum of market value plus current dividends of two firms identical in all respects other than dividend-payout ratios will be the same. The individual investor can retain and invest his own earnings, and do this as well as the corporation can for him.[8]

One point needs clarification, however. In our example, we have assumed that external financing involves the sale of new stock and that the effect of this sale on the market price of the stock offsets exactly the payment of dividends. What if the external financing involved debt? MM's position then rests upon their previous indifference thesis with respect to leverage: the real cost of debt is the same as the real cost of equity financing. Therefore, according to MM, the means of external financing used to offset the payment of dividends does not affect their hypothesis that dividends are irrelevant. Thus, we see the interdependency of MM's two positions. Dividend policy does not affect their thesis regarding leverage; in their position on dividends, the means of external financing is not a factor.

If dividends are irrelevant, a firm's cost of capital would be independent of its dividend-payout ratio. If both leverage and dividends are irrelevant, the firm would be indifferent as to whether investment opportunities were financed with debt, retained earnings, or a common stock issue. One method of financing would be as satisfactory as the next.

DIVIDENDS UNDER UNCERTAINTY

MM drop their assumption of complete certainty and consider the case of uncertainty. Despite their admission that D_1 and P_1 in Eq. (11-1) are subject to uncertainty, they conclude that dividend policy continues

---

[7]Miller and Modigliani, "Dividend Policy," p. 416.

[8]For illustrations of the arbitrage process for the dividend decision, see Wilbur G. Lewellen, *The Cost of Capital* (Belmont, Calif.: Wadsworth, 1969), pp. 54–57; and James E. Walter, *Dividend Policy and Enterprise Valuation* (Belmont, Calif.: Wadsworth, 1967), pp. 106–110.

to be irrelevant. Their conclusion is based upon the familiar arbitrage argument. Given two firms of identical business risk and the same prospective future earnings and investment policies, the market prices of the two firms must be the same if there is "symmetric market rationality."[9] Symmetric market rationality occurs when every market participant behaves rationally in preferring more wealth to less, and believes that other market participants behave in the same manner. According to MM, differences in current and future dividend policies cannot affect the market value of these two firms, for the present value of prospective dividends plus terminal value are the same. Even under uncertainty, then, MM continue to maintain that dividend policy is irrelevant, given the investment policy of the firm. Attacks upon the irrelevance doctrine have been centered on the case of uncertainty and imperfections in the markets.

ARGUMENTS FOR RELEVANCE

A number of arguments have been advanced in support of the contrary position—namely, that dividends are relevant under conditions of uncertainty.[10] In other words, the investor is not indifferent as to how the earnings stream is split between dividends and retained earnings. We shall examine these arguments under conditions of uncertainty but will keep intact MM's other assumptions—no transaction or flotation costs, the absence of taxes, and a given fixed investment policy of the firm. Later, all but the last of these assumptions will be removed when we investigate dividend policy under real-world conditions.

RESOLUTION OF UNCERTAINTY

It has been argued that the payment of current dividends resolves uncertainty in the minds of investors, and, therefore, an investor is not indifferent between dividends and capital gains. He prefers dividends. Gordon, for example, contends that uncertainty on the part of investors increases at an increasing rate with the distance in the future of prospective cash payments.[11] As a result, the discount rate, ρ_t, is said to rise

---

[9] Miller and Modigliani, "Dividend Policy," pp. 425–28.

[10] Lintner, "Dividends, Earnings, Leverage, Stock Prices and the Supply of Capital to Corporations," pp. 254–60, has classified uncertainty in several stages. *Fully idealized uncertainty* describes the situation in which information needed to formulate probability distributions of possible events is distributed uniformly among all market participants, and the probability distributions of possible events of all participants are identical. *Uncertainty with uniform information and diverse judgmental distributions*, as the name implies, recognizes that the subjective probability distributions formulated by market participants need not be identical. Finally, *generalized uncertainty* describes the situation in which both the "quality" and the "quantity" of information is not distributed uniformly. Lintner argues that only in the case of fully idealized uncertainty is dividend policy irrelevant.

[11] Myron J. Gordon, "Optimal Investment and Financing Policy," and "The Savings Investment and Valuation of a Corporation," *Review of Economics and Statistics*, 44 (February 1962), 37–51.

with the distance in the future, *t*. When a company cuts its dividend to finance investments, its near dividend is reduced, while distant dividends are increased. If the discount rate rises with the length of time in the future, the reduction in the near dividend is said to lead to a lower share price, all other things the same.

According to Gordon, investors are not indifferent between current dividends and the retention of earnings with the prospect of future dividends, capital gains, or both. They prefer the early resolution of uncertainty and are willing to pay a higher price for the stock that offers the greater current dividend, all other things held constant. This is not to say that the basic business risk of a firm's investments is affected by its dividend payout. Rather, it is contended that investors' *perception* of such riskiness, or their uncertainty, may be affected.[12]

A number of authors have taken issue with Gordon.[13] Even if current dividends are perceived as less risky than future ones, it is argued that stockholders are able to sell a portion of their shares to obtain the desired cash distribution.[14] In essence, investors are able to manufacture "homemade dividends" in the same way as they are "homemade leverage" in the case of the capital structure decision. Because "homemade" dividends supposedly are perfect substitutes for corporate dividends, the Gordon argument is said not to hold. The company is said not to be able to do something for investors that they cannot do for themselves; therefore, dividend policy is not a thing of value.

INFORMATIONAL CONTENT OF DIVIDENDS

The argument above is allied closely to the "informational content of dividends" argument. The latter argument implies that dividends have an impact on share price because they communicate information to investors about the firm's profitability. When a firm has a target payout ratio that is stable over time, and it changes this ratio, investors may believe that management is announcing a change in the expected future profitability of the firm. Accordingly, the price of the stock may react to this change in dividends.

Empirically, R. Richardson Pettit has lent support to the notion that the market does react to announcements of dividend changes—rising

[12] For amplification of this point, see Simon M. Keane, "Dividends and the Resolution of Uncertainty," *Journal of Business Finance & Accounting*, 1 (Autumn 1974), 389–93.

[13] See Michael Brennan, "A Note on Dividend Irrelevance and the Gordon Valuation Model," *Journal of Finance*, 26 (December 1971), 1115–21; Robert C. Higgins, "Dividend Policy and Increasing Discount Rates: A Clarification," *Journal of Financial and Quantitative Analysis*, 7 (June 1972), 1757–62; and Robert E. Krainer, "A Pedagogic Note on Dividend Policy," *Journal of Financial and Quantitative Analysis*, 6 (September 1971), 1147–54.

[14] Higgins, "Dividend Policy and Increasing Discount Rates."

when there is a significant increase in dividends, or payment for the first time, and falling when there is a significant decrease or omission.[15] He concluded that substantial information is conveyed by announcements of dividend changes and that these announcements convey significantly more information than earnings announcements. In another empirical study, Ross Watts finds a positive relationship between unexpected dividend changes and future earnings changes.[16] However, the relationship is weak. On the basis of this and other tests, Watts concludes that the information effect of dividends is very small—in contrast to Pettit's conclusion.

A somewhat different interpretation of the information effect is advanced by Simon M. Keane.[17] He suggests that the disclosure requirements by regulatory bodies, such as the Securities and Exchange Commission, are much greater for a company involved in a new issue of stock than they are for a company that finances with retained earnings. Because the company that pays a dividend and then issues stock must disclose more information about itself, the payment of dividends and resulting new equity issues results in less uncertainty in the minds of investors. This argument, then, is tied in with the previous one on the resolution of uncertainty.

MM do not deny the possibility of the information effect but continue to maintain that present and expected future earnings are what determine value. They assert that dividends are merely a reflection of these factors and do not in themselves determine value; therefore, the irrelevance proposition holds.[18] Thus, dividends are said to be used by investors as predictors of the firm's future performance; they convey management's expectation of the future. If subsequent observed behavior is consistent with the information conveyed previously, investors will come to rely upon dividends as predictors of what is to come.[19] However, the basic factor affecting value is not dividends but expectations of future performance.

PREFERENCE FOR CURRENT INCOME

Another aspect of the uncertainty question involves investors who have a preference for current income. Under the irrelevance proposition, MM would argue that these investors can sell stock on a periodic basis to

[15]"Dividend Announcements, Security Performance, and Capital Market Efficiency," *Journal of Finance*, 27 (December 1972), 993–1007. Pettit employs an abnormal performance measure to isolate risk-adjusted market movements and studies the 1964–68 period. See also Eugene Fama, Lawrence Fisher, Michael C. Jensen, and Richard Roll, "The Adjustment of Stock Prices to New Information," *International Economic Review* 10 (February 1969), 1–26.

[16]"The Information Content of Dividends," *Journal of Business*, 46 (April 1973), 191–211.

[17]"Dividends and the Resolution of Uncertainty," p. 392.

[18]Miller and Modigliani, "Dividend Policy," p. 428.

[19]See Walter, *Dividend Policy and Enterprise Valuation*, pp. 90–98.

obtain income. With perfect markets, the investor always could sell part of his holdings or reinvest the dividends to satisfy his desire for consumption. Over the long run, the investor should be able to obtain the same income as he would with regular dividends. However, with uncertainty, stock prices fluctuate. Certain investors may regard as unsatisfactory the alternative of selling a portion of their stock for income at fluctuating prices. As a result, they may have a definite preference for current dividends. In addition to the uncertainty of the selling price, the inconvenience of selling a small portion of stock periodically for income may be a factor. For this reason alone, certain investors might prefer current dividends to capital gains.

Brokerage fee (see p. 288)

The critical question is whether the "quality" of a dividend payment is greater than the "quality" of a capital gain. Proponents of the irrelevance proposition argue that there is no difference and, as a result, there is no systematic preference in the market as a whole for current dividends. Whereas certain investors may prefer dividends, others prefer capital gains. At the margin, the market is said to behave in a manner consistent with the irrelevance proposition. MM suggest:

> If, for example, the frequency distribution of corporate-payout ratios happened to correspond exactly with the distribution of investor preferences for payout ratios, then the existence of these preferences would clearly lead ultimately to a situation whose implications were different in no fundamental respect from the perfect market case. Each corporation would tend to attract to itself a "clientele" consisting of those preferring its particular payout ratio, but one clientele would be entirely as good as another in terms of the valuation it would imply for the firm.[20]

Essentially, the "clientele" argument is that if groups of investors have dividend preferences, corporations will adjust their dividend policies to take advantage of the situation. In equilibrium, the dividend policies of corporations will match the dividend desires of investor groups. No company would be able to affect its share price by altering its dividend policy.[21] In other words, if there were a net excess demand in the market for high-dividend-yielding stocks, corporations would recognize this excess demand and increase their payout ratios. The action of a number of companies doing this would eliminate the excess demand, thereby driving the market to equilibrium.

Thus, proponents of the irrelevance of dividends argue that the mere existence of dividend preferences by various investor clienteles

[20] Miller and Modigliani, "Dividend Policy," p. 429.

[21] See Fischer Black and Myron Scholes, "The Effects of Dividend Yield and Dividend Policy on Common Stock Prices and Returns," *Journal of Financial Economics*, 1 (May 1974), 1–5. In testing a modification of the capital-asset pricing model to include a variable to measure the deviation of a stock's dividend yield from that of the market portfolio, they find the coefficient of the variable to be insignificant. Stocks with high payout ratios did not provide returns significantly different from those with low payout ratios. The authors interpret this finding as being consistent with the idea that dividend policy does not matter.

does not negate their position. As long as the "supply" of dividends by companies matches the demand for them by investor groups, their argument will hold. However, this argument depends on corporations' having full knowledge of the demands of investors for dividends. It also depends on there being no capital market imperfections that impede the adjustment of corporate dividend payouts when the market is not in equilibrium. (For example, flotation costs on new stock issues, which we consider shortly, represent such an impediment.) Because of these factors, the case for the exact correspondence of the distribution of demand for dividends with that of supply is tenuous.

SALE OF STOCK AT A LOWER PRICE

The irrelevance doctrine also rests upon the assumption that the sale of stock by the firm to replace the dividend will be at the current price. In order to sell the stock, however, the firm must appeal to new investors or to existing stockholders to increase their holdings. With divergent investor expectations, Lintner contends that the equilibrium price of a share of stock will decline as the firm sells additional stock to replace dividends.[22] In other words, there is a downward-sloping demand curve for the stock. Those investors holding the stock believe that its value is at least as great as the prevailing price. However, investors who do not hold the stock believe that the value is less than this price. In order to entice them into buying a new issue of stock, the issuing price must be lower than the prevailing price.

Thus, "the payment of an added cash dividend . . . requires that ownership . . . be transferred to others whose expectations justify *their* holding (buying) the stock only at a lower price, so that *this* shift in finance-mix and current dividend *reduces* the (conditional) expected *aggregate* market value of the company's equity *ceteris paribus.*"[23] With underpricing, the firm will need to sell more shares to replace the dividend. This dilution is said to cause a lower discounted value per share after financing than was true in the case of our irrelevance example. Thus, a downward-sloping demand curve for new issues of stock implies a preference toward retention, as opposed to paying higher dividends.

MARKET IMPERFECTIONS

We now consider other factors that were assumed away by MM. Any attack on MM, however, must be based upon factors other than the ones

---

[22] Lintner, "Dividends, Earnings, Leverage, Stock Prices and the Supply of Capital to Corporations," pp. 256–59.
[23] Ibid., p. 258.

we take up now. Nevertheless, the market imperfections we discuss are important in evaluating the effect of dividends upon valuation in the real world.

Tax effect   When we allow for taxes, there is a variety of effects. The most important is due to capital gains being taxed at a lower rate than dividends. Moreover, the capital gains tax is deferred until the investor actually sells his stock. Thus, there is a strong bias in favor of capital gains as opposed to dividends, and this bias favors the retention of earnings.[24] Suppose a corporation pays a substantial dividend and expands by selling stock on a privileged-subscription basis to existing stockholders. These stockholders receive dividends, which are taxed at the ordinary income tax rate, and then purchase more stock. If the corporation had retained the earnings, the tax would have been avoided. The stockholder could realize value on his investment by selling some of his shares and paying only a capital gains tax. The effect of the tax differential must be qualified to take account of the growing number of tax-free institutional investors. For these investors, the tax effect would not influence their preference for dividends or capital gains.

In his extensive study of dividend-payout ratios, Brittain found that for the 1920–60 period corporate payout ratios tended to vary inversely with the differential between tax rates on ordinary income and capital gains.[25] In other words, rising tax rates tended to depress dividends. This finding is consistent with stockholders' preferring lower dividends when the differential increases, and with corporations adjusting their dividend policies to the desires of their stockholders.

Other tax laws favor current dividends over capital gains. Individuals are able to exclude the first $100 of dividend income; such income is not taxed. Presumably, this tax provision creates a preference for current dividends on the part of small investors. For corporate investors, intercompany dividends are taxed at a rate below that applicable to capital gains. Accordingly, there would be a preference for current dividends on the part of these investors. However, the two effects described here are overshadowed by the differential tax on dividends and capital gains, which, as stated earlier, creates a preference for capital gains.

---

[24] In testing the price behavior of stocks when they go ex-dividend in relation to the magnitude of dividend for a large sample of companies, Elton and Gruber found an inverse relationship between the dividend payout ratio and the implied tax bracket of marginal investors. They interpret this result as consistent with a clientele effect where investors in high tax brackets show a preference for capital gains over dividends and vice versa. Edwin J. Elton, and Martin J. Gruber, "Marginal Stockholder Tax Rates and the Clientele Effect," *Review of Economics and Statistics*, 52 (February 1970), 68–74.

[25] *Corporate Dividend Policy*, Chapter 4.

Flotation costs   The irrelevance proposition is based upon the idea that, given the investment policy of the firm, funds paid out by the firm must be replaced by funds acquired through external financing. The introduction of flotation costs favors the retention of earnings in the firm. For each dollar paid out in dividends, the firm nets less than a dollar after flotation costs per dollar of external financing. Moreover, the smaller the size of the issue, the greater in general the flotation costs as a percentage of the total amount of funds raised. In addition, stock financing is "lumpy" in the sense that small issues are difficult to sell even with high flotation costs. The fact that common stock financing is less than perfectly divisible in practice favors the retention of earnings.

**Transaction
costs and
divisibility
of securities**

Transaction costs involved in the sale of securities tend to restrict the arbitrage process in the same manner as that described for debt. The stockholder who desires current income must pay a brokerage fee on the sale of a portion of his stock if the dividend paid is not sufficient to satisfy his current desire for income. This fee varies inversely, per dollar of stock sold, with the size of the sale. For a small sale, the brokerage fee can be rather significant percentage-wise. Because of this fee, stockholders with consumption desires in excess of current dividends will prefer that the company pay additional dividends. Perfect capital markets also assume that securities are infinitely divisible. The fact that the smallest integer is one share may result in "lumpiness" with respect to selling shares for current income. This too acts as a deterrent to the sale of stock in lieu of dividends. On the other hand, the stockholder not desiring dividends for current consumption purposes will need to reinvest his dividends. Here again transaction costs and divisibility problems work to the disadvantage of the stockholder, although in the opposite direction.

Thus, transaction costs and divisibility problems cut both ways. However, there is reason to believe that in recent years the net impact of these factors has created a slight bias on the side of a preference for current dividends. Many companies now have automatic dividend reinvestment plans. These plans allow the stockholder to specify a reduction in the amount of dividends he is to receive. This reduction is then used to purchase additional shares of stock in the company.[26] The reinvestment is administered by a bank in behalf of the company and is automatic. Transaction costs are lower than what a stockholder could do on his own, and there is virtually no inconvenience involved. Because of the increasing use of automatic dividend reinvestment programs, the

---

[26] For a survey of the use of these plans, see Richard H. Pettway, and R. Phil Malone, "Automatic Dividend Reinvestment Plans for Nonfinancial Corporations," *Financial Management*, 2 (Winter 1973), 11–18.

reinvest dividends as opposed to the one who desires greater current
income. As a result, transaction costs overall may result in a net preference in the market for current dividends, all other things the same.

**Other legal
impediments**
Certain institutional investors are restricted by law
as to the types of common stock in which they can
invest. The prescribed list of eligible securities is
determined in part by the duration over which dividends have been paid.
If a company does not pay a dividend or has not paid dividends over a
sufficiently long period of time, certain institutional investors are not
able to invest in the stock. Universities, on the other hand, sometimes
have restrictions on the expenditure of capital gains from their endow-
ment. Though these two influences are small in aggregate, they work in
the direction of a preference for current income as opposed to capital
gains.

Of the market imperfections taken up in this section, the differential
tax effect on dividends and capital gains is by far the strongest. As
mentioned previously, this imperfection creates a preference for the
retention of earnings in the firm.

**OPTIMAL
DIVIDEND POLICY**

A company should endeavor to establish a dividend policy that will
maximize shareholder wealth. In theory, the optimal dividend payout
should be determined in keeping with the firm's investment opportunities and any preference that investors have for dividends as opposed to
capital gains. Insight into such a preference can best be gained through
an empirical study of the relationship between share price and dividend
payout for a sample of similar companies. The following key arguments
support the notion that investors overall have a systematic preference
for current dividends over capital gains: the desire for current income in
the form of dividends; the net impact of transaction and inconvenience
costs; and legal restrictions on institutional investors, which constrain
their investment into stocks with consistent dividend-paying records.
Even without the last two factors, many investors are likely to view the
receipt of current income from the sale of stock as unsatisfactory, owing
to the uncertainty associated with the selling price.

Offsetting these factors is the more favorable tax treatment of
capital gains relative to that of dividends. This factor, of course, creates
a preference for capital gains as opposed to current dividends. Whether
there is a net preference on the part of investors for dividends as
opposed to capital gains or vice versa is determined to a large extent by
the combined influence of the desire for current income, transaction
costs, restrictions on investors, and differential tax rates.

If there exists a net preference among investors for capital gains as

[handwritten margin note: DIVIDENDS preferred to CAPT'L GAINS]

[handwritten margin note: CAPT'L GAINS preferred to DIVIDENDS]

opposed to dividends, the firm's dividend policy would be strictly a residual decision determined by the profitability of its investment opportunities. Only if the firm had earnings remaining after financing all "acceptable" investment opportunities would it distribute dividends to stockholders. Justification for paying a dividend in excess of unused earnings requires a net preference among investors for current dividends as opposed to capital gains, and that this net preference be sufficiently strong to offset the difference in "cost" between retained earnings and new equity financing. Flotation costs and underpricing, of course, make the sale of common stock a more "expensive" form of financing than the retention of earnings. Therefore, both a net preference of investors for current dividends as opposed to capital gains as well as a sufficient magnitude of net preference are required.

ILLUSTRATION OF DIVIDEND POLICY AND INVESTMENT OPPORTUNITIES

To illustrate this concept, suppose a firm had a capital structure consisting entirely of equity and had enough acceptable investment opportunities to just exhaust its earnings.[27] Suppose further that, on the basis of an empirical test, it determined that investors had a net preference for current dividends and that share price initially could be raised by increasing the payout ratio, all other things remaining the same. This phenomenon is illustrated by the upper curve in Figure 11-1. We see that share price increases at a decreasing rate with dividend payout until eventually it turns down. This pattern is consistent with the preference for current dividends being quite important to investors when dividends are first declared. However, as more dividends are paid, it becomes less important vis-à-vis the tax disadvantage of dividends relative to capital gains. Eventually, the tax disadvantage causes the net preference line to turn down.

Any net preference for current dividends must be balanced against the difference in "cost" between financing with common stock and with retained earnings. Recall that the difference is attributable to underpricing and flotation costs. Given our assumptions, if a dividend is paid, it must be financed with common stock. If either there is a net preference for capital gains as opposed to current dividends, or there is a net preference for current dividends but this net preference does not offset

---

[27] In reality, the acceptance criterion may be affected by the dividend policy employed. However, we assume for simplicity that the last acceptable project provides a return significantly in excess of the required rate of return, while the next most profitable project provides a return significantly below the required return.

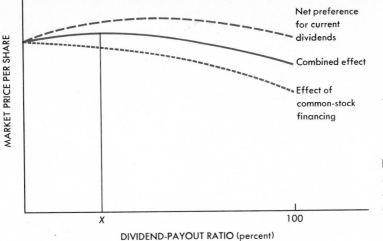

flotation costs
+ underpricing
← more expensive

FIG. 11·1
*Hypothetical relationship
between share price
and dividend payout*

the difference in "cost" between common-stock financing and financing with retained earnings, the firm in our example should pay no dividends. Suppose that, on the basis of a study, the firm determined that the relationship between share price and the payout ratio, attributable to the difference in cost between common-stock and retained earnings financing, could be depicted by the lower curve in Figure 11-1. The greater the payout ratio, of course, the greater the common-stock financing that is necessary. The line would be expected to decline because of flotation costs and underpricing, both of which cause increased dilution relative to that which would occur if stock could be sold at the current price with no flotation costs. If the amount of underpricing increases with the amount of financing, the line might decline at an increasing rate, as illustrated in the figure.

The combined influence of these two factors determines the relationship between the share price and the payout ratio, holding other things constant. The optimal dividend payout would be the one that maximized share price, point X in the figure. Thus, the optimal dividend-payout ratio is determined by balancing any net preferences of investors for current dividends as opposed to capital gains with the flotation cost and underpricing disadvantage of common-stock financing. Recall that in our example we assumed the firm had acceptable investments exactly equal to its earnings. In other words, there were no residual funds and the dividend paid came from the sale of common stock.

If the firm does not have enough attractive investment projects to utilize its entire earnings, the optimal payout ratio is affected by this factor as well. Under such circumstances, the firm should determine the portion of earnings that cannot be employed profitably in investment projects. These earnings should be earmarked for payment to stockholders in the form of dividends. The firm should then analyze, on the basis of the considerations discussed above, whether it should pay an even higher dividend than that dictated by the amount of funds left over after investment. When this has been decided, the amount of dividend and the dividend-payout ratio can be determined. In other words, the dividend paid may come from both residual earnings and the sale of common stock.

A FINAL PERSPECTIVE

In conclusion, if dividend policy is not relevant, a firm should choose its dividend policy solely in keeping with its long-run investment opportunities. At the point at which the return on investment is less than the cost of capital, the firm should stop investing and should pay the unused funds out as dividends. The growth company that expands faster than its growth in earnings would pay no dividends; whereas a firm in a shrinking industry might have a 100 percent dividend payout or even a liquidating dividend. The firm need not pay out the exact unused portion of earnings every period. Some years, the payout may be more; other years, it may be less. Indeed, the firm may want to stabilize the absolute amount of dividends paid from period to period but in such a manner that over the long run the total earnings retained, plus the senior securities the increasing equity base will support, correspond to the amount of profitable investment opportunities available. Dividend policy would still be a passive decision variable determined by the amount of investment opportunities.

For the firm to be justified in paying a dividend larger than that dictated by the amount of profitable investment opportunities, there must be a net preference of investors for current dividends as opposed to capital gains. Moreover, this net preference must more than offset the fact that owing to flotation costs and underpricing, common stock is a more expensive form of financing than is the retention of earnings. Although empirical evidence concerning the effect of dividends on the market price of a stock is far from clear in this regard, many companies appear to behave as if dividends are relevant.[28] For example, a number

---

[28] In comparing the valuation of firms that both paid dividends and engaged in new equity financing with other firms in an industry sample, James C. Van Horne and John G. McDonald, "Dividend Policy and New Equity Financing," *Journal of Finance*, 26 (May 1971), 507–19, found some support for the existence of a net preference by investors for current dividends as opposed to capital gains. Both electric utility and electronic industry samples were tested, but the evidence would have to be classified as only providing crude insight into the question.

of growth companies that expand at a rate faster than their growth in earnings pay small dividends. If these companies believed dividends were irrelevant, they would retain all their earnings. A number of other companies that pay significant dividends go to the capital markets for additional equity capital rather than retain a greater portion of earnings. Examples include public utilities and airlines. Whereas these actions do not support the idea that dividends are relevant, they do indicate that many companies behave as though they were. The dividend-payout ratio that these firms believe is optimal is greater than that dictated by investment opportunities alone.

SUMMARY

The critical question in dividend policy is whether dividends have an influence upon the value of the firm, given its investment decision. If dividends are irrelevant, as Modigliani and Miller believe, the firm should retain earnings only in keeping with its investment opportunities. If there are not sufficient investment opportunities to provide expected returns in excess of the cost of capital, the unused funds should be paid out as dividends.

The key issue is whether dividends are more than just a means of distributing unused funds. If they do affect the value of the common stock, dividend policy becomes more than a passive variable determined solely by the investment opportunities available. The firm could affect shareholder wealth by varying its dividend-payout ratio; as a result there would be an optimal dividend policy.

In this chapter, we have examined the various arguments for and against the relevance of dividends. If dividends are relevant, the net preference of investors for current dividends as opposed to capital gains must be balanced against the difference in cost between the sale of stock and the retention of earnings in determining the optimal dividend-payout ratio.

Unfortunately, empirical evidence on the relevance of dividends has been little more than suggestive. Nevertheless, we know that many companies behave as if dividends do matter and can affect shareholder wealth. In the next chapter, we extend our analysis of the dividend payout and examine other aspects of dividend policy.

PROBLEMS

1. Financial data are shown below on two companies. What differences are reflected in these data that give insight into dividend policy and valuation?

fairly stable

erratic

	Cleveland Machine Tool Company			Fox Electronics Company		
	Earnings per Share	Dividends per Share	Range P/E Ratio	Earnings per share	Dividends per Share	Range P/E Ratio
1977	$3.02	$1.50	12–18	$1.18	$0.15	25–32
1976	3.19	1.50	9–14	1.02	0.10	25–35
1975	3.10	1.25	13–18	0.81	0.10	30–40
1974	2.90	1.25	10–17	0.72	0.10	30–40
1973	1.06	1.25	13–17	0.48	0.05	35–45
1972	2.03	1.25	14–18	0.41	0.05	40–50
1971	2.87	1.25	15–23	0.29	0.05	45–55
1970	2.13	1.25	11–16	0.20	0.04	40–60
1969	1.32	1.00	8–13	0.14	0.00	30–45
1968	2.21	1.00	10–15	0.13	0.00	40–50

2. Malkor Instruments Company treats dividends as a residual decision. It expects to generate $2 million in net earnings after taxes in the coming year. The company has an all-equity capital structure and its cost of equity capital is 10 percent. The company treats this cost as the opportunity cost of retained earnings. Because of flotation costs and underpricing, the cost of common stock financing is higher; it is 11 percent.

(a) How much in dividends (out of the $2 million in earnings) should be paid if the company has $1.5 million in projects whose expected return exceeds 10 percent?

(b) How much in dividends should be paid if it has $2 million in projects whose expected return exceeds 10 percent?

(c) How much in dividends should be paid if it has $3 million in projects whose expected return exceeds 11 percent? What else should be done?

3. The Mann Company belongs to a risk class for which the appropriate capitalization rate is 10 percent. It currently has outstanding 100,000 shares selling at $100 each. The firm is contemplating the declaration of a $5 dividend at the end of the current fiscal year, which just began. Answer the following questions based on the Modigliani and Miller model and the assumption of no taxes.

(a) What will be the price of the stock at the end of the year if a dividend is not declared? What will it be if one is?

(b) Assuming that the firm pays the dividend, has net income of $1 million, and makes new investments of $2 million during the period, how many new shares must be issued?

(c) Is the MM model realistic with respect to valuation? What factors might mar its validity?

4. The Combine Corporation has 1 million shares outstanding, earns net income of $3 million, and pays dividends of $2 million. The shareholders of Combine have a 60 percent normal tax rate, a 25 percent capital

gains tax rate, and value Combine by the Graham and Dodd formula of $P = M\left(\dfrac{E}{3} + D\right)$, with a multiple ($M$) of 12.

(a) At what price does Combine sell?

(b) If all of the above data remained constant every year, what after-tax return would Combine shareholders earn?

(c) If Combine desired to raise $1 million in equity funds, show the long-run effects upon current shareholders of (1) cutting the dividend, or (2) selling stock at 90 percent of the current market price. Assume the new equity would raise earnings by $200,000.

5. The Eureka Mining Company consists of one mine, which has a remaining useful life of five years. The owners feel that no new shafts should be sunk for at least this long; indeed, they probably will not continue in this business after five years. Since the initiation of the company, total cash flows have been paid out in dividends. All of the firm's stockholders were original investors, have a marginal tax rate of 40 percent, and require an after-tax return of 10 percent. The mine will generate the following income during each of the next five years:

Net operating income	$25,000
Less: Depreciation and depletion	5,000
Net income before taxes	$20,000
Less: Taxes @ 22%	4,400
Net income	$15,600

(a) Compute the total market value of Eureka if all available funds were paid in dividends at the end of the year they became available.

(b) Compute the total market value assuming that Eureka invests its available funds at the end of each year in notes yielding 5.13 percent, which mature at the end of year 5; at the end of this time, Eureka will be liquidated.

(c) Instead of notes, assume that Eureka chooses to invest at the end of each year in 8.27 percent preferred stock, which will be redeemed at cost at the end of year 5. Compute the total market value of Eureka (still assuming liquidation at the end of year 5).

Hint: (1) 5.13% × 78% = 4%.

(2) Dividends received by corporations are 85 percent tax exempt.

SELECTED REFERENCES

Black, Fischer, and Myron Scholes, "The Effects of Dividend Yield and Dividend Policy on Common Stock Prices and Returns," *Journal of Financial Economics,* 1 (May 1974), 1–22.

Brennan, Michael, "A Note on Dividend Irrelevance and the Gordon Valuation Model," *Journal of Finance,* 26 (December 1971), 1115–23.

Brigham, Eugene F., and Myron J. Gordon, "Leverage, Dividend Policy, and the Cost of Capital," *Journal of Finance,* 23 (March 1968), 85–104.

Brittain, John A., *Corporate Dividend Policy.* Washington, D.C.: Brookings Institution, 1966.

Elton, Edwin J., and Martin J. Gruber, "Marginal Stockholder Tax Rates and the Clientele Effect," *Review of Economics and Statistics,* 52 (February 1970), 68–74.

Fama, Eugene F., "The Empirical Relationships between the Dividend and Investment Decisions of Firms," *American Economic Review,* 64 (June 1974), 304–18.

Fama, Eugene F., and Harvey Babiak, "Dividend Policy: An Empirical Analysis," *Journal of the American Statistical Association,* 63 (December 1968), 1132–61.

Friend, Irwin, and Marshall Puckett, "Dividends and Stock Prices," *American Economic Review,* 54 (September 1964), 656–82.

Gordon, Myron J., *The Investment, Financing and Valuation of the Corporation.* Homewood, Ill.: Richard D. Irwin, 1962.

———, "Optimal Investment and Financing Policy," *Journal of Finance,* 18 (May 1963), 264–72.

Higgins, Robert C., "The Corporate Dividend-Saving Decision," *Journal of Financial and Quantitative Analysis,* 7 (March 1972), 1527–41.

———, "Dividend Policy and Increasing Discount Rate: A Clarification," *Journal of Financial and Quantitative Analysis,* 7 (June 1972), 1757–62.

Keane, Simon M., "Dividends and the Resolution of Uncertainty," *Journal of Finance & Accounting,* 1 (Autumn 1974), 389–93.

Krainer, Robert E., "A Pedagogic Note on Dividend Policy," *Journal of Financial and Quantitative Analysis,* 6 (September 1971), 1147–54.

Lintner, John, "Distribution of Income of Corporations among Dividends, Retained Earnings, and Taxes." *American Economic Review,* 46 (May 1956), 97–113.

———, "Optimal Dividends and Corporate Growth under Uncertainty," *Quarterly Journal of Economics,* 88 (February 1964), 49–95.

———, "Security Prices, Risk and Maximal Gains from Diversification," *Journal of Finance,* 20 (December 1965), 587–615.

Litzenberger, Robert H., "Capital Budgeting and Dividend Decisions under Proportional Flotation Costs and Proportional Brokerage Fees," Research Paper No. 233, Stanford Graduate School of Business, 1974.

Miller, Merton H., and Franco Modigliani, "Dividend Policy, Growth, and the Valuation of Shares," *Journal of Business,* 34 (October 1961), 411–33.

———, "Some Estimates of the Cost of Capital to the Electric Utility Industry," *American Economic Review,* 56 (June 1966), 333–91.

Pettit, R. Richardson, "Dividend Announcements, Security Performance, and Capital Market Efficiency," *Journal of Finance,* 27 (December 1972), 993–1007.

Pettway, Richard H., and R. Phil Malone, "Automatic Dividend Reinvestment Plans of Nonfinancial Corporations," *Financial Management,* 2 (Winter 1973), 11–18.

Pogue, Thomas F., "A Cross-Section Study of the Relationship between Dividends and Investment," *Yale Economic Essays,* 2 (Fall 1971), 181–218.

Porterfield, James T. S., "Dividends, Dilution, and Delusion," *Harvard Business Review,* 37 (November–December 1959), 156–61.

———, *Investment Decisions and Capital Costs,* Chapter 6. Englewood Cliffs, N.J.: Prentice-Hall, 1965.

Pye Gordon, "Preferential Tax Treatment of Capital Gains, Optimal Dividend Policy, and Capital Budgeting," *Quarterly Journal of Econonomics,* 86 (May 1972), 226–42.

Stiglitz, Joseph E., "On the Irrelevance of Corporate Financial Policy," *American Economic Review,* 64 (December 1974), 851–66.

Van Horne, James C., and John G. McDonald, "Dividend Policy and New Equity Financing," *Journal of Finance,* 26 (May 1971), 507–19.

Walter, James E., "Dividend Policies and Common Stock Prices," *Journal of Finance,* 11 (March 1956), 29–41.

———, *Dividend Policy and Enterprise Valuation.* Belmont, Calif.: Wadsworth, 1967.

Watts, Ross, "The Information Content of Dividends," *Journal of Business,* 46 (April 1973), 191–211.

Whittington, G., "The Profitability of Retained Earnings," *Review of Economics and Statistics,* 54 (May 1972), 152–60.

DIVIDEND POLICY of the FIRM

Given its approximate long-run investment requirements, the firm is able to adopt a long-run dividend-payout ratio. This ratio should be determined in keeping with the objective of maximizing shareholder wealth. As discussed in the preceding chapter, its determination will depend upon the expected magnitude of acceptable investment opportunities, the perceived value to investors of dividends as opposed to capital gains, and the difference in cost between common-stock financing and the retention of earnings. Although the dividend-payout ratio is a major aspect of the dividend policy of the firm, there are other aspects that may affect valuation. In this chapter, we consider the stability of dividends, certain factors that influence the dividend-payout ratio from the standpoint of the firm, stock dividends and stock splits, the repurchase of stock, and the procedural and legal elements of dividend policy.

STABILITY OF DIVIDENDS

In addition to the percentage of dividend payout of a company over the long run, investors may value stable dividends over this period. All other things being the same, the market price of the stock of a company may be higher if it pays a stable dividend over time than if it pays out a fixed percentage of earnings. To illustrate, suppose Company *A* has a long-run dividend-payout ratio of 50 percent of earnings. Suppose further that it has the policy of paying out this percentage every year, despite the fact that its earnings are cyclical. The dividends of Company *A* are shown in Figure 12-1. Company *B*, on the other hand, has exactly the same earnings and a long-run dividend-payout ratio of 50 percent, but it maintains a relatively stable dividend over time. It changes the

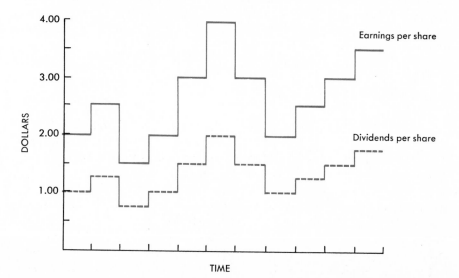

FIG. 12·1
Hypothetical dividend policy of Company **A**

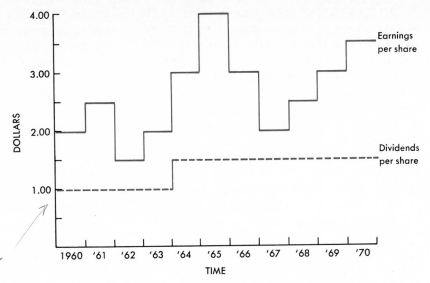

FIG. 12·2
Hypothetical dividend policy of Company **B**
(Economic Report of the President, 1975)

absolute amount of dividend only in keeping with the underlying trend of earnings. The dividends of Company *B* are shown in Figure 12-2.

Over the long run, the total amount of dividends paid by these two firms is the same. However, the market price per share of Company *B* may be higher than that of Company *A*, all other things being the same. Investors may well place a positive utility on dividend stability and pay a premium for the company that offers such stability. To the extent that investors value dividend stability, the overall dividend policy of Company *B* would be better than that of Company *A*. This policy includes not only the percentage of dividend payout in relation to earnings but also the manner in which the actual dividends are paid. Rather than vary dividends directly with changes in earnings per share, Company *B* raises the dividend only when reasonably confident a higher dividend can be maintained.

VALUATION OF STABILITY

There are several reasons why investors may value stable dividends and pay a premium for the stock of the company providing such stability. These include the informational content of dividends, the desire of investors for current income, and certain legal considerations.

Informational content   As we said in the preceding chapter, dividends may serve to resolve uncertainty in the minds of investors. When earnings drop and a company does not cut its dividend, the market's confidence in the stock may be bolstered over what it would be if the dividend were cut. The stable dividend may convey to investors management's view that the future of the company is better than the drop in earnings suggests. Thus, management may be able to influence the expectations of investors through the informational content of dividends. Management, however, cannot "fool" the market permanently. If there is a downward trend in earnings, a stable dividend will not convey forever an impression of a rosy future. Moreover, if a firm is in an unstable business with wide swings in earnings, a stable dividend cannot give the illusion of underlying stability.

Current income desires

A second factor favoring stable dividends is that investors who desire a specific periodic income will prefer a company with stable dividends to one with unstable dividends, even though both companies may have the same pattern of earnings and long-run dividend payout. Although the investor can always sell a portion of his stock for income when the dividend is not sufficient to meet his current needs, many investors have an aversion to "dipping into principal." Moreover, there are transaction and inconvenience costs. Finally, when a company reduces its dividend, earnings usually are down and the market price of the stock depressed. As a result, the investor would have to sell his stock on unfavorable terms. Overall, it would seem that income-conscious investors place a positive utility on stable dividends.

Legal considerations

Finally, a stable dividend may be advantageous from the legal standpoint of permitting certain institutional investors to invest in the stock. Various governmental bodies prepare legal lists of securities in which pension funds, savings banks, trustees, insurance companies, and others may invest. In order to qualify, a company must have an uninterrupted pattern of dividends. A cut in, or omission of, the dividend may result in the removal of a company from these legal lists.

The arguments presented in support of the notion that stable dividends have a positive effect upon the market price of the stock are only suggestive. There is little in the way of empirical evidence to shed light on the question. Although studies of individual stocks often suggest that stable dividends buffer the market price of the stock when earnings turn down, there have been no comprehensive studies of a large sample of stocks dealing with the relationship between dividend stability and valuation. Nevertheless, most companies strive for stability in their dividend payments. This occurrence is illustrated in Figure 12-3, where total corporate dividends and net earnings after taxes are shown for the post-World War II period. Overall, corporations behave in a manner that is consistent with a belief that stable dividends have a positive effect on

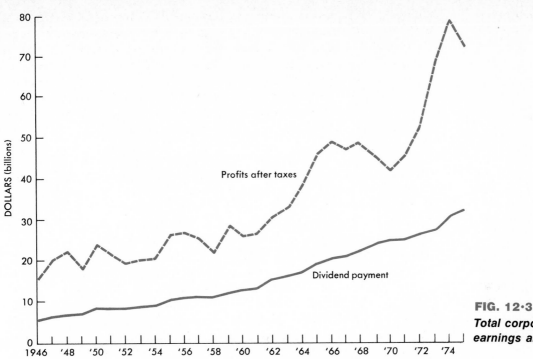

FIG. 12·3
Total corporate earnings and dividends

value. From the standpoint of public policy, dividend stability acts as a built-in stabilizer, for it tends to cushion the effect of changes in income on aggregate demand over economic cycles.[1]

TARGET PAYOUT RATIOS

It would appear that a number of companies follow the policy of a target dividend-payout ratio over the long run. Lintner contends that dividends are adjusted to changes in earnings, but only with a lag.[2] When earnings increase to a new level, dividends are increased only when it is felt that the increase in earnings can be maintained. In addition, there appears to be a definite reluctance on the part of companies to cut the absolute amount of their cash dividend. Both of these factors explain the lag in dividend changes behind changes in earnings. Given a lag relationship, retained earnings will increase relative to

[1] See John A. Brittain, *Corporate Dividend Policy* (Washington, D.C.: Brookings Institution, 1966), p. 212.
[2] See John Lintner, "Distribution of Income of Corporations," *American Economic Review*, 46 (May 1956), 97–113.

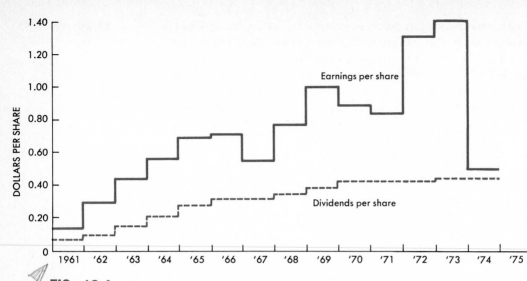

FIG. 12·4   *Coleman Company, dividends and earnings per share, 1961–1974*
(change to Lifo method of inventory valuation reduced 1974 net income by sixty cents
a share)

lagged effect

dividends in an economic upturn. In a contraction, however, retained earnings will decrease relative to dividends. Empirically, the lag of dividend changes behind changes in earnings has been verified by several investigators, using Lintner's target payout ratio model.[3]

To illustrate the use of a target payout ratio and stable dividends, consider the case of Coleman Company. This company makes outdoor recreation equipment and central heating and air-conditioning units. These lines of business are somewhat cyclical, with resulting swings in earnings. However, the company maintained stable and increasing dividends in the sixties and early seventies; it seems to raise dividends once management and the board of directors are confident that the earnings can be sustained. The dividends per share and earnings per share for the company are shown in Figure 12-4. (Note the effect of the switch to Lifo for inventory purposes—earnings per share were reduced by sixty cents in 1974.)

REGULAR AND EXTRA DIVIDENDS

One way for a company to increase its cash distribution in periods of prosperity is to declare an *extra* dividend in addition to the *regular* quarterly or semiannual dividend. By declaring an extra dividend, the

[3] See Brittain, *Corporate Dividend Policy,* Chapters 2–7; and Eugene F. Fama and Harvey Babiak, "Dividend Policy: An Empirical Analysis," *Journal of the American Statistical Association,* 63 (December 1968), 1132–61.

company attempts to prevent investors from expecting that the dividend represents an increase in the established dividend rate. The declaration of an extra dividend is particularly suitable for companies with fluctuating earnings. General Motors, for example, frequently declares extra dividends in good car years. The use of the extra dividend enables the company to maintain a stable record of regular dividends but also to distribute to stockholders some of the rewards of prosperity. By paying extra dividends only when earnings are higher than usual, the company will not lead investors to count on the increased dividends in future periods. However, a company cannot pay extra dividends continuously without conveying to the market some impression of permanency. As soon as a certain level of dividends is recurrent, investors begin to expect that level regardless of the distinction between regular and extra dividends.

So far, we have related the dividend policy of a firm to the investment opportunities of that firm, to the magnitude and stability of earnings, to the possible preference of investors for dividends relative to capital gains, and to the fact that common stock is a more expensive form of financing than is the retention of earnings. However, a number of other considerations influence a company in the dividend policy it undertakes. These considerations tend to be of a more practical nature than those discussed so far.

OTHER CONSIDERATIONS

LIQUIDITY

The liquidity of a company is an important consideration in many dividend decisions. As dividends represent a cash outflow, the greater the cash position and overall liquidity of a company, the greater its ability to pay a dividend.[4] A company that is growing and profitable may not be liquid, for its funds may go into fixed assets and permanent working capital. Because the management of such a company usually desires to maintain some liquidity cushion to give it flexibility and a protection against uncertainty, it may be reluctant to jeopardize this position in order to pay a large dividend. The liquidity of the company, of course, is determined by the firm's investment and financing decisions. The investment decision determines the rate of asset expansion and the firm's need for funds; and the financing decision determines the way in which this need will be financed.

---

[4]Brittain, *Corporate Dividend Policy*, pp. 184–87, found that for a sample of forty large firms over the 1920–60 period, dividends were related positively to corporate liquidity.

ABILITY TO BORROW

A liquid position is not the only way to provide for flexibility and thereby protect against uncertainty. If a firm has the ability to borrow on comparatively short notice, it may be relatively flexible. This ability to borrow can be in the form of a line of credit or a revolving credit from a bank, or simply the informal willingness on the part of a financial institution to extend credit. In addition, flexibility can come from the ability of a firm to go to the capital markets with a bond issue. The larger and more established a company, the better its access to the capital markets. The greater the ability of the firm to borrow, the greater its flexibility, and the greater its ability to pay a cash dividend. With ready access to debt funds, management should be less concerned with the effect that a cash dividend has upon its liquidity.

CONTROL

If a company pays substantial dividends, it may need to raise capital at a later time through the sale of stock in order to finance profitable investment opportunities. Under such circumstances, the controlling interest of the company may be diluted if controlling stockholders do not or cannot subscribe for additional shares. These stockholders may prefer a low dividend payout and the financing of investment needs with retained earnings.

Control can work two ways, however. In the case of a company being sought by another company or by individuals, a low dividend payout may work to the advantage of the "outsiders" seeking control. The outsiders may be able to convince stockholders that the company is not maximizing shareholder wealth and that they (the outsiders) can do a better job. Consequently, companies in danger of being acquired may establish a high dividend payout in order to please stockholders.

NATURE OF STOCKHOLDERS

When a firm is closely held, management usually knows the dividend desires of its stockholders and may act accordingly. If most stockholders are in high tax brackets and prefer capital gains to current income, the firm can establish a low dividend payout. The low payout, of course, would be predicated upon having profitable investment opportunities in which to employ the retained earnings. The corporation with a large number of stockholders does not know the dividend desires of its stockholders. It can judge these desires only in a market context.

A company may have profitable investment opportunities, but these opportunities may occur too sporadically for the company to be justified in retaining earnings. For example, a firm may know that it will need to build a major extension on its existing plant in about six years. If it retains earnings to finance this plant expansion, the funds will not be used for some period of time. During this period, the company will invest the funds in short-term securities yielding less than the required rate of return on retained earnings. However, shareholder wealth might be better maximized by paying out the intermediate earnings as dividends and raising the capital six years later with a stock issue. The sale of stock is a more desirable means than retained earnings by which to raise a large block of capital at one time.

RESTRICTIONS IN BOND INDENTURE OR LOAN AGREEMENT

The protective convenants in a bond indenture or loan agreement often include a restriction on payment of dividends.[5] This restriction is employed by the lender(s) to preserve the company's ability to service debt. Usually, it is expressed as a maximum percentage of cumulative earnings. When such a restriction is in force, it naturally influences the dividend policy of the firm. There are times when the management of a company welcomes a dividend restriction imposed by lenders because it does not then have to justify to stockholders the retention of earnings. It need only point to the restriction.

INFLATION

Inflation also may have an influence upon dividend policy. With rising prices, funds generated from depreciation are not sufficient to replace and/or restore existing assets as they wear out or become obsolete.[6] Consequently, a case can be made for retaining earnings simply to preserve the earning power of the firm.[7] This decision must be based upon considerations taken up in the preceding chapter concerning investment policy and valuation.

[5] For a more detailed examination of these restrictions, see Chapter 18.

[6] See James C. Van Horne and William F. Glassmire, Jr., "The Impact of Unanticipated Changes in Inflation on the Value of Common Stocks," *Journal of Finance*, 27 (December 1972), 1081–92.

[7] *Economic depreciation* is defined as the amount of investment needed to keep the earning power of an asset the same. This amount may differ significantly from *accounting depreciation*. See Eugene M. Lerner and Willard T. Carleton. *A Theory of Financial Analysis* (New York: Harcourt, Brace & Jovanovich, 1966), Chapter 4.

In this section, we discuss stock dividends and stock splits. In an economic sense, the two are very similar, although typically they are used for different purposes. Only from an accounting standpoint is there a significant difference.

STOCK DIVIDENDS

A stock dividend simply is the payment of additional stock to stockholders. It represents nothing more than a recapitalization of the company; a stockholder's proportional ownership remains unchanged. To illustrate, suppose a company had the following capital structure before issuing a stock dividend:

Common stock ($5 par, 400,000 shares)	$ 2,000,000
Capital surplus	1,000,000
Retained earnings	7,000,000
Net worth	$10,000,000

Now, suppose the company pays a 5 percent stock dividend, amounting to 20,000 additional shares of stock, and that the fair market value of the stock is $40 a share. For each twenty shares of stock owned, the stockholder receives an additional share. The balance sheet of the company after the stock dividend would be

Common stock ($5 par, 420,000 shares)	$ 2,100,000
Capital surplus	1,700,000
Retained earnings	6,200,000
Net worth	$10,000,000

With a stock dividend, $800,000, ($40 × 20,000 shares), is transferred from retained earnings to the common stock and capital surplus accounts. Because the par value stays the same, the increase in number of shares is reflected in a $100,000 increase in the common stock account ($5 par × 20,000 shares). The residual of $700,000 goes into the capital surplus account. The net worth of the company remains the same.

Because the number of shares of stock outstanding is increased by 5 percent, earnings per share of the company are reduced proportionately. Suppose that total net profit after taxes were $1 million. Before the stock dividend, earnings per share would be $2.50, ($1 million/400,000). After the stock dividend, earnings per share are $2.38, ($1 million/420,000). Thus, the stockholder has more shares of stock but lower earnings per share. His proportion of total earnings available to common stockholders remains unchanged.

**Value to
investor**   If the company pays no cash dividend, what does
the stockholder receive with a stock dividend? In
theory, he receives nothing but an additional stock
certificate. His proportionate ownership of the company is unchanged.
Presumably, the market price of the stock will drop, all other things
being equal, so that the total market value of his holdings stays the same.
For example, if he held 100 shares of stock previously, and market price
per share were $40, the total value of his holdings would be $4,000.
After the stock dividend, the price of the stock should drop by
$40(1 − 1.00/1.05), or by $1.90. The total value of his holdings then would
be $38.10 × 105, or $4,000. Under these conditions, the stock dividend
does not represent a thing of value to the stockholder. He simply has an
additional stock certificate evidencing ownership.

$$\left(\text{MKT Price}\right)\left(1 - \frac{\text{old hldgs}}{\text{new}}\right)$$

$$40\left(1 - \frac{100}{105}\right) = 1.90$$

$$38.10 \times 105 = 4000$$

To the extent that the investor wishes to sell a few shares of stock for
income, the stock dividend may make it easier for him to do so. Without
the stock dividend, of course, he could also sell a few shares of his
original holdings for income. In either case, the sale of stock represents
the sale of principal and is subject to the capital gains tax. However, it
is probable that certain investors do not look upon the sale of a stock
dividend as a sale of principal. To them, the stock dividend represents a
windfall gain; they can sell it and still retain their original holdings. The
stock dividend may have a favorable psychological effect on these
stockholders.

The stock dividend can also be a thing of value to the investor if the
company maintains the same cash dividend per share after the stock
dividend as before. Suppose an investor owns 100 shares of a company
paying a $1 dividend and that the company declares a 10 percent stock
dividend and, at the same time, announces that the cash dividend per
share will remain unchanged. The investor then will have 110 shares;
and total cash dividends will be $110 rather than $100, as before. In this
case, a stock dividend increases his total cash dividends. Whether this
increase in cash dividend has a positive effect upon shareholder wealth[8]
will depend upon the tradeoff between current dividends and retained
earnings, which we discussed in the last chapter. Clearly, the stock
dividend in this case represents a decision by the firm to increase
modestly the amount of cash dividends.

Use of the stock dividend per se may convey some information.
Stock dividends typically are associated with growth companies. Under
these circumstances, the dividend may connote to investors that man-

---

[8] In an extensive study of the effect of stock dividends on market value, Barker concluded
that the stock dividend was beneficial only when the cash dividend was increased. C.
Austin Barker, "Evaluation of Stock Dividends," *Harvard Business Review*, 36 (July 1958),
99–114. Unfortunately, Barker's study suffers from his not holding other factors constant in
his comparisons.

agement expects earnings to continue to grow and to more than offset the dilution in earnings per share arising from the increase in the total number of shares. The underlying effect on value is growth, however, and not the stock dividend itself.

Advantages and disadvantages   Frequently, a stock dividend is employed to "conserve cash." Instead of increasing the cash dividend as earnings rise, a company may desire to retain a greater portion of its earnings and declare a stock dividend. The decision then is to lower the dividend-payout ratio, for as earnings rise and total cash dividends remain the same, the payout ratio will decline. Whether shareholder wealth is increased by this action will depend upon considerations taken up in the preceding chapter. The decision to retain a higher proportion of earnings, of course, could be accomplished without a stock dividend. However, the stock dividend may tend to please certain investors by virtue of its informational content as well as its psychological impact. In addition, if the cash dividend per share is kept the same, total cash dividends will increase slowly in keeping with the increase in the number of shares.

In the discussion of advantages so far, the decision to issue a stock dividend has been based upon the availability of profitable investment opportunities. The percentage of cash dividend payout was reduced in order to finance a portion of these opportunities with retained earnings. Certain companies, however, have employed the stock dividend as a means of replacing the cash dividend because of financial difficulty. In these situations, the stock dividend should not connote the prospect of favorable earnings, but financial deterioration, and it should be so evaluated. It is doubtful whether many investors are fooled by the substitution.

The use of a stock dividend by a firm may also serve to keep the market price of the stock within a popular trading range. Certain companies do not like to see the market price of their stocks above a certain amount—say $60 a share—because a high price will not appeal to small investors. Consequently, they will endeavor to keep the price below a desired ceiling either by using stock dividends or, more commonly, by means of stock splits. Increasing the total number of shares outstanding may increase the total number of stockholders, resulting in a greater overall popularity of the stock.

The principal disadvantage of stock dividends to the firm is that they are much more costly to administer than cash dividends. Another disadvantage is that small periodic stock dividends, perhaps 2 or 3 percent, may tend to distort downward the company's perceived growth in earnings. Whereas investment analysts adjust earnings per share for stock splits and significant stock dividends, many do not do so for small stock dividends. If earnings per share are not adjusted, the measured growth in earnings per share will be less than the true increase in earnings for the investor who held his stock over the period measured.

STOCK SPLITS

With a stock split, the number of shares are increased through a proportional reduction in the par value of the stock. Suppose that the capital structure of a company before a two-to-one stock split were

Common stock ($5 par, 400,000 shares)	$ 2,000,000
Capital surplus	1,000,000
Retained earnings	7,000,000
Net worth	$10,000,000

After the split, the capital structure is

Common stock ($2.50 par, 800,000 shares)	$ 2,000,000
Capital surplus	1,000,000
Retained earnings	7,000,000
Net worth	$10,000,000

With a stock dividend, the par value is not reduced; whereas with a split, it is. As a result, the common stock, capital surplus, and retained earnings accounts remain unchanged. The net worth, of course, also stays the same; the only change is in the par value of the stock. Except in accounting treatment, the stock dividend and stock split are very similar. A stock split, however, is usually reserved for occasions when a company wishes to achieve a substantial reduction in the market price per share. The principal purpose of a split is to place the stock in a more popular trading range. The stock of a super-growth company can rather quickly sell in excess of several hundred dollars a share unless it is split periodically and the total number of shares increased accordingly.

As was true of the stock dividend, the stock split does not represent a thing of value to the investor. He has more shares than before, but his proportional ownership of the company remains unchanged. The market price of the stock should decline proportionately, so that the total value of his holdings stays the same. Again, however, the split may have a favorable informational content. The announcement of the split may indicate to investors that management believes that earnings will continue to grow. As a result, the market price per share may increase upon the announcement of the split, or the rumor of an announcement, and remain higher.[9] However, the underlying cause for the increase in market price is growth and not the split itself.

Very seldom will a company maintain the same cash dividends per share after a split as it did before. However, it may increase the effective dividends to stockholders. For example, suppose a company splits its stock two for one and establishes a dividend rate of $1.20 a share, whereas before the rate was $2.00 a share. A stockholder owning 100 shares before the split would receive $200 in cash dividends per annum. After the split, he would own 200 shares and would receive $240 in dividends. The market price of the stock (on an after-split basis) may react favorably to the increase in cash dividends.

Reverse split Rather than increasing the number of shares of stock outstanding, a company may want to reduce the number. This reduction can be accomplished with a *reverse split*. In our example above, suppose that there were a one-to-four reverse split, instead of the two-to-one straight stock split. For each four shares held, the stockholder would receive one share in exchange. The par value per share would become $20, and there would be 100,000 shares outstanding rather than 400,000. Reverse stock splits are employed to increase the market price per share when the stock is considered to be selling at too low a price. Many companies have an aversion to seeing the price of their stock fall below $10 per share. If, due to financial difficulty or other reasons, the price should fall into this range, the market price per share can be increased with a reverse split. The reverse split is regarded by many as an admission by a company that it is in financial difficulty. However, financial difficulty is not always the reason for the split, and the stock market's reaction to it depends primarily upon the company's past and expected future earnings.[10]

REPURCHASE OF STOCK

In recent years, the repurchase of stock has become increasingly popular. A number of large companies have turned to it. There are several reasons for its popularity. Some companies repurchase stock in

---

[9] This occurrence is supported by the empirical work of Keith B. Johnson, "Stock Splits and Price Change," *Journal of Finance*, 21 (December 1966), 675–86. In testing the same data, however, W. H. Hausman, R. R. West, and J. A. Largay, "Stock Splits, Price Changes, and Trading Profits: A Synthesis," *Journal of Business*, 45 (January 1971), 69–77, concluded that the superior price performance of stocks that split occurred prior to the announcement of the split. Their results indicated that buying a stock on the announcement of the split does not lead to price appreciation greater than the appreciation expected by underlying valuation effects. This finding is similar to that of Eugene F. Fama, Lawrence Fisher, Michael Jensen, and Richard Roll, "The Adjustment of Stock Prices to New Information," *International Economic Review*, 10 (February 1969), 1–22, who tested the 1927–59 period.

[10] See Richard R. West and Alan B. Brouilette, "Reverse Stock Splits," *Financial Executive*, 38 (January 1970), 12–17.

order to have it available for stock options. In this way, the total number of shares is not increased with the exercise of the options. Another reason for repurchase is to have shares available for the acquisition of other companies. In other situations, however, stock is repurchased with the full intention of retiring it. Under these circumstances, repurchase of stock may be treated as a substitute for dividends.

REPURCHASING AS PART OF
A DIVIDEND DECISION

If a firm has excess cash and insufficient profitable investment opportunities to justify the use of these funds, it may be in the shareholders' best interests to distribute the funds. The distribution can be accomplished either by the repurchase of stock or by paying the funds out in increased dividends. In the absence of personal income taxes and transaction costs, it should make no difference theoretically to stockholders, which of the two alternatives is chosen. With repurchase, fewer shares remain outstanding, and earnings per share rise. As a result, the market price per share should rise as well. In theory, the capital gain arising from repurchase should equal exactly the dividend that otherwise would have been paid.

To illustrate, suppose that a company has the following earnings and market price per share:

Net profit after taxes	$2,000,000
Number of shares outstanding	500,000
Earnings per share	$4.00
Market price per share, ex-dividend	$60.00
Price/earnings ratio	15

Suppose further that the company is considering the distribution of $1.5 million, either in cash dividends or in the repurchase of its own stock. If investors are expecting the cash dividend, the value of a share of stock before the dividend is paid will be $63—that is, $3 a share in expected dividends ($1.5 million/500,000) plus the $60 market price. Suppose, however, that the firm chooses to repurchase its stock and makes a tender offer to stockholders at $63 a share. It then will be able to repurchase $1.5 million/$63, or 23,810 shares. Earnings per share will be

$$EPS = \$2,000,000/476,190 = \$4.20$$

If the price/earnings ratio stays at 15, the total market price per share will be $63 ($4.20 × 15), the same total value as under the dividend alternative. Thus, the amount of distribution to stockholders is $3 per share, whether dividends or repurchase of stock (and subsequent capital gain) is used. If stockholders are indifferent between dividends and capital gains, the value of the stock is not influenced by the way the funds are returned to stockholders. We have seen in the preceding chapter, however, that this indifference is open to question. If investors have a systematic preference either for current dividends or for capital gains, the value of the firm may be affected by the method of distribution.

The benefit arising from the repurchase of stock is that the total number of shares is reduced so that earnings per share (and dividends per share if a constant dividend-payout ratio is maintained) are increased. If the price/earnings ratio remains unchanged, the market price of the stock will increase.

In our example, the equilibrium repurchase price to offer was $63 a share. If a lower price were offered, stockholders who sold their shares would suffer a decrease in wealth relative to those who retained their stock. A higher price would result in a redistribution of wealth in favor of those who sold their shares. The equilibrium price the firm should offer in a repurchase is[11]

$$P^* = P_x + \frac{D}{S} \tag{12-1}$$

where P_x = market price per share on an ex-dividend basis

D = aggregate amount the firm wishes to distribute

S = number of shares outstanding prior to the distribution

With a differential tax rate on dividends and capital gains, however, repurchase of stock offers a considerable tax advantage over payment of dividends. The market-price increase resulting from a repurchase of stock is subject to the capital gains tax; whereas dividends are taxed at the higher ordinary income tax rate. It is important to recognize that if an investor manufactures a "homemade" dividend by selling off sufficient stock to match the cash dividend that otherwise would have been paid, the proceeds realized are not entirely subject to the capital gains tax. Only the excess of the price realized over original cost is subject to taxation. Capital gains arising from the repurchase are not taxed on the remainder of the investor's holdings until such stock is actually sold. In essence, the bulk of the capital gains tax is postponed. For tax reasons, then, the investor is better off financially if the firm elects to distribute unused funds via the stock repurchase route than through cash dividends.[12]

[11] See Edwin Elton and Martin Gruber, "The Effect of Share Repurchases on the Value of the Firm," *Journal of Finance*, 23 (March 1968), 136–37.

[12] If existing stockholders are equivalent with respect to tax treatment, their wealth is enhanced by an amount equal to the difference between the marginal income tax rate and marginal capital gains tax rate, times the aggregate amount of cash the firm wishes to distribute (ibid., pp. 138–39). Elton and Gruber go on to explore modifications of this amount due to the postponement and incidence of the capital gains tax, and to various types of costs associated with paying a dividend and undertaking a repurchase. With the heterogeneous tax treatment of stockholders, the preferred method of distribution will depend upon the composition of stockholders.

The repurchase of stock is particularly advantageous when the firm has a large amount of unused funds to distribute. To pay the funds out through an extra dividend would result in a substantial tax to stockholders. The tax effect could be alleviated somewhat by paying the funds out as extra dividends over a period of time, but this action might result in investors' counting on the extra dividend. The firm must be careful not to undertake a steady program of repurchase in lieu of paying dividends. The Internal Revenue Service is likely to regard such a program as an attempt to allow stockholders to avoid the payment of taxes on dividends; accordingly, it may impose a penalty.[13] Hence, it is important that the repurchase of stock be somewhat of a "one-shot" nature and not be used as a substitute for regular dividends or even for recurring extra dividends.

INVESTMENT OR FINANCING DECISION?

Some regard the repurchase of stock as an investment decision instead of a dividend decision. Indeed, in a strict sense, it is. However, stock held in the treasury does not provide an expected return as other investments do. No company can exist by investing only in its own stock. The decision to repurchase should involve distribution of unused funds when the firm's investment opportunities are not sufficiently attractive to employ those funds, either now or in the foreseeable future. Therefore, the repurchase of stock cannot be treated as an investment decision as we define the term.

Repurchase may be regarded as a financing decision, however, provided its purpose is to alter the capital structure proportions of the firm. By issuing debt and repurchasing stock, a firm can immediately change its debt-to-equity ratio toward a greater proportion of debt. In this case, the repurchase of stock is a financing decision, because the alternative is to not pay out dividends.[14] Only when there is excess cash can the repurchase of stock be treated as a dividend decision.

METHOD OF REPURCHASE

The two most common methods of repurchase are through a tender offer and through the purchase of stock in the marketplace. With a tender offer, the company makes a formal offer to stockholders to

[13] See Harold Bierman, Jr., and Richard West, "The Acquisition of Common Stock by the Corporate Issuer," *Journal of Finance*, 21 (December 1966), 687–96.

[14] Results of an empirical study by Allan Young, "Financial, Operating and Security Market Parameters of Repurchasing," *Financial Analysts Journal*, 25 (July–August 1969), 124, suggest that a number of companies use stock repurchase to effect major capitalization changes. Overall, however, Young's results are consistent with the fact that repurchasing companies have less favorable operating performances than nonrepurchasing companies, which in turn is consistent with a lack of investment opportunities. Thus, the evidence is consistent with stock repurchase for most companies being a dividend decision.

purchase so many shares, typically at a set price. This bid price is above the current market price; stockholders can elect either to sell their stock at the specified price or to continue to hold it. In open-market purchases, a company buys its stock through a brokerage house in the same manner as does any other investor. If the repurchase program is gradual, its effect is to put steady upward pressure on the market price per share. This upward pressure, of course, is of benefit to stockholders. In general, the transaction costs to the firm in making a tender offer are much higher than those incurred in the purchase of stock in the open market.

Before the company repurchases stock, it is important that stockholders be informed of the company's intentions. In a tender offer, these intentions are announced by the offer itself. Even here, however, it is important that the company not withhold other information. For example, it would be unethical for a mining company to withhold information of a substantial ore discovery while making a tender offer to repurchase shares.

In open-market purchases, it is expecially important to disclose the company's repurchase intentions. Otherwise, stockholders may sell their stock not knowing that a repurchase program is under way that will increase earnings per share. Given full information about the amount of repurchase and the objective of the company, the stockholder can sell his stock if he so chooses. Without proper disclosure, the selling stockholder may well be penalized.[15] When the amount of stock repurchased is substantial, a tender offer is particularly suitable, for it gives all stockholders equal treatment.

PROCEDURAL AND LEGAL ASPECTS

DECLARATION OF DIVIDENDS

When the board of directors of a corporation declares a cash dividend, it specifies a *date of record*. Holders of record on that date are entitled to the dividend declared. After the date of record, the stock is said to trade *ex-dividend*, for investors that purchase it are not entitled to receive the declared dividend. Theoretically, the market price of the stock should decline by the amount of the dividend when the stock goes ex-dividend. Because other factors influence the market price of the stock, this effect is sometimes difficult to measure. Once a dividend is declared, stockholders become creditors of the company until the dividend is actually paid; the declared but unpaid dividend is a current liability of the company.

---

[15] For a discussion of the ethics surrounding repurchase, see Richard Stevenson, "Corporate Stock Reacquisitions," *Accounting Review*, 41 (April 1966), 312–17.

Although the legal restrictions we discuss below are unimportant in most dividend decisions, some companies are affected by them. We have already considered one type of legal restriction—namely, the restriction on dividends imposed in a bond indenture or loan agreement. Other legal restrictions have to do with capital impairment, insolvency, and excess accumulation of cash.

Capital restriction
Although state laws vary considerably, most states prohibit the payment of dividends if these dividends impair capital. *Capital* is defined in some states as the par value of the common stock. For example, if a firm had one million shares outstanding with a $2 par value, total capital would be $2 million. If the net worth of a company were $2.1 million, the company could not pay a cash dividend totaling $200,000 without impairing capital.

Other states define capital to include not only the par value of the common stock but also the capital surplus. Under such statutes, dividends can be paid only out of retained earnings. The purpose of the capital impairment laws is to protect creditors of a corporation. For a relatively new corporation, these laws may afford creditors a degree of protection. However, for established companies that have been profitable in the past and have built up retained earnings, substantial losses will usually have been incurred before the restriction has an effect. By this time, the situation may be sufficiently hopeless that the restriction gives creditors little protection.

Insolvency
Some states prohibit the payment of cash dividends if the company is insolvent. *Insolvency* is defined either in a legal sense, as liabilities exceeding assets, or in a technical sense, as the firm's being unable to pay its creditors as obligations come due. Because the ability of the firm to pay its obligations is dependent upon its liquidity rather than upon its capital, the technical insolvency restriction gives creditors a good deal of protection. When cash is limited, a company is restricted from favoring stockholders to the detriment of creditors.

Excess accumulation of cash
The Internal Revenue Code prohibits the undue retention of earnings. Although *undue retention* is defined vaguely, it usually is thought to be retention significantly in excess of the present and future investment needs of the company. The purpose of the law is to prevent companies from retaining earnings for the sake of avoiding taxes. For example, a company might retain all its earnings and build up a substantial cash and marketable-securities position. The entire company

then could be sold, and stockholders would be subject only to a capital gains tax. If the excess earnings were distributed as dividends, the dividends would be taxed as ordinary income. If the IRS can prove unjustified retention, it can impose penalty tax rates on the accumulation. Whenever a company does build up a substantial liquid position, it has to be sure that it can justify the retention of these funds to the IRS. Otherwise, it may be in order to pay the excess funds out to stockholders as dividends.

SUMMARY

The stability of dividends is felt by many to have a positive effect upon the market price of the stock. Stable dividends may tend to resolve uncertainty in the minds of investors, particularly when earnings per share drop. They also may have a positive utility to investors interested in current periodic income. Many companies appear to follow the policy of a target dividend-payout ratio, increasing dividends only when it is felt that an increase in earnings can be sustained. The use of an extra dividend permits a cyclical company to maintain a stable record of regular dividends while paying additional dividends whenever earnings are unusually high.

Other considerations that affect the cash-dividend policy of the firm include the liquidity of the company; its ability to borrow; the desire to maintain control; the nature of the company's stockholders; the timing of investment opportunities; dividend restrictions in a bond indenture or loan agreement; and the impact of inflation on the replacement of assets.

A stock dividend represents the payment of additional stock to stockholders. It is used frequently as a means to conserve cash and to reduce the cash dividend-payout ratio of the firm. Theoretically, the stock dividend does not represent a thing of value to the stockholder unless cash dividends per share remain unchanged or are increased. However, stock dividends may have informational content with respect to earnings and may serve to keep the market price per share in a popular trading range. A much more effective device for reducing market price per share is a stock split. With a split, the number of shares is increased by the terms of the split—for example, a three-to-one split means that the number of shares is tripled.

A company's repurchase of its own stock should be treated as a dividend decision when the firm has funds in excess of present and foreseeable future investment needs. It may distribute these funds either by dividends or by the repurchase of stock. In the absence of a tax differential between dividends and capital gains, the monetary value of the two alternatives should be about the same. With the tax differential, there is a considerable tax advantage to the repurchase of stock. Because of objections by the Internal Revenue Service, however, repurchase of stock cannot be used in lieu of regular dividends. Repurchases can be accomplished either with a tender offer or through purchases in the open market. In either case, the repurchase intentions of the company should be made clear to stockholders.

Finally, we discussed in this chapter the procedure by which dividends are declared and various legal aspects that upon occasion may influence the dividend policy of the firm.

1.

The Sherill Corporation capital structure Dec. 30, 19X1

Common stock ($1 par, 1,000,000 shares)	$1,000,000
Excess over par*	300,000
Retained earnings	1,700,000
Net worth	$3,000,000

*Also called capital surplus.

The firm earned $300,000 after taxes in 19X1, and paid out 50 percent of this in cash dividends. The price of the firm's stock on Dec. 30 was $5.

(a) If the firm declared a stock dividend of 3 percent on Dec. 31, what would the reformulated capital structure be?

(b) If the firm declared a 50 percent stock dividend rather than the 3 percent dividend, what would the reformulated capital structure be? (*Hint:* In the case of a large stock dividend [over 25 percent], the reformulated capital structure should be calculated on a book value, and not a market value, basis.)

(c) Assuming the firm paid no stock dividend, how much would earnings per share for 19X1 be? How much would dividends per share be?

(d) Assuming a 3 percent stock dividend, what would EPS and DPS be for 19X1? Assuming a 50 percent stock dividend?

(e) What would the price of the stock be after the 3 percent dividend? After the 50 percent dividend?

2.

Zoppo Manufacturers capital structure Dec. 30, 19X1

Common stock ($100 par, 300,000 shares)	$ 30,000,000
Excess over par	15,000,000
Retained earnings	55,000,000
Net worth	$100,000,000

On Dec. 31, Zoppo split the stock 2-for-1 and then declared a 10 percent stock dividend. The price of the stock on Dec. 30 was $500. Reformulate the capital structure of the firm.

3. The Sampson Company is owned by several wealthy New York businessmen, all of whom are in the 70 percent marginal income tax bracket. The firm earned $3,500,000 after taxes this year. With one million shares outstanding, earnings per share were thus $3.50. The stock has recently traded at $72 per share, among the current shareholders. Two dollars of this value is accounted for by investor anticipation of a cash dividend. As financial manager of Sampson, you have contemplated the alternative of repurchasing the company stock by means of a tender offer at $72 per share.

   (a) How much stock could the firm repurchase if this alternative were selected?

   (b) Ignoring taxes, which alternative should be selected?

   (c) Considering taxes, which alternative should be selected?

   (d) What might preclude the firm from choosing the preferred alternative?

4. The Axalt Corporation and the Baxalt Corporation have had remarkably similar earnings patterns over the last five years. In fact, both firms have had identical earnings per share. Further, both firms are in the same industry, produce the same product, and face the same business and financial risks. In short, these firms are carbon copies of each other in every respect but one: Axalt pays out a constant percentage of its earnings (50 percent) in dividends, while Baxalt has paid a constant cash dividend. The financial manager of the Axalt Corporation has been puzzled, however, by the fact that the price of his firm's stock has been generally lower than the price of Baxalt's stock, even though in some years Axalt's dividend was substantially larger than Baxalt's.

   (a) What might account for this condition?

   (b) What might be done by both companies to increase the market prices of their stock?

	Axalt			Baxalt		
Year	EPS	Div.	Mkt. Price	EPS	Div.	Mkt. Price
19X1	$1.00	.50	$6	$1.00	.23	$4⅞
19X2	.50	.25	4	.50	.23	4⅜
19X3	− .25	nil	2	− .25	.23	4
19X4	.30	.15	3	.30	.23	4¼
19X5	.50	.25	3½	.50	.23	4½

5. The Xavier Cement Company has hired you as a financial consultant to advise the company with respect to its dividend policy. The cement industry has been very stable for some time, and the firm's stock has not appreciated significantly in market value for several years. However,

the rapidly growing southwestern market provides an excellent opportunity for this old, traditionally midwestern cement manufacturer to undertake a vigorous expansion program into a new market area. To do so, the company has decided to sell common stock for equity capital in the near future. The company expects its entrance into the southwestern market to be extremely profitable—returning approximately 25 percent on investment each year. Below you will find data on earnings, dividends, and common-stock prices.

	19X1	19X2	19X3	19X4	Anticipated 19X5
Earn./share	$ 4.32	$ 4.17	$ 4.61	$ 4.80	$ 4.75
Cash avail./share	$ 6.00	$ 5.90	$ 6.25	$ 6.35	$ 6.25
Dividend/share	$ 2.90	$ 2.80	$ 3.00	$ 3.20	?
Payout ratio	67%	67%	65%	67%	?
Avg. market price	$60.00	$58.00	$60.00	$67.00	$66.00
P/E ratio	14/1	14/1	13/1	14/1	14/1

What dividend policy recommendations would you make to the company? Specifically, what payout would you recommend for 19X5? Justify your position.

6. The Davis Company, a large manufacturing concern, is a rapidly growing corporation. It has consistently earned over 20 percent on its investment in assets, and prospects for the future appear to be equally good. In the past, the company has retained about 30 percent of its earnings, paying out 70 percent in dividends. The firm's management has justified this payout policy on two grounds: (1) that a company exists for purposes of paying dividends to stockholders, and (2) that the dividends paid by the company have a favorable effect on the price of the company's stock.

   (a) Evaluate the management's justification of its dividend policy in light of the fact that most of the firm's stockholders are middle-aged businessmen in rather high marginal income tax brackets.

   (b) What other factors would you, as a financial manager, take into consideration in deciding the appropriate dividend policy in addition to those considered by the Davis management?

SELECTED REFERENCES

Bierman, Harold Jr., and Richard West, "The Acquisition of Common Stock by the Corporate Issuer," *Journal of Finance,* 21 (December 1966), 687–96.

Brittain, John A., *Corporate Dividend Policy,* Washington, D.C.: Brookings Institution, 1966.

Ellis Charles D., "New Framework for Analyzing Capital Structure," *Financial Executive,* 37 (April 1969), 75–86.

Elton, Edwin J., and Martin J. Gruber, "The Cost of Retained Earnings—Implications of Share Repurchase," *Industrial Management Review,* 9 (Spring 1968), 87–104.

———, The Effect of Share Repurchases on the Value of the Firm," *Journal of Finance,* 23 (March 1968), 135–50.

———, "Marginal Stockholder Tax Rates and the Clientele Effect," *Review of Economics and Statistics,* 52 (February 1970), 68–74.

Fama, Eugene F., and Harvey Babiak, "Dividend Policy: An Empirical Analysis," *Journal of the American Statistical Association,* 63 (December 1968), 1132–61.

Fama, Eugene F., Lawrence Fisher, Michael Jensen, and Richard Roll, "The Adjustment of Stock Prices to New Information," *International Economic Review,* 10 (February 1969), 1–21.

Griffin, Paul A., "Published Earnings, Dividend Announcements and Analysts' Forecasts," *Journal of Finance,* 31 (May 1976).

Hausman, W. H., R. R. West, and J. A. Largay, "Stock Splits, Price Changes, and Trading Profits: A Synthesis," *Journal of Business,* 45 (January 1971), 69–77.

Johnson, Keith B., "Stock Splits and Price Changes," *Journal of Finance,* 21 (December 1966), 675–86.

Lintner, John, "Distribution of Income of Corporations," *American Economic Review,* 46 (May 1956), 97–113.

Millar, James A., and Bruce D. Fielitz, "Stock Splits, Stock Dividends and Share Price: Some Empirical Evidence," Paper presented at the Finance Management Association Meetings, San Antonio, October 1972.

Stevenson, Richard, "Corporate Stock Reacquisitions," *Accounting Review,* 41 (April 1966), 312–17.

Stewart, Samuel S., Jr., "Should a Corporation Repurchase Its Own Stock?" *Journal of Finance,* forthcoming.

West, Richard R., and Harold Bierman, Jr., "Corporate Dividend Policy and Preemptive Security Issues," *Journal of Business,* 42 (January 1968), 71–75.

West, Richard R., and Alan B. Brouilette, "Reverse Stock Splits," *Financial Executive,* 38 (January 1970), 12–17.

MANAGEMENT
of LIQUIDITY
and
CURRENT ASSETS

WORKING-CAPITAL MANAGEMENT and EFFICIENT MARKET CONSIDERATIONS

In Parts I through III, we considered the valuation of the firm under varying assumptions as to the perfection of capital markets. While the discussion involved investment in assets and financing in general, the implied focus was on fixed assets and long-term financing. By tradition perhaps more than anything else, a split has evolved between consideration of current assets–short-term financing and fixed assets–long-term financing. *Current assets*, by accounting definition, are assets normally converted into cash within one year. Working-capital management is usually described as involving the administration of these assets— namely, cash and marketable securities, receivables, and inventories— and the administration of current liabilities. Administration of *fixed assets* (assets normally not converted into cash within the year), on the other hand, is usually considered to fall within the realm of capital budgeting, whereas administration of long-term financing involves capital structure considerations.

In our view, this split is unfortunate, for it has tended to cloud the valuation of the firm as a whole. There is no question but that from the standpoint of the day-to-day operations of the typical financial manager, the management of current assets and liabilities occupies the bulk of his attention. Unfortunately, this repetitive concentration has tended to result in a myopic approach to such management. Most of the work dealing with working-capital management has been confined to the left-hand side of the balance sheet, where it has been directed to optimizing the levels of cash and marketable securities, of receivables, and of inventories.[1] For the most part, the optimization process is in isolation of the optimization of other current assets and of the overall valuation of the firm.

On the asset side, the separation in treatment of current and fixed assets is often justified on the basis of differences in their nature. Fixed assets are said to be "lumpy" in the sense that they involve the commitment of funds to a specific asset over an extended period of time, during which the asset is thought to have limited marketability. In contrast, current assets are often viewed as a continuum of possible investment levels as opposed to investment in a specific form or type of liquid asset, receivable, or inventory. While this distinction has some validity, we feel it has been exaggerated and has resulted in an isolation of current-asset decisions from fixed-asset decisions and from the overall valuation of the firm. On the liability side, much less distinction exists in theory as well as in practice between current and long-term liabilities. Here the important variable is maturity, and the breakdown between current and long-term liabilities is arbitrary.

Conceptually, it does not make sense to divorce the various components of working-capital management from the more fundamental

---

[1] For an excellent compilation of articles dealing with the subject, see Keith V. Smith, *Management of Working Capital* (New York: West Publishing, 1974).

decisions of investment and financing. In practice, however, we must recognize that many firms do separate working-capital management from other aspects of financial management. In recent years, there have evolved some highly sophisticated models for cash, receivables, and inventory management. Here the benefits associated with a particular level of current asset are balanced against the risk-adjusted cost of maintaining it. While these models provide efficient decision rules, virtually all of them optimize in a partial equilibrium sense. It is clear that what is needed is an understanding of current-asset and liability decisions in light of the overall valuation of the firm.

In this chapter, we endeavor to present this conceptual understanding. In this regard, we categorize the various components of working-capital management according to the avenues by which they impact valuation. These categories are liquidity, receivables and inventories, and current liabilities. As the chapter unfolds, we will see that decisions reached in these areas determine the amount of working capital the firm maintains. However, the latter emerges as a by-product; it does not represent an active decision in itself. The discussion in this chapter is purposely general so as to provide a conceptual overview for judging working-capital decisions in relation to the valuation of the firm. Hopefully, this overview will give a better perspective for decisions involving specific current assets and liabilities, which we examine in the remaining chapters of this part and the next.

LIQUIDITY AND ITS ROLE

Liquidity may be defined as the ability to realize value in money, the most liquid of assets. It has two dimensions: (1) the time necessary to convert an asset into money; and (2) the degree of certainty associated with the conversion ratio, or price, realized for the asset. While most assets have a degree of liquidity, we will focus on the most liquid assets of the firm—cash and marketable securities. Liquidity management, then, involves determining the total amount of these two types of assets the firm will hold.[2] Implied is that we hold constant the credit policies and procedures of the firm, its inventory management and control, and the administration of its fixed assets, for decisions here affect the overall liquidity of the firm. Thus, a narrow definition of liquidity is taken in order to simplify our discussion of certain principles.

LIQUIDITY WHEN PERFECT CAPITAL MARKETS EXIST

Recall from Parts I through III that under the assumptions of perfect capital markets, a firm could not alter its value by varying its capital structure, its dividend policy, and the diversification of the assets

---

[2] The split between the two types of assets is taken up in the subsequent chapter.

it holds. If we invoke these assumptions again, the degree of liquidity of the firm also would be a matter of indifference to equityholders. Presumably, investors would manage their portfolios of common stocks and other assets, as well as their liabilities, in such a way as to satisfy their utility for liquidity. As a result, the liquidity of individual firms would not be a factor enhancing shareholder wealth. In essence, the argument is that the firm is unable to do something for investors that they cannot do for themselves. The same argument applies to the irrelevance of capital structure decisions (where investors are able to undertake "homemade" leverage by borrowing on their own), of dividend decisions (where investors are able to manufacture "homemade" dividends by selling a portion of their holdings), and of diversification of asset decisions (where investors are able to diversify on their own).

Implied in the assumptions of perfect capital markets is that if the firm should become technically insolvent,[3] and unable to pay its bills, creditors are able to step in instantaneously and realize value either by liquidating assets or by running the company themselves. If the assets are sold, assumed is that they are employed productively without delay or inefficiency in other areas of the economy. When we allow for the costs of bankruptcy, a market imperfection, liquidity may become a desirable characteristic affecting value. Recall from our earlier discussion of bankruptcy costs in Chapter 9 that there are two dimensions to such costs. The first is the "shortfall" arising from the liquidation of assets at "distress" prices below their economic values. The second is the out-of-pocket fees paid to lawyers, trustees in bankruptcy, referees, receivers, liquidators, and so forth. Embodied in the "shortfall" phenomenon is the fact that considerable delays are involved in bankruptcy proceedings during which time the firm and its value can continue to deteriorate. With respect to out-of-pocket costs, certain studies show that administrative costs approximate 20 percent of the estate.[4] Although the documentation of bankruptcy costs is sketchy, there appear to be a number of inefficiencies in bankruptcy proceedings which make administrative costs high.

LIQUIDITY MANAGEMENT WITH BANKRUPTCY COSTS

In effect, bankruptcy costs represent a drain in the system to suppliers of capital. This drain obviously works to the disadvantage of equityholders, who have a residual claim on assets in liquidation. More-

---

[3] *Technical insolvency* occurs whenever a firm is unable to meet its cash obligations. It differs from *insolvency* in a legal sense, which is defined as the point at which the assets of the firm are less than its liabilities, and, as a result, it has a negative net worth. See James E. Walter, "Determination of Technical Insolvency," *Journal of Business*, 30 (January 1957), 30–43.

[4] See, for example, David T. Stanley and Marjorie Girth, *Bankruptcy: Problem, Process, Reform* (Washington, D.C.: Brookings Institution, 1971).

over, creditors may pass on all or part of the ex ante costs of bankruptcy in the form of higher interest rates on loans than would be the case in the absence of such costs. This obviously also works to the disadvantage of equityholders. Investors are unable to diversify away the costs of bankruptcy. However, the firm can reduce the probability of bankruptcy by maintaining liquidity.

This reduction may benefit stockholders, particularly if by avoiding bankruptcy and its associated costs in one period through maintaining liquidity, future states are likely to prevail where bankruptcy does not occur. Under these circumstances, bankruptcy costs could be avoided altogether, and considerable benefits would accrue to stockholders as residual owners of the firm. Thus, the firm may be able to do something for stockholders that they cannot do for themselves. If bankruptcy is merely postponed, bankruptcy costs will eventually be incurred. Whether or not stockholders benefit in this case depends on the circumstances, but it is clear that if they do benefit it will be to a much lesser degree than in the previous case.

As liquidity is increased, the probability of technical insolvency can be reduced. The benefits associated with this reduction will depend on the magnitude of bankruptcy costs avoided. To illustrate with a simple example, suppose we have a two-period model. Assume the initial probabilities of insolvency and the bankruptcy costs shown in the upper panel of Table 13-1. Let us suppose further that if insolvency occurs, creditors will initiate bankruptcy proceedings and liquidate the company. As a result, bankruptcy costs will be incurred. We assume then that

Table 13·1   Illustration of bankruptcy costs

	Period 1			Period 2	
State	**Probability**	**Present Value of Bankruptcy Costs**	**State**	**Probability**	**Present Value of Bankruptcy Costs**
Zero Liquidity					
Insolvency	.2	$1,000			
Insolvency	.2	$500			
Solvency	.6	0	Insolvency	.1	$500
			Solvency	.9	0
$20,000 Liquidity					
Insolvency	.1	$750			
Solvency	.9	0	Insolvency	.1	$1,000
			Insolvency	.2	$500
			Solvency	.7	0
$40,000 Liquidity					
Insolvency	.1	$750			
Solvency	.9	0	Insolvency	.2	$700
			Solvency	.8	0

where R_k = required rate of return for investment project k

$\quad i$ = risk-free rate

$\quad R_m$ = expected rate of return on the market portfolio

$\quad \sigma_m$ = standard deviation of the probability distribution of possible returns for the market portfolio

$\quad \sigma_k$ = standard deviation of the probability distribution of possible returns for project k

$\quad r_{km}$ = correlation between rates of return for proposal k and the market portfolio

The term $(r_{km}\sigma_k\sigma_m)$ is the covariance of returns for project k with those of the market portfolio, whereas $(R_m - i)/\sigma_m^2$ represents the market equilibrium relationship between excess returns and risk. As we know from before, Eq. (13-4) can be expressed as

$$R_k = i + (R_m - i)\beta_k \qquad \text{(13-5)}$$

where β_k is a measure of the responsiveness of excess market returns on the project to excess returns on the market portfolio. This term is known as the beta of the asset, and it portrays the degree of systematic risk. According to the capital-asset pricing model, the relevant risk of an investment project is its systematic risk. This is the risk that the investor in the firm's stock cannot avoid through efficient diversification of the securities he holds.

The reader is referred to Chapter 7 for an illustration of how this approach may be used in practice. Our purpose here is to suggest that the same principles that hold for the valuation of fixed assets hold for the valuation of receivables and inventories. According to the assumptions embodied in the capital-asset pricing model, an investment project should have the same required rate of return regardless of the particular firm that undertakes it. This is illustrated in Figure 13-1, where the market-determined relationship between expected return and systematic risk is shown by the diagonal line. For a level of systematic risk equal to, say, y, the required return is found by tracing up to the diagonal line and then over to the vertical axis to point x. Thus, the project requires an expected return of x or greater in order for it to be acceptable. Just because a particular project has the same required rate of return for all firms does not mean that it is equally valuable to all of them. Due to expertise and operating efficiencies, some firms will be able to generate greater profitability from the project than will other firms.

Projects that are comprised entirely of receivables, or of inventories, can be evaluated using this approach. An example of the former is a decision of whether or not to lower credit standards, where the latter might involve a decision to stock a greater number of parts. The advantage of the approach is that it allows consideration of projects with

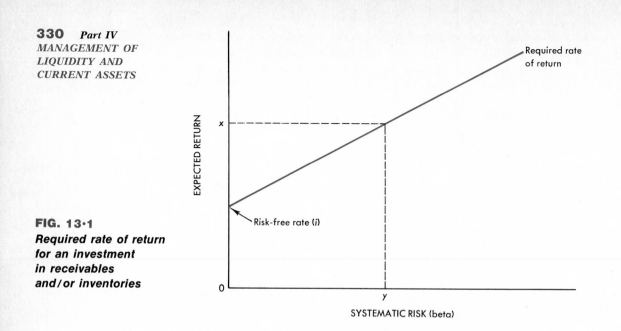

FIG. 13·1
*Required rate of return
for an investment
in receivables
and/or inventories*

greatly different risks. A separate required rate of return is determined for each project, and this return is based on the systematic risk of the project in a market context. The lower the risk, the lower the required rate of return.

This is particularly important when it comes to projects comprised heavily of receivables and/or inventories. As these assets frequently are less risky than fixed assets, they would require a lower return. The virtue of the approach is in specifying a required rate of return low enough to take account of the project's inherent safety.

THE EFFECT OF IMPERFECTIONS

In Chapter 7, we contrasted the evaluation of risky investments in a capital-asset pricing model context relative to a firm-risk context. In this regard, we suggested that to the extent the assumptions associated with perfect capital markets do not hold in practice, residual risk, or the risk that cannot be diversified away by the investor, becomes important. When market imperfections, such as bankruptcy costs, exist, rational investors become concerned with the total risk of the firm, not just its systematic risk. Total risk, of course, is comprised of both systematic and residual risk. We then suggested the use of dual investment hurdle rates—the required return in a capital-asset pricing model context and the required return in a total firm-risk context. The more the real-world conditions involved approximate those of perfect capital markets, the greater the reliance that would be placed on the capital-asset pricing model approach; whereas the greater the imperfections that can be identified, the greater the reliance that would be placed on the total firm-risk approach.

In general, we might expect to find fewer imperfections involved in connection with a receivable investment than we would in connection with an inventory and/or a fixed-asset investment, and in certain cases fewer imperfections involved in connection with an inventory investment than in connection with a fixed-asset investment. Receivables are a financial asset rather than a real asset. In general, fewer imperfections are evident in financial markets than in product markets. If financial markets were perfect, the firm could not expect to earn an excess return on the investment in receivables. That is, it could not expect to earn a return above the required return line in Figure 13-1. Under these circumstances, it would make no difference whether receivables were held as an investment or sold in the market.[7] Only with imperfections in financial markets can excess returns above the required return be earned by the firm on its investment in receivables.

In contrast to receivables, inventories represent a real asset, the same as fixed assets. However, there is reason to believe that there may be somewhat fewer imperfections in the product market for inventories than in that for fixed assets. Obviously, there are a number of exceptions to this statement, but inventories are portable and have other characteristics that give rise to fewer imperfections. The important thing to be gleaned from this discussion is that if a case can be made for the use of the capital-asset pricing model approach for evaluating fixed assets, an equally strong if not stronger case can be made for its use with receivables and inventories. In other words, the imperfections that drive one in the direction of placing greater reliance on the evaluation of risky investments in a firm-risk context are likely to be less in the case of receivables and inventories.

While one may want to use both the capital-asset pricing model approach and the firm-risk approach to evaluating investments in receivables and/or inventories, the hurdle rate derived in the former case takes on considerable importance. It is the economic justification for setting a required rate of return for a particular type of asset which is lower than that of the firm as a whole. Decisions reached over time on investment projects of which receivables and inventories are a part will determine, of course, the level of investment in these two assets. We turn now to the liability side of the balance sheet and examine the last facet of what has been "characterized" working-capital management.

---

[7]See John J. Pringle and Richard A. Cohn, "Steps toward an Integration of Corporate Financial Planning," in Keith V. Smith, *Management of Working Capital* (New York: West Publishing, 1974), pp. 369–75.

For purposes of analysis we assume that the firm has an established policy with respect to payment for purchases, labor, taxes, and other expenses. As a result, payables and accruals represent passive decision variables; they change in keeping with changes in the level of production or service offered and, in the case of taxes payable, with a change in income before taxes. In a sense, this component of current liabilities represents built-in financing; it tends to rise as the firm expands and fall as the firm contracts.

In contrast, the other component of current liabilities, which we call the active component, should be determined as part of more basic decisions involving determination of the maturity composition and other conditions of the firm's debt. By other conditions, we mean such things as whether or not the debt is secured, the type of security, the type of call feature, and whether or not it is convertible. Determination of the total amount of debt the firm should maintain was taken up in Chapters 9 and 10, when we examined the capital structure of the firm. Our concern now is with the type of debt that should be used.

THE VALUE IMPLICATIONS OF DEBT MATURITY AND OTHER CONDITIONS

If perfect financial markets are assumed, not only is the debt-versus-equity question irrelevant, but so are the maturity and other conditions of the debt. Under this assumption, all of the firm's financial liabilities would have the same cost on a certainty-equivalent basis.[8] This statement follows from our previous discussion of arbitrage in efficient financial markets. As the argument is a familiar one by this time, we need not repeat it. If imperfections exist in financial markets, however, different financial liabilities may have different certainty-equivalent costs. Such imperfections as taxes, transaction costs, flotation costs, bankruptcy costs, costs of information, and legal constraints on investing by certain institutions may make the maturity and other conditions of a firm's debt relevant considerations when it comes to their impact on value. While we would not expect the impact of market imperfections here to be as important as they are for the question of debt-versus-equity, nonetheless some effect may exist which causes different financial liabilities to have somewhat different certainty-equivalent costs.

Unfortunately, the differential impact of various financial liabilities has not received nearly the attention in the literature as has the debt-versus-equity question. There has been a reasonable amount of research on the call feature and some on the maturity structure of corporate debt.[9] While most of this work supports the notion of efficient markets,

---

[8] See Pringle and Cohn, "Steps toward an Integration," for a discussion of this point.

[9] See Chapter 21 for a review of the work on the call feature, and Chapter 17 for a discussion of maturity.

the empirical tests involved are not precise enough to pick out the subtle effects of market imperfections. About the only conclusion one can reach is that if imperfections make these factors (maturity and call feature) a thing of value, the impact is slight. There has been virtually no work on the effect of different types of secured positions on the value of debt. With bankruptcy costs, we would expect in theory at least that variations in the type of secured position would have an effect on the debt's value. The same principle would apply to the various protective covenants included in the loan agreement or bond indenture. These covenants give the lender greater flexibility to effect changes should the borrower's financial condition deteriorate.[10]

Clearly, much more work needs to be done on the subject. In this book, we allow for the possibility that differences in maturity and other conditions *may* result in differences, albeit slight, in the certainty-equivalent costs to a company of the various debt instruments available. We assume, therefore, that these factors may be relevant considerations when it comes to structuring the financial liabilities of the firm. To assume otherwise would negate the need to examine the features of various financial instruments. In Part V, we explore the various real-world conditions associated with short- and intermediate-term debt in the hope of obtaining a better understanding of their valuation implications.

The important thing to realize in closing this section is that the amount of current liabilities the firm maintains is the result of more fundamental decisions concerning the maturity composition of its debt. Any debt with a maturity of one year or less, by accounting definition, is a current liability. However, the active component of current liabilities should not be determined in isolation, but rather as part of an overall determination of the best combination of financial liabilities for the firm. The amount of debt that falls into current liabilities is incidental.

IMPLICATIONS FOR WORKING CAPITAL

In the preceding sections of this chapter, we have presented a conceptual overview for reaching decisions concerning cash and marketable securities, receivables, inventories, and current liabilities. This overview was in keeping with an objective of maximizing the overall value of the firm. Once decisions are reached concerning these areas, the level of working capital, by definition, is also determined. However, the latter is not determined in any active decision sense, but rather falls out as a residual from the decisions made above.

Thus, working capital—current assets less current liabilities—has no economic meaning in the sense of implying some type of normative

[10] For a discussion of the various protective covenants, see Chapter 18. See also James C. Van Horne, "Optimal Initiation of Bankruptcy Proceedings by Debt Holders," *Journal of Finance*, 31 (June 1976).

behavior. According to this line of reasoning, it is largely an accounting artifact. Working-capital management, then, is a misnomer; the working capital of the firm is not managed. Instead, the term is used to describe a category of management decisions affecting specific types of current assets and current liabilities. In turn, those decisions should be rooted in the overall valuation of the firm.

SUMMARY

In this chapter, we took up the valuation of the firm as it pertains in particular to the current assets and liabilities of the firm. We argued that in theory it does not make sense to separate decisions involving specific current assets and liabilities from the overall investment and financing decisions of the firm. Thus, the distinction between current and fixed assets and between current and long-term liabilities is largely an accounting one. In practice, however, there are some characteristics associated with current assets that differentiate them somewhat from fixed assets, and these were explored.

The various components of working capital were categorized along functional lines and analyzed in keeping with the valuation of the firm in a market context. These components were liquidity, receivables and inventories, and current liabilities. We saw that theoretical justification for maintaining liquidity rests on the presence of bankruptcy costs. Given these costs, liquidity management can be a thing of value. Receivables and inventories can be evaluated in much the same manner as fixed assets by using the capital-asset pricing model. The advantage of this approach is that it allows determination of a required rate of return in keeping with the inherent safety, or lack thereof, of receivables and inventories. We also explored the degree of imperfections in the markets for these two assets and the implications for the use of the capital-asset pricing model approach.

The last area of concern was the current liabilities of the firm. The amount of current liabilities the firm maintains falls out as a by-product of fundamental decisions involving capital structure, and the maturity and other conditions of the debt. We then touched on the degree of imperfections in the market for financial liabilities and the implications of such imperfections. Once decisions are reached in these three areas, the level of working capital of the firm emerges as a residual.

In the subsequent chapters of Part IV, we explore the cash and marketable securities, receivables, and inventories of the firm in more detail. The analysis will purposely be partial equilibrium in nature, since most of the analytical work to date has been in this vein and managerial decisions are framed in this manner. However, the conceptual overview presented in this chapter will transcend our discussion. Hopefully, it will provide the reader with the ability to transform, or link, the decision-making problems presented in the subsequent chapters to their valuation underpinnings.

1. The Andersen Corporation has a sales level of $280,000 with a 10 percent net profit margin before interest and taxes. To generate this sales volume, the firm maintains a fixed-asset investment of $100,000. Currently, the firm maintains $50,000 in current assets.

    (a) Determine the asset turnover for the firm. Compute the rate of return on assets.

    (b) What would be the rate of return if management assumed a more conservative attitude and increased current assets by $50,000?

    (c) What would be the rate of return if management assumed a less conservative attitude and decreased current assets by $25,000?

    (d) Appraise the significance of increases and decreases in the level of current assets.

2. The Amos Company has determined that the distribution of expected net cash flows (available to meet current liabilities) for the next three months is approximately normal with a mean of $500,000 and a standard deviation of $350,000. The firm now earns 16 percent on its investment in nonliquid assets; by investing in marketable securities, it could earn only 4 percent. It has been estimated that lengthening the maturity of the firm's outstanding debt ($6 million) could reduce the outflow of cash in the following manner:

Added Length of Maturity	Reduced Cash Outflow
One year	$250,000
Two years	375,000
Three years	450,000
Four years	500,000
Five years	535,715
Six years	562,500
Seven years	583,333

    Lengthening the maturity by five years or less would cost the company an additional 1 percent annually, while lengthening it by six or seven years would result in a 2 percent annual increase in interest costs.

    (a) Assuming that the management of the Amos Company is willing to tolerate a 5 percent probability of running out of cash, by how much should it increase its liquid assets (or decrease cash outflows)?

    (b) There are three alternatives that will reduce the probability of running out of cash to 5 percent:

    (1) Increase liquid assets
    (2) Lengthen maturity of debt
    (3) A combination of (1) and (2)
    Which alternative is best from the standpoint of management?

3. The George T. Booker Company is considering increasing its inventory investment in glass fibers by $200,000 in order to give customers better service. It has found in the past that the sale of such fibers closely parallels the Gross National Product. On the basis of this observation, Mr. Booker, the company's president, feels that the underlying risk of

the inventory investment is "about that of a typical stock listed on the New York Stock Exchange."

At present the rate on Treasury bills is 5 percent, and in recent years the average return on Standard & Poor's 500-stock index has been 10 percent. The Booker Company has an all-equity capital structure and intends to finance all new investment proposals entirely with equity.

(a) On the basis of this information, what is the required rate of return on the investment?

(b) On what does this required return depend? Is it a realistic acceptance criterion to employ?

SELECTED REFERENCES

Archer, Stephen H., "A Model for the Determination of Firm Cash Balances," *Journal of Financial and Quantitative Analysis,* 1 (March 1966). 1–11.

Bierman, H., K. Chopra, and J. Thomas, "Ruin Considerations: Optimal Working Capital and Capital Structure," *Journal of Financial and Quantitative Analysis,* 10 (March 1975), 119–28.

Bildersee, John S., "Working Capital, Risk, Growth and Diversification" Working Paper No. 8-74, Rodney L. White Center for Financial Research, University of Pennsylvania, 1974.

Budin, Morris, and Robert J. Van Handel, "A Rule-of-Thumb Theory of Cash Holdings by Firm," *Journal of Financial and Quantitiative Analysis,* 10 (March 1975), 85–108.

Chervany, Norman L., "A Simulation Analysis of Causal Relationships within the Cash Flow Process," *Journal of Financial and Quantitative Analysis,* 5 (December 1970), 445–68.

Cossaboom, Roger A., "Let's Reassess the Profitability-Liquidity Tradeoff," *Financial Executive,* 39 (May 1971), 46–51.

Glautier, M.W.E., "Towards a Reformulation of the Theory of Working Capital," *Journal of Business Finance,* 3 (Spring 1971), 37–42.

Knight, W. D., "Working Capital Management—Satisficing versus Optimization," *Financial Management.* 1 (Spring 1972), 33–40.

Mehta, Dileep R., *Working Capital Management.* Englewood Cliffs, N.J.: Prentice-Hall, 1974.

Merville, L. J., and L. A. Tavis, "Optimal Working Capital Policies: A Chance-Constrained Programming Approach," *Journal of Financial and Quantitative Analysis,* 8 (January 1973), 47–60.

———,"A Total Real Asset Planning System," *Journal of Financial and Quantitative Analysis,* 9 (January 1974), 107–15.

Smith, Keith V., *Management of Working Capital.* New York: West Publishing, 1974.

Stancill, James McN., *The Management of Working Capital.* Scranton, Pa.: Intext, 1971.

Tinsley, P. A., "Capital Structure, Precautionary Balances, and Valuation of the Firm: The Problem of Financial Risk," *Journal of Financial and Quantitative Analysis,* 5 (March 1970), 33–62.

Van Horne, James C., "A Risk-Return Analysis of a Firm's Working-Capital Position," *Engineering Economist,* 14 (Winter 1969), 71–89.

Walker, Ernest W., "Towards a Theory of Working Capital," *Engineering Economist,* 9 (January–February 1964), 21–35.

Walter, James E., "Determination of Technical Solvency," *Journal of Business,* 30 (January 1957), 30–43.

MANAGEMENT
of CASH
and MARKETABLE
SECURITIES

Our concern in the preceding chapter was with the valuation implications for liquidity, receivables and inventories, and current liabilities. In this and the subsequent two chapters, we examine the firm's investment in specific current assets. Our purpose is to investigate ways in which these assets can be managed efficiently so as to contribute to the overall objective of the firm. This chapter is devoted to cash management and the investment of excess funds in marketable securities. In the last two decades, we have witnessed ever-increasing sophistication in cash management by corporations. The trend has been toward reducing cash—the firm's most liquid asset—to a minimum; the funds released are invested in earning assets. This trend can be attributed to rising interest rates on securities, which make the opportunity cost of holding cash more expensive, to innovations in cash management, and to economies of scale in cash management as corporations grow larger.

Keynes has identified three motives for holding cash: the transactions motive, the precautionary motive, and the speculative motive.[1] The transactions motive is the need for cash to meet payments arising in the ordinary course of business. These payments include such things as purchases, labor, taxes, and dividends. The precautionary motive for holding cash has to do with maintaining a cushion or buffer to meet unexpected contingencies. The more predictable the cash flows of the business, the less precautionary balances that are needed. Ready borrowing power to meet emergency cash drains also reduces the need for this type of balance. It is important to point out that not all of the firm's transactions and precautionary balances need be held in cash; indeed, a portion may be held in marketable securities—near-money assets.

The speculative motive relates to the holding of cash in order to take advantage of expected changes in security prices. When interest rates are expected to rise and security prices to fall, this motive would suggest that the firm should hold cash until the rise in interest rates ceases. When interest rates are expected to fall, cash may be invested in securities; the firm will benefit by any subsequent fall in interest rates and rise in security prices. For the most part, companies do not hold cash for the purpose of taking advantage of expected changes in interest rates. Consequently, we concentrate only upon the transactions and precautionary motives of the firm, with these balances held both in cash and in marketable securities.

CASH MANAGEMENT

In this section, we analyze various collection and disbursement methods by which a firm can improve its cash management efficiency. These methods constitute two sides of the same coin; they exercise a

---

[1] John Maynard Keynes, *The General Theory of Employment, Interest, and Money* (New York: Harcourt, Brace & Jovanovich, 1936), pp. 170–74.

joint impact on the overall efficiency of cash management. We consider first the acceleration of collections, or reducing the delay between the time a customer pays his bill and the time the check is collected and becomes usable funds for the firm. A number of methods have been employed to speed up this collection process and maximize available cash. These methods are designed to do one or all of the following: (1) speed the mailing time of payments from customers to the firm; (2) reduce the time during which payments received by the firm remain uncollected funds; and (3) speed the movement of funds to disbursement banks.

CONCENTRATION BANKING

Concentration banking is a means of accelerating the flow of funds of a firm by establishing strategic collection centers. Instead of a single collection center located at the company headquarters, multiple collection centers are established. The purpose is to shorten the period between the time a customer mails in his payment and the time when the company has the use of the funds. Customers in a particular geographic area are instructed to remit their payments to a collection center in that area. The selection of the collection centers usually is based upon the geographic areas served and the volume of billings in a given area. When payments are received, they are deposited in the collection center's local bank. Surplus funds are then transferred from these local bank accounts to a concentration bank or banks. A bank of concentration is one with which the company has a major account—usually a disbursement account. For example, a company headquartered in New York City might have but one concentration bank, a New York bank. Concentration banking is one way to reduce the size of the float, the difference between the amount of deposit and the amount of usable funds in a bank. A company usually cannot withdraw a deposit until the bank actually collects the checks. Until collected, the deposited checks represent float.[2]

"*Float*"

[2] Checks deposited with a bank usually are processed for collection by that bank through the Federal Reserve System, through a correspondent bank, or through a clearing-house system of a group of banks in a particular city. A check becomes collected funds when it is presented to the drawee bank and actually paid by that bank. In order to streamline the availability of credit, however, the Federal Reserve has established a schedule specifying the availability of credit for all checks deposited with it for collection. This schedule is based upon the average time required for a check deposited with a specific Federal Reserve bank to be collected in a particular geographic area of the country. The maximum period for which credit is deferred is two business days. This means that a check deposited with a Federal Reserve bank for collection at a distant point would become available credit for the depositing bank two days later. Correspondent banks frequently set up deferment schedules based upon the Federal Reserve schedule. From the standpoint of a company, the length of the float depends upon the time it takes the bank to obtain available credit on checks processed for collection. In turn, this time will depend upon where the drawee banks are located.

An illustration To illustrate concentration banking and the transfer of funds, we examine the case of an actual large company with over twenty collection centers. At the time of the study, each collection center billed customers in its area and made daily deposits in its local bank of payments received from customers. On the average, the checks deposited in a bank were collected in one and one-fourth days. In other words, the company had use of the funds one and one-fourth days after deposit. In each of its local banks, the company maintained sufficient collected balances to compensate the bank for the costs of servicing the account.

A daily *wire transfer* arrangement was used to transfer collected balances in excess of compensating balances to one of several concentration banks. The managers of the collection centers initiated the transfer on the basis of a daily report of estimated collected balances from their local banks. Because the wire transfers were made through the Federal Reserve System, the funds transferred became available immediately at the concentration banks.

This method of transfer differs from a *depository transfer check* arrangement for the movement of funds, whereby a depository check is drawn on the local bank, payable to a concentration bank. Funds are not immediately available at the concentration bank, for the check must be collected through the usual channels. Whereas a transfer check costs only about $0.10 to process, it is not as fast as a wire transfer, which costs about $1.50. The delay must be analyzed in relation to the difference in cost. For small transfers, a wire transfer is too costly compared with a depository transfer check and should not be used. The earnings possible on investing the released funds simply do not cover the differential in cost.[3]

The advantage of a system of decentralized billings and collections over a centralized system is twofold. (Recall that we compare a system of multiple collection centers with a single collection center located at company headquarters.)

1. The time required for mailing is reduced. Because the collection center bills customers in its area, these customers usually receive their bills earlier than if the bills were mailed from the head office. In turn, when customers pay their bills, the mailing time to the nearest collection center is shorter than the time required for the typical remittance to go to the head office. The company estimated that there was a saving of approximately one day in mailing time from the customer to the company.

2. The time required to collect checks is reduced, because remittances deposited in the collection center's local bank usually are drawn on banks in that general area. The company estimated that the average

[3] See Frederick W. Searby, "Use Your Hidden Cash Resources," *Harvard Business Review*, 46 (March–April 1968), 74–75.

collection period would be two and one-fourth days if all remittances were deposited in the company's head office bank, compared with one and one-fourth days under the present system. At the margin, then, the company was able to speed up the collection of customer checks by one day.

Thus, the company was able to accelerate overall collections by two days; one day was gained by reducing the mailing time and one day by reducing the time during which deposited checks remain uncollected. At the time of the study, average daily remittances by customers were $2.1 million. By saving two days in the collection process, approximately $4.2 million in funds were released for investment elsewhere. With a high level of interest rates, it is not difficult to see the opportunity cost of tying up funds. However, profits from the investment of the released funds must be compared with any additional costs of a decentralized system over a centralized one. Also, it is important to consider any differences between the two systems in total compensating balances. The greater the number of collection centers, the greater the number of local bank accounts that must be maintained.

LOCK-BOX SYSTEM

Another means of accelerating the flow of funds is a lock-box arrangement. With concentration banking, remittances are received by a collection center and deposited in the bank after processing. The purpose of a lock-box arrangement is to eliminate the time between the receipt of remittances by the company and their deposit in the bank. A lock-box arrangement usually is on a regional basis, with the company choosing regional banks according to its billing patterns. Before determining the regions to be used, a feasibility study is made of the availability of checks that would be deposited under alternative plans. In this regard, operation research techniques have proved useful in the selection of lock-box sites.[4] If a company divided the country into five sections on the basis of a feasibility study, it might pick New York City for the Northeast, Atlanta for the Southeast, Chicago for the Midwest, Dallas for the Southwest, and San Francisco for the West Coast.

The company rents a local post office box and authorizes its bank in each of these cities to pick up remittances in the box. Customers are billed with instructions to mail their remittance to the lock box. The bank picks up the mail several times a day and deposits the checks in the company's account. The checks are microfilmed for record purposes

---

[4]See Ferdinand K. Levy, "An Application of Heuristic Problem Solving to Accounts Receivable Management," *Management Science*, 12 (February 1966), 236–44; and Robert F. Calman, *Linear Programming and Cash Management/CASH ALPHA* (Cambridge, Mass.: M.I.T. Press, 1968), Chapter 4.

and cleared for collection. The company receives a deposit slip and a list of payments, together with any material in the envelope. This procedure frees the company from handling and depositing the checks.

The main advantage of a lock-box system is that checks are deposited at banks sooner and become collected balances sooner than if they were processed by the company prior to deposit. In other words, the lag between the time checks are received by the company and the time they actually are deposited at the bank is eliminated. The principal disadvantage of a lock-box arrangement is the cost. The bank provides a number of services additional to the usual clearing of checks and requires compensation for them, usually preferring increased deposits. Because the cost is almost directly proportional to the number of checks deposited, lock-box arrangements usually are not profitable if the average remittance is small.

The appropriate rule for deciding whether or not to use a lock-box system, or, for that matter, concentration banking, is simply to compare the added cost of the most efficient system with the marginal income that can be generated from the released funds. If costs are less than income, the system is profitable; if not, the system is not a profitable undertaking. The degree of profitability depends primarily upon the geographical dispersion of customers, the size of the typical remittance, and the earnings rate on the released funds. Although there is disagreement as to what earnings rate to use, the most appropriate rate for our purpose is the rate on marketable securities. Because a decision as to the total amount of liquid assets to maintain was considered in Chapter 13, our present decision affects mainly the proportion of cash to marketable securities, not their sum. Thus, the opportunity cost of tying up funds in cash is the return foregone on marketable securities.

OTHER PROCEDURES

Frequently, firms give special attention to the handling of large remittances so that they may be deposited in a bank as quickly as possible. This special handling may involve personal pickup of these checks or the use of airmail or special delivery. When a small number of remittances account for a large proportion of total deposits, it may be worthwhile to initiate controls to accelerate the deposit and collection of these large checks. The firm should exercise tight control over interbank transfers of cash and transfers between various units of the company, such as divisions or subsidiaries. Excessive funds may be tied up in various divisions of the firm.

Some companies maintain too many bank accounts, thereby creating unnecessary pockets of idle funds. A company that has an account in every city where it has either a sales office or a production facility might be able to reduce cash balances considerably if it were to eliminate some of these accounts. The banking activities of a sales office can often be handled from a larger account with little loss in service or availability of funds. Even though small accounts may create a degree of goodwill with bankers, they make little sense in the overall cash management of the firm. By closing such unnecessary accounts, a firm may be able to release funds that it then can put to profitable use.

CONTROL OF DISBURSEMENTS

In addition to accelerating collections, effective control of disbursements can result in a faster turnover of cash. Whereas the underlying objective of collections is maximum acceleration, the objective in disbursements is to slow them down as much as possible. The combination of fast collections and slow disbursements will result in maximum availability of funds.

For a company with multiple banks, it is important to be able to shift funds quickly to those banks from which disbursements are made, to prevent excessive balances from building up temporarily in a particular bank. Operating procedures for disbursements should be well established. If cash discounts are taken on accounts payable, procedures should aim toward eliminating or minimizing the loss of discounts due to clerical inefficiencies. The timing of payments is important. For maximum use of cash, payments should be made on the due dates, not before and not after.

A company can delay disbursements through the use of drafts. Unlike an ordinary check, the draft is not payable on demand. When it is presented to the issuer's bank for collection, the bank must present it to the issuer for acceptance. The funds then are deposited by the issuing firm to cover payment of the draft. The advantage of the draft arrangement is that it delays the time the firm actually has to have funds on deposit to cover the draft. Consequently, it allows the firm to maintain smaller deposits at its banks.

Another way of maximizing cash availability is "playing the float." In this case, float is the difference between the total dollar amount of checks drawn on a bank account and the balance shown on the bank's books. It is possible, of course, for a company to have a negative balance on its books and a positive bank balance, because checks outstanding have not been collected from the account on which they are drawn. If the size of float can be estimated accurately, bank balances can be reduced and the funds invested to earn a positive return.

Many companies maintain a separate account for payroll disbursements. In order to minimize the balance in this account, one must predict when the payroll checks issued will be presented for payment. If payday falls on a Friday, for example, not all of the checks will be cashed on that day. Consequently, the firm need not have funds on deposit to

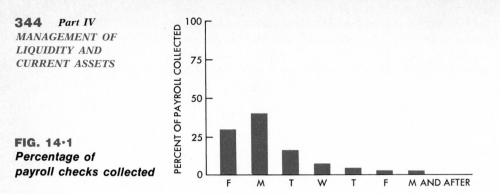

FIG. 14·1
Percentage of
payroll checks collected

cover its entire payroll.[5] Even on Monday, some checks will not be presented due to delays in their deposit. Based upon its experience, the firm should be able to construct a distribution of when, on the average, checks are presented for collection. An example is shown in Figure 14-1. With this information, the firm can approximate the funds it needs to have on deposit to cover payroll checks.

However, this information is not enough. The firm also needs to know the magnitude of possible deviations from expected outcomes. On the first day, Friday, suppose the firm expects the probability distributions of possible outcomes shown in Figure 14-2. The actual balance maintained will depend upon the risk tolerances of management. If management is willing to tolerate insufficient cash with a 2 percent probability, it would maintain approximately 39 percent of the total payroll on deposit on Friday. The outcome on the second day depends upon what happened the first day. For example, if a small percentage of employees present checks for collection on Friday, the percentage presented for collection on Monday and succeeding days will be larger than would otherwise be the case. Consequently, it is necessary to develop a series of conditional probabilities of outcomes, given the outcome on preceding days. If transfers from the general account can be consummated rapidly, there is no reason why a firm cannot predict ahead one day at a time. As a result, the complexity of the problem is reduced; only one probability distribution need be projected at a time. Similar to the payroll account, many firms establish a separate account for dividends. Here too the idea is to predict when such checks will be presented for payment so as to minimize the cash balance in the account.[6]

As mentioned earlier, optimizing cash availability involves acceler-

---

[5] See James McN. Stancill, *The Management of Working Capital* (Scranton, Pa.: Intext, 1971), pp. 19–22.

[6] See Stancill, *Management of Working Capital*, pp. 20–21.

ating collections as much as possible and delaying payments as long as is realistically possible. Because delaying payments may damage the firm's credit standing, the resulting cost to the firm must be taken into account. In the future, we can expect to see further improvements in money payments. As we move toward a "checkless society," the time funds remain uncollected becomes shorter. In a checkless society where transfers are made through computers, payments will be immediate. There will be no uncollected funds, for one party's account will be debited the instant another's is credited. Although the firm's deposits will be collected faster, so too will the checks it writes. Whether it gains or loses will depend upon the typical float on checks deposited relative to the float on checks written.

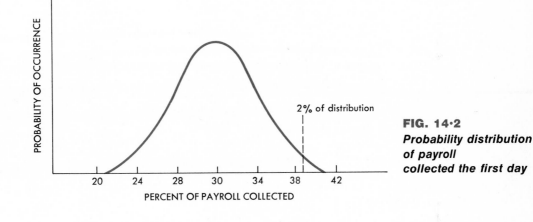

FIG. 14·2
*Probability distribution
of payroll
collected the first day*

COMPENSATING BALANCES

Establishing a minimum level of cash balances depends in part upon the compensating balance requirements of banks. These requirements are set on the basis of the profitability of the accounts. A bank begins by calculating the average collected balances shown on the bank's books over a period of time. As brought out before, this balance often is higher than the cash balance shown on the company's books. From the average collected balance, the bank subtracts the percentage of deposits it is required to maintain at the Federal Reserve, around 17 percent. The residual constitutes the earnings base on which income is generated. Total income is determined by multiplying the base times the earnings rate of the bank. This rate fluctuates in keeping with money market conditions.

Reserve Req't.

Once the income from an account is determined, the cost of the account must be computed. Most banks have a schedule of costs on a per item basis for such transactions as transfers and processing checks. The account is analyzed for a typical month during which all transactions are multiplied times the per item cost and totaled. If the total cost is less than the total income from the account, the account is profitable; if more, it is unprofitable. The minimum average level of cash balances required is the point at which the account is just profitable. Because banks differ in the earnings rate they use as well as in their costs and method of account analysis, the determination of compensating balances varies. The firm, therefore, may be wise to shop around and determine the bank that requires the lowest compensating balances for a given level of activity. If a firm has a lending arrangement with a bank, the firm may well be required to maintain balances in excess of those required to compensate the bank for the activity in its account. Because we consider compensation for a lending arrangement in Chapter 17, no discussion of this form of compensation will be undertaken at this time.

In recent years, there has been a trend toward paying cash for services rendered by a bank instead of maintaining compensating balances. The advantage to the firm is that it may be able to earn more on funds used for compensating balances than the fee for the services. The higher the interest rate in the money markets, the greater the opportunity cost of compensating balances and the greater the advantage of service charges. It is an easy matter to determine if the firm would be better off with service charges as opposed to maintaining compensating balances. One simply compares the charges with the earnings on the funds released. Most banks resist placing normal services, such as clearing checks, on a fee basis. Nevertheless, an increasing number of bank services are being offered on such a basis. The balances maintained at a bank and the services the bank performs should be analyzed carefully. If deposits are more than compensating, funds may be tied up unnecessarily.[7]

---

[7]Linear programming has been used to structure a firm's banking relations and to determine a minimum level of cash balances. See Calman, *Linear Programming and Cash Management/CASH ALPHA*. The objective function of his model is to minimize the total cost of the banking system to the firm, subject to various levels of activities requiring banking services. Gerald A. Pogue, Russell B. Faucett, and Ralph N. Bussard, "Cash Management: A Systems Approach," in Keith V. Smith, *Management of Working Capital* (New York: West Publishing, 1974), pp. 77–90, approach the problem in a similar manner, as does Bernell K. Stone, "Allocating Credit Lines, Planned Borrowing, and Tangible Services over a Company's Banking System," *Financial Management*, 4 (Summer 1975), 65–78, although additional factors are considered. For an extensive linear-programming model that deals with cash management of the firm as a whole, see Yair E. Orgler, *Cash Management* (Belmont, Calif.: Wadsworth, 1970), Chapters 3–6; and Orgler, "An Unequal-Period Model for Cash Management Decisions," *Management Science*, 16 (October 1969), 77–92. The objective function encompasses payments, short-term financing, and security transactions. This function is maximized subject to managerial and institutional constraints, including minimum cash balance requirements.

Given the overall level of transactions and precautionary balances, we wish to consider the appropriate split between cash and marketable securities. Because these securities can be converted into cash on very short notice, they serve the precautionary need of the firm to hold cash. The level of cash, which in turn determines the level of marketable securities given our assumptions, should be the *greater* of two constraints. The first is the compensating balance requirement of a commercial bank. This requirement is expressed in terms of an average cash balance over some period of time rather than a minimum below which cash cannot fall. The second constraint is self-imposed, and it is determined by the need for cash, the predictability of this need, the interest rate on marketable securities, and the fixed cost of effecting a transfer between marketable securities and cash. This constraint should be determined apart from the first constraint, and, as suggested, the optimal level of cash is the greater of the two constraints. Because we have already discussed the determination of the compensating balance constraint, we turn now to the second constraint.

If the future were known with certainty, it would be an easy matter to determine the optimal split between cash and marketable securities. Projected cash would be invested as long as the interest earnings exceeded transactions and inconvenience costs, and as long as the delays in conversion between cash and marketable securities did not hinder the firm in paying its bills. If transactions and inconvenience costs were zero and conversion between the two assets were instantaneous, the firm would hold no cash. It simply would sell securities to pay its bills. When transactions and inconvenience costs are positive, however, the firm will want to hold cash when the expected holding period for investment is not long enough to earn sufficient interest to offset them.[8] By the same token, with conversion delays, the firm may need to hold cash. Thus, even if future cash flows were known with certainty, a firm would probably hold some cash.

INVENTORY MODEL

Under conditions of certainty, one simple model for determining the optimal average amount of transaction cash is the economic order quantity formula (EOQ) used in inventory management (see Chapter 16). It provides a useful conceptual foundation for the cash management problem.[9] In the model, the carrying cost of holding cash, namely the

compensating balance

skip 347-358

[8] See D. E. Peterson, *A Quantitative Framework for Financial Management* (Homewood, Ill.: Richard D. Irwin, 1969), pp. 212–19.

[9] The model was first applied to the problem of cash management by William J. Baumol, "The Transactions Demand for Cash: An Inventory Theoretic Approach," *Quarterly Journal of Economics*, 66 (November 1952), 545–56. It has been further refined and developed by a number of others.

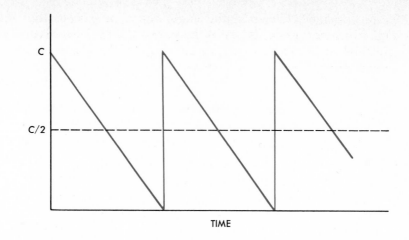

FIG. 14·3

Inventory model
applied to cash
management

interest foregone on marketable securities, is balanced against the fixed cost of transferring marketable securities to cash or vice versa. The model is illustrated by the sawtooth lines in Figure 14-3.

In the figure, we assume that the firm has a steady demand for cash over some period of time, say one month. The firm obtains cash during this period by selling marketable securities. Suppose it starts out with C dollars in cash, and when this amount is expended, it replenishes it by selling C dollars of marketable securities. Thus, the transfer of funds from securities to cash occurs whenever cash touches zero. If a cushion is desired or if there are lead times to effect a transaction, the threshold for initiating a transfer can be higher. The principle is the same regardless of whether or not a cushion is used.

The objective is to specify the value of C, which minimizes total costs—that is, the sum of the fixed costs associated with transfers and the opportunity cost of earnings foregone by holding cash balances. These costs can be expressed as

$$b\left(\frac{T}{C}\right) + i\left(\frac{C}{2}\right) \qquad (14\text{-}1)$$

where b is the fixed cost of a transaction that is assumed to be independent of the amount transferred, T is the total demand for cash over the period of time involved, and i is the interest rate on marketable securities for the period involved (assumed to be constant). T/C represents the number of transactions during the period, and when it is multiplied times the fixed cost per transaction, we obtain the total fixed cost for the period. $C/2$ represents the average cash balance, and when it is multiplied times the interest rate, we obtain the earnings foregone by virtue of holding cash. The larger the C, the larger the average cash balance, $C/2$, and the smaller the average investment in securities and earnings from these securities. Thus, there is a higher opportunity cost of interest income foregone. However, the larger the C, the fewer the transfers, T/C, which occur and the lower the transfer costs. The object is to balance these two costs so that total costs are minimized.

The optimal level of C is found to be

$$C^* = \sqrt{\frac{2bT}{i}} \qquad (14\text{-}2)$$

when the derivative of Eq. (14-1) with respect to C is set equal to zero. Thus, cash will be demanded in relation to the square root of the dollar volume of transactions. This phenomenon implies that as the level of cash payments increases, the amount of transaction cash the firm needs to hold increases by a lesser percentage. In other words, economies of scale are possible. The implication is that the firm should try to consolidate individual bank accounts into as few as possible in order to realize economies in cash management. We see from Eq. (14-2) that C^* varies directly with the fixed cost, b, and inversely with the interest rate on marketable securities, i.[10] However, the relationship is dampened by the square-root sign in both cases.

To illustrate the use of the EOQ formula, consider a firm with estimated cash payments of $6 million for a one-month period where these payments are expected to be steady over the period. The fixed cost per transaction is $100 and the interest rate on marketable securities is 6 percent per annum, or 0.5 percent for the one-month period. Therefore,

$$C = \sqrt{\frac{2bT}{i}} = \sqrt{\frac{2(100)(6{,}000{,}000)}{.005}} = \$489{,}898$$

Thus, the optimal transaction size is $489,898 and the average cash balance $489,898/2 = $244,949. This means the firm should make $6,000,000/$489,898 = 12 + transactions of marketable securities to cash during the month.

It is useful now to consider in more detail the two costs involved. The interest rate is fairly straightforward; it simply represents the rate of interest on securities that would be sold to replenish cash. In most cases, this is the rate on short-term money market instruments and not the average rate of return on all marketable securities. The fixed cost associated with a transaction is more difficult to measure because it consists of both explicit and implied costs. Included are the fixed component of transaction costs, the time it takes the treasurer or other official to place

---

[10] For a study involving the effect changing interest rates have on the relative level of cash held by the firm, see Morris Budin and Robert J. Van Handel, "A Rule-of-Thumb Theory of Cash Holdings by Firms," *Journal of Financial and Quantitative Analysis,* 10 (March 1975), 85–108.

an order with an investment banker, the time he consumes in recording the transaction, the secretarial time needed to type the transaction and the purchase order, the time needed to record the transaction on the books, and the time needed to record the safekeeping notification. Given a number of transactions, the procedures for placing an order can be streamlined to reduce the average fixed cost per transaction. Nevertheless, these costs do exist and too often are either overlooked or underestimated.

One limitation to the use of the EOQ model is that cash payments are assumed to be steady over the period of time specified. Only if this assumption is a reasonable approximation of the situation is the model applicable. When cash payments become lumpy, it may be appropriate to reduce the period for which calculations are made so that expenditures during the period are relatively steady. The EOQ model can be applied also when receipts are continuous and there are discontinuous large payments. The decision to be made then would be the optimal purchase size of marketable securities.

Another limitation to the use of the model is that cash payments are seldom completely predictable. For modest degrees of uncertainty, one need only add a cushion so that a transfer from marketable securities to cash is triggered at some level of cash above zero. In general, the EOQ model gives the financial manager a benchmark for judging the optimal cash balance. It does not have to be used as a precise rule governing his behavior. The model merely suggests what would be the optimal balance under a set of assumptions. The actual balance may be more if the assumptions do not entirely hold.

STOCHASTIC MODELS

In those cases where the uncertainty of cash payments is large, the EOQ model may not be applicable and other models should be used to determine optimal behavior. If cash balances fluctuate randomly, one can apply control theory to the problem. Assume that the demand for cash is stochastic and unknown in advance. We then can set control limits such that when cash reaches an upper limit a transfer of cash to marketable securities is consummated, and when it hits a lower limit a transfer from marketable securities to cash is triggered. As long as the cash balance stays between these limits, no transactions take place.

How the limits are set depends in part upon the fixed costs associated with a securities transaction and the opportunity cost of holding cash. As before, we assume these costs are known and that the fixed cost of selling a marketable security is the same as that for buying it. In essence, we want to satisfy the demand for cash at the lowest possible total cost. Although there are a number of applications of control theory to the problem, we discuss a relatively simple one. The Miller-Orr model

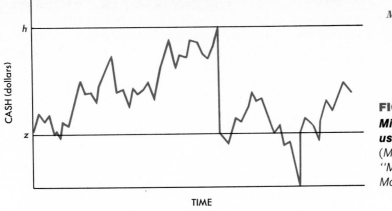

FIG. 14·4
Miller-Orr model
using control limits
(*Miller and Orr,*
"Model of the Demand for
Money by Firms.")

specifies two control limits—h dollars as an upper bound and zero dollars as a lower bound.[11] The model is illustrated in Figure 14-4. When the cash balance touches the upper bound, $h - z$ dollars of marketable securities are bought and the new balance becomes z dollars. When the cash balance touches zero, z dollars of marketable securities are sold and the new balance again becomes z. This is illustrated in the figure. The minimum bound can be set at some amount higher than zero, and h and z would move up in the figure. However, we will use zero as the lower bound for purposes of illustration, recognizing that a firm can set the lower bound at some positive amount. This obviously would be necessary if there were delays in transfer.

The solution for the optimal values of h and z depend not only upon the fixed and opportunity costs but also upon the degree of likely fluctuation in cash balances. The optimal value of z, the return-to-point for security transactions, is

$$z = \sqrt[3]{\frac{3b\sigma^2}{4i}} \qquad (14\text{-}3)$$

where b = fixed cost associated with a security transaction

σ^2 = variance of daily net cash flows

i = interest rate per day on marketable securities

The optimal value of h is simply $3z$. With these control limits set, the model minimizes the total costs (fixed and opportunity) of cash management. Again, the critical assumption is that cash flows are random. The average cash balance cannot be determined exactly in advance, but

---

[11] See Merton H. Miller and Daniel Orr, "A Model of the Demand for Money by Firms," *Quarterly Journal of Economics*, 80 (August 1966), 413–35.

it is approximately $(z + h)/3$. As experience unfolds, however, it can be easily calculated.[12]

The Miller-Orr model is one of a number of control-limit models designed to deal with the cash management problem under the assumption of stochastic cash flows.[13] As long as cash remains within specified limits, no transactions take place.[14] Thus, we have considered

[12] In a second article, Miller and Orr, "The Demand for Money by Firms: Extension of Analytic Results," *Journal of Finance*, 23 (December 1968), 735–59, extend the model to allow for two types of securities—long-term and short-term. On the supposition that the control of cash has little effect on the choice between long- and short-term securities, they assume that the amount of funds to be transferred between cash and marketable securities is independent of the mix of securities.

Miller and Orr assume also that long-term securities are riskier than short-term ones and, accordingly, provide a higher return. In addition, transaction costs are higher. Transfers between cash and marketable securities occur in short-term securities unless certain control limits are breached. If cash balances exceed the upper limit, h, and a transfer to short-term securities exceeds the upper control limit, H, for these securities, long-term securities should be purchased. More specifically, a cash transfer of $h - z$ should be used to purchase long-terms. Moreover, the firm also should sell $X - Z$ of short-term securities and purchase an equal amount of long-terms, where X is the actual level of short holdings and Z is the lower control limit for short holdings. If cash balances equal zero and actual short holdings are less than the lower cash-holding control limit, z, short holdings are deemed excessively low. The firm then should sell $z + Z - X$ worth of long-term securities and buy $Z - X$ worth of shorts. The residual, z, would go into cash. All other transactions between cash and marketable securities involve short-term securities.

"The frequency of trade in longs is determined entirely by the values assigned to H and Z, the control levels on the shorts accounts, and is independent of h and z, the control levels on the cash account." (Ibid., p. 750.) Thus, cash transfers occur in the same manner as with the two-asset model. Optimal values of the policy variables are found to be

$$z = \sqrt[3]{\frac{3b_s m^2 t}{4i}} \qquad Z = \sqrt{\frac{3b_l m^2 t}{4(i_l - i_s)}}$$

where b_s and b_l are transaction costs for trades in short- and long-term securities, respectively, and i_s and i_l are average yields on short- and long-term securities. As before, $h = 3z$ and $H = 3Z$. Because the numerator for Z is larger than that for z and because the denominator is smaller, the frequency of transactions involving long-term securities is less than that for transactions in short-term securities.

[13] See Gary D. Eppen and Eugene F. Fama, "Solutions for Cash-Balance and Simple Dynamic-Portfolio Problems," *Journal of Business*, 41 (January 1968), 94–112; Eppen and Fama, "Cash Balance and Simple Dynamic Portfolio Problems with Proportional Costs," *International Economic Review*, 10 (June 1969), 119–33; Eppen and Fama, "Three-Asset Cash Balance and Dynamic Portfolio Problems," *Management Science*, 17 (January 1971), 311–19; Edwin H. Neave, "The Stochastic Cash Balance Problem with Costs for Increases and Decreases," *Management Science*, 16 (March 1970), 472–90; Nadia M. Girgis, "Optimal Cash Balance Levels," *Management Science*, 15 (November 1968), 130–40; Suresh P. Sethi and Gerald L. Thompson, "Application of Mathematical Control Theory to Finance: Modeling Simple Dynamic Cash Balance Problems," *Journal of Financial and Quantitative Analysis*, 5 (December 1970), 381–94; Martin Weitzman, "A Model of the Demand for Money by Firms: Comment," *Quarterly Journal of Economics*, 82 (March 1968), 161–64; Andrew H. Y. Chen, Frank C. Jen, and Stanley Zionts, "Portfolio Models with Stochastic Cash Demands," *Management Science*, 19 (November 1972), 319–32; and Mark I. Abed, "The Stochastic Cash Balance Problem" (unpublished Ph.D. dissertation, University of California, Berkeley, 1972).

[14] Peter A. Frost, "Banking Services, Minimum Cash Balances, and the Firm's Demand for Money," *Journal of Finance*, 25 (December 1970), 1029–39, extends the stochastic cash management model to incorporate varying levels of banking services. If the bank's supply function of services varies with the level of deposits, Frost contends that the minimum cash balance and the transaction balance must be determined simultaneously.

two models for determining the optimal level of cash. The EOQ model assumes cash flows are predictable, while the control-limit model assumes they are random. The average cash balance suggested by the second model will be higher than that suggested by the first for obvious reasons.

PROBABILITY MODEL

Usually, the cash flows of a firm are neither completely predictable nor stochastic. Rather, they are predictable within a range. This occurrence calls for formulating the demand for cash as a probability distribution of possible outcomes. For simplicity, we assume a one-period model. Suppose that at the beginning of each week the treasurer analyzes the firm's cash and marketable securities positions for the subsequent week relative to cash projections for that week. The frequency of analysis will depend upon the dispersion of projected cash flows, the degree to which cash flows are correlated over time, and the cost of the review.

Assuming that reviews once a week are appropriate, we assume that the average yield on short-term marketable securities, such as Treasury bills, is 0.08 percent per week. This return applies to both existing investments and any additional investments. Because the investment is for a short term and there is no default risk, we assume no risk of security price fluctuations. Also, we assume that the conversion between cash and marketable securities is instantaneous. Transaction costs are twofold: the commission involved in buying or selling the security, and the internal fixed costs of making a transaction.

For our illustration, we assume that the commission for both buying and selling a security is 0.03 percent and that the fixed cost per transaction is $40. We assume also that, based upon its analysis of minimum cash balances, the firm has established a strict policy of having at least a $3 million cash position at the end of each seven-day week and maintaining a minimum of approximately $3 million in cash during the week. However, it is possible for the firm to fall below this minimum temporarily during the week. We assume that the firm will not borrow to maintain the minimum cash level as long as it has marketable securities that can be sold either at the end of the week or during the week.

Our concern, then, is with finding the proper split between cash and marketable securities, on the basis of cash projections. Suppose that at the beginning of a given week, the firm has a cash balance of $3.2 million and short-term investments totaling $1.8 million. Moreover, the probable cash balances one week hence without the purchase or sale of securities are estimated as follows:

Amount (in millions)	$2.9	$3.0	$3.1	$3.2	$3.3	$3.4
Probability of occurrence	0.10	0.10	0.20	0.30	0.20	0.10

These cash balance estimates are based upon the firm's cash projection and upon its past experience and knowledge of possible variations in cash flow.

The model illustrated   The job now is to analyze the cash projections in relation to the other information at hand, to determine the optimal holding of marketable securities for the forthcoming week. The minimum level of marketable securities that might be held is $1.7 million. Under this alternative, there is no

Table 14·1   Expected earnings from holding securities

(1)	(2)	(3)	(4)	(5)
Marketable Security Level (in millions)	Gross Earnings for Week 0.0008(1)	Buying Costs*	Probability of Having to Sell Amount	Probability
$1.7	$1,360	—	$100,000	1.00
1.8	1,440	—	100,000	0.10
1.9	1,520	$ 70	200,000	0.10
			100,000	0.10
2.0	1,600	100	300,000	0.10
			200,000	0.10
			100,000	0.20
2.1	1,680	130	400,000	0.10
			300,000	0.10
			200,000	0.20
			100,000	0.30
2.2	1,760	160	500,000	0.10
			400,000	0.10
			300,000	0.20
			200,000	0.30
			100,000	0.20
2.3	1,840	190	600,000	0.10
			500,000	0.10
			400,000	0.20
			300,000	0.30
			200,000	0.20
			100,000	0.10

probability that the cash balance at the end of the week will be less than $3 million. Therefore, a lower level of security holdings would make no sense. This alternative would require the sale of $100,000 of existing securities, involving fixed costs of $40 and a commission of $30: ($100,000 × 0.0003). The expected net earnings under this alternative are shown in the first row of Table 14-1. From the $1,360 in gross earnings for the week ($1.7 million × 0.0008), we subtract the cost of selling $100,000 of existing securities, or $70, to obtain expected net earnings of $1,290.

The second alternative is to maintain the present $1.8 million in

Table 14·1   Expected earnings from holding securities (*Cont.*)

(6)	*(7)*	*(8)*	*(9)*	*(10)*
*Selling Costs**	*Expected Fixed Costs and Earnings Lost on Account of Sale Before End of Week*	*Total Expected Selling Costs* $(5) \times (6 + 7)$	*Total Expected Costs* $(3) + (8)$	*Expected Net Earnings* $(2) - (9)$
$ 70	—	$ 70.00	$ 70.00	$1,290.00
70	—	7.00	7.00	1,433.00
100	$ 10.00	11.00		
70	—	7.00		
		$ 18.00	88.00	1,432.00
130	32.50	$ 16.25		
100	10.00	11.00		
70	—	14.00		
		$ 41.25	141.25	1,458.75
160	72.00	$ 23.20		
130	32.50	16.25		
100	10.00	22.00		
70	—	21.00		
		$ 82.45	212.45	1,467.55
190	133.00	$ 32.30		
160	72.00	23.20		
130	32.50	32.50		
100	10.00	33.00		
70	—	14.00		
		$135.00	295.00	1,465.00
220	220.00	$ 44.00		
190	133.00	32.30		
160	72.00	46.40		
130	32.50	48.75		
100	10.00	22.00		
70	—	7.00		
		$200.45	390.45	1,449.55

* Includes commission of 0.0003 times amount of transaction plus fixed cost of $40 per transaction.

securities. Under this alternative, there is a 10 percent probability that $100,000 of securities will have to be sold at the end of the period in order to restore the cash balance to $3 million at the end of the week. As shown in the second row of Table 14-1, the expected cost of selling these securities is the probability of having to sell $100,000 in securities times the fixed costs and transaction costs, or 0.10 [$40 + 0.0003(100,000)], or $7. This amount is subtracted from gross earnings to obtain expected net earnings of $1,433 for the week.

At this point in our illustration, we must consider more specifically the fact that securities might have to be sold during the week in order to maintain approximately $3 million in cash. Suppose that the firm had found from past experience that the probability of having to sell a portion of the securities during the week increases with the total amount of securities that had to be sold (shown in column (4) of Table 14-1). In other words, the need to sell securities during the week increases with the amount of the total cash drain. No longer is it sufficient simply to sell securities at the end of the week in order to maintain a cash balance of approximately $3 million; securities need to be sold during the week. If securities are sold during the week, the firm incurs on a marginal basis an additional fixed cost of $40 plus the opportunity cost of interest lost during the remainder of the week.[15] Let us assume that management is able to estimate accurately the probability that securities will have to be sold during the week.

Suppose that if the total amount having to be sold by the end of the week is $100,000, management estimates that there is no probability that any portion of this amount will have to be sold before the end of the week. However, if the total amount that must be sold is $200,000, management might estimate a 0.10 probability that half the total amount will have to be sold during the week. Assume also that on the average, the securities will have to be sold on the second day and that three-quarters of the weekly gross earnings—0.06 percent—will be lost on the securities sold. Thus, there will be an additional fixed cost of $40, and $60 in interest will be lost ($100,000 × 0.0006). Therefore, the expected fixed costs and earnings lost on the securities sold are 0.10($100), or $10. If the total amount of securities to be sold were $300,000, there might be a 0.25 probability that one-half of this amount would need to be sold on the second day. Again, the additional fixed cost incurred is $40, but the interest lost is now ($150,000 × 0.0006), or $90. Thus, the expected additional cost is 0.25($130), or $32.50. Similarly, if we tabulate the probabilities for other amounts of securities sold during the week, we might obtain a schedule like that shown in Table 14-2. It can be seen from the table that expected costs increase with the total amount of

---

[15] Note that the transaction costs are already accounted for in Table 14-1 in the sale of securities at the end of the week (column (6)).

**Table 14·2   Expected fixed costs and earnings lost
on account of sale before end of week**

Total Amount of Securities Sold (Column (4) of Table 14-1)	Additional Fixed Cost	Interest Lost*	Total Additional Costs	Probability	Expected Additional Costs
$100,000	$ 0	$ 0	$ 0	0	$ 0
200,000	40	60	100	0.10	10.00
300,000	40	90	130	0.25	32.50
400,000	40	120	160	0.45	72.00
500,000	40	150	190	0.70	133.00
600,000	40	180	220	1.00	220.00

*0.0006 (one-half amount in first column).

securities that must be sold. The expected additional costs shown in the last column of Table 14-2 are incorporated in column (7) of Table 14-1.

Taking into account the additional costs associated with selling securities before the end of the week, we can consider the third alternative—a security level of $1.9 million. For this level of security holdings, the firm must acquire an additional $100,000 of securities at a cost of $70, [$40 + 0.0003($100,000)]. Moreover, there is a 0.10 probability that it will have to sell $200,000 of securities and a 0.10 probability that it will have to sell $100,000 of securities in order to restore the cash balance to $3 million at the end of the week. The costs of selling the securities at the end of the week are [$40 + 0.0003(200,000)], or $100, and [$40 + 0.0003(100,000)], or $70, respectively. If the firm has to sell $200,000 in securities at the end of the week, there is a 0.10 probability that one-half of this amount will have to be sold during the week. As calculated in the preceding paragraph, the expected marginal cost of this occurrence is $10; this amount is shown in column (7) of Table 14-1. When we multiply the sum of the costs shown in columns (6) and (7) by their respective probabilities of occurrence and add the products, we obtain total expected selling costs of $18. This amount is added to the buying costs to obtain total expected costs of $88. Subtracting this amount from gross earnings for the week, we obtain expected net earnings of $1,432 for the week.

When we carry these calculations through for all possible levels of security holdings, we obtain the results shown in the remaining rows of Table 14-1. The table tells us the expected net earnings for each level of security holdings for the week. We see that the optimal level of security holdings for the week is $2.1 million, resulting in expected net earnings of $1,467.55. Consequently, the company should purchase $300,000 in additional securities. To increase security holdings another $100,000 to $2.2 million would involve marginal expected costs in excess of marginal gross earnings and therefore would not be profitable.

The optimal security level for the following week would be determined in a similar manner one week later, based upon the cash position and security level at that time and upon cash projections for the subsequent week. Decisions with respect to the level of cash and marketable securities would be made on a week-to-week basis.

OPTIMAL LEVEL OF CASH

The above model is but one of many probability models that can be used to determine the proper level of cash. Many of the assumptions can be modified depending upon the circumstances. Where these optimization models do not offer improvement over simpler decision rules, they should not be used.[16] Their purpose is to assist one in determining the appropriate level of investment in marketable securities. Given the level of total liquid assets, determination of an appropriate level of cash will also determine the level of investment in marketable securities.

The optimal level of average cash balances will be the greater of two constraints: the compensating balance requirement imposed by a bank, and the average level of cash suggested by an appropriate cash-marketable securities model. In most cases, the former will exceed the latter. However, when the fixed costs of a security transaction are high, the opportunity cost of holding cash is low, and/or cash flows are subject to great fluctuation, the average cash balance suggested by an appropriate model may be higher than that required by the bank. Therefore, average balances in excess of those considered compensating should be maintained.

**INVESTMENT IN
MARKETABLE
SECURITIES**

Once the firm has determined an optimal cash balance, the residual of its liquid assets are invested in marketable securities. In the models examined, we assumed a given yield and no risk of fluctuations in market price. These assumptions are realistic for very short-term, high-grade securities used as a buffer to replenish cash. However, firms frequently hold securities with lesser characteristics for less immediate needs. In this section, then, we examine the types of marketable securities available to a company as near-money investments, allowing for varying yields and for fluctuations in market price. First, however, we

---

[16]For an analysis of the potential savings arising from the use of such models vis-à-vis simple heuristic cash management rules, see Hans G. Daellenbach, "Are Cash Management Optimization Models Worthwhile?" *Journal of Financial and Quantitative Analysis,* 9 (September 1974), 607–26. Only if fixed transaction costs are relatively large does Daellenbach find the use of optimization models to be worthwhile.

need to explore the reasons for differences in yields on different securities. These yield differentials exist because of differences in default risk, in marketability, in length of time to maturity, and in taxability.[17]

DEFAULT RISK

When we speak of default risk we mean the risk of default on the part of the borrower in the payment of principal or interest. Investors are said to demand a risk premium to invest in other than default-free securities.[18] The greater the possibility that the borrower will default on his obligation, the greater the financial risk and the premium demanded by the marketplace. Treasury securities are usually regarded as default-free, and other securities are judged in relation to them. For example, U.S. government agency issues might be rated next to Treasury securities in credit-worthiness. For all practical purposes, these securities are default-free. The credit-worthiness of other obligations is frequently judged on the basis of security ratings. Moody's Investors Service and Standard & Poor's, for example, grade corporate and municipal securities as to their quality. The greater the default risk of the borrower, the greater the yield of the security should be, all other things held constant. By investing in riskier securities, the firm can achieve higher returns, but it faces the familiar tradeoff between expected return and risk.

MARKETABILITY

Marketability of a security relates to the ability of the owner to convert it into cash. There are two dimensions: the price realized and the amount of time required to sell the asset. The two are interrelated in that it is often possible to sell an asset in a short period of time if enough price concession is given. For financial instruments, marketability is judged in relation to the ability to sell a significant volume of securities in a short period of time without significant price concession. The more

---

[17]Callability also affects the yield to maturity. Because the marketable securities position of most firms is confined to short-term securities, it usually is not an important factor. The call feature, however, is analyzed in Chapter 21 from the standpoint of an issuer of long-term debt.

[18]For empirical investigations of default-risk premiums, see Lawrence Fisher, "Determinants of Risk Premiums on Corporate Bonds," *Journal of Political Economy,* 67 (June 1959), 217–37; Ramon E. Johnson, "Term Structure of Corporate Bond Yields," *Journal of Finance,* 22 (May 1967), 313–45; and Ray C. Fair and Burton G. Malkiel, "The Determination of Yield Differentials between Debt Instruments of the Same Maturity," *Journal of Money, Credit and Banking,* 4 (November 1971), 733–49. For a more extended discussion of default risk, see James C. Van Horne, *The Function and Analysis of Capital Market Rates* (Englewood Cliffs, N.J.: Prentice-Hall, 1970), Chapter 5.

marketable the security, the greater the ability to execute a large transaction near the quoted price. In general, the lower the marketability of a security, the greater the yield necessary to attract investors. Thus, the yield differential between different securities of the same maturity is caused not only by differences in default risk but also by differences in marketability.

MATURITY

The relationship between yield and maturity can be studied graphically by plotting yield and maturity for securities differing only in the length of time to maturity. In practice, this means holding constant the degree of default risk. For example, we could study the yield-maturity relationship for default-free Treasury securities. An example of the yield-maturity relationship for Treasury securities on two separate dates is shown in Figure 14-5. Maturity is plotted on the horizontal axis and yield on the vertical; their relationship is described by a yield curve fitted to the observations.

Generally, when interest rates are expected to rise, the yield curve is upward-sloping, whereas it is humped and downward-sloping when they are expected to fall significantly. However, the yield differential between

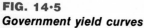

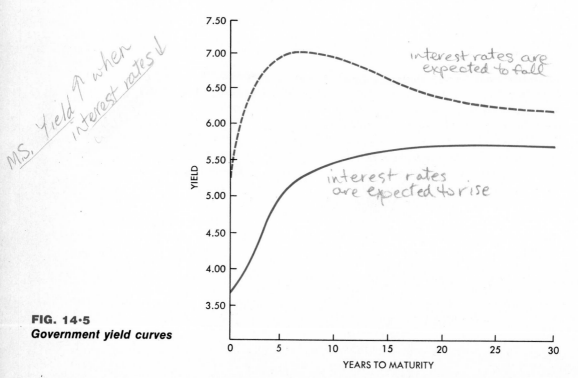

FIG. 14·5
Government yield curves

short- and long-term securities is greater for the steepest upward-sloping yield curve than the negative difference is for the steepest downward-sloping yield curve. In other words, there is a tendency toward positive-sloped yield curves. Most economists attribute this tendency to the presence of risk for those who invest in long-term securities vis-à-vis short-term securities. In general, the longer the maturity, the greater the risk of fluctuation in the market value of the security. Consequently, investors need to be offered a risk premium to induce them to invest in long-term securities. Only when interest rates are expected to fall significantly are they willing to invest in long-term securities yielding less than short- and intermediate-term securities.[19]

Some firms try to take advantage of an upward-sloping yield curve by "riding the yield curve," which involves selling securities before they mature. By investing in 180-day Treasury bills, for example, and selling them before maturity, a firm may be able to obtain a significantly higher return for the holding period than by holding the bills to maturity. If 180-day bills yield 6 percent and 90-day bills 5 percent, and the firm buys the 180-day bills now and sells them 90 days later at a yield of 5 percent, its return per annum for the holding period is 7.2 percent. This example assumes that the yield curve does not change over the holding period. Ignoring transaction costs, the investor buys the 180-day bills at a price of $97, at which price they yield 6 percent to maturity, and sells them 90 days later for $98.75, where they yield 5 percent to maturity. Thus, he realizes a holding-period yield of $(1.75/97)(360/90) = 7.2$ percent.

A second aspect of "riding the yield curve" involves taking advantage of expected shifts in interest rates. If interest rates are expected to fall, the firm will invest in long-term securities because these securities tend to have the greatest increase in market price when interest rates are falling. When the interest rate cycle is thought to have bottomed out, long-term securities will be sold and the firm will invest in very short-term securities, to assure a minimum of market-price decline if interest rates rise. Playing the yield curve in this manner involves risk, because expectations may prove to be wrong. Consequently, a firm that holds marketable securities as near-money investments to meet possible cash drains should be careful not to undertake such an operation on too large a scale.

TAXABILITY

Another factor affecting observed differences in market yields is the differential impact of taxes. The most important tax, and the only one we shall consider, is the income tax. The interest income on all but one

[19]For a much deeper discussion of this concept, see Van Horne, *Function and Analysis of Capital Market Rates*, Chapter 4.

category of securities is taxable to taxable investors. Interest income from state and local government securities is tax-exempt; as a result, they sell in the market at lower yields to maturity than Treasury and corporate securities of the same maturity. A differential impact on yields arises also because interest income is taxed at the ordinary tax rate, while capital gains on securities held more than six months are taxed at the more favorable capital gains tax rate. As a result, fixed-income securities that sell at a discount because of a low coupon rate in relation to prevailing yields are attractive to taxable investors. The reason is that part of the yield to maturity is a capital gain. Because of the desirability of discount bonds, their yield to maturity tends to be lower than the yield on comparable bonds with higher coupon rates. The greater the discount, the greater the capital gains attraction and the lower its yield relative to what it would be if the coupon rate were such that the security sold at par.

We have considered four factors that explain yield differentials on different securities: default risk, marketability, maturity, and taxability. By analyzing securities in terms of these concepts, one is able to determine what he has to give up in order to obtain a higher yield. In this way, a systematic analysis of marketable securities is possible so that a portfolio is formed in keeping with the objectives of the firm.

TYPES OF MARKETABLE SECURITIES

In this section, we describe briefly the more prominent marketable securities available for investment. Space prohibits the discussion of longer-term investments in this book, although corporations do invest excess funds in long-term securities that mature in the near future.

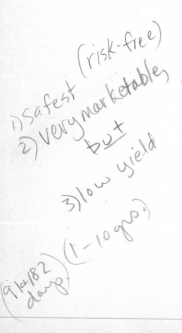

Treasury securities

U.S. Treasury obligations constitute the largest segment of the money markets. The principal securities issued are bills, tax-anticipation bills, notes, and bonds. Treasury bills are auctioned weekly by the Treasury with maturities of 91 days and 182 days. In addition, nine-month and one-year bills are sold periodically. Treasury bills carry no coupon but are sold on a discount basis. These securities are extremely popular with companies as short-term investments, in part because of the large amount outstanding. The market is very active, and the transaction costs involved in the sale of Treasury bills in the secondary market are small.

The original maturity on Treasury notes is one to ten years, whereas the original maturity on Treasury bonds is over ten years. With the passage of time, of course, a number of these securities have maturities of less than one year and serve the needs of short-term investors. Notes and bonds are coupon issues, and there is an active market for them. Overall, Treasury securities are the safest and most marketable investments. Therefore, they provide the lowest yield for a given maturity of the various instruments we consider.

Chapter 14 **363**
MANAGEMENT OF CASH AND MARKETABLE SECURITIES

Agency securities

Obligations of various agencies of the federal government are guaranteed by the agency issuing the security and not usually by the U.S. government as such. Principal agencies issuing securities are the Federal Housing Administration and the Government National Mortgage Association (Ginnie Mae). In addition, there are a number of government-sponsored, quasi-private agencies. The securities of these agencies are not guaranteed by the federal government, nor is there any stated "moral" obligation. In final analysis, however, there is an implied backing. It would be hard to imagine the federal government allowing them to fail. Major government-sponsored agencies include the Banks for Cooperatives, Federal Home Loan Banks, Federal Intermediate Credit Banks, Federal Land Banks, and the Federal National Mortgage Association (Fannie Mae). Although agency issues are being increasingly accepted by the investment community, they still provide a modest yield advantage over Treasury securities of the same maturity. These securities have a fairly high degree of marketability; they are sold in the secondary market through the same security dealers as are Treasury securities. With the sharp increase in agency financing in recent years, marketability has been enhanced considerably. Maturities range from a month up to approximately fifteen years. However, about one-half of the securities outstanding mature in less than a year.

[handwritten margin note:) Hi marketability (1mo-15yrs.) — 2nd-ary mkt]

Bankers' acceptances

Bankers' acceptances are drafts that are accepted by banks, and they are used in the financing of foreign and domestic trade. The credit-worthiness of bankers' acceptances is judged relative to the bank accepting the draft, not the drawer. Acceptances generally have maturities of less than 180 days and are of very high quality. They are traded in an over-the-counter market dominated by five principal dealers. The rates on bankers' acceptances tend to be slightly higher than rates on Treasury bills of like maturity; and both are sold on a discount basis.

[handwritten margin note: (< 180 days) (OTC mkt.) — higher yield than Treasury bills]

Commercial paper

Commercial paper consists of short-term unsecured promissory notes issued by finance companies and certain industrial concerns. Commercial paper can be sold either directly or through dealers. Many large sales finance companies have found it profitable, because of the volume, to sell their paper directly to investors, thus bypassing dealers. Among companies selling paper on this basis are the C.I.T. Financial Corporation, Ford Motor Credit Company, General Motors Acceptance Corporation (GMAC), and Sears Roebuck Acceptance Corporation.

[handwritten margin note: Direct sales $25,000 + up — higher yield than Treasury (30-270 days) — No secondary mkt]

Paper sold through dealers is issued by industrial companies and smaller finance companies. The dealer organization for commercial paper is dominated by three firms. Overall, the total volume of paper sold through dealers is considerably less than the total volume sold directly. Dealers screen potential issuers very carefully as to their credit-worthiness. In a sense, the dealer stands behind the paper he places with investors.

Rates on commercial paper are somewhat higher than rates on Treasury bills of the same maturity and about the same as the rates available on bankers' acceptances. Paper sold directly, however, generally commands a lower yield than paper sold through dealers. Usually, commercial paper is sold on a discount basis, and maturities generally range from 30 to 270 days. Most paper is held to maturity, for there is essentially no secondary market. However, direct sellers of commercial paper will often repurchase the paper on request. Arrangements may also be made through dealers for repurchase of paper sold through them. Commercial paper is sold only in fairly large denominations, usually of at least $25,000.

Repurchase agreements

In an effort to tap new sources of financing, government security dealers offer repurchase agreements to corporations. The repurchase agreement, or "repo," as it is called, is the sale of short-term securities by the dealer to the investor whereby the dealer agrees to repurchase the securities at a specified future time. The investor receives a given yield while he holds the security. The length of the holding period itself is tailored to the needs of the investor. Thus, repurchase agreements give the investor a great deal of flexibility with respect to maturity. Rates on repurchase agreements are related to the rates on Treasury bills, federal funds, and loans to government security dealers by commercial banks. There is little marketability to the instrument, but the usual maturity is only a few days. Because the instrument involved is a U.S. Treasury security, there is no default risk.

Negotiable certificates of deposit

Negotiable time certificates of deposit are a short-term investment that originated in 1961. The certificate (CD) is evidence of the deposit of funds at a commercial bank for a specified period of time and at a specified rate of interest. The most common denomination is $100,000, so its appeal is limited to large investors. Money-market banks quote rates on CD's; these rates are changed periodically in keeping with changes in other money-market rates. The maximum rate that banks are allowed to pay, however, is regulated by the Federal Reserve System under Regulation Q. Yields on CD's are greater than those on Treasury bills and repos and about the same as those on bankers' acceptances and commercial paper. Original maturities of CD's generally range from 30 to

360 days. A fair secondary market has developed for the CD's of the large money-market banks, so such CD's are marketable. Default risk is that of the bank failing, a possibility that is low in most cases.

Portfolio management

The decision to invest excess cash in marketable securities involves not only the amount to invest but also the type of security in which to invest. To some extent, the two decisions are interdependent. Both should be based upon an evaluation of expected net cash flows and the certainty of these cash flows. If future cash-flow patterns are known with reasonable certainty, the portfolio may be arranged so that securities will be maturing on approximately the dates when the funds will be needed. Such a cash-flow pattern gives the firm a great deal of flexibility in maximizing the average return on the entire portfolio, for it is unlikely that significant amounts of securities will have to be sold unexpectedly. If future cash flows are fairly uncertain, the most important characteristics of a security become its marketability and risk with respect to fluctuations in market value. Treasury bills and short-term repos are perhaps best suited for the emergency liquidity needs of the firm. Higher yields can be achieved by investing in longer-term, less marketable securities with greater default risk. Although the firm should always be concerned with marketability, some possibility of loss of principal is tolerable provided the expected return is high enough. Thus, the firm faces the familiar tradeoff between risk and return.

The larger the security portfolio, the more chance there is for specialization and economies of operation. A large enough security portfolio may justify a staff whose sole responsibility is managing the portfolio. Such a staff can undertake research, plan diversification, keep abreast of market conditions, and continually analyze and improve the firm's position. When investment is made a specialized function of the firm, the number of different securities considered for investment is likely to be diverse. Moreover, continual effort can be devoted to achieving the highest yield possible in keeping with the cash needs of the firm. Trading techniques in such a firm tend to be very sophisticated. For companies with smaller security positions, however, there may be no economic justification for a staff. Indeed, a single individual may handle investments on a part-time basis. For this type of company, the diversity of securities in the portfolio will probably be limited.

Although diversification of the short-term marketable security portfolio of a firm might be desirable, there is far less opportunity for such diversification than there is with a portfolio of common stocks.[20] *Diversification* is usually defined as the reduction of the dispersion of possible returns from a portfolio relative to the expected return from the portfolio. This reduction is achieved by investing in securities not having

[20] See Chapter 3 for a review of portfolio analysis and selection.

high degrees of covariance among themselves. Unfortunately, there is a high degree of correlation in the price movements of money-market instruments over time. Consequently, they are ill-suited for purposes of diversification. As a result, the objective of most firms is to maximize overall return subject to maintaining sufficient liquidity to meet cash drains. Because of differences in the ability to diversify, the management of a firm's marketable security portfolio differs considerably from the management of a portfolio of common stocks.

SUMMARY

The firm has three motives for holding liquid assets: the transactions motive, the precautionary motive, and the speculative motive. Our concern is with only the first two of these motives. In the management of cash, we should attempt to accelerate collections and handle disbursements so that maximum cash is available. Collections can be accelerated by means of concentration banking, a lock-box system, and certain other procedures. Disbursements should be handled so as to give maximum transfer flexibility and the optimum timing of payments.

Given the total level of liquid assets, comprised of cash and marketable securities, the firm must determine the optimal split between these two assets. The optimal level of cash, which in turn determines the optimal level of marketable securities, is the greater of (1) the compensating balance requirement of a commercial bank, and (2) the optimal level determined by an appropriate model. The first constraint is rather straightforward and its determination was discussed in depth. With respect to the second constraint, the optimal level of cash depends upon the predictability of future cash flows, their volatility, the fixed cost of a security transaction, and the carrying cost of holding cash—that is, the interest rate foregone on marketable securities. Several models were examined for determining an optimal level of average cash balances under varying assumptions as to the predictability and pattern of future cash flows.

There are a number of marketable securities in which the firm can invest. These securities can be evaluated in relation to their default risk, marketability, maturity, and taxability. Depending upon the cash-flow pattern of the firm and other considerations, a portfolio can be selected in keeping with these characteristics. Specific securities considered included Treasury securities, government agency securities, bankers' acceptances, commercial paper, repurchase agreements, and certificates of deposit. It was shown that the management of a firm's portfolio of marketable securities is considerably different from the management of a portfolio of common stocks.

1. The Zindler Company currently has a centralized billing system. Payments are made by all customers to the central billing location. It requires, on the average, four days for customers' mailed payments to reach the central location. Further, an additional one and one-half days are required to process payments before a deposit can be made. The firm has a daily average collection of $500,000.

   The company has recently considered the possibility of initiating a lock-box system. It has been estimated that such a system would reduce the time required for customers' mailed payments to reach the receipt location by two and one-half days. Further, the processing time could be reduced by an additional day, because each lock-box bank would pick up mailed deposits twice daily.

   (a) Determine the reduction in cash balances that can be achieved through the use of a lock-box system.

   (b) Determine the opportunity cost of the present system, assuming a 5 percent return on short-term instruments.

   (c) If the annual cost of the lock-box system will be $75,000, should such a system be initiated?

2. The List Company, which can earn 7 percent on money-market instruments, currently has a lock-box arrangement with a New Orleans bank for its southern customers. The bank handles $3 million a day in return for a compensating balance of $2 million.

   (a) The List Company has discovered that it could divide the southern region into a southwestern region (with $1 million a day in collections, which could be handled by a Dallas bank for a $1 million compensating balance) and a southeastern region (with $2 million a day in collections, which could be handled by an Atlanta bank for a $2 million compensating balance). In each case, collections would be one-half day quicker than with the New Orleans arrangement. What would be the annual savings (or cost) of dividing the southern region?

   (b) In an effort to retain the business, the New Orleans bank has offered to handle the collections strictly on a fee basis (no compensating balance). What would be the maximum fee the New Orleans bank could charge and still retain List's business?

3. The Schriver Company plans to have $1 million in steady cash outlays for next year. The firm believes that it will face an opportunity interest rate of 5 percent and will incur a cost of $100 each time it borrows (or withdraws). Cash outlays are expected to be steady over the year. Using the inventory model:

   (a) Determine the transactions demand for cash (the optimal borrowing or withdrawal lot size) for the Schriver Company.

   (b) What is the total cost for the use of cash needed for transactions demand?

   (c) What will be the cash cycle for the firm (velocity)?

   (d) What would be the average cash balance for the firm?

4. Assume that the Schriver Company (problem 3) began the year with $1 million in cash.

(a) How much would initially be invested in securities?

(b) How much would be invested in securities after 231 days?

5. The Verloom Berloop Tulip Bulb Company has experienced a stochastic demand for its product with the result that cash balances fluctuate randomly. The standard deviation of daily net cash flows, σ, is $1,000. The company wishes to make the transfer of funds from cash to marketable securities and vice versa as automatic as possible. It has heard that this can be done by imposing upper and lower bound control limits. The current interest rate on marketable securities is 6 percent. The fixed cost associated with each transfer is $100 and transfers are instantaneous.

(a) What are the optimal upper and lower bound control limits? (Assume a 360-day year.)

(b) What happens at these control limits?

6. The Excelsior Manufacturing Company follows a policy of determining its cash needs on a weekly basis and investing surplus cash in Treasury bills. The firm must maintain a minimum cash balance of $10 million throughout the week. It can obtain 0.10 percent per week on Treasury bills, though a commission of 0.02 percent must be paid on each purchase and each sale. A fixed cost of $100 per transaction is also incurred. The firm can purchase or sell bills in minimum lots of $500,000.

As of March 7, the firm had $10 million in cash and $7 million in Treasury bills. The cash budget for the week ending March 14 indicates the following net receipt distribution:

Probability	.10	.20	.30	.20	.20
Amount	$-$1,000,000	$-$500,000	0	$+$500,000	$+$1,000,000

Assuming that the firm will not borrow to maintain the minimum level of cash balances as long as it has marketable securities on hand:

(a) Determine the optimum level of security holdings for the week.

(b) Why do you get the results you obtain? Do you suspect that the optimum level might not be attainable in this situation?

(c) How much expected net income will be earned on the security holdings?

Note: It is assumed that the sale of securities during the week will result in a loss of one-half the interest that would be received if the securities were held for the entire week.

(This problem involves extensive computations. Typical time to work it is somewhat over one hour.)

7. Assume the initial position of the Excelsior Manufacturing Company on March 7. Further, assume that all conditions outlined in problem 6 prevail except the following:

(a) Treasury bills yield 0.08 percent per week.

(b) Commissions are 0.03 percent per transaction.

(c) The sale of securities during the week will result in a 75 percent loss of the interest that would be received if the securities were held for the entire week.

    (1) Determine the optimum level of security holdings for the week.

    (2) Should bills be purchased or sold? In what quantity?

    (3) How much expected net income will be earned on the security holdings?

    (4) How much expected net income would be earned if an amount $500,000 below the optimum were held? An amount $500,000 above the optimum?

8. The James Company has excess cash to invest for thirty days; it has narrowed the choice of money-market instruments to Treasury bills and commercial paper. Because of the greater risk associated with commercial paper, the expected return is higher but the dispersion of possible returns is also greater than in the case of Treasury bills. It is assumed that the returns on each instrument are normally distributed and perfectly positively correlated with each other (for example, if the bill return is $\mu_{TB} + 1\sigma_{TB}$, the paper return will be $\mu_{CP} + 1\sigma_{CP}$).

    (a) If $\mu_{TB} = 6$ percent and $\sigma_{TB} = 0.25$ percent, while $\mu_{CP} = 6.5$ percent and $\sigma_{CP} = 0.75$ percent (all expressed on an annual basis), what is the probability that Treasury bills will offer a higher effective yield over the period?

    (b) If the James Company has decided not to invest in commercial paper unless it will offer a superior yield to Treasury bills 90 percent of the time, what should the company do?

    (c) Rework parts (a) and (b), assuming $\sigma_{CP} = 0.5$ percent.

9. *Research Project*

    Examine quotations in *The Wall Street Journal* for each of the following money-market instruments:

    (a) Treasury bills

    (b) Bankers' acceptances

    (c) Certificates of deposit

    (d) Commercial paper

    (e) Government agency issues

Evaluate the yield-risk tradeoff for each instrument. Consider the appropriateness of each of these securities for the corporation's short-term investment account.

SELECTED REFERENCES

Abed, Mark I., "The Stochastic Cash Balance Problem," Ph.D. Dissertation, University of California, Berkeley, 1972.

An Analytical Record of Yields and Yield Spreads. New York: Salomon Brothers, 1976.

Archer, Stephen H., "A Model for the Determination of Firm Cash Balances," *Journal of Financial and Quantitative Analysis,* 1 (March 1966), 1–11.

Baumol, William J., "The Transactions Demand for Cash:

An Inventory Theoretic Approach," *Quarterly Journal of Economics,* 65 (November 1952), 545–56.

Baxter, Nevins D., "Marketability, Default Risk, and Yields on Money-Market Instruments," *Journal of Financial and Quantitative Analysis,* 3 (March 1968), 75–85.

Budin, Morris, and A. T. Eapen, "Cash Generation in Business Operations: Some Simulation Models," *Journal of Finance,* 25 (December 1970), 1091–1107.

Barro, Robert J., "Integral Constraints and Aggregation in an Inventory Model of Money Demand," *Journal of Finance,* 31 (March 1976), 77–88.

Budin, Morris, and Robert J. Van Handel, "A Rule-of-Thumb Theory of Cash Holdings by Firms," *Journal of Financial and Quantitative Analysis,* 10 (March 1975), 85–108.

Calman, Robert F., *Linear Programming and Cash Management/CASH ALPHA.* Cambridge, Mass.: M.I.T. Press, 1968.

Daellenbach, Hans G., "Are Cash Management Optimization Models Worthwhile?" *Journal of Financial and Quantitative Analysis,* 9 (September 1974), 607–26.

Elton, Edwin J., and Martin J. Gruber, *Finance as a Dynamic Process,* Chapter 3. Englewood Cliffs, N.J.: Prentice-Hall, 1975.

Eppen, Gary D., and Eugene F. Fama, "Cash Balance and Simple Dynamic Portfolio Problems with Proportional Costs," *International Economic Review,* 10 (June 1969), 110–33.

———, "Solutions for Cash-Balance and Simple Dynamic-Portfolio Problems," *Journal of Business,* 41 (January 1968), 94–112.

———, "Three-Asset Cash Balance and Dynamic Portfolio Problems," *Management Science,* 17 (January 1971), 311–19.

Frost, Peter A., "Banking Services, Minimum Cash Balances and the Firm's Demand for Money," *Journal of Finance,* 25 (December 1970), 1029–39.

Levy, Ferdinand K., "An Application of Heuristic Problem Solving to Accounts Receivable Management," *Management Science,* 12 (February 1966), 236–44.

Mehta, Dileep R., *Working Capital Management,* Chapters 6–8. Englewood Cliffs, N.J.: Prentice-Hall, 1974.

Miller, Merton H., and Daniel Orr, "The Demand for Money by Firms: Extension of Analytic Results," *Journal of Finance,* 23 (December 1968), 735–59.

———, "A Model of the Demand for Money by Firms," *Quarterly Journal of Economics,* 80 (August 1966), 413–35.

Neave, Edwin H., "The Stochastic Cash-Balance Problem with Fixed Costs for Increases and Decreases," *Management Science,* 16 (March 1970), 472–90.

Orgler, Yair E., *Cash Management.* Belmont, Calif.: Wadsworth, 1970.

———, "An Unequal-Period Model for Cash-Management Decisions," *Management Science,* 16 (October 1969), 77–92.

Peterson, D. E., *A Quantitative Framework for Financial Management,* Chapter 8. Homewood, Ill.: Richard D. Irwin, 1969.

Searby, Frederick W., "Use Your Hidden Cash Resources," *Harvard Business Review,* 46 (March–April 1968), 74–75.

Sethi, Suresh P., and Gerald L. Thompson, "Application of Mathematical Control Theory to Finance: Modeling Simple Dynamic Cash Balance Problems," *Journal of Financial and Quantitative Analysis,* 5 (December 1970), 381–94.

Smith, Keith V., *Management of Working Capital,* Section 2. New York: West Publishing, 1974.

Stancill, James McN., *The Management of Working Capital,* Chapters 2 and 3. Scranton, Pa.: Intext, 1971.

Stone, Bernell K., "Cash Planning and Credit-Line Determination with a Financial Statement Simulator: A Cash Report on Short-Term Financial Planning," *Journal of Financial and Quantitative Analysis,* 8 (November 1973), 711–30.

———, "Allocating Credit Lines, Planned Borrowing, and Tangible Services over a Company's Banking System," *Financial Management,* 4 (Summer 1975), 65–78.

Tobin, James, "The Interest Elasticity of Transactions Demand for Cash," *Review of Economics and Statistics,* 37 (August 1956), 241–47.

Van Horne, James, *The Function and Analysis of Capital Market Rates.* Englewood Cliffs, N.J.: Prentice-Hall, 1970.

———, "Interest-Rate Expectations, the Shape of the Yield Curve, and Monetary Policy," *Review of Economics and Statistics,* 48 (May 1966), 211–15.

———, "Interest-Rate Risk and the Term Structure of Interest Rates," *Journal of Political Economy,* 73 (August 1965), 344–51.

Vogel, Robert C., and G. S. Maddala, "Cross-Section Estimates of Liquid Asset Demand by Manufacturing Corporations," *Journal of Finance,* 22 (December 1967), 557–75.

Weitzman, Martin, "A Model of the Demand for Money by Firms: Comment," *Quarterly Journal of Economics,* 82 (March 1968), 161–64.

Whalen, E. L., "An Extension of the Baumol-Tobin Approach to the Transactions Demand for Cash," *Journal of Finance,* 23 (March 1968), 113–34.

MANAGEMENT of ACCOUNTS RECEIVABLE

Accounts receivable represent the extension of open-account credit by one firm to other firms and to individuals. For many companies, accounts receivable are an extremely important investment and require careful analysis. The purpose of this chapter is to examine this vital function and the means by which receivables can be managed efficiently. We consider first the credit and collection policies of the firm as a whole and then discuss credit and collection procedures for the individual account.

Actually, the two facets are closely related. For example, credit policy involves a tradeoff between the profits on sales that give rise to receivables on one hand and the cost of carrying these receivables plus bad-debt losses on the other. Credit analysis is instrumental in determining the amount of credit risk to be accepted. In turn, the amount of risk accepted affects the slowness of receivables, and the resulting investment in receivables, as well as the amount of bad-debt losses. Collection procedures also affect these factors. Thus, the credit and collection procedures of the firm are essential to the firm's overall credit and collection policies.

CREDIT AND COLLECTION POLICIES

Although the level of accounts receivable is affected importantly by the influence of economic conditions on credit sales, it is determined also by policy decisions. Economic conditions, of course, are largely beyond the control of the financial manager. As with other current assets, however, he can vary the level of receivables in keeping with the tradeoff between profitability and risk. By increasing the level of receivables through lower quality standards, for example, the financial manager hopes to stimulate demand, which, in turn, should lead to higher profits. However, there is a cost to carrying the additional receivables as well as a greater risk of bad-debt losses. It is this tradeoff we wish to examine.

The policy variables we consider include the quality of the trade accounts accepted, the length of the credit period, the cash discount given, any special terms given, such as seasonal datings, and the collection program of the firm. Together, these elements largely determine the average collection period and the proportion of bad-debt losses. We analyze each element in turn, holding constant certain of the others as well as an exogenous variables that affect the average collection period and the percentage of bad-debt losses. In addition, we assume that the evaluation of risk is sufficiently standardized so that degrees of risk for different accounts can be compared objectively.

CREDIT STANDARDS

Credit policy can have a significant influence upon sales. If competitors extend credit liberally and we do not, our policy may have a dampening effect upon the marketing effort. Trade credit is one of many factors that influence the demand for a firm's product. Consequently, the degree to which trade credit can promote demand depends upon what other factors are being employed. In theory, the firm should lower its quality standard for accounts accepted as long as the profitability of sales generated exceeds the added costs of the receivables. What are the costs of relaxing credit standards? One type of cost is the enlarged credit department and the clerical expenses involved in checking additional accounts and servicing the added volume of receivables. We assume for now that these costs are deducted from the profitability of additional sales to give a net profitability figure for computational purposes. Another cost comes from the increased probability of bad-debt losses. However, we postpone consideration of this cost to a subsequent section; we assume for now that there are no bad-debt losses.

Finally, there is the cost of the additional investment in receivables, resulting from (1) increased sales and (2) a slower average collection period. If new customers are attracted by the relaxed credit standards, collecting from these customers is likely to be slower than collecting from existing customers. In addition, a more liberal extension of credit may cause certain existing customers to be less conscientious in paying their bills on time. Those who decide credit policy must consider this possibility.

To determine the profitability of a more liberal extension of credit, we must know the profitability of additional sales, the added demand for products arising from the relaxed credit standards, the increased slowness of the average collection period, and the required return on investment. Suppose a firm's product sells for $10 a unit, of which $7 represents variable costs before taxes, including credit department costs. Current annual sales are $2.4 million, represented entirely by credit sales. The firm is considering a more liberal extension of credit, which will result in a slowing in the average collection period from one to two months. However, existing customers are not expected to alter their payment habits. The relaxation in credit standards is expected to produce a 25 percent increase in sales, to $3 million annually.[1] This $600,000 increase represents 60,000 additional units if we assume that the price per unit stays the same. Finally, assume that the required rate of return on investment in receivables is 20 percent before taxes.

Given this information, our evaluation is reduced to a tradeoff between the added profitability on the additional sales and the required return on the additional investment in receivables, and we are able to make the calculations shown in Table 15-1. Inasmuch as the profitability on additional sales, $180,000, exceeds the required return on the additional investment, $42,000, the firm would be well advised to relax its credit standards. An optimal credit policy would involve extending trade

[1] In estimating the effect of a change in credit policy on demand, it is important to take into account the reaction of competitors to this change. Their reaction will affect demand over the long run.

Table 15·1   Profitability versus required return

Profitability of additional sales	=	$3 × 60,000 units = $180,000
avg. Present level of receivables *(1mo.)*	=	(Annual sales/Receivable turnover)
T.O = 12		$2.4 million/12 = $200,000
avg Level of receivables after change *(2 mos)* in credit policy T.O = $\frac{12}{72}$ < 6	=	$3 million/6 = $500,000
Additional receivables	=	$300,000
Additional investment in receivables	=	Additional receivables × Variable costs as a percent of sales $300,000 × 0.7 = $210,000
Required return on additional investment	=	0.20 × $210,000 = $42,000

credit more liberally until the marginal profitability on additional sales equals the required return on the additional investment in receivables.

Obviously, there are many practical problems in affecting a change in credit policy, particularly in estimating the outcomes. In our example, we have worked with only the expected values of additional demand and of the slowing of the average collection period. It is possible, and desirable, to attach probability distributions to the increased demand and to the increased slowness in receivables and evaluate a range of possible outcomes. For simplicity of discussion, however, we shall not incorporate these dimensions into our example.

Another assumption is that we can produce 60,000 additional units at a variable cost of $7 a unit; that is, we do not have to increase our plant. After some point, we are no longer able to meet additional demand with existing plant and would need to add plant. This occurrence would necessitate a change in analysis, for there would be a large block of incremental costs at the point where the existing plant could produce no more units. One implication to all of this is that the firm should vary its credit quality standards in keeping with the level of production. As capacity is approached, quality standards might be increased. When production sags and the firm operates at a level below capacity, the lowering of credit quality standards becomes more attractive, all other things the same. Implied also in our analysis is that the conditions described will be permanent. That is, increased demand as a function of lowering credit quality standards as well as price and cost figures will remain unchanged. If the increase in sales that results from a change in credit policy were a one-shot as opposed to a continuing occurrence, we would need to modify our analysis accordingly.

CREDIT TERMS

Credit period   Credit terms involve both the length of the credit period and the discount given. The terms "2/10, net 30" mean that a 2 percent discount is given if the bill is paid before the tenth day after the date of invoice; payment is due by the thirtieth day.

The credit period, then, is thirty days. Although the customs of the industry frequently dictate the terms given, the credit period is another means by which a firm may be able to affect product demand—hoping to increase demand by extending the credit period. As before, the tradeoff is between the profitability of additional sales and the required return on the additional investment in receivables. Assume for the purpose of illustration that our example involves lengthening the credit period from thirty to sixty days instead of relaxing credit standards. Assume also that by lengthening the credit period, the firm expects sales to increase by 25 percent and the average collection period to increase from one to two months. Because the quality of account being accepted is the same, we assume that there is no change in bad-debt losses—in other words, that there are no losses. The analysis is the same as in Table 15-1. As seen, such a policy would be advantageous to the company because the profitability on additional sales—$180,000—exceeds the required return on the additional investment in receivables—$42,000.

Discount given and the discount period

Varying the discount involves an attempt to speed up the payment of receivables. To be sure, the discount also may have an effect upon demand and upon bad-debt losses. However, we assume that the discount offered is not regarded as a means of cutting price and thereby affecting demand,[2] and that the discount offered does not affect the amount of bad-debt losses. Holding constant these factors, we must determine whether a speedup in collections would more than offset the cost of an increase in the discount. If it would, the present discount policy should be changed.

Suppose, for example, that the firm has annual credit sales of $3 million and an average collection period of two months, and that the sales terms are net 45 days, with no discount given. Assume further that the annual turnover of receivables is six times. Consequently, the average receivable balance is $500,000. Now, suppose that by instigating terms of 2/10, net 45, the average collection period is reduced to one month and that 50 percent of the customers (in dollar volume) take advantage of the 2 percent discount. The opportunity cost of the discount to the firm is .02 × 0.5 × $3 million, or $30,000 annually. However, the turnover of receivables has improved to twelve times a year, so that average receivables are reduced from $500,000 to $250,000.

Thus, the firm realizes $250,000 from accelerated collections. The value of the funds released is their opportunity cost. If we assume a 20 percent rate of return, the opportunity saving is $50,000. In this case the opportunity saving arising from a speedup in collections is greater than

---

[2]If a price effect does occur, it will depend upon the elasticity of demand. The greater the discount, the lower the effective price to the customer who takes discounts and the greater his demand. However, the relevant range of discount changes is quite small. Unless demand is highly elastic, the effect on demand will be small.

the cost of the discount. Consequently, the firm should adopt a 2 percent discount. If the speedup in collections had not resulted in sufficient opportunity savings to offset the cost of discount, the discount policy should not be changed. It is possible, of course, that discounts other than 2 percent may result in an even greater difference between the opportunity savings and the cost of the discount.

In addition to the size of the discount offered, the length of the discount period also may affect the average collection period. Here, the effect is not as clear as before. When a firm lengthens the discount period, two forces influence the average collection period. If the credit period is held constant, certain customers will be tempted to take the discount where previously they did not do so. This practice will tend to shorten the average collection period. On the other hand, customers who have been taking the discount and paying at the end of the discount period will now postpone payment until the end of the new discount period, thereby lengthening the average collection period. Whether the first force dominates the second will depend upon the mix of payment habits of the firm's customers. Given estimates of the likely effect of a change in the discount period on the average collection period, the firm can balance this effect with the increased dollar cost associated with more customers taking the discount. For all practical purposes, the discount period is variable within only a narrow range. The minimum period for mailing invoices and receipt of checks is about ten days. To increase it significantly beyond ten days defeats its purpose. In reality, then, the discount period is not an important decision variable.

Seasonal datings

Another aspect of the credit terms given to customers involves seasonal datings. During periods of slack sales, firms will sometimes sell to customers without requiring payment for some time to come. This extension of the credit period is known as seasonal dating. Seasonal datings may be employed to stimulate demand from customers who cannot pay until later in the season. Because datings can be tailored to the cash flow of the customer, they can play an important role in selling the goods. Again, we should compare the profitability of additional sales with the required return on the additional investment in receivables to determine whether datings are an appropriate means by which to stimulate demand.

Datings also can be used to avoid inventory carrying costs. If sales are seasonal and production is steady throughout the year, there will be buildups in finished goods inventory during certain times of the year. Storage involves warehousing costs; therefore, it may be profitable to give datings in order to move the goods and avoid these costs. If warehousing costs plus the required rate of return on investment in inventory exceed the required rate of return on the additional investment in receivables, it is worthwhile to give datings.

In the above examples, we assumed no bad-debt losses. Our concern in this section is not only with the slowness of collection but also with the portion of the receivables defaulting. Different credit policies will involve both of these factors. Suppose that we are considering the present credit policy (sales of $2,400,000) together with two new ones and that these policies are expected to produce the following results:

	Present Policy	Policy A	Policy B
Additional demand (percentage)	0	25	35
Average collection period	1 month	2 months	3 months
Default losses (percentage)	1	3	6

We assume that after six months an account is turned over to a collection agency and that, on the average, 1 percent of the total receivable volume under the present credit policy is never received by the firm, 3 percent is never received under policy A, and 6 percent is never received under policy B.

If we go through the same type of calculations as in the earlier example, we obtain the results shown in Table 15-2 for policies A and B. The profitability of the two credit policies in relation to the required return on investment can be summarized as follows:

	Policy A	Policy B
Profitability of additional sales less additional bad-debt losses, Present Policy to Policy A	$114,000	
Profitability of additional sales less additional bad-debt losses, Policy A to Policy B		$(32,400)
Required return on additional investment	42,000	43,400
	$ 72,000	$(75,800)

Consequently, we would want to adopt Policy A but would not want to go so far in relaxing our credit standards as Policy B. As we see, the marginal benefit is positive in moving from the present policy to Policy A, but negative in going from Policy A to Policy B. It is possible, of course, that a relaxation of credit standards that fell on one side or the other of Policy A would provide an even greater marginal benefit; the optimal policy is the one that provides the greatest marginal benefit.

Table 15·2   Profitability versus required return and bad-debt losses

	Policy A	Policy B
Annual sales	$3,000,000	$3,240,000
Turnover of receivables	6	4
Level of receivables after change in credit policy	$ 500,000	$ 810,000
Additional receivables	$ 300,000	$ 310,000
Additional investment in receivables above present investment*	$ 210,000	
Additional investment in receivables above Policy A investment*		$ 217,000
Required return on additional investment (20%)	$ 42,000	$ 43,400
Additional sales above present sales (units)	$ 60,000	
Additional sales above Policy A sales (units)		$ 24,000
Profitability of additional sales	$ 180,000	$ 72,000
Bad-debt losses (percent of annual sales)	$ 90,000	$ 194,400
Additional bad-debt losses above present losses ($24,000)	$ 66,000	
Additional bad-debt losses above Policy A losses ($90,000)		$ 104,400
Profitability of additional sales less additional bad-debt losses	$ 114,000	$ (32,400)

*(Additional receivables) (Variable cost per unit/Selling price per unit)

Another approach to the problem might be to combine the probability of bad-debt losses with the probability of slowness of collection for each customer. Such an approach would be practical only if the size of the account is reasonably large. For a customer with a $10,000 receivable, we might formulate the probability distribution of expected collections shown in Table 15-3.

Table 15·3   Possible time of receipt: single account

Time Received after Billing	Probability	Expected Collections
1 month	0.50	$ 5,000
2 months	0.20	2,000
3 months	0.10	1,000
4 months	0.05	500
5 months	0.05	500
6 months	0.05	500
Bad-debt loss	0.05	500
	1.00	$10,000

For this customer, there is a .05 probability that the account will not be paid after six months and that it will be charged off as a bad-debt loss.[3] For other customers, we could construct similar probability distributions. If the probability distributions were independent, a total probability distribution could be obtained simply by totaling the expected collections for each month for all accounts.[4] For our hypothetical firm, the probability distribution for all accounts, totaling $500,000, might be that shown in Table 15-4. By calculating probability distributions for all accounts at different times of the year and comparing actual results with expected results, we could obtain fairly exact information as to the average investment in receivables and the average collection period for these receivables.

Table 15·4   Possible time of receipts: all accounts

Time Received after Billing	Probability	Expected Collections
1 month	0.60	$300,000
2 months	0.15	75,000
3 months	0.10	50,000
4 months	0.05	25,000
5 months	0.04	20,000
6 months	0.02	10,000
Bad-debt loss	0.04	20,000
	1.00	$500,000

COLLECTION POLICY

The overall collection policy of the firm is determined by the combination of collection procedures it undertakes. These procedures include such things as letters sent, phone calls, personal calls, and legal action, and they are described later in this chapter. One of the principal policy variables is the amount expended on collection procedures.

[3] Cyert, Davidson, and Thompson have made an interesting application of Markov chains to estimating the probability of a bad-debt loss for an account at various future dates. R. M. Cyert, H. J. Davidson, and G. L. Thompson, "Estimation of the Allowance for Doubtful Accounts by Markov Chains," *Management Science*, 8 (April 1962), 287–303. For similar applications, see William Beranek, *Analysis for Financial Decisions* (Homewood, Ill.: Richard D. Irwin, 1963), pp. 308–20; and Edwin J. Elton and Martin J. Gruber, *Finance as a Dynamic Process* (Englewood Cliffs, N.J.: Prentice-Hall, 1975), Chapter 4.

[4] For an examination of the predictive accuracy of expected bad-debt ratios for customers under varying degrees of correlation between default losses for such customers, see James C. T. Mao and Carl Erik Sarndal, "Controlling Risks in Accounts Receivable Management," *Journal of Business Finance & Accounting*, 1 (Autumn 1974), 395–403.

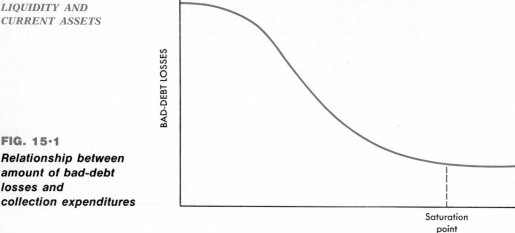

Within a range, the greater the relative amount expended, the lower the proportion of bad-debt losses and the shorter the average collection period, all other things the same.

The relationships, however, are not linear. Initial collection expenditures are likely to cause little reduction in bad-debt losses. Additional expenditures begin to have a significant effect in reducing the amount of bad-debt losses. Beyond a point, however, additional expenditures tend to have little effect in further reducing these losses. The hypothesized relationship between expenditures and bad-debt losses is shown in Figure 15-1. Likewise, the relationship between the average collection period and the level of collection expenditures is likely to be similar to that shown in the figure.

If sales are independent of the collection effort, the appropriate level of collection expenditure again involves a tradeoff—this time between the level of expenditure on the one hand and the reduction in the cost of bad-debt losses and reduction in investment in receivables on the other. Suppose that we are considering the present collection program in relation to two new ones and that the programs were expected to produce these results:

	Present Program	Program A	Program B
Annual collection expenditures	$116,000	$148,000	$200,000
Average collection period	2 months	1½ months	1 month
Percentage of default	3	2	1

Assume that present sales are $2.4 million and that they are not expected to change with changes in the collection effort. If we go through the same type of reasoning as we did for the discount policy where receivables were reduced and for bad-debt losses, we obtain the results in Table 15-5. In the last three rows of the table, we see that the opportunity saving resulting from a speedup in collections plus the reduction in bad-debt losses exceeds the additional collection expenditures in going from the present program to Program *A*, but not in going from Program *A* to Program *B*. As a result, the firm should adopt Program *A* but not increase collection expenditures to the extent of Program *B*.

In the example above, we have assumed that demand is independent of the collection effort. In most cases, however, sales are likely to be affected adversely if the collection efforts of the firm become too intense and customers become increasingly irritated. If they do, we must take into account the relationship between the collection effort and demand. Reduction in demand can be incorporated into the marginal analysis of collection expenditures in the same manner as was the increase in demand accompanying a relaxation in credit standards. In addition, if

Table 15·5 Evaluation of collection programs

	Present Program	Program A	Program B
Annual sales	$2,400,000	$2,400,000	$2,400,000
Turnover of receivables	6	8	12
Average receivables	$ 400,000	$ 300,000	$ 200,000
Reduction in receivables from present level		$ 100,000	
Reduction in receivables from Program A level			$ 100,000
Return on reduction in receivables (20 percent)		$ 20,000	$ 20,000
Bad-debt losses (percent of annual sales)	$ 72,000	$ 48,000	$ 24,000
Reduction in bad-debt losses from present losses		$ 24,000	
Reduction in bad-debt losses from Program A losses			$ 24,000
Opportunity saving on reduced receivables plus reduction in bad-debt losses		$ 44,000	$ 44,000
Additional collection expenditures from present expenditures		$ 32,000	
Additional collection expenditures from Program A expenditures			$ 52,000

the collection effort has an effect on the percentage of total sales taking a cash discount, this factor must be considered. With increased collection efforts, for example, more customers might take the cash discount.

CREDIT AND COLLECTION POLICIES— SUMMARY

We see that the credit and collection policies of a firm involve several decisions as to (1) the quality of account accepted, (2) the credit period, (3) the cash discount given, (4) any special terms such as seasonal datings, and (5) the level of collection expenditures. In each case, the decision should involve a comparison of what is to be gained by a change in policy with the cost of the change. Optimal credit and collection policies would be those that resulted in the marginal gains equaling the marginal costs.

To maximize profits arising from credit and collection policies, the firm should vary these policies jointly until an optimal solution is achieved. That solution will determine the best combination of credit standards, credit period, cash discount policy, special terms, and level of collection expenditures. In this regard, sensitivity analysis might be used to judge the impact of a change in policies upon profits. Once functional relationships have been specified for the relationship between a particular policy and marginal sales, average collection period, and bad-debt losses, the policy can be varied from one extreme to the other, holding constant other factors. This variation gives insight into the impact of a change in policy upon profits.

For most policy variables, profits increase at a decreasing rate up to a point and then decrease as the policy is varied from no effort to an extreme effort. This relationship is depicted in Figure 15-2 for the quality of account rejected. When there are no credit standards, that is, when all applicants are accepted, sales are maximized. However, the maximization of sales is offset by large bad-debt losses as well as by the opportunity cost of carrying a very large receivable position. As credit standards are initiated and applicants rejected, revenue from sales declines, but so do the average collection period and bad-debt losses. Because the latter two decline initially at a faster rate than do sales, profits increase. As credit standards are tightened increasingly, however, sales revenue declines at an increasing rate. At the same time, the average collection period and bad-debt losses decrease at a decreasing rate. Fewer and fewer bad credit risks are eliminated. Because of the combination of these influences, total profits of the firm increase at a diminishing rate with stricter credit standards up to a point, after which they decline. The optimal policy with respect to credit standards is represented by point X in the figure. In turn, this policy determines the level of accounts receivable held by the firm.

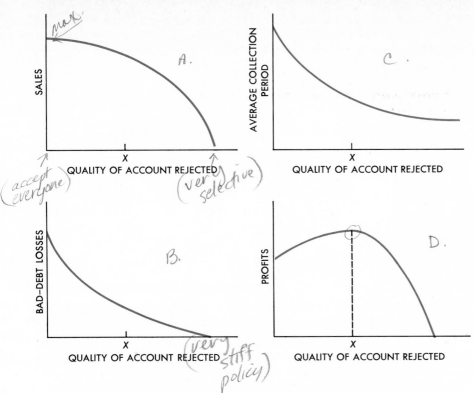

max.

A.

SALES

X
QUALITY OF ACCOUNT REJECTED

(accept
everyone)

(very
selective)

C.

AVERAGE COLLECTION PERIOD

X
QUALITY OF ACCOUNT REJECTED

B.

BAD-DEBT LOSSES

X
QUALITY OF ACCOUNT REJECTED

(very
stiff
policy)

D.

PROFITS

X
QUALITY OF ACCOUNT REJECTED

FIG. 15·2
Relationship of sales,
average collection period,
bad-debt losses, and
profits to the quality
of account rejected

To the extent that decisions with respect to credit standards, the credit period, the discount given, special terms offered, and the level of collection expenditures exercise a joint influence upon profits, this interdependency must be recognized in formulating the functional relationships. With assumed relationships specified, the firm can use sensitivity analysis to experiment with different credit and collection policies in order to determine the optimal set of policies. The optimal set establishes the credit terms given, the collection procedures followed, and the cutoff point on quality of account accepted.[5]

In cases where some of the underlying parameters change, sensitivity analysis proves valuable in formulating new credit and collection policies. For example, if the marginal profit per unit of sales declines due to increased competition, the optimal set of policies is likely to change. Lower profits per unit of sale may not justify the present level of

---

[5] Greer develops a model to maximize profits based upon the number of credit applicants accepted by a creditor. Functional relationships are derived linking the number of accounts accepted to most of the factors we discussed. By differentiating the profit function with respect to the number of applicants accepted and setting the expression equal to zero, one can solve for the number of applicants that maximizes profits. Although somewhat unrealistic for trade credit, the model is useful for a retail company trying to determine a credit policy for charge accounts. Carl C. Greer, "The Optimal Credit Acceptance Policy," *Journal of Financial and Quantitative Analysis*, 2 (December 1967), 399–415.

receivables carried nor the present loss rate. As a result, new credit and collection policies might be in order. Through sensitivity analysis, management could determine the new set of policies that will maximize profit.

The analysis in the last several sections has purposely been rather general, to provide insight into the important concepts of credit and collection policies. Obviously, a policy decision should be based upon a far more specific evaluation than that contained in the examples above. Estimating the increased demand and increased slowness of collections that might accompany a relaxation of credit standards is extremely difficult. Nevertheless, management must make estimates of these relationships if it is to appraise realistically its existing policies.

EVALUATING THE CREDIT APPLICANT

Having established the terms of sale to be offered, the firm must evaluate individual credit applicants and consider the possibilities of a bad debt or slow payment. The credit evaluation procedure involves three related steps: obtaining information on the applicant; analyzing this information to determine the applicant's credit-worthiness; and making the credit decision. The credit decision, in turn, establishes whether credit should be extended and what the maximum amount of credit should be.

SOURCES OF INFORMATION

Though there are a number of sources of credit information, there necessarily are expenses incurred in collecting it. For some accounts, especially small ones, the cost of collecting comprehensive credit information may outweigh the potential profitability of the account. The firm extending credit may have to be satisfied with a limited amount of information on which to base a decision. Later in this chapter, we present a sequential investigation process whereby a firm may weigh the cost of collecting and analyzing additional information in relation to the expected benefits to be derived from it. In addition to cost, the firm must consider the time it takes to investigate a credit applicant. A shipment to a prospective customer cannot be delayed unnecessarily pending an elaborate credit investigation. Thus, the amount of information collected needs to be considered in relation to the time and expense required. Depending upon these considerations, the credit analyst may use one or more of the following sources of information.[6]

---

[6] For a good practical discussion of the ways a company should go about a credit investigation, see Robert S. Morrison, *Handbook for Manufacturing Entrepreneurs*, 2nd ed. (Cleveland: Western Reserve Press, 1974), Chapter 50.

Financial statement
One of the most desirable sources of information for credit analysis is a financial statement that the seller may request from his customer at the time of the prospective sale. Some companies are perfectly willing to provide statements to suppliers, whereas others may refuse to do so. There is frequently a correlation between a company's refusal to provide a statement and weaknesses in its financial position. When possible, it is helpful to obtain interim statements, particularly for companies having seasonal patterns of sales. Needless to say, audited statements are far better than unaudited figures.

Credit ratings and reports
In addition to financial statements, credit ratings are available from various mercantile agencies. Dun & Bradstreet, Inc., is perhaps the best known and most comprehensive of these agencies. It provides credit ratings to subscribers for a vast number of business firms throughout the nation. A key to its individual ratings is shown in Figure 15-3. As we see in the figure, D & B ratings give the credit analyst an indication of the esti-

New Key to Ratings
(Effective May 1, 1971)

ESTIMATED FINANCIAL STRENGTH			COMPOSITE CREDIT APPRAISAL			
			HIGH	GOOD	FAIR	LIMITED
5A	Over	$50,000,000	1	2	3	4
4A	$10,000,000 to	50,000,000	1	2	3	4
3A	1,000,000 to	10,000,000	1	2	3	4
2A	750,000 to	1,000,000	1	2	3	4
1A	500,000 to	750,000	1	2	3	4
BA	300,000 to	500,000	1	2	3	4
BB	200,000 to	300,000	1	2	3	4
CB	125,000 to	200,000	1	2	3	4
CC	75,000 to	125,000	1	2	3	4
DC	50,000 to	75,000	1	2	3	4
DD	35,000 to	50,000	1	2	3	4
EE	20,000 to	35,000	1	2	3	4
FF	10,000 to	20,000	1	2	3	4
GG	5,000 to	10,000	1	2	3	4
HH	Up to	5,000	1	2	3	4

CLASSIFICATION FOR BOTH ESTIMATED FINANCIAL STRENGTH AND CREDIT APPRAISAL

FINANCIAL STRENGTH BRACKET

	EXPLANATION
1 $125,000 and Over	When only the numeral (1 or 2) appears, it is an indication that the estimated financial strength, while not definitely classified, is presumed to be within the range of the ($) figures in the corresponding bracket and that a condition is believed to exist which warrants credit in keeping with that assumption.
2 20,000 to 125,000	

NOT CLASSIFIED OR ABSENCE OF RATING

The absence of a rating, expressed by two hyphens (--), is not to be construed as unfavorable but signifies circumstances difficult to classify within condensed rating symbols. It suggests the advisability of obtaining a report for additional information.

Dun & Bradstreet.®
Business Information Systems, Services and Sciences

FIG. 15·3
Dun & Bradstreet key to ratings

mated size of net worth and a credit appraisal for companies of a particular size, ranging from "high" to "limited." D & B also indicates when the information available is insufficient to provide a rating for a given business.

In addition to its rating service, D & B provides credit reports on business firms. These reports contain a brief history of the company and its principal officers, the nature of the business, certain financial information, and a trade check of suppliers as to the length of their experience with the company and as to whether payments are discount, prompt, or past due. The quality of the D & B reports varies with the information available externally and the willingness of the company being checked to cooperate with the D & B reporter. In addition to Dun & Bradstreet, there are a number of credit agencies that specialize in a particular line of business or in geographic areas, such as New York or Chicago.

Bank checking Another source of information for the firm is a credit check through a bank. Many banks have large credit departments that undertake, as a service, credit checks for their customers. By calling or writing the bank(s) of account of the company being checked, a firm's bank is able to obtain information as to the average cash balance carried, loan accommodations, experience, and sometimes financial information. Because banks generally are more willing to share information with other banks than with a direct inquirer, it usually is best for the firm to initiate the credit check through its own bank rather than to inquire directly.

Exchange of information Credit information frequently is exchanged among companies selling to the same customer. Through various credit organizations, credit men in a particular area become a closely knit group. A company is able to check other suppliers as to their experience with an account. Useful information includes the length of time they have had the account, the maximum credit extended, the amount of the line of credit, and whether payments are prompt or slow. In addition, there are various clearing houses of credit information. The largest of these is the National Association of Credit Management; credit information is provided by this agency in the form of a report.

The company's own experience In addition to these sources, a company's own experience with an account is extremely important.

A study of the promptness of past payments, including any seasonal patterns, for example, is very useful. Frequently, the credit department will make written assessments of the quality of the management of a company to whom credit may be extended. These assessments are very important, for they pertain to the first of the famous "three C's" of credit: *character, collateral,* and *capacity.* For a prospective customer, the salesman is frequently able to supply useful information based on his impressions of the management and operations. Caution is necessary in interpreting this information, however, because a salesman has a natural bias toward granting credit and making the sale.

CREDIT ANALYSIS AND DECISION

Having collected credit information, the firm must undertake a credit analysis of the applicant and determine if he falls above or below the minimum quality standard. If financial statements are provided, the analyst should make a ratio analysis, as described in Chapter 25. As suggested in that chapter, empirical studies may be undertaken to determine which financial ratios have the greatest predictive power. The analyst will be particularly interested in the applicant's liquidity and ability to pay bills on time.

In addition to analyzing financial statements, the credit analyst will consider the financial strength of the firm, the character of the company and its management, and various other matters. He then attempts to determine the ability of the applicant to service trade credit. In this regard, he assesses the probability of an applicant's not paying on time and of a bad-debt loss. On the basis of this information, a decision is reached as to whether the applicant falls below the minimum quality standard.

One tool finding increasing utilization in this regard is *discriminant analysis.* This statistical technique is described in the appendix to this chapter, so we will not go into a detailed description here. On the basis of a weighted overall score provided by this technique, an applicant is judged to be a "good" or a "bad" credit risk. Discriminant analysis has been used with success in consumer credit and other forms of installment lending, where various characteristics of an individual are quantitatively rated and a credit decision made on the basis of the total score.[7] Numerical rating systems also are being used by companies extending trade credit. With the overall growth of trade credit, a number of companies are finding it worthwhile to screen out "clear" accept and reject applicants. In other words, routine credit decisions are delegated

---

[7]See James H. Myers and Edward W. Forgy, "The Development of Numerical Credit Evaluation Systems," *Journal of the American Statistical Association,* 58 (September 1963), 799–806; Sylvia Lane, "Submarginal Credit Risk Classification," *Journal of Financial and Quantitative Analysis,* 7 (January 1972), 1379–85; William P. Poggess, "Screen-Test Your Credit Risks," in Keith V. Smith, ed., *Working Capital Management,* (New York: West Publishing, 1974), pp. 109–20; and Robert O. Edmister and Gary G. Schlarbaum, "Credit Policy in Lending Institutions," *Journal of Financial and Quantitative Analysis,* 9 (June 1974), 335–56.

to subordinates to make on the basis of a numerical score. Marginal applicants, which fall between "clear" accept or reject signals, can then be analyzed in detail by the credit analyst.[8] In this way, a company is able to achieve greater efficiency in its credit investigation process, utilizing trained credit analysts to the best advantage.

SEQUENTIAL INVESTIGATION PROCESS

Most credit investigations involve a sequential analysis where the collection of information and its analysis are interrelated. In general, the riskier the credit applicant, the more information the analyst will want to have. The cost of acquiring this information, however, must be balanced against the expected benefits to be derived from the order. A credit decision for an individual account may take one of three courses of action: accept, reject, or obtain additional information.[9] For the last alternative, the expected value of additional information must exceed the cost of acquiring it.

To illustrate a sequential investigation process, suppose the following stages of credit investigation were open to a company:

1. Consult past experience to see if the firm has had previous experience with the account and, if it has, what has been that experience.
2. Order a Dun & Bradstreet report on the applicant and evaluate it.
3. Undertake credit checks with banks and trade creditors.

Stages 2 and 3 could be broken down into additional steps. For example, a firm might first seek a credit rating from Dun & Bradstreet and, on the basis of that rating, decide whether or not to order a report. For stage 3 it might check banks first and then, depending upon the outcome of the bank check, check trade creditors. Moreover, the number of trade creditors checked might be a sequential function. An additional stage might be a personal interview by the credit analyst with the company placing the order. For simplicity of illustration, we consider only three stages but recognize that the sequential investigation process could be expanded to take account of additional stages.

These three stages are broken down into various quality categories. For stage 1, an order is classified into one of the following categories, depending upon what the investigation of past experience reveals:[10]

---

[8] In addition to the appendix, see Dileep R. Mehta, *Working Capital Management* (Englewood Cliffs, N.J.: Prentice-Hall, 1974), Chapter 1, for a detailed discussion of this technique.

[9] This section draws upon Dileep Mehta, "The Formulation of Credit Policy Models," *Management Science*, 15 (October 1968), 30–50.

[10] Ibid., p. 33.

a. Good. A good account is one in which the customer consistently pays within the credit period.

b. Fair. This rating is given to a customer who frequently pays beyond the credit period but usually is no more than forty-five days delinquent. Moreover, the customer keeps the firm informed and pays according to plan.

c. Poor. A poor account is one where the customer is often more than forty-five days delinquent. In addition, the customer does not keep the firm informed and usually is inconsistent in payments.

d. New. A new order.

When a report is ordered from Dun & Bradstreet, the credit analyst evaluates it and the financial statements contained therein. On the basis of this evaluation, he assigns a letter rating of either A, B, C, or D. A is the highest grade and indicates that the prospects for the customer paying within the credit period are excellent. On the other end of the spectrum, D is the lowest rating and indicates that there is a high degree of probability the customer either will be delinquent in payment or will not pay at all. Similarly, for stage 3, a letter rating of A through D is assigned on the basis of credit checks with banks and trade creditors. In the investigation process, it is important that each stage be treated as independent of the preceding stage. In other words, credit checks should be evaluated independently of the evaluation of the D & B report.

When an order is received, the credit department must make a decision as to whether or not to accept it. It would of course be desirable to undertake stages 1 through 3 for all orders, but each involves a cost. To investigate past experience, someone must check the credit file and accounts receivable ledger and categorize the applicant into one of four quality categories. For stage 2, the firm must pay for the D & B report. In addition, the credit analyst must devote time to analyzing the report and to assigning a letter rating. This analysis also involves a cost. The last stage, credit checkings, involves a considerable cost, for the credit analyst must either call or write bank(s) and trade creditors and inquire of their experience. Additionally, he must analyze the information and assign a letter rating. Suppose that the costs for the various stages of investigation are the following:

		Cost
Stage 1	Past experience	$ 1
Stage 2	D & B report	8
Stage 3	Credit checkings	15

These costs will be compared shortly with the expected value of information provided by each stage.

EXPECTED BENEFITS AND COSTS

First, however, we must establish the expected benefits to be derived from an order. Assume that the firm makes but one product and that the marginal profit from each unit sold is $10 and the marginal cost to produce it $15. Moreover, suppose that the required return on investment in receivables is 15 percent on a before-tax basis. Given this information, the firm must estimate the average collection period, the average collection costs, and the probability of bad-debt loss for each of the possible quality categories. These estimates should be based upon actual experience during a sample period in which the firm undertakes all stages of investigation for each credit applicant but extends open-book credit to all. As experience unfolds for an account, the firm records the collection period, the collection cost, and whether or not it was a bad debt. On the basis of experience with a number of accounts over the sample period, it computes an average collection period, average collection costs, and the percentage of bad debt for each quality category of applicants. An example of this information for stage 1 is presented in Table 15-6. If future orders are not expected to differ significantly from the orders constituting the sample, the firm may use the information in this table to assess the profitability of an order.[11]

It now is possible to compute the expected cost of accepting an order:

$$\text{Acceptance cost} = \text{Probability of bad debt(Variable cost per unit)}X + (\text{Required return})(\text{Average collection period}/360)(\text{Variable cost per unit})X + \text{Average collection cost} \quad (15\text{-}1)$$

where X is the number of units ordered. For our hypothetical example,

Table 15·6   Estimates of collection period, collection costs, and bad debts for stage 1

Stage	Average Collection Period	Average Collection Costs	Probability of Bad-Debt Loss
Past experience:			
Good	28.5 days	0.775	0.0175
Fair	52.5	2.775	0.1560
Poor	87.0	9.000	0.3375
New account	59.3	3.560	0.2060

[11] It is essential that future orders correspond closely to those in the sample; otherwise, the estimates of profitability of an order will not be reliable.

Acceptance cost = (Probability of bad debt)(15X) + 0.15(Average
collection period/360)(15X) + Average collection cost

Recall that variable costs were assumed to be $15 per unit and the
required rate of return 15 percent. Thus, the acceptance cost embodies
the costs of bad-debt losses, carrying receivables, and collection. Because collection costs are assumed to be fixed, they do not vary with the
size of the order. The expected cost of rejecting an order is

$$\text{Rejection cost} = (1 - \text{Probability of bad debt})(\text{Marginal profit per unit})X \qquad (15\text{-}2)$$

which, for our example, is

$$\text{Rejection cost} = (1 - \text{Probability of bad debt})10X$$

The rejection cost is simply the probability of payment times the marginal profit foregone on the order.

To illustrate the calculation of acceptance and rejection costs,
suppose that there is an order for X units and that as a matter of policy
the firm always investigates past experience. The expected costs of
acceptance and rejection for a poor account are

$$\begin{aligned}
\text{Acceptance cost} &= 0.3375(15X) + 0.15(87/360)(15X) + \$7.00 \\
&= 5.606X + \$9.00 \\
\text{Rejection cost} &= 0.6625(10X) = 6.625X
\end{aligned}$$

Similarly, we can compute the expected costs of acceptance and rejection for the other quality categories in the first stage. These costs are
shown in Figure 15-4.

From the information in Figure 15-4, we can determine that for the

FIG. 15·4 *Investigation of past experience cost structure*

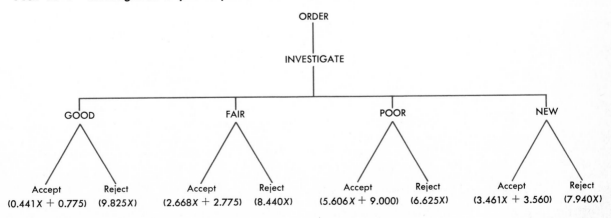

poor category, the cost of acceptance exceeds the cost of rejection for orders of eight units or less. When $X \geq 9$, however, the cost of acceptance is less. If past experience (stage 1) were the only stage of investigation, an order that fell into the poor category would be rejected if it were for eight units or less and accepted if it were for nine units or more. For the good, fair, and new-order categories, the cost of acceptance is less than the cost of rejection for all $X \geq 1$. Therefore, an order that fell into any of these categories would be accepted if examining past experience were the only stage of investigation.

SEQUENTIAL STAGES OF INVESTIGATION

With additional stages of investigation, however, we must decide whether to investigate further or to accept or reject the order on the basis of the information we have. A decision to go on to the next stage of investigation depends upon the benefits expected to be derived from the additional information in relation to its cost. In a nutshell, we want to establish whether the added information will improve our chances of making a correct decision.[12]

Stage 2 involves analyzing a D & B report. Assume for now that only the first two stages of investigation are open to the company. On the basis of an evaluation of the D & B report, the credit analyst assigns a letter grade ranging from *A* through *D*. When this information is combined with that in the preceding stage, the probabilities as well as the average collection periods, average collection costs, and probabilities of bad-debt losses change. New estimates of them should be based upon the sample discussed earlier. Suppose that on the basis of this sample, the firm found the conditional probabilities, average collection periods, average collection costs, and probabilities of bad-debt losses to be those shown in Table 15-7. Note that when the combination of past experience and D & B report analysis is less desirable, the factors shown in the last three columns are worse.

Similar to Figure 15-4, the expected costs of acceptance and rejection can be determined for the combinations shown in Table 15-7; and they are shown in Table 15-8. Given this information, we are able to determine whether the firm should go beyond the investigation of past experience to analyze a D & B report. The crux of the decision involves comparing the expected benefits derived from the additional information with the cost of acquiring it. In turn, the magnitude of benefits depends upon the size of the order.

---

[12]The new information has value only if we change our previous accept-reject decision on the basis of it. See Harold Bierman, Jr., Charles P. Bonini, and Warren H. Hausman, *Quantitative Analysis for Business Decisions* (Homewood, Ill.: Richard D. Irwin, 1969), Chapters 4–9.

Table 15·7   **Estimates of collection period, collection costs and bad-debt loss for D & B report analysis, given the investigation of past experience**

Good Past Experience D & B Report	Conditional Probability of Occurrence	Average Collection Period	Average Collection Cost	Probability of Bad-Debt Loss
A	0.70	25 days	0.50	0.00
B	0.15	30	1.00	0.02
C	0.10	40	1.50	0.07
D	0.05	50	2.50	0.15
Fair Past Experience D & B Report				
A	0.20	30 days	1.00	0.03
B	0.40	45	2.00	0.10
C	0.25	60	3.50	0.20
D	0.15	90	6.00	0.40
Poor Past Experience D & B Report				
A	0.05	40 days	1.50	0.05
B	0.25	60	3.50	0.15
C	0.35	80	8.00	0.30
D	0.35	120	15.00	0.55
New Order D & B Report				
A	0.20	32 days	1.20	0.04
B	0.30	48	2.40	0.12
C	0.30	65	4.00	0.22
D	0.20	95	7.00	0.48

AN ILLUSTRATION

To illustrate the investigation process, assume an order for ten units is received and that the firm has investigated its past experience and found it to be poor. For a cost of $8, it can go to the next stage of investigation and analyze a D & B report. The question is whether it is worthwhile for it to do so. From Figure 15-4, we know the order would be accepted if past experience were the only stage of investigation—the reason is that for orders of nine or more units, the cost of acceptance is less than the cost of rejection. We now must determine if the additional

**Table 15·8   Costs of acceptance and
rejection for D & B report analysis**

Good Past Experience D & B Report	Cost of Acceptance	Cost of Rejection
A	0.16X + 0.50	10.0X
B	0.49X + 1.00	9.8X
C	1.30X + 1.50	9.3X
D	2.56X + 2.50	8.5X

Fair Past Experience D & B Report		
A	0.64X + 1.00	9.7X
B	1.78X + 2.00	9.0X
C	3.38X + 3.50	8.0X
D	6.56X + 6.00	6.0X

Poor Past Experience D & B Report		
A	1.00X + 1.50	9.5X
B	2.63X + .3.50	8.5X
C	5.00X + 8.00	7.0X
D	9.00X + 15.00	4.5X

New Order D & B Report		
A	0.90X + 1.20	9.6X
B	2.10X + 2.40	8.8X
C	3.71X + 4.00	7.8X
D	7.79X + 7.00	5.2X

information arising from a D & B report analysis will cause us to change our decision. Only if it will does the additional information have value. The cost of acceptance and the cost of rejection for an order of ten units, given poor past experience, can be derived from Table 15-8; and they are found to be:

D & B Report Grade	Cost of Acceptance	Cost of Rejection
A	$ 11.50	$95.00
B	26.30	85.00
C	58.00	70.00
D	105.00	45.00

Thus, if ten units are ordered, the cost of acceptance exceeds the cost of rejection only if the D & B analysis grade turns out to be *D*. Under these circumstances, the firm would reject the order, where before the order would have been accepted. Consequently, there is value in obtaining the additional information. The expected net benefit is the difference between the cost of acceptance avoided and the cost of rejection incurred, times the conditional probability of occurrence. For our example, the expected net benefit is

$$(105.00 - 45.00)0.35 = \$21.00$$

Inasmuch as this figure exceeds the cost of investigation of $8, an analysis of a D & B report should be undertaken. When $X = 9$, it also is found that the expected benefits associated with a stage 2 investigation exceed the $8 cost.

There still remains the question of whether it is worthwhile to undertake a D & B report analysis if the order is for eight units or less. Here, the order would be rejected on the basis of past experience alone. We must determine if additional information will cause us to change that decision. If the order were for five units, the expected costs of acceptance and rejection would be:

MANAGEMENT OF
ACCOUNTS RECEIVABLE

D & B Report Grade	Cost of Acceptance	Cost of Rejection
A	$ 6.50	$47.50
B	16.65	42.50
C	33.00	35.00
D	60.00	22.50

If a D & B report analysis were undertaken, the firm could avoid the cost of rejection for cases of grades A, B, and C. However, it would incur the lesser cost of acceptance in all three cases. Because the order would be rejected on the basis of past experience alone, there is no benefit to be derived from grade D, inasmuch as the cost of acceptance exceeds the cost of rejection. Again, the value of additional information comes only if it causes us to change a decision. The expected net benefit to the firm is determined by multiplying the differences between the costs of rejection and acceptance for the first three cases times their respective conditional probabilities of occurrence:

$$(47.50 - 6.50)0.05 + (42.50 - 16.65)0.25 + (35.00 - 33.00)0.35 = \$9.21$$

Because the expected net benefit exceeds the cost of undertaking a D & B report analysis, the investigation of a D & B report is worthwhile. However, when an order is for four units, the expected benefit, $7.50, is less than the cost of investigation of $8.00. Therefore, an order for four units from a poor account should be rejected.

As a general decision rule, then, the firm should reject any order for five units or less if an investigation of past experience reveals the account to have been poor. No further investigation should be undertaken. If the order is for six or more units, however, the firm should undertake an analysis of a D & B report because the expected benefit of the additional information exceeds its cost. Depending upon the outcome of this investigation, the order will be either accepted or rejected.[13]

Similarly, decision rules can be formulated for other categories of past experience. For good past experience, the cost of acceptance in Table 15-8 is less than the cost of rejection for all $X \geq 1$. Therefore, there is no benefit to be derived from further investigation. The previous acceptance decision will not be changed. As a result, the firm should accept all orders where an investigation of past experience reveals that experience to have been good.

For an account judged to be fair by past experience, the cost of acceptance exceeds the cost of rejection in Table 15-8 only if the D & B report analysis grade turns out to be D. Under these circumstances, the expected net benefit is

$$(6.56X + 6.00 - 6.0X)0.15$$

For an analysis of a D & B report to be worthwhile, the expected net benefit must exceed the cost of investigation of $8.00. To be indifferent, we must have the following equality:

$$(6.56X + 6.00 - 6.0X)0.15 = 8.00$$

Transposing and solving for X:

$$0.56X + 6.00 = 8.00/0.15$$
$$0.56X = 53.33 - 6.00$$
$$X = 84.5$$

Thus, only if the order size is eighty-five units or more will an analysis of a D & B report benefit the firm. If an order judged to be fair by past experience is for less than eighty-five units, it should be accepted without such analysis.

---

[13]This decision rule and the others presented assume a linear utility function with respect to money. As discussed in Chapter 2, there is a serious question as to whether a manager behaves in this fashion. If his utility function could be specified, the sequential investigation process could be expressed in utile values in a manner similar to the analysis in Chapter 2. However, given the relatively small size of investment in the individual account, a linear utility function is not unreasonable to assume.

For a new account, the cost of acceptance exceeds the cost of rejection only for grade D in Table 15-8. The expected benefit is

$$(7.79X + 7.00 - 5.2X)0.20$$

To be indifferent, the expected benefit must equal the cost of investigation:

$$(7.79X + 7.00 - 5.2X)0.20 = 8.00$$

Transposing and solving for X:

$$2.59X + 7.00 = 8.00/0.20$$
$$2.59X = 40.00 - 7.00$$
$$X = 12.7$$

Consequently, only if the order size is thirteen units or more should the firm analyze a D & B report for a new order. If the order is for less than this number, it should be accepted without credit investigation.

Our example could be extended to take account of the last stage of investigation—a checking of banks and trade suppliers. However, because our example is already rather long, we shall limit it to the first two stages of the investigation process. Because the desirability of additional information diminishes with each successive stage, one can visualize that the number of times where the additional information would be worthwhile would be less for credit checkings than for the D & B report analysis. One final point has to do with the procedure used to solve the problem. For purposes of illustration, we have solved it in descending stages of analysis. However, it often makes more sense to work backward from the last stage to the first. Those readers familiar with dynamic programming have probably already discovered that the problem lends itself to this optimization technique.

Implications   The sequential investigation process presented illustrates one means by which a firm can reach a credit decision with a minimum of investigation cost. Rather than perform all stages of investigation regardless of the size of the order and the firm's past experience, the firm should undertake investigation in stages and go to a new stage only when the expected net benefits of the additional information exceed the cost of acquiring it. When past experience has been favorable, there may be little need for further investigation. We saw that decision rules can be established whereby an order is investigated only if it meets certain size constraints and falls into a particular category in the preceding stage of investigation. Because the stages of credit investigation are sequential, added sophistication is introduced only when it is beneficial to do so. In this manner, the firm can make optimal credit decisions with respect to acceptance, rejection, or further investigation.

The decision rules used in a sequential investigation process will vary according to the marginal profit and marginal cost of the product, the cost of bad debts, the average collection period, and the average collection costs. To the extent that these factors change over time, the firm will need to formulate new decision rules. As experience changes and the sample on which estimates are made is no longer valid, the firm will need to revise its probability estimates and its estimates of costs and bad-debt losses in Tables 15-6 and 15-7. Perhaps the most suitable means for review is to extend credit to all applicants on a periodic basis. With this experience recorded, new estimates of the average collection period and costs, the probability of bad-debt losses, and the probabilities of occurrence can be formulated. The more stable the experience over time, the less frequent the need for periodic review. If the underlying system is basically unstable, however, a sequential investigation process is not well suited for the problem at hand. Yet, for most situations it represents a meaningful application of decision theory to credit analysis.

LINE OF CREDIT

Another means of control for repeat orders is to establish a line of credit for an individual account. A line of credit is a maximum limit on the amount the firm will permit to be owing at any one time. In essence, it represents the maximum risk exposure that the firm will allow itself to undergo for an account. In the sequential investigation method illustrated above, single orders were evaluated. With a line of credit, multiple orders are assumed. The principle, however, is the same. Likely profits from present and future sales must be balanced against the likely collection period, collection costs, and probability of bad-debt losses over time. The latter three depend upon the magnitude of the line of credit offered rather than upon the size of order. As before, probability concepts can be applied in order to analyze the tradeoff between expected benefits and expected costs and to determine an appropriate line of credit for the customer.

The establishment of a credit line streamlines the procedure for shipping goods, for one need only determine whether an order brings the amount owed by a customer in excess of the line. If not, the order is shipped; if so, an incremental credit decision must be reached. The line itself must be reevaluated periodically in order to keep abreast of developments in the account. What was a satisfactory risk exposure today may be more or less than satisfactory a year from today. Despite comprehensive credit procedures, there will always be special cases that must be dealt with individually. Here, too, however, the firm can streamline the operation by defining responsibilities clearly.

COLLECTION PROCEDURES

In addition to credit procedures for the individual account, the firm must establish clear-cut collection procedures for past due or delinquent accounts. The initial question to be answered is, How past due should an account be allowed to go before collection procedures are initiated? Because a receivable is only as good as the likelihood that it will be paid, a firm cannot afford to wait too long before initiating collection procedures. On the other hand, if it initiates procedures too soon, it may anger reasonably good customers who, for some reason, fail to make payments by the due date. Procedures, whatever they are, should be firmly established. Initially, a letter is usually sent, followed, perhaps, by additional letters that become ever more serious in tone. Next may come a telephone call from the credit manager and then, perhaps, one from the company's attorney. Some companies have collection men who make personal calls on the account.[14]

If all else fails, the account may be turned over to a collection agency. The agency's fees are quite substantial—frequently, one-half the amount of the receivable—but such a procedure may be the only feasible alternative, particularly for a small account. Direct legal action is costly, sometimes serves no real purpose, and may only force the account into bankruptcy. When payment cannot be collected, compromise settlements may provide a higher percentage of collection.[15]

Similar to our analysis of the amount of collection expenditures in the aggregate, the amount spent on an individual account must be evaluated in relation to the likely benefits. In short, the firm should not spend $25 to collect a $15 account. The expected benefits should exceed the collection costs. Suppose that Z-REX Corporation was owed $1,000 from a delinquent customer. With a $60 collection expenditure, Z-REX expects the following:

Collection	Probability	Expected Outcome
$ 0	0.5	$ 0
100	0.2	20
200	0.1	20
300	0.1	30
400	0.1	40
		$110

Because the expected value of benefits, $110, exceeds the amount expended, $60, the collection effort provides an expected value of net

[14] For an evaluation of alternative collection policies using the Markov process, see Mehta, *Working Capital Management*, Chapter 2.

[15] For an extended discussion of these settlements, see Chapter 24.

benefits of $50. Of course, other collection efforts may result in even higher net benefits and they should be explored. Past experience may tell a firm what the optimal collection procedure is relative to profitability.

CREDIT INSURANCE

To protect against unusual bad-debt losses in extending trade credit, a firm may take out credit insurance. Although the firm cannot insure against losses incurred normally in the industry (known as primary losses), it can insure against above-normal losses. Insurance companies usually restrict coverage to certain acceptable risks, as determined by Dun & Bradstreet ratings. In addition, these companies usually insist upon *coinsurance,* the participation of the collecting firm in a portion of the bad-debt loss—usually 10 to 20 percent. The insistence upon coinsurance safeguards the insurance company from the firm's becoming excessively liberal in the granting of credit. The cost of credit insurance varies directly with the risk of the accounts accepted and is calculated as a percentage of sales. The decision to use credit insurance depends upon the probability of extreme credit losses and the ability of the firm to bear these losses, as well as the amount of premiums.

USE OF ELECTRONIC DATA PROCESSING EQUIPMENT

Computers have been used a great deal in credit management. Their use provides certain essential up-to-date information needed for analysis. All of the information previously placed on receivable ledgers can be placed on punched cards or tapes. As a result, the credit department has very quick access to this information. At frequent intervals, it can obtain a trial balance that gives a summary of all billings, payments, discounts taken, and amounts still owed. Also, it can obtain an aging of accounts showing the total amounts owed the firm, the portion that is current, the portion that is up to thirty days past due, that which is thirty to sixty days past due, and so forth.

In addition, the computer can be programmed to provide complete reports on all delinquent accounts, and delinquency letters can be sent out mechanically at regular intervals. Frequent reports on past-due accounts, which were not possible before the computer, alert the credit manager to problems as they develop. As a result, he is able to stay on top of them and take corrective action. Formerly, the situation might have deteriorated during the information lag. Management also may want to be informed when an account approaches the line of credit established for it, and computers can provide this information easily.

The computer helps the credit manager by providing timely and accurate information on the status of accounts. The payment history of a customer can be drawn from storage and printed out in seconds. Included in this history is information such as the date the account was opened, the amount owed currently, the customer's credit line, any numerical credit ratings, and the promptness of past payments. Special reports can be prepared that involve categorization or comparisons. For example, if several companies in the same industry are slow in their payments at a particular time of the year, management might want to know the firm's experience with all other companies in that particular industry. Such information enables the credit manager to analyze and deal with the problem more effectively. In another situation, management might wish to compare incoming orders from a particular customer with his payment history. This information also can be provided quickly.

Indeed, the computer can provide a vast array of detailed information, previously impractical to obtain, that may be useful not only to the credit manager but to other management as well. In addition to processing data, the computer can be programmed to make certain routine credit decisions.[16] In particular, small orders from good accounts can be approved by the computer without the order ever going to a credit analyst. All in all, electronic data processing can make a significant contribution to the credit department. As their volume of receivables grows, many firms find computer processing to be the only feasible means by which to handle receivables.

[16]For a discussion of credit decision making by simulation, see Roger L. Sisson and Norman L. Statland, "The Future of Computers in Credit Management," *Credit and Financial Management*, 65 (November 1963), 40,44.

SUMMARY

Credit and collection policies encompass the quality of accounts accepted, the credit period extended, the cash discount given, certain special terms, and the level of collection expenditures. In each case, the credit decision involves a tradeoff between the additional profitability and the cost resulting from a change in any of these elements. For example, by liberalizing the quality requirements for accounts, the firm might hope to make more on the additional sales than the cost of carrying the additional receivables plus the additional bad-debt losses. To maximize profits arising from credit and collection policies, the firm should vary these policies jointly until an optimal solution is obtained. This variation can be accomplished through simulation once the functional relationships are specified. The firm's credit and collection policies, together with its credit and collection procedures, determine the magnitude and quality of its receivable position.

In evaluating a credit applicant, the credit analyst is concerned with obtaining financial and other information about the applicant, analyzing this information, and reaching a credit decision. A sequential analysis process using decision theory was presented whereby the firm can reach a decision with respect to accepting an order, rejecting it, or obtaining additional information. Obtaining additional information is justified only when the expected benefits of the information exceed its cost. In turn, expected benefits arise only if the information allows us to correct a previously wrong decision. Because the stages of investigation are sequential, added sophistication in credit analysis is undertaken only when it is profitable to do so.

If the account is new, the firm must decide whether or not to accept the order. With repeat orders, the firm usually must decide upon the maximum credit to extend. This maximum, known as a line of credit, is based upon the credit-worthiness of the applicant. Collection procedures should be firmly established and applied consistently. The length of time an account may be delinquent before collection procedures are initiated will depend upon the billing terms and the nature of the account. To protect against unusual credit losses, a firm may take out credit insurance. We reviewed briefly some of the applications of electronic data processing to credit management. The uses of the computer are many and are likely to increase in importance.

Study!

APPENDIX

APPLICATION OF DISCRIMINANT ANALYSIS TO THE SELECTION OF ACCOUNTS

Discriminant analysis is a statistical tool by which we can decide which prospective accounts to accept or reject, on the basis of certain relevant variables.[17] This type of analysis is similar to regression analysis but assumes that the observations come from two or more different universes. In our case, these universes consist of good and bad accounts. Suppose that we start with an evaluation of only two characteristics of trade credit applicants: the size of the company and its quick, or acid-test, ratio. For purposes of experiment, we extend open-book credit to all new credit applicants for a sample period. For each account, we record

[17] For a discussion of discriminant analysis, see Gerhard Tintner, *Econometrics* (New York: John Wiley, 1952), pp. 96–102; and E. J. Williams, *Regression Analysis* (New York: John Wiley, 1959), Chapter 10.

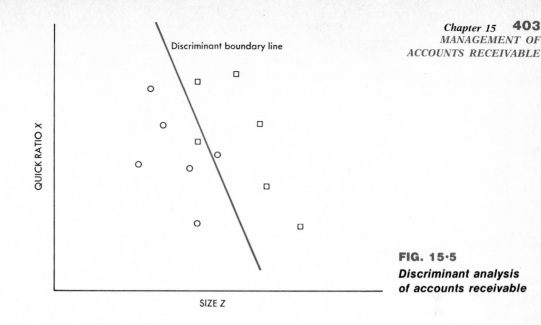

Discriminant boundary line

QUICK RATIO X

SIZE Z

FIG. 15·5
Discriminant analysis
of accounts receivable

the size of the firm, its quick ratio, and whether or not after a length of time it defaults in payment. If the account defaults, it is classified as a bad account; if it pays on time, it is classified as a good account. With this information, we are able to undertake a linear discriminant analysis with two independent variables. We wish to determine the predictive value of these variables for the behavior of the dependent variable, whether the account is good or bad.

Suppose that we plot quick ratios and size for each account on a scatter diagram, obtaining the results shown in Figure 15-5.[18] The circles represent bad accounts; the squares represent good accounts. Using the two independent variables, our objective is to find the linear boundary line that discriminates best between good and bad accounts. We need to find the parameters, or weights, of the following discriminant function:

$$f = a(X) + b(Z) \qquad \text{(15A-1)}$$

where X is the quick ratio of the firm, Z is its size, and a and b are the parameters we wish to compute. Our purpose is to obtain parameter values such that the average value of f_g in Eq. (15A-1) for good accounts will be significantly larger than the average value of f_b for bad accounts.

[18]This example is similar to one used by William F. Massy, "Statistical Analysis of Relations between Variables," in Ronald E. Frank, Alfred A. Kuehn, and William F. Massy, *Quantitative Techniques in Marketing Analysis* (Homewood, Ill.: Richard D. Irwin, 1962), pp. 95–100.

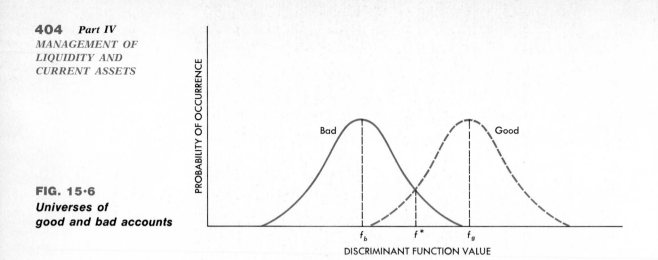

FIG. 15·6
Universes of
good and bad accounts

This notion is illustrated in Figure 15-6, where the discriminant function value is along the horizontal axis and the probability of occurrence is along the vertical. In the figure, two universes of credit applicants are shown, good to the right and bad to the left. The average value, f_b, for bad accounts is seen to be much lower than the average value, f_g, for good accounts. However, we see also that there is an area of overlap between the two universes. In general, the smaller the area of overlap, the better the ability of discriminant analysis to predict good and bad accounts.[19]

The coefficients a and b in Eq. (15A-1) can be computed mathematically from the sample data by

$$a = \frac{Szzdx - Sxzdz}{SzzSxx - Sxz^2} \tag{15A-2}$$

$$b = \frac{Sxxdz - Sxzdx}{SzzSxx - Sxz^2} \tag{15A-3}$$

where Sxx and Szz represent the variances of variables X and Z, respectively, and Sxz is the covariance of variables X and Z. The difference between the average of X's for good accounts and the average of X's for bad accounts is represented by dx. Similarly, dz represents the difference between the average of Z's for good accounts and the average of Z's for bad accounts. When we solve for a and b, we obtain the parameters of the linear discriminant function in Eq. (15A-1). The ratio a/b determines the slope of the discriminant boundary line.

We now need to determine the minimum cutoff value of the func-

[19] See D. E. Peterson, *A Quantitative Framework for Financial Management* (Homewood, Ill.: Richard D. Irwin, 1969), pp. 285–89.

tion. The idea is to refuse credit to those accounts with values of f below the cutoff value and extend credit to those with f values above the cutoff value. In theory, we wish to find the discriminant function value in Figure 15-6 denoted by f^*. Using this value for cutoff purposes will minimize the prediction of good accounts when they are bad and the prediction of bad accounts when they are good. To determine the cutoff value in practice, we start by calculating the f_i for each account, given the parameters of Eq. (15A-1). For our example, suppose that we obtained the f_i values, arranged in ascending order of magnitude, shown in Table 15A-1.

We see that there is an area of overlap for accounts 6, 12, 11, and 4. We know that the cutoff value must lie between 1.65 and 1.91. For simplicity, we may want to use the midpoint, 1.78, as our cutoff value. Given the cutoff value, we are able to draw the discriminant boundary line in Figure 15-5 that discriminates best between good and bad accounts. We note, however, that two of the accounts, 11 and 12, are misclassified, given this cutoff value. Account 11 is classified as a good account when, in fact, it was bad; while account 12 is classified as a bad account when, in fact, it was good. Rather than assign a strict cutoff value, it may be better to allow for misclassification and designate the area between 1.65 and 1.91 as uncertain, requiring further analysis. In theory, this area would correspond to the area of overlap in Figure 15-6.

If we have reason to believe that new credit applicants will not differ significantly from the relationships found for the sample accounts, discriminant analysis can be used as a means for selecting and rejecting credit sale customers. If we use a minimum cutoff value, we will reject all sales in which the f_i value for the credit applicant is less than 1.78 and accept all sales in which the f_i value exceeds 1.78. If a range is used, we will accept all sales in which the prospective customer has an f_i value in excess of 1.91 and reject applicants with f_i values below 1.65. For applicants with f_i values lying between these two values, we might want

Table 15A·1   Values of f_i

Account Number	Good or Bad	f_i
7	Bad	0.81
10	Bad	0.97
2	Bad	1.36
3	Bad	1.44
6	Bad	1.65
12	Good	1.77
11	Bad	1.83
4	Good	1.91
1	Good	2.12
8	Good	2.19
5	Good	2.34
9	Good	2.48

to obtain additional credit information, along with information as to the profitability of the sale, before making a decision.

Although the example we used is simple, it illustrates the potential of discriminant analysis in selecting or rejecting credit applicants.[20] Discriminant analysis can be extended to include a number of other independent variables. In fact, additional independent variables should be added as long as the benefits of greater predictability exceed the costs of collecting and processing the additional information. For discriminant analysis to have predictive value, the credit applicants being analyzed must correspond to the sample applicants on whom the discriminant-function parameters are based. Where the parameters are no longer realistic, a new sample must be drawn. As experience provides new information, it is important to assess continually the validity of the parameters.

Where a linear discriminant function does not fit the data, it is possible to develop nonlinear functions. Discriminant analysis is sufficiently flexible to be a practical means for evaluating accounts. Because the information is processed on a high-speed computer, time spent on clerical work and credit analysis can be reduced. Credit analysts can concentrate on only those marginal accounts falling in an uncertain area. Discriminant analysis offers an efficient means by which a company can meet the mounting demands on its credit department.

PROBLEMS

1. In order to increase sales from their present annual level of $240,000, the Heap Corporation is considering a more liberal credit policy. Currently, the firm has an average collection period of thirty days; however, it is believed that as the collection period is lengthened, sales will increase by the following amounts:

Credit Policy	Increase in Average Collection Period	Increase in Sales
A	15 days	$10,000
B	30 days	15,000
C	45 days	17,000
D	60 days	18,000

[20] Edward I. Altman, "Financial Ratios, Discriminant Analysis and the Prediction of Corporate Bankruptcy," *Journal of Finance*, 23 (September 1968), 589–609, and Robert O. Edmister, "An Empirical Test of Financial Ratio Analysis for Small Business Failure Prediction," *Journal of Financial and Quantitative Analysis*, 7 (March 1972), 1477–93, employ multiple discriminant analysis effectively in predicting corporate failure prior to its occurrence. These studies are described in Chapter 24.

The firm has the following cost pattern at present:

Price of the only product manufactured	$1.00
Variable costs per unit (before taxes)	.60
Average costs per unit (current)	.80

.40 Profit.

If the firm requires a pretax return on investment of 20 percent, which credit policy should be pursued? (Assume a 360-day year.)

2. If the only information available to the Heap Corporation (problem 1) was that an increase in the average collection period by sixty days would increase sales by $18,000, would the firm increase the collection period?

3. The Heap Corporation (problem 1) has estimated that the following pattern of bad-debt experience will prevail if it initiates more liberal credit terms:

Increase in Average Collection Period	Percent Default
15 days	3%
30 days	6%
45 days	10%
60 days	15%

The current bad-debt loss is 1 percent. Given the other assumptions in problem 1, which credit policy should be pursued?

4. Recalculate problem 3, assuming the following pattern of bad-debt experience:

Increase in Average Collection Period	Percent Default
15 days	1.5%
30 days	2.0%
45 days	4.0%
60 days	8.0%

5. The Chickee Corporation has a 12 percent opportunity cost of funds and currently sells on terms of net 10, EOM. This means that goods shipped before the end of the month must be paid for by the 10th of the following month. The firm has sales of $10 million a year, which are 80 percent on credit and spread evenly over the year. Currently, the average collection period is sixty days. If Chickee offered terms of 2/10, net 30, 60 percent of its customers would take the discount, and the collection period would be reduced to forty days. Should Chickee change its terms from net/10, EOM to 2/10, net 30?

6. The Pottsville Manufacturing Corporation is considering extending trade credit to the San Jose Company. Examination of the records of San Jose has produced the following financial statements.

San Jose Company balance sheet (in millions)

	19X1	19X2	19X3
Assets:			
Current assets:			
Cash	$ 1.5	$ 1.6	$ 1.6
Receivables	1.3	1.8	2.5
Inventories (at lower of cost or market)	1.3	2.6	4.0
Other	.4	.5	.4
Total current assets	$ 4.5	$ 6.5	$ 8.5
Fixed assets:			
Buildings (net)	2.0	1.9	1.8
Machinery and equipment (net)	7.0	6.5	6.0
Total fixed assets	$ 9.0	$ 8.4	$ 7.8
Other assets	1.0	.8	.6
Total assets	$14.5	$15.7	$16.9
Liabilities:			
Current liabilities:			
Notes payable (8½%)	$ 2.1	$ 3.1	$ 3.8
Trade payables	.2	.4	.9
Other payables	.2	.2	.2
Total	$ 2.5	$ 3.7	$ 4.9
Term loan (8%)	4.0	3.0	2.0
Total	$ 6.5	$ 6.7	$ 6.9
Net worth			
Common stock	5.0	5.0	5.0
Preferred stock (6½%)	1.0	1.0	1.0
Retained earnings	2.0	3.0	4.0
Total liabilities and net worth	$14.5	$15.7	$16.9

San Jose Company income statement (in millions)

	19X1	19X2	19X3
Net credit sales	$15.0	$15.8	$16.2
Cost of goods sold	11.3	12.1	13.0
Gross profit	$ 3.7	$ 3.7	$ 3.2
Operating expenses	1.1	1.2	1.2
Net profit before taxes	$ 2.6	$ 2.5	$ 2.0
Tax	1.3	1.2	1.0
Profit after taxes	$ 1.3	$ 1.3	$ 1.0
Dividends	.3	.3	.0
	$ 1.0	$ 1.0	$ 1.0

ble Management," *Journal of Business Finance & Accounting,* 1 (Autumn 1974), 395–403.

Marrah, George L., "Managing Receivables," *Financial Executive,* 38 (July 1970), 40–44.

Mehta, Dileep, "The Formulation of Credit Policy Models," *Management Science,* 15 (October 1968), 30–50.

———, "Optimal Credit Policy Selection: A Dynamic Approach," *Journal of Financial and Quantitative Analysis,* 5 (December 1970), 421–44.

———, *Working Capital Management,* Chapters 1–3. Englewood Cliffs, N.J., Prentice-Hall, 1974.

Mitchner, Morton, and Raymond P. Peterson, "An Operations-Research Study of the Collection of Defaulted Loans," *Operations Research,* 5 (August 1957), 522–45.

Morrison, Robert S., *Handbook for Manufacturing Entrepreneurs,* 2nd ed., Chapter 50. Cleveland: Western Reserve Press, 1974.

Myers, James H., and Edward W. Forgy, "The Development of Numerical Credit Evaluation Systems," *Journal of the American Statistical Association,* 58 (September 1963), 799–806.

Peterson, D. E., *A Quantitative Framework for Financial Management,* Chapter 10. Homewood, Ill.: Richard D. Irwin, 1969.

Schiff, Michael, "Credit and Inventory Management," *Financial Executive,* 40 (November 1972), 28–33.

Schiff, Michael, and Zvi Lieber, "A Model for the Integration of Credit and Inventory Management," *Journal of Finance,* 29 (March 1974), 133–40.

Schwartz, Robert A., "An Economic Model of Trade Credit," *Journal of Financial and Quantitative Analysis,* 9 (September 1974), 643–58.

Shapiro, Alan, "Optimal Inventory and Credit Granting Strategies under Inflation and Depreciation," *Journal of Financial and Quantitative Analysis,* 7 (January 1973), 37–46.

Sisson, Roger L., and Norman L. Statland, "The Future of Computers in Credit Management," *Credit and Financial Management,* 67 (May 1965), 13–15.

Smith, Keith V., *Management of Working Capital,* Section 3. New York: West Publishing, 1974.

Welshans, Merle T., "Using Credit for Profit Making," *Harvard Business Review,* 45 (January–February 1967), 141–56.

Wrightsman, Dwayne, "Optimal Credit Terms for Accounts Receivable," *Quarterly Review of Economics and Business,* 9 (Summer 1969), 59–66.

INVENTORY MANAGEMENT

Inventories, like receivables, represent a significant portion of most firms' assets and, accordingly, require substantial investments. In order that this investment not become unnecessarily large, inventories must be managed efficiently. Our purpose is to investigate briefly the means by which efficient management can be achieved and to relate these methods to financial management.

Inventories provide a very important link in the production and sale of a product. For a company engaged in manufacturing, a certain amount of inventory is absolutely necessary in the actual production of the product; this inventory is known as "goods in process." Although other types of inventory—namely, in-transit, raw-materials, and finished-goods inventory—are not absolutely necessary in the strictest sense, they are extremely important if the firm is to be at all flexible. For example, inventory in transit, that is, inventory between various stages of production or storage, permits efficient production scheduling and utilization of resources. Without this type of inventory, each stage of production would be dependent upon the preceding stage's finishing its operation on a unit of production. As a result, there probably would be delays and considerable idle time in certain stages of production. Thus, there is an incentive for the production area of the firm to maintain large in-transit inventory.

Raw-materials inventory gives the firm flexibility in its purchasing. Without it, the firm must exist on a hand-to-mouth basis, buying raw material strictly in keeping with its production schedule. Moreover, the purchasing department often is able to take advantage of quantity discounts. By so doing, raw-materials inventory may be bloated temporarily. Finished-goods inventory allows the firm flexibility in its production scheduling and in its marketing effort.[1] Production does not need to be geared directly to sales. Given the desire of the marketing department to fill orders promptly, large inventories allow efficient servicing of customer demands. If a certain product is temporarily out of stock, present as well as future sales to the customer may be lost. Thus, there is an incentive to maintain large stocks of all three types of inventory.

The advantages of increased inventories, then, are several. The firm can effect economies of production and purchasing and can fill customer orders more quickly. In short, the firm is more flexible. The obvious disadvantages are the total cost of holding the inventory, including storage and handling costs, and the required return on capital tied up in the investment in inventory. Inventories, like accounts receivable, should be increased as long as the resulting savings exceed the total cost of holding the added inventory. The balance finally reached depends upon the estimates of actual savings, the cost of carrying addi-

---

[1] See John F. Magee, "Guides to Inventory Policy: Functions and Lot Sizes," *Harvard Business Review*, 34 (January–February 1956), 49–60.

tional inventory, and the efficiency of inventory control. Obviously, this balance requires coordination of the production, marketing, and finance areas of the firm in keeping with an overall objective.

INVENTORY CONTROL

For a given level of inventory, the efficiency of inventory control affects the flexibility of the firm. Two essentially identical firms with the same amount of inventory may have significantly different degrees of flexibility in operations due to differences in inventory control. Inefficient procedures may result in an unbalanced inventory—the firm may frequently be out of certain types of inventory, and overstock other types, necessitating excessive investment. These inefficiencies ultimately have an adverse effect upon profits. Turning the situation around, differences in the efficiency of inventory control for a given level of flexibility affect the level of investment required in inventories. The less efficient the inventory control, the greater the investment required. Similarly, excessive investment in inventories affects profits adversely. Thus, the effects of inventory control on flexibility and on the level of investment required in inventories represent two sides of the same coin. Our purpose in the subsequent sections is to examine various principles of inventory control.

ECONOMIC ORDER QUANTITY

The economic order quantity (EOQ) is an important concept in the purchase of raw materials and in the storage of finished-goods and in-transit inventories. In our analysis, we wish to determine the optimal order quantity for a particular item of inventory, given its forecasted usage, ordering cost, and carrying cost. Ordering can mean either the purchase of the item or its production. Assume for the moment that the usage of a particular item of inventory is known with certainty. More-over, assume that this usage is stationary or steady throughout the period of time being analyzed. In other words, if usage is 2,600 items for a six-month period, 100 items would be used each week. While the EOQ model can be modified to take account of increasing and decreasing usage over time,[2] we do not get into this added degree of complexity.

We assume that ordering costs, O, are constant regardless of the size of the order. In the purchase of raw materials or other items, these costs represent the clerical costs involved in placing an order as well as certain costs of receiving and checking the goods once they arrive. For finished-goods inventories, ordering costs involve scheduling a production

[2] For such a modification, see Dileep R. Mehta, *Working Capital Management* (Englewood Cliffs, N.J.: Prentice-Hall, 1974), pp. 81–89.

run. For in-transit inventories, ordering costs are likely to involve nothing more than record keeping. The total ordering cost for a period is simply the number of orders for that period, times the cost per order.

Carrying costs per period, C, represent the cost of inventory storage, handling, and insurance, together with the required rate of return on the investment in inventory. These costs are assumed to be constant per unit of inventory, per unit of time. Thus, the total carrying cost for a period is the average number of units of inventory for the period, times the carrying cost per unit. In addition, we assume for now that inventory orders are filled without delay. Because out-of-stock items can be replaced immediately, there is no need to maintain a buffer or safety stock. Though the assumptions made up to now may seem overly restrictive, they are necessary for an initial understanding of the conceptual framework that follows. Subsequently, we will relax some of them.

If the usage of an inventory item is perfectly steady over a period of time and there is no safety stock, average inventory (in units) can be expressed as

$$\text{Average inventory} = \frac{Q}{2} \qquad (16\text{-}1)$$

where Q is the quantity (in units) ordered and is assumed to be constant for the period. The above problem is illustrated in Figure 16-1. Although the quantity demanded is a step function, we assume for analytical purposes that it can be approximated by a straight line. We see that zero inventory always indicates that further inventory must be ordered.

The carrying cost of inventory is the carrying cost per unit, times the

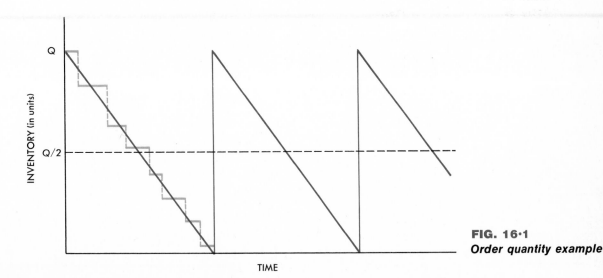

FIG. 16·1
Order quantity example

average number of units of inventory, or $CQ/2$. The total number of orders for a period of time is simply the total usage (in units) of an item of inventory for that period, S, divided by Q. Consequently, total ordering costs are represented by the ordering cost per order, times the number of orders, or SO/Q. Total inventory costs, then, are the carrying costs plus ordering costs, or

$$T = \frac{CQ}{2} + \frac{SO}{Q} \tag{16-2}$$

We see from Eq. (16-2) that the higher the order quantity, Q, the higher the carrying costs but the lower the total ordering costs. The lower the order quantity, the lower the carrying costs but the higher the total ordering costs. We are concerned with the tradeoff between the economies of increased order size and the added cost of carrying additional inventory.

In order to determine the optimal order quantity, Q^*, we differentiate Eq. (16-2) with respect to Q and set the derivative equal to zero, obtaining[3]

$$Q^* = \sqrt{\frac{2SO}{C}} \tag{16-3}$$

This equation is known as the economic lot-size formula.[4] To illustrate its use, suppose that usage of an inventory item is 2,000 units during a 100-day period, ordering costs are $100 an order, and the carrying costs

---

[3]The steps are $\dfrac{dT}{dQ} = \dfrac{C}{2} - \dfrac{SO}{Q^2} = 0$

$$CQ^2 - 2SO = 0$$

$$Q^2 = \frac{2SO}{C}$$

$$Q = \sqrt{\frac{2SO}{C}}$$

[4]This formula also holds if there is a variable component to order costs, provided the component is a linear function of order size. Given a linear relationship, total variable costs for the period of time being analyzed are VS, where V is variable cost per unit ordered. Total costs then become

$$T = \frac{CQ}{2} + VS + \frac{SO}{Q}$$

When we differentiate this expression with respect to Q, we see that VS does not enter in and that the optimal order quantity is $\sqrt{\dfrac{2SO}{C}}$

are $10 per unit per 100 days. The optimal economic order quantity, then, is

$$Q^* = \sqrt{\frac{2(2,000)(100)}{10}} = 200 \text{ units}$$

With an order quantity of 200 units, the firm would order (2,000/200), or ten times, during the period under consideration or, in other words, every ten days. We see from Eq. (16-3) that Q^* varies directly with total usage, S, and order cost, O, and inversely with the carrying cost, C. However, the relationship is dampened by the square-root sign in both cases. As usage increases, then, the optimal order size and the average level of inventory increase by a lesser percentage. In other words, economies of scale are possible.

In our example, we have assumed that inventory can be ordered with no delay. However, there is usually a time lapse in procurement between the time a purchase order is placed and the time the inventory is actually received, or in the time it takes to manufacture an item after an order is placed. This lead time must be considered. If it is constant and known with certainty, however, the optimal order quantity is not affected. In the above example, the firm would still order 200 units at a time and place ten orders during the specified time period, or every ten days. If the lead time for delivery were three days, the firm simply would place its order seven days after delivery of the previous order.

The EOQ function is illustrated in Figure 16-2. In the figure, we plot ordering costs, carrying costs, and total costs—the sum of the first two

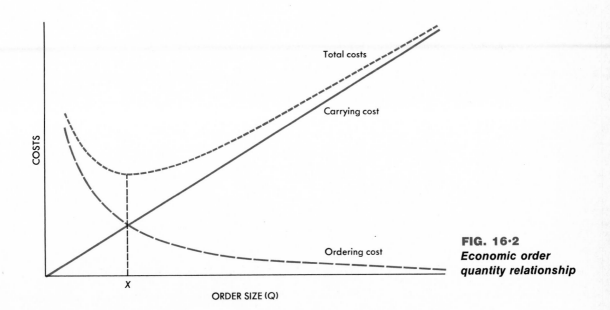

FIG. 16·2
Economic order quantity relationship

costs. We see that whereas carrying costs vary directly with the size of the order, ordering costs vary inversely with the size of the order. The total cost line declines at first as the fixed costs of ordering are spread over more units. The total cost line begins to rise, however, when the decrease in average ordering cost is more than offset by the additional carrying costs. Point *X*, then, represents the economical order quantity, which minimizes the total cost of inventory.

The EOQ formula taken up in this section is a very useful tool for inventory control. In purchasing raw materials or other items of inventory, it tells us the amount to order and the best timing of our orders. For finished-goods inventory, it enables us to exercise better control over the timing and size of production runs. In general, the EOQ model gives us a rule for deciding when to replenish inventories and the amount to replenish. All inventory models, no matter how complex, address themselves to this problem of the timing and magnitude of replenishment.[5]

QUANTITY DISCOUNTS

Frequently, the firm is able to take advantage of quantity discounts in ordering. Because these discounts affect the price per unit, they also influence the economic order quantity. However, the basic EOQ framework should still be used as a point of departure for analyzing the problem. In our example, we assumed 2,000 units of usage during a 100-day period, order costs of $100 an order, and carrying costs of $10 per unit per 100 days, resulting in an economic order quantity of 200 units. Suppose now that a quantity discount of $0.10 a unit in price is available if the firm increases its order size to 250 units, whereas currently it enjoys no discount. To determine whether or not the discount is worthwhile, we must analyze the benefits in relation to the costs involved.

The savings available to the firm in lower purchase price are

$$\text{Savings} = \text{Discount per unit} \times \text{Usage} \\ = 0.10 \times 2{,}000 = \$200 \tag{16-4}$$

The cost is the additional carrying cost less savings in ordering costs that result from fewer orders being placed. The additional carrying cost, where Q' is the new order size required, is

$$\frac{(Q' - Q^*)C}{2} = \frac{(250 - 200)10}{2} = \$250$$

[5] See Harvey M. Wagner, *Principles of Operations Research with Applications to Managerial Decisions* (Englewood Cliffs, N.J.: Prentice-Hall, 1969), pp. 786–89.

The saving in ordering costs is

$$\frac{SO}{Q^*} - \frac{SO}{Q'} = \frac{(2,000)(100)}{200} - \frac{(2,000)(100)}{250} = \$200$$

Therefore, the net increase in costs is $250 − $200, or $50, for going from an order quantity of 200 units to 250 units. Because the net cost is less than the benefits to be derived, $200, the firm should use an order quantity of 250 units. Similarly, other problems involving quantity discounts can be analyzed in this manner. The economic order quantity formula serves as a point of departure for balancing the benefits against the costs of a change in order size.

UNCERTAINTY AND SAFETY STOCKS

In practice, the demand or usage of inventory generally is not known with certainty; usually it fluctuates during a given period of time. Typically, the demand for finished-goods inventory is subject to the greatest fluctuation. In general, the usage of raw-materials inventory and in-transit inventory, both of which depend upon the production scheduling, is much more predictable. In addition to demand or usage, the lead time required to receive delivery of inventory once an order is placed is usually subject to some variation. Owing to these fluctuations, it is not feasible in most cases to allow expected inventory to fall to zero before a new order is expected to be received, as could be done when usage and lead time were known with certainty.

Most firms maintain some margin of safety, or safety stock; otherwise, they may be unable to satisfy the demand for an item of inventory at a particular time. There are opportunity costs to being out of stock. In the case of finished-goods inventory, the customer is likely to become irritated and may take his business elsewhere. In the case of raw-materials and in-transit inventories, the cost of being out of stock is a stoppage in production and the resulting inefficiencies that occur. While this opportunity cost is measured more easily than that associated with finished-goods inventory, a stockout of the latter has a cost; and the firm must recognize it.

PROPER LEVEL OF SAFETY STOCK

The decision to maintain a safety stock involves balancing the cost of stockouts with the cost of carrying additional inventory. If we know the probability distribution of future demand or usage, we can assess this balance. Suppose, for example, that the usage of an inventory item over a ten-day period is expected to be the following:

Usage (in units)	50	100	150	200	250	300	350
Probability	0.04	0.08	0.20	0.36	0.20	0.08	0.04

Moreover, assume an economic order quantity of 200 units every ten days, steady usage, 200 units of inventory on hand at the beginning of the period, and three days lead time required to procure inventory. This lead time is known with certainty, and a new order is always placed at the end of the eighth day for delivery at the end of the eleventh day. If the firm carries no safety stock, there will be no stockouts if usage is 200 units or less. However, if usage proves to be 250 units instead of 200 units, there will be a stockout of 50 units. Similarly, if usage is 300 units or 350 units, there will be stockouts of 100 units and 150 units, respectively.

If we know the cost per unit of stockout, we can calculate the expected cost of stockouts and then compare this cost with the cost of carrying additional inventory. Included in the stockout cost are the loss of profit associated with the order not being filled as well as the intangible loss of customer goodwill. The extreme with respect to dissatisfaction is that the customer will cease to do business with the firm altogether. Suppose that we are able to estimate the stockout cost and that it is $6 a unit, and that the average carrying cost for the ten-day period is $1 per unit. In Table 16-1, we show the expected stockout cost, carrying cost, and total cost for various levels of safety stock. We see that the optimal safety stock is 50 units, the level at which the total cost is lowest. Rather

Table 16·1   Expected costs associated with various safety stocks

Safety Stock	Stockout	Stockout Cost ($6 per unit)	Probability	Expected Stockout Cost	Carrying Cost	Total Cost
150 units	0	$ 0	0	$ 0	$150	$150
100 units	50	300	0.04	12	100	112
50 units	100	600	0.04	24		
	50	300	0.08	24		
				$ 48	50	98
0 units	150	900	0.04	36		
	100	600	0.08	48		
	50	300	0.20	60		
				$144	0	144

than estimate a cost of stockout, some firms simply specify a maximum probability of running out of stock. If the hypothetical firm in our example did not want the probability of stockout to be more than 5 percent, it would maintain a safety stock of 100 units. In this way, it could meet all demand except that for 350 units, where there is a 4 percent probability of occurrence.

UNCERTAINTY OF LEAD TIME

Suppose that the lead time required for procurement, like demand or usage, is subject to a probability distribution and is expected to vary, with the following probabilities:

Lead time	2 days	3 days	4 days
Probability	0.25	0.50	0.25

For simplicity of illustration, assume that the usage of inventory on the eleventh day is the same as the average usage during the previous ten. If the probability distributions for usage and lead time are independent, we can calculate their joint probability of occurrence. These calculations are shown in Table 16-2. The last column of the table shows the number of units of stockout if no safety stock is held and there are 200 units of inventory on hand at the beginning of the period. From the table, we see that if usage is 200 units, but lead time is four days instead of three, there is a stockout of 20 units, assuming usage to be 20 units on the eleventh day. Similarly, we are able to calculate the number of units of stockout for other combinations of usage and lead time, in keeping with the above assumptions. For example, if usage is 300 units, or 30 units a day, and lead time is four days, the stockout is 130 units or the sum of the stockout occasioned by additional usage, 100 units, and by the additional lead time, 30 units.

Given the information in the last two columns of Table 16-2, together with the cost per unit of stockout and the carrying cost of inventory, we can determine the optimal level of safety stock for the period in a manner similar to that shown in Table 16-1. These calculations are shown in Table 16-3. We see from the table that the optimal safety stock is 70 units, the level at which the expected stockout cost plus carrying cost is lowest. If the firm did not wish to use the cost-of-stockout approach but wished to specify a maximum stockout probability instead, and this probability were 5 percent, it would maintain a safety stock of 115 units.

Table 16·2 Joint probabilities of usage and lead time

Usage		Lead Time		Joint Probability	Stockout (in units)
Units	Probability	Days	Probability		
50	0.04	2	0.25	0.01	None
		3	0.50	0.02	None
		4	0.25	0.01	None
100	0.08	2	0.25	0.02	None
		3	0.50	0.04	None
		4	0.25	0.02	None
150	0.20	2	0.25	0.05	None
		3	0.50	0.10	None
		4	0.25	0.05	None
200	0.36	2	0.25	0.09	None
		3	0.50	0.18	None
		4	0.25	0.09	20
250	0.20	2	0.25	0.05	25
		3	0.50	0.10	50
		4	0.25	0.05	75
300	0.08	2	0.25	0.02	70
		3	0.50	0.04	100
		4	0.25	0.02	130
350	0.04	2	0.25	0.01	115
		3	0.50	0.02	150
		4	0.25	0.01	185

Table 16·3 Determination of total cost

Safety Stock	Incremental Stockout	Incremental Stockout Cost ($6 per unit)	Cumulative Probability	Incremental Expected Stockout Cost	Cumulative Expected Stockout Cost	Carrying Cost	Total Cost
185	0	$ 0	0	$ 0	$ 0	$185	$185.00
150	35	210	0.01	2.10	2.10	150	152.10
130	20	120	0.03	3.60	5.70	130	135.70
115	15	90	0.05	4.50	10.20	115	125.20
100	15	90	0.06	5.40	15.60	100	115.60
75	25	150	0.10	15.00	30.60	75	105.60
70	5	30	0.15	4.50	35.10	70	105.10
50	20	120	0.17	20.40	55.50	50	105.50
25	25	150	0.27	40.50	96.00	25	121.00
20	5	30	0.32	9.60	105.60	20	125.60
0	20	120	0.41	49.20	154.80	0	154.80

Because the probabilistic analysis taken up in the preceding section is cumbersome, many people find it unfeasible for a multiperiod problem. Instead, they propose using an order point, whereby an order is placed once inventory reaches so many units.[6] The firm specifies an acceptable stockout percentage and then calculates an order point based upon this percentage, as well as upon other factors. The optimal order point is the level of inventory at which we should order the economic order quantity of additional stock. It is the point at which forecasted usage of an item of inventory, given a stockout tolerance, would just exhaust the existing inventory during the lead time required to procure additional inventory.

$$\text{Order point}^* = S(L) + F\sqrt{SR(L)} \qquad (16\text{-}5)$$

where S is the usage, L is the lead time required to obtain additional inventory once an order is placed, R is the average number of units per order, and F is a stockout acceptance factor.

If 300 units were ordered during a period of time, with twenty orders, R would be fifteen. The stockout acceptance factor is based upon the probability distribution of usage. If demand or usage is distributed according to a Poisson distribution,[7] F can be determined as in Figure 16-3. For example, if the stockout acceptance percentage is specified as 10 percent, we see from the figure that this percentage corresponds to an acceptance factor of 1.29.

To illustrate the use of Eq. (16-5), suppose that we consider a problem in which usage, S, is 100 units per month, lead time, L, is one-half month, the average number of units per customer order, R, is five, and the acceptable stockout percentage is 10 percent. The optimal order point, then, would be

$$100(\tfrac{1}{2}) + 1.29\sqrt{(100)(5)(\tfrac{1}{2})} = 70 \text{ units}$$

Thus, the firm should reorder when inventory reaches 70 units. We note that the order point includes a safety stock, which is determined by the stockout acceptance percentage we specify. If there were no safety stock, the order point would be at 50 units, or one-half of one month's usage. The one-half month takes into account the lead time required to actually receive inventory once an order is placed. The order point

---

[6] See Arthur Snyder, "Principles of Inventory Management," *Financial Executive*, 32 (April 1964), 13–21. This section is based upon his article, although the concept of an order point is found in most of the literature on inventory theory.

[7] For a discussion of Poisson probability distributions, see William Feller, *Probability Theory and its Applications*, 2nd ed. (New York: John Wiley, 1957), pp. 142–49.

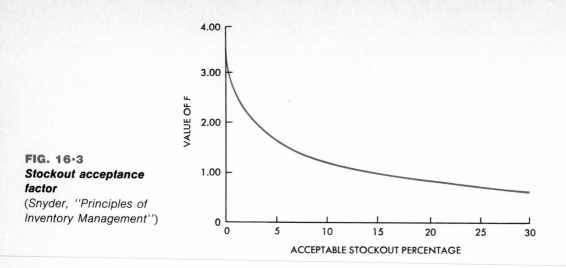

formula given in Eq. (16-5) minimizes the investment in inventory relative to an acceptable level of stockout. The concept of the order point can be extended to situations where usage is normally distributed[8] or distributed according to some other distribution.

The concept itself is illustrated in Figure 16-4 in conjunction with an economic order quantity. If demand is reasonably steady over a long period of time, the firm might employ the EOQ formula and order the same amount of inventory whenever the level of inventory touched the order point. In the figure, the order quantity is represented by the vertical distances and is the same for each order. The lead time for actual delivery of inventory is assumed to be known with certainty and to be the same for each order. However, usage is assumed to be subject to uncertainty. As a result, the time intervals T_1, T_2, T_3, and T_4 are not equal; and the low points in the level of inventory are not the same. Indeed, during period T_2, inventory reaches zero and the firm is out of stock until the new order is received.

The inventory system illustrated in Figure 16-4 is known as a "two-bin system," in which a constant replenishment order is placed whenever a critical level of inventory is reached. One might think of it as using stock from the regular bin and when this bin is exhausted, using stock from the safety bin and at the same time placing a replenishment order. The system combines the economic order quantity with the order point concept to produce an optimal control system when the firm is faced with lead times and uncertain usage. We see that if the size of the order point is reduced, less inventory is held on the average and carrying costs

[8] For an analysis of the order point when usage is assumed to be normally distributed, see Harold Bierman, Jr., Charles P. Bonini, and Warren H. Hausman, *Quantitative Analysis for Business Decisions* (Homewood, Ill.: Richard D. Irwin, 1969), Chapter 12.

are reduced. However, the probability of stockout is increased. Likewise, when the order quantity is reduced, carrying costs are reduced and the probability of stockout increased. Because total costs are affected by both the order point and the order quantity, an optimal control system must embody both of these factors.

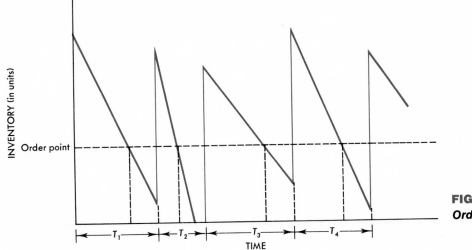

FIG. 16·4
Order-point example

The inventory control methods described in the last several sections give us a means for determining an optimal level of inventory, as well as how much should be ordered and when. These tools are necessary for managing inventory efficiently and balancing the advantages of additional inventory against the cost of carrying this inventory. With the use of computers, great improvements in inventory control have been made and are continuing to be made. Unfortunately, a review of the many applications of operations research to inventory management is beyond the scope of this book.[9]

Although inventory management usually is not the direct operating responsibility of the financial manager, the investment of funds in inventory is a very important aspect of financial management. Consequently, the financial manager must be familiar with ways to control inventories effectively so that capital may be allocated efficiently. The greater the opportunity cost of funds invested in inventory, the lower the optimal level of average inventory and the lower the optimal order

**INVENTORY
CONTROL AND
THE FINANCIAL
MANAGER**

[9]For such a review, see Arthur F. Veinott, Jr., "The Status of Mathematical Inventory Theory," *Management Science*, 12 (July 1966), 745–77.

quantity, all other things held constant. This statement can be verified by increasing the carrying costs, C, in Eq. (16-3). The EOQ model can also be useful to the financial manager in planning for inventory financing.

When demand or usage of inventory is uncertain, the financial manager may try to effect policies that will reduce the average lead time required to receive inventory once an order is placed. The lower the average lead time, the lower the safety stock needed and the lower the total investment in inventory, all other things held constant. The greater the opportunity cost of funds invested in inventory, the greater the incentive to reduce this lead time. In the case of purchases, the purchasing department may try to find new vendors that promise quicker delivery or place pressure on existing vendors for faster delivery. In the case of finished goods, the production department may be able to schedule production runs for faster delivery by producing a smaller run. In either case, there is a tradeoff between the added cost involved in reducing the lead time and the opportunity cost of funds tied up in inventory.

The opportunity cost of funds is the link by which the financial manager ties inventory management to the overall objective of the firm. In this regard, inventory can be treated as an asset to which capital is committed like any capital-budgeting project. Different items of inventory may involve different risks, and these differences can be incorporated into an analysis of risk similar to that for capital budgeting. As discussed in Chapter 13, the essential difference between a capital asset and inventory is that the former typically involves a discrete investment, while the latter represents a continuum of possible investments. Our discussion in this chapter has focused on determining an optimal *level* of investment. We know that the greater the efficiency with which the firm manages its inventory, the lower the required investment and the greater the shareholder wealth, all other things the same.

SUMMARY

The optimal level of inventories should be judged in relation to the flexibility inventories afford. If we hold constant the efficiency of inventory management, the lower the level of inventories, the less the flexibility of the firm. The higher the amount of inventories, the greater the flexibility of the firm. In evaluating the level of inventories, management must balance the benefits of economies of production, purchasing, and increased product demand against the cost of carrying the additional inventory. Of particular concern to the financial manager is the cost of funds invested in inventory.

The efficiency of inventory control very much affects the flexibility of the firm, given a level of inventory. Conversely, given a degree of flexibility, efficiency affects the level of inventory investment. In this chapter, we have examined several tools of inventory control. One is the economic order quantity (EOQ), whereby we determine the optimal size of order to place, on the basis of the demand or usage of the inventory, the ordering costs, and the carrying costs. Under conditions of uncertainty, the firm usually must provide for a safety stock, owing to fluctuations in demand for, or usage of, inventory and in lead times. Another tool—the order point formula—tells us the optimal point at which to reorder a particular item of inventory. Together, these tools provide the means for determining an optimal average level of inventory for the firm.

PROBLEMS

1. A college book store is attempting to determine the optimal order quantity for a popular book on financial management. The store sells 5,000 copies of this book a year at a retail price of $12.50, although the publisher allows the store a 20 percent discount from this price. The store figures that it costs $1 per year to carry a book in inventory and $100 to prepare an order for new books.
   (a) Determine the total costs associated with ordering one, two, five, ten, and twenty times a year.
   (b) Determine the economic order quantity.

2. The Hedge Corporation manufactures only one product, planks. The single raw material used in making planks is the dint. For each plank manufactured, twelve dints are required. Assume that the company manufactures 150,000 planks per year, that demand for planks is perfectly steady throughout the year, that it costs $200 each time dints are ordered, and that carrying costs are $8 per dint per year.
   (a) Determine the economic order quantity of dints.
   (b) What are total inventory costs for Hedge (carrying costs plus ordering costs)?
   (c) How many times per year would inventory be ordered?

3. Favorite Foods Inc. buys 50,000 boxes of ice cream cones every two months to service steady demand for the product. Order costs are $100 per order and carrying costs are $0.40 per box.
   (a) Determine the optimal order quantity.
   (b) The vendor now offers Favorite Foods a quantity discount of $0.02 per box if it buys cones in order sizes of 10,000 boxes. Should Favorite Foods avail itself of the quantity discount?

4. The Seguro Corporation has determined that its only raw material has an economic order quantity of 1,000 units every thirty days. Further, the firm knows with certainty that a four-day lead time is required for

ordering. It has been estimated that the following inventory usage distribution will prevail each month:

Usage (in units)	900	950	1,000	1,050	1,100	1,150	1,200	1,250
Probability	.06	.14	.30	.16	.13	.10	.07	.04

If stockouts would cost the firm $10 per unit, and the average monthly carrying cost is $1 per unit:

(a) Determine the optimal safety stock.

(b) What is the probability of being out of stock?

5. The Seguro Corporation (problem 4) has found that the lead time required for procurement is not known with certainty but is, in fact, subject to risk. The following lead time distribution has been estimated:

Lead time	3 days	4 days	5 days	6 days
Probability	.20	.30	.30	.20

Assuming that the probability distributions for usage and lead time are independent, that 1,000 units of inventory were on hand at the beginning of the month, and that daily inventory usage does not vary, what is the optimal safety stock?

(*Note:* This problem involves rather extensive computations. Typical time involved is somewhat over one hour.)

6. The Apex Company has a policy of reordering raw materials when inventory levels reach a certain point. The firm has determined that it uses 50,000 units of inventory per month, that a lead time of ten days is required, that 5,000 orders necessitating equal raw-materials usage are filled on the average each month, and that the stockout-acceptance percentage is 10 percent (demand is Poisson distributed).

(a) What is the optimal order point?

(b) What would be the order point with no safety stock?

7. Wilstat is contemplating a change in inventory policy. Currently, the firm has an inventory turnover of twenty-four times a year. Sales have been holding steady at $250,000 per year. Variable costs are 70 percent of the total sales dollar. The company feels that if it were to increase inventories, it could avoid certain stockouts that now occur and, as a result, increase sales. The required rate of return before taxes is 20 percent. The company estimates the following relationship between inventory turnover and sales:

Inventory turnover	24	12	6	4	3
Sales	$240,000	$252,000	$261,000	$266,000	$270,000

Using the marginal analysis procedure developed in the preceding chapter (accounts receivable), determine the optimal inventory policy.

SELECTED REFERENCES

Ammer, Dean S., "Materials Management as a Profit Center," *Harvard Business Review,* 47 (January–February 1969), 72–89.

Beranek, William, "Financial Implications of Lot-Size Inventory Models," *Management Science,* 13 (April 1967), 401–8.

Bierman, Harold, Jr., Charles P. Bonini, and Warren H. Hausman, *Quantitative Analysis for Business Decisions,* Chapters 10–12. Homewood, Ill.: Richard D. Irwin, 1969.

Brown, Robert G., *Decision Rules for Inventory Management.* New York: Holt, Rinehart & Winston, 1967.

Buffa, Elwood S., *Production-Inventory Systems: Planning and Control.* Homewood, Ill.: Richard D. Irwin, 1968.

Hadley, G., and T. M. Whitin, *Analysis of Inventory Systems.* Englewood Cliffs, N.J.: Prentice-Hall, 1963.

Haley, Charles W., and Robert C. Higgins, "Inventory Control Theory and Trade Credit Financing," *Management Science,* 20 (December 1973), 464–71.

Hausman, Warren H., and L. Joseph Thomas, "Inventory Control with Probabilistic Demand and Periodic Withdrawals," *Management Science,* 18 (January 1972), 265–75.

Hillier, Frederick S., and Gerald J. Lieberman, *Introduction to Operations Research,* Chapter 12. San Francisco: Holden-Day, 1967.

Magee, John F., "Guides to Inventory Policy," I–III, *Harvard Business Review,* 34 (January–February 1956), 49–60; (March–April 1956), 103–16; and (May–June 1956), 57–70.

Mehta, Dileep R., *Working Capital Management,* Chapters 4–5. Englewood Cliffs, N.J.: Prentice-Hall, 1974.

Schiff, Michael, and Zvi Lieber, "A Model for the Integration of Credit and Inventory Management," *Journal of Finance,* 29 (March 1974), 133–40.

Shapiro, Alan, "Optimal Inventory and Credit-Granting Strategies under Inflation and Devaluation," *Journal of Financial and Quantitative Analysis,* 7 (January 1973), 37–46.

Smith, Keith V., *Management of Working Capital,* Section 4. New York: West Publishing, 1974.

Snyder, Arthur, "Principles of Inventory Management," *Financial Executive,* 32 (April 1964), 13–21.

Stancill, James McN., *The Management of Working Capital,* Chapter 5. Scranton, Pa.: Intext, 1971.

Starr, Martin K., and David W. Miller, *Inventory Control— Theory and Practice.* Englewood Cliffs, N.J.: Prentice-Hall, 1962.

Veinott, Arthur F., Jr., "The Status of Mathematical Inventory Theory," *Management Science,* 12 (July 1966), 745–77.

Wagner, Harvey M., *Principles of Operations Research— with Applications to Managerial Decisions,* Chapters 9, 19, and Appendix II. Englewood Cliffs, N.J.: Prentice-Hall, 1969.

SHORT-TERM and INTERMEDIATE-TERM FINANCING

V

UNSECURED SHORT-TERM FINANCING

CONCEPTUAL UNDERPINNINGS

In Chapter 13, we considered the current liabilities of the firm as part of its overall financing decision. Involved was not only the question of debt versus equity but also questions about the maturity composition of the debt and about conditions associated with the debt. (An example of the latter is whether or not the debt is secured and, if so, the type of security.) Decisions reached with respect to these issues determine the amount of current liabilities of the firm. We suggested that if capital markets were perfect, stockholders would be indifferent as to the maturity and type of debt the firm employed. Put another way, the firm would be unable to affect the value of its equity by altering the maturity composition and types of debt contracts employed. Accordingly, there would be no reason to proliferate the types and maturities of debt; one debt strategy would be as good as the next.

If imperfections exist in financial markets, however, it will be in the stockholders' interest that the firm "package" its debt instruments in such a way as to take advantage of these imperfections. The more important imperfections affecting debt financing are flotation costs, bankruptcy costs, costs of information, and restrictions on lenders. Since these imperfections were described earlier in Parts II and III, we touch now on their implications for the problem at hand.

If flotation costs are fixed, either in whole or in part, this creates a bias toward less frequent financing, larger offerings of debt each time, and longer maturities. In other words, the presence of fixed costs results in economies of scale with respect to debt offerings. The existence of bankruptcy costs creates a bias in favor of lower levels of debt obligations coming due in the near future, that is, longer maturities. To the extent that there are costs of information, these costs affect the sources of financing the firm is able to tap. If the cost of information is somewhat fixed to either the lender or the borrower, this creates a bias toward fewer types of debt arrangements. For example a medium-sized firm may be unable to sell its debt in a public offering simply because the cost of information to ultimate investors is sufficiently high as to make debt issues of less than $10 million unfeasible. Instead, the firm will go to a commercial bank or an institutional lender such as an insurance company where it need negotiate with only one party. If the relationship is continuous over time, the cost of information per financing can be reduced. Thus, economies of scale in information affect the sources of debt financing the firm is able to tap.

Restrictions, or institutional constraints, on lenders affect the type of loans they can make. These constraints may be caused by such things as legal restrictions or tax differences, or they may simply be self-imposed. Commercial banks tend to make short- to intermediate-term loans, for example, owing to regulations on their investment behavior. To the extent that a firm is small and, because of the cost-of-information argument, restricted to bank financing, the maturity composition of its debt may be shorter than would otherwise be the case. Other examples of imperfections could be cited, but these examples are sufficient to give one an idea as to the direction of their impact.

In Part V, we assume implicitly that imperfections exist in financial markets, without necessarily arguing that they are substantial. As a result, the way the firm "packages" its debt financing is important. That is, by varying the maturity composition and conditions of its debt, the firm may be able to affect its value, albeit the impact is likely to be modest. For our purposes in this chapter, the most important aspect of a firm's debt is its maturity.

HEDGING APPROACH TO MATURITY COMPOSITION

If the firm adopts a hedging approach to financing, each asset would be offset with a financing instrument of the same approximate maturity. This approach to financing is similar to hedging in the commodity futures market. For example, a miller having a contract to deliver processed grain three months from now at an established price may purchase a futures contract for delivery of the grain he needs three months hence. Thus, the miller hedges against the uncertainty of changes in the price of grain by having a contract to buy grain on approximately the same date in the future as he will need it. With a hedging approach to financing, short-term or seasonal variations in current assets—less accounts payable and accruals—would be financed with short-term debt; the permanent component of current assets would be financed with long-term debt or equity. This policy is illustrated in Figure 17-1.

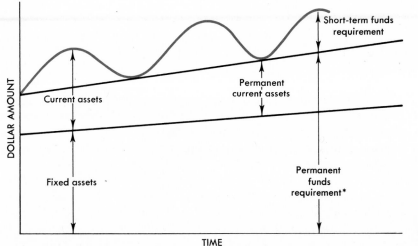

FIG. 17·1
Funds requirement

*Financed by long-term debt, equity, and the permanent component of current liabilities (accounts payable and accruals)

If current assets fluctuate in the manner shown in the figure, only the short-term fluctuations shown at the top of the figure would be financed with short-term debt. To finance short-term requirements with long-term debt would necessitate the payment of interest for the use of funds during times when they were not needed. This occurrence could be illustrated if we drew a straight line to represent the total amount of long-term debt and equity across the seasonal humps at the top of Figure 17-1. It is apparent that financing would be employed in periods of seasonal lull when it was not needed. With a hedging approach to financing, the borrowing and payment schedule for short-term financing would be arranged so as to correspond to the expected swings in current assets, less payables and accruals. Fixed assets and the permanent component of current assets would be financed with long-term debt, equity, and the permanent component of current liabilities.

A hedging approach to financing suggests that apart from current installments on long-term debt, a firm would show no current borrowings at the seasonal troughs in Figure 17-1. Short-term borrowings would be paid off with surplus cash. As the firm moved into a period of seasonal funds needs, it would borrow on a short-term basis, again paying the borrowings off as surplus cash was generated. In this way, financing would be employed only when it was needed. Permanent funds requirements would be financed with long-term debt and equity. In a growth situation, permanent financing would be increased in keeping with increases in permanent funds requirements.

MATURITY OF DEBT

Although an exact synchronization of the schedule of expected future net cash flows and the payment schedule of debt is appropriate under conditions of certainty, it usually is not under uncertainty. Net cash flows will deviate from expected flows in keeping with the business risk of the firm. As a result, the schedule of maturities of the debt contracts is very important in the risk-profitability tradeoff. We assume that the firm will not arrange its debt obligations so that the composite maturity schedule calls for payments of principal and interest before expected net cash flows are available. The question, however, is what margin of safety should be built into the maturity schedule in order to allow for adverse fluctuations in cash flows. The shorter the maturity schedule of the debt, the greater the risk that the firm will be unable to meet principal and interest payments. The longer the maturity schedule, the less risky the financing of the firm, all other things held constant.

The composite maturity schedule of debt for a firm will depend upon management's risk preferences. Generally, the longer the maturity schedule of debt in relation to expected net cash flows, the less the risk of inability to meet principal and interest payments. However, the longer

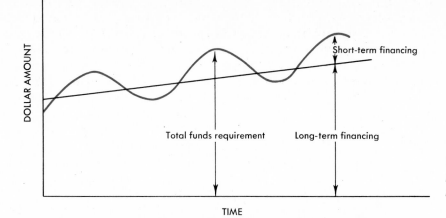

FIG. 17·2
Funds requirement:
margin of safety

Cost of LT financing
is greater than ST ✗

the maturity schedule, the more costly the financing is likely to be. For one thing, the explicit cost of long-term financing usually is more than that of short-term financing.[1] In periods of high interest rates, however, the rate on short-term corporate borrowings may exceed that on long-term borrowings. Over a reasonable period of time, however, the firm typically pays more for long-term borrowings, particularly if they are negotiated privately. In addition to the generally higher costs of long-term borrowings, the firm may well pay interest on debt over periods of time when the funds are not needed. Thus, there usually is an inducement to finance funds requirements on a short-term basis.[2]

Consequently, we have the familiar tradeoff between risk and profitability. The margin of safety, or lag between expected net cash flows and payments on debt, will depend upon the risk preferences of management. In turn, its decision as to the maturity breakdown of the firm's debt will determine the portion of current assets financed by current liabilities and the portion financed on a long-term basis.

To allow for a margin of safety, management might decide upon the proportions of short-term and long-term financing shown in Figure 17-2. Here, we see, the firm finances a portion of its expected seasonal funds requirement, less payables and accruals, on a long-term basis. If the expected net cash flows do occur, it will pay interest on debt during seasonal troughs when the funds are not needed. Thus the firm can

---

[1] We ignore at this time consideration of implicit costs that might be associated with short-term financing. These costs are analyzed in Chapters 9 and 10.

[2] For an analysis of the optimal mix of short- and long-term debt to finance cyclical funds requirements where these requirements are known, as are the costs of the two methods of financing, see D. J. Aigner and C. M. Sprenkle, "On Optimal Financing of Cyclical Cash Needs," *Journal of Finance*, 28 (December 1973), 1249–54. The optimal mix is the least cost mix, and Aigner and Sprenkle show that it is independent of the shape of the funds requirements curve.

reduce the risk of cash insolvency by increasing the maturity schedule of its debt.

With this general framework in mind, we are now able to examine in detail specific methods of short-term financing. The major sources are trade credit, commercial paper, and short-term loans. The first two as well as unsecured short-term loans are considered in this chapter; secured short-term loans are taken up in the next. We wish to see how these sources of short-term financing may be used to finance seasonal and temporary fluctuations in funds requirements, as well as the more permanent needs of the firm.

TRADE CREDIT

Trade credit is a form of short-term financing common to almost all businesses. In fact, it is the largest source of short-term funds for business firms collectively. In an advanced economy, most buyers are not required to pay for goods upon delivery but are allowed a short deferment period before payment is due. During this period, the seller of the goods extends credit to the buyer. Because suppliers generally are more liberal in the extension of credit than are financial institutions, trade credit is an important source of funds for small companies in particular.

There are three types of trade credit: open account, notes payable, and trade acceptances. By far the most common type is the open-account arrangement. With this arrangement, the seller ships goods to the buyer along with an invoice that specifies the goods shipped, the price, the total amount due, and the terms of the sale. Open-account credit derives its name from the fact that the buyer does not sign a formal debt instrument evidencing the amount that he owes the seller. The seller extends credit based upon his credit investigation of the buyer (see Chapter 15).

In some situations, promissory notes are employed instead of open-account credit. In this case, the buyer is asked to sign a note that evidences his debt to the seller. The note itself calls for the payment of the obligation at some specified future date. Promissory notes have been used in such lines of business as furs and jewelry. This arrangement is employed where the seller wants the buyer to recognize his debt formally. For example, a seller might request a promissory note from a buyer if the latter's open account became past due.

A trade acceptance is another arrangement by which the indebtedness of the buyer is recognized formally. Under this arrangement, the seller draws a draft on the buyer ordering him to pay the draft at some date in the future. The seller will not release the goods until the buyer accepts the time draft.[3] When the buyer accepts the draft, he designates

---

[3] If the instrument is a sight draft, the buyer is ordered to pay the draft upon presentation. Under this arrangement, trade credit is not extended.

a bank at which the draft will be paid when it comes due. At that time, the draft becomes a trade acceptance; and, depending upon the credit-worthiness of the buyer, it may possess some degree of marketability. If the trade acceptance is marketable, the seller of the goods can sell it at a discount and receive immediate payment for the goods. At final maturity, the holder of the acceptance presents it to the designated bank for collection.

TERMS OF SALE

Because the use of promissory notes and trade acceptances is rather limited, the subsequent discussion will be confined to open-account trade credit. With this type of credit, the terms of the sale are an important consideration. These terms, which are specified in the invoice, may be placed in several broad categories according to the net period within which payment is expected and according to the terms of the cash discount.

**COD and CBD—
no extension
of credit**
COD terms mean cash on delivery of the goods. The only risk that the seller undertakes in this type of arrangement is that the buyer may refuse the shipment. Under such circumstances, the seller will be stuck with the shipping costs. Occasionally, a seller might ask for cash before delivery (CBD) to avoid all risk. Under either COD or CBD terms, the seller does not extend credit. CBD terms must be distinguished from progress payments, which are very common in certain industries. With progress payments, the buyer pays the manufacturer at various stages of production prior to the actual delivery of the finished product. Because large sums of money are tied up in work in progress, aircraft manufacturers request progress payments from airlines in advance of the actual delivery of aircraft.

**Net period—
no cash
discount**
When credit is extended, the seller specifies the period of time allowed for payment. For example, the terms "net 30" indicate that the invoice or bill must be paid within thirty days. If the seller bills on a monthly basis, it might require such terms as "net/15 EOM," which means that all goods shipped before the end of the month must be paid for by the fifteenth of the following month.

**Net period
with
cash discount**
In addition to extending credit, the seller may offer a cash discount if the bill is paid during the early part of the net period. The terms "2/10, net 30" indicate that the buyer is offered a 2 percent discount if the bill is paid within ten days; if he does not pay within ten days, he must pay the full amount of the bill within thirty days. A cash

discount differs from a trade discount and from a quantity discount. With a trade discount, one type of customer (a wholesaler, for example) is given a lower price on goods purchased than is another type of customer, say a retailer. With a quantity discount, a customer is given a discount if the shipment is above a certain amount. Under most circumstances, a cash discount is offered as an incentive to the buyer to pay early. In Chapter 15, we considered the question of the optimal cash discount to be offered by a seller.

Datings   Datings are used frequently in a seasonal business, where the seller wishes to encourage customers to place their orders before a heavy selling period. For example, a manufacturer of lawn mowers may give seasonal datings specifying that any shipment to a dealer in the winter or spring does not have to be paid for until summer. The arrangement is beneficial to the seller because, with earlier orders, he can gauge his demand more realistically and schedule production more efficiently. Also, the seller does not have to store certain finished-goods inventory. The advantage of datings to the buyer is that he does not have to pay for the goods until he is able to sell them. Under this arrangement, credit is extended for a longer than normal period of time.

TRADE CREDIT AS A MEANS OF FINANCING

We have seen that trade credit is a source of funds, because the buyer does not have to pay for goods until after they are delivered. If the firm automatically pays its bills a certain number of days after the date of invoice, trade credit becomes a built-in source of financing that varies with the production cycle. As the firm increases its production and corresponding purchases, accounts payable increase and provide part of the funds needed to finance the increase in production. As production decreases, accounts payable tend to decrease. Although the variation of accounts payable with production may not be directly proportional, on account of shortages or gluts in inventory on hand, there is a strong degree of correspondence.

If a firm adheres strictly to the practice of paying its bills at a given time after invoice, trade credit is not a discretionary source of financing. It is entirely dependent upon the purchasing plans of the firm, which, in turn, are dependent upon its production cycle. In examining trade credit as a discretionary form of financing, we want to consider specifically situations in which (1) a firm does not take a cash discount but pays on the last day of the net period, and (2) a firm pays its bills beyond the net period.

In this section, we assume that the firm foregoes a cash discount but does pay its bill on the final due date of the net period. If no cash discount is offered, there is no cost for the use of credit during the net period. By the same token, if a firm takes the discount, there is no cost for the use of trade credit during the discount period. However, if a cash discount is offered and it is not taken, there is a definite opportunity cost. For example, if the terms of sale are 2/10, net 30, the firm has the use of funds for an additional twenty days if it does not take the cash discount but pays on the final day of the net period. In the case of a $100 invoice, it would have the use of $98 for twenty days. The annual interest cost is[4]

$$\frac{2}{98} \times \frac{360}{20} = 36.7 \text{ percent}$$

Thus, we see that trade credit can be a very expensive form of short-term financing when a cash discount is offered.

The cost of trade credit declines the longer the net period is in relation to the discount period. For example, had the terms in the above example been 2/10, net 60, the annual interest cost would have been

$$\frac{2}{98} \times \frac{360}{50} = 14.7 \text{ percent}$$

The relationship between the annual interest cost of trade credit and the number of days between the end of the discount period and the end of the net period is shown in Figure 17-3. In the figure, we assume 2/10 discount terms. We see that the cost of trade credit decreases at a decreasing rate as the net period increases. The point is that if a firm does not take a cash discount, its cost of trade declines the longer it is able to postpone payment.

The following terms have been used by tufters in the carpet and floor covering industry:[5]

5/10, 4/70, net 71

These terms mean that if a firm pays within ten days after invoicing, it is entitled to a 5 percent cash discount; while if it pays between day 10 and day 70, it is entitled to a 4 percent discount. The final due date is seventy-one days after invoicing. If a purchaser pays on day 70, it

---

[4] For ease of calculation, 360 rather than 365 is used as the number of days in the year.
[5] This example is drawn from John J. Brosky, *The Implicit Cost of Trade Credit and Theory of Optimal Terms of Sale* (New York: Credit Research Foundation, 1969), p. 3.

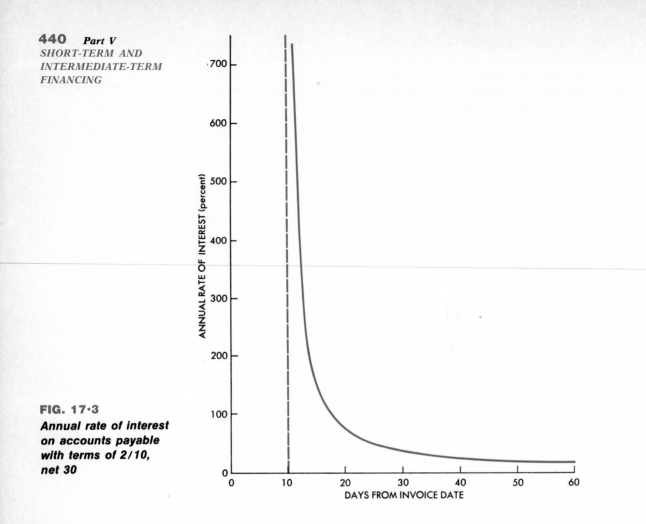

FIG. 17·3

Annual rate of interest on accounts payable with terms of 2/10, net 30

foregoes a 1 percent higher discount for the use of funds from day 10 to day 70. If the invoice is for $100, the annual interest cost is

$$\frac{1}{95} \times \frac{360}{60} = 6.3 \text{ percent}$$

Thus, the cost of foregoing the 5 percent discount in favor of the 4 percent one is relatively low in this case, and trade credit is an attractive means of financing. With these terms, the seller creates a powerful incentive to pay on the seventieth day. No one should pay on the final due date, for the cost of credit for the day is astronomical, as can be easily determined.

STRETCHING ACCOUNTS PAYABLE

In the preceding section, we assumed that payment was made at the end of the due period. However, a firm may postpone payment beyond this period; we shall call this postponement "stretching" accounts payable or "leaning on the trade." The cost of stretching accounts payable is twofold: the cost of the cash discount foregone and the possible deterioration in credit rating. In Chapter 15, we discussed the rating system of such credit agencies as Dun & Bradstreet. If a firm stretches its payables excessively so that trade payables are significantly delinquent, its credit rating will suffer. Suppliers will view the firm with apprehension and may insist upon rather strict terms of sale if, indeed, they sell at all. Also, banks and other lenders do not regard excessive slowness in the trade very favorably in assessing a company. Although it is difficult to measure, there is certainly an opportunity cost to a deterioration in a firm's credit reputation.

Notwithstanding the possibility of a deteriorating credit rating, it may be possible to postpone certain payables beyond the net period without severe consequences. Suppliers are in business to sell goods, and trade credit may be a very important sales tool. A supplier may well be willing to go along with a certain stretching of his payables, particularly if the risk of bad-debt loss is negligible. If the funds requirement of the firm is seasonal, suppliers may not view the stretching of payables in an unfavorable light during periods of peak requirements, provided that the firm is current in the trade during the rest of the year. However, there may be an indirect charge for this extension of credit in the form of higher prices. The firm should be particularly careful to consider this possibility in evaluating the cost of stretching accounts payable.

Periodic and reasonable stretching of payables is not necessarily bad per se. It should be evaluated objectively in relation to its cost and in relation to alternative sources of short-term credit. When a firm does stretch its payables, effort should be made to keep suppliers fully informed of its situation. A large number of suppliers will allow a firm to stretch payables if the firm is honest with the supplier and consistent in its payments. Sometimes a firm with seasonal funds requirements is able to obtain a dating from a supplier. When a firm obtains a dating, it does not stretch its payables; as long as it pays the bill by the final date, no deterioration in its credit ratings is likely.

ADVANTAGES OF TRADE CREDIT

The firm must balance the advantages of trade credit as a discretionary source of financing without any explicit cost against the cost of foregoing a cash discount and the opportunity cost associated with a possible deterioration in credit reputation if it stretches its payables. There are several advantages of trade credit as a form of short-term financing. Probably the major advantage is its ready availability. The accounts payable of most firms represent a continuous form of credit. There is no need to arrange financing formally; it is already there. If the firm is now taking cash discounts, additional credit is readily available by not paying existing accounts payable until the end of the net period. There is no need to negotiate with the supplier; the decision is entirely up to the firm. In the case of stretching accounts payable, it will become necessary, after a certain degree of postponement, to negotiate with the supplier.

In other types of short-term financing, it is necessary to negotiate formally with the lender over the terms of the loan. The lender may impose restrictions on the firm and seek a secured position. Restrictions are possible with trade credit, but they are not nearly as likely. With other sources of short-term financing, there may be a lead time between the time the need for funds is recognized and the time the firm is actually able to borrow them. Trade credit is a more flexible means of financing. The firm does not have to sign a note, pledge collateral, or adhere to a strict payment schedule on the note. A supplier views an occasional delinquent payment with a far less critical eye than does a banker or other lender.

Trade credit is advantageous to small firms that have difficulty obtaining credit elsewhere, or cannot obtain it at all. Typically, a higher percentage of the total liabilities of a small firm is comprised of trade credit than is true of a large firm. In periods of tight money, it has been contended that large firms obtain credit more easily than small firms do. However, small firms still have access to trade credit as a means of financing; often this credit comes from large suppliers who, in turn, avail themselves of other sources of financing. On balance, it appears that trade credit in the economy flows from firms with easy access to the capital markets, or with idle money balances, to firms with little access to the capital markets. To the extent that the former category consists predominantly of large, well-established firms while the latter consists of smaller, newer firms, trade credit serves as an "escape" valve for the small firm in times of tight money.[6]

The advantages of using trade credit must be weighted against the

---

[6] For an excellent analysis of this question, see Robert A. Schwartz, "An Economic Analysis of Trade Credit," *Journal of Financial and Quantitative Analysis*, 9 (September 1974), 643–57. See also Arthur B. Laffer, "Trade Credit and the Money Market," *Journal of Political Economy*, 78 (March–April 1970); Allan H. Meltzer, "Monetary Policy and the Trade Credit Practices of Business Firms," in Commission on Money and Credit, *Stabilization Policies* (Englewood Cliffs, N.J.: Prentice-Hall, 1963), p. 494; Meltzer, "Mercantile Credit, Monetary Policy and the Size of Firms," *Review of Economics and Statistics*, 42 (November 1960), 429–37; and Thomas Mayer, "Trade Credit and the Discriminatory Effects of Monetary Policy," *National Banking Review* (June 1966), pp. 543–45.

cost. As we have seen, the cost may be very high when all factors are
considered. Many firms utilize other sources of short-term financing in
order to be able to take advantage of cash discounts. The savings in cost
over other forms of short-term financing, however, must offset the
flexibility and convenience of trade credit. For certain firms, moreover,
there simply are no alternative sources of short-term credit.

WHO BEARS THE COST?

It is important to recognize that trade credit involves a cost for the
use of funds over time. In the previous sections, it was implied that there
is no explicit cost to trade credit if the buyer pays the invoice during the
discount period or during the net period, if no cash discount is given.
Although this supposition is valid from the standpoint of marginal
analysis, it overlooks the fact that somebody must bear the cost of trade
credit, for the use of funds over time is not free. The burden may fall on
the supplier, the buyer, or both parties. The supplier may be able to pass
the cost on to the buyer in the form of higher prices.

In the case of a product for which demand is elastic, however, the
supplier may be reluctant to increase prices and may end up absorbing
most of the cost of trade credit. Under other circumstances, the supplier
is able to pass the cost on to the buyer. The buyer should determine who
is bearing the cost of trade credit; if he finds that he is bearing the cost,
he may want to consider other suppliers to see if he can do better
elsewhere. In addition, the buyer should recognize that the cost of trade
credit changes over time. In periods of rising interest rates and tight
money, suppliers may raise the price of their products to take account of
the rising cost of carrying receivables. This rise in price should not be
confused with other rises caused by changing supply and demand
conditions in the product markets.

COMMERCIAL PAPER

Large, well-established companies sometimes borrow on a short-
term basis through commercial paper. Commercial paper consists of
unsecured short-term negotiable promissory notes sold in the money
market. Because these notes are unsecured and are a money-market
instrument, only the most credit-worthy companies are able to use
commercial paper as a source of short-term financing. The development
of the commercial paper market in this country began in the colonial
period. Its explosive growth in the sixties and seventies (see Table 17-1)
was closely associated with the growth of the economy as a whole and
the growth of installment financing of durable goods. In addition, the
growth in commercial paper financing in the late sixties and 1973–74 was

Table 17·1   Commercial paper rates and amounts outstanding, 1960–1975

| | Commercial Paper Outstanding at Dec. 31 (in millions) | | | Commercial Paper Avg. Interest Rate for Year | | |
	Total	Dealer Placed	Directly Placed	Dealer Placed 4–6 Mos.	Directly Placed 3–6 Mos.	Prime Rate on Bank Loans at June 30
1960	$ 4,497	$ 1,358	$ 3,139	3.85%	3.54%	5.00%
1965	9,058	1,903	7,155	4.38	4.27	4.50
1967	16,535	4,901	11,634	5.10	4.89	5.50
1969	31,624	11,817	19,807	7.83	7.16	8.50
1970	33,071	10,650	22,421	7.72	7.23	8.00
1971	32,126	10,095	22,031	5.11	4.91	5.50
1972	34,721	11,212	23,509	4.69	4.52	5.25
1973	41,073	10,926	30,147	8.15	7.40	7.50
1974	49,144	10,787	38,357	9.87	8.62	11.75
1975(o)	50,437	10,929	39,508	6.33	6.16	7.00

Source: *Federal Reserve Bulletins.*

attributable in part to the fact that banks curtailed credit in general and credit to finance companies in particular. Borrowers then turned to the commercial paper market as an alternative source of financing.

MARKET FOR COMMERCIAL PAPER

The commercial paper market is composed of two parts: the dealer market and the direct placement market.[7] Industrial firms, utilities, and medium-sized finance companies sell commercial paper through dealers. The dealer organization is composed of a half-dozen major dealers, who purchase commercial paper from the issuer and, in turn, sell it to investors. The typical commission a dealer earns is one-eighth percent, and maturities on dealer-placed paper generally range from one to six months. The market is a highly organized and sophisticated one; paper is sold in denominations ranging from $25,000 to several million dollars. Although the dealer market has been characterized in the past by a significant number of issuers who borrow on a seasonal basis, the trend definitely is toward financing on a revolving or more permanent basis.

Table 17-1 shows the surge in commercial paper placed through dealers during the 1965 through 1969 period. This growth resulted in part from industrial firms and utilities discovering commercial paper as an appropriate alternative source of funds in periods of tight money. During these periods, commercial banks were not able to accommodate

[7] For a discussion of commercial paper from the standpoint of a short-term investor, see Chapter 14.

their demand for loans; therefore, the utilities and industrial firms were forced to seek other sources of short-term financing.

Since the 1920s, a number of large sales finance companies, such as General Motors Acceptance Corporation and C.I.T. Financial Corporation, have bypassed the dealer organization in favor of selling their paper directly to investors. These issuers tailor both the maturity and the amount of the note to the needs of investors, most of which are large corporations with excess cash. Maturities on directly placed paper can range from as little as a few days up to nine months. Unlike many industrial issuers, finance companies use the commercial paper market as a permanent source of funds. With the development of the direct-placement market, pockets of idle investment funds have been tapped for short-term financing purposes. As shown in Table 17-1, directly placed paper has recently accounted for 60 to 80 percent of the total commercial paper outstanding. The growth in direct paper was caused by the increased demand for consumer credit along with the substitution of commercial paper for bank credit by large finance companies.

CHARACTERISTICS FOR THE BORROWER

The principal advantage of commercial paper as a source of short-term financing is that it is generally cheaper than a short-term business loan from a commercial bank. Usually, the rate on prime commercial paper is 0.25 percent to 2 percent lower than the prime rate for bank loans to the highest-quality borrower. The differential tends to increase in periods of easy money and to decrease in periods of tight money. It is important to recognize that commercial paper rates fluctuate considerably in keeping with money-market conditions. Table 17-1 shows the average rates for dealer-placed and directly placed commercial paper as well as the prime rate on business loans since 1960. In assessing commercial paper as a means of financing, the firm should weigh the relative cost and availability in comparison with alternative sources of funds. In this comparison, the cost of bank credit should be adjusted upward for compensating-balance requirements.

Many companies consider commercial paper a desirable supplement to bank credit. Ideally, a company would borrow heavily through commercial paper when the interest-rate differential was wide and borrow more from banks when the differential narrowed. This strategy would result in the lowest average interest cost and the maximum flexibility. However, commercial banks do not look favorably on credit requests only in periods of tight money. Switching from commercial paper to bank borrowings is possible, but a company must be careful not to impair relations with its bank. The commercial paper market is highly impersonal. If a firm cannot borrow from a commercial bank, it is at the mercy of the market. Therefore, it is important to maintain lines of credit at commercial banks in order to backstop adverse money-market conditions.

In addition to cost advantages, another reason commercial paper is used is that the legal limitations on the size of a loan that a commercial bank can extend preclude satisfying the requirements of the large finance companies. For example, the maximum loan a national bank can make to a single borrower is 10 percent of its capital and surplus. The total borrowing requirements of the three largest sales finance companies exceed the legal lending limits of the fifty largest banks in this country. Consequently, these companies must turn to other sources of short-term financing—namely, direct investors.

UNSECURED SHORT-TERM LOANS

For expository purposes, it is convenient to separate business loans into two categories: unsecured loans and secured loans. Almost without exception, finance companies do not offer unsecured loans, simply because a borrower who deserves unsecured credit can borrow at a lower cost from a commercial bank. Consequently, our discussion of unsecured loans will involve only commercial banks. Secured loans will be examined in the next chapter.

Short-term, unsecured bank loans typically are regarded as "self-liquidating" in that the assets purchased with the proceeds generate sufficient cash flows to pay the loan in less than a year. At one time, banks confined their lending almost exclusively to this type of loan. Fortunately, banks now provide a wide variety of business loans, tailored to the specific needs of the borrower. Still, the short-term, self-liquidating loan is an important source of business financing. It is particularly popular in financing seasonal buildups in accounts receivable and inventories. Unsecured short-term loans may be extended under a line of credit, under a revolving-credit agreement, or on a transaction basis. The debt itself is evidenced formally by a promissory note signed by the borrower, showing the time and amount of payment and the interest to be paid.

LINE OF CREDIT

A line of credit is an arrangement between a bank and its customer with respect to the maximum amount of unsecured credit the bank will permit the firm to owe at any one time. Usually, credit lines are established for a one-year period and are subject to one-year renewals. Frequently, lines of credit are set for renewal after the bank receives the audited annual report and has had a chance to review the progress of the borrower. For example, if the borrower's year-end statement date is December 31, a bank may set its line to expire sometime in March. At

Second National Bank
Palo Alto, California

March 23, 1977

Mr. Joseph A. Ralberg
Vice President & Treasurer
Barker Manufacturing Corporation
Palo Alto, California

Dear Mr. Ralberg:

Based upon our analysis of your year-end audited statements,
we are pleased to renew your $1 million unsecured line of
credit for the forthcoming year. Borrowings under this
line will be at a rate of one-half percent (½%) over the
prime rate.

This line is subject to only the understanding that your
company will maintain its financial position and that it
will be out of bank debt for at least 45 days during the
fiscal year.

Yours very truly,

John D. Myers
Vice President

FIG. 17·4
Sample letter
extending line of credit

that time, the bank and the company would meet to discuss the credit
needs of the firm for the coming year in light of its past year's performance. The amount of the line is based upon the bank's assessment of the
credit-worthiness of the borrower and upon his credit needs. Depending
upon changes in these conditions, a line of credit may be adjusted at the
renewal date, or before, if conditions necessitate a change.

The cash budget, perhaps, gives the best insight into the borrower's
short-term credit needs. For example, if maximum or peak borrowing
needs over the forthcoming year are estimated at $800,000, a company

might seek a line of credit of $1 million to give it a margin of safety. Whether the bank will go along with the request, of course, will depend upon its evaluation of the credit-worthiness of the firm. If the bank agrees, the firm then may borrow on a short-term basis—usually ninety days—up to the full $1-million line. Because banks tend to regard borrowing under lines of credit as seasonal or temporary financing, they usually require that the borrower be out of bank debt at some time during the year. Frequently, the borrower will be required to "clean up" bank debt for at least thirty days during the year. The understanding between the bank and the borrower with respect to a "cleanup," of course, is subject to negotiation. The "cleanup" itself is evidence to the bank that the loan is truly seasonal in nature and not a portion of the permanent financing of the firm.

Despite its many advantages to the borrower, a line of credit does not constitute a legal commitment on the part of the bank to extend credit. The borrower is usually informed of the line by means of a letter indicating that the bank is willing to extend credit up to a certain amount. An example of such a letter is shown in Figure 17-4. This letter is not a legal obligation of the bank to extend credit. If the credit-worthiness of the borrower should deteriorate over the year, the bank may not want to extend credit and would not be required to do so. Under most circumstances, however, a bank feels bound to honor a line of credit.

REVOLVING-CREDIT AGREEMENT

A revolving-credit agreement represents a legal commitment on the part of the bank to extend credit up to a maximum amount. While the commitment is in force, the bank must extend credit to the borrower any time he wishes to borrow, provided total borrowings do not exceed the maximum amount specified. If the revolving credit is for $1 million, and $700,000 is already owing, the borrower can borrow an additional $300,000 at any time. For the privilege of having this formal commitment, the borrower usually is required to pay a commitment fee on the unused portion of the revolving credit. For example, if the revolving credit is for $1 million, and borrowing for the year averages $400,000, the borrower will be required to pay a commitment fee on the $600,000 unused portion. If the fee is 0.5 percent, the cost of this privilege will be $3,000 for the year. Revolving-credit agreements frequently extend beyond one year. Because lending arrangements of more than a year must be regarded as intermediate rather than short-term credit, we shall examine revolving credits more extensively in Chapter 18. The purpose of introducing them at this time is to illustrate the formal nature of the arrangement in contrast to the informality of a line of credit.

Borrowing under a line of credit or under a revolving-credit arrangement is not appropriate when the firm needs short-term funds for only one purpose. For example, a contractor may borrow from a bank in order to complete a job. When the contractor receives payment for the job, he pays the loan. For this type of loan, a bank evaluates each request by the borrower as a separate transaction. In these evaluations, the cash-flow ability of the borrower to pay the loan usually is of paramount importance.

COMPENSATING BALANCES

In addition to charging interest on loans, commercial banks often require the borrower to maintain demand-deposit balances at the bank in direct proportion to either the amount of funds borrowed or the amount of the commitment. These minimum balances are known as compensating balances. The amount required in the compensating balance varies according to the particular bank and the borrower, but many banks require balances equal to 15 percent of a line of credit. If the line is $1 million, the borrower will be required to maintain average balances of at least $150,000 during the year. The effect of a compensating-balance requirement is to raise the effective cost of borrowing if the borrower is required to maintain balances above the amount the firm would maintain ordinarily.

To the extent that a compensating-balance requirement does not require the borrower to maintain balances above those that it would maintain ordinarily, such a requirement does not raise the effective cost of borrowing. However, if balances above the ordinary must be maintained, the effective cost of borrowing is raised.[8] For example, suppose we borrow $1 million at 8 percent and are required to maintain $100,000 more in balances than we would ordinarily. We would then have use of only $900,000 of the $1 million loan. The effective annual interest cost is $80,000/$900,000 = 8.88 percent, rather than 8 percent.

Compensating-balance requirements may increase the liquidity position of the borrower from the bank's point of view. As a last resort, the bank can exercise its legal right of offset and apply the balances on deposit to pay off the loan or a portion of the loan. The compensating balance required of a firm may vary somewhat in keeping with credit availability in general. When money is tight and loan demand high, commercial banks are able to enforce higher compensating-balance requirements than they are when credit is readily available.

---

[8] For an analysis of the relationship between interest cost, compensating balances, activity in the account, and loan costs to the bank, see Bernell K. Stone, "The Cost of Bank Loans," *Journal of Financial and Quantitative Analysis*, 7 (December 1972), 2077–86.

There is some indication that the notion of compensating balances for loans is lessening somewhat in importance. Increasingly, banks are becoming more profit- as opposed to deposit-oriented and, accordingly, are "fine tuning" their profitability analyses of customer relationships. This movement has led a number of banks to prohibit the use of balances to support both account activity and lending arrangements. With the rapid and significant fluctuation in the cost of funds to banks in recent years, some banks are making loans without compensating-balance requirements. The interest rate charged is higher and more in line with the bank's incremental cost of obtaining funds. The movement toward more sophisticated profitability analysis is likely to reduce further, though certainly not eliminate, the imposition of compensating-balance requirements in connection with lending arrangements.[9]

INTEREST RATES

Unlike interest rates on such impersonal money-market instruments as Treasury bills, bankers' acceptances, and commercial paper, most business loans are determined through personal negotiation between the borrower and the lender(s). In some measure, banks try to vary the interest rate charged according to the credit-worthiness of the borrower; the lower the credit-worthiness, the higher the interest rate. Interest rates charged also vary in keeping with money-market conditions. One measure that varies with underlying market conditions is the *prime* rate. The prime rate is the lowest rate typically charged on business loans to large, well-established, and financially sound companies. The rate itself is usually set by large money-market banks and is relatively uniform throughout the country. In the past, the rate changed only slowly over time in keeping with underlying changes in market conditions. This phenomenon is evident in Figure 17-5 up to the mid-sixties.

After the mid-sixties, the prime rate changed much more rapidly. Several factors were responsible. For one thing, there was a greater volatility in overall market rates of interest. The early- to mid-sixties was a period of unprecedented stability in interest rates. This stability has not been witnessed since. Another factor is the cost of funds to banks. Over the years, time deposits and other liabilities on which interest is paid have increased significantly in relation to demand deposits. As a result, fluctuations in market rates of interest cause greater volatility in the cost of funds to banks than was true in years gone by. Finally, certain banks have instigated "floating" prime rates. The "floating" prime is in keeping with changes in money-market rates. For example, the rate might be 0.5 percent above the commercial paper rate, with adjustments occurring

---

[9] For further discussion of this issue, see Paul S. Nadler, "Compensating Balances and the Prime at Twilight," *Harvard Business Review*, 50 (January–February 1972), 112–20.

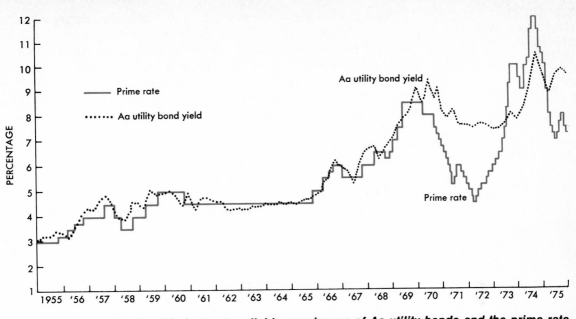

FIG. 17·5 *Relationship between callable new issues of Aa utility bonds and the prime rate*

on a weekly basis. The "floating" prime not only has resulted in those banks adjusting their prime rates more frequently than before but has brought pressure on "nonfloating" prime banks to change their rates more frequently than might otherwise be the case. All of these factors have resulted in frequent changes in the prime rate in recent years, as evidenced in Figure 17-5.

Given a prime rate for companies of the highest credit-worthiness, other borrowers are charged rates above the prime. For example, a bank might extend a line of credit to a company at a rate of 0.5 percent above prime. If the prime rate is 7.5 percent, the borrower will be charged an interest rate of 8 percent. If the prime rate changes to 7 percent, the borrower will pay 7.5 percent.

The interest-rate differential between the prime rate and the rate charged to a borrower will depend upon the relative bargaining power of the borrower and the bank. Supposedly, this differential should reflect only the borrower's credit-worthiness in relation to that of a "prime-risk" borrower. However, other factors influence the differential. The balances maintained and other business the borrower has with a bank (such as trust business) may be important considerations. A good customer who has maintained very attractive balances in the past may be able to obtain a more favorable interest rate than will a firm of equal credit-worthiness that has carried rather meager balances in the past. Although the prime rate reflects national credit conditions, many banks extend credit only in a specific geographic area. To the extent that credit conditions in that area differ from national conditions, the interest-rate differential from the prime rate will be affected. In addition, a bank that is aggressively seeking a relationship with a company may be willing to extend credit at a rate slightly lower than it might charge normally.

Thus, the interest rate charged on a short-term loan will depend upon the prevailing prime rate, the credit-worthiness of the borrower, his present and prospective relationship with the bank, and, sometimes, upon other considerations. Because of the fixed costs involved in credit investigation and in the processing of a loan, we would expect the interest rate on small loans to be higher than the rate on large loans.

Methods of computing interest rates

There are two ways in which interest on a loan may be paid: on a collect basis and on a discount basis. When paid on a collect basis, the interest is paid at the maturity of the note; when paid on a discount basis, interest is deducted from the initial loan. To illustrate, suppose we have a $10,000 loan at 7 percent interest for one year. The effective rate of interest on a collect note is

$$\frac{\$700}{\$10,000} = 7.00 \text{ percent}$$

On a discount basis, the effective rate of interest is not 7 percent but

$$\frac{\$700}{\$9,300} = 7.53 \text{ percent}$$

Discount → deduct fr. total

When we pay on a discount basis, we have the use of only $9,300 for the year but must pay back $10,000 at the end of that time. Thus, the effective rate of interest is higher on a discount note than on a collect note. We should point out that most bank business loans are on a collect-note basis.

SUMMARY

Trade credit can be an important source of short-term financing for the firm. However, it is a discretionary source of financing only if a firm does not have a strict policy with respect to the number of days after invoice a bill is paid. When a cash discount is offered but not taken, the cost of trade credit is the cash discount foregone. However, the longer the period between the end of the discount period and the time the bill is paid, the less this opportunity cost. "Stretching" accounts payable involves postponement of payment beyond the due period. The opportunity cost of stretching payables is the possible deterioration in the firm's credit rating. The firm must balance the costs of trade credit against its advantages and the costs of other short-term credit. The major advantage of trade credit is the flexibility it gives the firm.

Commercial paper is used only by well-established, high-quality companies. The evidence of debt is an unsecured short-term promissory note that is sold in the money market. Commercial paper is sold either through dealers or directly to investors. The latter method is used by large sales finance companies, and about two-thirds of commercial paper is placed in this manner. The principal advantage of commercial paper is that its yield typically is less than the rate of interest a company would have to pay on a bank loan. When used properly, it therefore is a very desirable source of short-term funds.

Short-term loans can be divided into two types, unsecured loans and secured loans. Unsecured credit is usually confined to bank loans under a line of credit, under a revolving-credit agreement, or on a transaction basis. Typically, banks require balances to compensate for a lending arrangement. If the borrower is required to maintain balances above those that it would maintain ordinarily, the effective cost of borrowing is increased. Interest rates on business loans are a function of the existing prime rate, the creditworthiness of the borrower, and the profitability of the relationship for the bank.

LINEAR PROGRAMMING APPROACH TO SHORT-TERM FINANCING

APPENDIX

Robichek, Teichroew, and Jones have developed an extensive linear-programming model for making short-term financing decisions.[10] Because the type of approach they propose has considerable merit, we describe it briefly in this appendix. The first step is the preparation of a cash budget in which total receipts less total disbursements are tabulated for each future period. Disbursements include payments for purchases and other disbursements. Given beginning cash, the minimum amount of cash the firm desires to hold, and total receipts less total disbursements, a cumulative cash deficit or surplus can be determined for each future period in the manner described in Chapter 26.

The financial manager has available to him a number of alternatives by which the cumulative cash deficit can be financed or excess cash invested. These alternatives carry certain costs per period and are

[10] See A. A. Robichek, D. Teichroew, and J. M. Jones, "Optimal Short-Term Financing Decision," *Management Science*, 12 (September 1965), 1–36; and Alexander A. Robichek and Stewart C. Myers, *Optimal Financing Decisions* (Englewood Cliffs, N.J.: Prentice-Hall, 1965), Chapter 7. For a somewhat different approach with a focus on portfolio considerations, see Manak C. Gupta, "Optimal Financing Policy for a Firm with Uncertain Fund Requirements," *Journal of Financial and Quantitative Analysis*, 8 (December 1973), 731–47.

subject to constraints. The alternatives assumed to be available are the following:

1. Unsecured borrowings under a line of credit. This line sets the upper limit on borrowings. An additional constraint pertains to the need to maintain compensating balances.

2. Accounts-receivable loan. This type of loan has an upper constraint and is limited to a percentage of the face value of accounts receivable pledged.

3. Stretching accounts payable. The cost of this alternative is the discount foregone. Stretching of accounts is limited to two periods and is further constrained by a limitation on the percentage of payables that can be stretched in any one period. In addition to the explicit cost of cash discount foregone, the authors assume an implicit cost of ill will to creditors if payables are stretched more than one period.

4. Term loan from a bank. This type of loan is constrained, having a minimum and a maximum amount, and is subject to a fixed installment payment schedule. There are additional constraints on the maximum amount of total borrowings. Here, too, the authors assume an implicit cost.

5. Investment of excess cash. The financial manager may invest excess cash in any given period at a specified rate of return.

The objective function of the linear-programming problem is to show how to provide the funds needed, as shown by the cash budget, at the minimum total cost. This objective function is subject to the constraints listed under the financial alternatives. When the multiperiod linear-programming problem is solved,[11] we obtain the optimal financing strategy for each period of the planning horizon under consideration. The optimal amounts of unsecured borrowings, accounts-receivable financing, stretching of payables, term loan, and investment of excess cash are specified for each period, together with the cost of this optimal financing procedure. By evaluating the dual variables, management obtains insight into the opportunity cost of the various constraints.[12] This approach provides the financial manager with a decision-making tool for solving rather complex short-term financing problems.

In a similar manner, Mao, Peterson, and Orgler propose linear-programming models to deal with financing decisions.[13] Of these, Peterson's is the most comprehensive because he incorporates into the short-run operating plan of the firm the following sources of short-term financing: accounts payable, a bank line of credit, secured financing based upon

---

[11] See Robichek, Teichroew, and Jones, "Optimal Short-Term Financing Decision," pp. 21–25.

[12] For a detailed evaluation of dual variables in connection with a different linear-programming problem, see the appendix to Chapter 18.

[13] James C. T. Mao, *Quantitative Analysis of Financial Decisions* (London: Macmillan, 1969), pp. 527–47; D. E. Peterson, *A Quantitative Framework for Financial Management* (Homewood, Ill.: Richard D. Irwin, 1969), Chapter 7; and Yair E. Orgler, *Cash Management* (Belmont, Calif.: Wadsworth, 1970), Chapters 3–6.

accounts receivable and/or inventories, and the sale of commercial paper.

The most serious shortcoming of a linear-programming approach to short-term financing is the need to project future cash flows as though they were known with certainty. This treatment eliminates from consideration possible deviations from expected outcomes as well as the flexibility of financing instruments to deal with unexpected cash demands or surpluses. The approach suffers also from the need to formulate certain implicit costs as constraints. For example, borrowings may not be limited in any absolute sense to a specific amount. Rather, the explicit and implicit costs simply may increase at an increasing rate, so that beyond a point borrowing is no longer feasible. By necessity, a linear-programming approach tries to "force" these costs into constraints. Where the alternative sources of financing are few, a more appropriate method may be simply a comparison of explicit costs, with the financial manager assessing implicit costs on the basis of probabilistic cash-budget information. When short-term financing problems are complex, however, a linear-programming approach provides a rigorous tool for obtaining a solution. As long as its limitations are recognized, the tool can be useful.

PROBLEMS

1. Determine the annual percentage interest cost for each of the following terms of sale, assuming the firm does not take the cash discount but pays on the final day of the net period (assume a 360-day year):

   (a) 1/20, net 30 ($500 invoice) $\frac{5}{495} \cdot \frac{360}{10} = 36.4\%$

   (b) 2/30, net 60 ($1,000 invoice) $\frac{20}{980} \cdot \frac{360}{30} = 24.5\%$ $\qquad \frac{2}{98} \times \frac{360}{5} = 146.9\%$

   (c) 2/5, net 10 ($100 invoice)

   (d) 3/10, net 30 ($250 invoice) $\frac{7.50}{242.50} \cdot \frac{360}{20} = 55.7\%$

2. Does the dollar size of the invoice affect the annual interest cost of not taking discounts? Illustrate with an example. No

3. Recompute problem 1, assuming a ten-day stretching of the payment date. What is the major advantage of stretching? What are the disadvantages?

4. The Dud Company purchases raw materials on terms of 2/10, net 30. A review of the company's records by the owner, Mr. Dud, revealed that payments are usually made fifteen days after purchases are received. When asked why the firm did not take advantage of its discounts, the bookkeeper, Mr. Grind, replied that it cost only 2 percent for these funds, whereas a bank loan would cost the firm 6 percent.

   $\frac{2}{98} \times \frac{360}{20} = 36.7\%$

   (a) What mistake is Grind making?

   (b) What is the real cost of not taking advantage of the discount?

   (c) If the firm could not borrow from the bank and was forced to resort to the use of trade-credit funds, what suggestion might be made to Grind that would reduce the annual interest cost?

5. The Fox Company is able to sell $1 million of commercial paper every

three months at a rate of 7 percent and a placement cost of $3,000 per issue. The dealers require Fox to maintain $200,000 in bank balances, which would otherwise not be held. Fox has a 40 percent tax rate. What is the after-tax cost of funds from commercial paper to Fox?

6. The Sphinx Supply Company needs to increase its working capital by $100,000. It has decided that there are essentially three alternatives of financing available. They are:

   (a) Forego cash discounts, granted on a basis of 3/10, net 30.

   (b) Borrow from the bank at 8 percent. This alternative would necessitate maintaining a 25 percent compensating balance.

   (c) Issue commercial paper at 7½ percent. The cost of placing the issue would be $500 each six months.

   Assuming the firm would prefer the flexibility of bank financing, and provided the additional cost of this flexibility is no more than 1 percent, which alternative should be selected?

7. ABC Corporation borrows $100,000 for one year at 8 percent interest from a bank.

   (a) What is the effective interest cost if the loan is on a discount basis?

   (b) What is the effective interest cost if the bank requires compensating balances of 20 percent but the loan is on a collect basis?

SELECTED REFERENCES

Brosky, John J., *The Implicit Cost of Trade Credit and Theory of Optimal Terms of Sale.* New York: Credit Research Foundation, 1969.

Crane, Dwight B., and William L. White, "Who Benefits from a Floating Prime Rate?" *Harvard Business Review,* 50 (January–February 1972), 121–29.

Gibson, W. E., "Compensating Balance Requirements," *National Banking Review,* 2 (March 1965), 298–311.

Gupta, Manak C., "Optimal Financing Policy for a Firm with Uncertain Fund Requirements," *Journal of Financial and Quantitative Analysis,* 8 (December 1973), 831–47.

Hayes, Douglas A., Bank Lending Policies: Domestic and International. Ann Arbor, Mich.: University of Michigan, 1971.

Jaffee, Dwight M., and Franco Modigliani, "A Theory and Test of Credit Rationing," *American Economic Review,* 59 (December 1969), 850–72.

Joss, Robert L., "The Market for Commercial Paper," PhD. dissertation, Stanford University, 1970.

King, Alfred M., *Increasing the Productivity of Company Cash,* Chapter 12. Englewood Cliffs, N.J.: Prentice-Hall, 1969.

Laffer, Arthur B., "Trade Credit and the Money Market," *Journal of Political Economy,* 78 (March–April 1970).

Meltzer, Allan H., "Mercantile Credit, Monetary Policy, and Size of Firms," *Review of Economics and Statistics,* 42 (November 1960), 429–37.

Nadiri, M. I., "The Determinants of Trade Credit in the U.S. Total Manufacturing Sector," *Econometrica,* 37 (July 1969), 408–23.

Nadler, Paul S., "Compensating Balances and the Prime at Twilight," *Harvard Business Review,* 50 (January–February 1972), 112–20.

Robichek, A. A., D. Teichroew, and J. M. Jones, "Optimal Short-Term Financing Decision," *Management Science,* 12 (September 1965), 1–36.

Schadrack, Frederick C., Jr., "Demand and Supply in the Commercial Paper Market," *Journal of Finance,* 25 (September 1970), 837–52.

Schwartz, Robert A., "An Economic Analysis of Trade Credit," *Journal of Financial and Quantitative Analysis,* 9 (September 1974), 643–58.

Smith, Keith V., *Management of Working Capital,* Section 5. New York: West Publishing, 1974.

Stone, Bernell K., "Allocating Credit Lines, Planned Borrowing, and Tangible Services over a Company's Banking System," *Financial Management,* 4 (Summer 1975), 65–78.

———, "The Cost of Bank Loans," *Journal of Financial and Quantitative Analysis,* 7 (December 1972), 2077–86.

SECURED LOANS and INTERMEDIATE-TERM DEBT

In this chapter, we extend our examination of short-term loans to consider secured types of lending arrangements. The principal characteristic of short-term loans is that they are self-liquidating over a period of time of less than a year. Frequently, these types of loans are employed to finance seasonal and temporary funds requirements. Intermediate-term financing, on the other hand, is employed to finance more permanent funds requirements, such as underlying buildups in receivables and inventories, as well as to provide flexibility in a period of uncertainty. In the second part of the chapter, we examine various types of intermediate-term loans. In the following chapter, we consider lease financing, another means of intermediate-term financing.

SECURED CREDIT

Many firms cannot obtain credit on an unsecured basis, either because they are new and unproven or because their ability to service debt is not regarded as adequate by bankers. In order to make a loan, lenders require security so as to reduce their risk of loss. With security, lenders have two sources of loan payment: the cash-flow ability of the firm to service the debt, and, if that source fails for some reason, the collateral value of the security. Most lenders will not make a loan unless the firm has sufficient expected cash flows to make proper servicing of debt probable. To reduce their risk further, however, they require security as well.

COLLATERAL VALUE

The excess of the market value of the security pledged over the amount of the loan determines the lender's margin of safety. If the borrower is unable to meet his obligation, the lender can sell the security to satisfy the claim. If the security is sold for an amount exceeding the amount of the loan and interest owed, the difference is remitted to the borrower. If the security is sold for less, the lender becomes a general, or unsecured, creditor for the amount of the difference. Because secured lenders do not wish to become general creditors, they usually seek security with a market value sufficiently above the amount of the loan to minimize the likelihood of their not being able to sell the security in full satisfaction of the loan. However, the degree of security protection a lender seeks varies with the credit-worthiness of the borrower, the security the borrower has available, and the financial institution making the loan. Before discussing various short-term secured lending arrangements, we must examine briefly the means by which a lender protects himself under the Uniform Commercial Code.

It is important to understand the implications of the Uniform Commercial Code for secured lending. Article 9 of the Code deals with security interests of lenders, the specific aspect with which we are concerned. Prior to the adoption of the Code, procedures by which a lender perfected a valid lien on collateral were complex and differed greatly among states. Article 9 consolidated rules governing security devices into one meaningful body of laws.[1] Because the lending arrangements discussed in subsequent sections involve security interests under the Uniform Commercial Code, we need to define certain terms in this section.

Whenever a lender requires collateral of a borrower, he obtains a *security interest* in the collateral. The collateral may be accounts receivable, inventory, equipment, or other assets of the borrower. The security interest in the collateral is created by a *security agreement*, also known as a *security device*. This agreement is signed by the borrower and lender and contains a description of the collateral. An example of a security agreement is illustrated in Figure 18-2. In order to "perfect" a security interest in the collateral, the lender must file a copy of the security agreement or a financing statement with a public office of the state in which the collateral is located. Frequently, this office is that of the secretary of state. The filing gives public notice to other parties that the lender has a security interest in the collateral described. Before accepting collateral as security for a loan, a lender will search the public notices to see if the collateral has been pledged previously in connection with another loan. Only the lender with a valid security interest in the collateral has a prior claim on the assets and can sell the collateral in settlement of his loan.

ASSIGNMENT OF ACCOUNTS RECEIVABLE

RECEIVABLE LOANS

Accounts receivable represent one of the most liquid assets of the firm, and, consequently, they make desirable security for a loan. From the standpoint of the lender, the major difficulties with this type of security are the cost of processing the collateral and the risk of fraud. To illustrate the nature of the arrangement, we trace through a typical assignment of accounts-receivable loan. A company may seek a receivable loan from either a commercial bank or a finance company. Because the interest rate charged by a bank usually is less than that charged by a finance company, the firm will generally try to borrow first from a bank.

[1] See Lester E. Denonn, "The Security Agreement," *Journal of Commercial Bank Lending*, 50 (February 1968), 32–40.

Quality and size of receivables

In evaluating the loan request, the lender will analyze the quality of the firm's receivables in order to determine the amount he is willing to lend against these receivables. The greater the quality of the accounts the firm maintains, the greater the percentage the lender is willing to advance against the face value of the receivables pledged. A lender does not have to accept all the borrower's accounts receivable; usually, he will reject accounts that have low credit ratings or that are unrated. Also, government and foreign accounts usually are ineligible unless special arrangements are made. Depending upon the quality of the receivables accepted, a lender typically advances between 50 percent and 85 percent of their face value.

The lender is concerned not only with the quality of receivables but also with their size. The lender must keep records on each account receivable that is pledged; the smaller the average size of the accounts, the more it costs per dollar of loan to process them. Consequently, a firm that sells low-priced items on open account will generally be unable to obtain a receivable loan regardless of the quality of the accounts. The cost of processing the loan is simply too high. Occasionally a "bulk" assignment of receivables will be used to circumvent the problem. With a "bulk" assignment, the lender does not keep track of the individual accounts but records only the total amounts in the accounts assigned and the payments received. Because preventing fraud is difficult with a "bulk" assignment, the percentage advance against the face value of receivables is likely to be low—perhaps 25 percent.

Procedure

Suppose a lender has decided to extend a loan to a firm on the basis of a 75 percent advance against the face value of accounts receivable assigned. The firm then sends in a schedule of accounts showing the name of the account, the date of billing(s), and the amounts owed. An example of an assignment schedule is shown in Figure 18-1. The lender will sometimes require evidence of shipment, such as an invoice. Having received the schedule of accounts, the lender has the borrower sign a promissory note and a security agreement. The firm then receives 75 percent of the face value of the receivables shown on the schedule of accounts.

A receivable loan can be on either a nonnotification or a notification basis. Under the former arrangement, the customer of the firm is not notified that his account has been pledged to the lender. When the firm receives payment on the account, it forwards this payment, together with other payments, to the lender. The lender checks the payments against its record of accounts outstanding and reduces the amount the borrower owes by 75 percent of the total payments. The other 25 percent is credited to the borrower's regular checking account. With a nonnotification arrangement, the lender must take precautions to make sure the borrower does not withhold a payment check, using the funds himself.

SCHEDULE OF ACCOUNTS ASSIGNED

The undersigned hereby assigns to **WELLS FARGO BANK** the following accounts:

(LIST NAMES OR REFER TO ATTACHED)	GROSS AMOUNT	
Accounts receivable totalling_____		
evidenced by_____		
for (dates)_____		
Attached hereto and made a part hereof		
TOTAL		

The above accounts are assigned to **WELLS FARGO BANK** and a security interest is granted in accordance with the terms and conditions of the existing Continuing Security Agreement between undersigned and **WELLS FARGO BANK**, to which reference is made.

Date _____

Signed _____

By: _____

Schedule No. S _____

N503   —100/PAD—217—006

FIG. 18·1

Accounts-receivable assignment form

With a notification arrangement, the account is notified of the assignment, and remittances are made directly to the lender. Under this arrangement, the borrower cannot withhold payments. Most firms naturally prefer to borrow on a nonnotification basis; however, the lender reserves the right to place the arrangement on a notification basis.

Means of financing

An accounts-receivable loan is a more or less continuous financing arrangement. As the firm generates new receivables that are acceptable to the lender, they are assigned, adding to the security base against which the firm is able to borrow. New receivables replace the old, and the security base and the amount of loan fluctuate accordingly. A receivable loan is a very flexible means of secured financing. As receivables build up, the firm is able to borrow additional funds to finance this buildup. Thus, it has access to "built-in" financing. Many banks do not require compensating balances for receivable loans. Because the borrower frequently is rapidly growing, the burden of this requirement is felt to be unreasonable. Compensation comes in the form of a higher rate. Also, a "cleanup" of the loan is not required, because it is regarded as a more or less permanent source of financing.

At a commercial bank, the interest cost of borrowing against accounts receivable usually is 2 to 5 percent higher than the prime rate. In addition, many banks have a service charge of an additional 1 to 2 percent for processing this type of loan. Costs at commercial finance companies are higher; the total interest cost of a receivable loan may range from 12 to 24 percent.

FACTORING RECEIVABLES

In the assignment of accounts receivable, the firm retains title to the receivables. When a firm *factors* its receivables, however, it actually sells them to a factor. The sale may be either with or without recourse, depending upon the type of arrangement negotiated. The factor maintains a credit department and makes credit checks on accounts. Based upon its credit investigation, the factor may refuse to buy certain accounts that it deems too risky. By factoring, a firm frequently relieves itself of the expense of maintaining a credit department and making collections. Any account that the factor is unwilling to buy is an unacceptable credit risk unless, of course, the firm wants to assume this risk on its own and ship the goods. Factoring arrangements are governed by a contract between the factor and the client. The contract frequently is for one year with an automatic provision for renewal and can be canceled only with prior notice of thirty to sixty days. Although it is customary in a factoring arrangement to notify the customer that his account has been sold and that payments on the account should be sent directly to the factor, in some instances notification is not made. The customer continues to remit payments to the firm, which in turn, endorses them to the factor. These endorsements are frequently camouflaged to prevent the customer from learning that his account has been sold.

Factoring costs　For bearing risk and servicing the receivables, the factor receives a fee of around 1 to 3 percent of the face value of the receivables sold. This fee will vary according to the typical size of individual accounts, the volume of receivables sold, and the quality of the accounts. The typical fee is somewhat over 1 percent. We must recognize that the receivables sold to the factor will not be collected from the various accounts for a period of time. If the firm wishes to receive payment for the sale of its receivables before they are actually collected, it must pay interest on the advance. Advancing payment is a lending function of the factor in addition to his functions of risk bearing and of servicing the receivables. For this additional function, the factor requires compensation.

For example, if the receivables sold total $10,000, and the factoring fee is 2 percent, the factor will credit the firm's account with $9,800. If the firm wants to draw on this account before the receivables are collected, however, it will have to pay an interest charge—say 1 percent a month—for the use of the funds. If it wishes a cash advance of the full

$9,800, and the receivables are collected on the average, in one month, the interest cost will be approximately $0.01 \times \$9,800$, or \$98.[2] Thus, the total cost of factoring is composed of a factoring fee plus an interest charge if the firm draws upon its account before the receivables are collected. If the firm does not draw on its account until the receivables are collected, there is no interest charge. A third alternative is for the firm to leave its funds with the factor beyond the time when the receivables are collected and to receive interest on the account from the factor.

Flexibility   The typical factoring arrangement is continuous. As new receivables are acquired, they are sold to the factor, and the firm's account is credited. The firm then draws upon this account as it needs funds. Sometimes the factor will allow the firm to overdraw its account during periods of peak needs and thereby borrow on an unsecured basis. Under other arrangements, the factor may withhold a reserve from the firm's account as a protection against losses. There are about twenty old-line factors in the country, most of which are located in New York City. In recent years, commercial banks and bank holding companies have entered the factoring business and, accordingly, are a source of such financing. As with the old-line factors, most banks that factor are located on the eastern seaboard.[3]

Factoring, like the assignment of accounts receivable, affords the firm flexibility in its financing. As sales increase and the firm needs funds, financing becomes available automatically. This eliminates the uncertainty associated with the collection cycle. Consequently, the cash flows of the firm are more predictable. Factoring is widely used in the textile and apparel industries and has found acceptance in the shoe and furniture industries as well. While some people attach a stigma to the company that factors, in many quarters it is regarded as a perfectly acceptable method of financing. Its principal shortcoming is that it can be expensive. We must bear in mind, however, that the factor often relieves the firm of credit checkings, the cost of processing receivables, and collection expenses. For a small firm, the savings may be quite significant. All in all, factoring has found increasing acceptance as a means of financing, showing substantial growth in volume during the last fifteen years.

INVENTORY LOANS

Inventories also represent a reasonably liquid asset and are, therefore, suitable as security for a short-term loan. As with a receivable loan, the lender determines a percentage advance against the market value of

[2] The actual cash advance would be \$9,800 less the interest cost, or \$9,702.

[3] For an analysis of the entry of commercial banks into factoring, see Robert P. Shay and Carl C. Greer, "Banks Move into High-Risk Commercial Financing," *Harvard Business Review*, 46 (November–December 1968), 149–53, 156–61.

the collateral. This percentage varies according to the quality of the inventory. Certain inventories, such as grains, are very marketable and resist physical deterioration over time. The margin of safety required by the lender on a loan of this sort is fairly small, and the advance may be as high as 90 percent. On the other hand, the market for a highly specialized piece of equipment may be so narrow that a lender is unwilling to make any advance against its reported market value. Thus, not every kind of inventory can be pledged as security for a loan. The best collateral is inventory that is relatively standard and for which a ready market exists apart from the marketing organization of the borrower.

Lenders determine the percentage that they are willing to advance by considering marketability, perishability, market-price stability, and the difficulty and expense of selling the inventory to satisfy the loan. The cost of selling some inventory may be very high indeed. The lender does not want to be in the business of liquidating collateral, but he does want to assure himself that the collateral has adequate value in case the borrower defaults in the payment of principal or interest. As is true with most secured loans, however, the actual decision to make the loan will depend upon the cash-flow ability of the borrower to service debt. There are a number of different ways a lender can obtain a secured interest in inventories, and we consider each in turn. In the case of the first methods (floating lien, chattel mortgage, and trust receipt), the inventory remains in the possession of the borrower. In the last two methods (terminal warehouse and field warehouse receipts), the inventory is in the possession of a third party.

FLOATING LIEN

Under the Uniform Commercial Code, the borrower may pledge his inventories "in general" without specifying the specific inventory involved. Under this arrangement, the lender obtains a floating lien on all inventory of the borrower. This lien is very general and difficult to police on the part of the lender. Frequently, a floating lien is requested only as additional protection and does not play a major role in determining whether or not the loan will be made. Even if the lender does regard the collateral as important, he usually is willing to make only a moderate advance because he cannot exercise tight control over the collateral. The floating lien can be made to cover both receivables and inventories, as well as the collection of receivables. This modification gives the lender a lien on a major portion of a firm's current assets. In addition, the lien can be made to encompass almost any length of time so that it includes future as well as present inventory as security.[4]

[4] For further discussion, see J. Carson Quarles, "The Floating Lien," *Journal of Commercial Bank Lending*, 53 (November 1970), 51–58.

CHATTEL MORTGAGE

With a chattel mortgage, inventories are identified specifically either by serial number or by some other means. While the borrower holds title to the goods, the lender has a lien on inventory. This inventory cannot be sold unless the lender gives his consent. Because of the rigorous identification requirements, chattel mortgages are ill suited for inventory with rapid turnover and/or inventory that is not easily identified because of size or other reasons. They are well suited, however, for certain capital assets such as machine tools.

TRUST RECEIPT LOANS

Under a trust receipt financing arrangement, the borrower holds the inventory and proceeds from the sale of inventory in trust for the lender. This type of lending arrangement, known also as floor planning, has been used extensively by automobile dealers, equipment dealers, and consumer durable goods dealers. To illustrate trust receipt financing, suppose an automobile manufacturer ships cars to a dealer who, in turn, finances the payment for these cars through a finance company. The finance company pays the manufacturer for the cars shipped. The dealer signs a trust receipt security agreement, which specifies what can be done with the inventory. A copy of the security device used under a trust receipt arrangement is shown in Figure 18-2. The car dealer is allowed to sell the cars but must turn the proceeds of the sale over to the lender in payment of the loan. Inventory in trust, unlike inventory under a floating lien, is specifically identified by serial number or by other means. In our example, the finance company periodically audits the cars the dealer has on hand. The serial numbers of these cars are checked against those shown in the security agreement. The purpose of the audit is to see if the dealer has sold cars without remitting the proceeds of the sale to the finance company.

As the dealer buys new cars from the automobile manufacturer, a new trust receipt security agreement is signed that takes account of the new inventory. The dealer then borrows against this new collateral, which he holds in trust. Although there is tighter control over collateral with a trust receipt agreement than with a floating lien, there is still the risk of inventory being sold without the proceeds being turned over to the lender. Consequently, the lender must exercise judgment in deciding to lend under this arrangement. A dishonest dealer can devise numerous ways to fool the lender.

Many durable goods manufacturers finance the inventories of their distributors or dealers. Their purpose is to encourage dealers or distributors to carry reasonable stocks of goods. It is reasoned that the greater the stock, the more likely the dealer or distributor is to make a sale.

SECURITY AGREEMENT: FLOORING

DEALER'S
REFERENCE {   }

Pursuant to the California Uniform Commercial Code, the undersigned Borrower hereby grants to
_____
(Bank)

a security interest in the following described inventory, together with all replacements and substitutions thereof, all additions and accessions thereof, and all proceeds thereof.

YEAR	MAKE	ARTICLE	MODEL OR MOTOR NO.	SERIAL NO.	INVOICE NO.	COST	RELEASE PRICE	DATE RELEASED
								1.
								2.
								3.
								4.
								5.
								6.
								7.
								8.

1. BORROWER'S OBLIGATIONS: The security interest created hereby is given as security for the payment of $_____,
together with interest thereon payable _____ from date hereof at the rate of _____ percent per annum, provided that said rate of interest may be changed upon not less than _____ days notice to Borrower. Borrower hereby agrees to pay said
sum to Secured Party at its office as follows:
   _____ % of the cost of each unit of collateral on or before _____ , 19 _____ ;
   _____ % of the cost of each unit of collateral on or before _____ , 19 _____ ;
   and the balance of principal and interest on or before _____ , 19 _____ ,
unless the maturity is extended by Secured Party. This Agreement also secures all other Indebtedness of Borrower to Bank, including all
debts, obligations, or liabilities now or hereafter existing, absolute or contingent, and future advances.
2. LOCATION OF COLLATERAL: _____
3. USE OF COLLATERAL: The inventory Collateral of this agreement is to be held for ☐ Sale   ☐ Lease
4. INCORPORATION OF PROVISIONS ON REVERSE: All provisions on the reverse side are incorporated herein as if set forth fully at this
point.

Dated _____ , 19 _____

IF
CORPORATION
AFFIX
SEAL

By _____
SIGNATURE OF BORROWER(S) - TITLE

_____
BORROWER(S) - PRINT

_____
CHIEF PLACE OF BUSINESS OR RESIDENCE (INDIVIDUALS)

CBA-SA-3 (4-66)

ORIGINAL — TO BANK

FIG. 18·2   *A trust receipt security agreement*

Because the manufacturer is interested in selling his product, financing terms often are more attractive than they are with an "outside" lender.

TERMINAL WAREHOUSE RECEIPT LOANS

A borrower secures a terminal warehouse receipt loan by storing inventory with a public, or terminal, warehousing company.[5] The ware-

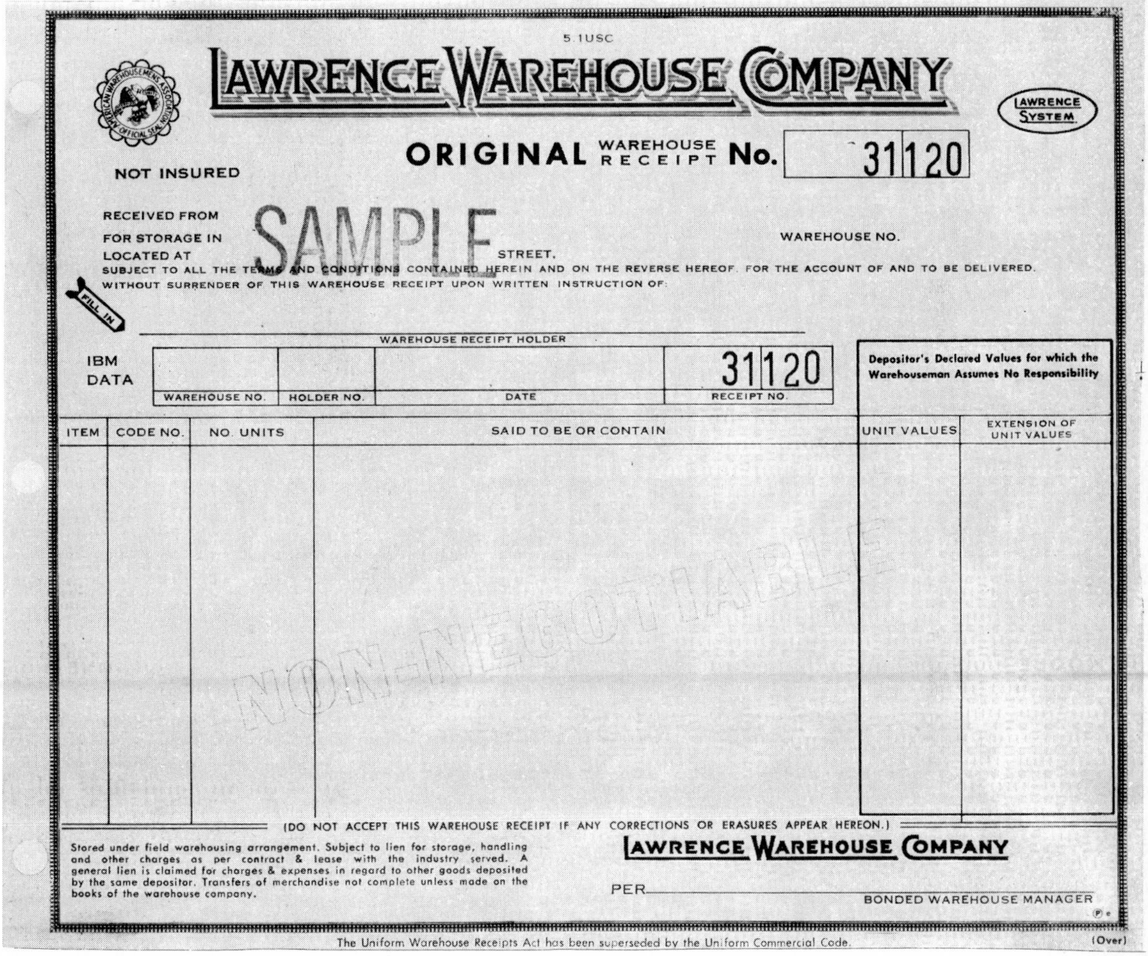

5 1USC

LAWRENCE WAREHOUSE COMPANY

LAWRENCE SYSTEM

NOT INSURED

ORIGINAL WAREHOUSE RECEIPT No. 31120

RECEIVED FROM

FOR STORAGE IN

LOCATED AT STREET, WAREHOUSE NO.

SAMPLE

SUBJECT TO ALL THE TERMS AND CONDITIONS CONTAINED HEREIN AND ON THE REVERSE HEREOF. FOR THE ACCOUNT OF AND TO BE DELIVERED, WITHOUT SURRENDER OF THIS WAREHOUSE RECEIPT UPON WRITTEN INSTRUCTION OF:

FILL IN

WAREHOUSE RECEIPT HOLDER

IBM DATA

WAREHOUSE NO.	HOLDER NO.	DATE	RECEIPT NO.
			31120

Depositor's Declared Values for which the Warehouseman Assumes No Responsibility

ITEM	CODE NO.	NO. UNITS	SAID TO BE OR CONTAIN	UNIT VALUES	EXTENSION OF UNIT VALUES

NON-NEGOTIABLE

(DO NOT ACCEPT THIS WAREHOUSE RECEIPT IF ANY CORRECTIONS OR ERASURES APPEAR HEREON.)

Stored under field warehousing arrangement. Subject to lien for storage, handling and other charges as per contract & lease with the industry served. A general lien is claimed for charges & expenses in regard to other goods deposited by the same depositor. Transfers of merchandise not complete unless made on the books of the warehouse company.

LAWRENCE WAREHOUSE COMPANY

PER

BONDED WAREHOUSE MANAGER

The Uniform Warehouse Receipts Act has been superseded by the Uniform Commercial Code. (Over)

FIG. 18·3 ***Warehouse receipt***

house company issues a warehouse receipt, which evidences title to specified goods that are located in the warehouse. An example of a warehouse receipt is shown in Figure 18-3. The warehouse receipt gives

[5] For an excellent discussion of warehouse receipts, see Robert W. Rogers, "Warehouse Receipts and Their Use in Financing," *Bulletin of the Robert Morris Associates,* 46 (April 1964), 317–27.

the lender a security interest in the goods, against which he makes a loan to the borrower. Under such an arrangement, the warehouseman can release the collateral to the borrower only when authorized to do so by the lender. Consequently, the lender is able to maintain strict control over the collateral and will release collateral only when the borrower pays a portion of the loan. For his own protection, the lender usually requires the borrower to take out an insurance policy with a loss-payable clause in favor of the lender.

Warehouse receipts may be either nonnegotiable or negotiable. A nonnegotiable warehouse receipt is issued in favor of a specific party—in this case, the lender—who is given title to the goods and has sole authority to release them. A negotiable warehouse receipt can be transferred by endorsement. Before goods can be released, however, the negotiable receipt must be presented to the warehouseman. A negotiable receipt is useful when title to the goods is transferred from one party to another while the goods are in storage. With a nonnegotiable receipt, the release of goods can be authorized only in writing. Most lending arrangements are based upon nonnegotiable receipts.

FIELD WAREHOUSE RECEIPT LOANS

In a terminal warehouse receipt loan, the goods are located in a public warehouse. Another arrangement, known as field warehousing, permits loans to be made against inventory that is located on the borrower's premises. Under this arrangement, a field warehousing company sets off a designated storage area on the borrower's premises for the inventory pledged as collateral. The field warehousing company has sole access to this area and is supposed to maintain strict control over it. (The goods that serve as collateral are segregated from the borrower's other inventory.) The field warehousing company issues a warehouse receipt as described in the preceding section, and the lender extends a loan based upon the collateral value of the inventory. The field warehouse arrangement is a useful means of financing when it is not desirable, either because of the expense or because of the inconvenience, to place the inventory in a public warehouse. Field warehouse receipt lending is particularly appropriate when a borrower must make frequent use of inventory. Because of the need to pay the field warehousing company's expenses, the cost of this method of financing can be relatively high.

It is important to recognize that the warehouse receipt, as evidence of collateral, is only as good as the issuing warehousing company. When administered properly, a warehouse receipt loan affords the lender a high degree of control over the collateral. However, there have been sufficient examples of fraud to show that the warehouse receipt does not always evidence actual value. The warehouseman must exercise strict control. A grain elevator that is alleged to be full may, in fact, be empty. Upon close examination, we may find that barrels reported to contain chemical concentrate actually contain water.

As stated at the beginning of this chapter, intermediate-term financing is used to finance more permanent funds requirements than those associated with short-term loans. The means for payment of the loan usually come from the generation of cash flows over a period of years. As a result, most of these loans are paid in regular, periodic installments. We regard intermediate-term financing as involving final maturities of one to five years. These boundaries are arbitrary, although the one-year boundary is rather commonly accepted. The firm, of course, should choose those financial instruments that best serve its needs from the entire spectrum of maturities available. In this section, we examine various forms of intermediate-term debt. We begin by considering bank term loans, perhaps the most important source of intermediate-term financing for the firm.

INTERMEDIATE-TERM DEBT

ORDINARY TERM LOANS

An ordinary term loan is a business loan with an original, or final, maturity of more than one year, repayable according to a specified schedule. For the most part, these loans are repayable in periodic installments; for example, quarterly, semiannually, or yearly. The payment schedule of the loan usually is geared to the borrower's cash-flow ability to service the debt. Typically, this schedule calls for equal periodic installments, but it may be irregular with respect to amounts or may simply call for repayment in a lump sum at final maturity. Sometimes the loan is amortized in equal periodic installments except for the final payment, known as a "balloon" payment, which is larger than any of the others.

Maturity   Most bank term loans are written with original maturities in the one- to six-year range. Some banks are willing to make longer-term loans, but only rarely will a bank make a term loan with a final maturity of more than ten years. In recent years, however, banks have been making longer-term loans. Whereas a four- to six-year loan once was considered dangerous to a bank's liquidity, term loans in this maturity range now are common.

Interest costs   Generally, the interest rate on a term loan is higher than the rate on a short-term loan to the same borrower. For example, if a firm could borrow at the prime rate on a short-term basis, it might pay 0.25 percent to 0.50 percent more on a term loan. The interest rate on a term loan can be set in one of two ways: (1) a fixed rate that is effective over the life of the loan may be established at the outset, or (2) a variable rate may be set that is adjusted in keeping with changes in the prime rate. In addition to interest costs, the borrower is required to pay the legal expenses that the bank incurs in drawing up the loan agreement. Also, a commitment fee may be charged for the time during the commitment period when the loan is not taken down. For an ordinary term loan, these additional costs usually are rather small in relation to the amount of the loan. An indirect cost to the borrower is the need to maintain compensating balances, which we discussed in Chapter 17.

Advantages

The principal advantage of an ordinary bank term loan is flexibility. The borrower deals directly with the lender, and the loan can be tailored to the borrower's needs through direct negotiation. The bank usually has had previous experience with the borrower, so it is familiar with the company's situation. Should the firm's requirements change, the terms and conditions of the loan may be revised. It is considerably more convenient to negotiate with a single lender or a reasonably small group of lenders than with a large number of public security holders, as there are with a bond issue. In addition, the borrower can deal confidentially with a bank, or, for that matter, with any private lending institution, and does not have to reveal certain financial information to the public.

In many instances, bank term loans are made to small businesses that do not have access to the capital markets and cannot readily float a public issue. Large companies also may find it quicker and more convenient to seek a bank term loan than to float a public issue. A term loan can be arranged in several weeks, whereas a public issue takes a good deal longer.

Limitations

One of the limitations on the use of a bank term loan is the maturity. Banks seldom will make a term loan for more than ten years and often will want a shorter maturity. Another limitation is the restrictive provisions imposed in the loan agreement, which we will discuss in detail in this chapter. Although the borrower is restricted by these provisions, he probably would encounter them with an insurance company term-loan agreement or a bond indenture. A possible disadvantage of a bank term loan is the legal restriction on the maximum amount a bank can lend to a single borrower. However, many term loans are extended by a group of banks rather than a single bank. Except for the very largest of loans, the legal lending limit on banks is not a barrier.

When making term loans in the face of inflation, some banks ask for equity kickers in order to get a "piece of the action." These kickers usually take the form of stock purchase warrants, which enable the bank to purchase a number of shares of stock at a specified price. A percentage of net profit is another form of kicker, as is a percentage of the gross sales of a retail organization. These kickers, of course, work to the disadvantage of the borrower; they raise the effective cost of borrowing. If the firm is doing well, the effective cost can be very high indeed. A firm regarded as risky, however, may have little choice other than to provide a kicker. This may spell the difference between obtaining a loan or being refused term credit. Moreover, the kicker usually operates in only one direction. If the firm is doing poorly, the kicker it provides has negligible value and, accordingly, costs the firm very little. If the firm is doing well, the kicker will have value. However, the firm will also be in a better position to incur the added cost.

REVOLVING CREDITS

As we said in Chapter 17, a revolving credit is a formal commitment by a bank to lend up to a certain amount of money to a company over a specified period of time. The actual notes evidencing debt are short-term, usually ninety days; but the company may renew them or borrow additionally, up to the specified maximum, throughout the duration of the commitment. Many revolving-credit commitments are for three years, although it is possible for a firm to obtain a shorter commitment. As with an ordinary term loan, the interest rate is usually 0.25 to 0.50 percent higher than the rate at which the firm could borrow on a short-term basis under a line of credit. When a bank makes a revolving-credit commitment, it is legally bound under the loan agreement to have funds available whenever the company wants to borrow. The borrower usually must pay for this availability in the form of a commitment fee, perhaps 0.50 percent per annum, on the difference between the amount borrowed and the specified maximum.[6]

Because most revolving-credit agreements are for more than one year, they are regarded as intermediate-term financing. This borrowing arrangement is particularly useful at times when the firm is uncertain about its funds requirements. A revolving-credit agreement has the features of both a short-term borrowing arrangement and a term loan, for the firm can borrow a fixed amount for the entire duration of the commitment. Thus, the borrower has flexible access to funds over a period of uncertainty and can make more definite credit arrangements

---

[6] For an analysis of the optimal amount of revolving credit to establish, see Paul D. Berger and William K. Harper, "Determination of an Optimal Revolving Credit Agreement," *Journal of Financial and Quantitative Analysis*, 8 (June 1973), 491–97. In the article, the authors examine the tradeoff between the commitment fee cost, which is a linear function of the amount of the revolving credit, and the risk of borrowing needs exceeding the amount of revolving credit established.

when the uncertainty is resolved. Revolving-credit agreements can be set up so that at the maturity of the commitment, borrowings then owing can be converted into a term loan at the option of the borrower. To illustrate, suppose a company introduces a new product and is faced with a period of uncertainty over the next several years. To provide maximum financial flexibility, the company might arrange a three-year revolving credit that is convertible into a five-year term loan at the expiration of the revolving-credit commitment. At the end of three years, the company, hopefully, would know its funds requirements better. If these requirements are permanent, or nearly so, the firm might wish to exercise its option and take down the term loan.

LOAN AGREEMENTS

When a bank makes a term loan or revolving-credit commitment, it provides the borrower with available funds for an extended period of time. Much can happen to the financial condition of the borrower during that period. In order to safeguard itself, the lender requires the borrower to maintain its financial condition and, in particular, its current position at a level at least as favorable as when the commitment was made. The provisions for protection contained in a loan agreement are known as protective convenants. In this section, we examine these provisions from the standpoint of the lender. However, later in the section and in the appendix to this chapter, we examine how a firm can negotiate to lessen the restrictiveness of the provisions.

The loan agreement itself simply gives the bank legal authority to step in should the borrower default under any of the provisions. Otherwise, the bank would be locked into a commitment and would have to wait until maturity before being able to effect corrective measures. If the borrower should suffer losses or other adverse developments, he will default under a well-written loan agreement; the bank then will be able to act. The action usually takes the form of working with the company to straighten out its problems. Seldom will a bank demand immediate payment, although it has the legal right to do so in cases of default.

Formulation of provisions The formulation of the different restrictive provisions should be tailored to the specific loan situation. These provisions are the tools by which the banker fashions the overall protection of his loan. No one provision is able by itself to provide the necessary safeguards, but together with the other provisions, it is designed to assure overall liquidity and ability to pay a loan. The important protective convenants of a loan agreement may be classified as follows: (1) general provisions used in most loan agreements, which are variable to fit the situation; (2) routine provisions used in most agreements, which usually are not variable; and (3) specific provisions that are used according to the situation. Although we focus on a bank loan agreement, the protective covenants used and the philosophy underlying their use are the same for an insurance company loan agreement or the indenture for a bond issue.

**General
provisions**

The *working capital requirement* probably is the most commonly used and most comprehensive provision in a loan agreement. Its purpose is to preserve the company's current position and ability to pay the loan. Frequently, a straight dollar amount, such as $2 million, is set as the minimum working capital the company must maintain during the duration of the commitment. When the bank feels that it is desirable for a specific company to build working capital, it may increase the minimum working capital requirement throughout the duration of the loan. The establishment of a working capital minimum normally is based upon the amounts of present working capital and projected working capital, allowing for seasonal fluctuations. The requirement should not restrict the company unduly in the ordinary generation of profit. However, should the borrower incur sharp losses or spend too much for fixed assets, purchase of stock, dividends, redemption of long-term debt, and so forth, it would probably breach the working capital requirement.

The *cash dividend and repurchase-of-stock restriction* is another important restriction in this category. Its purpose is to limit cash going outside the business, thus preserving the liquidity of the company. Most often, cash dividends and repurchase of stock are limited to a percentage of net profits on a cumulative basis after a certain base date, frequently the last fiscal year-end prior to the date of the term-loan agreement. A less flexible method is to restrict dividends and repurchase of stock to an absolute dollar amount each year. In most cases, the prospective borrower must be willing to undergo a cash dividend and repurchase-of-stock restriction. If tied to earnings, this restriction still will allow adequate dividends as long as the company is able to generate satisfactory profits.

The *capital-expenditures limitation* is third in the category of general provisions. Capital expenditures may be limited to a fixed dollar amount each year. However, it probably is more common to limit annual capital expenditures either to depreciation or to a percentage thereof. The capital-expenditures limitation is another tool used by the banker to assure the maintenance of the borrower's current position. By limiting capital expenditures directly, the bank can be more sure that it will not have to look to liquidation of fixed assets for payment of its loan. Again, however, the provision should not be so restrictive as to prevent the adequate maintenance and improvement of facilities.

A *limitation on other indebtedness* is the last general provision. This limitation may take a number of forms, depending upon the circumstances. Frequently, a loan agreement will prohibit a company from incurring any other long-term debt. This provision protects the bank, inasmuch as it prevents future lenders from obtaining a prior claim on the borrower's assets. Usually a company is permitted to borrow within reasonable limits for seasonal and other short-term purposes arising in the ordinary course of business.

Routine provisions

The second category of restrictions includes routine, usually invariable, provisions found in most loan agreements. Ordinarily, the loan agreement requires the borrower to furnish the bank with financial statements and to maintain adequate insurance. Additionally, the borrower normally is required not to sell a substantial portion of its assets and is required to pay, when due, all taxes and other liabilities, except those contested in good faith. A provision forbidding the pledging or mortgaging of any of the borrower's assets is almost always included in a loan agreement; this important provision is known as a negative pledge clause.

Ordinarily, the company is required not to discount or sell its receivables. Moreover, the borrower generally is prohibited from entering into any leasing arrangement of property, except up to a certain dollar amount of annual rental. The purpose of this provision is to prevent the borrower from taking on a substantial lease liability, which might endanger its ability to pay the loan. A lease restriction also prevents the firm from leasing property instead of purchasing it and thereby getting around the limitations on capital expenditures and debt. Usually, too, there is a restriction on other contingent liabilities. The provisions in this category appear as a matter of routine in most bank loan agreements. Although somewhat mechanical, they are important because they close many loopholes and provide a tight, comprehensive loan agreement.

Special provisions

Special provisions are used in specific loan agreements by the banker in order to achieve a desired total protection of his loan. For instance, a loan agreement may contain a definite understanding regarding the use of the loan proceeds, so that there will be no diversion of funds to purposes other than those contemplated when the loan was negotiated. A provision for limiting loans and advances often is found in a bank term-loan agreement. Closely allied to this restriction is a limitation on investments, which is used to safeguard liquidity by preventing certain nonliquid investments.

If one or more executives are essential to a firm's effective operation, a bank may insist that the company carry life insurance on their lives. Proceeds of the insurance may be payable to the company or directly to the bank, to be applied to the loan. An agreement may also contain a management clause under which certain key individuals must remain actively employed in the company during the time the loan is owing. Aggregate executive salaries and bonuses sometimes are limited in the loan agreement to prevent excessive compensation of executives, which might reduce profits. This provision closes another loophole; it prevents large stockholders who are officers of the company from increasing their own salaries in lieu of paying higher dividends, which are limited under the agreement.

Negotiation of restrictions The provisions described above represent the most frequently used protective convenants in a loan agreement. From the standpoint of the lender, the aggregate impact of these provisions should be to safeguard the financial position of the borrower and its ability to pay the loan. Under a well-written agreement, the borrower cannot get into serious financial difficulty without defaulting under the agreement, thereby giving the bank legal authority to take action. Although the lender is instrumental in establishing the restrictions, the restrictiveness of the protective covenants is subject to negotiation between the borrower and the lender. The final result will depend upon the relative bargaining power of each of the parties involved. In the appendix to this chapter, a linear-programming approach for evaluating the opportunity costs of the protective covenant restrictions is presented. If it knows these opportunity costs, management is able to bargain more effectively over the restrictiveness of the covenants.

INSURANCE COMPANY TERM LOANS

Insurance companies and certain other institutional lenders, as well as banks, extend term loans to companies. The former establish protective covenants much as a bank does. However, there are important differences in the maturity of the loan extended and in the interest rate charged. In general, life insurance companies are interested in term loans with final maturities in excess of ten years. Because these companies do not have the benefit of compensating balances or other business from the borrower, and because their loans usually have a longer maturity than bank term loans, typically the rate of interest is higher. To the insurance company, the term loan represents an investment and must yield a return commensurate with the costs involved in making the loan, the risk, the maturity, and prevailing yields on alternative investments. Because an insurance company is interested in keeping its funds employed without interruption, it normally has a prepayment penalty, whereas ordinarily the bank does not. One of the simpler prepayment formulas calls for a premium of 0.25 percent for each year remaining to maturity.

Insurance company term loans generally are not competitive with bank term loans. Indeed, they are complementary, for they serve different maturity ranges. Sometimes a bank and an insurance company will participate in the same loan. The bank may take the early maturities, perhaps the first five years, with the insurance company taking the remaining maturities. Including an insurance company in the credit permits a longer maturity range than the bank can provide, and the bank can offer a lower interest rate on the early maturities. Usually, there will be only one loan agreement, drawn up jointly by the bank and the insurance company. A term loan of this sort may serve both the intermediate- and long-term funds requirements of the firm.

EQUIPMENT FINANCING

Equipment represents another asset of the firm that may be pledged to secure a loan. If the firm either has equipment that is marketable or is purchasing such equipment, it usually is able to obtain some sort of secured financing. Because such loans usually are for more than a year, we consider them in this chapter rather than under short-term secured loans. As with other secured loans, the lender is concerned with the marketability of the collateral. Depending upon the quality of the equipment, he will make a percentage advance against the equipment's market value. Frequently, the repayment schedule for the loan is set in keeping with the depreciation schedule of the equipment. For example, a trucking company will usually depreciate its tractors over four years and its trailers over six years. A lender might set a four-year installment payment schedule for a loan secured by tractors and a six-year schedule for a loan secured by trailers. In setting the repayment schedule, the lender wants to be sure that the market value of the tractor or trailer always exceeds the balance of the loan.

The excess of the expected market value of the equipment over the amount of the loan represents the margin of safety, which will vary according to the specific situation. In the case of the rolling stock of a trucking company, the collateral is movable and reasonably marketable. As a result, the advance may be as high as 80 percent. Less marketable equipment, such as that with a limited use, will not command as high an advance. A certain type of lathe, for example, may have a thin market, and a lender might not be willing to advance more than 50 percent of its reported market value. Some equipment is of such a special-purpose nature that it has no value for collateral purposes. Frequently, the lender either will have its own appraiser or will hire an appraiser to estimate the approximate value of a piece of equipment if it should have to be sold. As with other collateral, the lender is interested not only in the estimated market price of the equipment but also in the cost of selling it.

Sources of equipment financing

Sources of equipment financing include commercial banks, finance companies, and the sellers of equipment. Because the interest charged by a finance company on an equipment loan usually is higher than that charged by a commercial bank, a firm will turn to a finance company only if it is unable to obtain the loan from a bank. The seller of the equipment may finance the purchase either by holding the secured note itself or by selling the note to its captive finance subsidiary. The interest charge will depend upon the extent to which the seller uses financing as a sales tool. If he uses it extensively, he may charge only a moderate interest rate and may make up for part of the cost of carrying the notes by charging higher prices for the equipment. The borrower must consider this possibility in judging the true cost of financing. Equipment loans may be secured either by a chattel mortgage or by a conditional sales contract arrangement.

Chattel mortgage

A chattel mortgage is a lien on property other than real estate. The borrower signs a security agreement, which gives the lender a lien on the equipment specified in the agreement. In order to perfect the lien, the lender files a copy of the security agreement or a financing statement with a public office of the state in which the equipment is located. Given a valid lien, the lender can sell the equipment if the borrower defaults in the payment of principal or interest on the loan.

Conditional sales contract

With a conditional sales contract arrangement, the seller of the equipment retains title to it until the purchaser has satisfied all the terms of the contract. The buyer signs a conditional sales contract security agreement under which he agrees to make periodic installment payments to the seller over a specified period of time. These payments usually are monthly or quarterly. Until the terms of the contract are satisfied completely, the seller retains title to the equipment. Thus, the seller receives a down payment and a promissory note for the balance of the purchase price upon the sale of the equipment. The note is secured by the contract, which gives the seller the authority to repossess the equipment if the buyer does not meet all the terms of the contract.

The seller may either hold the contract himself or sell it, simply by endorsing it, to a commercial bank or finance company. The bank or finance company then becomes the lender and assumes the security interest in the equipment. If the buyer should default under the terms of the contract, the bank or finance company could repossess the equipment and sell it in satisfaction of its loan. Often, the vendor will sell the contract to a bank or finance company with recourse. Under this arrangement, the lender has the additional protection of recourse to the seller in case the buyer defaults.

SUMMARY

Many firms are unable to obtain unsecured credit and are required by the lender to pledge security. In giving a secured loan, the lender looks first to the cash-flow ability of the company to service debt and, if this source of loan repayment should fail, to the collateral value of the security. To provide a margin of safety, a lender usually will advance somewhat less than the market value of the collateral. The percentage advance varies according to the quality of the collateral pledged and the control the lender has over this collateral. Accounts receivable and inventory are the principal assets used to secure short-term business loans. Receivables may either be pledged to secure a loan or sold to a factor. Inventory loans can be under a general lien, under a trust receipt, or under terminal warehouse or field warehouse receipt arrangements.

Intermediate-term financing generally is thought to include maturities of one to five years. There are a number of sources of intermediate-term financing. Commercial banks, insurance companies, and other institutional investors make term loans to business firms. Banks also provide financing under a revolving-credit arrangement, which represents a formal commitment on the part of the bank to lend up to a certain amount of money over a specified period of time.

Lenders who offer unsecured credit usually impose restrictions on the borrower. These restrictions are called protective covenants and are contained in a loan agreement. If the borrower defaults under any of the provisions of the loan agreement, the lender may initiate immediate corrective measures. On a secured basis, firms can obtain intermediate-term financing by pledging equipment that they own or are purchasing. Banks, finance companies, and sellers of the equipment are active in providing this type of secured financing.

Typically, intermediate-term financing is self-liquidating. For this reason, it resembles short-term financing. However, intermediate-term financing also can satisfy more permanent funds requirements and, in addition, can serve as an interim substitute for long-term financing. If a firm wishes to float long-term debt or issue common stock but conditions are unfavorable in the market, the firm may seek intermediate-term debt to bridge the gap until long-term financing can be undertaken on favorable terms. Thus, intermediate-term debt may give a firm flexibility in the timing of long-term financing. It also can provide flexibility when the firm is uncertain as to the size and nature of its future funds requirements. As uncertainty is resolved, intermediate-term financing can be replaced by a more appropriate means of financing. (A bank revolving credit is well suited for providing this type of flexibility.) The most important use of intermediate-term financing, however, is to provide credit when the expected cash flows of the firm are such that the debt can be retired steadily over a period of several years and the size of the need precludes long-term financing. Even though it sometimes is linked to a particular asset, such as a piece of equipment, intermediate-term financing must be considered in relation to the firm's total funds requirements.

A METHOD FOR EVALUATING RESTRICTIONS UNDER A LOAN AGREEMENT[7]

When a company enters into a bond indenture or loan agreement, certain restrictions usually are placed on it. These restrictions, known as protective covenants, may have a significant influence on the firm's profits, making the bargaining strategy of the company very important. But to bargain effectively over the restrictiveness of the protective covenants, management must know the impact that the covenants have on profits. In this appendix, a method is proposed for determining the opportunity costs of the restrictions imposed under the indenture or agreement. These opportunity costs represent the additional profit a company could make if a restriction were relaxed. The framework for analysis is a linear-programming model for capital-budgeting and financing decisions, using a hypothetical company as an example. Sensitivity analysis is employed to determine the opportunity costs of the restrictions and to give management the information it needs to formulate its bargaining strategy.

STATEMENT OF THE PROBLEM

We assume that the company's objective is to maximize net-present value arising from various investment proposals. There are, of course, many difficulties in forecasting the cash flows expected from an investment proposal as well as in determining the required rate of return to be used as the discount factor. However, we shall assume that cash flows are known with certainty and the company can measure its required rate of return accurately.

Table 18A·1 Investment proposals available

Proposal	Proportion of Working Capital to Fixed Assets	Maximum Amount of Investment	Profitability Index
1	1:4	$350,000	0.18
2	2:1	225,000	0.06
3	1:1	170,000	0.13
4	3:1	200,000	0.09
5	1:2	150,000	0.15
6	4:1	250,000	0.07
7	1:3	300,000	0.08

[7]Adapted from James Van Horne, "A Linear-Programming Approach to Evaluating Restrictions under a Bond Indenture or Loan Agreement," *Journal of Financial and Quantitative Analysis*, 1 (June 1966), 68–83.

Assuming that all outlays are made at the time of the investment decision, net-present value per dollar of investment in a proposal can be determined by the profitability index. For our purposes, the profitability index is interpreted as the net-present value of all outlays and inflows, divided by the amount of initial cash outlay. Table 18A-1 shows seven investment proposals available to our hypothetical company, all having positive profitability indexes, and involving varying proportions of working capital and fixed assets. We assume that the company may invest in each proposal at any level between zero and the stated maximum.[8]

We assume also that the size of the capital budget is limited to $800,000, financed by $400,000 in retained earnings represented by excess cash and $400,000 in debt. The debt portion may be divided between short-term and long-term borrowings. In addition, when the firm finances investment proposals with equal amounts of retained earnings and borrowings, the relative proportions of borrowings and equity remain unchanged. Thus, we assume that the financing of investment proposals leaves the cost of capital used as a discount factor virtually unchanged.[9] The problem, as stated so far, involves weighing the alternative investment proposals in Table 18A-1 so as to maximize the value of the firm. If there were no protective-covenant constraints imposed on the company, we would expect it to invest, in descending order of profitability, $350,000 in investment proposal 1, $150,000 in proposal 5, $170,000 in proposal 3, and $130,000 in proposal 4. Investment in these proposals, totaling $800,000, would result in the maximum possible increase in net-present value—that is, $119,300.

We now consider the constraints imposed by the terms of the bond indenture or loan agreement; these are the constraints that we shall evaluate later. The problem will involve a single-stage decision at a point in time to invest and to borrow, subject to liquidity and other financial constraints. To simplify the problem, we assume that the impact of the restrictions occurs at the time of the decision.

---

[8] In the model, we have assumed the divisibility of investment proposals. If a proposal is nonfractional, investment must be either zero or some absolute amount; and a dichotomy exists. Problems of this sort having "either-or" conditions may be solved by integer programming. See George B. Dantzig, "On the Significance of Solving Linear Programming Problems with Some Integer Variables," *Econometrica*, 28 (January 1960), 30–44; and Ralph E. Gomory, "Outline of an Algorithm for Integer Solutions to Linear Programs," *Bulletin of the American Mathematical Society*, 64 (September 1958), 275–78.

Although the direct problem is straightforward when integer-valued variables are involved, there may be complications in interpreting values for the dual variables. For exposition of the dual-variable problem in integer programming, see Ralph E. Gomory and William J. Baumol, "Integer Programming and Pricing," *Econometrica*, 28 (July 1960), 521–50; and H. Martin Weingartner, *Mathematical Programming and the Analysis of Capital Budgeting Problems*, copyright H. Martin Weingartner, Chapter 5.

[9] We are assuming that the acceptance of an investment proposal or group of proposals does not alter the business-risk complexion of the firm, as perceived by suppliers of capital.

The first protective covenant we consider is *a minimum working capital constraint.* If minimum working capital is $2,250,000 and existing working capital $2,500,000, investment in fixed assets (a use of working capital) could exceed long-term borrowings (a source of working capital) by only $250,000. A *capital-expenditures constraint,* the second covenant, involves a limitation on the amount of funds that may be invested in fixed assets. We assume in this example that capital expenditures are limited to $500,000.

Protective covenants dealing with long-term debt may take a number of forms. We shall use only one—*a percentage limitation of long-term debt to working capital*—but additional constraints may be fashioned to fit the situation. We assume this percentage to be 80 percent.

The last protective-covenant constraint we consider is a *cash dividend restriction.* This restriction is most often expressed as a limitation on the proportion of dividends to annual earnings on a cumulative basis. In our example, the percentage limitation is assumed to be 50 percent, and it becomes effective at the time of the investment decision, there being no accumulated earnings available for dividend payments. Therefore, dividends must not exceed 50 percent of book earnings on existing projects plus book earnings generated from investment in the projects under consideration.

These protective covenants are by no means the only possible restrictions that may be imposed in a bond indenture or loan agreement. However, the covenants considered do represent some of the more widely used restrictions. In molding the above restrictions into linear-programming constraints, we use the limits imposed in the indenture or agreement. Where a constraint is binding in the final program, the company would be at the verge of violation under the specific covenant involved. It might be appropriate, therefore, to allow for a margin of safety. If, for example, the minimum working capital requirement in the indenture or loan agreement is $1,250,000, we might want to use $1,350,000 in formulating the linear-programming constraint. Other restrictions likewise can be reformulated to permit a margin of safety.

FORMULATION OF PROBLEM

Given the information in Table 18A-1, the objective function for our hypothetical company would be

$$
\begin{aligned}
\text{Max. } Z = {} & .18X_{11} + .06X_{21} + .13X_{31} + .09X_{41} + .15X_{51} + .07X_{61} \\
& + .08X_{71} + .18X_{12} + .06X_{22} + .13X_{32} + .09X_{42} \\
& + .15X_{52} + .07X_{62} + .08X_{72} \quad\quad\quad\quad \text{(18A-1a)}
\end{aligned}
$$

where X_{11} through X_{71} represent investment in working capital for the seven proposals and X_{12} through X_{72} represent investment in fixed assets. Structural constraints are introduced by virtue of the ceilings on investment, the relative proportions of working capital and fixed assets, and the need to finance the proposals with retained earnings and debt. For constraints relating to ceilings on investment, we have

$$X_{11} + X_{12} \leqq 350,000 \qquad \text{(18A-1b)}$$
$$X_{21} + X_{22} \leqq 225,000 \qquad \text{(18A-1c)}$$
$$X_{31} + X_{32} \leqq 170,000 \qquad \text{(18A-1d)}$$
$$X_{41} + X_{42} \leqq 200,000 \qquad \text{(18A-1e)}$$
$$X_{51} + X_{52} \leqq 150,000 \qquad \text{(18A-1f)}$$
$$X_{61} + X_{62} \leqq 250,000 \qquad \text{(18A-1g)}$$
$$X_{71} + X_{72} \leqq 300,000 \qquad \text{(18A-1h)}$$

The structural constraints relating to proportions of working capital and fixed assets are

$$4X_{11} - X_{12} = 0 \qquad \text{(18A-1i)}$$
$$X_{21} - 2X_{22} = 0 \qquad \text{(18A-1j)}$$
$$X_{31} - X_{32} = 0 \qquad \text{(18A-1k)}$$
$$X_{41} - 3X_{42} = 0 \qquad \text{(18A-1l)}$$
$$2X_{51} - X_{52} = 0 \qquad \text{(18A-1m)}$$
$$X_{61} - 4X_{62} = 0 \qquad \text{(18A-1n)}$$
$$3X_{71} - X_{72} = 0 \qquad \text{(18A-1o)}$$

The last set of structural constraints is

$$\sum_{i=1}^{7}\sum_{j=1}^{2} X_{ij} - \sum_{l=1}^{3} Y_l = 0 \qquad \text{(18A-1p)}$$

$$\sum_{l=1}^{3} Y_l \leqq 800,000 \qquad \text{(18A-1q)}$$

$$\sum_{l=1}^{2} Y_l - Y_3 = 0 \qquad \text{(18A-1r)}$$

where Y_1 is the amount of short-term borrowings, Y_2 the amount of long-term borrowings, and Y_3 the amount of retained earnings used to finance the investment proposals.

As taken up in the previous section, there are four protective-covenant constraints for our hypothetical example. The first, the *minimum*

$$\sum_{i=1}^{7} X_{i2} - Y_2 \leq 250,000 \qquad (18A\text{-}1s)$$

where \$250,000 represents existing working capital less minimum or required working capital. The *capital-expenditures constraint* may be expressed as

$$\sum_{i=1}^{7} X_{i2} \leq 500,000 \qquad (18A\text{-}1t)$$

If long-term debt cannot exceed 80 percent of working capital under the *long-term debt to working capital constraint,* we have

$$WC - \sum_{i=1}^{7} X_{i2} + Y_2 \geq 1\frac{1}{4} LTD + 1\frac{1}{4} Y_2$$

where *WC* is existing working capital, and *LTD* is existing long-term debt. If existing working capital is \$2,500,000, as before, and existing long-term debt is \$1,720,000, by transposing and multiplying through by −1, we obtain

$$\sum_{i=1}^{7} X_{i2} + \frac{1}{4} Y_2 \leq WC - 1\frac{1}{4} LTD \leq 350,000 \qquad (18A\text{-}1u)$$

With the *cash dividend restriction,* dividends are limited to 50 percent of book earnings on existing projects and proposals under consideration. The first-year profit (or loss) per dollar of investment for the seven investment proposals under consideration is shown as follows:

Proposal	1	2	3	4	5	6	7
First-year profit (loss) per dollar of investment	(0.08)	0.10	(0.04)	(0.03)	(0.09)	(0.02)	0.05

We assume that the company desires to pay, at the end of the first year, cash dividends totaling \$200,000 and that book first-year earnings on existing projects, exclusive of proposals under consideration, will be $425,000. We have as a constraint:

$$0.08X_{11} - 0.10X_{21} + 0.04X_{31} + 0.03X_{41} + 0.09X_{51} + 0.02X_{61}$$
$$- 0.05X_{71} + 0.08X_{12} - 0.10X_{22} + 0.04X_{32} + 0.03X_{42} + 0.09X_{52}$$
$$+ 0.02X_{62} - 0.05X_{72} \leqq Y - 2C \qquad \text{(18A-1v)}$$

where Y equals first-year earnings on existing projects, and C equals the cash dividend the company desires to pay. Thus, $Y - 2C = \$425,000 - 2(\$200,000) = \$25,000$. It would be possible to reformulate this constraint for additional years. For simplicity, we assume that book profits for all investment proposals under consideration are positive beyond the first year and that the lowest total combination of book profits in any one year is more than twice the cash dividend the company desires to pay. Consequently, the dividend restriction is of concern only in the first year.

The complete problem may be expressed as

$$\text{Max. } Z = \sum_{i=1}^{7} \sum_{j=1}^{2} C_i X_{ij} \qquad \text{(18A-2)}$$

subject to

$$\sum_{i=1}^{7} \sum_{j=1}^{2} A_{kij} X_{ij} + \sum_{l=1}^{3} A_{kl} Y_l \leqq b_k$$

and the nonnegative requirement:

$$X_{ij} \text{ and } Y_l \geqq 0 \text{ for all } ijl.$$

SOLUTION OF PROBLEM

A computer program was used to solve this problem, and optimal values of the direct-problem variables and the dual variables are shown in Table 18A-2.[10] The values for the direct-problem variables tell us that we should invest $169,500 in investment proposal 1, $54,750 in proposal 2, $170,000 in proposal 3, $200,000 in proposal 4, and $205,750 in proposal 6. Moreover, the company should borrow $320,000 on a short-term basis

---

[10] For each direct problem there is a dual problem that makes use of the same data as are employed in the direct problem. The dual theorem of linear programming states that the optimal solutions to the direct and the dual problems are the same. For explanation of the dual method, see A. Charnes and W. W. Cooper, *Management Models and Industrial Applications of Linear Programming*, Vol. I (New York: John Wiley, 1961), or other texts dealing with linear programming.

Table 18A·2 Optimal values for example problem

Direct				Dual			
$X_{11} =$	33,900	$X_{32} =$	85,000	$W_1 =$	0	$W_{12} = 0.04671$	
$X_{21} =$	36,500	$X_{42} =$	50,000	$W_2 =$	0	$W_{13} = 0.03150$	
$X_{31} =$	85,000	$X_{52} =$	0	$W_3 = 0.00758$		$W_{14} = 0.09792$	
$X_{41} =$	150,000	$X_{62} =$	41,150	$W_4 = 0.00954$		$W_{15} = 0.03333$	
$X_{51} =$	0	$X_{72} =$	0	$W_5 =$	0	$W_{16} = 0.03333$	
$X_{61} =$	164,600	$Y_1 =$	320,000	$W_6 =$	0	$W_{17} =$	0
$X_{71} =$	0	$Y_2 =$	80,000	$W_7 =$	0	$W_{18} = 0.03150$	
$X_{12} =$	135,600	$Y_3 =$	400,000	$W_8 = 0.03150$		$W_{19} =$	0
$X_{22} =$	18,250			$W_9 = 0.05250$		$W_{20} = 0.12600$	
				$W_{10} = 0.07875$		$W_{21} = 0.25833$	
				$W_{11} = 0.03937$			

and $80,000 on a long-term basis. Substituting into Eq. (18A-1a), the increase in net-present value resulting from this optimal solution is $88,297.50.

From Table 18A-2 it can be seen that the optimal investment policy under the protective-covenant constraints differs considerably from what would be optimal without the constraints. As mentioned previously, the optimal policy without constraints would call for investment of $350,000 in investment proposal 1, $170,000 in proposal 3, $130,000 in proposal 4, and $150,000 in proposal 5; and this policy would result in a $119,300 increase in net-present value. Thus, the restrictions have a marked effect on the optimal investment policy of the company. For example, under the protective-covenant restrictions, the company would invest $54,750 in the least profitable proposal, 2, and invest nothing in the second most profitable, 5. The $119,300 increase in net-present value represents the limit of increase in net-present value attainable with relaxation of the protective-covenant constraints. In the analysis that follows, it is useful to relate the increase in net-present value arising from relaxation of an individual restriction to this limit.

EVALUATING THE RESTRICTIONS

The dual-variable values in Table 18A-2 enable us to determine the opportunity costs of certain protective-covenant constraints imposed under the bond indenture or loan agreement. Knowledge of these costs is extremely important to management in formulating negotiation strategy. For example, what will be the effect if the minimum working capital requirement is relaxed? If this constraint is binding or critical in the final program, the dual variable for the restriction will be more than zero; if not, it will be zero. Thus, for the working capital constraint, $W_{18} = 0.0315$ signifies that if required working capital is decreased by $1, the company will be able to increase net-present value $0.0315 if the dollar is optimally employed.[11] We see in Table 18A-2 that the capital expenditures limitation is not binding in the final program, for $W_{19}^* = 0$. The constraint, as formulated in inequality (18A-1t), would be critical only if investments in fixed assets increased by $170,000, bringing total investment in fixed assets to $500,000.

For the limitation of long-term debt to 80 percent of working capital (inequality (18A-1u)), the value $W_{20}^* = 0.126$ denotes that a $1 increase in $(WC - 1\frac{1}{4} LTD)$, if used optimally, would result in a $0.126 increase in net-present value.[12] More important than the effect of changes in $(WC - 1\frac{1}{4} LTD)$ is the effect that changes in the maximum percentage of long-term debt to working capital have on the optimal solution. For example, what would be the effect if the percentage limitation is relaxed from 80 percent to 100 percent? Inequality (18A-1u) would become

$$\sum_{i=1}^{7} X_{i2} \leqq WC - LTD \qquad (18A-3)$$

where $WC - LTD$ is $2,500,000 - $1,720,000 = $780,000. If optimal adjustment is made to this relaxation of the percentage limitation, net-present value would increase by $22,223.55, to $110,521.05.[13]

For the dividend constraint (inequality (18A-1v)), $W_{21}^* = 0.25833$. If $Y - 2C$, where Y is first-year earnings on existing projects and C is the total cash dividend the company desires to pay at the end of the first year, were to increase by $1, net-present value would increase $0.25833 if the $1 were employed optimally.[14] What effect does the payment of

---

[11] Optimal use would involve investing an additional $0.30 in proposal 1 and $0.15 in proposal 2, decreasing by $0.45 the investment in proposal 6, increasing short-term borrowings by $0.80, and decreasing long-term borrowings by $0.80. The dual variable, $W_{18} = 0.0315$, is valid only within certain limits. We can increase short-term debt and decrease long-term debt by only $80,000 before inequality (18A-1q) and the nonnegative requirement become binding. On the other hand, investment in proposal 6 can increase only $44,250 before inequality (18A-1g) becomes binding. Consequently, $W_{18}^* = 0.0315$ remains valid for $151,666.67 \leqq (WC - min. WC) \leqq $350,000.

[12] Optimal employment of a $1 increase in the right-hand side of inequality (18A-1u) would involve a $1.20 increase in proposal 1, a $0.60 increase in proposal 2, a $1.80 decrease in proposal 6, an $0.80 decrease in short-term borrowings, and an $0.80 increase in long-term borrowings. The value $W_{20}^* = 0.126$ remains valid for $325,416.67 \leqq (WC - 1\frac{1}{4}LTD) \leqq $464,305.55. At $325,416.67, inequality (18A-1g) becomes binding and precludes further investment in proposal 6; at $464,305.55, further reductions in investment proposal 6 would not be possible.

[13] Optimal adjustment would involve increasing investment in proposal 1 by $180,500 to $350,000, increasing investment in proposal 2 by $129,460.53 to $184,210.53, eliminating the investment of $200,000 in proposal 4, investing $95,789.47 in proposal 5, eliminating the investment of $205,750 in proposal 6, decreasing short-term borrowings by $160,263.16, and increasing long-term borrowings by the same amount.

[14] Optimal employment would involve a $1.67 increase in proposal 1, a $7.50 decrease in proposal 2, and a $5.83 increase in proposal 6. As can be determined, $W_{21}^* = 0.25833$ remains valid for $2,300 \leqq Y - 2C \leqq $32,300. Below $2,300, inequality (18A-1c) becomes binding on further increases in proposal 2. Above $32,300, further decreases in proposal 2 are not possible.

dividends have on the firm's net-present value? Given the amount of the first-year earnings on existing projects and the limitation of dividends to 50 percent of earnings, the company may increase net-present value by $0.25833 for each $0.50 decrease in total cash dividends it pays at the end of the first year. Thus, given the dividend restriction, management is able to determine the effect that the payment of dividends has on net-present value.[15]

Perhaps the more important consideration is the effect that the percentage limitation has on profitability, given the dividend the company desires to pay. If the limitation is increased from 50 percent to 66.67 percent, what would be the effect on net-present value? The right-hand side of the constraint, inequality (18A-1v), would become

$$425,000 - 1.5(200,000) = 125,000$$

If optimal adjustment is made to this relaxation in the dividend restriction, net-present value will increase by $18,858.33.[16]

IMPLICATIONS

Through sensitivity analysis, we may evaluate the effect on the optimal solution of given changes in the protective-covenant constraints. The sensitivity of the optimal solution to changes in these parameters was determined without our having to solve one or a series of new problems. Equipped with knowledge of the opportunity costs of the various restrictions, management can bargain more rationally and effectively, giving ground when the restrictions involved have small opportunity costs or none and driving a hard bargain on those restrictions having high opportunity costs.

This knowledge is important to management if there is a possibility that the covenants under an existing indenture or agreement might be relaxed through negotiation with the lender(s). Changing protective covenants is much more likely under a loan agreement in which there is only one or a relatively small number of lenders than it is under a bond indenture. Knowledge of the opportunity costs involved in various restrictions is perhaps even more valuable in the initial negotiation of protective covenants to be imposed under an indenture or agreement.

[15] We ignore the problem of deviations from desired dividends having an effect on the cost of capital by assuming that the moderate changes in dividends under consideration will not affect the cost of capital.

[16] Optimal adjustment would involve increasing investment in proposal 1 by $12,166.67 to $181,666.67, eliminating the $54,750 investment in proposal 2, and increasing investment in proposal 6 by $42,583.33 to $248,333.33.

1. The Barnes Corporation has just acquired a large account. As a result, it needs an additional $75,000 in working capital immediately. It has been determined that there are three feasible sources of funds:

   (a) Trade credit: the company buys about $50,000 of materials per month on terms of 2/30, net 90. Discounts are taken.

   (b) Bank loan: the firm's bank will loan $100,000 at 9 percent. A 20 percent compensating balance will be required.

   (c) A factor will buy the company's receivables ($100,000 per month), which have a collection period of sixty days. The factor will advance up to 75 percent of the face value of the receivables for an annual charge of 8 percent. The factor will also charge a 2 percent fee on all receivables purchased. It has been estimated that the factor's services will save the company a credit department expense and bad-debt expense of $1,500 per month.

   Which alternative should be selected?

2. The Sphartz Company has estimated the following net cash-flow pattern for the first three months of next year as follows:

January	+$150,000
February	− 200,000
March	− 300,000

   These flows exclude consideration of gains secured from investing and costs associated with obtaining short-term funds. Further, it is assumed that all flows are effected at the *end* of the month.

   The firm may obtain funds when needed from the following sources:

   Short-Term Revolving Credit Agreement: The firm may borrow up to $500,000. The monthly fee for the privilege is $\frac{1}{10}$ percent on the unused portion. It is believed that a borrowing rate of 8 percent will prevail for the next three months. As of December 31, $200,000 of this amount was unused.

   Trade Credit: The firm purchases approximately $100,000 of materials each month on terms 2/30, net 60. Currently, the firm is taking its discounts.

   Factoring: The firm can borrow up to 90 percent of its average factor balance ($200,000 per month) at a rate of $\frac{3}{4}$ percent per month. The firm factors all of its receivables each month at a 2 percent fee in order to keep this line of financing open. The firm saves $3,000 per month by not maintaining a credit department.

   The firm may invest surplus funds in bankers' acceptances yielding 7 percent. The commission cost of these purchases (and sales) is $\frac{2}{10}$ percent. Assuming the firm now has (Dec. 31) and must maintain a cash balance of $100,000, determine the optimum borrowing-investing pattern for the firm for the next three months. (Be sure to adjust cash flows for gains secured from investing and costs associated with obtaining short-term funds.)

3. The Bone Company has been factoring its accounts receivable for the

past five years. The factor charges a fee of 2 percent and will lend up to 80 percent of the volume of receivables purchases for an additional $\frac{3}{4}$ percent per month. The firm typically has sales of $500,000 per month, 70 percent of which are on credit. By using the factor, two savings are effected:

(a) $2,000 per month that would be required to support a credit department, and

(b) A bad-debt expense of 1 percent on credit sales.

The firm's bank has recently offered to lend the firm up to 80 percent of the face value of the receivables shown on the schedule of accounts. The bank would charge 8 percent per annum interest plus a 2 percent processing charge per dollar of receivables lending. The firm extends terms of net 30, and all customers who pay their bills do so by the thirtieth of the month. Should the firm discontinue its factoring arrangement in favor of the bank's offer if the firm borrows, on the average, $100,000 per month on its receivables?

4. The Sharpless Corporation is in financial difficulty. In order to continue operations, the firm must raise $100,000 in working capital. The firm is unable to secure bank credit, though a commercial sales company has agreed to lend the company up to $100,000 secured by a warehouse receipt. The loan will carry an annual interest charge of 20 percent. The additional cost of maintaining a field warehouse arrangement to issue negotiable receipts is $2,000 per year.

   A second alternative open to the firm is stretching its trade credit. The firm purchases on terms of 2/10, net 30. Stretching beyond the due date will result in a 3 percent per month penalty charge, though it is believed that stretching beyond the due date by over 60 days may impair the firm's ability to get trade credit.

   (a) If the firm purchases $80,000 of raw materials every thirty days, how much will discount losses and stretching penalties cost the firm each month after the required $100,000 is raised?

   (b) Which form of financing is cheaper?

5. The Kedzie Cordage Company needs to finance a seasonal bulge in inventories of $400,000. The funds are needed for six months. The company is considering the following possibilities:

   (a) Warehouse receipt loan from a finance company. Terms are 12 percent with an 80 percent advance against the value of the inventory. The warehousing costs are $7,000 for the six-month period. The residual financing requirement, which is $400,000 less the amount advanced, will need to be financed by foregoing cash discounts on its payables. Standard terms are 2/10, net 30. However, the company feels it can postpone payment until the fortieth day without adverse effect.

   (b) A floating lien arrangement from the supplier of the inventory at an effective interest rate of 20 percent. The supplier will advance the full value of the inventory.

   (c) A field warehouse loan from another finance company at an interest rate of 10 percent. The advance is 70 percent and field warehousing costs amount to $10,000 for the six-month period. The residual financing requirement will need to be financed by foregoing cash discounts on payables as in the first alternative. Which is the least costly method of financing the inventory needs of the firm?

6. The Bell Corporation has indentures that require mortgage debt to be no more than 50 percent of all other junior debt and net worth, senior debentures to be no more than 75 percent of all other junior debt and net worth, subordinated debentures to be no more than 25 percent of all securities junior to it, and preferred stock to be no more than 30 percent of common. Bell is currently at these limits and will always return to them through the immediate sale of securities.

   If $5 million of subordinated debentures were converted into common, what net gain in total liabilities and net worth would take place?

7. The McDonald Company wishes to buy a $1.2 million piece of equipment over a two-year period. The bank has offered to loan the required money on the basis of a two-year note with a $300,000 amortization payment every six months. The loan would require a compensating balance equal to 15 percent of the outstanding balance and would bear an interest rate of 10 percent. The seller of the equipment has offered McDonald a conditional sales contract with four equal semi-annual payments. How large could the payments be before McDonald would find the bank loan more attractive?

8. The Dale Boot Company is contemplating investing in a project that will generate the following net cash flows (after taxes):

Year	0	1	2	3
Net cash flow (end of year)	−4,000,000	+1,000,000	+2,000,000	+3,000,000

The company has decided to finance the project through intermediate-term debt and is considering two possibilities:

(a) Utilize an additional $4 million of the firm's three-year revolving bank credit. Currently $3 million of the $8 million commitment is in use. The bank charges 1 percent over prime and a $\frac{1}{2}$ percent commitment fee on the unused portion. Interest is paid at the end of the year. No additional compensating balances are required. The company expects the prime rate, now 7 percent, to increase to 8 percent at the end of year 1, and to remain at that level through year 3.

(b) Privately place a $4 million unsecured note with California-Sierra Mutual Life Insurance Co. The interest cost is $8\frac{1}{4}$ percent with a 0.5 percent placement fee. The note calls for payment of $1 million at the end of years 1 and 2, and $2 million at the end of year 3. Which financing arrangement is preferred? Why?

9. The Chain Corporation needs $10 million for the next ten years. The prime rate is now 6 percent; it is expected to ascend gradually to 8 percent at the end of year 5 and then descend gradually back to 7 percent at the end of year 10. Chain has the following alternative sources of financing:

   (a) Ten one-year bank loans at prime with a 20 percent compensating balance. The interest cost would be computed on the basis of the average prime rate for the year.

   (b) Two five-year notes placed with an insurance company. The interest cost would be set at 1 percent above the prime rate at the time the note was negotiated.

   (c) One ten-year bond sold publicly (total costs of issue = 3 percent of gross proceeds) now at an interest rate of 7.25 percent.

   If the Chain Corporation has a 50 percent tax rate, which alternative should be selected?

10. *Research Project*

    Examine several bond indentures and/or loan agreements (if available). What major restrictions are imposed? Do you note any differences in the restrictions outlined in bond indentures as opposed to those in loan agreements? Why might these differences exist? Do you find any correlation between the maturity length of the instrument and the number (and degree) of the restrictions? What might account for your findings?

SELECTED REFERENCES

Abraham, Alfred B., "Factoring—The New Frontier for Commercial Banks," *Journal of Commercial Bank Lending,* 53 (April 1971), 32–43.

Berger, Paul D., and William K. Harper, "Determination of an Optimal Revolving Credit Agreement," *Journal of Financial and Quantitative Analysis,* 8 (June 1973), 491–98.

Credit and Financial Management, 75 (December 1973). A special issue devoted to factoring.

Denonn, Lester E., "The Security Agreement," *Journal of Commercial Bank Lending,* 50 (February 1968), 32–40.

Hayes, Douglas A., Bank Lending Policies: Domestic and International. Ann Arbor, Mich.: University of Michigan, 1971.

Middleton, J. William, "Term Lending—Practical and Profitable," *Journal of Commercial Banking Lending,* 50 (August 1968), 31–43.

Quarles, J. Carson, "The Floating Lien," *Journal of Commercial Bank Lending,* 53 (November 1970), 51–58.

Rogers, Dean E., "An Approach to Analyzing Cash Flow for Term Loan Purposes," *Bulletin of the Robert Morris Associates,* 48 (October 1965), 79–85.

Rogers, Robert W., "Warehouse Receipts and Their Use in Financing," *Bulletin of the Robert Morris Associates,* 46 (April 1964), 317–27.

Van Horne, James, "A Linear-Programming Approach to Evaluating Restrictions under a Bond Indenture or Loan Agreement," *Journal of Financial and Quantitative Analysis,* 1 (June 1966), 68–83.

Van Horne, James C., "Optimal Initiation of Bankruptcy Proceedings by Debt Holders," *Journal of Finance,* 31 (June 1976).

LEASE
FINANCING

A *lease* is a means by which a firm can acquire the economic use of an asset for a stated period of time.[1] This financing device has developed rapidly in the decades of the sixties and seventies with a wide variety of applications, as well as a substantial increase in the sheer volume of transactions. In this chapter, our concern is with financial leases rather than with operating leases. A *financial lease* is a noncancelable contractual commitment on the part of a lessee to make a series of payments to a lessor for the use of an asset. The lessee acquires most of the economic values associated with outright ownership of the asset, even though the lessor retains title to it. With a financial lease, the lease period generally corresponds to the economic life of the asset. In addition, the total payments the lessee agrees to make must exceed the purchase price of the asset.[2] The distinguishing feature between a financial and an operating lease is cancelability; an operating lease can be canceled by giving proper notice, whereas a financial lease cannot. An example of an operating lease is one for telephone service.

Because of the contractual nature of a financial lease obligation, it must be regarded as a form of financing. It is used in place of other methods of financing to acquire the use of an asset. An alternative method of financing might be to purchase the asset and finance its acquisition with debt. Both the lease payment and the payment of principal and interest on debt are fixed obligations that must be met. Inability to meet these obligations will result in financial embarrassment. Thus, lease financing and debt financing are very similar from the standpoint of analyzing the ability of the firm to service fixed obligations.

In lease financing, the nature of the obligations of the lessor and the lessee is specified in the lease contract. This contract contains

1. The basic lease period during which the lease is noncancelable.

2. The timing and amounts of periodic rental payments during the basic lease period.

3. Any option to renew the lease or to purchase the asset at the end of the basic lease period. Otherwise the lessor takes possession of the asset and is entitled to any residual value associated with it.

4. Provision for the payment of the costs of maintenance and repairs, taxes, insurance, and other expenses. With a "net lease," the lessee pays all of these costs. Under a "maintenance lease," the lessor maintains the asset and pays the insurance.

---

[1] The development of most of this chapter assumes that the reader has covered Parts II and III.

[2] See Richard F. Vancil, "Lease or Borrow: New Method of Analysis," *Harvard Business Review*, 39 (September–October 1961), 122–36.

There are three main types of lease financing: a sale and leaseback arrangement, the direct acquisition of an asset under a lease, and leveraged leasing. Virtually all lease-financing arrangements fall into one of these three categories. In this section, we briefly describe these categories; in the subsequent sections, we present a framework for the analysis of lease financing and we discuss the basic valuation implications.

SALE AND LEASEBACK

Under a sale and leaseback arrangement, a firm sells an asset it owns to another party, and this party leases it back to the firm. Usually, the asset is sold at approximately its market value. The firm receives the sales price in cash and the economic use of the asset during the basic lease period. In turn, it contracts to make periodic lease payments and, of course, gives up title to the asset. As a result, the lessor realizes any residual value the asset might have at the end of the lease period, whereas before this would have been realized by the firm. Lessors engaged in sale and leaseback arrangements include insurance companies, other institutional investors, finance companies, and independent leasing companies.

DIRECT LEASING

Under direct leasing, a company acquires the use of an asset it did not own previously. For example, a firm simply may lease an asset from the manufacturer: IBM leases computers; Kearney & Trecker Corporation leases machine tools. Indeed, a number of capital goods are available today on a lease-financed basis. There are a wide variety of direct leasing arrangements available to meet the various needs of the firm. The major types of lessors are manufacturers, finance companies, banks, independent leasing companies, special-purpose leasing companies, and partnerships. For leasing arrangements involving all but the first, the vendor sells the asset to the lessor and he, in turn, leases it to the lessee. In certain cases, economies of scale are possible in the purchase of capital assets by the lessor. These economies may be passed on to the lessee in the form of lower lease payments.

Since 1963, commercial banks have been allowed to engage in direct leasing; their entry represents an important development in the leasing industry. Independent leasing companies, such as Boothe Leasing and Nationwide Leasing, finance the purchase of a wide variety of equipment. In doing so, they frequently borrow from banks, securing the loan with the assignment of the lease payments. Special-purpose leasing companies confine their operations to certain types of assets; computer leasing companies, for example, mainly lease computer hardware and peripheral equipment. In recent years, high-tax-bracketed individuals

Chapter 19 **495**
LEASE FINANCING

peripheral equipment. In recent years, high-tax-bracketed individuals have formed partnerships for the purpose of purchasing equipment and leasing it to companies. The tax shield afforded by accelerated depreciation charges and interest paid on borrowings is more valuable to them than to a corporation. As a result, both the lessor and the lessee may benefit. Much more will be said about this when we take up the economic benefits associated with leasing.

LEVERAGED LEASING

In recent years, a special form of leasing has developed in conjunction with the financing of assets requiring large capital outlays. It is known as *leveraged leasing*. In contrast to the two parties involved in the forms of leasing previously described, there are three parties involved in leveraged leasing: (1) the lessee, (2) the lessor, or equity participant, and (3) the lender. We examine each in turn.[3]

From the standpoint of the lessee, there is no difference between a leveraged lease and any other type of lease. The lessee contracts to make periodic payments over the basic lease period and, in return, is entitled to the use of the asset over that period of time. The role of the lessor, however, is changed. The lessor acquires the asset in keeping with the terms of the lease arrangement. This acquisition is financed in part by an equity investment by the lessor of, say, 20 percent (hence the name *equity participant*). The remaining 80 percent is provided by a long-term lender or lenders. The loan is usually secured by a mortgage on the asset, as well as by the assignment of the lease and lease payments.[4] The lessor, however, is the borrower.

As owner of the asset, the lessor is entitled to deduct all depreciation charges associated with the asset, as well as utilize the entire investment tax credit. The cash-flow pattern for the lessor typically involves (1) a cash outflow at the time the asset is acquired, which represents its equity participation less the investment tax credit; (2) a period of cash inflows represented by lease payments and tax benefits, less payments on the debt (principal and interest); and (3) a period of net cash outflows where, because of declining tax benefits, the sum of lease payments and tax benefits falls below the debt payments due. If there is any residual value at the end of the lease period, this of course represents a cash inflow to the lessor.

---

[3] For a discussion of leveraged leasing, see "FASB Discussion Memorandum: Accounting for Leases" (Stamford, Conn.: Financial Accounting Standards Board, July 2, 1974), Sec. VIII; Robert C. Wiar, "Economic Implications of Multiple Rates of Return in the Leveraged Lease Context," *Journal of Finance*, 28 (December 1973), 1275–86; and E. Richard Packham, "An Analysis of the Risks of Leveraged Leasing," *Journal of Commercial Bank Lending*, 57 (March 1975), 2–29.

[4] Sometimes in addition the lessee guarantees the debt.

**Table 19·1   Illustration of cash flows to lessor
in a leveraged lease**

End of Year	(1) Initial Equity Participation ($100,000) less Investment Tax Credit ($35,000)	(2) Lease Payment Receipt	(3) Depreciation	(4) Loan Interest Payment
0	$(65,000)			
1	—	$115,000	$166,667	$40,000
2	—	115,000	133,333	33,448
3	—	115,000	100,000	26,241
4	—	115,000	66,667	18,313
5	—	115,000	33,333	9,593

To illustrate, suppose that A. B. Chance Company leased an asset from the Third National Bank. The asset cost $500,000, and lease payments of $115,000 are required at the end of each of the next five years. The lessor puts up $100,000 in "equity participation" and borrows the remaining $400,000 through mortgage bonds which are placed with a group of large individual investors. These bonds bear an interest rate of 10 percent, and loan payments of $105,519 are required at the end of each of the next five years. These payments embody both principal and interest, the latter of which is deductible for tax purposes. Depreciation is on the sum-of-the-years'-digits basis where $5/15$, $4/15$, $3/15$, $2/15$, and $1/15$ of the purchase price of the asset are deductible at the end of each of the five years. We assume that an investment tax credit of 7 percent is realized at the time the asset is acquired. (The actual credit would be less, but for simplicity 7 percent is assumed.) Finally, let us assume no residual value at the end of the lease period and a tax rate for the lessor of 40 percent.

Given these considerations, the cash flows to the lessor are shown in Table 19-1. In the last column, we see that the cash flow is negative at time 0, followed by positive flows for years 1–3, and negative flows for years 4 and 5. The declining cash flows are of course due to decreasing tax benefits, which in turn are caused by the decrease in depreciation and in interest payments.

In some leveraged lease situations, the negative cash flow in later periods is sufficiently large so that the sum total of cash flows for all years is negative. This gives rise to the calculation of multiple internal rates of return when the lessor goes to compute his return.[5] (This

[5] For a discussion of this problem as well as the presentation of a possible approach, see Wiar, "Economic Implications of Multiple Rates of Return in the Leveraged Lease Context."

Table 19·1 (*cont.*)

(5)	(6)	(7)	(8)
Taxable Income (2) − (3) − (4)	Taxes* (5) × 0.4	Total Loan Payment	Cash Flows (1) + (2) − (6) − (7)
			$(65,000)
$(91,667)	$[36,667]	$105,519	46,148
(51,781)	[20,712]	105,519	30,193
(11,241)	[4,496]	105,519	13,977
30,020	12,008	105,519	(2,527)
72,074	28,830	105,519	(19,349)

*Brackets indicate a tax credit.

problem and the need to determine the "economic" return were addressed in Appendix A in Chapter 4.) It is important to note that the reversal in signs for cash flows to the lessor from positive to negative is one of the distinguishing features of a leveraged lease.

The leveraged lease may at first seem more complicated than either the sale and leaseback arrangement or direct leasing. However, it reduces to certain basic concepts, which, from the standpoint of the lessee, can be analyzed in the same manner as for any lease. Therefore, we will not treat it separately in the rest of this chapter. It should be emphasized, however, that leveraged leasing has increasingly been used in the financing of large capital assets, and its growth has paralleled that of project financing.

ACCOUNTING FOR LEASES

In recent years, the accounting treatment of leases has involved greater and greater disclosure. Where once leases did not have to be disclosed, rulings by the Accounting Principles Board and its successor, the Financial Accounting Standards Board, have resulted in enough disclosure that the financial statement user is able to judge the impact of this contractual obligation in the same way as he is the impact of debt payments. Therefore, the attraction of lease financing as an "off balance sheet" method of financing has diminished from the standpoint of the firm.

The omission of consideration of the lease obligation can of course have a favorable, and deceptive, effect upon the financial condition of a firm, as depicted by financial ratios, over what would be the case if the asset were purchased and financed with debt. For one thing, the company that leases would show a faster turnover of its assets and better earning power than an identical company that engaged in debt financing. Moreover, it would appear to have less financial risk under the leasing alternative. The debt-to-equity ratio would be less, and the coverage ratio of times interest earned higher. Close analysis of the financial statement, however, would show that the better financial ratios of the lease-financed company were an illusion. The lease payments represent just as much a contractual obligation on the part of the company as does the payment of principal and interest on debt.

At the time of this writing, the accounting treatment of leases was undergoing change. At the very least, the lease obligation must be disclosed in a footnote to the audited financial statements. However, the Financial Accounting Standards Board has come out with a proposal that calls for capitalization on the balance sheet of certain types of leases. By *capitalization*, it is meant that annual lease payments are capitalized at an appropriate discount rate and the capitalized liability is shown on the balance sheet, together with the amortized value of the asset. The proposal is complex, but in principle it classifies certain types of leases as capital leases which must be shown on the balance sheet.[6]

A lease is regarded as a capital lease if it satisfies any one of the following conditions:

1. The lease transfers title to the asset to the lessee by the end of the lease period.
2. The lease contains an option to purchase the asset at a bargain price.
3. The lease period is equal to or greater than 75 percent of the estimated economic life of the asset.
4. The estimated fair value of the asset at the end of the lease period is less than 25 percent of what it was at the beginning.
5. The asset is of special purpose for the lessee and would not be readily marketable to others.

If a lease meets one or more of these conditions, it would need to be capitalized on the asset side of the balance sheet. The amount reflected would be the present value of minimum lease payments over the lease period, using the lessee's incremental borrowing rate as the discount rate. The associated lease obligation would be shown on the liability side of the balance sheet, with the present value of payments due within one year being reflected as current liabilities and the present value of payments due after one year being shown as non-current liabilities.

In addition, the firm would need to show captions on the balance sheet for operating leases. An operating lease is any lease which does not meet one of the five criteria listed above for a capital lease. The same present-value information would need to be shown for operating leases,

---

[6] *Accounting for Leases Exposure Draft* (Stamford, Conn.: Financial Accounting Standards Board, August 26, 1975).

with the exception that it would be reflected under a caption as opposed to under the asset or liability columns. With a combination of capital and operating leases, the balance sheet might look like the following:

Assets		Liabilities	
Leased Property:		**Current:**	
Capital leases less		Obligations under	
accumulated depreciation	$1,000	capital leases	$150
Operating leases ($2,250)		**Long-term:**	
		Obligations under	
		capital leases	850
		Commitments under	
		operating leases	
		($2,250)	

For both capital and operating leases, more detailed information would be required in footnotes. Relevant information here would include the gross amounts of leases by major property categories, a schedule by years of future minimum lease payments required, the range and weighted average of discount rates used to reduce these payments to present value, and a general description of the leasing arrangements. The latter would include a discussion of the terms of renewal or purchase option, any restrictions on the company, the basis on which any contingent rental payments were determined, and the relative importance of the lease arrangements to the company.

If this proposal ultimately is made a final ruling by the Financial Accounting Standards Board, it will cause the reflection of many leased assets and their associated contractual obligations on the balance sheet. The board is the accounting profession's rule-making body. Accountants must conform to its rulings if they are to give unqualified opinions on the financial statements of the companies they audit. If leases are shown on the balance sheet, it will permit an easier analysis of the contractual nature of the obligation by creditors and investors. The obligation is less likely to be overlooked, as can sometimes now occur when it is "buried" in a footnote. As a result, one of the purported advantages of leasing as opposed to borrowing will cease to exist. Whether or not it ever was an advantage with respect to the valuation of the firm is problematical.

Whether lease financing or borrowing is favored will depend upon the patterns of cash outflows for each financing method and upon the opportunity cost of funds. A number of different methods may be used to compare the two alternatives. In this section, we illustrate some of the

ANALYSIS OF LEASING AND BORROWING ALTERNATIVES

more important, using a hypothetical example.[7] We assume that the firm has decided to invest in a project on the basis of considerations taken up in Part II. In other words, the investment-worthiness of the project is evaluated separately from the specific method of financing to be employed.[8] We assume also that the firm has determined an appropriate capital structure and that this structure calls for financing the project with a fixed-income obligation—either debt or lease financing. Our concern is with determining the least costly alternative.

EXAMPLE

For comparative purposes, each method of analysis we consider will be illustrated with the same example. Suppose a firm has decided to acquire an asset costing $200,000 and having an expected economic life of ten years, after which the asset is not expected to have any residual value. Once the investment decision is made, the question becomes, Is it better to finance the asset by leasing or by borrowing? If leasing is used, the lessor requires that cost of the asset be completely amortized over the ten-year period and that it yield a 9 percent return. As is customary, lease payments are to be made in advance—that is, at the end of the year prior to each of the ten years. The amount of annual lease payment may be calculated by solving the following equation for x:

$$\$200,000 = \sum_{t=0}^{9} \frac{x}{(1.09)^t}$$

$$\$200,000 = x + 5.9852x \qquad (19\text{-}1)$$

$$x = \frac{\$200,000}{6.9852}$$

$$x = \$28,600$$

Because lease payments are made in advance, we solve for the annual lease payment that equates the cost of the asset, $200,000, with the present value of one lease payment at time 0, plus the present value

[7]This analysis assumes the lease is noncancelable over the basic lease period. For cancelable leases, it is necessary to estimate the probability distribution of possible termination dates and determine the expected cost of leasing on the basis of this distribution. For such an approach, see David O. Jenkins, "Purchase or Cancellable Lease," *Financial Executive*, 38 (April 1970), 26–31.

[8]For an analysis in which the leasing contract is viewed as an investment rather than a financing decision, see Robert W. Johnson and Wilbur G. Lewellen, "Analysis of the Lease-or-Buy Decision," *Journal of Finance*, 27 (September 1972), 815–24. They hold that the lease is a long-term acquisition of services and that the relevant comparison is lease versus buy, not lease versus borrow. For a comparison of various methods for analyzing leasing versus borrowing, see Richard S. Bower, "Issues in Lease Financing," *Financial Management*, 2 (Winter 1973), 25–34.

of nine lease payments at the end of each of the next nine years. Because the discount rate is 9 percent, we find in Table A-2 at the end of the book that the present-value discount factor for an even stream of cash flows for nine years, discounted at 9 percent, is 5.9852. Therefore, the annual lease payment necessary to amortize the cost of the asset completely and to return the lessor 9 percent is $28,600.

If the asset is purchased, the firm is able to deduct depreciation charges for tax purposes as well as avail itself of the investment tax credit. If straight-line depreciation is used, annual depreciation charges are $20,000. The investment tax credit is available at the time the asset is placed into service. For a moment of digression, this credit was conceived in 1962 to provide an incentive to corporations and individuals to invest in capital assets. The credit was later repealed, reinstated, and repealed, and reistated once again in 1971 in a counter-cyclical manner designed to stimulate or dampen modernization, depending on the phase of the economy. Since 1971, it has remained in effect. The maximum permanent credit available at the time of this writing was 7 percent on qualified property with a useful life of seven or more years; the effective percentage is less if the useful life is less than seven years. In the Tax Reduction Act of 1975, the maximum credit was increased to 10 percent on a temporary basis. In the example that follows we assume a 7 percent investment tax credit; however, the example can easily be reworked for a 10 percent credit.

Back to our example then, assume that a 7 percent credit is applicable and the asset is placed in service at the time of purchase. As a result, $14,000 is deductible at time 0. This deduction effectively lowers the purchase price by $14,000 to $186,000, if the asset is purchased.[9] Assume also that (1) if the firm were to borrow it would be able to do so at a 10 percent rate, (2) the effective federal income tax rate is 50 percent for the firm involved, and (3) the operating costs borne by the firm are the same whether the asset is purchased or leased.

PRESENT-VALUE ANALYSIS OF ALTERNATIVES

The first method of analysis we consider is a comparison of the present values of cash outflows for each of the alternatives. According to this method, whichever alternative has the lowest present value is the most desirable. Recall that the firm will make annual lease payments of $28,600 if the asset is leased. Because these payments are an expense, they are deductible for tax purposes. However, they are deductible only in the year for which the payment applies. For example, the $28,600

---

[9]We assume at this time that the firm is able to use the tax credit in its entirety to offset taxes it would otherwise pay. As we shall see later in the chapter, some firms are unable to completely utilize the tax credit, and this affects the relative desirability of leasing.

**Table 19·2   Schedule of cash outflows:
leasing alternative**

End of Year	*(1)* Lease Payment	*(2)* Tax Shield	*(3)* Cash Outflow after Taxes *(1 − (2)*	*(4)* Present Value of Cash Outflows *(5%)*
0	$28,600	—	$28,600	$ 28,600
1–9	28,600	$14,300	14,300	101,642
10	—	14,300	−14,300	−8,779
				$121,463

payment at the end of year 0 represents a prepaid expense and is not deductible for tax purposes until year 1. Similarly, the other nine payments are not deductible until the following year.

As leasing is analogous to borrowing, an appropriate discount rate for discounting the after-tax cash flows might be the after-tax cost of borrowing. The use of this rate assumes that the firm's future taxable income will be sufficient so as to fully utilize the tax shield associated with lease payments. It also assumes that the tax rate will not change. While these assumptions are not unreasonable approximations of reality for many firms, it is important to point out that there is disagreement as to the appropriate discount rate to employ.[10]

Given the assumptions above, we are able to derive a schedule of cash outflows after taxes and compute their present value. These computations are shown in Table 19-2. The present value of the total cash outflows under the leasing alternative is seen to be $121,463. This figure, then, must be compared with the present value of cash outflows under the borrowing alternative.

If the asset is purchased, the firm is assumed to finance it entirely with a 10 percent unsecured term loan. Moreover, we assume that the loan payment schedule is of the same configuration as the lease payment schedule. In other words, loan payments are assumed to be payable at the beginning as opposed to the end of each year. This assumption places the loan on an equivalent basis with the lease and allows us to compare "apples" with "apples," as most lease arrangements call for payment in advance.[11] Recall that if the asset is purchased, an invest-

---

[10] See Bower, "Issues in Lease Financing," p. 31; and Myron J. Gordon, "A General Solution to the Buy or Lease Decision: A Pedagogical Note," *Journal of Finance*, 29 (March 1974), 245–46.

[11] If the loan payments were payable at the end of the year while lease payments were payable at the beginning, the earlier payments under the lease alternative would in theory at least release capacity for raising funds by other means of financing earlier than under the debt alternative. See Richard S. Bower, Frank C. Herringer, and J. Peter Williamson, "Lease Evaluation," *Accounting Review*, 41 (April 1966), 257–65.

ment tax credit of $14,000 is available at the outset. Therefore, the effective cost of the asset and the amount to be financed is $200,000 − $14,000 = $186,000. A loan of this amount is taken out at time 0 and is payable over ten years at annual payments of $27,519 at the beginning of each year.[12] The proportion of interest in each payment depends upon the unpaid balance of the principal amount owing during the year. For example, the principal amount owing during year 1 is $186,000 − $27,519 = $158,481; the annual interest for that year is $15,848.[13] Table 19-3 shows the amount of debt payments, and the proportion represented by interest.

Given annual interest and depreciation, we are able to compute the cash outflows after taxes for the borrowing alternative; these outflows are shown in Table 19-4. Because both depreciation and interest are deductible for tax purposes, they provide a tax shield equal to their sum times the tax rate. When this shield is deducted from the total payment of $27,519, we obtain the cash outflow after taxes at the end of each year. Finally, we compute the present value of these outflows, and they are found to total $108,709. As this present value is less than that for the lease alternative, $121,463, the firm should acquire the asset through debt financing.

This conclusion arises despite the fact that the implied interest rate embodied in the lease payments, 9 percent, is less than the explicit interest rate on the debt, 10 percent. The major relative advantage of purchasing the asset and financing it with debt is the realization of the investment tax credit at the outset. This credit effectively reduces the

Table 19·3 Schedule of debt payments

End of Year	Interest Plus Principal Payments	Principal Amount Owing at End of Year	Annual Interest
0	$27,519	$158,481	$ 0
1	27,519	146,810	15,848
2	27,519	133,972	14,681
3	27,519	119,850	13,397
4	27,519	104,316	11,985
5	27,519	87,229	10,432
6	27,519	68,433	8,723
7	27,519	47,757	6,843
8	27,519	25,014	4,776
9	27,516	0	2,502

[12] This amount is computed in the same manner as in Eq. (19-1), using 10 percent instead of 9 percent as the discount factor. At the end of year 10, nothing is owing.

[13] For ease of illustration, we round to the nearest dollar throughout. This results in the final debt payment in Table 19-3 being slightly less than would otherwise be the case.

purchase price and the amount of debt to be incurred. In the case of the lease, the lessor is entitled to the investment tax credit. This advantage may be passed off in part to the lessee in the form of lease payments lower than would otherwise be the case. While the lower interest rate embodied in the lease payments in our example reflects this occurrence, it is not sufficient to cause the lease alternative to be more attractive. More will be said about how much of the tax credit and the tax benefits associated with depreciation are passed off to the lessee in the form of lower lease payments when we take up the economics of leasing in the last section of the chapter. For now, our concern is with the analysis of the alternatives and not with the underlying economics.

Another factor that favors the debt alternative is the deductibility of interest payments for tax purposes. Because the amount of interest embodied in a "mortgage-type" debt payment is high at first and declines with successive payments, the tax benefits associated with these payments follow the same pattern over time. From a present-value standpoint, this pattern benefits the firm relative to the pattern of lease payments, which typically are constant over time. (The reader should compare Table 19-2 with Table 19-3 for amplification of this point.)

In our example, we assumed straight-line depreciation. If the company uses accelerated depreciation, it obtains a greater tax shield in the early years and a lower one in later years. As a result, cash outflows after taxes in the early years are reduced relative to cash outflows in later years, and the present value under the borrowing alternative is decreased. For example, if sum-of-the-years'-digits depreciation is employed, the present value of cash outflows under the borrowing alternative becomes $103,080, in contrast with $108,709 when straight-line depreciation is used. Thus, accelerated depreciation makes borrowing

Table 19·4   Schedule of cash outflows: debt alternative

End of Year	(1) Loan Payment	(2) Interest	(3) Depreciation	(4) Tax Shield [(2) + (3)]0.5	(5) Cash Outflows after Taxes (1) − (4)	(6) Present Value of Cash Flows (5%)
0	$27,519	$ 0	$ 0	$ 0	$27,519	$27,519
1	27,519	15,848	20,000	17,924	9,595	9,138
2	27,519	14,681	20,000	17,340	10,179	9,233
3	27,519	13,397	20,000	16,699	10,820	9,347
4	27,519	11,985	20,000	15,992	11,527	9,483
5	27,519	10,432	20,000	15,216	12,303	9,561
6	27,519	8,723	20,000	14,362	13,157	9,818
7	27,519	6,843	20,000	13,421	14,098	10,019
8	27,519	4,776	20,000	12,388	15,131	10,241
9	27,516	2,502	20,000	11,251	16,271	10,489
10	0	0	20,000	10,000	(10,000)	(6,139)
						$108,709

more attractive than it is with straight-line depreciation. It should be pointed out, however, that a lessor also is able to use accelerated depreciation. In turn, the lessor may pass on some of the benefits inherent in its use to the lessee in the form of lower lease payments.

Recall that we assumed the project had no residual value at the end of ten years. If it were expected to have an after-tax residual value, this value should simply be treated as a cash inflow at the end of year 10. This inflow would be reflected at the end of year 10 in column (5) of Table 19-4. Thus, the likely occurrence of a residual, or salvage, value involves only a simple modification of the procedure. In all cases, it makes the borrowing alternative more attractive.

INTERNAL-RATE-OF-RETURN ANALYSIS

Instead of computing the present value of cash outflows for the two financing alternatives, we could compute the internal rates of return. This approach avoids the problem of having to choose a rate of discount. In general, businessmen feel more comfortable in comparing percentages than they do in comparing present values. For these reasons as well as others presented later, the author has a preference for the internal-rate-of-return method of analysis. Variations of this method have been used by Beechy, Doenges, Findlay, Mitchell, Roenfeldt and Osteryoung, and Wyman.[14]

To begin with consideration of the lease, the after-tax cost of leasing can be determined by solving the following equation for r:

$$A_o - \sum_{t=0}^{n-1} \frac{L_t}{(1+r)^t} + \sum_{t=1}^{n} \frac{T(L_{t-1} - P_t)}{(1+r)^t} - ITC = 0 \qquad (19\text{-}2)$$

where A_o = cost of the asset to be leased

n = number of periods to the end of the lease

L_t = lease payment at the end of period t

T = corporate tax rate

P_t = depreciation in period t that would be applicable if the asset were owned

ITC = amount of investment tax credit

[14]Thomas H. Beechy, "Quasi-Debt Analysis of Financial Leases," *Accounting Review*, 44 (April 1969), 375–81; Beechy, "The Cost of Leasing: Comment and Correction," *Accounting Review*, 45 (October 1970), 769–73; Conrad R. Doenges, "The Cost of Leasing," *Engineering Economist*, 17 (Fall 1971), 31–44; M. Chapman Findlay III, "A Sensitivity Analysis of IRR Leasing Models," *Engineering Economist*, 20 (Summer 1975), 231–42; G. B. Mitchell, "After-Tax Cost of Leasing," *Accounting Review*, 45 (April 1970), 308–14; Rodney L. Roenfeldt and Jerome S. Osteryoung, "Analysis of Financial Leases," *Financial Management*, 2 (Spring 1973), 74–87; and Harold E. Wyman, "Financial Lease Evaluation under Conditions of Uncertainty," *Accounting Review*, 48 (July 1973), 489–93. All of these articles are well summarized and analyzed in Bower, "Issues in Lease Financing."

In this construct, the cost of leasing is the rate of discount that equates the present value of lease payments, net of their tax shields, together with the tax shields for depreciation and the investment tax credit, which would occur if the asset were purchased, with the cost of the asset. In other words, the cost of leasing includes not only the lease payments but the depreciation tax deductions as well as investment tax credit foregone by virtue of leasing the asset as opposed to purchasing it. These two tax benefits, which are associated with owning an asset, represent opportunity costs if the asset is leased. As we shall see in the last section of this chapter, they represent the focal point around which lease financing by the firm should be negotiated.

Using our previous example and assuming straight-line depreciation, the information necessary to solve for the after-tax cost of leasing is shown in Table 19-5. The last column represents the cash-flow stream. When we solve for the rate of discount that equates the negative cash flows with the positive ones in this column, we find it to be 6.81 percent. This figure then serves as the after-tax cost of lease financing, and it should be compared with the after-tax cost of debt financing to determine which method results in the lower cost of financing. The after-tax cost of debt financing is merely the before-tax cost times 1 minus the tax rate. With the before-tax interest cost of 10 percent and a tax rate of 0.5 for our example problem, the after-tax cost of debt financing is $10.00(1 - 0.5) = 5.00$ percent. According to this method of analysis, then, borrowing is the preferred alternative because its effective yield is less than that for the leasing alternative.

In summary, the internal-rate-of-return method of analysis permits a simple comparison of the after-tax costs of the lease and borrowing alternatives. Whichever alternative has the lowest rate would be selected according to this method. Again, this assumes that decisions have

Table 19·5 Schedule of cash flows—lease analysis

End of Year	(1) Cost of Asset	(2) L_t Lease Payment	(3) P_t Depreciation	(4) Tax Shield $T(L_{t-1} - P_t)$	(5) Investment Tax Credit	(6) Cash Flow (1) − (2) + (4) − (5)
0	$200,000	$28,600	—	—	$14,000	$157,400
1	—	28,600	$20,000	4,300	—	(24,300)
2	—	28,600	20,000	4,300	—	(24,300)
3	—	28,600	20,000	4,300	—	(24,300)
4	—	28,600	20,000	4,300	—	(24,300)
5	—	28,600	20,000	4,300	—	(24,300)
6	—	28,600	20,000	4,300	—	(24,300)
7	—	28,600	20,000	4,300	—	(24,300)
8	—	28,600	20,000	4,300	—	(24,300)
9	—	28,600	20,000	4,300	—	(24,300)
10	—	—	20,000	4,300	—	4,300

already been reached with respect to acquiring the asset and to financing it with a fixed-income type of instrument—either debt or a lease. Implied is that either method of financing has the same effect on the capacity of the firm to raise additional funds.

BOWER-HERRINGER-WILLIAMSON METHOD

In yet another approach to evaluating lease versus borrowing, Bower, Herringer, and Williamson (BHW) divide the payments streams into two parts: the cash flows associated with financing and the cash flows associated with tax savings.[15] As in our present-value example, they assume that the loan payment schedule is of the same configuration as the lease payment schedule. This assumption places the loan on an equivalent basis with the lease.

Analyzing the cash flows associated with financing first, Bower, Herringer, and Williamson measure the incremental impact of a loan by subtracting the present value of lease payments from the present value of loan payments, where both are discounted at the debt rate. For our example problem, the present value of loan payments in Table 19-3 is $186,000 if a 10 percent discount rate is used. Recall that the investment tax credit of $14,000 reduced the amount of debt financing from $200,000 to $186,000. The present value of the lease payments is determined by discounting the lease payments in column (1) of Table 19-2 by 10 percent, and it is found to be $193,307. Given these present values, the *financial disadvantage* of leasing is determined as follows:

Present value of loan payments	**$186,000**
Present value of lease payments	193,307
Financial advantage (disadvantage)	$ (7,307)

The next step is to determine the incremental present value of the tax savings associated with leasing. If we use the straight-line depreciation example, we begin by subtracting the tax shield for the borrowing alternative in Table 19-4 from that for the leasing alternative in Table 19-2. The difference represents the decrease in the firm's tax payments, which is associated with leasing as opposed to borrowing. The calculations are shown in Table 19-6. When these decreases in tax payments are discounted by the cost of capital rate, we obtain what BHW call the *operating advantage* of the lease. If the cost of capital is, say, 13 percent,

[15]"Lease Evaluation," pp. 257–65.

Table 19·6 Calculation of decrease in tax payments with leasing

End of Year	(1) Leasing Tax Shield*	(2) Borrowing Tax Shield†	(3) Decrease in Tax Payments with Leasing (1) − (2)	(4) Present Value of Decreases (13%)
1	$14,300	$17,924	−$3,624	−$3,207
2	14,300	17,340	− 3,040	− 2,381
3	14,300	16,699	− 2,399	− 1,663
4	14,300	15,992	− 1,692	− 1,038
5	14,300	15,216	− 916	− 497
6	14,300	14,362	− 62	− 30
7	14,300	13,421	879	374
8	14,300	12,388	1,912	719
9	14,300	11,251	3,049	1,015
10	14,300	10,000	4,300	1,267
				−$5,441

*From Table 19-2.
†From Table 19-4.

the present value of the decreased tax payments is found to be −$5,441 for our example problem.

The decision to lease or borrow is made on the basis of whether the operating advantage of the lease exceeds its financial disadvantage. If so, lease financing should be used; if not, debt financing should be employed. In our case, there is an actual operating disadvantage associated with leasing. Therefore, the latter holds and debt financing should be employed, according to this analysis.

The BHW method of analysis is similar to the *basic interest rate* approach of Richard F. Vancil.[16] Like BHW, Vancil separates the financing effect of leasing from its tax-savings effect. Holding constant the amount of financing, he discounts the tax savings associated with the noninterest portions of the two payments streams by the cost of capital. Whichever financing alternative has the lower present value is preferred.

A critical factor in both the BHW and the Vancil approaches is the discount rate employed. As discussed earlier, a case can be made for using the after-tax cost of debt. BHW justify the use of the cost of capital as the discount rate on the basis that investors and creditors, in their valuation of the firm, recognize the difference in tax savings between the two methods. Because investors and creditors determine the overall

[16]"Lease or Borrow: New Method of Analysis," *Harvard Business Review*, 39 (September–October 1961), 138–59.

value of the firm, BHW view the average cost of capital as the appropriate discount rate.[17] Whether investors and creditors evaluate differences in tax savings in this manner is open to serious doubt. In addition, there is the conceptual problem of the cost of capital depending in part upon the decision to lease or borrow. An inconsistency arises in using the cost of capital as the discount rate to evaluate this decision. While the problem is not important when the project being financed is relatively small, the problem is important if the project is large. In essence, the tax savings that result from a financing decision are evaluated as though they were an investment.

Because of these problems a case can be made for the use of the internal-rate-of-return method proposed in the preceding section. By comparing effective yields for the two financing alternatives, one does not have to choose a discount rate. This approach avoids intermingling investment and financing decisions by treating the problem as one of financing alone. Nonetheless, if differences in taxes are valued in the market at an implied interest rate higher than the effective interest yield computed, the method will give biased results. To the extent that these differences are valued at a rate that approximates the firm's cost of capital, the BHW method would be preferred. Under most circumstances, the two methods will provide identical decisions.

This concludes our presentation of various methods for analyzing leasing versus borrowing. In recent years, a number of articles have been written on this subject, and no attempt is made in this chapter to present all views. By and large, the methods proposed are variations of the three methods presented. In the final section of this chapter, we explore reasons why lease financing might be a thing of value for the corporation and discuss how one can focus one's analysis on the factors that give rise to such value. First, however, we wish to consider two special lease situations and how they might be analyzed using the methods of analysis already described.

ANALYSIS WHEN PURCHASE PRICE DIFFERS FROM CASH-EQUIVALENT PRICE

In the methods of analysis considered so far, we have assumed that the purchase price of the asset is the same to the lessee as it is to the lessor. However, there are situations where the lessor and lessee work from different cost bases; this occurrence requires a special analysis. For example, the manufacturer of a capital asset such as a computer may be

[17]For an analysis of the minor differences between the Vancil and Bower-Herringer-Williamson approaches, see M. Chapman Findlay III, "Financial Lease Evaluation: Survey and Synthesis" (paper presented at the Eastern Finance Association Meetings, Storrs, Conn., April 12, 1973).

willing to sell it outright or to lease it under a noncancelable lease. The selling price for outright purchase may differ from the cash-equivalent price the manufacturer uses to determine lease payments. By varying the selling price relative to the cash-equivalent price or vice versa, the manufacturer can encourage or discourage leasing. Similarly, in a third-party lease, the selling price by the manufacturer to the lessor may be different—usually lower—than the selling price to the potential lessee. To evaluate situations of this sort, the firm should determine the cash-equivalent price used by the lessor. Given this price, the firm then can evaluate leasing versus borrowing with one of the methods described earlier.

To illustrate, suppose that Carter Electronics Corporation is considering acquiring a quality-control testing machine from DSS Manufacturing Company. The purchase price of the machine is $20,000, and it is expected to have an economic life of five years, with no residual value at the end of that time. When Carter Electronics discounts the expected future cash benefits after taxes by the required rate of return, it finds that the present value of these benefits exceeds $20,000. Therefore, acquisition of the machine with an outright purchase is considered worthwhile. However, DSS also offers the company the opportunity to lease the machine for five years, with annual lease payments of $5,189, payable at the end of the year prior to each of the five years. If Carter Electronics believes the interest rate being used by DSS in calculating the lease payments is 9 percent, Carter could compute the cash-equivalent price by solving the following equation for X:

$$X = \sum_{t=0}^{4} \frac{\$5,189}{(1.09)^t}$$

$$X = 5,189(1 + 3.2397) = \$22,000$$

(19-3)

In this equation, 3.2397 is the present value of $1 received at the end of each year for four years. As one payment is made at the end of year 0, we must add one to it. Thus, the cash-equivalent price of $22,000 exceeds the purchase price of $20,000. DSS Manufacturing appears to be discouraging leasing relative to outright purchase.

The difference between the two figures—$2,000—must be incorporated into our analysis of leasing versus borrowing. If the internal-rate-of-return method is used, the schedule of cash flows for the lease alternative should be based on a cost or value of the asset of $20,000 instead of $22,000 and lease payments of $5,189 per year. As the lease payments are higher than they would be if the cash-equivalent price equaled the purchase price of $20,000, the lease alternative will have a higher effective yield than it would have if the two prices were the same. Thus, the difference between the two prices is incorporated in the comparison of effective yields. As before, the preferred method is the one with the lower effective yield. If the BHW method of analysis is used, the difference between the purchase price and the cash-equivalent price is automatically embodied in the financial disadvantage. Because lease payments are higher than they would be if the two prices were the same, the present value of these payments also will be higher. As a result, the financial disadvantage will be greater.

If the cash-equivalent price were less than the purchase price, the two methods of analysis described also would take account of the difference in this direction. Thus, the methods proposed previously allow us to analyze situations where the purchase price of an asset differs from the cash-equivalent price being used by the lessor.

ANALYSIS OF AN ASSET THAT CAN ONLY BE LEASED

Occasionally, the firm must evaluate an asset that can only be acquired by leasing. For example, use of certain dock facilities by ocean freighters can be obtained only through a long-term lease. An alternative purchase price is not available. In situations of this sort, the firm does not choose between leasing or borrowing; the only decision is whether or not to lease. As a result, the investment and financing decisions are inextricably intertwined.

Although no method of analysis is entirely satisfactory, perhaps the best approach is to determine the merit of the project as an investment. The first step is to compute the cash-equivalent price of the lease alternative, beginning by establishing an interest rate that is consistent with other current leasing arrangements. The cash-equivalent price is the present value of all required lease payments discounted by this rate. The next step is to compute the present value of expected future cash benefits associated with the project, discounted at the required rate of return. Obviously, these benefits should be estimated only for the duration of the lease period. If the present value of the expected future cash benefits exceeds the cash-equivalent price, the project is worthwhile, and the firm should enter into the lease.[18] If the present value of the cash benefits is less than the cash-equivalent price, the project should be rejected.

If the project is accepted, obviously it can be financed only by leasing. Implied then in our method of analysis is that lease financing does not alter the firm's cost of capital. In other words, the firm must be able to balance this method of financing with others so that it maintains

[18] We assume that the acceptance of the project does not change the business-risk complexion of the firm (see Part II). Under no circumstances should the lease payments be deducted from the expected cash benefits and the project judged on the basis of whether or not the present value of the residuals is positive.

a desired capital structure. If, for some reason, this balancing is not possible, perhaps because the project is large, then the effect of financing the project on the firm's cost of capital must be taken into account.

THE ECONOMICS OF LEASING

We have saved our discussion of the economics of leasing until the last. Hopefully the reader has acquired an understanding of leasing and how it might be analyzed in relation to debt financing. In this section, we focus on the factors that give rise to leasing's being a thing of value in the capital markets. These are shown to be differences in effective taxes paid by lessors and lessees and differences in the protection afforded the lender and the lessor in bankruptcy. In the end, we will show how a firm can concentrate its evaluation on these factors to determine whether lease financing is appropriate for its situation.

LEASE FINANCING IN PERFECT CAPITAL MARKETS

It is useful to begin by assuming that capital markets are perfect. As taken up in Part III and in other parts of the book, this implies that there are no transaction costs, information is costless and readily available to all, securities are infinitely divisible, there are no bankruptcy costs, and there are no taxes. Under these assumptions, and the implied perfect competition among financial markets that results, it can be shown that the debt and lease obligations of a firm will be valued by lenders and lessors in the same manner.[19] The costs of debt and lease financing will therefore be the same, and the firm would be indifferent between the two as methods of financing.

When we relax the assumptions of perfect capital markets, however, debt and lease instruments may not be valued in the same manner. As a result, their costs to the firm may differ. The introduction of transaction costs, information costs, and less than infinite divisibility of securities results in impediments to arbitraging between financial instruments. However, these imperfections do not have a systematic effect in the sense that they favor leasing or favor debt financing all of the time. Rather, arbitrage between the markets is impeded, and consequently it may be possible for the firm to take "advantage" of the situation by issuing one type of instrument or the other. However, the advantage is likely to be small and extremely difficult to predict in practice. Therefore,

---

[19]In James C. Van Horne, "Leasing as a Form of Financial Intermediation," Research Paper (Stanford Graduate School of Business, 1975), this is demonstrated using a state-preference model. As the model is complicated, it is not presented here. However, the conclusion logically follows from all of our earlier discussion of the impact of the perfect market assumption on the valuation of financial instruments.

we do not concentrate on these imperfections. In contrast, differences in
bankruptcy costs and taxes affect things in a systematic manner and
their effect is predictable as to direction. To these factors we now turn.

Chapter 19 **513**
LEASE FINANCING

BANKRUPTCY COSTS TO THE LENDER OR LESSOR

One "advantage" to a lease relative to debt from the standpoint of a
supplier of capital is that the lessor enjoys a superior position in liquidation.[20] Because the lessor owns the asset, he is able to take it back when
conditions of default occur. Although the lender can secure his loan with
the asset involved, it is more difficult and costly to gain possession of it
in the event of default. As we know from our analysis of capital structure
decisions and liquidity decisions earlier in the book, there are costs
associated with the initiation of bankruptcy proceedings. In addition to
out-of-pocket costs, there are delays to the secured lender in taking over
the asset involved; these delays have an obvious opportunity cost.
Neither the out-of-pocket costs nor the delays affect the lessor nearly to
the extent that they do the secured lender. If the lender has an unsecured loan, of course, he becomes a general creditor in the event of
bankruptcy and the settlements typically are low.

The riskier the firm that seeks financing, the greater the incentive for
the supplier of capital to make the arrangement a lease rather than a
loan. While certain suppliers of capital are either lenders or lessors but
not both, others engage in both types of accommodations. A case in
point is the bank holding company. The author is familiar with situations
where loans have been converted to leases when the risk of default has
increased significantly. The purpose, of course, is simply to improve
one's position should liquidation occur. In the total scheme of things,
there is less "external drain" due to bankruptcy costs with lease financing than there is with debt financing. To the extent that any of the ex ante
costs of bankruptcy avoided by leasing instead of borrowing are passed
on to the lessee in the form of lower lease payments than would otherwise be the case, the firm might have an incentive to lease as opposed to
borrow.[21]

Although the superior position of the lessor in bankruptcy relative to
that of the lender is one reason for the development of the leasing
industry, it is not the dominant one. But it is important and should not be
overlooked, as it often distinguishes a lease from a loan in the eyes of a
supplier of capital. Moreover, the importance of this factor varies over
time. As the default risk of companies in general increases, as it might in

---

[20] See Chapter 24 for a discussion of bankruptcy proceedings.

[21] This advantage may be offset by the fact that leasing sometimes introduces an additional
intermediary with a resulting increment in administrative costs.

a recession, this factor becomes more important. As a result, the incentive for lease financing increases, and we would expect to see a greater amount of it.

THE EFFECT OF DIFFERING TAXES

The dominant economic reason for the existence of leasing, however, is differences in the tax benefits associated with the ownership of an asset among companies, financial institutions, and individuals. The greater the divergence in tax benefits from owning an asset among economic units in an economy, the greater the attraction of lease financing overall, all other things the same. We know from our previous discussion that the tax benefits associated with owning an asset are the investment tax credit, which is realized when the asset is placed into service, and the tax shield afforded by the deduction of depreciation over the depreciable life of the asset.

If the effective tax benefits associated with owning an asset were the same for all economic units in the economy, and if capital markets were perfect in every other way, debt and lease obligations would be valued in the same manner. As a result, their costs would be the same. If the lessor did not pass on all of the tax benefits associated with the ownership of the asset to the prospective lessee in the form of lower lease payments than would otherwise be the case, the prospective lessee could simply purchase the asset and finance it with debt. In this way, it could avail itself of all of the tax benefits. Therefore, it is not the existence of taxes *per se* which gives rise to leasing being a thing of value, but it is due to a situation where different companies, financial institutions, and individuals have different abilities to realize the tax benefits associated with owning an asset.

Such differences are due to (1) different tax rates among economic units in the economy and (2) different levels of past and current income among economic units. Examples of the former include differences in personal and corporate income tax rates, as well as differences in tax rates among various individuals and corporations. An example of the latter is a company with a tax-loss carry forward which pays little or no taxes on profits. Another example is a situation where the investment tax credit is so large that it exceeds the taxes that the firm otherwise would pay. As a result, part of the tax credit goes unutilized.

To the extent that a firm that pays little or no taxes is able to lease an asset from another party that pays high taxes, it may be able to avail itself of part of the tax benefits associated with ownership through lease payments that are lower than they would otherwise be. In turn, the lessor is able to use the full tax credit which might not otherwise be available to it. As a result, both parties gain.

Example of the analysis of divergent tax benefits

To illustrate, suppose that W. Barclay and Company, a food producer and processor, wishes to acquire the use of a large and highly sophisticated crop bundler, which has an economic life of eight years. No salvage value is expected at the end of that time. The machine and electronic accessories cost $1 million and are subject to a 7 percent investment tax credit, or $70,000 at the outset. Unfortunately, Barclay has had several loss years and currently has a tax-loss carry forward of $200,000, which can be applied against future profits up to five years. If unutilized, the tax credit may be carried forward for a period up to seven years.

Suppose further that Barclay has entered into a contract to supply corn at a price that guarantees Barclay a profit over the next eight years. These before-tax profits are as follows, and they are expected with a high degree of certainty:[22]

			Profit (in thousands)				
19—1	19—2	19—3	19—4	19—5	19—6	19—7	19—8
$100	$120	$140	$170	$200	$250	$300	$300

Barclay is considering financing the machine either with debt or with lease financing, both from the Third National Bank of Wabash, Indiana. If debt, the rate would be 10 percent and the loan would be payable $170,404 annually at the beginning of each of the next eight years.[23] In other words, payments are due in advance, the same as with leasing. The schedule of debt payments is shown in Table 19-7. Because of the

Table 19·7 Schedule of debt payments for Barclay and Company example

End of Year	Interest Plus Principal Payments	Principal Amount Owing at End of Year	Annual Interest
19_0	$170,404	$829,596	$ 0
19_1	170,404	742,152	82,960
19_2	170,404	645,963	74,215
19_3	170,404	540,155	64,596
19_4	170,404	423,767	54,016
19_5	170,404	295,740	42,377
19_6	170,404	154,910	29,574
19_7	170,404	0	15,491

[22] Profit projections assume the machine in question is acquired, but they do not include financing charges associated with its acquisition or depreciation charges.

[23] This amount is computed in the same manner as Eq. (19-1), using a 10 percent rate and eight years.

Table 19·8 Cash outflows for Barclay and Company using a loan

End of Year	(1) Loan Payment	(2) Interest	(3) Depreciation SYD	(4) Expected Profit before Interest and Depreciation	(5) Expected Profit after Interest and Depreciation (4) − (2) − (3)
19_0	$170,404	$ 0			
19_1	170,404	82,960	$222,222	$100,000	$(205,182)
19_2	170,404	74,215	194,444	120,000	(148,659)
19_3	170,404	64,596	166,667	140,000	(91,263)
19_4	170,404	54,016	138,889	170,000	(22,905)
19_5	170,404	42,377	111,111	200,000	46,512
19_6	170,404	29,574	83,333	250,000	137,093
19_7	170,404	15,491	55,555	300,000	228,954
19_8	—	—	27,778	300,000	272,222

advanced payments, the amount owed at time 0 is $1,000,000 − $170,404 = $829,596.

Assume that the tax rate for corporations is 22 percent on the first $25,000 in income and 48 percent on amounts in excess of $25,000. We then show in Table 19-8 tax and loan payment cash outflows for Barclay and Company over the next eight years. Because no taxes are expected to be paid until the eighth year, the investment tax credit of $70,000 expires and, consequently, goes unutilized. Moreover, because of the previous tax-loss carry forward as well as negative profits for the first several years, the company is unable to fully utilize the tax advantages associated with depreciation and interest payments on the debt. As shown, part of the tax-loss carry forward expires in 19__5, so the firm loses altogether some of the tax advantage. In other words, the tax benefit is not merely postponed, which works to one's disadvantage on a present-value basis, but part of it is lost forever.

In contrast, the Third National Bank, which has agreed to make the loan at a 10 percent rate, is not similarly affected. The bank is very profitable, and its marginal tax rate is 48 percent. If it were to buy the asset and lease it to Barclay and Company, it would be able to reap the full advantage of the investment tax credit and accelerated depreciation. The tax benefits to the bank on a cash basis arising from the arrangement would be those shown in Table 19-9. From this table, it is obvious that the bank could charge a rate of interest much lower than 10 percent if it were to lease to the company as opposed to lending it money.

Suppose, for example, that the bank agreed to charge an implied rate of interest of 2 percent. This corresponds to annual lease payments of $133,833, payable at the beginning of each of the next eight years.[24]

---

[24] As before, this amount is computed using Eq. (19-1).

Table 19·8 (cont.)

(6)	(7)	(8)	(9)	(10)
Tax-Loss Carry Forward Utilized	Remaining Tax-Loss Carry Forward	Expected Taxable Income	Expected Taxes†	Cash Outflows (1) + (9)
	$200,000			$170,404
—	405,182	$ 0	—	170,404
—	553,841	0	—	170,404
—	645,104	0	—	170,404
—	668,009	0	—	170,404
$46,512	468,009*	0	—	170,404
137,093	262,827*	0	—	170,404
228,954	33,873	0	—	170,404
33,873	0	238,349	$107,908	107,908

* At the end of five years, the unutilized carry forward expires.
† 22 percent on first $25,000; 48 percent on profits above that.

The after-tax cash flows to the bank arising from such a lease are shown in Table 19-10. These cash flows are comprised of lease receipts plus tax benefits, less the taxes paid on interest earnings. The internal rate of return for the cash flows shown in the last column of the table is 17.20 percent. Thus, with an initial cash outlay of $796,167, ($1 million less the initial lease receipt of $133,833 less the investment tax credit of $70,000), the bank is able to earn a return of 17.20 percent after taxes.

This return compares with an after-tax return of .10(1 − .48) = 5.20 percent for a loan involving an initial cash outlay of $829,596, ($1 million less the initial loan payment of $170,404). Obviously, it is better off with the lease even though the implied interest rate embodied in the lease receipts is much less than the explicit interest rate on the loan. The reason is that the bank is able to avail itself of the investment tax credit

Table 19·9 Schedule of tax benefits to the lessor—Third National Bank

End of Year	(1) Investment Tax Credit	(2) Accelerated Depreciation	(3) Tax Shield (2) × 0.48	(4) After-Tax Cash Benefits (1) + (3)
19_0	$70,000			$70,000
19_1	—	$222,222	$106,667	106,667
19_2	—	194,444	93,333	93,333
19_3	—	166,667	80,000	80,000
19_4	—	138,889	66,667	66,667
19_5	—	111,111	53,333	53,333
19_6	—	83,333	40,000	40,000
19_7	—	55,555	26,666	26,666
19_8	—	27,778	13,333	13,333

Table 19·10   Schedule of cash flows to the lessor—Third National Bank

End of Year	(1) Purchase of Asset	(2) Lease Receipts	(3) Interest Portion of Lease Receipt	(4) Taxes on Interest (3) × 0.48	(5) Cash Benefits* after Taxes	(6) Cash Flows after Taxes (1) + (2) − (4) + (5)
19_0	$(1,000,000)	$133,833			$ 70,000	$(796,167)
19_1	—	133,833	$17,323	$8,315	106,667	232,185
19_2	—	133,833	14,993	7,197	93,333	219,969
19_3	—	133,833	12,616	6,056	80,000	207,777
19_4	—	133,833	10,192	4,892	66,667	195,608
19_5	—	133,833	7,719	3,705	53,333	183,461
19_6	—	133,833	5,197	2,495	40,000	171,338
19_7	—	133,833	2,624	1,260	26,666	159,239
19_8	—	—	—	—	13,333	13,333

*From Table 19-9.

and the tax benefits associated with accelerated depreciation. These are not available to it in the case of a loan.[25]

Barclay and Company also benefits from the lease arrangement in that the present value of its incremental cash outflows is lower than it is with the loan. In Table 19-11, the cash outflows under the lease arrangement are shown.[26] When the cash outflows in column (8) are related to the purchase price of $1 million at time 0, the internal rate of return is

Table 19·11   Cash outflows for Barclay and Company using a lease

End of Year	(1) Lease Payment	(2) Expected Profit before Lease Payments	(3) Expected Profit after Lease Payments (2) − (1)	(4) Tax-Loss Carry Forward Utilized	(5) Remaining Tax-Loss Carry Forward	(6) Expected Taxable Income	(7) Expected Taxes†	(8) Cash Outflow (1) + (7)
19_0	$133,833				$200,000			$133,833
19_1	133,833	$100,000	$(33,833)	—	233,833	$ 0	$ 0	133,833
19_2	133,833	120,000	(13,833)	—	247,666	0	0	133,833
19_3	133,833	140,000	6,167	$6,167	241,499	0	0	133,833
19_4	133,833	170,000	36,167	36,167	205,332	0	0	133,833
19_5	133,833	200,000	66,167	66,167	47,666*	0	0	133,833
19_6	133,833	250,000	116,167	47,666	0	68,501	26,380	160,213
19_7	133,833	300,000	166,167	0	0	166,167	73,260	207,093
19_8	—	300,000	300,000	0	0	300,000	137,500	137,500

*At the end of five years, the unutilized carry forward expires.
†22 percent on first $25,000; 48 percent on profits above that.

[25] In this analysis, we ignore the fact that in the event of bankruptcy, the bank enjoys a better position as a lessor than it does as a lender. This factor makes leasing even more attractive.

[26] One might note that while part of the loss carry forward expires, much less expires than in the case of the loan (Table 19-8).

found to be 6.95 percent. This rate compares with an internal rate of return for the cash outflows under the loan arrangement (column (10) of Table 19-8) of 11.29 percent. Thus, Barclay is better off with lease financing than it is with debt financing.

The relative advantage is due to the fact that the company is unable to avail itself of the investment tax credit and some of the accelerated depreciation tax benefits associated with owning the asset. In turn, this is caused by poor earnings in the past and the low earnings projected in the near future. As the Third National Bank is able to avail itself of all the tax benefits associated with ownership, it is willing to pass some of them on to Barclay and Company in the form of lower lease payments than would otherwise be the case. In this situation, the company should go with lease as opposed to debt financing.

A SUMMING UP

This example illustrates how both the lessee and the lessor can gain through a lease-financing arrangement. While the example is purposely extreme, it illustrates the principal economic foundation for the existence of leasing and the leasing industry. Again, this reason is differences among companies, financial institutions, and individuals in their ability to realize the tax benefits associated with owning an asset. Leasing permits the firm with little such ability to realize a greater portion of these benefits than it is able to do on its own. How much greater a realization depends upon the supply and demand for lease financing among economic units in the economy.

A lessor is unlikely to give up all of the tax benefits because realization of such benefits by the company seeking financing depends on its favorable tax situation. By the same token, competition among lessors will assure that part of the benefits will be transferred to the lessee in the form of lower lease payments than would otherwise be the case. The exact sharing of the tax benefits is negotiable, but it will depend on equilibrium conditions in the capital markets. Our example showed how a firm can concentrate its analysis on the important tax considerations when approaching the question of whether to lease or borrow.

For the consistently profitable company, lease financing may make little sense. To the extent that a third-party lessor is involved, an added financial intermediary is introduced. This additional intermediation adds administrative costs which must be passed off to the lessee. As a result, lease financing may be more costly than debt financing. For the marginally profitable firm or for the firm that has had a temporary setback and expects to pay little in the way of taxes in the near future, however, lease financing may hold substantial promise. The economic benefits passed off to the lessee are reflected in the amount of periodic lease payments relative to the cost of the asset involved, or simply the implied interest cost. By concentrating on this cost and the economic benefits associated with leasing relative to those for borrowing, a firm is able to determine whether lease financing is promising, to better "shop around" among lessors, and to better negotiate the lease. Indeed, the decision will be grounded in sound economic reasoning if such an analysis is undertaken.

In the United States, a sophisticated market has developed in the leasing of such large and expensive assets as airplanes, ships, railroad cars, and computers. Commercial banks, because of their profitability and relatively high tax brackets, have come to dominate the field as lessors. As would be expected, the lessees of such assets are primarily companies that have relatively low profitability and are unable to take full advantage of the tax benefits. Perhaps the most important illustration of this arrangement is the lease financing of jet airplanes by airlines. The profitability of these companies has been relatively low or negative in recent years, and therefore they are unable to take full advantage of the tax benefits available, particularly the investment tax credit. Lease financing enables them to realize a significant portion of these benefits. In addition to commercial banks, partnerships of high-tax-bracketed individuals are frequently formed to buy an asset and lease it to a company. This form of arrangement has grown in importance in recent years, and we can expect it to continue.

Although divergent tax situations among companies, financial institutions, and individuals are the principal foundation on which the leasing industry rests, we should not lose track of the superior position of the lessor relative to that of the lender in bankruptcy. This factor also has contributed to the growth of lease financing. Together these factors are reflected in differences in the "true" cost between lease and debt financing, a comparison that the reader should now be in a position to make.

SUMMARY

Lease financing involves the acquisition of the economic use of an asset through a contractual commitment to make periodic lease payments to a lessor who owns the asset. Because of this contractual obligation, leasing is regarded as a method of financing similar to borrowing. Leasing can involve the direct acquisition of an asset under a lease, a sale and leaseback arrangement whereby the firm sells an asset it owns and leases it back from the buyer, or a leveraged lease.

Several methods were analyzed for evaluating lease financing in relation to debt financing. The decision to lease or borrow can be made on the basis of which alternative has the lowest present value of cash outflows or the lowest after-tax internal rate of return. Because the latter does not require specifying a discount rate, it is preferred by many. Another method of analysis calls for the separation of differences in explicit financing costs from differences in taxes, with the two methods of financing compared according to their present values. Consideration was given to situations in which the purchase price of the asset differs from its cash-equivalent price under leasing, and also to the case where leasing is the only means by which an asset can be acquired.

In the final section, we took up the economics of leasing. The foundation for the growth in leasing was shown to be (1) differences in the protection afforded the lessor and the lender in the event of bankruptcy, and (2) differences in the ability of companies, financial institutions, and individuals to take advantage of the tax benefits associated with owning an asset. The impact of both of these factors varies over time with changes in perceived default risk, in bankruptcy costs, in federal, state, and local tax rates, and in the overall profitability of companies. As a result, the relative importance of lease financing in the economy can change over time.

Of the two factors, the second is by far the more important, and we concentrated our attention on it. It was shown that firms that pay low taxes may be able to reap significant economic benefit from lease as opposed to debt financing. By leasing an asset from a lessor that pays substantial taxes, the firm is able to realize part of the tax benefits associated with the investment tax credit and accelerated depreciation through lease payments that are lower than would otherwise be the case. It was shown that both parties can gain by the lease arrangement. A framework was presented for analyzing the incremental tax benefits that may be achieved through lease as opposed to debt financing. By concentrating one's attention on the important economic variables, far more rational decisions are possible with respect to lease financing than those that have been based on the "accounting" effect or on the "sales pitch" of many a leasing company.

PROBLEMS

1. The Carver Paper Company has decided to acquire a $300,000 pulp quality control device, which has a useful life of ten years after which no salvage value is expected. The device would be depreciable on a sum-of-the-years'-digits basis with $^{10}/_{55}$ depreciation in the first year, $^{9}/_{55}$ in the second, down to $^{1}/_{55}$ in the last year. The investment tax credit is in effect, and a 7 percent credit is applicable at the time the device is acquired and placed into service.

The company is trying to determine whether it is better to finance the acquisition with debt or with a lease arrangement. If debt, the interest rate would be 10 percent and debt payments would be due at the very beginning of each of the ten years. The company is in a 50 percent tax bracket. If the acquisition is financed with a lease, lease payments of $33,000 would be required at the beginning of each year.

What is the present value of cash outflows for each of these financing alternatives, using the after-tax cost of debt? Which alternative is preferable?

2. The Kraus Corporation, which has a 40 percent tax rate, wishes to acquire a $100,000 stamping machine, which would be depreciated on a straight-line basis with an eight-year life and no salvage value. An investment tax credit of 7 percent is available at the time the asset is acquired. It would be possible to lease the machine for $15,000 per year, payable in advance; it also would be possible to borrow at a 10 percent rate. Using an internal-rate-of-return analysis, determine the better alternative.

3. In problem 2, describe what would happen if sum-of-the-years'-digits instead of straight-line depreciation were used. (Merely explain; do not work out.) Describe what would happen if the tax rate were 60 percent instead of 40 percent.

4. **Hardt Corporation balance sheet (in millions)**

Current assets	**$10**
Fixed assets (30 years, straight-line depreciation)	30
Total assets	$40
Current liabilities	$ 5
Long-term debt (8%)	15
Total debt	$20
Net worth	20
Total liabilities	$40

Income Statement

Sales	$100,000,000
Operating income	8,200,000
Depreciation	1,000,000
Interest	1,200,000
Net income before taxes	$ 6,000,000
Taxes (50%)	3,000,000
Net income	$ 3,000,000

The Hardt Corporation is contemplating the sale and leaseback of $10 million of fixed assets. The proceeds would be used to retire debt. The annual lease payments would be $1 million.

(a) Reformulate the financial statements under the assumption that this transaction took place.

(b) Show the effects of this sale upon the following ratios:
   (1) Asset turnover
   (2) Return on assets
   (3) Debt to net worth
   (4) Times interest earned

(c) What is the real impact of this transaction? Has the corporation's fundamental position improved?

5. The Xenia-Youngstown Zipper Company (XYZ) has decided to invest in a computer-controlled measuring device costing $120,000. The device has an economic life of seven years, after which no salvage value is expected. The company must determine whether it is better to finance the acquisition through debt or leasing. XYZ expects profits before taxes of $10,000 next year, $20,000 the following year, $30,000 the third year, and $40,000 each year thereafter (before depreciation on the device). It has a high degree of confidence in these estimates. The tax rate is 22 percent on the first $25,000 in profits and 48 percent on amounts over that. The company has had break-even operations during the previous three years. Finally, the machine is subject to a 7 percent investment tax credit.

If the machine is financed with debt, the Atticks National Bank of Youngstown is willing to extend a loan for the full purchase price at an 11 percent rate of interest payable in equal annual amounts over seven years. The bank also has a leasing division and has indicated that it is willing to lease finance the acquisition for XYZ over the seven-year period. The bank is and has been quite profitable, and it is in a 48 percent tax bracket. Describe in words whether lease or debt financing is likely to be more favorable for XYZ. Why? Is the bank likely to want to accommodate the company more on a lease basis or on a debt basis?

SELECTED REFERENCES

Accounting for Leases Exposure Draft. Stamford, Conn.: Financial Accounting Standards Board, August 26, 1975.

Beechy, Thomas H., "The Cost of Leasing: Comment and Correction," *Accounting Review,* 45 (October 1970), 769–73.

——, "Quasi-Debt Analysis of Financial Leases," *Accounting Review,* 44 (April 1969), 375–81.

Bower, Richard S., "Issues in Lease Financing," *Financial Management,* 2 (Winter 1973), 25–34.

Bower, Richard S., Frank C. Herringer, and J. Peter Williamson, "Lease Evaluation," *Accounting Review,* 41 (April 1966), 257–65.

Cooper, Kerry, and Robert H. Strawser, "Evaluation of Capital Investment Projects Involving Asset Leases," *Financial Management,* 4 (Spring 1975), 44–49.

Doenges, R. Conrad, "The Cost of Leasing," *Engineering Economist,* 17 (Fall 1971), 31–44.

Elam, Rick, "The Effect of Lease Data on the Predictive Ability of Financial Ratios," *Accounting Review,* 50 (January 1975), 25–43.

"FASB Discussion Memorandum: Accounting for Leases," Stamford, Conn.: Financial Accounting Standards Board, July 2, 1974.

Ferrara, William L., "Should Investment and Financing Decisions Be Separated?" *Accounting Review,* 41 (January 1966), 106–14.

Ferrara, William L., and Joseph F. Wojdak, "Valuation of Long-Term Leases," *Financial Analysts Journal,* 25 (November–December 1969), 29–32.

Findlay, M. Chapman, III, "Financial Lease Evaluation: Survey and Synthesis," Paper presented at the Eastern Finance Association Meetings, Storrs, Conn., April 12, 1973.

——, "A Sensitivity Analysis of IRR Leasing Models," *Engineering Economist,* 20 (Summer 1975), 231–42.

Gordon, Myron J., "A General Solution to the Buy or Lease Decision: A Pedagogical Note," *Journal of Finance,* 29 (March 1974).

Gritta, Richard D., "The Impact of the Capitalization of Leases on Financial Analysis," *Financial Analysts Journal,* 30 (March–April 1974), 1–6.

Johnson, Robert W., and Wilbur G. Lewellen, "Analysis of the Lease-or-Buy Decision," *Journal of Finance,* 27 (September 1972), 815–23.

Keller, Thomas F., and Russell J. Peterson, "Optimal Financial Structure, Cost of Capital, and the Lease-or-Buy Decision," *Journal of Business Finance & Accounting,* 1 (Autumn 1974), 405–14.

Mitchell, G. B., "After-Tax Cost of Leasing," *Accounting Review,* 45 (April 1970), 308–14.

Myers, Stewart C., David A. Dill, and Alberto J. Bautista, "An Exact Solution to the Lease vs. Borrow Problem," Research Paper, London Graduate School of Business, 1975.

Packham, E. Richard, "An Analysis of the Risks of Leveraged Leasing," *Journal of Commercial Bank Lending,* 57 (March 1975), 2–29.

Roenfeldt, Rodney L., and Jerome S. Osteryoung, "Analysis of Financial Leases," *Financial Management,* 2 (Spring 1973), 74–87.

Schall, Lawrence D., "The Lease-or-Buy and Asset Acquisition Decisions," *Journal of Finance,* 29 (September 1974), 1203–14.

Vancil, Richard F., "Lease or Borrow: New Method of Analysis," *Harvard Business Review,* 39 (September–October 1961), 122–36.

Wiar, Robert C., "Economic Implications of Multiple Rates of Return in the Leverage Lease Context," *Journal of Finance,* 28 (December 1973), 1275–86.

Wyman, Harold E., "Financial Lease Evaluation under Conditions of Uncertainty," *Accounting Review,* 48 (July 1973), 489–93.

LONG-TERM FINANCING

VI

INVESTMENT BANKING and COMMON STOCK

In Part III, the focus of our analysis was primarily on the theoretical aspects of long-term financing—both external and internal. By and large, methods of financing were categorized broadly into the equity and nonequity portions of the capital structure of the firm. In this part, we explore in detail the specific methods of external long-term financing. We are concerned with the way a firm employs these various methods, their features, various valuation concepts, and, when appropriate, the integration of certain aspects of a method into the theory discussed previously. This chapter explores the role of investment banking in long-term financing, the institutional aspects of common stock, and the issuance of common stock through a rights offering to existing shareholders. In Chapter 21, we take up long-term bond issues, private placements, and preferred stock, while in Chapter 22 our concern is with convertible securities and warrants.

INTRODUCTION

The raising of funds externally automatically involves a company in the financial markets. Because conditions in these markets affect the cost and availability of alternative methods of financing, obviously the financing decision is affected. By virtue of their interdependence with this decision, the investment and dividend decisions are affected as well. Consequently, it is very important that the financial manager keep abreast of financial market conditions. The more frequent the need of the firm to finance externally, of course, the closer the attention that he will need to pay. Extensive evaluation of interest rates and equity returns in financial markets is beyond the scope of this book; however, such an analysis is available in a supplementary volume.[1]

When a business firm finances its investment in real assets externally, it ultimately obtains funds from savings-surplus economic units in the economy. A savings-surplus unit can be either a business, a household, or a government whose current savings (current income less current consumption) exceeds its investment in real assets for the period under consideration. A savings-deficit unit, on the other hand, is one whose investment in real assets exceeds its current savings. If the investment in real assets always equaled the current savings for all economic units in an economy, there would be no need for any economic unit to obtain funds externally or for money and capital markets. In a modern economy, the investment in real assets for most economic units differs from their savings. Some units save more than they invest; others invest more than they save. As a result, we have money and capital markets. The more diverse these economic units are in their patterns of investment in real assets and savings, the greater the need for

[1] See James C. Van Horne, *The Function and Analysis of Capital Market Rates* (Englewood Cliffs, N.J.: Prentice-Hall, 1970).

financial markets and the greater the amount of financial assets in the economy. Although *ex post* investment must equal *ex post* savings for the economy as a whole, there can be considerable divergence between savings and investment for the individual economic unit.

One of the functions of the money and capital markets is to allocate efficiently the flow of funds from savings-surplus economic units to savings-deficit units. The allocation of these funds occurs primarily on the basis of interest rates—the price of money. The efficiency of a country's money and capital markets is instrumental in the channeling of savings to the most promising investment opportunities and in the growth and development of a viable economy. The more varied the vehicles by which savings can flow from ultimate savers to ultimate users of funds, the more efficient the financial markets of an economy tend to be. In this regard, we are concerned specifically with the way business firms obtain funds—in particular long-term funds—to finance the excess of their investment in real assets over current savings for the period.

Our emphasis will be on the *primary* market for corporate securities; that is, the sale of new securities by the firm to investors. This market differs from the *secondary* market, where existing securities are bought and sold among investors. It is important to understand that a viable secondary market enhances the efficiency of the primary market because it provides marketability to the original investor. As a result, the primary security is more attractive than it would be in the absence of a secondary market. The secondary market also gives management of a company information about the costs of debt and equity funds, providing the backdrop for the valuation concepts advanced in this book. We do not want to leave the impression that the secondary market is unimportant. Our focus in this chapter is simply upon understanding the role of the primary market as it pertains to corporate securities.

INVESTMENT BANKING

The efficient functioning of financial markets requires a number of financial institutions.[2] One of these institutions is the investment banker, who acts as middleman in the distribution of new securities to the public. His principal function is to buy the securities from the company and then resell them to investors. For this service, the investment banker receives the difference, or spread, between the price he pays for the security and the price at which the securities are resold to the public. Because most companies make only occasional trips to the capital market, they are not specialists in the distribution of securities. To sell securities on their own would be both costly and risky. On the other hand, investment banking firms have the know-how, the contacts, and

[2] For a theoretical discussion of the efficiency of financial markets and savings flows, see ibid., Chapters 1 and 2.

the sales organization necessary to do an efficient job of marketing securities to investors. Because they are continually in the business of buying securities from companies and selling them to investors, investment bankers can perform this service at a lower cost than can the individual firm.

Public Offering

COMPETITIVE BIDDING VERSUS NEGOTIATED OFFERING

A security offering through an investment banker to investors other than the firm's own stockholders (known as a public offering) can be either on a competitive bid basis or on a negotiated basis. When new securities are sold by competitive bidding, the company issuing the securities invites bids from investment bankers. Frequently, two or more investment banking firms join together for purposes of bidding on a security issue; the combination is known as a syndicate. The purpose underlying the formation of a syndicate is to spread the risk and to obtain a larger overall selling organization. The issuing company specifies the date that sealed bids will be received, and competing syndicates submit bids at the specified time and place. The syndicate with the highest bid wins the security issue. At that time, it pays the company the difference between its good-faith deposit and the bid price and then attempts to resell the issue at a higher price to investors.

With a negotiated offering, the company issuing the securities selects an investment banking firm and works directly with that firm in determining the essential features of the issue. Together, they discuss and negotiate a price for the security and the timing of the issue. Depending upon the size of the issue, the investment banker may invite other firms to join it in sharing the risk and selling the issue. If a company has satisfactory experience with an investment banking firm, it usually will use the same firm for subsequent security issues.

From the standpoint of the issuing company, the key consideration in deciding between a competitive offering and a negotiated offering is the likely net price paid to it. Advocates of competitive offerings argue that the competition between bidding syndicates results in a higher price to the company and a lower profit spread to the investment banker than does a negotiated offering. For this reason, certain types of companies are required to issue securities on a competitive bid basis. For example, Rule 50 of the Public Utility Holding Company Act of 1935 mandates that utility holding companies receive at least two bids. Similarly, many state public utility commissions require that public utilities in their states issue securities by competitive bidding, unless an exemption is sought by the utility and approved by the commission. In addition, railroads are required by the Interstate Commerce Commission to use competitive bidding in the sale of their securities.

Advocates of negotiated offerings argue that such underwritings allow the investment banker more time to locate investors and to place the issue, which in turn results in a more favorable price than is possible under a competitive bidding situation. In particular, this is said to be important in times of "demoralized" markets where security prices are falling, as well as in the case of a very large issue. In a "demoralized" market, certain investment bankers may refuse to enter into a competitive bid syndicate. Their absence, together with the reluctance of others to bid aggressively, could result in a lower net price to the company than would be the case with a negotiated offering.

Unfortunately, there has been little empirical testing of competitive versus negotiated offerings with respect to corporate securities. Various studies of municipal bonds suggest that the issuer receives a higher net price with competitive bids than with a negotiated offering.[3] Two studies of corporate bonds suggest that the underwriter profit spread is lower for competitive bid offerings than it is for negotiated offerings.[4] In another study of public utility bond issues for the 1961–70 period, it was found that the underwriter spread was lower for the negotiated offering method during periods of unstable market conditions, whereas it was lower for the competitive bid method in stable periods.[5] Overall, then, what limited evidence is available on corporate bonds is mixed and it pertains only to underwriter compensation, not to the net price paid to the company. Intuitively, many would contend that competition should result in a higher price to the company on average. However, we must allow for the difficulty of placing securities in a "demoralized" market.

FUNCTIONS OF THE INVESTMENT BANKER—UNDERWRITING

One of the key functions the investment banker performs is that of bearing risk. When an investment banker buys a security issue, he *underwrites* the sale of the issue by giving the company a check for the

---

[3]Reuben A. Kessel, "A Study of the Effects of Competition in the Tax-Exempt Bond Market," *Journal of Political Economy*, 79 (August 1971), 706–38; Richard R. West, "New Issue Concessions on Municipal Bonds: A Case of Monopsony Pricing," *Journal of Business*, 38 (April 1965), 135–48; and West, "Determinants of Underwriters' Spreads on Tax-Exempt Bond Issues," *Journal of Financial and Quantitative Analysis*, 2 (September 1967), 241–63.

[4]Avery B. Cohan, *Cost of Flotation and Long-Term Corporate Debt* (Chapel Hill, N.C.: University of North Carolina Press, 1961); and Louis H. Ederington, "Uncertainty, Competition, and Costs of Corporate Bond Underwriting," *Journal of Financial Economics*, 2 (March 1975), 71–94. In contrast, Keith B. Johnson, T. Gregory Morton, and M. Chapman Findlay, III, "An Empirical Analysis of the Flotation Cost of Corporate Securities," *Journal of Finance*, 30 (September 1975), 1129–33, do not find the distinction between negotiated and competitive offerings to be significant in explaining flotation costs. Their sample consisted of 160 corporate bond issues during 1971 and 1972.

[5]Gary D. Tallman, David F. Rush, and Ronald W. Melicher, "Competitive versus Negotiated Underwriting Costs of Regulated Industries," *Financial Management*, 3 (Summer 1974), 49–55.

purchase price. At that time, the company is relieved of the risk of not being able to sell the issue to investors at the established price. If the issue does not sell well, either because of an adverse turn in the market or because it is overpriced, the underwriter, and not the company, takes the loss. Thus, the investment banker insures, or underwrites, the risk of adverse market price fluctuations during the period of distribution.

Typically, the investment banker with whom a company discusses the offering does not handle the underwriting alone. In order to spread risk and obtain better distribution, he invites other investment bankers to participate in the offering. The originating house usually is the manager and has the largest participation. Other investment bankers are invited into the syndicate, and their participations are determined primarily on the basis of their ability to sell securities.[6] For the risk-bearing function of the offering, these investment bankers are compensated by an underwriting profit.

Underwriting commission To illustrate the compensation of investment bankers, we turn to an example. Figure 20-1 shows the cover of the prospectus for a $150 million issue of $8\frac{7}{8}$ percent mortgage bonds of Southern California Edison Company. The issue was on a competitive bid basis, and the winning syndicate was comprised of fifty-one investment banking firms. The comanagers, Blyth Eastman Dillon & Co.; Halsey, Stuart & Co.; Kidder, Peabody & Co.; Merrill Lynch, Pierce, Fenner & Smith; and Salomon Brothers had the largest participations—$21.3 million, $10 million, $12 million, $28 million, and $28 million, respectively. Other participations ranged from $8 million down to $150,000. We see in the figure that the syndicate bought the bonds from the company for $147,772,500, or $985.15 per bond. In turn, it priced the bonds to the public at $992.50 per bond, or $148,875,000 in total. The spread of $7.35 per bond represents the gross commission to the syndicate for underwriting the issue, for selling it, and for covering the various expenses incurred.

Of the total spread of $7.35 per bond, $3.35, or 46 percent, represents the gross underwriting profit. The remaining 54 percent represents the selling concession, which we discuss shortly. This breakdown between underwriting and selling profits is typical for corporate bonds. A portion of the gross underwriting profit goes to the originating houses as managers of the offering. Although this figure is not given for the Southern California Edison issue, the typical fee is 15 to 20 percent of the total spread. After the bonds are sold, total underwriting profits less expenses and managers' fee are distributed to members of the syndicate on the basis of their percentage participation. It should be noted that the amount of underwriting profit to a member of a syndicate after expenses

---

[6]For a discussion of the traditions by which syndicates are formed, see Samuel L. Hayes III, "Investment Banking: Power Structure in Flux," *Harvard Business Review*, 49 (March–April 1971), 136–52.

$150,000,000

SOUTHERN CALIFORNIA EDISON COMPANY

8⅞%

FIRST AND REFUNDING MORTGAGE BONDS, SERIES FF, DUE 2000

The New Bonds will be redeemable at the option of the Company on 30 days' notice at prices set forth herein, but are not redeemable prior to March 1, 1980 through funds borrowed by the Company at an effective annual interest cost of less than 9.026%.

Interest Payable September 1 and March 1   Due March 1, 2000

Application will be made to list the New Bonds on the American Stock Exchange. Listing is subject to meeting the requirements of the Exchange including those relating to distribution of the New Bonds.

THESE SECURITIES HAVE NOT BEEN APPROVED OR DISAPPROVED BY THE SECURITIES AND EXCHANGE COMMISSION NOR HAS THE COMMISSION PASSED UPON THE ACCURACY OR ADEQUACY OF THIS PROSPECTUS. ANY REPRESENTATION TO THE CONTRARY IS A CRIMINAL OFFENSE.

	Price to Public(1)	Underwriting Discounts and Commissions(2)	Proceeds to Company(1)(3)
Per Unit	99.250%	0.735%	98.515%
Total	$148,875,000	$1,102,500	$147,772,500

(1) Plus accrued interest from March 1, 1975 to date of delivery and payment.

(2) The Company has agreed to indemnify the several Purchasers against certain civil liabilities, including liabilities under the Securities Act of 1933.

(3) Before deducting expenses payable by the Company estimated at $250,000.

The New Bonds are offered by the several Purchasers named herein subject to prior sale, when, as and if issued and accepted by the Purchasers and subject to their right to reject any orders for the purchase of the New Bonds, in whole or in part. It is expected that the New Bonds will be ready for delivery on or about March 13, 1975, in New York City.

BLYTH EASTMAN DILLON & CO.
INCORPORATED

HALSEY, STUART & CO. INC.
AFFILIATE of BACHE & CO. INCORPORATED

KIDDER, PEABODY & CO.
INCORPORATED

MERRILL LYNCH, PIERCE, FENNER & SMITH
INCORPORATED

SALOMON BROTHERS

The date of this Prospectus is March 6, 1975.

FIG. 20·1   *Prospectus of the Southern California Edison Company*

and the managers' fee is not particularly large. In our example, it probably is around $2 a bond. The principal reward from participation comes from selling the securities.

Divided and undivided accounts
Underwriting syndicates can be of two types: divided and undivided. A *divided account* is one in which the liability of members is limited to their percentage participation. If the member sells all the securities alloted to him under his participation, he has no liability, regardless of whether or not other members are able to sell their allotments. With an *undivided account,* each member is liable for his percentage participation in the unsold securities of the syndicate, regardless of the number of securities the individual member sells. If a member of a syndicate has a 20 percent participation in an offering involving 40,000 bonds, and 10,000 remain unsold at the termination of the syndicate, the member would be responsible for 2,000 bonds. His liability would be the same whether he had sold 20,000 bonds or none. It is important to recognize that virtually all syndicates involved in corporate securities are undivided. The principal use of divided accounts is in municipal securities.

Best efforts offering
Instead of underwriting a security issue, an investment banker may sell the issue on a *best efforts* basis. Under this arrangement, the investment banker agrees only to sell as many securities as he can at an established price. The investment banker has no responsibility for securities that are unsold. In other words, he bears no risk. Investment bankers frequently are unwilling to underwrite a security issue of a small company. For these companies, the only feasible means by which to place securities may be through a best efforts offering.

Making a market
On occasion, the underwriter will make a market for a security after it is issued. In the case of a public offering of common stock for the first time, making a market is extremely important to investors. In making a market, the underwriter maintains a position in the stock and stands ready to buy and sell it at bid and ask prices he quotes. These quotations are based upon underlying supply and demand conditions. With a secondary market, the stock has greater liquidity to investors; this appeal enhances the success of the original offering.

SELLING THE SECURITIES

The second major function of the investment banker is that of selling the securities to investors. As we discussed earlier, investment bankers are invited into syndicates and their participations are determined primarily on the basis of their ability to distribute securities. For this function, an investment banker is rewarded by a selling concession of so many dollars a bond. In the case of the Southern California Edison offering, the selling concession was $4 per bond, or 54 percent of the total spread of $7.35. The ultimate seller can be either a member of the underwriting syndicate or a qualified outside security dealer. In order to earn the full concession, however, he must be a member of the syndicate. An outside security dealer must purchase the bond(s) from a member, obtaining only a dealer concession, which is less than the full selling concession. In our example, the outside dealer concession was $2.50 per bond out of a total selling concession of $4.00.

In a negotiated offering, the underwriters begin to line up prospective buyers before the actual offering date. A preliminary prospectus stating certain facts about the issue and the company is printed and given to interested investors. At this time, a price has not been established for the securities; the prospectus is known as a "red herring" because it contains, printed in red, a statement to the effect that a registration statement has been filed with the Securities and Exchange Commission but has not as yet been approved. Upon approval of the registration, the offering price to the public is established, and a final prospectus is printed. At that time, security salesmen seek orders from investors. If the issue is priced fairly, it will be sold within a matter of a day or two or, perhaps, even within a few hours. Sometimes "hot" issues are sold out in advance to preorder subscribers. Upon the sale of all the securities, the underwriting syndicate is dissolved.

ADVISING

In a negotiated offering, such as our example, the originating house is able to advise the company on a wide variety of matters pertinent to the success of the offering. For a company that makes infrequent trips to the capital markets, this advice can be very valuable, for the matters considered include the timing of the issue, its pricing, and features that are desirable to assure a successful sale. Because of his expertise and experience in the market, the investment banker is able to recommend the best package of terms for the particular issue under consideration. When the sale of securities is by competitive bid, the issuer does not receive the benefit of this advice because the underwriter enters the picture only after the bid is accepted and the price determined. Advice from investment bankers may be of a continuing nature, with the company consulting a certain investment banker or a group of bankers regularly.

In a negotiated offering, the issuing company and the investment banker determine the price. The investment banker would like to see a price low enough to assure a successful sale, but he is aware that if the price is too low, the issuing company will be dissatisfied. An investment banker can ill afford dissatisfied customers, for news of such dissatisfaction spreads quickly in the financial community. Moreover, the issuing company must agree to the price recommended by the underwriter. Otherwise, of course, there can be no offering.

In the case of bonds, the issue will be priced in relation to the price of other new issues of the same grade. For example, if the bond being issued were rated Baa, comparisons would be made with other Baa new issues. The underwriter and the issuing company must assess the tone of the market with respect to expectations as to future interest rates. In addition to recent interest rate movements in the money and capital markets, they consider the forthcoming supply of new issues, the expected future of the economy, and expectations as to monetary and fiscal policy. Typically, a new issue will have to be sold at a lower price and higher yield to maturity than a seasoned issue of the same maturity and grade. In a competitive bidding situation, the syndicate will consider these same factors in determining the bid it will submit.[7] The syndicate wants to submit a bid high enough to win the issue but low enough to be able to sell the issue readily to investors. For the negotiated issue, the underwriter wants a price that is high enough to satisfy the issuer but low enough to make the probability of a successful sale to investors reasonably high.

For a common-stock issue, the problem of pricing is perhaps more difficult because of the greater volatility of the stock market. When a company already has stock outstanding that is held by the public, the principal factor that governs the price of any new issue is the market price of the existing stock. The new issue will need to be underpriced in order to sell, however. The degree of underpricing will depend upon the volatility of the stock and the tone of the market. When it becomes known in the marketplace that a company is going to offer new stock, downward pressure usually is exerted on the market price of the outstanding stock. This pressure reflects investors' concern over dilution in earnings per share. Pressure usually develops on the day the new issue is announced, or before, if rumors of the new issue are out. This pressure contributes to the problem of underpricing the issue properly. With a negotiated offering where stock already is held by the public, the price usually is not established until the night before the offering.

[7] See Ernest Bloch, "Pricing a Corporate Bond Issue: A Look Behind the Scenes," *Essays in Money and Credit,* Federal Reserve Bank of New York (December 1964), pp. 72–76.

If a company is issuing stock to the public for the first time, the pricing problem is much more difficult because there is no current market price to serve as a benchmark. For privately held companies that are going public, a comparison with similar companies usually is made to determine the appropriate price/earnings ratio. For this comparison, regression studies and other types of statistical analyses may be helpful. However, some companies may be so specialized that comparison with other companies is very difficult. The pricing of these issues is usually resolved by consideration of such essentials as present earnings, the growth rate, the volatility of earnings, and the company's underlying risk to investors. For a company going public for the first time, the underwriter and the company may agree on a price well before the offering. Because there is no secondary market for existing shares, it is not necessary to delay pricing to the last minute.[8]

It is important to recognize that there exists a tradeoff between the price per share to the public and the underwriting spread. The higher the price, the greater the risk that the investment banker will be unable to sell the entire issue or that the distribution period will be prolonged. As a result of this greater risk, greater compensation is needed in the form of the spread between the price paid to the company and the reoffering price to the public.[9] The important thing to the company, of course, is the net price it is paid by the underwriter. In addition to this factor, it has been found that the underwriter spread varies inversely with the number of bidders and with the size of the issue. The first relationship is attributable to increased competition, while the second is due to economies of scale in underwriting.[10]

FLOTATION COSTS

The flotation costs of a new issue of securities tend to vary with the size and the type of the issue. These costs include the underwriting spread, registration expenses, and other out-of-pocket expenses. Unfortunately, we have little in the way of empirical evidence on flotation costs. The results of a survey for the 1963–65 period showed that the larger the issue, the lower the cost of flotation as a percentage of gross

---

[8] For an analysis of the price performance and return to investors on new issues of common stock, see J. G. McDonald and A. K. Fisher, "New-Issue Stock Price Behavior," *Journal of Finance,* 27 (March 1972), 97–102.

[9] For an empirical investigation of this tradeoff with respect to unseasoned issues of common stock, see Dennis E. Logue and John R. Lindvall, "The Behavior of Investment Bankers: An Econometric Investigation," *Journal of Finance,* 29 (March 1974), 203–15.

[10] For a theoretical investigation of the relationship between underwriter uncertainty in bidding for an issue, the offer price, and the underwriter spread, as well as an empirical test of the interrelationship, see Louis H. Ederington, "Uncertainty, Competition, and Costs in Corporate Bond Underwriting," *Journal of Financial Economics,* 2 (March 1975), 71–94.

in particular—essentially are fixed, the larger the issue, the lower their
percentage cost. The underwriter also has certain "fixed" expenses.
Thus, the larger the issue, the smaller the underwriting expense percentagewise. Additionally and more importantly, there usually is an
inverse relationship between the size of an issue and the quality of the
issuing company. The study also showed that the relative cost of flotation is highest for a common-stock issue and lowest for a debt issue—a
fact not surprising in view of the differences in underwriting risk.

In a more recent study, Keith B. Johnson, T. Gregory Morton, and
M. Chapman Findlay, III, used a large sample of corporate bond and
common stock issues during the years 1971 and 1972 to test certain
explanatory variables.[12] With flotation costs as the dependent variable,
they found that the size of the issuer was the most significant variable in
both cases (the larger the issuer, the lower the flotation costs percentagewise). For bond issues, other significant variables were a surrogate
for seasoning, a risk surrogate, whether or not warrants were attached,
and variables for the type of offering (direct placement, underwriting, or
best efforts). For stock issues, other significant variables were the type of
offering (underwriting or rights offering), and variables reflecting seasoning.

GOVERNMENT REGULATIONS

Both the federal and state governments regulate the sale of new
securities to the public. A company issuing securities must comply with
these regulations. Of the two regulatory bodies, the federal authority is
far more encompassing in its influence.

**Federal
regulation**
With the collapse of the stock market in 1929 and
the subsequent depression, there came a cry for the
protection of investors from misinformation and
fraud. Congress undertook extensive investigations and, in the end,
proposed federal regulation of the securities industry. The Securities Act
of 1933 dealt with the sale of new securities and required the full
disclosure of information to investors. The Securities Exchange Act of
1934 dealt with the regulation of securities already outstanding. More-

[11] *Cost of Flotation of Registered Equity Issues, 1963–65,* Securities and Exchange Commission (Washington, D.C.: Government Printing Office, March 1970); and Irwin Friend, James
R. Longstreet, Morris Mendelson, Ervin Miller, and Arleigh P Hess, Jr., *Investment Banking
and the New Issues Market* (Cleveland: World Publishing, 1967), pp. 408–09. For an earlier
study, see Avery Cohan, *Cost of Flotation of Long-Term Corporate Debt since 1935* (Chapel
Hill, N.C.: University of North Carolina Press, 1961).

[12] "An Empirical Analysis of the Flotation Cost of Corporate Securities," *Journal of
Finance,* 30 (September 1975), 1129–33.

over, it created the Securities and Exchange Commission to enforce the two acts.

Almost all corporations selling securities to the public must register the issue with the SEC. Certain types of corporations, such as railroads, are exempt because they are regulated by other authorities. In addition, a corporation selling $300,000 or less in new securities is required to file only a limited amount of information with the SEC. Other corporations, however, must file a detailed registration statement, which contains such information as the nature and history of the company, the use of the proceeds of the security issue, financial statements, the management and directors and their security holdings, competitive conditions and risks, legal opinions, and a description of the security being issued. Along with the registration statement, the corporation must file a copy of the *prospectus*, which is a summary of the essential information in the registration statement. As mentioned previously, this prospectus is known as a "red herring" because it has not yet been approved by the SEC. The prospectus must be available to prospective investors and others who request it.

The SEC reviews the registration statement and the prospectus to see that all the required information is presented and that it is not misleading. If the SEC is satisfied with the information, it approves the registration, and the company then is able to sell the securities. If not, it issues a *stop order*, which prevents the sale of the securities. Most deficiencies can be corrected by the company, and approval will usually be given eventually, except in cases of fraud or misrepresentation. For serious violations of the 1933 Securities Act, the SEC is empowered to go to court and seek an injunction. It should be pointed out that the SEC is not concerned with the investment value of the securities being issued, only with the presentation of complete and accurate information. The investor must make his own decision based upon that information. The security being issued may well be a highly speculative one subject to considerable risk. As long as the information is correct, the SEC will not prevent its sale.

The minimum period required between the time a registration statement is filed and the time it becomes effective is twenty days, sometimes known as a "cooling-off" period. During this time, investors can evaluate the information in the prospectus and reach a decision. The usual time lapse, however, is longer, around forty days.

The SEC regulates the sale of securities in the secondary markets in addition to the sale of new issues. In this regard, it regulates the activities of the security exchanges, the over-the-counter market, investment bankers and brokers, the National Association of Security Dealers, and investment companies. In its regulatory capacity, the SEC seeks to prevent fraudulent practices, excessive commissions, and other abuses affecting the investment public.

State regulation Individual states have security commissions that regulate the issuance of new securities in their states. Like the SEC, these commissions seek to prevent the fraudulent sale of securities. The laws providing for state regulation of securities are known as "blue-sky" laws, because they attempt to prevent the false promotion and sale of securities representing nothing more than "blue sky." State regulations are particularly important when the amount of the issue is $300,000 or less and not subject to the rigorous scrutiny of the SEC. Unfortunately, the laws of the individual states vary greatly in their effectiveness. Some states are strict, but others are fairly permissive, with the result that misrepresentative promotion can thrive.

INSTITUTIONAL ASPECTS OF COMMON STOCK

The common stockholders of a corporation are its residual owners; collectively, they own the company and assume the ultimate risk associated with ownership. Their liability, however, is restricted to the amount of their investment. In the event of liquidation, these stockholders have a residual claim on the assets of the company after the claims of all creditors and preferred stockholders are settled in full. Common stock, like preferred stock, has no maturity date, and a stockholder can liquidate his investment by selling his stock in the secondary market.

FEATURES OF COMMON STOCK

Authorized, issued, and outstanding shares The corporate charter of a company specifies the number of *authorized* shares of common stock, the maximum that the company can issue without amending its charter. Although amending the charter is not a difficult procedure, it does require the approval of existing stockholders, which takes time. For this reason, a company usually likes to have a certain number of shares that are authorized but unissued. These unissued shares allow flexibility in granting stock options, pursuing mergers, and splitting the stock. When authorized shares of common stock are sold, they become *issued* stock. *Outstanding* stock is the number of shares issued that actually are held by the public; the corporation can buy back part of its issued stock and hold it as *Treasury* stock.

Par value A share of common stock can be authorized either with or without par value. The par value of a stock is merely a stated figure in the corporate charter and is of little economic significance. However, a company should not issue stock at a price less than par value, because stockholders are liable to creditors for the difference between the price they paid and the par value. Consequently, the par values of most stocks are set at fairly low figures relative to their market values. Suppose a company sold 10,000 shares of new common stock at $45 a share and that the par value of the stock was $5 per share. The equity portion of the balance sheet would be:

Common stock ($5 par value)	$ 50,000
Capital surplus	400,000
Net worth	$450,000

Stock can be authorized without par value, in which case the stock is carried on the books at the market price at which it is sold or at some stated value. The difference between the issuing price and the stated value is reflected as capital surplus.

Book value and liquidating value

The book value of a share of stock is the net worth of a corporation less the par value of preferred stock outstanding, divided by the number of shares outstanding. Suppose the equity portion of the balance sheet of a company is as follows:

Preferred stock ($100 par value)	$10,000,000
Common stock ($5 par value)	5,000,000
Capital surplus	10,000,000
Retained earnings	16,000,000
Net worth	$41,000,000

The book value of a share of common stock is $31 million/1 million shares = $31 per share. Theoretically, the book value of a share of stock should correspond to the liquidating value of the company, but this situation seldom occurs. Only if the assets of a corporation can be liquidated for the book values shown on the financial statement will book value per share correspond to the liquidating value per share. Even then, if liquidating costs are high, the liquidating value per share will be less than book value per share. For most companies, the liquidating value per share is less than book value per share because many of the assets can be liquidated only at distress prices. However, some companies carry certain assets—notably, land and mineral rights—at modest values on their books relative to the market value of the asset. For these companies, the liquidating value per share may be significantly higher than the book value. Sometimes investors calculate the net working capital per share in order to obtain a more conservative estimate of the possible liquidating value of a company.

RIGHTS OF STOCKHOLDERS

**Right
to income**
Common stockholders are entitled to share in the earnings of the company only if cash dividends are paid. Stockholders prosper from the market value appreciation of their stock, but they are entirely dependent upon the board of directors for the declaration of dividends that give them income from the company. Thus, we see that the position of a common stockholder differs markedly from that of a creditor. If the company fails to pay contractual interest and principal payments to creditors, the creditors are able to take legal action to assure that payment is made or the company is liquidated. Stockholders, on the other hand, have no legal recourse to a company for not distributing profits. Only if management, the board of directors, or both are engaged in fraud may they take their case to court and, possibly, force the company to pay dividends. With stock options, however, the goals of management are likely to approximate those of stockholders.

Voting power
Inasmuch as the common stockholders of a company are its owners, they are entitled to elect a board of directors, In a large corporation, stockholders usually exercise only indirect control through the board of directors they elect. The board, in turn, selects the management; and management actually controls the operations of the company. With a proprietorship, partnership, or small corporation, the owners usually control the operations of the business directly. With a large corporation, however, there may be times when the goals of management differ from those of the common stockholders. The only recourse of a stockholder to management is through the board of directors. Because common stockholders often are widely dispersed geographically and, therefore, disorganized, management can often exercise effective control of a large corporation if it controls only a small percentage of the stock outstanding. By proposing a slate of directors that is favorable to its own interests, management is able to maintain control. An outside stockholder, however, does have the right to expect that the directors will administer the affairs of the corporation properly in his behalf. If the directors act in a manner that results in personal gain, a stockholder can sue to recover. These suits are known as *derivative suits*. However, derivative suits are infrequent, partly because many states require that the stockholder bear the legal expenses of the corporation if he loses the suit. These laws were instigated to prevent stockholders from undertaking derivative suits at the least provocation.

Proxies
Each common stockholder is entitled to one vote for each share of stock he owns. Because most stockholders do not attend the annual meeting, they may vote by proxy. A proxy is simply a form by which the stockholder assigns his right to

vote to another person or persons. The SEC regulates the solicitation of proxies and also requires companies to disseminate information to its stockholders through proxy mailings. Prior to the annual meeting, management solicits proxies from stockholders to vote for the recommended slate of directors and for any other proposals requiring stockholder approval. If stockholders are satisfied with the company, they generally sign the proxy in favor of management, giving written authorization to management to vote their shares. If a stockholder does not vote his shares, the number of shares voted at the meeting and the number needed to constitute a majority are lower. Because of the proxy system and the fact that management is able to mail information to stockholders at the company's expense, management has a distinct advantage in the voting process. As a result, it usually is able to perpetuate existing practices if it so chooses.

However, outsiders can seize control of a company through a proxy contest. Obviously, outsiders would not attempt a takeover if management controlled a large percentage of shares outstanding. When an outside group undertakes a proxy raid, it is required to register its proxy statement with the Securities and Exchange Commission to prevent the presentation of misleading or false information. The outside group attempts to persuade stockholders to sign a proxy giving them the authority to vote the stockholders' shares.

In a proxy contest, the odds favor existing management to win the contest. It has both the organization and the use of the company's resources to carry on the proxy fight. Insurgents are likely to be successful only when the earnings performance of the company has been bad and management obviously ineffective. The lower the rate of return, profit margins, dividend payout, and percentage of stock owned by management, the greater the probability of success for the insurgents.[13] In recent years, proxy contests have been relatively infrequent. To a large extent, they have been replaced by tender offer takeover bids, a topic considered in Chapter 23.

Voting procedures

Depending upon the corporate charter, the board of directors is elected either under a *majority voting system* or under a *cumulative voting system*. Under the former system, each stockholder has one vote for each share of stock he owns, and he must vote for each director position that is open. For example, if a stockholder owns 100 shares, he will be able to cast 100 votes for each director's position open. Because each person seeking a position on the board must win a majority of the total votes cast for that position, the system precludes minority interests from electing directors.

---

[13] See Richard M. Duvall and Douglas V. Austin, "Predicting the Results of Proxy Contests," *Journal of Finance*, 20 (September 1965), 464–71. They use discriminant analysis with the four variables mentioned above to predict the results.

If management can obtain proxies for over 50 percent of the shares voted, it can select the entire board.

Under a cumulative voting system, a stockholder is able to accumulate his votes and cast them for less than the total number of directors being elected. His total number of votes is the number of shares he owns times the number of directors being elected. For example, if a stockholder owns 100 shares, and twelve directors are to be elected, he will be entitled to cast 1,200 votes. He can cast these votes for whatever number of directors he chooses, the maximum being 1,200 votes for one director.

A cumulative voting sytem, in contrast to the majority system, permits minority interests to elect a certain number of directors. The minimum number of shares necessary to elect a specific number of directors is determined by

$$\frac{\text{Total shares outstanding times specific number of directors sought}}{\text{Total number of directors to be elected plus one}} + 1 \qquad (20\text{-}1)$$

For example, if there are 3 million shares outstanding, the total number of directors to be elected is fourteen, and if a minority group wishes to elect two directors, it will need at least the following number of shares:

$$\frac{3,000,000 \times 2}{14 + 1} + 1 = 400,001$$

As is evident, cumulative voting gives minority interests a better opportunity to be represented on the board of directors of a corporation. Because the system is more democratic, a number of states require that companies in the state elect directors in this way. Even with cumulative voting, however, management sometimes can preclude minority interests from obtaining a seat on the board of directors by reducing the number of directors. For example, suppose the minority group above actually owns 400,001 shares. With fourteen directors to be elected, the group can elect two directors. However, if the board is reduced to six members, the minority group can elect no directors because the minimum number of shares needed to elect a single director is

$$\frac{3,000,000 \times 1}{6 + 1} + 1 = 428,572$$

Another method used to thwart a minority interest from obtaining representation is to stagger the terms of the directors so that only a portion is elected each year. For example, if a firm had twelve directors and the term was four years, only three would be elected each year. As a result, a minority group would need considerably more shares voted in its favor to elect a director than it would if all twelve directors came up for election each year.

**Right to
examine books**
A stockholder legally is entitled to inspect the books and records of a corporation. However, this access is limited, for most corporations feel that the audited financial statement is sufficient to satisfy the requirement. To obtain more specific information, the stockholder may have to take his case to court in order to prove the necessity for obtaining this information. Stockholders are also entitled to a list of the stockholders of the corporation and their addresses. This list is vital to an insurgent group in a proxy contest. However, management may engage in delaying tactics by contending that the stockholder list will be misused. In these situations, the stockholder may have to go to court and demonstrate sufficient cause for obtaining the information. Upon a court order, management is required to provide the list.

CLASSIFIED COMMON STOCK

A company may have more than one class of common stock. Its common stock can be classified with respect to the claim on income and as to voting power. For example, the Class A common of a company may have no voting privilege but may be entitled to a prior claim to dividends, while the Class B common has voting rights but a lower claim to dividends. Usually, the promoters of a corporation and its management will hold the Class B common stock, whereas the Class A common is sold to the public. Actually, the Class A shares in this example are no more than a form of preferred stock. However, the Class A stock usually is given some voting power, but not as much as the Class B stock per dollar of investment. One incentive is that the New York Stock Exchange will not list a nonvoting stock, and other exchanges will do so only with reluctance.

Suppose, for example, that the Class A and Class B common stockholders of a company are entitled to one vote per share, but that the Class A stock is issued at an initial price of $20 a share. If $2 million is raised in the original offering through the issuance of 80,000 shares of Class A common for $1.6 million and 200,000 shares of Class B common for $400,000, the Class B stockholders will have over twice the number of votes as the Class A holders, despite the fact that their original investment is only one quarter as large. Thus, the Class B holders have effective control of the company. Indeed, this is the purpose of classified stock.

For this control, the Class B holders must be willing to give something up in order to make the Class A stock attractive to investors. Usually, they take a lower claim to dividends and a lower claim on assets. An appropriate balance must be struck between voting power and the claim to dividends and assets if the company is to bargain effectively for

Class A equity funds. Sometimes, the Class B common simply is given to the promoters of a corporation without any cash investment on their part.

Ford Motor Company example

An example of a company with classified common stock is the Ford Motor Company. At December 31, 1974, the issued shares of capital stock for the company were:

	Shares Issued
Class B (voting)	12,089,395
Common stock (voting)	81,500,338
	93,589,733

The Class B stock is owned by members of the Ford family and constitutes 40 percent of the total voting power of the company. The common is held by the general public and has 60 percent of the voting power of the company. The common stock was owned originally by the Ford Foundation, but the stock has been sold to the general public. A holder of common stock of Ford is entitled to one vote for each share he owns. A holder of Class B common is entitled to that number of votes per share that will make the voting power of the Class B common 40 percent of the total voting power of the corporation. At December 31, 1974, this number was

$$\frac{81,500,338}{12,089,395} \times \frac{0.40}{0.60} = 4.49 \text{ votes}$$

Each shareholder of Class B stock was entitled to 4.49 votes per share at the end of 1974. Thus, members of the Ford family retain substantial voting power in the company despite the fact that they hold far fewer shares than does the general public. All shares of common and Class B stock share equally in dividends and equally in their claim on assets in the event of liquidation.[14] The use of classified capital stock in this case affects only the voting power.

SELLING COMMON STOCK THROUGH A PRIVILEGED SUBSCRIPTION

Instead of selling a security issue to the general public, many firms offer the securities first to existing shareholders on a privileged-subscription basis. Frequently, the corporate charter requires that a new issue of common stock or an issue of securities convertible into common be offered first to existing shareholders because of their preemptive right.

[14]*Annual Report,* Ford Motor Company, 1974; and *Prospectus* to Ford Motor Company Stock, November 20, 1963.

PREEMPTIVE RIGHT

Under a preemptive right, an existing commonstockholder has the right to preserve his proportionate ownership in the corporation. If the corporation issues additional common stock, he must be given the right to subscribe to the new stock so that he maintains his pro rata interest in the company. Suppose an individual owns 100 shares of a corporation and the company decides to increase by 10 percent the number of shares outstanding through a new common-stock offering. If the stockholder has a preemptive right, he must be given the option to buy ten additional shares so that he can preserve his proportionate ownership in the company. Various states differ with respect to laws regarding preemptive rights. However, the majority of the states provide that a stockholder does have a preemptive right unless the corporate charter otherwise denies it.

OFFERING THROUGH RIGHTS

When a company sells securities by privileged subcription, each stockholder is mailed one right for each share of stock he holds. With a common-stock offering, the rights give him the option to purchase additional shares according to the terms of the offering. The terms specify the number of rights required to subscribe for an additional share of stock, the subscription price per share, and the expiration date of the offering. The holder of rights has three choices: he can exercise them and subscribe for additional shares; he can sell them, because they are transferable; or he can simply do nothing and let them expire. The last usually occurs only if the value of a right is negligible and/or if the stockholder owns but a few shares of stock. Generally, the subscription period is thirty days or less. If a stockholder wishes to buy a share of additional stock but does not have the necessary number of rights, he may purchase additional rights. For example, suppose a person presently owns eighty-five shares of stock in a company, and the number of rights required to purchase one additional share is ten. Given his eighty-five rights, he can purchase only eight full shares of stock. He can, however, buy the ninth share by purchasing an additional five rights.

In a rights offering, the board of directors establishes a date of record. Investors that buy the stock prior to that date receive the right to subscribe to the new issue. The stock is said to sell with *rights-on* through the date of record. After the date of record, the stock is said to sell *ex-rights;* that is, the stock is traded without the rights attached. An investor who buys the stock after this date does not receive the right to subscribe to additional stock.

VALUE OF RIGHTS

The market value of a right is a function of the present market price of the stock, the subscription price, and the number of rights required to purchase an additional share of stock. The theoretical market value of one right after the offering is announced but while the stock is still selling rights-on is

$$R_o = \frac{P_0 - S}{N + 1} \qquad (20\text{-}2)$$

where R_o = market value of one right when stock is selling rights-on

P_0 = market value of a share of stock selling rights-on

S = subscription price per share

N = number of rights required to purchase one share of stock

For example, if the market price of a stock is $100 a share and the subscription price $90 a share, and it takes four rights to buy an additional share of stock, the theoretical value of a right when the stock is selling rights-on would be

$$R_o = \frac{100 - 90}{4 + 1} = \$2 \qquad (20\text{-}3)$$

We note that the market value of the stock with rights-on contains the value of one right.

When the stock goes ex-rights, the market price theoretically declines, for investors no longer receive the right to subscribe to additional shares. The theoretical value of one share of stock when it goes ex-rights is

$$P_x = \frac{(P_0 \times N) + S}{N + 1} \qquad (20\text{-}4)$$

where P_x = market price of stock when it goes ex-rights. For our example,

$$P_x = \frac{(100 \times 4) + 90}{4 + 1} = \$98 \qquad (20\text{-}5)$$

From this example we see that, theoretically, the right does not represent a thing of value to the stockholder. His stock is worth $100 before the date of record; after the date of record, it is worth $98 a share. The decline in market price is offset exactly by the value of the right. Thus, theoretically, the stockholder does not benefit from a rights offering; the right represents merely a return of capital. Another way to look at a rights offering is to equate it with a stock dividend to existing stockholders coupled with a new stock issue to which these stockholders have the first right to subscribe.[15] The fall in stock price caused by the rights offering, $P_o - P_x$, is the same as the fall in price caused by a stock dividend. In neither case does the stockholder receive a thing of value.

The theoretical value of a right when the stock sells ex-rights is

$$R_x = \frac{P_x - S}{N} \tag{20-6}$$

where $R_x =$ the market value of one right when the stock is selling ex-rights. If, in our example, the market price of the stock is $98 when it goes ex-rights,

$$R_x = \frac{98 - 90}{4} = \$2 \tag{20-7}$$

or the same value as before.

It is important to recognize that the actual value of a right may differ somewhat from its theoretical value on account of transaction costs, speculation, and the irregular exercise and sale of rights over the subscription period. There is an old adage on Wall Street that says a stockholder should sell his rights early in the subscription period because at that time they have the maximum value. The high value, as the reasoning goes, is due to hesitation on the part of many stockholders either to exercise or to sell their rights in the early days of the subscription period. This hesitation is said to reflect a "wait and see" attitude. As a result, there is a shortage of rights early in the subscription period; and the market price of the right rises relative to its theoretical value. The opposite occurs near the end of the subscription period; stockholders are said to unload rights.

Although this behavior may seem logical enough, empirical studies have not revealed any distinct price pattern of rights over the subscription period.[16] One reason is that arbitrage limits the deviation of actual value from theoretical value. If the price of a right is significantly higher than its theoretical value, stockholders will sell their rights and purchase the stock in the market. Such action will exert downward pressure on

---

[15] Haim Levy and Marshall Sarnat, "Risk, Dividend Policy, and the Optimal Pricing of a Rights Offering," *Journal of Money, Credit and Banking*, 3 (November 1971), 840–41. See also Simon M. Keane, "The Significance of the Issue Price in Rights Issues," *Journal of Business Finance*, 4, No. 3 (1972), 40.

[16] See Robert M. Soldofsky and Craig R. Johnson, "Rights Timing," *Financial Analysts Journal*, 23 (July–August 1967), 101–104.

the market price of the right and upward pressure on its theoretical value. The latter occurs because of the upward pressure on the market price of the stock. If the price of the right is significantly lower than its theoretical value, arbitragers will buy the rights, exercise their option to buy stock, and then sell the stock in the market. This occurrence will exert upward pressure on the market price of the right and downward pressure on its theoretical value. These arbitrage actions will continue as long as they are profitable.

In the rights formulas presented, it is assumed implicitly that the relative earning power and risk complexion of the firm do not change as a result of the investment of funds raised in the offering. Implied also is that the firm's capital structure does not change—that is, it employs the same financing mix as before. If these conditions do not hold, the market price of the common stock may well behave in a manner out of keeping with its previously computed theoretical value.

THE SUCCESS OF THE OFFERING

One of the most important aspects of a successful rights offering is the subscription price. If the market price of the stock should fall below the subscription price, stockholders obviously will not subscribe to the stock, for they can buy it in the market at a lower price. Consequently, a company will set the subscription price at a value lower than the current market price to reduce the risk of the market price's falling below it. We know that the stock should fall in price when it goes ex-rights. Its new theoretical value is determined by Eq. (20-4); and we see that it depends importantly upon N, the number of rights required to purchase one share of stock. The greater the N, the less the theoretical price decline when the stock goes ex-rights. Thus, the risk that the market price will fall below the subscription price is inversely related to N.[17] To illustrate, suppose the following were true:

$$P_x = \frac{(P_o \times N) + S}{N+1}$$

	Company A	Company B
Market value per share rights-on, P_o	$60.00	$60.00
Subscription price, S	$46.00	$46.00
Number of rights needed to purchase one share, N	1	10
Theoretical value of one share ex-rights, P_x	$53.00	$58.73

[17] See Levy and Sarnat, "Risk, Dividend Policy, and the Optimal Pricing of a Rights Offering," pp. 840–49.

We see that Company *A* will have a greater decline in value per share when its stock goes ex-rights than will Company *B*. All other things the same, there is a greater probability, or risk, that Company *A*'s stock will fall below the subscription price of $46 than there is that Company *B*'s stock will fall below it.

Amount of discount

Apart from the number of rights required to purchase one share, the risk that the market price of a stock will fall below the subscription price is a function of the volatility of the company's stock, the tone of the market, expectations of earnings, and other factors. To avoid all risk, a company could set the subscription price so far below the market price that there is virtually no possibility that the market price will fall below it. The greater the discount from the current market price, the greater the value of the right, and the greater the probability of a successful sale of stock, all other things the same.[18] As long as the stockholder does not allow his rights to expire, theoretically he neither gains nor loses by the offering. Therefore, it might seem feasible to set the subscription price at a substantial discount in order to assure a successful sale.

However, the greater the discount, the more shares that will have to be issued to raise a given amount of money, and the greater the dilution in earnings per share. This dilution may be a relevant consideration, for the investment community analyzes closely the growth trend in earnings per share. Significant underpricing of the new issue may excessively dampen the growth trend in earnings per share and result in a lower price/earnings ratio in the market. Although theoretically the stockholder should be equally well off regardless of the subscription price set, in practice the market value of his stock holdings may suffer if there is excessive dilution in reported earnings per share. Obviously, this would be an imperfection in the market, but imperfections on occasion can be important.

Moreover, if the firm wishes to maintain the same dividend per share, underpricing, which results in more shares being issued, will increase the total amount of dividends the company will need to pay and lower its coverage ratio. The disadvantages of underpricing must be balanced against the risk of the market price's falling below the subscription price. The primary consideration in setting the subscription price is to reduce the probability of this occurrence to a tolerable level. If, then, the subscription price results in excessive dilution, the company should consider a public issue, wherein the amount of underpricing usually is less.

[18]Peter W. Bacon, "The Subscription Price in Rights Offerings," *Financial Management*, 1 (Summer 1972), 59–64, in a test of rights offerings for the 1965–68 period, found at least some support for the notion that the relative size of the subscription discount influenced positively the success of the offering, as measured by the ratio of the number of shares subscribed for to the number of shares offered.

There are other factors that influence the success of
a rights offering. The size of the capital outlay in

relation to a stockholder's existing ownership of the stock is important.[19]
Stockholders are likely to be more willing to subscribe to an issue
amounting to a 10 percent addition to the stock they presently hold than
to an issue amounting to a 50 percent addition. The mix of existing
stockholders may also be a factor. If a substantial number of stockholders hold only a few shares, the success of the offering may be less
than if most stockholders held units of 100 shares. The breakdown
between institutional and individual investors may also bear upon the
success of the rights offering. The current trend and tone of the stock
market are extremely important. If the trend is upward and the market is
relatively stable in this upward movement, the probability of a successful sale is quite high. The more uncertain the stock market, the greater
the underpricing that will be necessary in order to sell the issue. In fact,
there are times when the market is so unstable that an offering will have
to be postponed.

STANDBY ARRANGEMENT

A company can insure the complete success of a rights offering by
having an investment banker or a group of investment bankers "stand
by" to underwrite the unsold portion of the issue. For this standby
commitment, the underwriter charges a fee that varies with the risk
involved in the offering. Often the fee consists of two parts: a flat fee,
and an additional fee for each unsold share of stock that the underwriter
has to buy. From the standpoint of the company issuing the stock, the
greater the risk of an unsuccessful sale, the more desirable a standby
arrangement, although it also is more costly.[20]

PRIVILEGED SUBSCRIPTION VERSUS PUBLIC ISSUE

By offering stock first to existing stockholders, the company taps
investors who are familiar with the operations of the company. As a
result, a successful sale is probable. The principal sales tool is the
discount from the current market price, whereas with a public issue, the
major selling tool is the investment banking organization. Because the
issue is not underwritten, the flotation costs of a rights offering are lower
than the costs of an offering to the general public. Moreover, many
stockholders feel that they should be given the first opportunity to buy

[19] See Harry G. Guthmann and Herbert E. Dougall, *Corporate Financial Policy*, 4th ed.
(Englewood Cliffs, N.J.: Prentice-Hall, 1962), p. 414.

[20] For an analysis of an underwriter's risk in a standby agreement, see Levy and Sarnat,
"Risk, Dividend Policy, and the Optimal Pricing of a Rights Offering," pp. 842–45. For an
excellent analysis of its use from the standpoint of the company, see Keane, "Significance
of the Issue Price in Rights Issues," pp. 40–45.

new common shares. Offsetting these advantages is the fact that a rights offering generally will have to be sold at a lower price than will an issue to the general public. Also, a public offering will result in a wider distribution of shares. Management can request stockholders with preemptive rights to waive them so that the company can sell stock to the general public. If the argument is persuasive enough or if management controls enough stock, the preemptive right may be waived.

SUMMARY

When companies finance their long-term needs externally, they may obtain funds from the capital markets. If the financing involves a public offering, the company usually will use the services of an investment banking firm. The investment banker's principal functions are risk-bearing, or underwriting, and selling the securities. For these functions, the investment banking firm is compensated by the spread between the price it pays for the securities and the price at which it resells the securities to investors. With a negotiated offering, the investment banker provides an additional service in advising the company as to the pricing and timing of the issue and as to procedures and features involved in the issue. With an offering on a competitive bid basis, the issue is sold to the investment banker or syndicate of investment bankers that submits the highest bid.

The common stockholders of a corporation are its owners. As such, they are entitled to share in the residual earnings of the company if cash dividends are paid. As owners, however, they have only a residual claim on assets in the event of liquidation. Common stockholders are also entitled to a voice in management through the board of directors they elect. These directors can be elected under a majority voting system or a cumulative voting system; the latter system allows minority interests to obtain representation on the board of directors. The use of different classes of common stock allows the promoters and management of a corporation to retain voting control without having to make a large capital contribution.

A company may give its existing stockholders the first opportunity to purchase a new security issue on a privileged-subscription basis. This type of issue is known as a rights offering, because existing stockholders receive one right for each share of stock they hold. A right represents an option to buy the new security at the subscription price, and it takes a specified number of rights to purchase the security. Depending upon the relationship between the current market price of the stock and the subscription price, a right usually will have a market value. Both security offerings to the general public and offerings on a privileged-subscription basis must comply with federal and state regulations. The enforcement agency for the federal government is the Securities and Exchange Commission, whose authority encompasses both the sale of new securities and the trading of existing securities in the secondary market.

1. The Homex Company wishes to raise $5 million in additional equity capital. After consideration is given to the potential difficulty of selling the shares, the investment banker decides that the selling concession should be between 3 percent and 4 percent of the value of the issue. When the risks of underwriting are evaluated, it is decided that the selling concession should constitute between 50 percent and 60 percent of the gross spread. If the management fee (which constitutes part of the underwriting profit) is taken to be 15 percent of the gross spread, answer the following questions:

   (a) Assuming that the selling concession is set at 4 percent of gross proceeds and 50 percent of the gross spread, what would be the dollar value of the management fee, net underwriting profit, selling concession, and gross spread on the Homex underwriting?

   (b) Rework (a), assuming that the selling concession were set at 3 percent of gross proceeds and 60 percent of the gross spread.

   (c) Assuming that the managing underwriter underwrote 25 percent and sold 20 percent of the issue, what would be his total compensation under case (a) above? Under case (b)?

   (d) Assuming this problem to be somewhat realistic, what are its implications for the financial manager of Homex?

2. The Tabbot Corporation, a rather new and speculative concern, wishes to sell stock. Its investment banker, the First Salem Corporation, offers the following two alternatives:

   (1) First Salem will make a firm underwriting of 1 million shares @ $4.00 per share, for a gross spread of 8 percent.

   (2) First Salem will attempt, for a $200,000 fee, a best efforts distribution, @ $4.50 per share, to the public with a gross spread of 8 percent on those shares sold. First Salem expects sales at this price to have an approximately normal distribution, with a mean of 900,000 shares and a standard deviation of 100,000 shares.

      (a) What are the expected proceeds to Tabbott under each alternative?

      (b) What is the approximate probability that the best efforts distribution would yield more to Tabbot than the firm underwriting?

3. D. Sent, a disgruntled stockholder of the Zebec Corporation, desires representation on the board. The Zebec Corporation, which has ten directors, has 1 million shares outstanding.

   (a) How many shares would Sent have to control to be assured of one directorship under a majority voting system?

   (b) Recompute (a), assuming a cumulative voting system.

   (c) Recompute (a) and (b), assuming the number of directors was reduced to five.

4. Joe Miller has formed a company that can earn a 12 percent return after taxes, although no investment has yet been made. Joe plans to take $100,000 in $1 par value stock for his promotion efforts. All financing for the firm will be in stock, and all earnings will be paid in dividends.

   (a) Suppose that Joe desires to keep 50 percent control of the company after he has acquired new financing. He can do this by taking his stock in the form of $1 par value Class B, with two votes per share; while selling $1 par value Class A stock, with one vote per share, to the public. In order to buy Class A stock, however, the investors would require a dividend formula that would give them a 10 percent return. How many Class A shares would be issued? What dividend formula would meet the investors' requirements? What dividend payment would be left for Joe's Class B shares?

(b) Suppose that, if Joe were willing to lose control of the company, he could have just one class of common stock and sell the same amount to the public as he could Class A in (a) above. In such a case the investors would only require an 8 percent rate of return. What would be the dividend formula and Joe's return in this case? Comparing this answer with that obtained in (a) above, what is Joe paying to retain control?

(c) Rework (b) above under the assumption that the investors would require 9 percent. What must Joe do?

5. The stock of the Dunbar Company is selling for $150 per share. If the company were to issue rights to subscribe for one additional share of stock, at $125 a share, for each nine held, compute the following:

(a) The theoretical value of a right when the stock is selling rights-on

(b) The theoretical value of one share of stock when it goes ex-rights

(c) The theoretical value of a right when the stock sells ex-rights and the actual market price goes to $143 per share

6. The stock of the National Corporation is selling for $50 per share. The company then issues rights to subscribe to one new share at $40 for each five shares held.

(a) What is the theoretical value of a right when the stock is selling rights-on?

(b) What is the theoretical value of one share of stock when it goes ex-rights?

(c) What is the theoretical value of a right when the stock sells ex-rights at $50?

(d) Joe Speculator has $1,000 at the time National stock goes ex-rights at $50 per share. He feels that the price of the stock will rise to $60 by the time the rights expire. Compute his return on his $1,000 if he (1) buys National stock at $50, or (2) buys the rights at the price computed in (c) above if his price expectations are valid.

7. Instead of a rights offering, National Corporation (see problem 6) could undertake a public offering at $45 per share with a 6 percent gross spread. National currently has 1 million shares outstanding and earns $4 million a year. All earnings are paid in dividends. In either case, National would sell enough shares to raise $1 million, which would be invested at an after-tax return of 10 percent.

(a) Compute the earnings per share, dividends per share, and market price of the stock (assuming a 12.5 P/E ratio) for (1) the rights offering and (2) the public offering alternatives.

(b) Mr. Brown owns one share of National stock. On a rights offering, he will sell the right (assume for $2) and use the proceeds to reduce his investment to $48. On a public offering, he would not buy any more shares. Compute Mr. Brown's earnings and dividend return on his investment and his price gain or loss on his investment under each of the two financing alternatives facing National.

SELECTED REFERENCES

Bacon, Peter W., "The Subscription Price in Rights Offerings," *Financial Management* (Summer 1972), 59–64.

Baumol, William J., *The Stock Market and Economic Efficiency.* New York: Fordham University Press, 1965.

Bear, Robert M., and Anthony J. Curley, "Unseasoned Equity Financing," *Journal of Financial and Quantitative Analysis,* 10 (June 1975), 311–26.

Bloch, Ernest, "Pricing a Corporate Bond Issue: A Look behind the Scenes," *Essays in Money and Credit,* pp. 72–76. New York: Federal Reserve Bank of New York, 1964.

Brown, J. Michael, "Post-Offering Experience of Companies Going Public," *Journal of Business* (January 1970), 10–18.

Cohan, Avery, *Cost of Flotation of Long-Term Corporate Debt since 1935.* Chapel Hill, N.C.: University of North Carolina Press, 1961.

Dougall, Herbert E., *Capital Markets and Institutions,* 3rd ed. Englewood Cliffs, N.J.: Prentice-Hall, 1974.

Duvall, Richard M., and Douglas V. Austin, "Predicting the Results of Proxy Contests," *Journal of Finance,* 20 (September 1965), 467–71.

Ederington, Louis H., "Negotiated versus Competitive Underwritings of Corporate Bonds," *Journal of Finance,* forthcoming.

————, "Uncertainty, Competition, and Costs in Corporate Bond Underwriting," *Journal of Financial Economics,* 2 (March) 1975), 71–94.

Eibott, Peter, "Trends in the Value of Individual Stockholdings," *Journal of Business,* 47 (July 1974), 339–48.

Evans, G. H., Jr., "The Theoretical Value of a Stock Right," *Journal of Finance,* 10 (March 1955), 55–61.

Firth, Michael, "The Information Content of Large Investment Holdings," *Journal of Finance,* 30 (December 1975), 1265–82.

Furst, Richard W., "Does Listing Increase the Market Price of Common Stocks?" *Journal of Business,* 43 (April 1970), 174–80.

Hayes, Samuel L., III, "Investment Banking: Power Structure in Flux," *Harvard Business Review,* 49 (March–April 1971), 136–52.

Johnson, Keith B., T. Gregory Morton, and M. Chapman Findlay III, "An Empirical Analysis of the Flotation Cost of Corporate Securities 1971–1972," *Journal of Finance,* 30 (September 1975), 1129–33.

Keane, Simon M., "The Significance of the Issue Price in Rights Issues," *Journal of Business Finance,* 4, No. 3 (1972), 40–45.

Levy, Haim, and Marshall Sarnat, "Risk, Dividend Policy, and the Optimal Pricing of a Rights Offering," *Journal of Money, Credit, and Banking,* 3 (November 1971), 840–49.

Logue, Dennis E., "On the Pricing of Unseasoned Equity Issues: 1965–1969," *Journal of Financial and Quantitative Analysis,* 8 (January 1973), 91–104.

Logue, Dennis E., and John R. Lindvall, "The Behavior of Investment Bankers: An Econometric Investigation," *Journal of Finance,* 29 (March 1974), 203–16.

Lowe, H. D., "The Classification of Corporate Stock Equities," *Accounting Review,* 36 (July 1961), 425–33.

McDonald, J. G., and A. K. Fisher, "New Issue Stock Price Behavior," *Journal of Finance,* 27 (March 1972), 97–102.

Nelson, J. Russell, "Price Effects in Rights Offerings," *Journal of Finance,* 20 (December 1965), 647–50.

Soldofsky, Robert M., "Classified Common Stock," *Business Lawyer* (April 1968), pp. 899–902.

Soldofsky, Robert M., and Craig R. Johnson, "Rights Timing," *Financial Analysts Journal,* 23 (July–August 1967), 101–4.

Stoll, Hans R., and Anthony J. Curley, "Small Business and the New Issues Market for Equities," *Journal of Financial and Quantitative Analysis,* 5 (September 1970), 309–22.

Tallman, Gary D., David F. Rush, and Ronald W. Melicher, "Competitive versus Negotiated Underwriting Costs for Regulated Industries," *Financial Management,* 3 (Summer 1974), 49–55.

Thompson, Howard E., "A Note on the Value of Rights in Estimating the Investor Capitalization Rate," JF 28 (March 1973), 157–60.

Van Horne, James C., *The Function and Analysis of Capital Market Rates.* Englewood Cliffs, N.J.: Prentice-Hall, 1970.

————, "New Listings and Their Price Behavior," *Journal of Finance,* 25 (September 1970), 783–94.

————, "Implied Fixed Costs in Long-Term Debt Issues," *Journal of Financial and Quantitative Analysis,* 8 (December 1973).

Weston, C. R., "Adjustment to Future Dividend Rates in the Prediction of Ex-Rights Prices," *Journal of Business Finance & Accounting,* 1 (Autumn 1974), 335–41.

Wiesen, Jeremy L., *Regulating Transactions in Securities,* St. Paul, Minn,; West Publishing, 1975.

Young, Alan, and Wayne Marshall, "Controlling Shareholder Servicing Costs," *Harvard Business Review,* 49 (January–February 1971), 71–78.

LONG-TERM DEBT and PREFERRED STOCK

In Chapters 9 and 10, the theoretical aspects of fixed-income securities were analyzed in conjunction with the use of equity capital. Our discussion was framed in terms of fixed-income securities in general rather than in terms of specific types of instruments as we considered the question of the optimal split between debt and equity. In this chapter, we examine the wide spectrum of long-term debt instruments available to the firm as well as evaluate the features of preferred stock.

FEATURES OF DEBT

The holders of a company's long-term debt, of course, are creditors. Generally, they cannot exercise control over the company and do not have a voice in management. However, if the company violates any of the provisions of the debt contract, these holders may be able to exert some influence upon the direction of the company. In addition to not having voting power, holders of long-term debt do not participate in the residual earnings of the company; instead, their return is fixed. Also, a debt instrument has a specific maturity, whereas a share of common or preferred stock does not. In liquidation, the claim of debtholders is before that of preferred and common stockholders. Depending upon the nature of the debt instrument, however, there may be differences in the priority of claim among the various creditors of a company.

SOME DEFINITIONS

The fixed return of a long-term debt instrument is denoted by the *coupon rate*. For example, a 7.5 percent debenture indicates that the issuer will pay the bondholder $75 per annum for every $1,000 face value bond he holds. The yield to maturity on a bond is determined by solving for the rate of discount that equates the present value of principal and interest payments with the current market price of the bond. (See the appendix to Chapter 2 for the mathematics of bond interest.) The yield on a bond is the same as the internal rate of return for an investment project.

With a bond issue to the public, a qualified *trustee* is designated by the company to represent the interests of the bondholders. The obligations of a trustee are specified in the Trust Indenture Act of 1939, administered by the Securities and Exchange Commission. His responsibilities are: to authenticate the bond issue as to its legality at the time of issuance; to watch over the financial condition and behavior of the borrower to make sure all contractual obligations are carried out; and to initiate appropriate actions if the borrower does not meet any of these obligations. The trustee is compensated directly by the corporation; this compensation adds to the cost of borrowing.

The legal agreement between the corporation issuing the bonds and the trustee, who represents the bondholders, is defined in the _indenture_. The indenture contains the terms of the bond issue as well as the restrictions placed upon the company. These restrictions, known as _protective covenants_, are very similar to those contained in a term-loan agreement. Because we analyzed protective covenants in detail in Chapter 18 and the appendix to that chapter, it is not necessary to describe these restrictions here. The terms contained in the indenture are established jointly by the borrower and the trustee. If the issue is a negotiated underwriting, the underwriter also will be involved. Naturally, the borrower does not want the terms to be unduly restrictive. Nevertheless, he is mindful of the need to appeal to investors and to conform to certain legal requirements. If the corporation defaults under any of the provisions of the indenture, the trustee, on behalf of the bondholders, can take action to correct the situation. If not satisfied, he then can call for the immediate payment of all outstanding bonds.

RETIREMENT

The retirement of bonds may be accomplished in a number of ways. For example, bonds may be retired by payment at final maturity, by conversion if the bonds are convertible, by calling the bonds if there is a call feature, or by periodic repayment. Periodic repayment of the debt is possible if the bond issue is either a sinking-fund issue or a serial bond issue. Conversion is taken up in the next chapter, and the calling of bonds is examined later in this chapter. We turn now to a discussion of sinking-fund and serial bonds.

Sinking funds   If a bond issue has a sinking fund, the corporation makes periodic sinking-fund payments to the trustee. In turn, the trustee uses these funds to purchase or redeem bonds and retire them. This operation generally is favorable to bondholders because it tends to support the market price of the bonds and assures the steady repayment of the issue. The trustee can retire bonds in two ways. He can purchase them in the open market. To prevent the purchase of bonds at too high a price, however, most sinking-fund bond issues provide for a _call price_, which enables the trustee to call the bonds for redemption. Usually, bonds are called on a lottery basis by their serial numbers, which are published in the _Wall Street Journal_ and other papers. The trustee will purchase the bonds in the open market as long as the market price is less than the call price; when the market price exceeds the call price, he will call the bonds. For example, if the market price of a bond is $99.75 and the call price is $101.25, the trustee will purchase the necessary bonds in the market.

The amount of required sinking-fund payment may be either fixed or variable, depending upon the terms in the indenture. Under the former arrangement, the corporation makes fixed, equal periodic payments to the trustee. As the bonds are retired, the interest on the outstanding bonds becomes less and less. These fixed sinking-fund payments do not necessarily have to retire all the bonds by final maturity. For example, a $20 million, twenty-year bond issue might call for annual sinking-fund payments of only $500,000. Thus a $10 million "balloon" payment at final maturity would be required to retire the remaining bonds.

Variable periodic sinking-fund payments are those that are not equal in amount. These payments may be tied to the earnings of the corporation, so that the greater the earnings, the greater the sinking-fund payment. This type of arrangement obviously is appealing to a company and its stockholders. In periods of poor earnings, the company is not constrained by the need to make a fixed sinking-fund payment. Bondholders, of course, would prefer fixed payments, because these payments assure a steady reduction of the debt over time. If the borrower cannot meet these payments, he would be in clear default under the terms of the indenture. This default enables the trustee to take corrective actions. In the case of variable sinking-fund payments, the borrower would not be in default, and the trustee would be powerless to take corrective measures. The amount of sinking-fund payment may vary also with the number of years to final maturity. For some bond issues, the amount of sinking-fund payment may increase over the years; for others, it may decrease. Variable sinking-fund payments are employed less often than are fixed payments.

Serial bonds

All sinking-fund bonds in an issue mature on the same date, although specific bonds are retired before that date. Serial bonds, however, mature periodically until final maturity. For example, a $20 million issue of serial bonds might have $1 million of the bonds maturing each year for twenty years. With a serial bond issue, the investor is able to choose the maturity that best suits his needs. Thus, a bond issue of this type appeals to a wider group of investors than an issue in which all the bonds have the same maturity.

TYPES OF DEBT FINANCING

DEBENTURES

The term *debenture* usually applies to the unsecured bonds of a corporation; the investor looks to the earning power of the corporation as his security. Because these general credit bonds are not secured by specific property, in the event of liquidation the holder becomes a general creditor. Although the bonds are unsecured, debenture holders are protected by the restrictions imposed in the indenture. One of the more important of these restrictions is a negative pledge clause, which precludes the corporation from pledging its assets to other creditors. This provision safeguards the investor in that the borrower's assets will not be impaired in the future. Because debenture holders must look to the general credit of the borrower to meet principal and interest payments, only well-established and credit-worthy companies are able to issue debentures.

SUBORDINATED DEBENTURES

Subordinated debentures represent debt that ranks behind senior debt with respect to the claim on assets. In the event of liquidation, subordinated debenture holders would receive settlement only if all senior creditors were paid the full amount owed them. However, these holders still would rank ahead of preferred stockholders in the event of liquidation. The existence of subordinated debentures works to the advantage of senior holders, because these holders are able to assume the claims of the subordinated debenture holders. To illustrate, suppose a corporation is liquidated for $600,000 and that it had $400,000 in straight debentures outstanding, $400,000 in subordinated debentures outstanding, and $400,000 in obligations owed to general creditors. One might suppose that the straight debenture holders and the general creditors would have an equal and prior claim in liquidation—that is, each would receive $300,000. However, the straight debenture holders are entitled to the subordinated debenture holders' claims, giving them $800,000 in total claims. As a result, they are entitled to two-thirds of the liquidating value, or $400,000, whereas general creditors are entitled to only one-third, or $200,000.

Because subordinated debentures are subordinate to all existing and future debt, senior creditors regard them as equity when evaluating the financial condition of the company. In fact, subordinated debt usually is employed to increase the equity base and support further borrowing. Finance companies have made extensive use of this type of debt in their capital structure. The increasing popularity of the instrument stems in part from the fact that interest payments are deductible for tax purposes, whereas dividends on preferred stock, the closest substitute method of financing, are not.

Because of the nature of the claim, a straight subordinated debenture issue has to provide a yield significantly higher than a regular debenture issue in order to be attractive to investors. Frequently, however, subordinated debentures are convertible into common stock and therefore may sell at a yield that actually is less than what the company would have to pay on an ordinary debenture. From the standpoint of a creditor, the equity base of the firm is the same whether the issue remains as subordinated debentures or is converted into common stock.

MORTGAGE BONDS

A mortgage bond issue is secured by a lien on specific assets of the corporation—usually fixed assets. The specific property securing the bonds is described in detail in the mortgage, which is the legal document giving the bondholder a lien on the property. As with other secured lending arrangements, the market value of the collateral should exceed the amount of the bond issue by a reasonable margin of safety. If the corporation defaults in any of the provisions of the bond indenture, the trustee, on behalf of the bondholders, has the power to foreclose. In a foreclosure, the trustee takes over the property and sells it, using the proceeds to pay the bonds. If the proceeds are less than the amount of the issue outstanding, the bondholders become general creditors for the residual amount.

A company may have more than one bond issue secured by the same property. For example, a bond issue may be secured by a *second mortgage*. In the event of foreclosure, the first-mortgage bondholders must be paid the full amount owed them before there can be any distribution to the second-mortgage bondholders. For the obvious reason of lack of appeal to investors, second-mortgage bonds seldom are used. When they are, the connotation usually is that financing has reached a rather desperate state.

A mortgage may be either *closed-end* or *open-end*. When a mortgage is closed, additional bonds cannot be issued under that lien. In order to raise additional funds through mortgage bonds, the company must mortgage additional properties. The result is frequently a hodgepodge of mortgage bond issues outstanding. Under an open-end mortgage, however, the company can issue additional bonds under an existing lien. This arrangement allows the company to issue various series of bonds at different times under the same lien. In this respect, it gives the company considerable flexibility in its financing. In order to protect the position of the bondholders of earlier series, certain restrictions usually are imposed that limit the amount of additional debt. These restrictions include a maximum percentage on the amounts of bonds in relation to the value of the property securing these bonds and a minimum earning power of the company in relation to the bonds outstanding. Public utilities and railroads have used open-end mortgages rather extensively and with notable success.

Some mortgage bond issues have an *after-acquired clause*. Under this clause, the lien covers acquisitions of property after the initial bond issue. The after-acquired clause affords investors additional protection, because any property acquired in the future is added to the lien. If the mortgage is open-end, which is almost always the case in this situation, the after-acquired clause does not restrict the company from additional mortgage financing. It merely assures existing bondholders that future bondholders will have exactly the same claim on assets as they do. It is important to recognize that even with a mortgage bond issue, investors look to the earning power of the corporation as the primary test of credit-worthiness.

COLLATERAL TRUST BONDS

A collateral trust bond is secured by stocks or bonds pledged by the corporation to the trustee. In the case of default, the trustee can sell the securities and pay the bondholders. Usually the securities held in collateral trust are securities of some other corporation. To a large extent, the quality of these securities determines the attractiveness of the collateral trust bonds to investors. This type of bond issue, sometimes employed in the past, now is used very infrequently.

INCOME BONDS

With an income bond, a company is obligated to pay interest only when it is earned. There may be a cumulative feature in the issue where unpaid interest in a particular year accumulates. If the company does generate earnings, it will have to pay the cumulative interest to the extent that earnings permit. However, the cumulative obligation usually is limited to no more than three years. As should be evident, this type of security offers the investor a rather weak promise of a fixed return. Nevertheless, the income bond is still senior to preferred and common stock as well as to any subordinated debt. Moreover, the interest payment is deductible for tax purposes, unlike preferred stock dividends. Because income bonds are not popular with investors, they have been used principally in reorganizations.[1]

EQUIPMENT TRUST CERTIFICATES

Although equipment trust financing is a form of lease financing, the certificates themselves represent an intermediate- to long-term fixed-income investment. This method of financing is used by railroads to finance the acquisition of "rolling stock." Under this method, the railroad arranges with a trustee to purchase equipment from a railway equipment manufacturer. The railroad signs a contract with the manufacturer for the construction of specific equipment. When the equipment is delivered, equipment trust certificates are sold to investors. The

---

[1] For a discussion of income bonds, see Bowman Brown, "Why Corporations Should Consider Income Bonds," *Financial Executive*, 35 (October 1967), 74–78; and Frank A. Halford, "Income Bonds," *Financial Analysts Journal*, 20 (January–February 1964), 73–79.

proceeds of this sale, together with the down payment by the railroad, are used to pay the manufacturer for the equipment. Title to the equipment is held by the trustee, who in turn leases the equipment to the railroad. Lease payments are used by the trustee to pay a fixed return on the certificates outstanding—actually a dividend—and to retire a specified portion of the certificates at regular intervals. Upon the final lease payment by the railroad, the last of the certificates is retired, and title to the equipment passes to the railroad.

The duration of the lease varies according to the equipment involved, but fifteen years is rather common. Because rolling stock is essential to the operation of a railroad and it has a ready market value, equipment trust certificates enjoy a very high standing as fixed-income investments. As a result, railroads are able to acquire cars and locomotives on extremely favorable financing terms. In addition to railroads, airlines use a form of equipment trust certificate to finance jet aircraft. Usually these certificates are sold to institutional investors; however, some issues are sold to the public.

CONVERTIBLE BONDS

A convertible bond is one that may be converted at the option of the holder into a certain number of shares of common stock of the corporation. The number of shares into which the bond is convertible is specified in the bond, and these shares remain unissued until actual conversion. Because we consider convertible securities in depth in Chapter 22, they are not discussed at this time.

PROJECT FINANCING

The term *project financing* is now being used to describe a variety of financing arrangements for large individual investment projects. Often a separate legal entity is formed which owns the project. Suppliers of capital then look to the earnings stream of the project for repayment of their loan or for the return on their equity investment. With the energy problems of recent years, there has come the need to finance not only large explorations of gas, oil, and coal but also tankers, port facilities, refineries, and pipelines. Other projects include alumina plants, fertilizer plants, and nuclear plants. These projects require huge amounts of capital, but such financing is often beyond the reach of a single company. Sometimes a consortium of companies is formed to finance the project. Part of the capital comes from equity participations by the companies, and the rest comes from lenders and/or lessors.

If the loan or lease is on a nonrecourse basis, the lender or lessor pays exclusive attention to the size of the equity participation and to the economic feasibility of the project. In other words, the lender or lessor can only look to the project for payout, so the larger the equity cushion and the greater the confidence that can be placed in the projections, the better the project. Sometimes the project's sponsors guarantee its completion, which simply assures the lendor or lessor that the project will be completely built. After its completion, however, the supplier of capital is on his own. Repayment must come from the project's earnings, so the economic feasibility of the project continues to be of major concern.[2] In still another type of arrangement, each sponsor may guarantee his share of the project's obligations. Under these circumstances, the lender or lessor places emphasis on the credit-worthiness of the sponsors as well as on the economic feasibility of the project.

For the sponsors of the project, there are several types of sharing rules. In a "take-or-pay" arrangement, each sponsor agrees to purchase a specific percentage of the output of the project and to pay that percentage of the operating costs of the project plus debt-servicing charges. When pipelines are involved, the type of sharing rule is frequently a "through put" arrangement. Here each sponsor is required to ship through the facility a certain amount, or percentage, of product. If the total shipped is insufficient to cover the expenses of running the facility, sponsors are assessed additional amounts to cover the shortfall. The amount of assessment is proportional to their participation. The maturity of the loan or lease corresponds to the likely ability of the project to generate cash over time. Although the financing need not be long-term, in most cases it extends over a period of eight or more years.

Actually, the term *project financing* conveys nothing more than the financing of a large project. The methods of financing are no different from those we have studied. They include debt and lease financing. What is different is the size and complexity of the financing. It is tailored to the needs of the sponsors as well as to the needs of potential suppliers of capital. Tax considerations become very important in tailoring the financing to the best advantage of all parties. In addition, certain environmental restrictions must be observed, and these influence the type of financing undertaken. When the project is located on foreign soil, political risks arise. These may be reduced by guarantees from the Export-Import Bank or from some other government agency. Nonetheless, foreign projects are complicated by different laws and political risks than those that prevail for domestic projects.

As indicated earlier, project financing has become significant in recent years because of the need to finance large energy-related investments. Their size necessitates financing apart from the sponsoring company's main line of business. This is particularly true when several

---

[2] For further discussion of these two kinds of arrangements, see Grover R. Castle, "Project Financing—Guidelines for the Commercial Banker," *Journal of Commercial Bank Lending*, 57 (April 1975), 14–30.

sponsors enter into a consortium in order to spread risk. The key, then, is that the project stands alone in the sense that the sponsoring companies are liable for no more than their equity participations. With the continuing energy needs and the large amounts of capital financing such needs require, project financing is likely to become increasingly important in the future.

FREQUENCY OF DEBT FINANCING

Once the firm has decided on an appropriate capital structure, its long-term debt requirements are determined by a forecast of its investment needs. Given these requirements over some interval of time, say three years, the question becomes, What is the optimal size and frequency of debt issues? For purposes of illustrating a method for determining the optimal size and frequency, assume for now that the amount of long-term debt required is known with certainty and that the use of these funds is steady over the interval involved. Assume further that the company wishes to go to the market with debt issues of the same size over this interval. The situation described is not unusual for such steady users of debt as public utilities. The idea is to determine the optimal size of debt issue, S, which in turn determines the frequency of financing. For example, if the total amount of debt financing required over the next three years were $60 million and the optimal value of S were found to be $15 million, the company would finance four times, or once every nine months. We turn now to a specific model for determining the optimal issue size.

AN ISSUE SIZE MODEL

If interest rates over the interval y were not expected to change, the optimal debt issue size could be determined using the economic order quantity formula employed in inventory management.[3] The essential ingredients of the model are the flotation costs and the carrying costs. The flotation costs of a debt issue usually include a fixed and a variable component. If the variable component is a constant percentage of the amount of funds raised, total flotation costs over the interval y can be expressed as

$$\text{Flotation costs} = \frac{FD}{S} + VD \qquad (21\text{-}1)$$

[3] See Chapter 16. The model also is used in conjunction with cash management in Chapter 14. See also Harold Bierman, Jr., "The Bond Issue Size Decision," *Journal of Financial and Quantitative Analysis*, 1 (December 1966), 1–14, for an application of the model to the problem at hand. Bierman modifies the basic approach outlined above to allow for bank borrowings. This allowance gives the firm the ability to finance funds gaps on a short-term basis.

where F is the fixed cost per issue of long-term debt, D is the total amount of funds raised during the interval y, D/S is the number of issues during the interval, and V is the variable cost of flotation per dollar of funds raised. Fixed costs include such things as executive and other time consumed in the offering, legal fees, accounting costs, registration costs, and printing costs; while variable costs pertain mainly to underwriting costs.

In addition to flotation costs, a carrying cost is involved. Because the use of funds is steady over the period, there are excess funds over parts of the period. Excess funds are assumed to be invested in short-term securities. The carrying cost can be thought of as the difference between the rate paid on the long-term debt and the rate the company is able to earn on the temporary investment of excess funds in short-term securities such as Treasury bills. We assume for now that interest rates on the two types of instruments are not only known but constant over the interval y.[4] Thus, total carrying costs for the interval are $(S/2)(L - B)$, where $S/2$ is the average investment in short-term securities, L is the rate of interest on long-term debt issues, and B is the rate of interest earned on Treasury bills. Both of these rates are expressed in terms of the interval of time involved.

Our objective is to minimize total costs over the interval y where these costs are depicted by

$$\Theta = \frac{FD}{S} + VD + \frac{S(L - B)}{2} \qquad (21\text{-}2)$$

Differentiating this expression with respect to S and setting the derivative equal to zero, we obtain

$$S^* = \sqrt{\frac{2FD}{L - B}} \qquad (21\text{-}3)$$

which is simply the economic lot-size formula. Given our assumptions, it tells us the issue size that minimizes total fixed and carrying costs over interval y.[5]

To illustrate its use, suppose that Bartlow Manufacturing Company estimates that it will need $50 million in long-term debt funds over the next three years, that the fixed component of flotation costs is $100,000, and that the long-term interest rate on debt issued is 8 percent, while

[4]This assumption is relaxed later in this section when we consider changing interest rates.

[5]Robert H. Litzenberger and David P. Rutenberg, "Size and Timing of Corporate Bond Flotations," *Journal of Financial and Quantitative Analysis*, 7 (January 1972), 1343–60, extend this basic model to consider situations in which the firm's annual demand for long-term debt funds is stochastic and stationary, deterministic and nonstationary, and stochastic and nonstationary. As a point of reference, demand in the above problem is assumed to be deterministic and stationary.

the rate on short-term securities is 6 percent. $L - B$ then becomes $(.08 - .06)3$, or $.06$. (It is necessary to convert annual rates to correspond to the 3-year interval.) Given these factors, the optimal issue size is

$$S^* = \sqrt{\frac{(2)(100,000)(50,000,000)}{.06}} = \$12,909,270$$

With an optimal issue size of $12,909,270, the company should issue long-term debt about every 9.3 months.[6]

ALLOWANCE FOR CHANGING INTEREST RATES

One obvious deficiency in the model outlined above is that interest rates on long-term debt and short-term securities are assumed to be constant throughout the interval. If interest rates are expected to change, both the timing and the frequency of debt financing are affected. For example, suppose interest rates were expected to rise steadily over the interval. Under these circumstances the firm should increase the size of debt issued currently, all other things the same. On the other hand, if interest rates were expected to fall, it should postpone the issue or decrease its size, all other things the same. With a change in interest rates, not only is the interest cost of long-term debt affected, but the relationship between the rate the company pays and what it is able to earn on short-term securities (the carrying cost) may be affected as well. Not to take account of expected changes in these two factors is likely to result in a suboptimal decision.

Thus, the firm should balance the fixed cost of issuing debt against expectations of the future course of interest rates as well as against carrying costs in deciding on the optimal size of debt issue. Because the rate of interest at which long-term debt is issued affects not only interest costs during interval y but also interest costs through maturity, the relevant consideration is the present value of all future interest payments.[7] (An appropriate discount rate might be the average of the interest rates on the company's long-term debt expected to prevail over interval y.)

The objective of the firm should be to minimize the sum of fixed costs, carrying costs, and the present value of interest payments. This

---

[6]This duration is determined by

$$36 \text{ months}/(50,000,000/12,909,270) = 9.3 \text{ months}$$

[7]We assume here that the issue is not called. Also assumed is that a debt issue is priced at face value so that the coupon rate equals the rate of interest in the market.

sum is represented as

$$\Theta = \frac{FD}{S} + VD + \sum_{x=0}^{(D/S)-1} \left[\frac{C_x}{D/S}\right]\frac{S}{2} + \sum_{x=0}^{(D/S)-1} \left[\frac{P_x}{D/S}\right]S \qquad (21\text{-}4)$$

where F = fixed cost per long-term debt issue

D = total demand for long-term debt funds during interval y

S = issue size

D/S = number of issues during interval y

$\dfrac{C_x}{D/S}$ = rate on long-term debt less rate on short-term investments expected to prevail $[x/(D/S)]$ $[y$ years] in the future, expressed in terms of $[1 - x/(D/S)]$ $[y$ years] to maturity

$\dfrac{P_x}{D/S}$ = present value of all future interest payments per \$1 of long-term debt issued $[x(D/S)]$ $[y$ years] in the future, discounted to the time of issuance[8]

The reader may find the expression of carrying cost and present value of interest costs to be somewhat puzzling. In these expressions, we simply need to specify the time of issuance. If $D/S = 1$, for example, the firm would borrow only once during interval y—at the outset—and the third and fourth terms would become $(C_o)(S/2)$ and $(P_o)(S)$, respectively. If $D/S = 2$, the third term would become $(C_o)(S/2) + C_{1/2(y \text{ years})}(S/2)$, where $C_{1/2(y \text{ years})}$ is the carrying cost expected to prevail one-half the way through interval y. The fourth term would be $P_o(S) + P_{1/2(y \text{ years})}(Q)$. Similarly, the carrying cost and present value of $\frac{1}{2}(y$ years) interest costs can be determined for other values of D/S. Thus, the first term on the right in Eq. (21-4) represents fixed costs over the interval y, the second term variable flotation costs over the interval, the third term is total carrying costs over the interval, and the last term is the total present value of all expected future interest payments on debt issued during the interval. The objective, of course, is to minimize Θ.

Once expectations are introduced, the EOQ formula becomes very difficult to differentiate. Perhaps the best method for determining the optimal issue size is simply to set S in Eq. (21-4) equal to 1, 2, 3, 4, 5, ..., n, solve for each of these S's and select the issue size that results in the minimum Θ. If expectations of future interest rates are stochastic, then $C_x/(D/S)$ and $P_x/(D/S)$ become stochastic and the problem can best be handled by simulation.

In summary, Eq. (21-4) provides a general framework by which the financial manager can approach the question of the optimal issue size for long-term debt. The model is meant not as a substitute for experience

---

[8] We assume that the length of time to maturity is the same for all issues.

but as a supplement to such experience in guiding the financial manager in the debt issue size decision. In particular, it places in proper perspective the fixed cost of an issue and the fact that the funds raised may not be used immediately. The firm needs to balance the fixed cost of an issue against the carrying cost of holding excess liquidity and against expectations as to the future course of interest rates. Where the assumptions of the model are not appropriate, it can be modified to accommodate different assumptions as to the demand for long-term debt funds, varying issue sizes, nonlinear variable costs, and so forth.

CALL PROVISION AND REFUNDING

Nearly all corporate bond issues provide for a call feature, which gives the corporation the option to buy back the bonds at a stated price before their maturity. The call price usually is above the par value of the bond and decreases over time. For example, a thirty-year bond issue might be callable at $106 ($1,060 per $1,000 face value bond) the first five years, $105 the second five years, and so on until the final five years, when it is callable at $101. Frequently, the call price in the first year is established at one year's interest above the face value of the bond. If the coupon rate is 8 percent, the initial call price may be $108 ($1,080 per $1,000 face value).

There are two types of call provision, according to when they can be exercised. Some issues state that the call privilege can be exercised immediately after issuance; with other issues, the call privilege is deferred for a period. The most widely used deferred call periods are five years for public utility bonds and ten years for industrial bonds. During this deferment period, the investor is protected from a call by the issuer.

The call provision gives the company flexibility in its financing. If interest rates should decline significantly, it can call the bonds and refinance the issue at a lower interest cost. Thus, the company does not have to wait until the final maturity to refinance. In addition, the provision may be advantageous to the company if it finds any of the protective covenants in the bond indenture to be unduly restrictive. By calling the bonds before maturity, the company can eliminate these restrictions. Of course, if the issue is refinanced with bonds, similar restrictions may be imposed.

VALUE OF CALL PRIVILEGE

Although the call privilege is beneficial to the issuing corporation, it works to the detriment of investors. If interest rates fall and the bond issue is called, they can invest in other bonds only at a sacrifice in yield to maturity. Consequently, the call privilege usually does not come free to the borrower. Its cost, or value, is measured at the time of issuance by the difference in yield on the callable bond and the yield that would be necessary if the security were noncallable. This value is determined by supply and demand forces in the market for callable securities. In equilibrium, the value of the call feature will be just sufficient to bring the demand for callable securities by investors into balance with the supply of callable securities by borrowers. In the equilibrating process, both borrowers and investors are influenced by expectations as to the future course of interest rates.

When interest rates are high and expected to fall, the call feature is likely to have significant value. Investors are unwilling to invest in callable bonds unless such bonds yield more than bonds that are noncallable, all other things the same. In other words, they must be compensated for assuming the risk that the bonds might be called. On the other hand, borrowers are willing to pay a premium in yield for the call privilege in the belief that yields will fall and that it will be advantageous to refund the bonds. In equilibrium, both the marginal borrower and the marginal investor will be indifferent as to whether the bond issue is callable or noncallable.[9]

When interest rates are low and expected to rise, the call privilege may have a negligible value in that the company might pay the same yield if there were no call privilege. For the privilege to have value, interest rate expectations must be such that there is a possibility that the issue will be called. If interest rates are very low and not expected to fall further, there is little probability that the bonds will be called. The key factor is that the borrower has to be able to refund the issue at a profit. In order for him to do so, interest rates have to drop significantly; for the issuer must pay the call price, which is usually at a premium above par value, as well as the flotation costs involved in refinancing. If there is no probability that the borrower can refund the issue at a profit, the call privilege is unlikely to have a value.

Empirical evidence with respect to the yield differential between immediate callable and deferred callable bonds suggests that the call privilege has the most value, and the most cost to the corporation when interest rates are high and are expected to fall.[10] By the same token, the call privilege has the greatest potential benefit to the corporation at these times. However, for this privilege, the corporation must pay a cost at the time the bonds are sold. We turn now to the question of refinancing an existing bond issue, given a call feature in the bond.

---

[9] See Gordon Pye, "The Value of the Call Option on a Bond," *Journal of Political Economy,* 74 (April 1966), 200–203.

[10] See references on Jen and Wert, Johnson and Klein, Kolodny, Pye, and Winn and Hess at the end of this chapter.

REFUNDING A BOND ISSUE

In this section, we analyze the profitability of refunding a bond issue before its maturity.[11] We assume that the decision to refund is based upon profitability alone; other considerations, such as removing restrictive protective covenants, are ignored. The refunding decision can be regarded as a form of capital budgeting; there is an initial cash outlay followed by future interest savings. These savings are represented by the difference between the annual cash outflow required under the old bonds and the net cash outflow required on the new, or refunding, bonds. Calculating the initial cash outlay is more complex. Consequently, it is best to use an example to illustrate the method of evaluation.

Suppose that a company has currently a $20 million, 8 percent debenture issue outstanding and that the issue still has twenty years to final maturity. In addition, assume that interest rates are significantly lower now than at the time of the original offering. As a result, the company can now sell a $20 million issue of twenty-year bonds at a coupon rate of 7 percent that will net it $19,600,000 after the underwriting spread.

For federal income tax purposes, the unamortized issuing expense of the old bonds, the call premium, and the unamortized discount of the old bonds, if they were sold at a discount, are deductible as expenses in the year of the refunding. Assume that the old bonds were sold originally at a slight discount from par value and that the unamortized portion now is $200,000. Moreover, the legal fees and other issuing expenses involved with the old bonds have an unamortized balance of $100,000. Finally, let us assume a call price on the old bonds of $105, issuing expenses on the new bonds of $150,000, a federal income tax rate of 50 percent, and a thirty-day period of overlap. The period of overlap is the lag between the time the new bonds are sold and the time the old bonds are called. This lag occurs because most companies wish to have the proceeds from the new issue on hand before they call the old issue. Otherwise, there is a certain amount of risk associated with calling the old issue and being at the mercy of the bond market in raising new funds. During the period of overlap, the company pays interest on both bond issues.

Framework for analysis With this rather involved background information in mind, we can calculate the initial cash outflow and the future cash benefits. The net cash outflow at the time of the refunding is as follows:

[11]This section draws heavily upon Oswald D. Bowlin, "The Refunding Decision: Another Special Case in Capital Budgeting," *Journal of Finance*, 21 (March 1966), 55–68.

Handwritten (top): $\dfrac{\$20\,mm}{\$100} = 200,000 \; \#\,of\,bonds$

Cost of calling old bonds (call price $105) *200K × $105 =*	→	$21,000,000
Net proceeds of new bond issue *(given)*		19,600,000
Difference		$ 1,400,000
Expenses:		
Issuing expense of new bonds	$ 150,000	
Interest expense on old bonds during overlap period	133,333	283,333
Gross cash outlay		$ 1,683,333
Less tax savings:		
Interest expense on old bonds during overlap period	133,333	
Call premium	1,000,000	
Unamortized discount on old bonds *(given)*	200,000	
Unamortized issuing expenses on old bonds *(given)*	100,000	
Total	$1,433,333	
Tax savings (50% of amount above)		716,667
Net cash outflow		$ 996,666

Handwritten: $\dfrac{\$20\,mm \times .08}{12} = 133,333$

Handwritten: $\$21\,mm - 20\,mm \;(or\; \$5 \times 200,000)$

Handwritten: (initially) 1 time investment

The annual net cash benefits may be determined by calculating the difference between the net cash outflow required on the old bonds and the net cash outflow required on the new or refunding bonds. The annual net cash outflow on the old bonds is:

Handwritten: $(8\% \times \$20\,MM)$

Interest expense 8%		$1,600,000
Less tax savings:		
Interest expense	$1,600,000	
Amortization of bond discount ($200,000/20)	10,000	
Amortization of issuing costs ($100,000/20)	5,000	
Total	$1,615,000	
Tax savings (50% of amount above)		807,500
Annual net cash outflow—old bonds		$ 792,500

The annual net cash outflow on the new bonds is:

Handwritten: $7\% \times \$20\,MM$

Interest expense 7%		$1,400,000
Less tax savings:		
Interest expense	$1,400,000	
Amortization of bond discount ($400,000/20)	20,000	
Amortization of issuing costs ($150,000/20)	7,500	
Total	$1,427,500	
Tax savings (50% of amount above)		713,750
Annual net cash outflow—new bonds		$ 686,250
Difference between annual net cash outflows ($792,500 − $686,250)		$ 106,250

Handwritten: net proceeds $\$20\,mm - 19,600,000 = \$400K$

Handwritten: (annually!) for 20 yrs.

Discounting   Thus, for an initial net cash outflow of $966,666, the company can achieve annual net cash benefits of $106,250 over the next twenty years. Because the net cash benefits occur in the future, they must be discounted back to present value. But what discount rate should be used? Certain authors advocate the use of the cost of capital. However, a refunding operation differs from other investment proposals. Once the new bonds are sold, the net cash benefits are known with certainty. From the standpoint of the corporation, the refunding operation is essentially a riskless investment project. The only risks associated with the cash flows are that of the firm defaulting in the payment of principal or interest. Because a premium for default risk is embodied in the market rate of interest, most agree that the appropriate discount rate is the cost of debt.[12]

However, there is disagreement as to whether the before-tax or the after-tax cost should be used. Myron J. Gordon argues that the before-tax cost of debt is the appropriate discount rate, even though the cash flows are after-tax.[13] The logic of his position is that the opportunity cost of the funds employed in the refunding is that which investors in the company require. Since an investor can earn the before-tax rate by buying the refunding bonds directly. Gordon argues that this rate is the appropriate opportunity cost.

Aharon R. Ofer and Robert A. Taggart, Jr., show that this is true only if the net refunding outlay is financed with equity.[14] If additional bonds are issued to finance the refunding outlay, stockholders will realize additional tax savings through the corporation, and the relevant discount rate becomes the after-tax cost of the refunding bonds. If the after-tax cost of the refunding bonds in our example, 3.5 percent, is used as the discount rate under the assumption that the initial outlay of $966,666 is financed with the sale of additional bonds, the net-present value of the refunding operation is found to be $543,400. As this amount is positive, the refunding operation would be worthwhile.[15] If the before-tax cost of the new bonds of 7 percent is used as the discount rate, the net-present value is found to be $158,947. Again the refunding operation would be worthwhile.[16] However, the worth of the operation obviously is less.

TIMING OF REFUNDING

We must recognize, however, that just because a refunding operation is found to be worthwhile, it should not necessarily be undertaken

[12] For a discussion of this issue, see Thomas H. Mayor and Kenneth G. McCoin, "The Rate of Discount in Bond Refunding," *Financial Management*, 3 (Autumn 1974), 54–58.

[13] "A General Solution to the Buy or Lease Decision: A Pedagogical Note," *Journal of Finance*, 29 (March 1974), 245–50.

[14] "Bond Refunding: A Clarifying Analysis," Working Paper (Graduate School of Management, Northwestern University, 1975). Ofer and Taggart also analyze the favorable effect of a refunding on the firm's debt capacity. They propose a means for analyzing the tax savings that result from the increase in debt capacity.

[15] We recall from Chapter 4 that the net-present value is the present value of net cash benefits less the initial cash outflow.

[16] For a study of the present values associated with actual bond refundings undertaken by public utilities, see A. M. Sibler, "Some Evidence on the Cash Flow Effects of Bond Refunding," *Financial Management*, 3 (Autumn 1974), 50–53.

right away. If interest rates are declining, and this decline is expected to continue, management may prefer to delay the refunding. At a later date, the refunding bonds can be sold at an even lower rate of interest, making the refunding operation even more worthwhile. The decision concerning timing must be based upon expectations of future interest rates. In determining whether or not to postpone refunding, the financial manager should also consider the dispersion and shape of the probability distribution of possible future interest rates. The greater the dispersion and the greater the skewness of the distribution to the right (toward higher interest rates), the less desirable it is to postpone the refunding, all other things the same.

Several writers have used dynamic programming models to deal with the optimal timing of a bond refunding. Weingartner[17] and Elton and Gruber[18] have viewed the problem as a multiperiod decision process, in which future interest rates are deterministic. Bierman[19] uses a two-period model in which probabilities of future interest rates are generated through Markov chains to decide whether to refund now or wait. Kalymon[20] extends this approach to the multiperiod case, in which future interest rates in each period are determined by a Markovian stochastic process. In an efficient market context, Kraus[21] presents a dynamic programming formulation involving a single refunding and a single-state variable. The essential feature of all of these models is that they provide guidelines for deciding each period whether to keep the existing bond or to refund it and issue a new bond. In this regard, the models supplement intuitive judgments as to the future course of interest rates.

Finally, two points should be raised with respect to the calculations in our example. First, most firms refund an existing issue with a new bond issue of a longer maturity. In our example, we assumed that the new bond issue has the same maturity as that of the old bond issue. Our analysis needs to be modified slightly when the maturity dates are different. The usual procedure is to consider only the net cash benefits

[17] H. Martin Weingartner, "Optimal Timing of Bond Refunding," *Management Science*, 13 (March 1967), 511–24.

[18] Edwin J. Elton and Martin J. Gruber, *Finance as a Dynamic Process* (Englewood Cliffs, N.J.: Prentice-Hall, 1975), Chapter 2.

[19] Harold Bierman, Jr., "The Bond Refunding Decision as a Markov Process," *Management Science*, 12 (August 1966), 545–51. In another paper, Harold Bierman, Jr., and Amir Barnea, "Expected Short-Term Interest Rates in Bond Refunding," *Financial Management*, 3 (Spring 1974), 75–80, use future interest rates reflected in the current term structure of interest rates to determine whether it is desirable to wait one or more periods to refund.

[20] Basil A. Kalymon, "Bond Refunding with Stochastic Interest Rates," *Management Science*, 18 (November 1971), 171–83.

[21] Alan Kraus, "The Bond Refunding Decision in an Efficient Market," *Journal of Financial and Quantitative Analysis*, 8 (December 1973), 793–806. Kraus shows that in this context the relevant time frame for expectations can be reduced to one period. The decision then is whether to refund immediately or to refund one period hence.

up to the maturity of the old bonds.[22] A second assumption in our example was that neither issue involved sinking-fund bonds or serial bonds. If either issue calls for periodic reduction of the debt, we must adjust our procedure for determining future net cash benefits.

PRIVATE PLACEMENTS

Rather than sell securities to the public, a corporation can sell the entire issue to a single institutional investor or a small group of such investors. This type of sale is known as a private or direct placement, for the company negotiates directly with the investor over the terms of the offering, eliminating the function of the underwriter. Some issues of common stock are placed privately, but the vast majority of private placements involve debt issues. Consequently, in the discussion that follows, we shall be concerned only with the direct placement of debt issues.

Private placements increased rapidly during the early sixties and accounted for about one-half of the total funds raised externally by corporations and for over three-fifths of the total debt issues by 1964. However, with the large increase in volume of corporate bond financing since 1965, the compositon of financing has shifted toward public offerings. In recent years, private placements have accounted for approximately one-fourth of the total funds raised externally by corporations. However, the percentage fluctuates from year to year. This variation in private placements relative to public offerings reflects in part the limited capacity of the private placement market to handle volume. When the total volume of corporate bond financing increases sharply, the capacity of institutional investors does not increase proportionately.[23] As a result, corporate borrowers must turn to public offerings for a larger portion of their requirements.

ADVANTAGES AND DISADVANTAGES

What are the reasons for private placements? We may gain some insight by studying their advantages and disadvantages.

---

[22] Mao, however, develops a model in which the expected interest rate on bonds at the time the outstanding issue matures is expressed in probabilistic terms. He then treats the probabilistic difference between the interest rate on these bonds and that on the refunding bonds as the interest savings or dissavings during the span between the two maturity dates. These savings or dissavings for the additional years are treated as future cash benefits and incorporated in the above model. James C. T. Mao, *Quantitative Analysis of Financial Decisions* (London: Macmillan, 1969), pp. 351–62.

[23] See Henry Kaufman, *The Changing Dimensions of the Corporate Bond Market* (New York: Salomon Brothers and Hutzler, 1967), p. 11.

Flexibility   One of the more frequently mentioned advantages of a private placement is the speed of the commitment. A public issue must be registered with the SEC, documents prepared and printed, and extensive negotiations undertaken; all this requires a certain lead time. In addition, the public issue always involves risks with respect to timing. With a private placement, the terms can be tailored to the needs of the borrower, and the financing can be consummated much more quickly. Because the issue is negotiated, the exact timing in the market is not a critical problem. The fact that there is but a single investor or small group of investors is attractive if it becomes necessary to change any of the terms of the issue. It is much easier to deal with a single investor than with a large group of public security holders.

Another advantage of a privately placed debt issue is that the actual borrowing does not necessarily have to take place all at once. The company can enter into an arrangement whereby it can borrow up to a fixed amount over a period of time. For this nonrevolving credit arrangement, the borrower usually will pay a commitment fee. This type of arrangement gives the company flexibility, allowing it to borrow only when it needs the funds. With a public issue, it is necessary to sell the entire issue at one time. Because the private placement does not have to be registered with the SEC, the company avoids making available to the public the detailed information required by the SEC.

Size of issue   Private placements allow medium-sized and sometimes small companies to sell a bond issue, whereas with a public offering the flotation costs would be prohibitive. Institutional investors are willing to invest in bonds of smaller companies, provided the company is credit-worthy. It is doubtful that institutional investors would seek an issue of less than $100,000 (and many insist upon a higher minimum), but we must remember that a $5 million bond issue is considered small as a public offering.

Cost of issue   There are two costs to consider in comparing a private placement of debt with a public offering: the initial cost and the interest cost. Because the negotiations usually are direct, private placement involves no underwriting or selling expenses. Frequently, however, a company seeks the services of an investment banker for advice in planning and negotiating the issue. Investment bankers have become increasingly involved as agents in private placements, thus offsetting to a certain degree the loss of underwriting and selling business. However, overall, the initial total cost of a private placement is significantly less than that of a public offering.[24]

---

[24]Avery B. Cohan, *Private Placements and Public Offerings: Market Shares Since 1935* (Chapel Hill, N.C.: School of Business Administration, University of North Carolina, 1961), Chapter 11.

The second aspect of the cost of a private placement of debt is the interest cost. Fragmentary evidence here indicates that the yield on private placements is significantly above that on public offerings. In addition to interest costs, institutional investors sometimes will request an equity "sweetener," such as warrants, to entice them to invest in the debt issue of a company. Although the exact cost of this "sweetener" is difficult to measure, it certainly adds to the total cost of a private placement.[25]

In summary, it would seem that the initial cost of a private placement of debt is less than that of a public offering. However, the interest cost and any additional compensation appear to be higher. For a long-term debt issue, the total cost is likely to be somewhat higher for a private placement than for a public offering. However, the difference in cost must be compared with the advantages of the private placement.

PREFERRED STOCK

Preferred stock is a hybrid form of financing, combining features of debt and common stock. In the event of liquidation, a preferred stockholder's claim on assets comes after that of creditors but before that of common stockholders. Usually, this claim is restricted to the par value of the stock. For example, if the par value of a share of preferred stock is $100, the investor will be entitled to a maximum of $100 in settlement of the principal amount. Although preferred stock carries a stipulated dividend, the actual payment of a dividend is a discretionary, rather than a fixed, obligation of the company. The omission of a dividend will not result in a default of the obligation or insolvency of the company. The board of directors has full power to omit a preferred stock dividend if it so chooses.

The maximum return to preferred stockholders usually is limited to the specified dividend, and these stockholders ordinarily do not share in the residual earnings of the company. Thus, if an investor owns 100 shares of 6 percent preferred stock, $100 par value, the maximum return he can expect in any one year, usually, is $600; and this return is at the discretion of the board of directors. The corporation cannot deduct this dividend on its tax return; this fact is the principal shortcoming of preferred stock as a means of financing. In view of the fact that interest payments on debt are deductible for tax purposes, the company that treats a preferred stock dividend as a fixed obligation finds the explicit cost to be rather high.

---

[25] For a discussion of the implications of equity "sweeteners" for institutional investors and borrowers, see Samuel L. Hayes III, "New Interest in Incentive Financing," *Harvard Business Review*, 44 (July–August 1966), 99–112.

CUMULATIVE FEATURE

Almost all preferred stocks have a cumulative feature, providing for unpaid dividends in any one year to be carried forward. Before the company can pay a dividend on its common stock, it must pay the dividends *in arrears* on its preferred stock. For example, suppose that the board of directors of a company omitted the preferred stock dividend on its 6 percent cumulative preferred stock for three consecutive years. If the stock has a $100 par value, the company would be $18 per share in arrears on its preferred stock. Before it can pay a dividend to its common stockholders, it must pay preferred stockholders $18 for each share of preferred stock held. It should be emphasized that just because preferred stock dividends are in arrears, there is no guarantee that they will ever be paid. If the corporation has no intention of paying a common-stock dividend, there is no need to clear up the arrearage on the preferred. The preferred stock dividend typically is omitted for lack of earnings, but the corporation does not have to pay a dividend if earnings are restored.

If the preferred stock dividends are in arrears, and the company wishes to pay a common-stock dividend, it may choose not to clear up the arrearage but to make an exchange offering to preferred stockholders. For example, suppose that the dividend arrearages on an issue of $100 par value preferred stock are $56 and that the market price of the stock is $74 a share. The company might offer preferred stockholders common stock in the company, valued at $110, for each share of preferred stock held. Although theoretically the preferred stockholder is asked to give up $156 ($100 par value plus $56 dividend arrearages), the exchange offering promises him $110 relative to a current preferred stock market value of only $74 per share. In order to eliminate the preferred stock, the company must obtain the approval of a required percentage of the stock outstanding, often two-thirds. Consequently, it probably will make its exchange offering contingent upon obtaining the required acceptance. If the incentive is attractive enough, preferred stockholders probably will accept the offer despite the fact that they are not satisfied to the full extent of the arrearages.[26]

If a preferred stock is noncumulative, dividends not paid in one year do not carry forward. As a result, a company can pay a common-stock dividend without regard to any dividends it did not pay in the past on its preferred stock. From the standpoint of an investor, a noncumulative

---

[26] In 1962, the Virginia Carolina Chemical Company offered preferred stockholders a package of prior-preferred stock, convertible preferred stock, and common stock worth about $150 for each share of $100 par value preferred stock they owned. The dividend arrearages on the preferred stock were $96 a share, giving a preferred stockholder a theoretical claim of $196 a share.

preferred stock is little more than an income bond. In fact, there is somewhat less uncertainty with income bonds, for the conditions under which interest will be paid are specified clearly, and bondholders have a prior claim on assets. Because of the obvious disadvantage to investors, noncumulative preferred stock issues are rare, although they may be used in reorganizations.

PARTICIPATING FEATURE

A participating feature allows preferred stockholders to participate in the residual earnings of the corporation according to some specified formula. For example, the preferred stockholder might be entitled to share equally with common shareholders in any common stock dividend beyond a certain amount. Suppose that a 6 percent preferred stock ($100 par value) were participating, so that the holders were entitled to share equally in any common-stock dividends in excess of $6 a share. If the common-stock dividend is $7, the preferred stockholder will receive $1 in extra dividends for each share of stock owned. The formula for participation can vary greatly. The essential feature is that preferred stockholders have a prior claim on income and an opportunity for additional return if the dividends to common stockholders exceed a certain amount. Unfortunately for the investor, practically all preferred stock issues are nonparticipating, with the maximum return limited to the specified dividend rate.

VOTING POWER

Because of their prior claim on assets and income, preferred stockholders normally are not given a voice in management unless the company is unable to pay preferred stock dividends during a specified period of time. For example, arrearages on four quarterly dividend payments might constitute such a default. Under such circumstances, preferred stockholders as a class will be entitled to elect a specific number of directors. Usually, the number is rather small in relation to the total. Moreover, by the time the preferred stockholders are able to obtain a voice in management, the company probably is in considerable financial difficulty. Consequently, the voting power that preferred stockholders are granted may be virtually meaningless.

Depending upon the agreement between the preferred stockholders and the company, they may obtain voting power under other conditions as well. The company may default under certain restrictions in the agreement similar to those found in a loan agreement or a bond indenture. One of the more frequently imposed restrictions is that dividends on common stock are prohibited if the company does not satisfy certain

financial ratios. We note, however, that default under any of the provisions of the agreement between the corporation and its preferred
stockholders does not result in the obligation's becoming immediately

Chapter 21 **581**
LONG-TERM DEBT AND
PREFERRED STOCK

payable, as does default under a loan agreement or bond indenture. The
preferred stockholders merely are given a voice in management and
assurance that common stock dividends will not be paid during the
period of default. Thus, preferred stockholders do not have nearly the
same legal power in default as do debtholders.

RETIREMENT OF PREFERRED STOCK

Preferred stock, like common stock, has no maturity. However, most
preferred stock issues are not regarded as a means of perpetual financing, because provision for retirement of the stock invariably is made.

Call feature   Practically all preferred stock issues have a stated
call price, which is above the original issuance price
and may decrease over time. Like the call feature on bonds, the call
feature on preferred stock affords the company flexibility. Because the
market price of a straight preferred stock tends to fluctuate in keeping
with interest-rate cycles, the value of the preferred stock call feature is
determined by the same considerations as is the call feature for bonds,
which we discussed earlier. However, with long-term debt, unlike with
preferred stock, there is a final maturity that assures the eventual
retirement of the issue. Without a call feature on preferred stock, the
corporation would be able to retire the issue only by the often more
expensive and less efficient methods of purchasing the stock in the open
market, inviting *tenders* of the stock from preferred stockholders at a
price above the market price, or offering the preferred stockholders
another security in its place.

Sinking fund   Many preferred stock issues provide for a sinking
fund, which partially assures an orderly retirement
of the stock. The trustee of the preferred stock issue may use the
sinking-fund payments to either buy stock in the open market or call a
portion of it. In either case, the stock is retired. A sinking fund is
advantageous to investors because the retirement process exerts upward
pressure on the market price of the remaining shares. Also, the coverage
ratio on the preferred stock dividend is improved as the number of
shares outstanding is reduced. The sinking fund works to the disadvantage of common stockholders because it represents another prior charge
and, therefore, contributes to the financial risk of the company from
their standpoint. A preferable arrangement for them would be a sinking-fund requirement wherein payments were variable in relation to
earnings. Because the sinking fund is beneficial to preferred stockhold-

ers, the company should be able to sell the issue at a lower dividend yield than if it provided for no sinking fund. Overall, sinking funds are used much less with preferred stock than with bonds.

Convertibility   Certain preferred stock issues are convertible into common stock at the option of the holder. Upon conversion, of course, the preferred stock is retired. Because practically all convertible securities have a call feature, the company can force conversion by calling the preferred stock if the market price of the preferred is significantly above the call price. Convertible preferred stock is used frequently in the acquisition of other companies.[27] In part, its use stems from the fact that the transaction is not taxable for the company that is acquired or its stockholders at the time of the acquisition. It becomes a taxable transaction only when the preferred stock is sold.[28] We shall examine convertible securities in much more detail in the next chapter.

FINANCING WITH PREFERRED STOCK

Nonconvertible preferred stock is not used extensively in financing; only public utilities employ it with any degree of regularity.[29] One of the principal drawbacks to its use is the fact that the preferred dividend is not tax deductible. With a 48 percent tax rate, the explicit cost of preferred stock is about twice that of bonds. As an investment, however, preferred stock may be more attractive to the corporate investor than bonds because 85 percent of the dividends received is not subject to taxation. As a result, many preferred stocks sell at a lower yield than do the bonds of the same company, despite their lower priority of claim. In fact, the average yield differential between high-grade industrial bonds and high-grade preferred stocks has narrowed over the post-World War II period to where now preferred stocks yield less on the average. Thus, the after-tax cost disadvantage of preferred stock financing has diminished somewhat during the last thirty years.

The advantage of preferred stock financing is that it is a flexible

---

[27] See Robert M. Soldofsky, "Convertible Preferred Stock: Renewed Life in an Old Form," *Business Lawyer* (July 1969), 1385–92.

[28] See Chapter 23 for a more detailed discussion of the tax effect.

[29] For a review of preferred stock financing, see Donald E. Fisher and Glenn A. Wilt, Jr., "Nonconvertible Preferred Stock as a Financing Instrument," *Journal of Finance,* 23 (September 1968), 611–24. One reason for the use of preferred stock by utilities is that the Securities and Exchange Commission stated in 1952 that the capital structure of an electric utility should not exceed 60 percent debt, and that common stock should not be less than 30 percent. Thus, the 10 percent residual could be filled by preferred stock. Another reason is that a public utility is able to pass off the higher explicit cost of preferred stock, as compared with that of debt, in the rates it charges. Public utility commissions allow utilities to base their rates on their overall measured cost of capital.

financing arrangement. The dividend is not a legal obligation on the part of the corporation issuing the securities; if earnings turn bad and the financial condition of the company deteriorates, the dividend can be omitted. With debt financing, interest must be paid regardless of whether earnings are good or bad. To be sure, companies that are accustomed to paying dividends on their common stock certainly regard the preferred dividend as a fixed obligation. Nevertheless, under dire circumstances, a company that omits its common stock dividend can also omit its preferred dividend.

Another advantage of a straight preferred stock issue is that it has no final maturity; in essence, it is a perpetual loan. Also, the majority of preferred stock issues do not require sinking-fund payments. Thus, a preferred stock issue gives a corporation flexibility by allowing it not to make principal payments or plan for refinancing. Moreover, from the standpoint of creditors, preferred stock adds to the equity base of the company and thereby strengthens its financial condition. The additional equity base enhances the ability of the company to borrow in the future. Although the explicit cost of preferred stock is considerably higher than that of bonds, the implied benefits discussed above may offset this cost. In addition, the implicit cost of preferred stock financing, from the standpoint of investors penalizing the price/earnings ratio of the common stock, may be somewhat less than that of debt financing. To the extent that investors are apprehensive over legal bankruptcy, they would regard debt as a riskier form of leverage. Unlike creditors, preferred stockholders cannot force a company into legal bankruptcy.[30]

[30] Gordon Donaldson, "In Defense of Preferred Stock," *Harvard Business Review,* 40 (July–August 1962), 123–36, defends rigorously the use of preferred stock as a means of financing under certain circumstances. He argues that when a company has utilized its debt capacity, it may be able to finance further with preferred stock because the preferred stock capacity of a company is distinct from its debt capacity.

SUMMARY

Our concern in this chapter has been with the various features and types of fixed-income securities. The decision to use such securities in the capital structure and the amount to be employed were considered in Chapters 9 and 10. The principal features of debt include the fixed return, the priority of claim on assets, the call privilege, and the method of retirement of the debt. We saw that periodic reduction of the debt can be accomplished by issuing either sinking-fund bonds or serial bonds.

In financing with long-term debt, the company must bargain with investors over the terms of the debt instrument. If the company wishes to include terms that are not beneficial to investors, it must be prepared to pay a higher yield in order to sell the instrument. For example, if debentures are subordi-

nated, investors will demand a higher yield than if the issue involves straight debentures. Another interesting aspect of the bargaining process between the borrower and investors relates to the call privilege. If interest rate expectations in the market are such that investors think that the issue may be called, the company will have to pay a higher yield for the privilege of being able to call it.

The size and frequency of long-term debt issues depend upon the fixed cost associated with an issue, upon the difference in yield between the rate of interest paid on the debt issue and the rate on short-term securities, and upon interest rate expectations. We examined a model for evaluating the tradeoff between these factors. In addition, a method was proposed for analyzing the refunding of a bond issue before maturity. This method treats the refunding operation as a riskless capital-budgeting project. Also examined was the timing of a refunding.

Rather than offer securities to the general public, a company may place them privately with an institutional investor. With a private placement, the company negotiates directly with the investor; there is no underwriting and no registration of the issue with the SEC. The private placement has the virtue of flexibility and affords the medium-sized and even the small company the opportunity to sell its securities.

Preferred stock is a hybrid form of security having characteristics of both debt and common stock. The payment of dividends is not a legal but a discretionary obligation, although many companies regard the obligation as fixed. Preferred stockholders' claims on assets and income come after those of creditors but before those of common stockholders. The return on their investment is almost always limited to the specified dividend; very seldom do preferred stockholders participate in the residual earnings of the company. Although they may have some voting power, this power generally is restricted to situations where the company has evolved itself into financial difficulty.

Because preferred stock has no final maturity, almost all recent issues have had call features that give the corporation financial flexibility. Retirement of the preferred stock can also be accomplished by a sinking fund, by convertibility, or by an exchange offering. The principal disadvantages of preferred stock are that the yield generally is higher than the yield on bonds and that the dividend is not tax deductible. Offsetting in some measure the difference in explicit costs between the two methods of financing are implicit benefits associated with debt capacity and financial flexibility. Despite these implicit benefits, however, preferred stock is little used as a method of financing.

1. The Lemand Corporation has $10 million of 8 percent mortgage bonds outstanding under an open-end indenture. The indenture allows additional bonds to be issued as long as all of the following conditions are met:

   (a) Pretax interest coverage [(income before taxes + bond interest)/ bond interest] remains greater than 4.

   (b) Net depreciated value of mortgaged assets remains twice the amount of mortgage debt.

   (c) Debt/equity ratio remains below 0.5.

   The Lemand Corporation has net income of $2 million and a 50 percent tax rate, $40 million in equity, and $30 million in depreciated assets, covered by the mortgage, which are depreciated at $2 million per year. Assuming that 50 percent of the proceeds of a new issue would be added to the base of mortgaged assets and that the company has no sinking-fund payments until next year, how much more 8 percent debt could be sold?

2. The Hirsch Corporation is in bankruptcy. Mortgaged assets have been sold for $5 million and other assets have yielded $10 million. Hirsch has $10 million in mortgage bonds, $5 million in subordinated (to the mortgage bonds) debentures, $15 million owed to general creditors, and $10 million par value of common stock. How would distribution of the $15 million in liquidating value be made?

3. Western States Electric Company needs to raise $200 million in long-term debt funds over the next three years. As the capital improvements that these funds will finance cannot be postponed and their cost is known, the $200 million figure is a certainty. Moreover, the use of funds will be steady over the three-year interval. The rate of interest on Treasury bills is currently 6 percent, and the company can raise long-term debt at $7\frac{1}{2}$ percent interest. Western States does not expect these rates to change over the three-year period. In a study of flotation costs about a year ago, the company found that fixed costs associated with an individual issue total $100,000.

   (a) If the size of debt issue were to be the same for each issue, what is the optimal issue size over the three-year period? What is the optimal frequency between financings?

   (b) From the formula for optimal issue size, what would happen if fixed costs increased?

   (c) What would happen if the rate on the long-term debt rose relative to the rate on Treasury bills?

4. The Laster Corporation wishes to borrow $10 million for ten years. It can issue either a noncallable bond at 8 percent interest or a bond callable at the end of five years for 9 percent. For simplicity, we assume that the bond will be called only at the end of year 5 and that both bonds are sold at par. The interest rate that is likely to prevail five years hence for a five-year bond can be described by a normal probability distribution with an expected value of 7 percent and a standard deviation of 1 percent.

(a) What is the probability that the absolute amount of total interest payments under the callable bonds and later issuance of five-year bonds will be less than that under the noncallable ten-year bonds?

(b) If the company can earn 14 percent before taxes on its funds, what is the probability that the callable bond alternative has a greater pretax present value than the noncallable bond alternative?

5. The U.S. Zither Corporation has $50 million of 10 percent debentures outstanding, which are due in thirty years. USZ could refund these bonds in the current market with new thirty-year bonds, sold to the public at par ($1,000) with a 9 percent coupon; total gross spread would be $2\frac{1}{2}$ percent of the issue. The old bonds have an unamortized discount of $1 million, unamortized legal fees and other expenses of $300,000, and a call price of 107. The tax rate is 50 percent. Treasury bills yield 6 percent, there is a two-month overlap, and issuing expenses are $200,000. Compute the present value of the refunding, using after-tax discount rates of 3 percent, 10 percent, and 15 percent.

6. The Kramer Corporation wishes to raise $10 million of debt for twenty years. It can sell bonds publicly with an 8 percent coupon and a 1.50 percent gross spread, or it can place an $8\frac{1}{2}$ percent note privately, with no other costs. Assuming that the Kramer Corporation would not repay the principal of either loan until maturity, would make annual interest payments, and is able to earn 12 percent before taxes on funds it employs, which plan would have the higher present value to the firm?

7. *Research Project*
Obtain copies of several bond indentures. Pay particular attention to the restrictive covenants concerning such things as dividends, working capital, additional debt, and nature of the business. Try to relate the cost of debt to the firm to the relative restrictiveness of these provisions. Does management pay extra for discretion? If it does, can these covenants truly be said to be nonquantifiable? How would you go about finding a measure of degree of restriction so that tradeoffs with interest could be made?

8. Eleven years ago the Delano Corporation sold 10,000 shares of 6 percent, $100 par preferred callable at 105. After a year of paying dividends on this stock, Delano fell upon hard times, with the result that each share is now $60 in arrears. Conditions have improved, however, so that the net income after taxes has risen to a normal level of $250,000. The 50,000 common shares would ordinarily sell at a P/E multiple of 12, but the preferred arrearages have caused the common to sell at $30. The preferred has been quoted at $120, although any buying pressure would cause this price to rise significantly. Delano has a 50 percent tax rate and is faced with the following alternatives:

(a) Exchange common for preferred on the basis of their market prices; or

(b) Call the preferred, and finance the transaction with a 9 percent debenture.

From the standpoint of current common shareholders, which alternative is preferable? What reservations do you have?

9. Lost Horizon Silver Mining Company has 200,000 shares of $7 cumulative preferred stock outstanding, $100 par value. The preferred stock has a participating feature. If dividends on the common stock exceed $1 per share, preferred stockholders receive additional dividends per share equal to one-half of the excess. In other words, if the common-stock dividend were $2, preferred stockholders would receive an additional dividend of $0.50. The company has 1 million shares of common outstanding. What would dividends per share be on the preferred stock and on the common stock if earnings available for dividends in three successive years were (a) $1,000,000, $600,000, and $3,000,000; (b) $2,000,000, $2,400,000, and $4,600,000; and (c) $1,000,000, $2,500,000, and $5,700,000. (Assume all of the available earnings are paid in dividends, but nothing more is paid.)

SELECTED REFERENCES

Ang, James S., "The Two Faces of Bond Refunding," *Journal of Finance,* 30 (June 1975), 869–74.

Bierman, Harold, Jr., "The Bond Refunding Decision as a Markov Process," *Management Science,* 12 (August 1966), 545–51.

Bierman, Harold, Jr., and Amir Barnea, "Expected Short-Term Interest Rates in Bond Refunding," *Financial Management,* 3 (Spring 1974), 75–79.

Bildersee, John S., "Some Aspects of the Performance of Non-Convertible Preferred Stocks," *Journal of Finance,* 28 (December 1973), 1187–1202.

Bowlin, Oswald D., "The Refunding Decision: Another Special Case in Capital Budgeting," *Journal of Finance,* 21 (March 1966), 55–68.

Brown, Bowman, "Why Corporations Should Consider Income Bonds," *Financial Executive,* 35 (October 1967), 74–78.

Cohan, Avery B., *Private Placements and Public Offerings: Market Shares since 1935.* Chapel Hill, N.C.: School of Business Administration, University of North Carolina, 1961.

Donaldson, Gordon, "In Defense of Preferred Stock," *Harvard Business Review,* 40 (July–August 1962), 123–36.

Elsaid, Hussein H., "The Function of Preferred Stock in the Corporate Financial Plan," *Financial Analysts Journal* (July–August 1969), 112–17.

Elton, Edwin J., and Martin J. Gruber, "Dynamic Programming Applications in Finance," *Journal of Finance,* 26 (May 1971), 473–505.

———, "The Economic Value of the Call Option," *Journal of Finance,* 27 (September 1972), 891–902.

———, *Finance as a Dynamic Process,* Chapter 2. Englewood Cliffs, N.J.: Prentice-Hall, 1975.

Fisher, Donald E., and Glenn A. Wilt, Jr., "Nonconvertible Preferred Stock as a Financing Instrument, 1950–1965," *Journal of Finance,* 23 (September 1968), 611–24.

Halford, Frank A., "Income Bonds," *Financial Analysts Journal,* 20 (January–February 1964), 73–79.

Jen, Frank C., and James E. Wert, "The Deferred Call Provision and Corporate Bond Yields," *Journal of Financial and Quantitative Analysis,* 3 (June 1968), 157–69.

———, "The Effect of Call Risk on Corporate Bond Yields," *Journal of Finance,* 22 (December 1967), 637–51.

———, "The Value of the Deferred Call Privilege," *National Banking Review,* 3 (March 1966), 369–78.

Johnson, Rodney, and Richard Klein, "Corporate Motives in Repurchases of Discounted Bonds," *Financial Management,* 3 (Autumn 1974), 44–49.

Kalymon, Basil A., "Bond Refunding with Stochastic Interest Rates," *Management Science,* 18 (November 1971), 171–83.

Kolodny, Richard, "The Refunding Decision in Near Perfect Markets," *Journal of Finance,* 29 (December 1974), 1467–78.

Kraus, Alan, "The Bond Refunding Decision in an Efficient Market," *Journal of Financial and Quantitative Analysis,* forthcoming.

Litzenberger, Robert H., and David P. Rutenberg, "Size and Timing of Corporate Bond Flotations," *Journal of Financial and Quantitative Analysis,* 8 (January 1972), 1343–59.

Mayor, Thomas H., and Kenneth G. McCoin, "The Rate of Discount in Bond Refunding," *Financial Management,* 3 (Autumn 1974), 54–58.

Ofer, Aharon, R., and Robert A. Taggart, Jr., "Bond Refunding: A Clarifying Analysis," Working Paper, Graduate School of Management, Northwestern University, 1975.

Pinches, George E., "Financing with Convertible Preferred Stock, 1960–1967," *Journal of Finance,* 25 (March 1970), 53–63.

Pinches, George E., and Kent A. Mingo, "A Multivariate Analysis of Industrial Bond Ratings," *Journal of Finance,* 28 (March 1973), 1–18.

——, "The Role of Subordination and Industrial Bond Ratings," *Journal of Finance,* 30 (March 1975), 201–6.

Pye, Gordon, "The Value of Call Deferment on a Bond: Some Empirical Results," *Journal of Finance,* 22 (December 1967), 623–36.

——, The Value of the Call Option on a Bond," *Journal of Political Economy,* 74 (April 1966), 200–205.

Sibler, A. M., "Some Evidence on the Cash Flow Effects of Bond Refunding," *Financial Management,* 3 (Autumn 1974), 50–53.

Stevenson, Richard A., "Retirement of Non-Callable Preferred Stock," *Journal of Finance,* 25 (December 1970), 1143–52.

Van Horne, James C., *The Function and Analysis of Capital Market Rates,* Chapters 4–6. Englewood Cliffs, N.J.: Prentice-Hall, 1970.

——, "Implied Fixed Costs in Long-Term Debt Issues," *Journal of Financial and Quantitative Analysis,* 8 (December 1973).

Weingartner, H. Martin, "Optimal Timing of Bond Refunding," *Management Science,* 13 (March 1967), 511–24.

Winn, Willis J., and Arleigh Hess, Jr., "The Value of the Call Privilege," *Journal of Finance,* 14 (May 1959), 182–95.

FINANCING with OPTIONS: the CONVERTIBLE SECURITY and WARRANT

Both convertible securities and warrants—the subject of this chapter—are forms of options. An *option*, as we will use the term, is merely a security that gives its owner the right to buy or sell the common stock of a company within a specific period of time. The price paid for the stock, or the price at which it is sold, is known as the *exercise price*, and it is stated in the contract. For example, we might have a "call" option to buy one share of stock of ABC Corporation at $10 through December 31 of the current year.[1] Thus, the option has an exercise price of $10 and an expiration date of December 31. The option itself may be traded in a market. If it is, its value will be closely related to the value of the associated stock—the two securities are close substitutes with respect to market price movements.

RELATION TO STOCK PRICE

In Figure 22-1, we illustrate the underlying theoretical relationship between the price of a share of common stock and the price of an option to buy that stock.[2] The 45-degree line represents the theoretical value of the option. It is simply the stock price less the exercise price of the option. When the price of the stock is less than the exercise price of the option, the option has a zero theoretical value; when more, it has a theoretical value on the line.

As long as there is some time to expiration, it is possible for the market value of an option to be greater than its theoretical value. The reason for this is the very nature of the contract—namely, it is an option that affords the holder flexibility with respect to the purchase of stock. To illustrate, suppose the current market price of ABC Corporation's stock were $10, which is equal to the exercise price. Theoretically, the option would have no value. However, if there is some probability that the price of the stock will exceed $10 before expiration, the option should have a positive value inasmuch as it *may* permit the holder to exercise it advantageously. To illustrate, suppose further that the option has thirty days to expiration and that trading occurs only at the end of that time. This assumption corresponds to the definition of a "European" option, which can only be exercised on a specified future date. Additionally, assume that there is a 0.3 probability that the stock will have a market price of $5 per share at the end of the thirty days, 0.4 that it will be $10, and 0.3 that it will be $15. The expected value of the option at the end of thirty days is thus

$$0(0.3) + 0(0.4) + (\$15 - \$10)(0.3) = \$1.50$$

---

[1] In contrast, a "put" option entitles the holder to sell stock at a specified exercise price through the expiration date. In the remainder of our discussion, we will be concerned only with call options.

[2] Throughout we assume that the option entitles the holder to buy one share of stock.

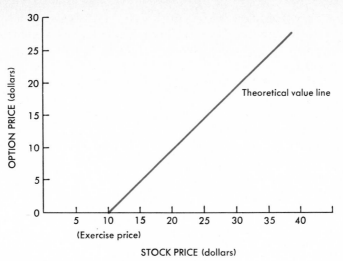

Chapter 22 **591**
FINANCING WITH
OPTIONS: THE
CONVERTIBLE
SECURITY AND
WARRANT

FIG. 22·1
*Theoretical value
of an option for
ABC Corporation stock*

Therefore, it is possible for an option whose associated stock value is less or equal to the exercise price to have a positive value. Because the option cannot go below zero in value, even when the stock price less the exercise price is negative, the option is frequently worth more than its theoretical value. How much more depends in part upon the time to expiration. Figure 22-2 illustrates the general relationship between stock prices and option prices for various terms to expiration.[3]

The highest value the option can take is the value of the stock, represented by the line X. This would presumably occur only if the option had a very long time to expiration, perhaps forever, and if the option was not expected to be exercised until far into the future. Under these circumstances, the present value of the exercise price to be paid in the future would approach zero. As a result, the value of the option would approach the value of the associated stock. The lowest value the option can take, of course, is its theoretical value, represented in the figure by zero up to the exercise price and by line Y for values of the stock greater than the exercise price. One might think of the theoretical value line as representing the values of an option with only a moment to expiration. Thus, lines X and Y constitute the boundaries for the value of an option in relation to the value of the associated stock.

For most options, however, the relationship lies between these two boundaries. In general, it can be described by a concave relationship where the value of the option commands the greatest premium over its theoretical value at approximately the exercise price and where the premium declines with increases in the value of the stock beyond that point. Because of the lesser investment required, an option will change in value by a greater percentage than will the stock. The largest per-

---

[3]Perhaps the first to draw attention to this type of presentation was Paul A. Samuelson, "A Rational Theory of Warrant Pricing," *Industrial Management Review*, 6 (Spring 1965).

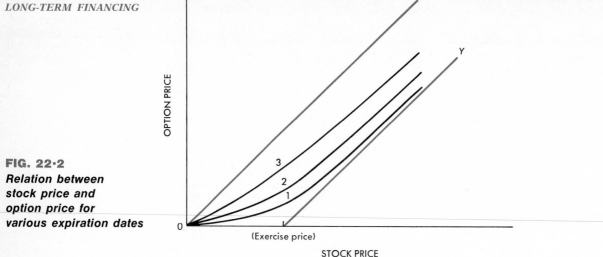

FIG. 22·2
Relation between stock price and option price for various expiration dates

centage change in option price relative to stock price occurs generally when the stock price is near the exercise price. To the left of the exercise price, downward changes in option price are buffered by the fact that the option price cannot go below zero. To the right of the exercise price, upward changes in option price are buffered percentagewise by the fact that the option is worth only its theoretical value upon ultimately being exercised. For these reasons, the option price typically commands the greatest premium over its theoretical value when the market price of the stock approximates the exercise price. In general, the longer the expiration date, the greater the value of the option relative to its theoretical value. The obvious reason is that there is more time in which the option *may* have value. As the expiration date approaches, the relationship between the option value and the stock value becomes more concave. In Figure 22-2, line 1 represents an option with a shorter time to expiration than that for line 2, and line 2 an option with a shorter time to expiration than that for line 3. The concepts behind the relationship between option prices and stock prices, shown in Figure 22-2, will be used in our examination of both convertible securities and warrants.

EQUILIBRIUM VALUE OF AN OPTION

From our discussion above, we know that an option affords its holder the opportunity to participate in movements in stock prices, but with a lower net investment than in the stock. Put another way, it is possible to get approximately the same "action" in dollar terms in either the stock or the option, but because the option requires less net invest-

Chapter 22 **593**
FINANCING WITH
OPTIONS: THE
CONVERTIBLE
SECURITY AND
WARRANT

ment, percentage movements in option prices will be greater than percentage changes in stock prices.[4] If the price of the option gets "out of line" with the price of the stock, there will be opportunity for arbitrage profit. One can take a hedged position by holding a share of stock long (owning it outright) and selling so many options short.

In a short sale, a person borrows the security from a brokerage house. (In so doing, he agrees to give it back within a specified period of time.) He then sells the borrowed security in the market. Eventually, of course, the security must be returned to the "lender." This is done by buying the security in the market and delivering it to the lender. Ignoring transaction costs, if the price at which the borrowed security is sold exceeds the price at which it is "bought back," the individual makes money;[5] if vice versa, he loses money.

A hedged position, then, might be one where an individual buys a share of stock outright and sells so many options short. By holding this combination, movements upward or downward in the price of the stock are offset by opposite movements in the value of the option position held short.[6] Therefore, the overall position (long in stock—short in options) is approximately risk-free. To the extent that excess returns are available on a fully hedged position, individuals will have an incentive to take such positions. The impact of their buying and selling stocks and options in order to establish hedged positions will affect relative prices in such a way as to drive out any excess returns that might be earned. In other words, arbitragers seek out situations where an option is undervalued relative to the stock, or vice versa, and they buy or sell until such time as the undervalued situation ceases to exist. As in any arbitrage example, the impact of buying and selling drives prices up or down until the excess return no longer exists.

To the extent that capital markets are efficient, Black and Scholes have shown that the expected return on a fully hedged position of stocks and options approximates the risk-free rate.[7] (In the appendix to this chapter, we present the Black-Scholes model.) In equilibrium, then, excess returns would not be possible, and stocks and options would be priced in the market in such a way that one would not be overvalued or undervalued relative to the other. To the extent that imperfections exist

[4] See Fischer Black, "Fact and Fantasy in the Use of Options" (unpublished paper, University of Chicago, 1974).

[5] This statement assumes that there are no imperfections involved in selling short, i.e., no margin is required on the part of the borrower of the security.

[6] As the price of the stock changes so will the relationship between a share of stock and the number of options necessary to maintain a fully hedged position. Therefore, this position must be continually adjusted. See the appendix to this chapter for more detail on this point.

[7] See Fischer Black and Myron Scholes, "The Pricing of Options and Corporate Liabilities," *Journal of Political Economy*, 81 (May–June 1973), 637–54. A similar conclusion was reached by Robert C. Merton, "A Rational Theory of Option Pricing," *Bell Journal of Economics and Management Science*, 4 (Spring 1973), 141–83.

in capital markets, however, a fully hedged position may not be possible, and returns in excess of the risk-free rate may be earned on the "partially" hedged position. With this general discussion of options in mind, we turn now to examine two specific types of options frequently employed by business firms in their financing—the convertible security and the warrant.

CONVERTIBLE SECURITIES

A *convertible security* is a bond or a share of preferred stock that can be converted at the option of the holder into the common stock of the same corporation. Once converted into common stock, the stock cannot be exchanged again for bonds or preferred stock. The ratio of exchange between the convertible security and the common stock can be stated in terms of either a *conversion price* or a *conversion ratio*. To illustrate, the Owens-Illinois, Inc., $4\frac{1}{2}$ percent convertible subordinated debentures ($1,000 face value), issued in November 1967, have a conversion price of $59, meaning that each debenture is convertible into 16.95 shares of common stock. We simply divide the face value of the security by the conversion price to obtain the conversion ratio, $1,000/59 = 16.95$. The conversion privilege can be stated either in terms of the conversion price or the conversion ratio.

The conversion terms are not necessarily constant over time. Many convertible issues provide for increases or "step-ups" in the conversion price at periodic intervals. For example, a $1,000 face value bond might have a conversion price of $100 a share for the first five years, $110 a share for the second five years, $120 for the third five, and so on. In this way, the bond converts into fewer shares of common stock as time goes by. Usually, the conversion price is adjusted for any stock splits or stock dividends that occur after the securities are sold. If the common stock were split two for one, for example, the conversion price would be halved. This provision protects the convertible bondholder and is known as an antidilution clause.

CONVERSION VALUE AND PREMIUM

The *conversion value* of a convertible security is the conversion ratio of the security times the market price per share of the common stock. If Owens-Illinois stock were selling for $60 per share, the conversion value of one convertible subordinated debenture would be $16.95 \times \$60$, or $1,017.

The convertible security provides the investor with a fixed return, in the case of a bond, or with a specified dividend, in the case of preferred stock. In addition, he receives an option to convert the security into common stock, and he thereby participates in the possibility of capital gains associated with being a residual owner of the corporation. Because of this option, the company usually is able to sell the convertible security at a lower yield than it would have to pay on a straight bond or preferred stock issue. At the time of issuance, the convertible security will be priced higher than its conversion value. The differential is known as the *conversion premium.* For example, the Owens-Illinois convertible subordinated debentures were sold to the public for $1,000 a bond. The market price of the common stock at the time of issuance (November 1967) was approximately $52. Therefore, the conversion value of each bond was $16.95 \times \$52$, or $881, and the differential of $119 between this value and the issuing price represented the conversion premium. Frequently, this premium is expressed as a percentage; in our example, the conversion premium is $119/$881 = 13.5 percent.

Almost without exception, convertible securities provide for a *call price.* As was true with the straight bond or preferred stock, the call feature enables the corporation to call the security for redemption. Few convertible securities, however, are ever redeemed. Instead, the purpose of the call usually is to force conversion when the conversion value of the security is significantly above its call price.

HOW SHOULD A CONVERTIBLE BE ANALYZED?

Because a convertible security is a bond or preferred stock at the time of issuance but is usually common stock later, it poses a certain amount of difficulty for the analyst examining the financial condition of the company. Convertible subordinated debt or convertible preferred stock can be treated as a part of the equity base by a creditor when he evaluates the financial condition of the issuer. In the event of liquidation, it makes no difference to the creditor if the issue is actually converted; for in either case he has a prior claim. The situation is different, however, in the case of a convertible bond that is not subordinated. As long as the bond is not converted, its holder would be a general creditor in the event of liquidation. Consequently, creditors tend to regard the convertible bond as debt until actual conversion takes place. For this reason, there is a strong incentive for the company to make the issue subordinated.

Investors in a company's common stock tend to recognize the *potential* dilution in their position before actual conversion takes place. To illustrate the dilution effect, suppose that a company issues $20 million in 6 percent convertible debentures and that the conversion price is $20 a share. The total number of additional shares upon conversion would be $20 million/$20 = 1 million shares. Assume further that the company has 3 million common shares outstanding and no other debt,

Chapter 22 595
FINANCING WITH
OPTIONS: THE
CONVERTIBLE
SECURITY AND
WARRANT

that it expects earnings before interest and taxes two years from now to be $10 million, and that the federal income tax rate is 50 percent. Earnings per share before and after conversion would be:

	Convertible Debentures Outstanding	Debentures Converted
Earnings before interest and taxes	$10,000,000	$10,000,000
Interest 6% debentures	$ 1,200,000	—
Profit before taxes	$ 8,800,000	$10,000,000
Taxes	$ 4,400,000	$ 5,000,000
Profit after taxes	$ 4,400,000	$ 5,000,000
Shares outstanding	3,000,000	4,000,000
Earnings per share	$1.47	$1.25

We see that upon future conversion, there is dilution in earnings per share in this example. We note also that upon conversion, the company no longer has to pay interest on the debentures; this factor has a favorable influence upon earnings per share. If earnings were low enough of course, the elimination of interest payments could result in an increase in earnings per share. However, this occurrence is the exception rather than the rule.

We should point out that it is necessary for companies to report earnings per share on a fully diluted basis. In May 1969, the Accounting Principles Board of the American Institute of Certified Public Accountants required "fully diluted" earnings per share to be shown on the income statement with equal clarity with "primary," or undiluted, earnings per share. Full dilution means the maximum possible dilution if all convertible securities were converted into common stock and all warrants or options to purchase common stock were exercised. As a result of this opinion by the Accounting Principles Board, which is binding on public accountants in certifying financial statements, the common-stock investor is not likely to overlook the potential dilution inherent in a company's financing with convertible securities and warrants.

FINANCING WITH CONVERTIBLES

Convertible securities, in most cases, are employed as deferred common-stock financing.[8] Technically these securities represent debt or preferred stock, but in essence they are delayed common stock. Companies that issue convertibles expect them to be converted in the future.

---

[8] For presentation of a different concept of convertible financing, see Wilbur G. Lewellen and George A. Racette, "Convertible Debt Financing," *Journal of Financial and Quantitative Analysis*, 8 (December 1973), 777–92. The authors argue that the principal benefit of convertible financing is the tax deductibility of interest payments. As a result, they conclude that convertibles are an inefficient source of financing, inferior to that of straight debt.

By selling a convertible security instead of common stock, they create less dilution in earnings per share, both now and in the future. The reason is that the conversion price on a convertible security is higher than the issuing price on a new issue of common stock.

To illustrate, suppose that the current market price of the common stock of ABC Corporation is $40 per share. If the company raises capital with an issue of common stock, it will have to underprice the issue in order to sell it in the market. Suppose that the company is able to sell the stock through underwriters and to realize net proceeds of $36 per share. If the company wishes to raise $18 million, the issue would involve 500,000 shares of additional stock. On the other hand, if ABC Corporation sells a convertible issue, it is able to set the conversion price above the current market price per share. If the conversion premium is 15 percent, the conversion price would be $46 per share. Assuming an $18 million issue of convertibles, the number of shares of additional stock after conversion would be

$$\frac{\$18 \text{ million}}{\$46} = 391,305$$

We see that potential dilution with a convertible issue is less than that with a common issue because fewer shares are being added.

As a financing strategy, management may wish to finance with convertible securities as opposed to common stock when its estimates of the firm's future are more favorable than those of the market. By so doing, it obtains lesser dilution for existing stockholders than it would if it financed with common stock. Once management's expectations are realized, the stock presumably will rise in price. Of course, the merit of such a strategy depends upon management's estimates of the future being more accurate than those of the market. When the stock is depressed in price, however, it may be wise to avoid both common stock and convertible financing. This situation will be discussed later in the chapter when we consider the timing of a convertible issue.

Another advantage to the company in using convertible securities is that the interest rate or preferred dividend rate typically is lower than the rate the company would have to pay on a straight bond or a straight preferred stock issue. The conversion feature makes the issue more attractive to investors. The greater the value of the conversion feature to investors, the lower the yield the company will need to pay in order to sell the issue. For companies with relatively low credit ratings but good prospects of growth, it may be extremely difficult to sell a straight issue of bonds or preferred stock. However, the market may regard a convertible issue of these companies in a favorable light, not because of its quality as a bond or as preferred stock but because of its quality as common stock. Convertible securities can be sold during periods of tight money when it is very difficult for even a credit-worthy company to sell

Chapter 22 **597**
FINANCING WITH
OPTIONS: THE
CONVERTIBLE
SECURITY AND
WARRANT

a straight bond or preferred stock. For these reasons, convertibles are attractive to many firms as a means of financing. Their use will be analyzed in the subsequent discussion.

FORCING OR STIMULATING CONVERSION

Companies usually issue convertible securities with the full expectation that these securities will be converted within a certain length of time. The investor can exercise his option voluntarily at any time and exchange the convertible security for common stock. However, he may simply prefer to hold the security, for its price will increase as the price of the common stock increases. In addition, he receives regular interest payments or preferred stock dividends. For these reasons and others discussed later in this chapter, many investors do not want to convert their security even though its conversion value is more than what they paid for it.

In order to force conversion, companies issuing convertible securities usually must call the issue. To do so, the market price of the security must be significantly higher than the call price, so that investors will convert rather than accept the lower call price. Many companies regard a 20 percent premium of conversion value over call price as a sufficient cushion for possible declines in market price and for enticing investors to convert their securities. Suppose that the conversion price of a convertible debenture ($1,000 face value) were $50 and that the call price were $1,080. For the conversion value of the bond to equal the call price, the market price of the stock must be $1,080/20, or $54 a share. If the bonds are called when the market price is $54, many investors might choose to accept the call price rather than convert. The company then would have to redeem many of the bonds for cash, in part defeating the purpose of the original financing. In order to assure almost complete conversion, it might wait to call the debentures until the conversion value of the bond is 20 percent above the call price, a value that corresponds to a common-stock market price of approximately $65 a share. At this price, the investor would suffer a significant opportunity loss if he accepted the call price.[9]

Other means are available to a company for "stimulating," as opposed to "forcing," conversion. By establishing an acceleration or "step-up" in the conversion price at steady intervals in the future, there is persistent pressure on bondholders to convert, assuming the conversion value of the security is relatively high. For example, if the conversion price is scheduled to increase from $50 to $56 at the end of next

---

[9] For a discussion of ways a company can notify bondholders of the call and to assure that a very high percentage exercise their option, see Alexander B. Miller, "How to Call Your Convertibles," *Harvard Business Review*, 49 (May–June 1971), 66–70.

month, convertible bondholders have an incentive to convert prior to that time, all other things the same. If the holder waits, he receives fewer shares of stock. Recognize that the "step-up" provision must be established at the time the convertible issue is sold. It cannot be used for purposes of stimulating conversion at a particular moment in time. Another means for stimulating conversion is to increase the dividend on the common stock, thereby making the common more attractive. In certain cases, the dividend income available on the associated common may exceed interest income on the convertible security. Although the two stimulants discussed above enhance conversion, invariably a portion of the convertible bondholders will not convert, owing to the downside protection of the bond, the superior legal claim on assets, and other reasons. Consequently, calling the issue may be the only means for assuring that the issue will be substantially converted.

Overhanging issue   If a company is unable to force or stimulate conversion because the market price of the stock has not risen sufficiently to entice the investor to convert, the convertible issue is said to be "overhanging." With an overhanging issue, the company is constrained in its ability to obtain new financing. It is difficult to sell another convertible security issue until the present one is converted. The overhanging issue creates apprehension in the market over the investment worthiness of any new issue of convertibles and may even create apprehension over the worthiness of a non-convertible security offering.

The risk of an overhanging issue and the loss of flexibility associated with such an issue may offset, at least in part, the advantage in issuing price of the convertible security over a common stock offering. With a common-stock offering, the firm obtains equity capital now. With a convertible security issue, it is uncertain when, if ever, the security will convert and the company will obtain equity capital. If it were not for this factor, the lesser dilution associated with a convertible issue as opposed to a common stock issue would always make the convertible issue more attractive.

CONVERTIBLE FINANCING FOR THE GROWTH COMPANY

Because issuing companies usually wish to force conversion within a reasonable length of time as well as avoid an overhanging issue, the convertible security is best suited for a growth company. The faster the increase in the market price of the company's stock, of course, the quicker the company will be in a position to force conversion. To illustrate, suppose R-Tronics, Inc., is able to sell a 6 percent convertible bond at a price of $1,000 to the public, with a conversion price of $50 and a call price of $1,060. This call price corresponds to a market price per share of $53. Suppose further that the price of the company's stock at the time of issuance is $44 per share. If R-Tronics has the policy of forcing conversion only when the conversion value of the bond is 20 percent in excess of the call price, it will need to wait until the stock rises to approximately $64 per share ($53 × 1.2). If the company is expected to have an annual growth in earnings per share of 30 percent in the foreseeable future, and if the price/earnings ratio is not expected to change, it will take less than eighteen months from the time of issuance for the stock to reach $64 per share. On the other hand, if the growth rate were expected to be only 5 percent per annum, it would take almost eight years for the stock to reach a value of $64 per share.

Thus, there is considerable question whether a company that envisions only modest growth should finance with convertible securities. With a growth rate of 5 percent in the example above, it takes an extremely long period of time before it is possible to force conversion. During this time, the company is less flexible in additional financing than it would be if it could "clear the decks" and force conversion. Moreover, investors have come to expect companies that issue convertible securities to be able to force conversion within several years after issuance. Not to be able to do so during this time is a sign that the stock has not performed as well as the company had expected originally. Thus, a company with prospects for little or no growth would be ill advised to use convertible securities as a method of financing. They are best suited for the growth company.

CONVERSION PREMIUMS AND TIMING

For most issues of convertibles, the conversion premium ranges from 10 to 20 percent. Recall that this premium is the percentage by which the issuing price of the convertible exceeds its conversion value. If a convertible bond were sold for $1,000 with a conversion price of $50, and if the market price of common at the time of issuance were $43 a share, the conversion premium would be $7/$43, or 16.3 percent. For a growth company, the conversion premium can be in the upper part of the 10–20 percent range, or perhaps even higher in the case of a super-growth stock. For companies with more moderate growth, however, the conversion premium may be closer to 10 percent. The range itself is established mainly by market tradition, in keeping, however, with the idea that the stock should be expected to rise in price so that it exceeds the conversion price within a reasonable period of time. The greater the growth in market price per share, the more quickly will the market price exceed the conversion price, all other things the same. Thus, the super-

Chapter 22 **601**
*FINANCING WITH
OPTIONS: THE
CONVERTIBLE
SECURITY AND
WARRANT*

growth company is able to command a higher conversion premium in the market than is a company with only moderate growth potential.

The higher the conversion premium, of course, the lower the dilution. If the company sets too high a conversion price, however, the issue will have to be sold as essentially a fixed-income security with a yield commensurate with what the company would pay on a straight debt or preferred stock issue. Under such circumstances, the issue cannot be considered delayed equity financing. The ability of the firm to force conversion simply is too uncertain. For this reason, there are practical limits as to how high a conversion premium can be set. For most situations, it is 20 percent or less.

The appropriate timing of a convertible issue must be evaluated in relation to the market for the company's common stock. If it is a poor time to sell common stock because of a depressed market price, it usually is also a poor time to sell a convertible, even though the convertible issue can be sold at a conversion price higher than the price at which a common-stock issue can be sold. This is due both to the depressed market price of the stock and to variations in the conversion premium with market psychology. Because the dilution associated with a convertible issue depends directly upon its conversion price, which in turn is primarily a function of the market price of the stock, it is obvious that considerable dilution occurs when the stock is depressed in price. In addition to this influence, the conversion premium at which the issue can be sold is likely to be lower when the stock is depressed than when it is buoyant. Because the conversion premium is a function of expected growth, and because investors are less likely to expect growth when the stock is depressed than when it is strong, the conversion premium normally will be lower in a depressed market. These factors will result in greater dilution, the more depressed the market price of the stock. Thus, we see that the appropriate timing of a convertible issue follows very closely the market behavior of the company's stock.

VALUE OF CONVERTIBLE SECURITIES

The value of a convertible security to an investor is twofold: its value as a bond or preferred stock, and its potential value as common stock. (Because the principles of valuation of a convertible bond and a convertible preferred stock are nearly the same, our subsequent discussion will refer to convertible bonds.) The investor obtains a hedge when he purchases a convertible bond. If the market price of the stock rises, the value of the convertible is determined largely by its conversion value. However, if the market for the stock turns down, the investor still holds a bond whose value provides a floor below which the price of the convertible is unlikely to fall.

BOND VALUE

The bond value of a convertible security is the price at which a straight bond of the same company would sell in the open market. It can be determined by solving the following equation for B:[10]

$$B = \sum_{t=1}^{n} \frac{I}{(1 + i)^t} + \frac{F}{(1 + i)^n} \tag{22-1}$$

where B = straight bond value of the convertible

I = annual interest payments determined by the coupon rate

F = face value of the bond

n = years to final maturity

i = market yield to maturity on a straight bond of the same company

For example, suppose that ABC Company has outstanding a 6 percent convertible debenture issue with a final maturity twenty years hence. Suppose further that if the company is to sell a straight twenty-year debenture in the current market, the bond will have to yield 8 percent to maturity to be attractive to investors. For a twenty-year bond with a 6 percent coupon to yield 8 percent to maturity, the bond has to sell at a discount. More specifically, the market price has to be $804 for each $1,000 face value bond.[11] Thus, the bond-value floor of ABC's convertible bond would be $804. This floor suggests that if the price of the common stock were to fall sharply so that the conversion feature had negligible value, the price of the convertible would fall only to $804. At that price, the security would sell as a straight bond in keeping with prevailing bond yields for that grade of security. (The above analysis requires one critical qualification: share price changes are independent of interest-rate changes.)

The bond-value floor of a convertible is not constant over time. It

---

[10] In this equation, we assume that interest payments are annual and paid at the end of the year. If payments are semiannual, the equation should be modified according to the discussion in the appendix to Chapter 2.

[11] Solving for Eq. (22-1)

$$B = \sum_{t=1}^{20} \frac{\$60}{(1.08)^t} + \frac{\$1,000}{(1.08)^{20}} = \$804$$

Fortunately, we need only consult a bond table to determine the market price. Given any three of the four variables above—namely, years to maturity, coupon rate, yield to maturity, and market price—we can determine quickly the fourth variable from the table. An example of a bond table is shown in the appendix to Chapter 2, where we take up the mathematics of bond interest.

varies with (1) interest rate movements in the capital markets and (2) changes in the financial risk of the company involved. If interest rates in general rise, the bond value of a convertible will decline. For example, if the yield to maturity on a straight bond in our example increases from 8 to 9 percent, the bond value of the convertible will drop from $804 to $726. Moreover, the company's credit rating can either improve or deteriorate over time. If it improves, and the company is able to sell a straight bond at a lower yield to maturity, the bond value of the convertible security will increase, all other things held constant. However, if the company's credit standing deteriorates and the yield on a straight bond increases, the bond-value floor will decline. Unfortunately for the investor, when the market price of the stock falls because of poor earnings, the company may have financial difficulty, in which case its credit standing will suffer. As a result, the straight bond value of the convertible may decline along with the decline in its conversion value, giving the investor less downside protection than he might have expected originally.[12]

PREMIUMS

Convertible securities usually sell at premiums over both their bond value and their conversion value. Recall that the conversion value of a convertible is simply the current market price per share of the company's common stock times the number of shares into which the security is convertible. The fact that the convertible bond provides the investor with a degree of downside protection, given the qualifications mentioned above, usually results in its selling at a market price somewhat higher than its conversion value. How much higher will depend upon the probability that the conversion value of the security will fall below its bond value. Suppose, in our example, that the conversion price is $50 a share and the current market price of the common stock is $60 a share. The conversion value of the $1,000 face value bond will be $1,200. If the stock falls to $25 a share, the conversion value of the bond will plummet to $500. Assuming a straight bond value of $804, however, the market price of the convertible would not be expected to fall below $804. Consequently, the investor can reduce his risk by investing in a convertible security rather than in the common stock of a corporation. In general, the more volatile the price movements of the stock, the more valuable is the downside protection afforded by the bond-value floor. For this reason as well as for additional reasons discussed later, the

[12]Mathematically, the straight bond value of a convertible security will rise over time, all other things held constant, if the face value of the convertible is above the straight bond value at the time of issuance. At final maturity, the straight bond value, of course, will equal the face value of the convertible. See the appendix to Chapter 2.

market price of a convertible security usually is above its conversion value. The difference is known as the *premium-over-conversion value.*

Moreover, a convertible bond usually will sell at a *premium-over-bond value,* primarily because of the conversion feature. Unless the market price of the stock is very low relative to the conversion price, the conversion feature usually will have value, in that investors may eventually find it profitable to convert the securities. To the extent that the conversion feature does have value, the convertible will sell at a premium over its straight bond value. The higher the market price of the common relative to the conversion price, the greater this premium.

RELATION BETWEEN PREMIUMS

The tradeoff between the two premiums depicts the value of the option to investors and is illustrated in Figure 22-3. On the horizontal axis is the market price of the common and on the vertical the value of the convertible security. It should be pointed out that the two axes are on different scales. If the conversion ratio were 20 to 1, for example, the horizontal axis might be in units of $10, while the vertical axis was in units of $200. The diagonal line, which starts at the origin, represents the conversion value of the bond, while the horizontal line represents its straight bond value. The curved line represents the market price of the convertible security. The distance between this line and the bond-value

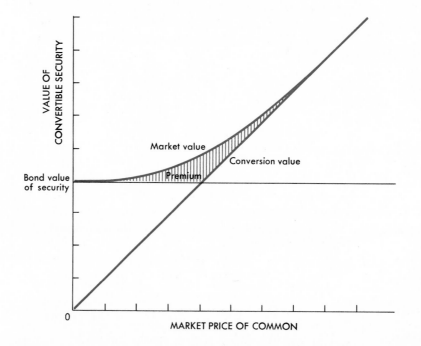

FIG. 22·3

Relation between bond value and conversion value premiums

Chapter 22 **605**
*FINANCING WITH
OPTIONS: THE
CONVERTIBLE
SECURITY AND
WARRANT*

line is the premium over bond value, while the distance between the market-price line and the conversion value line represents the premium-over-conversion value. Note the similarity of this figure with that for the value of an option—Figure 22-2.

We see that at relatively high common-stock price levels, the value of the convertible as a bond is insignificant. Consequently, its premium-over-bond value is high, whereas its premium-over-conversion value is negligible. The security sells mainly for its stock equivalent. Investors are unwilling to pay a significant premium-over-conversion value for several reasons. First, the greater the premium of market price of the convertible over its bond value, the less valuable the bond-value protection to the investor. If the bond-value floor of a convertible bond is $900, for example, there is considerably more downside protection if the market price of the convertible is $1,000 than if it is $2,000. Second, when the conversion value is high, the convertible may be called; and if it is, the investor will want to convert rather than redeem the bond for the call price. Upon conversion, of course, the bond is worth only its conversion value. Finally, if the company increases the dividend on its common stock, the fixed return on the convertible declines relative to the return available on the stock equivalent. This occurrence contributes also to a narrowing of the premium as conversion value increases.[13]

On the other hand, when the market value of the convertible is close to its straight bond value, the conversion feature has little value. At this level, the convertible security is valued primarily as a straight bond. Under these circumstances, the market price of the convertible is likely to exceed its conversion value by a substantial premium. Otherwise, the conversion feature would have a value, and the convertible security would sell at a premium over its bond value.

The principal reason for premiums in market price over both conversion value and bond value is the unusual appeal of a convertible as both a bond and a common stock. It offers the holder protection on the downside together with participation in upward movements in stock price. Thus, the distribution of possible outcomes is skewed to the right, and this characteristic finds favor with risk-averse investors. We note in Figure 22-3 that the premiums over both conversion value and bond value exist only within a range. At the far right of the figure, the convertible sells mainly for its common-stock equivalent and there is no premium-over-conversion value. There is, of course, a substantial premium-over-bond value. At the far left, the convertible sells as a bond with no premium-over-bond value but a substantial premium-over-conversion value. Because of the skewed nature of the distribution of possible outcomes, the convertible security should have more value the greater the volatility in the market price of the common. The investor has

---

[13] See Eugene F. Brigham, "An Analysis of Convertible Debentures: Theory and Some Empirical Evidence," *Journal of Finance,* 21 (March 1966), 37.

the downside protection of the bond-value floor in Figure 22-3 coupled with unlimited upside potential; thus, the greater the dispersion of the probability distribution of possible market prices, the higher the expected value of return.

Viewed in a different way, the convertible bond can be regarded as one of many investments available in a portfolio context. Recall from our discussion of the capital-asset pricing model in Chapter 3 that the expected return of a security in equilibrium can be expressed as

$$\bar{R}_c = i + \beta_c(\bar{R}_m - i) \tag{22-2}$$

where R_c is the expected return on convertible bond c, $\bar{R}_m$ is the expected return for the market portfolio, i is the risk-free rate, and β_c, or beta, represents the covariance between the convertible security and the market portfolio (Cov. R_c, R_m) divided by the variance of the market portfolio (σ_m^2). The beta is a measure of the systematic or undiversifiable risk of the convertible bond. Presumably, the benefit of the bond-value floor should be embodied in the convertible security's systematic risk.

In testing for the importance of this effect, James E. Walter and Agustin V. Que compared the betas for a sample of convertible bonds with the betas for the associated common stocks.[14] (The sample period was the 1960s and the Standard & Poor's 500-stock index was used as the market index.[15]) They found that betas for all but one of the convertible bonds were less than their common-stock counterparts. This evidence gives indication of the beneficial influence of the bond-value floor on systematic risk. However, the authors found that this benefit diminishes rapidly as the convertible's conversion value approaches and exceeds its straight bond value. Finally, Walter and Que undertook a number of simulations and found that the significance of the bond-value floor varies directly with the volatility of the associated common stock, as denoted by its beta. Thus, the Walter and Que study lends support to the notions embodied in Figure 22-3 and to our discussion.

OTHER REASONS FOR PREMIUMS

Although we have concentrated on the main reasons for premiums, other factors appear to have at least a modest influence on the premiums. The influence of these factors stems from the presence of certain impediments to the perfect market assumptions invoked earlier in our

---

[14] "The Valuation of Convertible Bonds," *Journal of Finance*, 28 (June 1973), 713–32. For a test in a similar vein which concentrates on the degree of systematic risk, see Edward H. Jennings, "An Estimate of Convertible Bond Premiums," *Journal of Financial and Quantitative Analysis*, 9 (January 1974), 33–56.

[15] See Chapter 3 for a more detailed discussion of the test involved.

discussion of options. For one thing, a convertible security sometimes is attractive to investors who operate on margin. In the past, the margin requirement on stock, which is set by the Federal Reserve, has been higher than that on convertible securities. This meant that market participants were able to borrow more for investment in convertible securities than they were for investment in stock. Thus the greater collateral-value attractiveness of convertibles resulted in a greater demand for convertibles than for stock; this demand, in turn, exerted upward pressure on the premiums. At the time of this writing, however, the margin requirement was the same for both types of securities, namely, 50 percent. This means that the maximum loan a person could obtain from a bank or investment house was 50 percent of the market value of the convertible securities or stock pledged. Therefore, the two types of securities had the same degree of collateral-value attractiveness.

Lower transaction costs on convertible bonds relative to those on common stocks also enhance the attractiveness of these bonds. An investor who wishes to acquire common stock of a company would incur lower transaction costs by purchasing a convertible bond and converting it into common stock than he would by purchasing the stock outright. This attraction should exert upward pressure on the premiums-over-conversion value and over-bond value. The duration of the convertible option also should affect the premiums. In general, the longer the duration, the more valuable the option.[16] Unlike other options, however, the duration until expiration is uncertain owing to the fact that the company can force conversion if the price of the common stock is high enough. The longest duration is the maturity of the security, but the actual duration typically is much shorter. Another factor is the dividend on the common. The greater the dividend, the greater the attraction of the common vis-à-vis the convertible security and the lower the premiums, all other things the same.

Yet another influence that may raise premiums is that certain institutional investors, such as life insurance companies, are very restricted with respect to investing in common stock.[17] By investing in convertible bonds, they gain the benefits of a common-stock investment without actually investing in common stock. All these influences account for the premiums at which convertible securities sell.

USE OF WARRANTS AND THEIR VALUATION

A *warrant* is an option to purchase a specified number of shares of common stock at a stated price. When the holder exercises the option, he surrenders the warrant. Warrants are employed customarily as "sweet-

[16] See Roman L. Weil, Jr., Joel E. Segall, and David Green, Jr., "Premiums on Convertible Bonds," *Journal of Finance*, 23 (June 1968), 445–47. See also Walter and Que, "Valuation of Convertible Bonds."

[17] See Brigham, "Analysis of Convertible Debentures," *Journal of Finance*, p. 153.

eners" to a public issue of bonds or debt that is privately placed.[18] The investor obtains not only the fixed return associated with debt but also an option to purchase common stock at a stated price. If the market price of the stock should rise, this option can be valuable. As a result, the corporation should be able to obtain a lower interest rate than it would otherwise. For companies that are marginal credit risks, the use of warrants may make the difference between being able and not being able to raise funds through a debt issue. Additionally, during periods of tight money, some financially sound companies may have to provide warrants in order to make their debt issues attractive to investors. In addition to a "sweetener" to debt financing, warrants also are used in the origination of a company as compensation to underwriters and venture capitalists.

FEATURES

The warrant itself contains the provisions of the option. It states the number of shares the holder can buy for each warrant he holds. For example, the Greyhound Corporation warrants provide an option to purchase one share of common stock for each warrant held; Braniff Airways warrants provide for the purchase of 3.18 shares for each warrant held. Another important provision is the price at which the warrant is exercisable. For example, Greyhound warrants are exercisable at $23.50 a share. The exercise price can be either fixed or "stepped up" over time. The Textron Inc., warrants, for example, are exercisable at $10.00 a share until May 1, 1979, and are exercisable at $11.25 after that time until their expiration in 1984.

Finally, the warrant must specify the date on which the option expires. Certain warrants, such as those of Alleghany Corporation, are perpetual, having no expiration date. Most warrants, however, have a stated expiration date. Warrants may be either detachable or non-detachable. Detachable warrants may be sold separately from the bond. Consequently, the bondholder does not have to exercise his option in order to obtain the value of the warrant. He simply can sell the warrant in the marketplace. Many detachable warrants are listed on the American Stock Exchange and a few on the New York Stock Exchange. A nondetachable warrant cannot be sold separately from the bond; it can be detached only when the bondholder exercises his option and purchases stock.

Because a warrant is only an option to purchase stock, the warrant holder is not entitled to any cash dividends paid on the common stock,

---

[18] For an analysis of the use of warrants in financing, see Samuel L. Hayes III and Henry B. Reiling, "Sophisticated Financing Tool: The Warrant," *Harvard Business Review,* 47 (January–February 1969), 137–50.

nor does he have voting power. If the common stock is split or a stock dividend is declared, the option price of the warrant usually is adjusted to take this change into account.

Chapter 22 **609**
*FINANCING WITH
OPTIONS: THE
CONVERTIBLE
SECURITY AND
WARRANT*

EXERCISE OF WARRANTS

Although warrants and convertible securities are similar in many respects, they differ with respect to the capitalization of the company after the option is taken. When convertible debentures are converted, new common stock is created, but the debentures are retired, and there is no infusion of new capital into the company. However, when warrants are exercised, the common stock of the company is increased, and the bonds still remain outstanding, assuming the warrants are detachable.

To illustrate the difference, let us compare the results of financing with convertible bonds and financing with a straight bond issue with warrants attached. Suppose that ABC Corporation is raising $20 million in debt funds with either a convertible debenture issue or a straight debenture with warrants attached. Assume that the convertible debenture issue has a coupon rate of 6 percent and a conversion price of $50, whereas the straight debenture issue has a 7 percent coupon rate. With the straight debenture, the investor receives one warrant entitling him to purchase three shares of common stock at $60 a share for each bond ($1,000 face value) purchased. The capitalization of the company before financing, after financing, and after complete conversion or exercise of the option, is shown in Table 22-1. We assume that the retained earnings of the company remain unchanged and that the straight debenture issue has neither matured nor been called.

Upon conversion of all the debentures, the total number of shares of common stock increases by 400,000. However, total capitalization stays at $55 million, for the debentures are retired. In the case of the deben-

Table 22·1   Capitalization of *ABC* Corporation (in millions)

	Before Financing	Convertible Debentures		Debentures With Warrants	
		Before Conversion	After Conversion	Before Exercise	After Exercise
Debentures		$20		$20	$20.0
Common stock					
($10 par value)	$10	10	$14	10	10.6
Capital surplus			16		3.0
Retained earnings	25	25	25	25	25.0
Net worth	$35	$35	$55	$35	$38.6
Total capitalization	$35	$55	$55	$55	$58.6

tures with warrants attached, the debentures remain outstanding after all the warrants are exercised. Exercising their options, the warrant holders purchase 60,000 shares of common stock at $60 a share, or $3.6 million in total. Consequently, the total capitalization of the company is increased by $3.6 million. Dilution, of course, is greater upon conversion of the convertible debentures (400,000 new shares) than upon exercise of the warrants (60,000 new shares).

A company cannot force the exercise of the warrant option as it can force the exercise of the conversion option by calling a convertible security. Consequently, it is unable to control when the warrant will be exercised and when there will be an infusion of new equity capital into the corporation. Only the expiration date sets a limit on how long the warrants can remain outstanding and unexercised.

VALUATION OF WARRANTS

The theoretical value of a warrant can be determined by

$$NP_s - E \tag{22-3}$$

where N = the number of shares that can be purchased with one warrant

E = the option price associated with the purchase of N shares

P_s = the market price of one share of stock

Note that this formula is exactly the same as that discussed earlier in the valuation of an option where $N = 1$. On July 15, 1975, the common stock of Occidental Petroleum closed at $22\frac{1}{8}$ per share. The exercise price for Occidental warrants was $16\frac{1}{4}$, which enabled the holder to purchase one share of common stock for each warrant held. Consequently, the theoretical value of an Occidental warrant on July 15, 1975, was

$$(1)(22\tfrac{1}{8}) - 16\tfrac{1}{4} = \$5\tfrac{7}{8}$$

The theoretical value of a warrant is the lowest level at which the warrant will generally sell. If, for some reason, the market price of a warrant were to go lower than its theoretical value, arbitragers would eliminate the differential by buying the warrants, exercising them, and selling the stock. A warrant is unlikely to sell below its theoretical value, and many warrants sell above that value. For example, the Occidental Petroleum warrants closed at $12\frac{1}{8}$ on July 15, 1975.

Chapter 22 **611**
*FINANCING WITH
OPTIONS: THE
CONVERTIBLE
SECURITY AND
WARRANT*

**Premium over
theoretical
value**

As in our earlier discussion of options in general, the primary reason that a warrant can sell at a price higher than its theoretical value is the opportunity for leverage. To illustrate the concept of leverage, consider the Textron warrants. For each warrant held, one share of common stock can be purchased, and the exercise price is $10. If the stock were selling at $12 a share, the theoretical value of the warrant would be $2. Suppose, however, that the common stock increased by 25 percent in price to $15 a share. The theoretical value of the warrant would go from $2 to $5, a gain of 150 percent.

The opportunity for increased gain is attractive to investors when the common stock is selling near its exercise price. For a given investment, the investor can buy a greater number of warrants than he can shares of common stock. If the stock moves up in price, he will make more money on his investment in warrants than he would on an equal investment in common stock. Of course, leverage works both ways; the percentage change can be almost as pronounced on the downside. There is some downside protection, however, because it is unlikely that the price of the warrant will drop to zero. In order for the market price to drop to zero, there would have to be no probability that the market price of the stock would exceed the exercise price during the option period.

Because of the opportunity for favorable leverage as well as because of certain other factors, the market prices of many warrants are higher than their theoretical values. In particular, this event occurs when the market price of the associated common stock, NP_s in Eq. (22-3), is near the exercise price. When the market price of the stock increases, however, the degree of leverage decreases. For example, on July 15, 1975, Textron common stock closed at $24\frac{3}{4}$ per share. At that price, the theoretical value of a warrant was

$$(1)(24\tfrac{3}{4}) - 10 = \$14\tfrac{3}{4}$$

If an investor were to purchase Textron warrants at $14\frac{3}{4}$ and the market price of the stock increased 25 percent from $24\frac{3}{4}$ to $30\frac{7}{8}$, the theoretical value of a warrant would increase 42 percent to $20\frac{7}{8}$. Thus, there is less opportunity for leverage when the market price of the associated common stock is high relative to the exercise price than when it is close to the exercise price. As a result, warrants tend to sell around their theoretical values when the market price of the common is relatively high. For example, the Textron warrants closed at $15\frac{1}{2}$ on July 15, 1975—slightly higher than their theoretical value.

The functional relationship between the market value of a warrant and the value of the associated common stock is shown in Figure 22-4. The theoretical value of the warrant is represented by the ~~white~~ brown line in the figure, and the actual market value by the dashed line. When the market value of the associated stock is less than the exercise price, the

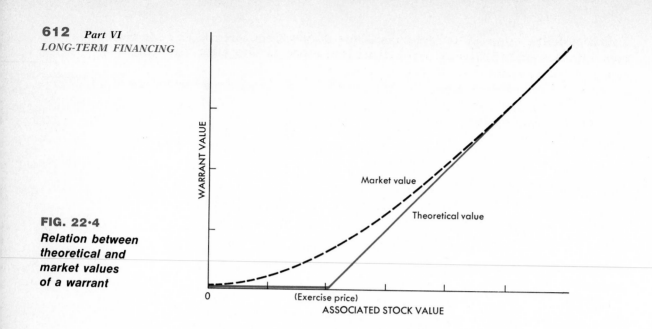

theoretical value of the warrant is zero. When the value of the associated common stock is greater than the exercise price, the theoretical value of the warrant is positive, as depicted by the solid diagonal line. Note again the similarity between this figure and Figure 22-2, which dealt with the valuation of options in general.

When the market value of the associated common stock is low relative to the exercise price, the actual market value of a warrant usually exceeds its theoretical value. However, as the market value of the associated stock rises, the market value of the warrant usually approaches its theoretical value. The exact shape of the actual value line in Figure 22-4 will depend in part upon the remaining length of the option, the payment of dividends on the common stock, the volatility of the common stock, the opportunity cost of funds to investors, and whether or not a warrant is listed on an exchange. Considering these factors in order, the shorter the length of time to expiration of the warrant, the less valuable the option to the investor and the more convex the actual value line—that is, the more it approaches the theoretical value line. This was analyzed in greater detail in our discussion of options in general. Because the investor in a warrant does not participate in dividends paid on the common, the greater the dividend on the common stock, the less attractive the warrant in relation to its associated stock. As a result, the greater the dividend, the more the actual value line would approach the theoretical value line.

Volatility works in the opposite direction; the more volatile the stock, the more valuable the warrant. To illustrate, suppose an investor were considering a warrant that permitted him to purchase one share of common stock at $20 a share. Suppose also that he expected the market price per share of common one period hence to be:[19]

Probability	.20	.30	.30	.20
Price	$ 5	$15	$25	$35

The expected value of the probability distribution is $20. This price suggests a theoretical value of the warrant of zero one period hence. However, because a warrant cannot sell at a negative price, its expected value of theoretical value is not zero but

$$.20(0) + .30(0) + .30(25 - 20) + .20(35 - 20) = \$4.50$$

Thus, the expected value of the warrant increases with the dispersion of the probability distribution to the right of the option price. The greater the expected volatility in market price for the stock, the greater the expected value of the warrant, all other things the same, and the higher the actual value line.

The opportunity cost of funds to the investor in warrants also may affect the actual value line. This opportunity cost can be either an external lending rate for the investor or his borrowing rate. The greater the value of funds to the investor, the more likely he is to prefer investing in the warrant than in the stock, because the warrant involves a lessser investment. As a result, the warrant is likely to rise in price relative to the price of the associated common stock, exerting upward pressure on the actual value line. The last factor, listing on a major exchange, presumably enhances marketability and results in a higher actual value line, all other things the same. All of these factors (length of the option, dividend paid on the common, volatility of the common, value of funds to investors, and listing) appear to affect the shape of the actual value line. They have been tested empirically, and the hypothesized relationships supported.[20] Although the principal determinant of warrant prices is the value of the associated common stock, additional factors have a modest influence on warrant valuation.

---

[19] This example comes from James C. Van Horne, "Warrant Valuation in Relation to Volatility and Opportunity Costs," *Industrial Management Review*, 10 (Spring 1969), 20–21.

[20] See Van Horne, "Warrant Valuation in Relation to Volatility and Opportunity Costs," 19–32; John P. Shelton, "The Relation of the Price of a Warrant to the Price of Its Associated Stock," *Financial Analysts Journal*, 23 (May–June and July–August 1967), 141–51 and 88–99; and David Rush and Ronald Melicher, "An Empirical Examination of Factors Which Influence Warrant Prices," *Journal of Finance*, 29 (December 1974), 1449–66.

SUMMARY

In this chapter, we have examined two types of options under which the holder can obtain common stock. The conversion feature enables the investor to convert a debt instrument or preferred stock into common stock, whereas a warrant attached to a bond enables the holder to purchase a specified number of shares of common stock at a specified price. With a warrant, the exercise of the option does not result in the elimination of the bonds. Convertibles tend to be used more than warrants in financing.

The value of the convertible in the marketplace is determined primarily by its value as a straight bond or preferred stock and its conversion value as common stock. For the corporation, convertibles represent delayed common-stock financing, and the timing of a convertible issue must be analyzed by the company in relation to the market for its common stock. There will be less dilution, for a given amount of financing, with a convertible issue than with a common-stock issue, assuming, of course, that the issue eventually converts. Offsetting in some measure this advantage is the risk of an "over-hanging" issue, which occurs when the company is unable to force conversion because the market price of the stock has not risen sufficiently to raise the conversion value of the security significantly above the call price.

Normally, warrants are employed as a "sweetener" to a public or private issue of debt. The market value of a warrant usually is higher than its theoretical value when the market value of the stock is close to the option price, because this situation gives an opportunity for favorable leverage to the investor. When the market price of the stock is high relative to the option price, warrants tend to sell at about their theoretical values. In addition to the market price of the associated common stock, certain other factors were discussed that appear to affect the value of warrants.

APPENDIX

BLACK-SCHOLES OPTION MODEL

In an important advance to the literature on valuation, Black and Scholes have developed a model for determining the equilibrium value of an option.[21] This model has both theoretical importance for evaluating debt claims in general and practical importance for identifying overvalued and undervalued options in the market.[22] Merton has ex-

---

[21] Black and Scholes, "Pricing of Options and Corporate Liabilities," pp. 637–54.

[22] For empirical testing of the model, see Fischer Black and Myron Scholes, "The Valuation of Option Contracts and a Test of Market Efficiency," *Journal of Finance*, 27 (May 1972), 399–417. See also Black, "Fact and Fantasy in the Use of Options."

tended the Black-Scholes model and in so doing has added clarity to its broad theoretical implications.[23] Because of the current as well as the likely future significance of this method for viewing valuation, we present the basic model in this appendix.

A number of assumptions are in order before we can begin:

1. Only "European" options are considered; that is, options that can be exercised only at maturity.

2. There are no transaction costs; options and stocks are infinitely divisible; and information is available to all without cost.

3. No imperfections exist in selling an option or a stock short.

4. The short-term interest rate is known and constant throughout the duration of the option contract. Market participants can both borrow and lend at this rate.

5. The stock pays no dividend.

6. Stock prices behave in a manner consistent with a random walk in continuous time. The variance of the return is constant over the life of the option contract and is known to market participants.

Given these assumptions, the equilibrium value of an option can be determined. Should the actual price of the option differ from that given by the model, a person would be able to establish a riskless hedged position and earn a return in excess of the short-term interest rate. As arbitragers entered the scene, the excess return would eventually be driven out and the price of the option would equal that value given by the model.

To illustrate a hedged position, suppose that the appropriate relationship between the option and the stock of XYZ Corporation were that shown in Figure 22-5. Suppose further that the current market price of the stock were $20 and the price of the option $7. At $20 a share, the slope of the line in Figure 22-5 is one-half. A hedged position could be undertaken by buying a share of stock for $20 and selling short two options at $7 each. The "net money" invested in this position is $20 − 2($7) = $6.

This combination of holding one share of stock long and two options short leaves the individual essentially hedged with respect to risk. If the stock drops slightly in value, the value of the short position goes up by approximately an equal amount. We say *approximately* because with changes in the price of the common and with changes in time, the ideal hedge ratio changes. With a stock price increase, for example, the slope of the line in Figure 22-5 increases. Therefore, fewer options would need

[23] Robert C. Merton, "A Rational Theory of Option Pricing," *Bell Journal of Economics and Management Science*, 4 (Spring 1973); and Merton, "On the Pricing of Corporate Debt," *Journal of Finance*, 29 (May 1974), 449–70.

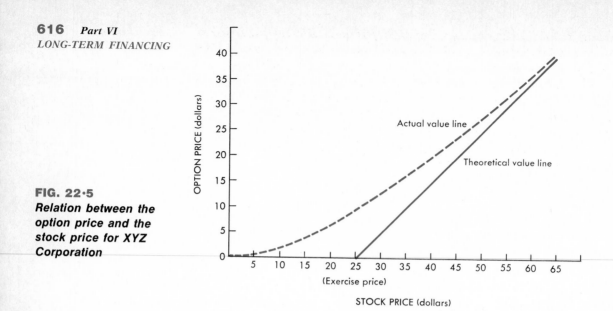

FIG. 22·5

Relation between the option price and the stock price for XYZ Corporation

to be sold short. If the stock price declines, the slope decreases and more options would need to be sold short to maintain a hedge. In addition, the line itself will shift downward as time goes on and the expiration date approaches. This was illustrated in Figure 22-2 earlier in the chapter. The downward shift due to the passage of time causes the line to be more concave and, therefore, its slope to be affected.

Thus, it is necessary to continually adjust one's short position in options for changes in the stock price and for changes in time if a riskless hedged position is to be maintained. Given the assumptions of the model, this of course is possible. In the real world with transaction costs, it is not possible to continuously adjust one's short position. Even here, however, the risk that will appear as a result of moderate changes in stock price or of the passage of time will be small. Moreover, it can be diversified away. For practical purposes, then, it is possible to maintain a hedged position that is approximately risk free.

Having illustrated a hedged position, we must return to our initial point. If the price of the option gets out of line with that of the stock, it will be possible for a person to earn more than the short-term rate on a hedged position. In the example above, the "net money" invested in the position was $6, [$20 − 2($7)]. As the total hedged position is riskless, the "net money" invested should provide a return equal only to the short-term rate. If for some reason the prices on the two instruments get "out of line" with each other, it would be possible to earn a return on the total position in excess of the short-term rate times the "net money" invested. In other words, excess returns would be possible on a position perfectly hedged for risk.

As a result, arbitragers would enter the picture and would borrow large sums of money, establish hedged positions and reap the excess returns available. This action would continue until the buying or selling pressure on the prices of the stock and the option drove such prices into "equilibrium" with each other. At such time, the return on the "net money" invested in a fully hedged position would once again be the short-term rate. Thus, there are equilibrating forces that cause a riskless hedge to provide a return equal to the short-term rate.

In this context, the equilibrium value of an option that entitles the holder to buy one share of stock is shown by Black and Scholes to be

$$w = xN(d_1) - ce^{-rt} N(d_2) \qquad \text{(22A-1)}$$

where x = the current price of the stock

c = the exercise price of the option

r = the short-term interest rate

t = the duration of the option to expiration

$N(d)$ = the value of the cumulative normal density function

$$d_1 = \frac{ln(x/c) + (r + 1/2\sigma^2)t}{\sigma\sqrt{t}}$$

$$d_2 = \frac{ln(x/c) + (r - 1/2\sigma^2)t}{\sigma\sqrt{t}}$$

ln = the natural logarithm

σ^2 = the variance rate of return on the stock

The important implication of this formula is that the value of the option is a function of the short-term interest rate, of the time to expiration, and of the variance rate of return on the stock, but it is not a function of the expected return on the stock.[24] As either or all of the terms for duration to expiration of the option, t, for the variance rate, σ^2, and for the short-term interest rate, r, increase, the value of the option in Eq. (22A-1) increases.[25] The reason for the first two relationships with option values is obvious from our discussion earlier in the chapter. The last is not so obvious. Recall that a person is able to take a position in options which will provide the same dollar movements as the associated stock, but with a lower net investment. The "difference" in net money in the option relative to the stock may be invested in short-term market instruments. The greater the return on these investments, therefore, the greater the attraction of the option relative to the stock, and the greater its value.[26]

Chapter 22 **617**
FINANCING WITH
OPTIONS: THE
CONVERTIBLE
SECURITY AND
WARRANT

---

[24] Black and Scholes, "Pricing of Options and Corporate Liabilities," p. 644.

[25] For an illustration of the individual and joint effect of these three terms on the value of the option using a hypothetical example, see Black, "Fact and Fantasy in the Use of Options."

[26] See Van Horne, "Warrant Valuation in Relation to Volatility and Opportunity Costs," pp. 21–23.

Another way to look at the matter is that the greater the interest rate, the lower the present value of exercise price that will need to be paid in the future if the option is exercised, and the greater the value of the option. Of the three factors affecting the value of the option, however, the short-term interest rate has the least impact.[27] With increases in t, r, and σ^2 in Eq. (22A-1), the value of the option approaches the value of a share of stock as a limit.[28]

With respect to solving the formula, we know the current stock price, the time to expiration, the exercise price, and the short-term interest rate. The key unknown, then, is the rate of variance. This must be estimated. The usual approach is to use the past volatility of the stock's return as a proxy for the future. Black and Scholes have tested their model using variance rates estimated from past data with some degree of success.[29] However, there are the usual statistical problems associated with predicting variance as well as the question of the volatility of returns being stationary over time. Clearly more work needs to be done in testing, but initial findings look promising.

Given the valuation equation for options, Black and Scholes derive the ratio of shares of stock to options necessary to maintain a fully hedged position. It is shown to be $N(d_1)$, which was defined earlier. Thus, the Black-Scholes model permits the quantification of the various factors that affect the value of an option. As we saw, the key factor is estimating the future volatility of the stock. In addition, the work of Black-Scholes and that of Merton provide us with a new and important way of looking at the equilibrium values of corporate liabilities. We can expect to see much more work in this vein in the future.

PROBLEMS

1. Eleven years ago Ardordyne issued 5 percent, 25-year convertible bonds at par. The bonds were convertible into common at $125 per share; the common was then selling at $100. The common was subsequently split two for one (the conversion price was adjusted) and currently sells at $47 with a $1.00 dividend. Nonconvertible bonds of similar quality currently yield 9 percent. What price would you be willing to pay for one of these bonds? On what rational basis might investors in different circumstances be willing to pay a price different from yours?

2. Using Eq. (22-3), compute the theoretical value of each of the following warrants:

---

[27] See Black, "Fact and Fantasy in the Use of Options," Appendix B. The statement assumes interest rate movements' having reasonable boundaries, say 5 percent in either direction.

[28] Black and Scholes, "Pricing of Options and Corporate Liabilities, p. 644.

[29] "Option Contracts and Market Efficiency."

Chapter 22 **619**
FINANCING WITH
OPTIONS: THE
CONVERTIBLE
SECURITY AND
WARRANT

	N	P	E
(a)	5	$100	$400
(b)	10	10	60
(c)	2.3	4	10
(d)	3.54	27⅛	35.40

3. (a) Compute the theoretical value of each of the following five warrants as a ratio of their option price:

	N	P	E
A	1	$10	$20
B	1	20	20
C	1	30	20
D	1	40	20
E	1	50	20

(b) Prepare a graph with warrant value/option price on the vertical axis and common-stock price/option price on the horizontal. Plot the theoretical value relationship computed in (a).

(c) Given the market values of the warrants below, fit a curve to them on the graph constructed in (b).

Warrant	Market Value
A	$ 3
B	7
C	15
D	23
E	30

(d) Explain the relationship between the theoretical and the actual value of a warrant.

4. The Beruth Company is contemplating raising $10 million by means of a debt issue. It has the following alternatives:
  (1) A 20-year, 6 percent convertible debenture issue with a $50 conversion price and $1,000 face value, or
  (2) A 20-year, 8 percent straight debt issue with a detachable warrant to purchase 4 shares for $50 a share attached to each $1,000 bond. The company has a 50 percent tax rate, and its stock is currently selling at $40 a share. Its net income before interest and taxes is a

constant 20 percent of its total capitalization, which currently appears as follows:

Common stock (par $5)	$ 5,000,000
Capital surplus	10,000,000
Retained earnings	15,000,000
Total	$30,000,000

(a) Show the capitalizations resulting from each alternative, both before and after conversion or exercise (a total of four capitalizations).

(b) Compute earnings per share currently and under each of the four capitalizations determined in (a).

(c) If the price of Beruth stock went to $75, determine the theoretical value of each warrant issued under option 2 above.

(d) Discuss the differences in the implicit costs of (1) straight debt, (2) convertible debt, and (3) debt with warrants.

5. The common stock of the Draybar Corporation earns $2.50 per share, has a dividend payout of ⅔, and sells at a P/E ratio of 16. Draybar wishes to offer $10 million of 7 percent, 20-year convertible debentures with an initial conversion premium of 20 percent and a call price of 105. Draybar currently has 1 million common shares outstanding and has a 50 percent tax rate.

(a) What is the conversion price?

(b) What is the conversion ratio per $1,000 debenture?

(c) What is the initial conversion value of each debenture?

(d) How many new shares of common must be issued if all debentures are converted?

(e) If Draybar can increase operating earnings by $1 million per year with the proceeds of the debenture issue, compute the new earnings per share and earnings retained before and after conversion.

(f) If the price of the stock is expected to increase at a compounded rate of 8 percent per year and Draybar wishes to allow for a 20 percent decline on the announcement of a call, how long will it be before the debentures can be called?

6. Assume that the Draybar Corporation (see problem 5) raised the $10 million through an issue of stock (total gross spread and expenses = 10 percent of gross proceeds of issue). How many new shares would have to be issued? If operating earnings were increased by $1 million through the use of the proceeds, compute the new earnings per share and earnings retention. Compare your answers with those obtained in 5(e) above.

7. Assume that the Draybar Corporation (see problem 5) could sell $10 million in straight debt at 9 percent as an alternative to the convertible issue.

Chapter 22 **621**
*FINANCING WITH
OPTIONS: THE
CONVERTIBLE
SECURITY AND
WARRANT*

(a) Compute the earnings per share and earnings retained after issuance of the straight debt under the assumption of a $1 million increase in operating earnings and compare your answer with those obtained in 5(e).

(b) Compute the bond value of the convertible debenture, assuming that interest is paid at the end of each year.

(c) Compute the premium-over-bond value at issuance of the convertible debenture.

SELECTED REFERENCES

Bacon, Peter W., and Edward L. Winn, Jr., "The Impact of Forced Conversion on Stock Prices," *Journal of Finance,* 24 (December 1969), 871–74.

Baumol, William J., Burton G. Malkiel, and Richard E. Quandt, "The Valuation of Convertible Securities," *Quarterly Journal of Economics,* 80 (February 1966), 48–59.

Bierman, Harold, Jr., "The Cost of Warrants," *Journal of Financial and Quantitative Analysis,* 8 (June 1973), 499–504.

Black, Fischer, "Fact and Fantasy in the Use of Options," unpublished paper, University of Chicago, September 1974.

Black, Fischer, and Myron Scholes, "The Pricing of Options and Corporate Liabilities," *Journal of Political Economy,* 81 (May–June 1973), 637–54.

———, "The Valuation of Option Contracts and a Test of Market Efficiency," *Journal of Finance,* 27 (May 1972), 399–417.

Brealey, Richard A., *Security Prices in a Competitive Market,* Chapters 16 and 17. Cambridge, Mass,: M.I.T. Press, 1971.

Brigham, Eugene F., "An Analysis of Convertible Debentures: Theory and Some Empirical Evidence," *Journal of Finance,* 21 (March 1966), 35–54.

Chen, Andrew H. Y., "A Model of Warrant Pricing in a Dynamic Market," *Journal of Finance,* 25 (December 1970), 1041–60.

Cox, John, "The Valuation of Financial Claims," *Journal of Finance,* 31 (May 1976).

Frank, Werner G., and Charles O. Kroncke, "Classifying Conversions of Convertible Debentures over Four Years," *Financial Management,* 3 (Summer 1974), 33–42.

Frank, Werner G., and Jerry J. Weygandt, "Convertible Debt and Earnings per Share: Pragmatism vs. Good Theory," *Accounting Review,* 45 (April 1970), 280–89.

Frankle, A. W., and C. A. Hawkins, "Beta Coefficients for Convertible Bonds," *Journal of Finance,* 30 (March 1975), 207–10.

Hayes, Samuel L., III, and Henry B. Reiling, "Sophisticated Financing Tool: The Warrant," *Harvard Business Review,* 47 (January–February 1969), 137–50.

Jennings, Edward H., "An Estimate of Convertible Bond Premiums," *Journal of Financial and Quantitative Analysis,* 9 (January 1974), 33–56.

Leabo, Dick A., and Richard L. Rogalski, "Warrant Price Movements and the Efficient Market Model," *Journal of Finance,* 30 (March 1975), 163–78,

Lewellen, Wilbur G., and George A. Racette, "Convertible Debt Financing," *Journal of Financial and Quantitative Analysis,* 7 (December 1973), 777–92.

Mehta, Dileep, "The Impact of Outstanding Convertible Bonds on Dividend Policy," *Journal of Finance,* 31 (May 1976).

Merton, Robert C., "On the Pricing of Corporate Debt," *Journal of Finance,* 29 (May 1974), 449–70.

———, "A Rational Theory of Option Pricing," *Bell Journal of Economics and Management Science,* 4 (Spring 1973), 141–83.

———, "Restrictions on Option Pricing," *Journal of Finance,* 31 (May 1976).

———, "Theory of Finance from the Perspective of Continuous Time," *Journal of Financial and Quantitative Analysis,* 10 (November 1975), 659–74.

Miller, Alexander B., "How to Call Your Convertible," *Harvard Business Review,* 49 (May–June 1971), 66–70.

Pinches, George E., "Financing with Convertible Preferred Stocks, 1960–1967," *Journal of Finance,* 25 (March 1970), 53–64.

Poensgen, Otto H., "The Valuation of Convertible Bonds," Parts I and II, *Industrial Management Review,* 6 and 7 (Fall 1965 and Spring 1966), 77–92 and 83–98.

Rush, David F., and Ronald W. Melicher, "An Empirical Examination of Factors Which Influence Warrant Prices," *Journal of Finance,* 29 (December 1974), 1449–66.

Samuelson, Paul A., "Rational Theory of Warrant Pricing," *Industrial Management Review,* 6 (Spring 1965), 13–31.

Samuelson, Paul A., and Robert C. Merton, "A Complete Model of Warrant Pricing that Maximizes Utility," *Industrial Management Review,* 10 (Winter 1969), 17–46.

Scholes, Myron S., "Taxes and the Pricing of Options," *Journal of Finance,* 31 (May 1976).

Shelton, John P., "The Relation of the Price of a Warrant to the Price of Its Associated Stock," *Financial Analysts Journal,* 23 (May–June and July–August 1967), 143–51 and 88–99.

Skerratt, L. C. L., "The Price Determination of Convertible Loan Stock: A UK Model," *Journal of Business Finance & Accounting,* 1 (Autumn 1974), 429–43.

Soldofsky, Robert M., "Yield-Rate Performance of Convertible Securities," *Financial Analysts Journal,* 27 (March–April 1971), 61–65.

Stone, Bernell K., "Warrant Financing," *Journal of Financial and Quantitative Analysis,* 11 (March 1976), 143–53.

Van Horne, James C., *The Function and Analysis of Capital Market Rates.* pp. 166–71. Englewood Cliffs, N.J.: Prentice-Hall, 1970.

———, "Warrant Valuation in Relation to Volatility and Opportunity Costs," *Industrial Management Review,* 10 (Spring 1969), 19–32.

Walter, James E., and Agustin V. Que, "The Valuation of Convertible Bonds," *Journal of Finance,* 28 (June 1973), 713–32.

Weil, Roman L., Jr., Joel E. Segall, and David Green, Jr., "Premiums on Convertible Bonds," *Journal of Finance,* 23 (June 1968), 445–63.

———, "Reply," *Journal of Finance,* 25 (September 1970), 931–33.

EXPANSION and CONTRACTION

VII

MERGERS and CONSOLIDATIONS

In Chapters 6 and 8, we considered the acquisition of another company as a capital-budgeting decision. Like an internally generated investment proposal, the acquisition requires an initial outlay, which is expected to be followed by future benefits. Our purpose in those chapters was to develop a conceptual framework for analyzing and evaluating the likely effect of an acquisition on the value of the firm in both firm-risk and market-risk contexts. In this chapter, we deal with some of the more practical aspects of external growth. Nonetheless, the framework developed in Chapters 6 and 8 underlies our discussion here. We turn now to some basic definitions.

A *merger* is a combination of two corporations where only one survives. The merged corporation goes out of existence, leaving its assets and liabilities to the acquiring corporation. A merger must be distinguished from a *consolidation*, which involves the combination of two or more corporations whereby an entirely new corporation is formed. All of the old companies cease to exist, and shares of their common stock are exchanged for shares in the new company. When two companies of about the same size combine, they usually consolidate. When the two companies differ significantly in size, usually a merger is involved. Though it is important to understand the distinction, the terms *merger* and *consolidation* tend to be used interchangeably to describe the combination of two companies.

METHODS OF COMBINATION

A merger or consolidation often begins with negotiations between the managements of the two companies.[1] Usually, the boards of directors of the companies are kept up to date on the negotiations. When initial agreement is reached as to terms, the respective boards must ratify these terms. Upon ratification, the agreement is submitted to the common stockholders of both companies for approval. Depending upon the corporate charter, an established majority—usually two-thirds—of the total shares is required. After approval by the common stockholders, the merger or consolidation can take place once the necessary papers are filed with the states in which the companies are incorporated.

One hurdle remains, however—that neither the Antitrust Division of the Department of Justice nor the Federal Trade Commission brings suit to block the combination. In order to actually block a merger or consolidation, the government, under Section 7 of the Clayton Act, must prove that a "substantial lessening of competition" might occur on account of it. Because the costs in executive time, legal expenses, and other expenses of waging an antitrust battle are so great, most companies want to be reasonably sure that they will not be challenged before going ahead with a combination.

[1] We defer consideration of a tender offer until later in this chapter.

ACCOUNTING TREATMENT

From an accounting standpoint, a combination of two companies is treated either as a *purchase* or as a *pooling of interests*. With a purchase, the acquired company is treated as an investment by the buyer. The excess of the price paid for the company above its net worth must be reflected as goodwill. Moreover, this goodwill usually is written off against future income, the logic being that it will be reflected in such income. Like any asset, an estimate must be made of its life; and goodwill is amortized over this period.[2] Thus, earnings are reduced by the amount of the charge. It is important to recognize that goodwill charges are not deductible for tax purposes. Therefore, the reduction of reported future earnings associated with this accounting treatment is viewed as a disadvantage by the acquiring firm.

In a pooling of interests, the balance sheets of the two companies are combined, with assets and liabilities simply being added together. As a result, goodwill is not reflected in the combination, and there is no charge against future income. Because reported earnings will be higher with the pooling-of-interests accounting treatment than they will be with the purchase treatment, most acquiring companies prefer it when the goodwill being acquired is substantial.

In August 1970, however, the Accounting Principles Board of the American Institute of Certified Public Accountants significantly restricted the conditions under which a pooling of interests could occur. The conditions that now must be met include:[3]

1. Each of the combined companies must be autonomous for at least two years prior to the pooling and independent of the others in the sense that no more than 10 percent of the stock is owned.

2. The combination must be consummated in a single transaction *or* in accordance with a specific plan within one year after the plan is initiated. In this regard, no contingent payments are permitted.

3. The acquiring corporation can issue only common stock, with rights identical to those of the majority of outstanding voting stock, in exchange for *substantially* all of the voting common stock of another company. Here, "substantially" means 90 percent or more.

4. The surviving corporation must not later retire or reacquire common stock issued in connection with the combination, must not enter into an arrangement for the benefit of former stockholders, and must not dispose of a significant portion of the assets of the combining companies for at least two years.

The most important condition is number 3, which states that common must be exchanged for common. Before, debt and other instruments

---

[2] The maximum period over which goodwill can be written off is forty years.

[3] *Opinions of the Accounting Principles Board,* No. 16 (New York: American Institute of Certified Public Accountants, August 1970).

could be used. The next most important is the prohibition of contingent payments. The result of these conditions is a significant reduction in the number of poolings of interest. Although there are certain inequities in the rules,[4] their overall effect is to reduce distortions in reported earnings per share caused by the pooling-of-interests accounting method.

PURCHASE OF ASSETS OR PURCHASE OF STOCK

The acquisition of another company can take place either by the purchase of assets or by the purchase of the common stock of the company being acquired. Under the former arrangement, the buying company may purchase all or a portion of the assets of another company and pay for this purchase either with cash or with its own stock. Frequently, the buyer acquires only the assets of the other company and does not assume its liabilities. If all the assets are purchased, the selling company is but a corporate shell. After the sale, its assets are composed entirely of cash or the stock of the buying company. The selling company can either hold the cash or stock or it can distribute the cash or stock to its stockholders as a liquidating dividend, after which the company is dissolved.

Thus, when its assets are purchased, the selling company can continue to exist if it holds the cash or stock arising from the sale. If it has cash, it may invest in other assets, such as a division of another company. Obviously, if only a portion of its assets are sold, the selling company will continue as a corporate entity. If paid in cash, the transaction is taxable to the selling company or its stockholders; that is, they must recognize the capital gain or loss on the sale of the assets at the time of the sale.[5] If payment is made in preferred or common stock, however, the transaction is not taxable at the time of sale. The capital gain or loss is recognized only when the stock is sold. A purchase of assets is easier to effect than a purchase of stock, for all that is needed on the part of the buying company is approval by the board of directors. The selling company, however, needs the approval of its stockholders.

When an acquiring company purchases the stock of another company, the latter is merged into the acquiring company. The company that is acquired ceases to exist, and the surviving company assumes all its assets and liabilities. As with a purchase of assets, the means of payment to the stockholders of the company being acquired can be either cash or stock. If cash, the transaction is taxable to the stockholders of the acquired company at the time of the acquisition. If stock, the transaction is not taxable to the stockholders until the stock is sold.

---

[4]See Arthur R. Wyatt, "Inequities in Accounting for Business Combinations," *Financial Executive*, 40 (December 1972), 28–35.

[5]Likewise, payment with a debt instrument of the acquiring company is also taxable at the time of sale.

DISSENTING STOCKHOLDERS

Although a combination generally depends only upon the approval of a required majority of the total number of shares outstanding, minority stockholders can contest the price paid for their stock. If a dissenting stockholder and the company fail to agree as to a just settlement on a voluntary basis, the stockholder can take his case to court and demand an appraisal of his shares and a settlement in cash. After a "fair market price" has been established by the court, the dissenting stockholder receives payment in cash for his shares. If the number of dissenting stockholders is large, they can cause considerable trouble. If the transaction is in stock, the demands for cash payments on the part of these stockholders may put a severe financial strain on the combination. Thus, most combinations depend not only upon obtaining approval of a required majority of stockholders but also upon minimizing the number of dissenting stockholders by making the offer attractive to all. Dissenting stockholders may be able to block the combination if they suspect that fraud is involved, even though the required majority of stockholders has approved it.

HOLDING COMPANIES

Instead of actually acquiring another company, a firm may purchase a portion of its stock and act as a holding company. By definition, a *holding company* owns sufficient voting stock to have a controlling interest in one or more other corporations. A holding company does not necessarily have to own 51 percent of the stock of another company in order to have control. For a widely held corporation, ownership of 20 percent or as little as 10 percent of the stock outstanding may constitute effective working control. The advantage of a holding company is that it allows a company to acquire control of another with a much smaller investment than would be necessary with a merger. Moreover, by acquiring only a portion of the stock, the holding company usually does not have to pay as high a price per share as it would if it sought to purchase all the stock. It may purchase the stock gradually without undue upward pressure on the market price of the stock. Another advantage of a holding company is the possibility that operating economies can be achieved through centralized management. One of the principal disadvantages of the holding company is that 15 percent of the dividends paid to it by the subsidiary is subject to taxation.[6] Thus, the holding company must pay a partial tax on dividends, and stockholders of the holding company also must pay a tax on dividends they receive.

---

[6]If the holding company owns 80 percent or more of the voting stock of the subsidiary, the dividend is not subject to taxation.

The partial tax could be avoided, of course, if the stockholders owned the operating companies directly.

Through pyramiding a series of holding companies, it is possible to obtain considerable leverage with respect to assets controlled and earnings. For example, suppose holding Company A owns 20 percent of holding Companies B, C, and D, which, in turn, own 20 percent controlling interest in nine operating companies. Thus, for every dollar of capital in each of the operating companies—$9 in all—Company A is able to control them with an investment of $0.36 ($0.20 \times 0.20 \times$ $9), or 4 percent of the total capital of the operating companies. As long as the operating companies are profitable and able to pay dividends to the holding companies, all may go well. However, in the 1920s, there tended to be excessive pyramiding of holding companies, particularly with respect to public utilities. In the 1930s the leverage of these companies magnified the losses, and a number of the pyramids crumbled. Because of the many abuses of holding companies, the Public Utility Holding Company Act of 1935 was passed to restrict the operation of holding companies in the public utility field.

REASONS FOR COMBINATION

The reasons for a combination are many and complex. Moreover, they are not mutually exclusive; more than one usually is involved in a combination. The ultimate purpose, of course, is to increase the market value per share of the firm. From Chapter 2, we know that share price can be expressed as

$$P_0 = \sum_{t=1}^{\infty} \frac{D_t}{(1 + k_e)^t} \tag{23-1}$$

where D_t is the dividend expected at the end of period t, and k_e is the required rate of return of investors in a stock of the risk involved. The case for a higher valuation after a merger than before must be based upon raising the level of expected future dividends per share in the numerator of Eq. (23-1), or lowering the required rate of return, k_e, in the denominator. The former primarily involves increasing earnings per share over what they otherwise would be, while the latter involves reducing the risk to investors. The reasons for combination that we examine in this section can be evaluated in relation to these two factors. Other more fundamental reasons were discussed in Chapter 8.

OPERATING ECONOMIES

Often, operating economies can be achieved through a combination of companies. Duplicate facilities can be eliminated, and marketing, purchasing, and other operations can be consolidated. For example, certain salesmen can be eliminated to avoid duplication of effort in a particular territory. The principal objective in a railroad merger is to realize economies of operation through elimination of duplicate facilities and runs. With an industrial company merger, a firm with a product that complements an existing product line can fill out that line and, hopefully, increase the total overall demand for the products of the acquiring company. The realization of operating economies is known as *synergism;* the fused company is of greater value than the sum of the parts—that is, $2 + 2 = 5$.

Operating economies can best be realized with a *horizontal merger,* in which two companies in the same line of business are combined. The economies achieved by this means result primarily from eliminating duplicate facilities and offering a broader product line in the hope of increasing total demand. A *vertical merger,* whereby a company either expands forward toward the ultimate consumer or backward toward the source of raw material, may also bring about economies. This type of merger gives a company more control over its distribution and purchasing. In the formation of U.S. Steel Corporation in 1900, one of the purposes was a complete vertical integration of steel from extraction of ore to the final sale of the product. There are few operating economies in a *conglomerate merger,* where two companies in unrelated lines of business are combined.[7]

A number of authors maintain that the possibility of operating economies is the only justification for a merger when the objective of a firm is to maximize shareholder wealth.[8] Their reasons essentially are those discussed in Chapter 8—namely, that investors are able to achieve the other benefits associated with mergers on their own. In particular, conglomerate mergers are felt to lack economic justification unless the acquiring company can manage more productively the assets of the companies being acquired. Only imperfections in the capital markets and/or irrational behavior on the part of investors can justify a merger in the absence of economies.[9]

MANAGEMENT ACQUISITION

Closely related to operating economies in this sense of raising expected future dividends per share over that they otherwise would be is

---

[7] For a different classification of acquisitions along the lines of financial, marketing, and manufacturing advantages as well as a framework for investigation, selection, negotiation, and integration, see Robert A. Howell, "Plan to Integrate Your Acquisitions," *Harvard Business Review,* 48 (November–December 1970), 66–76.

[8] See, for example, Dennis C. Mueller, "A Theory of Conglomerate Mergers," *Quarterly Journal of Economics,* 83 (November 1969), 652–53.

[9] In a test of 59 major industrial mergers, Robert A. Haugen and Terrence C. Langetieg, "An Empirical Test for Synergism in Merger," *Journal of Finance,* 30 (September 1975), 1003–14, find little evidence of synergism. Using a pairwise sample of merged firms and similar unmerged firms, the authors did not find that the merger altered the distribution of possible returns for the merged firm from that which existed before for the two separate firms.

the acquisition of management. If a firm finds that it is unable to hire top-quality management and that it has no one coming up through the ranks, it may seek a combination with another company having aggressive and competent management. The choice may be between gradual stagnation with an existing organization or combination with another company in order to obtain competent management and prospects for growth. To foster the long-run wealth of stockholders, the latter may be the only feasible alternative.

GROWTH

A company may not be able to grow at a fast or balanced enough rate by internal expansion and may find that its only way of achieving a desired growth rate is by acquiring other companies. The cost of growth by acquisition may well be cheaper than the real cost of internal growth; the numerous costs and risks involved in developing and embarking upon a new product line may be avoided through acquisition of a going concern. In addition, it usually is quicker to acquire new products and facilities through mergers than through internal development. An important aspect of external growth may be the acquisition of the research capabilities of another firm. Because research tends to be individually oriented, the acquiring company may be unable to develop such capabilities on its own. Closely related to research is the possession of basic patents. A company having certain patent rights may be extremely valuable for this reason alone.

Although these factors may lead to higher future earnings and growth, the critical factor is the price paid for the acquisition. If the company to be acquired is priced rationally in the market (that is, it is not undervalued or overvalued), its acquisition is unlikely to increase share price *unless* there is synergism. Unfortunately, in certain cases growth in sales, assets, and total earnings appears to have supplanted maximization of shareholder wealth as the primary goal of the firm. Robin Maris contends that because management's salaries, stock options, and prestige are more closely related to size than to profits, managers have considerable incentive to maximize growth.[10] If this is true, it is not difficult to understand the attractiveness of mergers in implementing such an objective, because in most cases growth can be achieved more easily through external acquisitions than through internal development.

[10] *The Economic Theory of Managerial Capitalism* (New York: Free Press, 1964). See also Mueller, "Theory of Conglomerate Mergers," pp. 644–48. In contrast, Wilbur G. Lewellen and Blaine Huntsman, "Managerial Pay and Corporate Performance," *American Economic Review*, 60 (September 1970), 710–20, find in an empirical study that executive compensation is influenced more strongly by profit and stock performance than by sales.

DIVERSIFICATION

Diversification is the motive in some mergers. By acquiring a firm in a different line of business, a company may be able to reduce cyclical instability in earnings. Although it is virtually impossible to find two companies with negative correlation in earnings, it is possible to find situations in which there is only moderate correlation. Related to the argument for diversification is the notion of spreading risk. For a small company the risk exposure of undertaking a new product line may be significant indeed. In fact, the potential loss may be so great in relation to the capital base of the company that management is unwilling to go ahead with the product development despite its considerable appeal. By combining with a larger company, however, the firm may be able to undertake the project, because the potential loss is not nearly as significant relative to the capital base of the surviving company.

To the extent that investors in a company's stock are averse to risk and are concerned only with the total risk of the firm, a reduction in earnings instability would have a favorable impact upon share price. Unlike the previous reasons for merging, the effect here is to reduce the rate of return that investors require in the denominator of Eq. (23-1). This argument assumes that investors evaluate risk solely in relation to the *total* risk of the firm. We know from Chapters 3 and 8, however, that investors are able to diversify risk on their own. If they evaluate risk in an overall market context, they will diversify at least as effectively on their own as the firm is able to do for them. Particularly when the stock of the company being acquired is publicly traded, there is no reason to believe that investors are not able to diversify their portfolios efficiently. Because the firm is unable to do something for them that they cannot do for themselves, diversification as a reason for merging is not a thing of value. Consequently, it would not lead to an increase in share price.

PERSONAL REASONS

In a tightly held company, the individuals who have controlling interest may want their company acquired by another company that has an established market for its stock. For estate tax purposes, it may be desirable for these individuals to hold shares of stock that are readily marketable and for which market-price quotations are available. The owners of a tightly held company may have too much of their wealth tied up in the company. By merging with a publicly held company, they obtain a marked improvement in their liquidity, enabling them to sell some of their stock and diversify their investments. Unlike the previous reasons we have investigated, this reason relates to specific stockholders as opposed to investors at large.

When two companies are combined, a ratio of exchange occurs that denotes the relative weighting of the firms. In this section, we consider the ratio of exchange with respect to the earnings, the market prices, and the book values of the stocks of the two companies involved. We assume that the combination is consummated in stock rather than in cash or debt. The objective in any merger should be to maximize the wealth of existing stockholders. In Chapters 6 and 8, we developed a framework for analyzing a prospective acquisition's risk-return tradeoff in both firm-risk and market-risk contexts. With this information, one can assess the probable impact of the acquisition on share price. In this section, we consider the effect of a prospective acquisition on certain financial relationships. Though these relationships are embodied in the framework presented in Chapters 6 and 8, many companies prefer to analyze them separately.

EARNINGS

In evaluating the possibility of an acquisition, it is important to consider the effect the merger has on the earnings per share of the surviving corporation. Suppose that Company A is considering the acquisition, by stock, of Company B. The financial data on the acquisition at the time it is being considered follow:

	Company A	Company B
Present earnings	$20,000,000	$5,000,000
Shares	5,000,000	2,000,000
Earnings per share	$ 4.00	$ 2.50
Price of stock	$64.00	$30.00
Price/earnings ratio	16	12

Assume that Company B has agreed to an offer of $35 a share to be paid in Company A stock. The exchange ratio, then, is $35/$64, or about 0.547 shares of Company A's stock for each share of Company B's stock. In total, 1,093,750 shares of Company A will need to be issued in order to acquire Company B. Assuming that the earnings of the component companies stay the same after the acquisition, earnings per share of the surviving company would be:

	Surviving Company A
Earnings	$25,000,000
Shares	6,093,750
Earnings per share	$4.10

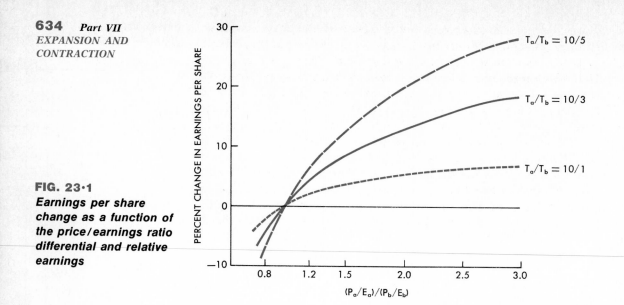

FIG. 23·1

*Earnings per share
change as a function of
the price/earnings ratio
differential and relative
earnings*

Thus, there is an immediate improvement in earnings per share for
Company *A* as a result of the merger. Company *B*'s former stockholders
experience a reduction in earnings per share, however. For each share of
B's stock they had held, they now hold 0.547 shares of *A*. Thus, the
earnings per share on each share of Company *B*'s stock they had held is
(0.547)(4.10), or $2.24, compared with $2.50 before.

Assume, however, that the price agreed upon for Company *B*'s stock
is $45 a share. The ratio of exchange, then, would be $45/$64, or about
0.703 shares of *A* for each share of *B*. In total, 1,406,250 shares would
have to be issued, and earnings per share after the merger would be:

	Surviving Company **A**
Earnings	$25,000,000
Shares	6,406,250
Earnings per share	$3.90

In this case, there is initial dilution in Company *A*'s earnings per share on
account of the acquisition of Company *B*.[11] Dilution in earnings per
share will occur anytime the price/earnings ratio paid for a company
exceeds the price/earnings ratio of the company doing the acquiring. In
our example, the price/earnings ratio in the first case was $35.00/$2.50,

[11]Company *B*'s former stockholders obtain an improvement in earnings per share.
Earnings per share on each share of stock they had held is $2.74.

or 14, and in the second case, it was $45.00/$2.50, or 18. Because the price/earnings ratio of Company A was 16, there was an increase in earnings per share in the first case and a decrease in the second.

Thus, both initial increases and decreases in earnings per share are possible. The *amount* of increase or decrease is a function of (1) the differential in price/earnings ratios, and (2) the relative size of the two firms as measured by total earnings.[12] The higher the price/earnings ratio of the acquiring company in relation to that of the company being acquired, and the larger the earnings of the acquired company in relation to those of the acquiring company, the greater the increase in earnings per share of the acquiring company. These relationships are illustrated in Figure 23-1 for three different earnings relationships. The a subscript for total earnings, T_a, and price/earnings ratio, P_a/E_a, denotes the acquiring company, while the b subscript for T_b and P_b/E_b denotes the company being acquired.

Future earnings

If the decision to acquire another company is based solely upon the initial impact on earnings per share, a company would never acquire another if there were an initial dilution in earnings per share. However, this type of analysis does not take into account the possibility of a future growth in earnings owing to the merger. If the earnings of Company B are expected to grow at a faster rate than those of Company A, a high ratio of exchange for the stock may be justified, despite the fact that there is initial dilution in earnings per share for stockholders of Company A. The superior growth in earnings of the acquired company may result eventually in higher earnings per share for these stockholders relative to earnings without the merger.

It is useful to graph likely future earnings per share with and without the acquisition. Figure 23-2 shows this for a hypothetical merger. The graph tells us how long it will take for the dilution in earnings per share to be eliminated, and for an accretion to take place. In this example, it is three years; earnings per share drop $0.30 initially, but this relative dilution is eliminated by the start of the fourth year. The greater the duration of dilution, the less desirable the acquisition is from the standpoint of the acquiring company. Some companies set a ceiling on the number of years dilution will be tolerated, and this ceiling serves as a constraint in establishing the exchange ratio to be paid in the acquisition.

Another drawback to using the initial impact on earnings per share as the sole criterion for judging the value of a merger is that the earnings of the surviving company are not necessarily an additive affair, such that

[12] See Walter J. Mead, "Instantaneous Merger Profit as a Conglomerate Merger Motive," *Western Economics Journal*, 7 (December 1969), 295–306.

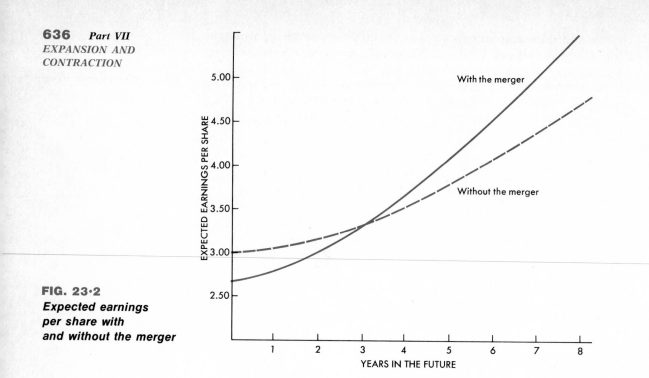

FIG. 23·2
*Expected earnings
per share with
and without the merger*

$2 + 2 = 4$. In many cases, there are *synergistic* effects, such that
$2 + 2 = 5$. Because of operating economies, increases in demand, and so
forth, earnings of the surviving company may be greater than the sum of
the earnings of the two companies without the merger. In our example,
suppose that total earnings three years after the merger are expected to
be $36 million for the surviving company, whereas total earnings of
Company *A* three years hence without the merger are expected to be $26
million. Assuming the price paid for Company *B*'s stock is $45 a share,
the expected earnings per share three years hence with and without the
merger are:

	With Merger	*Without Merger*
Expected earnings	$36,000,000	$26,000,000
Shares	6,406,250	5,000,000
Expected earnings per share	$5.62	$5.20

We see then that despite initial dilution, the acquisition of Company
B produces a favorable effect upon future earnings per share over and
above the expected growth in earnings per share for Company *A* without

the merger.[13] We can graph expected earnings per share, as in Figure 23-2, with and without the acquisition under the assumption of synergism. In fact, when an acquisition is being considered, graphs should be prepared under differing assumptions as to the exchange ratio. They also should be made under differing earnings assumptions for the combination; preparing multiple graphs gives management greater information on which to base negotiations.

Dividends per share   The ratio of exchange of dividends per share sometimes is considered in the evaluation of a merger. However, the dividend decision really is separate from the merger decision. The important variable is prospective earnings, for dividends are a function of these earnings. The acquiring company can alter its dividend-payout ratio if the prospect of a higher total dividend is enticing to the stockholders of the company being acquired. Justification for this action, however, must be based upon an analysis of its effect upon shareholder wealth (see Chapters 11 and 12).

MARKET VALUE

In addition to earnings, the major emphasis in the bargaining process is on the ratio of exchange of market prices per share. The market price of a publicly held stock is the focal judgment of investors as to the "intrinsic" value of that company. Accordingly, it reflects the earnings potential of the company, dividends, business risk, capital structure, asset values, and other factors that bear upon valuation. The ratio of exchange of market prices is simply

$$\frac{\text{Market price per share of acquiring company}}{\text{Market price per share of acquired company}} \times \text{Number of shares offered}$$

For example, if the market price of Company A is $60 per share and that of Company B is $30, and Company A offers a half share of its stock for each share of Company B, the ratio of exchange would be

$$\frac{\$60 \times 0.5}{\$30} = 1.00$$

[13] See J. Fred Weston, "Determination of Share Exchange Ratios in Mergers," in William W. Alberts and Joel E. Segall, eds., *The Corporate Merger* (Chicago: University of Chicago Press, 1966), pp. 117–38.

In other words, the stocks of the two companies would be exchanged on a one-to-one market-price basis. If the market price of the surviving company is relatively stable at $60 a share, each set of stockholders is about as well off as before with respect to market value. However, there is little enticement to the company being acquired to accept a one-to-one market-value ratio of exchange. Consequently, the acquiring company usually must offer a price in excess of the current market price per share of the company it wishes to acquire. Instead of a half share of stock, Company *A* might have to offer 0.667 shares, or $40 a share in current market value.

Even when the acquiring company offers a price in excess of the current market price of the company being acquired, its own stockholders could be better off with respect to market price per share. The reason is that there may be a difference in the price/earnings ratios of the two companies. Suppose that Company *B* is a moderate-sized company whose stock is traded in the over-the-counter market. Because, among other reasons, its stock is not particularly marketable, its price/earnings ratio is 10. Company *A*, on the other hand, has a price/earnings ratio of 18. Assume the following financial information:

	Company A	Company B
Present earnings	$20,000,000	$6,000,000
Shares	6,000,000	2,000,000
Earnings per share	$ 3.33	$ 3.00
Market price per share	$60.00	$30.00
Price/earnings ratio	18	10

With an offer of 0.667 shares of Company *A* for each share of Company *B*, or $40 a share in value, the market-price exchange ratio for Company *B* is

$$\frac{\$60 \times 0.667}{\$30} = 1.33$$

Stockholders of Company *B* are being offered a stock with a market value of $40 for each share of stock they own. Obviously, they benefit from the acquisition with respect to market price, because their stock was formerly worth $30 a share. However, the stockholders of Company *A* also stand to benefit, *if the price/earnings ratio of the surviving company stays at 18.* The market price per share of the surviving company after the acquisition, all other things held constant, would be:

	Surviving Company
Total earnings	$26,000,000
Number of shares	7,333,333
Earnings per share	$3.55
Price/earnings ratio	18
Market price per share	$63.90

The reason for this apparent bit of magic whereby the stockholders of both companies benefit is the difference in price/earnings ratios.

Under the conditions described above, companies with high price/earnings ratios would be able to acquire companies with lower price/earnings ratios and obtain an immediate increase in earnings per share, despite the fact that they pay a premium with respect to the market value exchange ratio. The key factor, however, is what happens to the price/earnings ratio after the merger. If it stays the same, the market price of the stock will increase. As a result, an acquiring company would be able to show a steady growth in earnings per share if it acquired a sufficient number of companies over time in this manner.[14] Recognize that this increase is not the result of operating economies or underlying growth but is due to the "bootstrap" increase in earnings per share through acquisitions. To the extent the marketplace values this illusory growth, a company presumably could increase shareholder wealth through acquisitions alone. However, in reasonably efficient capital markets it seems unlikely that the market will hold constant the price/earnings ratio of a company that cannot demonstrate growth potential in ways other than acquiring companies with lower price/earnings ratios. The acquiring company must be able to manage the companies it acquires if the benefit of acquisitions is to be lasting.

Thus, the acquiring company must consider the possibility that its price/earnings ratio will change with an acquisition. If the market is relatively free from imperfections and if synergism is not anticipated, we would expect the price/earnings ratio of the surviving firm to approach a weighted average of the two previous price/earnings ratios. Under these circumstances, the acquisition of companies with lower price/earnings ratios would not enhance shareholder wealth. In fact, if the market-price exchange ratio were more than one, shareholder wealth would decline. If synergism were expected, however, shareholder wealth could be increased through the acquisition.

[14]For further illustration of this process, see Mead, "Instantaneous Merger Profit," pp. 298–99.

Market values are unquestionably a major factor in most mergers; however, these values fluctuate greatly over time and in differing degrees for different companies. As a result, there may be considerable doubt as to just what the appropriate market value of a company is. Because of the fluctuation in market value, some companies vary their pursuit of acquisitions in keeping with the price of their stock. When the price is high, they may be aggressive in their pursuit of acquisitions; when it is relatively low, merger activity may dry up completely. Although certain mergers are based upon normalized market prices over a period of time, most are predicated upon the current market price. Consequently, fluctuations in this price are extremely important to the acquisition-minded company.

BOOK VALUE

Book value per share is rather meaningless as a basis for valuation in most mergers. Whereas once it was the dominant factor, book value per share is important now only when it is significantly above market value. When the purpose of an acquisition is to obtain the liquidity of another company, book value per share and working capital per share become important in the terms of the exchange. For example, Textron acquired American Woolen primarily for the latter's liquidity. American Woolen's book value per share was approximately $60, its working capital per share was $24, and its market price per share was $16. Textron paid $25 a share in cash. The ratios of exchange of book value per share of two companies is calculated in the same manner as is the ratio for market values. The importance of this ratio in bargaining is usually restricted to situations in which a company is acquired for its liquidity and asset values rather than for its earning power.

BOUNDARIES FOR NEGOTIATION

Once the financial relationships taken up in the preceding section have been analyzed, the acquiring firm is ready to begin negotiations. The financial relationships establish the boundaries within which negotiation can take place. To illustrate, suppose Company A were considering acquiring Company B.[15] The market price per share of Company A before the merger is

$$P_a = \frac{(P/E_a)Y_a}{N_a} \tag{23-2}$$

---

[15]This example is based upon Kermit D. Larson and Nicholas J. Gonedes, "Business Combinations: An Exchange-Ratio Determination Model," *Accounting Review*, 44 (October 1969), 720–28.

where P/E_a is the price/earnings ratio for Company A, Y_a is the total current earnings of that company, and N_a is the number of shares outstanding. For Company B, the market price per share is

$$P_b = \frac{(P/E_b)Y_b}{N_b} \qquad (23\text{-}3)$$

Expected market price per share after the combination is

$$P_{ab} = \frac{(P/E_{ab})(Y_a + Y_b)}{N_a + (ER)N_b} \qquad (23\text{-}4)$$

where P/E_{ab} is the expected price/earnings ratio after the merger, and ER is the exchange ratio; that is, the number of shares of Company A offered in exchange for one share of Company B. The estimate of P/E_{ab} should take account of any expected synergistic effects.

It is clear that stockholders in Company A will be dissatisfied if market price per share after the merger is less than that which prevailed before. Thus, the maximum exchange ratio that should be offered from their standpoint is the one that results in P_{ab} equaling P_a. Setting Eq. (23-2) equal to Eq. (23-4) and rearranging, Larson and Gonedes demonstrate that the maximum exchange ratio acceptable to Company A stockholders is[16]

$$ER_a = \frac{(P/E_{ab})(Y_a + Y_b) - (P/E_a)(Y_a)}{(P/E_a)(Y_a)(1/N_a)(N_b)} \qquad (23\text{-}5)$$

With this ratio of exchange, the expected market price per share after the merger would be the same as the market price per share before. Usually, the price/earnings ratio of the combined company, P/E_{ab}, is not known with any degree of certainty. Consequently, it is desirable to graph the maximum exchange ratio acceptable to Company A stockholders for a range of P/E_{ab}. An example is shown in Figure 23-3, and it is seen that ER_a is a linear function of P/E_{ab}. The greater P/E_{ab}, the greater the maximum exchange ratio acceptable to Company A stockholders. Thus, any exchange ratio on or below the straight line is acceptable.

In a similar manner, it is possible to graph the minimum exchange ratio acceptable to Company B stockholders. With this ratio, the market price of their holdings after the merger would equal the market price of their holdings before the merger, or $P_{ab} = P_b/ER$. Rearranging Eq. (23-4) and Eq. (23-3), one obtains the minimum exchange ratio acceptable to the stockholders of Company B.[17]

[16] Ibid., p. 724.
[17] Ibid., p. 725.

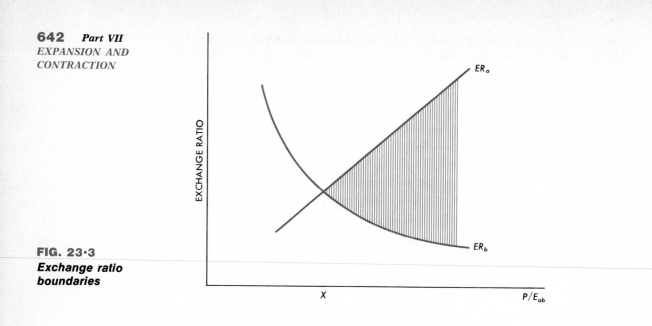

FIG. 23·3

Exchange ratio
boundaries

$$ER_b = \frac{(P/E_b)(Y_b/N_b)(N_a)}{(P/E_{ab})(Y_a + Y_b) - (P/E_b)(Y_b)} \qquad (23\text{-}6)$$

It is found that ER_b declines at a decreasing rate with P/E_{ab}. An example of this relationship also is shown in Figure 23-3. Stockholders of Company *B* would be satisfied only with an exchange ratio on or above the line.

Once these relationships are graphed, the resulting shaded area in the figure represents the boundaries for negotiation over the exchange ratio. With information of this sort, the management of Company *A* should try to bargain for an exchange ratio close to the ER_b line, while Company *B*'s management should strive for an exchange ratio close to the ER_a line. Boundary conditions shown in the figure establish the area in which fruitful negotiations are possible.

The exchange ratio finally settled upon depends upon the relative bargaining power of the two managements, as well as upon their expectations of the price/earnings ratio likely to prevail once the merger is consummated. Note that if the expected price/earnings ratio is to the left of point *X* in Figure 23-3, a merger of the two companies should not be undertaken. Neither set of shareholders is likely to gain, and one or both will suffer a decline in the market value of their holdings. At the intersection of the two lines, the price/earnings ratio for the surviving firm represents a weighted average of the price/earnings ratios of Companies *A* and *B* prior to the merger.[18] All price/earnings ratios to the right of point *X* are greater than the weighted average of the premerger price/

[18] Ibid., p. 726.

earnings ratios. In a market free from imperfections, these ratios would be due solely to the expectation of synergism. Under such circumstances, it is possible for both sets of stockholders to gain from the merger.

TENDER OFFERS

In our hypothetical examples, it is assumed that negotiations were confined to the managements and boards of directors of the companies involved. However, the acquiring company can make its appeal directly to the stockholders of the company it wishes to acquire through a *tender offer*. A tender offer is an offer to purchase shares of stock of another company at a fixed price per share from any stockholder who "tenders" his shares. The tender price is usually set significantly above the present market price in order to provide an incentive to stockholders to tender their shares. Use of the tender offer allows the acquiring company to bypass the management of the company it wishes to acquire and therefore, serves as a threat in any negotiations with that management. If management holds out for too high a price or otherwise balks at the offer of the acquiring company, that company can always make a tender offer.

The tender offer can also be used when there are no negotiations but when one company simply wants to acquire another. In a "surprise" tender offer, the acquiring company is careful not to reveal its intentions significantly in advance of the actual offer. The primary selling tool is the premium that is offered over the existing market price of the stock. As a rule of thumb, many suggest a premium of 20 percent, which is adjusted up or down depending upon the circumstances.[19] In addition, brokers are often given very attractive commissions for shares tendered through them. The tender offer itself is usually communicated through financial newspapers. Direct mailings are made to the stockholders of the company being bid for if the bidder is able to obtain a stockholders' list. Although a company is legally obligated to provide such a list, it usually is able to delay delivery long enough to frustrate the bidder.

From the standpoint of the company being bid for, a number of defensive tactics are available. First, management may try to persuade its stockholders that the offer is not in their best interests. Usually, the argument is that the bid is too low in relation to the true, long-run value of the firm. However, in the face of an attractive premium, the long run may be too distant. Some companies raise the cash dividend or declare a stock split in hopes of gaining stockholder support. Legal actions are often undertaken, more to delay and frustrate the bidder than with the expectation of winning. To the extent that the two firms are competitors, an antitrust suit may prove a powerful deterrent to the bidder. As a last

---

[19] See Samuel L. Hayes III and Russell A. Taussig, "Tactics in Cash Takeover Bids," *Harvard Business Review*, 45 (March–April 1967), 139–40.

FIG. 23·4
Tender offers

A bidder takes pains to keep his intentions secret until the last minute.
"Claude; Courtesy of *Fortune Magazine.*"

Management often seeks to foil a bidder by
quickly arranging a merger with another company.
"Claude; Courtesy of *Fortune Magazine.*"

Determined management opposition
can usually fend off an unwanted take-over bid.
"Claude; Courtesy of *Fortune Magazine.*"

resort, management of the company being bid for may seek a merger with a "friendly" company.[20] Some of the strategies involved in tender offers are depicted in Figure 23-4.

Although the use of tender offers increased dramatically in the sixties, it declined in importance in the seventies. In part, this decline was due to coinciding changes in security regulations and accounting

[20] For a more extensive discussion of these points, see ibid., pp. 124–48.

rules that tended to restrict the prospective acquirer.[21] There are many who oppose such restrictions because they believe tender offers contribute to corporate "democracy" and, thereby, serve a socially useful function. If management does not behave so as to maximize the value of the firm to its shareholders, there is always the danger of a tender offer from another company. Whereas stockholders may not have enough control to effect a change otherwise, a tender offer may bring about a change and increase shareholder wealth. In recent years, the tender offer has largely displaced the proxy contest as a means of obtaining control of a company.

[21] See Richard E. Cheney, "What's New on the Corporate Takeover Scene," *Financial Executive*, 40 (April 1972), 18–21.

SUMMARY

A company may grow internally, or it may grow externally through acquisitions. The objective of the firm in either case is to maximize existing shareholder wealth. Another company can be acquired through the purchase of either its assets or its stock. In turn, the means of payment can be cash, or it can be stock. When two companies combine and one loses its corporate existence, the combination is known as a merger; if two companies combine and form a new corporation, the combination is known as a consolidation. Other than merging or consolidating, one company can purchase effective working control of another company and act as a holding company.

There are a number of reasons for acquiring another company, all of which relate to expected return and risk. Among the more important are operating economies, acquisition of management, diversification, growth potential, financing, taxation, and personal motives of the owners. The relative valuation of two companies may be based upon earnings, market values, book values, or a combination of all three. Because the market price reflects the judgment of investors as to everything that affects value, it is the foundation upon which most exchange ratios are based.

Once financial relationships are analyzed, rational negotiations can take place. In this regard, it is useful to establish the exchange ratio boundaries for negotiations. Within these boundaries, the wealth of both sets of stockholders is enhanced. In cases where the acquiring company does not wish to negotiate with the management of a prospective company to be acquired, it can make a tender offer to purchase shares directly from the stockholders of that company.

1. The following data are pertinent for Companies A and B:

	Company A	Company B
Present earnings (in millions)	$20	$ 4
Shares (in millions)	10	7
Price/earnings ratio	18	10

(a) If the two companies were to merge and the exchange ratio were one share of Company A for each share of Company B, what would be the initial impact on earnings per share of the two companies? What is the market value exchange ratio? Is a merger likely to take place?

(b) If the exchange ratio were two shares of Company A for each share of Company B, what happens with respect to the above?

(c) If the exchange ratio were 1.5 shares of Company A for each share of Company B, what happens?

(d) What exchange ratio would you suggest?

2.

	Net Income	Number of Shares	Market Price per Share	Tax Rate
Nimbus Company	$5,000,000	1,000,000	$100	50%
Noor Company	1,000,000	500,000	20	50

The Nimbus Company wishes to acquire the Noor Company. If the merger were effected through an exchange of stock, Nimbus would be willing to pay a 25 percent premium for the Noor shares. If done for cash, the terms would have to be as favorable to the Noor shareholders; to obtain the cash, Nimbus would have to sell its own stock in the market.

(a) Compute the exchange ratio and the combined earnings per share if an exchange of stock were accomplished.

(b) If we assume that all Noor shareholders have held their stock for more than six months, have a 40 percent marginal tax rate, and paid an average of $14 for their shares, what cash price would have to be offered to be as attractive as the terms in (a) above?

(c) Why might the computation in (b) overstate the premium that would have to be paid to make the cash price comparable to the exchange of stock offer? Upon what factor would the size of premium depend?

(d) If the cash (see (b) above) were obtained by means of a stock issue at the current price (with total expenses of 10 percent), what would the earnings per share of new Nimbus be?

3. Suppose that the current balance sheets of Nimbus and Noor (see problem 2) are as follows:

	Nimbus	Noor
Cash	$ 10,000,000	$ 5,000,000
Accounts receivable	17,000,000	4,000,000
Inventories	20,000,000	5,000,000
Prepaid expenses	3,000,000	1,000,000
Total current assets	$ 50,000,000	$15,000,000
Fixed assets, net	100,000,000	10,000,000
Total assets	$150,000,000	$25,000,000
Notes payable	$ 15,000,000	—
Accounts payable	25,000,000	$ 8,000,000
Accrued wages and taxes	10,000,000	2,000,000
Total current liabilities	$ 50,000,000	$10,000,000
Long-term debt	50,000,000	5,000,000
Common stock	10,000,000	2,500,000
Capital surplus	20,000,000	2,500,000
Retained earnings	20,000,000	5,000,000
Total liabilities and net worth	$150,000,000	$25,000,000

(a) Derive the balance sheet of new Nimbus if the exchange of stock (see 2 a) were effected. Compute the old and new book value per share.

(b) Recompute (a), assuming instead that the Noor holders are paid in cash, as outlined in 2 (b) and (d). Assume that the Noor assets cannot be written up. Also compute an old and new net tangible assets per share.

4. Assume the exchange of Nimbus shares for Noor shares as outlined in problems 2 and 3 above.

(a) What is the ratio of exchange?

(b) Compare the earnings per Noor share before and after the merger. Compare the earnings per Nimbus share. On this basis alone, which group fared better? Why?

(c) What would you expect to happen to the share price of Nimbus after the merger? What would you expect to happen to the P/E ratio? Must they both move together?

(d) Why do you imagine that old Nimbus commanded a higher P/E than Noor? What should be the change in P/E ratio resulting from the merger? Does this conflict with your answer to (c)? Why?

(e) If the Nimbus Company is in a high-technology growth industry and Noor makes cement, would you revise your answers?

(f) In determining the appropriate P/E ratio for Nimbus, should the increase in earnings resulting from this merger be added as a growth factor?

(g) In light of the above discussion, do you feel that the Noor share-holders would have approved the merger if Noor stock paid a $1 dividend and Nimbus paid $3? Why?

5. Instead of an exchange of stock (see problem 2 b), suppose that Nimbus offered Noor shareholders a 5 percent preferred stock, con-vertible 20 percent above the market, at the same exchange ratio proposed for the common stock. Assume the common-stock dividend payments of problem 4 (g).

(a) If this transaction were viewed as an exchange of common stock, what is the effective exchange ratio?

(b) Compute the change in dividend income per Noor share after the exchange for Nimbus convertible preferred. Compute the change in dividend income after conversion into Nimbus common.

(c) Compute earnings per share for new Nimbus before and after conversion.

(d) Compute earnings retention before and after conversion, assuming the dividend remains the same.

6. The shares of the Navigation Company and the Matson Company have the following characteristics:

	Navigation	Matson
EPS	$ 4	$ 2
Growth in EPS expected forever	5%	10%
Number of shares (in millions)	10	3
Price per share	$40	$30

(a) If Navigation acquires Matson with an exchange of stock on the basis of their market values, what will be the new EPS?

(b) Graph Navigation EPS into the future with and without the acquisi-tion (assume no synergism).

(c) How long would it take to eliminate the dilution?

7. Let it be assumed that a holding company can always be set up with 50 percent debt at 8 percent and 20 percent preferred stock at 6 percent. Further assume that all companies pay a tax rate of 50 percent, the 85 percent intercorporate dividend exclusion applies in all cases, and that ownership of 40 percent of the stock of another company constitutes control. The shares of the Target Company can be obtained at their book value.

Target Company			
Total assets	$30,000,000	Debt (8%)	$15,000,000
		Preferred (6%)	5,000,000
		Common	10,000,000
			$30,000,000

(a) A group of investors has set up Holding Company *A* to acquire control of the Target Company. If the group holds all the equity of Holding Company *A*, how much money must they put up? If Target has operating earnings equal to 20 percent of total assets and pays all earnings in dividends, what return on investment will the group earn?

(b) Suppose the group sets up Holding Company *B* to acquire control of Holding Company *A*. If the group holds all the equity of *B*, how much money must they put up? If *A* pays all earnings in dividends, what return on investment will the group earn? How many dollars of operating assets does the group control per dollar of their own investment?

(c) How would your answers change if Target had operating earnings equal to 8 percent of total assets?

8. Reconsider Matson and Navigation (problem 6).

(a) Develop and graph the boundary conditions for the merger negotiations.

(b) If the P/E of the combined firm were estimated to be twelve times, what would be the possible range of exchange ratios?

(c) Rework part (b) with a P/E of 10.2.

9. Collect data on situations where one company made a tender offer for the shares of another, and management hurriedly conducted negotiations with a third company. Compare the terms of the two offers, especially with regard to the price of the offer. Did the offer endorsed by management always bear the highest price? Should this not be the case under the theory? Examine the other terms of the offers, including employment contracts, options, bonuses, and retirement provisions. Correlate management's endorsement with

(a) Those offers having the highest price, and then

(b) Those having the most favorable employment terms.

Which correlation is higher? Why? Finally, determine which offer was accepted by the stockholders. Correlate this with (a) those having the highest price, and (b) those endorsed by management. Which correlation is higher? Why?

SELECTED REFERENCES

Alberts, William W., and Joel E. Segall, eds., *The Corporate Merger.* Chicago: University of Chicago Press, 1966.

Appleyard, A. R., and G. K. Yarrow, "The Relationship between Take-over Activity and Share Valuation," *Journal of Finance,* 30 (December 1975), 1239–50.

Cohen, Manuel F., "Takeover Bids," *Financial Analysts Journal,* 26 (January–February 1970), 26–31.

Crowther, John F., "Peril Point Acquisition Prices," *Harvard Business Review,* 47 (September–October 1969), 58–62.

Cunitz, Jonathan A., "Valuing Potential Acquisitions," *Financial Executive,* 39 (April 1971), 16–28.

Gort, Michael, and Thomas E. Hogarty, "New Evidence on Mergers," *Journal of Law and Economics,* 13 (April 1970), 167–84.

Haugen, Robert A., and Terrence C. Langetieg, "An Empirical Test for Synergism in Merger," *Journal of Finance,* 30 (September 1975), 1003–14.

Hayes, Samuel L., III., and Russell A. Taussig, "Tactics in Cash Takeover Bids," *Harvard Business Review,* 45 (March–April 1967), 135–48.

Heath, John, Jr., "Valuation Factors and Techniques in Mergers and Acquisitions," *Financial Executive,* 40 (April 1972), 34–44.

Hexter, Richard M., "How to Sell Your Company," *Harvard Business Review,* 46 (May–June 1968), 71–77.

Higgins, Robert C., and Lawrence D. Schall, "Corporate Bankruptcy and Conglomerate Merger," *Journal of Finance,* 30 (March 1975), 93–114.

Hogarty, Thomas F., "The Profitability of Corporate Mergers," *Journal of Business,* 43 (July 1970), 317–27.

Howell, Robert A., "Plan to Integrate Your Acquisitions," *Harvard Business Review,* 48 (November–December 1970), 66–76.

Larson, Kermit D., and Nicholas J. Gonedes, "Business Combinations: An Exchange-Ratio Determination Model," *Accounting Review,* 44 (October 1969), 720–28.

Lev, Baruch, and Gershon Mandelker, "The Microeconomic Consequences of Corporate Mergers," *Journal of Business,* 45 (January 1972), 85–104.

Lewellen, Wilbur G., "A Pure Financial Rationale for the Conglomerate Merger," *Journal of Finance,* 26 (May 1971), 521–37.

Lorie, J. H., and P. Halpern, "Conglomerates: The Rhetoric and the Evidence," *Journal of Law and Economics,* 13 (April 1970), 149–66.

MacDougal, Gary E., and Fred V. Malek, "Master Plan for Merger Negotiations," *Harvard Business Review,* 48 (January–February 1970), 71–82.

Mandelker, Gershon, "An Empirical Analysis of the Gains from Mergers," *Journal of Finance,* 31 (May 1976).

——, "Risk and Return: The Case of Merging Firms," *Journal of Financial Economics,* 1 (December 1974), 303–35.

Mead, Walter J., "Instantaneous Merger Profit as a Conglomerate Merger Motive," *Western Economic Review,* 7 (December 1969), 295–306.

Melicher, Ronald W., and Thomas R. Harter, "Stock Price Movements of Firms Engaging in Large Acquisitions," *Journal of Financial and Quantitative Analysis,* 7 (March 1972), 1469–75.

Melicher, Ronald W., and David F. Rush, "Evidence on the Acquisition-Related Performance of Conglomerate Firms," *Journal of Finance,* 29 (March 1974), 141–50.

Mueller, Dennis C., "A Theory of Conglomerate Mergers," *Quarterly Journal of Economics,* 83 (November 1969), 643–59.

Reinhardt, Uwe E., *Mergers and Consolidations: A Corporate-Finance Approach.* Morristown: General Learning Press, 1972.

Reum, W. Robert., and Thomas A. Steele III, "Contingent Payouts Cut Acquisition Risks," *Harvard Business Review,* 48 (March–April 1970), 83–91.

Rockwell, Willard F., Jr., "How to Acquire a Company," *Harvard Business Review,* 46 (May–June 1968), 121–32.

Shad, John S. R., "The Financial Realities of Mergers," *Harvard Business Review,* 47 (November–December 1969), 133–46.

Shick, Richard A., "The Analysis of Mergers and Acquisitions," *Journal of Finance,* 27 (May 1972), 495–502.

Shick, Richard A., and Frank C. Jen, "Merger Benefits to Shareholders of Acquiring Firms," *Financial Management,* 3 (Winter 1974), 45–53.

Smalter, Donald J., and Roderic C. Lancey, "P/E Analysis in Acquisition Strategy," *Harvard Business Review,* 44 (November–December 1966), 85–95.

Weston, J. Fred, and Surendra K. Mansinghka, "Tests of the Efficiency of Conglomerate Firms," *Journal of Finance,* 26 (September 1971), 919–36.

Weston, J. Fred, Keith V. Smith, and Ronald E. Shrieves, "Conglomerate Performance Using the Capital Asset Pricing Model," *Review of Economics and Statistics* (November 1972), 357–63.

Wyatt, Arthur R., "Inequities in Accounting for Business Combinations," *Financial Executive,* 40 (December 1972), 28–35.

BUSINESS FAILURE and REORGANIZATION

Our analysis throughout most of this book has assumed that the firm is a going concern; nevertheless, we must not lose sight of the fact that some firms do fail. Recognition of failure is important both from the standpoint of internal management, and from the standpoint of a creditor with amounts owing from a company in distress. This point was brought into sharp perspective in the 1970s with the bankruptcy of such large companies as Penn Central and W. T. Grant. Previously, bankruptcy was regarded as a phenomenon restricted to small firms—the depression of the thirties being the last time major corporations had failed.

The word "failure" is vague, partly because there are varying degrees of failure. For example, a company is regarded as technically insolvent if it is unable to meet its current obligations. However, such insolvency may be only temporary and subject to remedy.[1] Insolvency in bankruptcy, on the other hand, means that the liabilities of a company exceed its assets; in other words, the net worth of the company is negative. Financial failure includes the entire range of possibilities between these extremes.

The remedies available to save a failing company vary in harshness according to the degree of financial difficulty. If the outlook is sufficiently hopeless, liquidation may be the only feasible alternative. However, many failing firms can be rehabilitated to the gain of creditors, stockholders, and society. Although the major purpose of a liquidation or rehabilitation is to protect creditors, the interests of the owners also are considered. (In the thirties, they were all but neglected.) Still, legal procedures favor creditors. Otherwise, they would hesitate to extend credit, and the allocation of funds in the economy would be less than efficient.

SIGNS OF FAILURE

Although the causes of financial difficulty are numerous, many failures are attributable either directly or indirectly to management. Usually, nonfinancial problems lead to losses, which, in turn, lead to financial strain and eventual failure. Very seldom is one bad decision the cause of the difficulty; usually the cause is a series of errors, and the difficulty evolves gradually. Because with most companies the signs of potential distress are evident prior to actual failure, a creditor may be able to take corrective actions before failure finally occurs.

In an extensive research study, William H. Beaver used financial ratios to predict failure.[2] The study encompassed a sample of seventy-nine relatively large firms which failed during the 1954–64 period.[3] For

---

[1] See James E. Walter, "Determination of Technical Insolvency," *Journal of Business*, 30 (January 1957), 30–43.

[2] "Financial Ratios as Predictors of Failure," *Empirical Research in Accounting: Selected Studies*, supplement to *Journal of Accounting Research* (1966), 71–111.

[3] *Failure* was defined as the inability of a firm to meet its financial obligations.

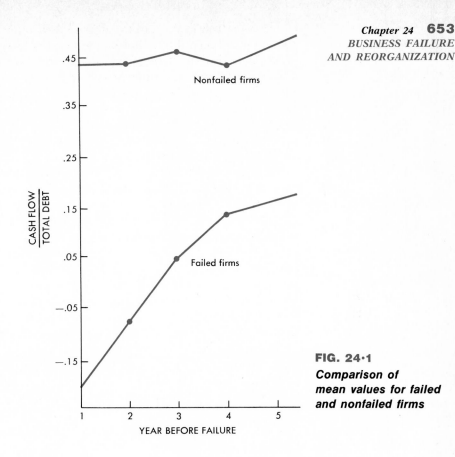

FIG. 24·1
*Comparison of
mean values for failed
and nonfailed firms*

each of these companies, another firm was selected that did not fail but was in the same industry and was of approximately the same size as the firm that failed. The data collected for the nonfailed companies were for the same years as those for the failed firms. These samples were used to test the predictive ability of thirty financial ratios. The mean values of the ratios for the two samples were compared over the five-year period prior to failure. An example of such a comparison, using the cash-flow/total-debt ratio, is shown in Figure 24-1. We see that the mean ratio for the failed firms differs significantly from that for the nonfailed firms. Not only is it lower, but it deteriorates markedly as failure approaches.

In addition to a comparison of mean values, Beaver tested the samples using a form of discriminant analysis and then went on to analyze the evidence using likelihood ratios. Although not all of the financial ratios examined predicted failure equally well, many showed excellent predictive power. In a companion article, Beaver investigated the ability to predict failure from the changes in market prices of stocks.[4]

---

[4]William H. Beaver, "Market Prices, Financial Ratios, and the Prediction of Failure," *Journal of Accounting Research*, 6 (Autumn 1968), 179–92.

He found that the median market price of the failed companies declined at an increasing rate as failure approached, relative to that for the nonfailed companies. The largest price decline occurred in the final year. Beaver concluded that investors adjust stock prices to the deteriorating condition of failing companies. Moreover, he found the evidence to be consistent with investors assessing the likelihood for failure on the basis of financial ratios.

In a similar type of study, Edward I. Altman employed multiple discriminant analysis to predict bankruptcy, using various financial ratios.[5] This statistical technique is described in the appendix to Chapter 15. Altman worked with a sample of thirty-three corporations that filed for bankruptcy during the 1946–65 period. Like Beaver, he collected a paired sample of thirty-three nonbankrupt firms on a stratified random basis. Starting with twenty-two financial ratios, he selected the five that did the best combined job of predicting bankruptcy. These ratios were used to discriminate between bankrupt and nonbankrupt firms, using data from one to five years prior to bankruptcy. As expected, the predictive accuracy of the multiple discriminant model declined with the number of years prior to bankruptcy. However, the model was able to forecast failure quite well up to two years before bankruptcy. Altman also tested the model with secondary samples of bankrupt and nonbankrupt firms. Using the parameter estimates obtained in the original sample, he found the model to have considerable predictive accuracy when used in conjunction with the secondary samples.

In his investigation, Altman, like Beaver, found that the financial ratios of bankrupt firms deteriorated as bankruptcy approached, the greatest deterioration occurring between the third and the second year. Altman concluded that through discriminant analysis, a creditor can predict potential bankruptcy successfully. In yet another study, Altman studied the railroad industry and found that certain liquidity, profitability, and leverage ratios were significantly worse for failing railroads than for the industry as a whole.[6] Moreover, the ratios for the former group deteriorated as bankruptcy approached.

Robert O. Edmister tested the usefulness of financial ratio analysis for predicting the failure of small businesses.[7] Similar to the others, he

[5] "Financial Ratios, Discriminant Analysis and the Prediction of Corporate Bankruptcy," *Journal of Finance*, 23 (September 1968), 589–609.

[6] "Railroad Bankruptcy Propensity," *Journal of Finance*, 26 (May 1971), 333–45. In a specific analysis of Penn Central, Roger F. Murray contends that evidence of deterioration was clearly evident prior to the actual collapse of Penn Central. "The Penn Central Debacle: Lessons for Financial Analysis," *Journal of Finance*, 26 (May 1971), 327–32.

[7] "An Empirical Test of Financial Ratio Analysis for Small Business Failure Prediction," *Journal of Financial and Quantitative Analysis*, 7 (March 1972), 1477–93. See also E. B. Deakin, "A Discriminant Analysis of Predictors of Business Failure," *Journal of Accounting Research*, 10 (Spring 1972), 167–79, for another study dealing with failure prediction. For an excellent overall discussion of this type of research, see Baruch Lev, *Financial Statement Analysis: A New Approach* (Englewood Cliffs, N.J.: Prentice-Hall, 1974), Part II.

employed multiple discriminant analysis and found it to be an accurate predictor of failure if ratios were averaged over a three-year span. Unlike the results of Beaver and Altman, however, an analysis based upon one year's financial statements was not sufficient to discriminate failing from nonfailing firms. Consecutive financial statements were necessary for the successful analysis of small-business failures. On the basis of the empirical studies described above, it would appear that signs of potential failure are evident well before actual failure occurs. For the creditor, the lag allows time to take corrective actions.

VOLUNTARY SETTLEMENTS

Despite difficulties caused by past mistakes, many companies can be preserved as going concerns and can make an economic contribution to society. Sometimes the rehabilitation is severe, in keeping with the degree of financial difficulty. Nevertheless, these measures may be necessary if the firm is to obtain a new lease on life. In this chapter, we consider the remedies available to a company in financial distress, beginning with remedies that are voluntary on the part of creditors and the company and then examining legal actions that can be taken in connection with a failing company. Our focus is different from that in Chapter 6, where we developed a decision rule for determining whether or not a firm should liquidate in whole or in part. Recall that the rule called for liquidating the firm when the expected return on its liquidating value was less than the required rate of return. Under such circumstances, the firm would not be expected to earn its economic keep; and liquidation would be in the best interest of all concerned.

In the remainder of this chapter, we take up the full spectrum of remedies available to a firm in financial distress. It is important to recognize that at the time this chapter was being written, Congress was considering a major reform of the Bankruptcy Act. In 1976, however, it was unclear which direction the proposed legislation would take and, if legislated, the date of transition to the new Bankruptcy Act. In what follows, then, we describe the remedies available to a failing firm under the existing Bankruptcy Act. In the last section of the chapter, we examine the major features of the proposed legislation and the ways in which it will change existing procedures.

EXTENSIONS

An extension involves nothing more than creditors extending the maturity of their obligations. In cases of temporary insolvency of a basically sound company, creditors may prefer to work the problem out with the company. By not forcing the issue with legal proceedings, creditors avoid considerable legal expense and the possible shrinkage of value in liquidation. Obviously, no one creditor is going to extend his obligation unless others do likewise. Consequently, the major creditors usually form a committee whose function is to negotiate with the company and to formulate a plan mutually satisfactory to all concerned.

We must point out, however, that no one creditor is obligated to go along with the plan. If there are dissenting creditors and they have small amounts owing, they may be paid off in order to avoid legal proceedings. The number of dissenters cannot be too large, for the remaining creditors must, in essence, assume their obligations. Obviously, the remaining creditors do not want to be left "holding the bag." If an extension is worked out, the creditors can institute controls over the company to assure proper management and to increase the probability of speedy recovery. In addition, they may elect to take security if marketable assets are available. The ultimate threat on the part of creditors is to initiate bankruptcy proceedings against the company and to force it into liquidation. By making an extension, however, they show an inclination to cooperate with the company.

COMPOSITION

A composition involves a pro rata settlement of creditors' claims in cash or in cash and promissory notes. The creditors must agree to accept a partial settlement in discharge of their entire claim. For example, a debtor may propose a settlement of sixty cents on the dollar. If creditors feel that the settlement is more than they could obtain in liquidation after legal expenses, they will probably accept. Even if it is somewhat less, they may still accept, because no company likes to be responsible for forcing another into bankruptcy. The settlement is a "friendly" one in the sense that legal proceedings are avoided.

As in an extension, however, the settlement must be agreed to by all creditors. Dissenting creditors must be paid in full, or they can force the company into bankruptcy. These creditors can be a considerable nuisance and may all but preclude a voluntary settlement. Overall, voluntary settlements can be advantageous to creditors as well as to the debtors, for they avoid legal expenses and complications.

OTHER ASPECTS OF VOLUNTARY SETTLEMENT

Creditors may agree to a voluntary settlement only if the present management is relieved of its responsibility. A creditors' committee may be appointed by creditors to control the operations of the company until the claims can be settled. The company enters into an agreement with creditors, giving them control of the company. One problem with this arrangement is the possibility of stockholder suits against the creditors for mismanagement of the company. Consequently, creditors are reluctant to become too active in the management of a failing company.

In certain circumstances, creditors may feel that the company should not be preserved, because further financial deterioration seems inevitable. When liquidation is the only realistic solution, it can be accomplished either through a private settlement or through bankruptcy proceedings. An orderly private liquidation is likely to be more efficient and result in a significantly higher settlement. A private settlement can also be through a formal assignment of assets to an appointed trustee. The trustee liquidates the assets and distributes the proceeds to creditors on a pro rata basis. Because the voluntary settlement must be agreed to by all creditors, it usually is restricted to companies with a limited number of creditors and securities outstanding that are not publicly held.

LEGAL PROCEDURES

Most legal procedures undertaken in connection with failing companies fall under the Bankruptcy Act of 1898, as amended by the Chandler Act of 1938. This act provides for both the liquidation of a company and for its reorganization.[8] In most cases, the courts take over the operation of the company and preserve the *status quo* until a decision is reached whether to liquidate the company or keep it alive through reorganization.

LIQUIDATION

If there is no hope for the successful operation of a company, liquidation is the only feasible alternative. The federal district court, then, declares the firm bankrupt and proceeds with a plan for orderly liquidation. Bankruptcy proceedings may be either voluntary or involuntary. With a voluntary bankruptcy, the company files a petition of bankruptcy with a federal district court. In an involuntary bankruptcy, three or more creditors with claims in excess of $500 initiate the action by filing a petition with the court. If the total number of creditors of a firm is less than twelve, any one creditor can file a petition. The federal court will declare the company an involuntary bankrupt if it violates one of the six acts of bankruptcy.[9]

---

[8] Before the thirties, companies were reorganized under equity receiverships. This process is no longer in use.

[9] The first act involves the concealment or removal of the bankrupt's property with the intent of defrauding creditors. The second act is the transfer of cash or other assets to one creditor in preference to others. The third act is the insolvent debtor's giving any creditor a lien on his property. The fourth act involves a general assignment by the debtor for the benefit of creditors. The fifth act occurs if the debtor, while insolvent, appoints a receiver or trustee to take charge of his property. The sixth act is an admission in writing by the debtor that he is unable to pay his debt and that he is willing to be adjudged a bankrupt.

Upon the declaration of bankruptcy, the court usually appoints a *referee* to take over the operation of the company temporarily and call a meeting of the creditors. At the meeting, claims of the creditors are proven, and the creditors are given the opportunity to appoint the *trustee in bankruptcy*. The trustee has the responsibility of liquidating the assets of the company and distributing liquidating dividends to the creditors. The conduct of the trustee in carrying out these responsibilities is under the supervision of the court.

In the distribution of the proceeds of a liquidation, the priority of claims must be observed. The administrative costs involved in the bankruptcy, taxes, and certain other claims must be paid before creditors are entitled to receive settlement. Secured creditors are entitled to the proceeds realized from the liquidation of specific assets on which they have a lien. If any balance of the claim is not realized from the sale of the collateral, these creditors become general creditors. General creditors are paid liquidating dividends on a pro rata basis from the total liquidation of unencumbered assets. If all of these claims are paid in full, liquidating dividends then can be paid to subordinated debtholders, to preferred stockholders, and, finally, to common stockholders. It is unlikely, however, that common stockholders will receive any distribution from a liquidation.

When a trustee cannot be appointed quickly, the court appoints a *receiver* to manage the operation of the company and conserve its assets until a trustee can be selected. After that, the procedure is the same as before. Upon the payment of all liquidating dividends, the bankrupt is discharged, thereby being relieved of any further claim. The principal objective of bankruptcy proceedings is an orderly liquidation of assets and an equitable distribution to creditors on a formal basis. The disadvantage of these proceedings is that they are slower and usually more expensive than a private liquidation. Some court-appointed officials are inefficient, being more concerned with their remuneration than with the proceeds available to creditors. As a result, a liquidation in bankruptcy may be less efficient than a private liquidation, providing creditors with a lower settlement. However, when creditors cannot come together in a voluntary manner, bankruptcy proceedings are the only recourse.

REORGANIZATION

It may be in the best interests of all concerned to reorganize a company rather than liquidate it. A reorganization is an effort to keep a company alive by changing its capital structure. The rehabilitation involves the reduction of fixed charges by substituting equity and limited-income securities for fixed-income securities.

Procedure

Most reorganizations of industrial and public utility companies occur under Chapter X of the Bankruptcy Act. Reorganization procedures are initiated in the same general manner as a liquidation in bankruptcy. The federal district court appoints a *trustee* to operate the debtor's business until a reorganization plan is put into effect.[10] If the debts of the company are in excess of $250,000, the court must appoint a "disinterested" trustee—that is, a party independent of the debtor. In addition to managing the operations of the debtor temporarily, the trustee must compile all the essential information required by the court, creditors, and—if the securities are publicly held—the SEC. Included is information pertaining to the value of assets, the nature of the liabilities, and the operating potential of the debtor from the standpoint of profitability.

Most important, the trustee is charged with the responsibility of drawing up a plan of reorganization. This plan is proposed after a thorough review of the situation and discussions with creditors and stockholders. Committees may be formed by the various classes of creditors and stockholders to represent and protect the interests of each class. The plan then is submitted to the court for hearings and approval. If liabilities exceed $3 million, and the securities are publicly held, the plan must also be submitted to the SEC. The SEC acts only in an advisory capacity to the court; it prepares a report on the proposed plan and submits it to the court. The final decision is that of the court.

If the court feels the reorganization plan is "fair, equitable, and feasible," it will approve the plan. All parties must be treated fairly and equitably; moreover, the plan must be workable with respect to the earning power and financial structure of the reorganized company. The reorganized company cannot have too great an amount of fixed financial charges in relation to its expected earning power. Upon approval by the court, the plan is submitted to the creditor and stockholder groups for approval. In order to become effective, it must be accepted by a two-thirds majority of each class of debtholders and by a simple majority of each class of stockholders. Upon approval by the majority of a particular class of security holders, the plan is binding on dissenters in that class.

The reorganization procedure for railroads is similar, except that the Interstate Commerce Commission plays an active role in the reorganization. Railroad reorganizations occur under Section 77 of the Bankruptcy Act and the Mahaffe Act of 1948. The reorganization plan must be submitted to the ICC, which approves the trustee. The ICC holds hearings and then either approves the proposed reorganization plan or submits its own plan to the court. The concern of the ICC is that the reorganization plan be compatible with the public's interest. The court,

---

[10]The company is declared a "debtor" in a reorganization as opposed to a "bankrupt" in a liquidation.

however, must approve the plan on the basis of whether it is fair, equitable, and feasible.

Reorganization plan

The difficult aspect of a reorganization is the recasting of the company's capital structure to reduce the amount of fixed charges. In formulating a reorganization plan, the trustee must carry out three steps. First, he must determine the total valuation of the reorganized company. This step, perhaps, is the most difficult and the most important. The technique favored by trustees is a capitalization of prospective earnings. For example, if future annual earnings of the reorganized company are expected to be $2 million, and the overall capitalization rate of similar companies averages 10 percent, a total valuation of $20 million would be set for the company. The valuation figure is subject to considerable variation owing to the difficulty of estimating prospective earnings and determining an appropriate capitalization rate. Thus, the valuation figure represents nothing more than a best estimate of potential value. Although the capitalization of prospective earnings is the generally accepted approach to valuing a company in reorganization, the valuation may be adjusted upward if the assets have substantial liquidating value. The common stockholders of the company, of course, would like to see as high a valuation figure as possible. If the valuation figure the trustee proposes is below the liquidating value of the company, common stockholders will argue for liquidation rather than reorganization.

Once a valuation figure has been determined, the next step is to formulate a new capital structure for the company to reduce fixed charges so that there will be an adequate coverage margin. To reduce these charges, the total debt of the firm is scaled down by being partly shifted to income bonds, preferred stock, and common stock. In addition to being scaled down, the terms of the debt may be changed. The maturity of the debt can be extended to reduce the amount of annual sinking-fund obligation. If it appears that the reorganized company will need new financing in the future, the trustee may feel that a more conservative ratio of debt to equity is in order to provide for future financial flexibility.

Once a new capital structure is established, the last step involves the valuation of the old securities and their exchange for new securities. Under an *absolute priority rule*, which is required in reorganization under Chapter X, all senior claims on assets must be settled in full before a junior claim can be settled. For example, in the exchange process, a bondholder must receive the par value of his bond in another security before there can be any distribution to preferred stockholders. The total valuation figure arrived at in step one sets an upper limit on the amount of securities that can be issued. Suppose that the existing capital structure of a company undergoing reorganization is as follows:

Debentures	**$ 9 million**
Subordinated debentures	**3 million**
Preferred stock	**6 million**
Common stock equity (at book value)	**10 million**
	$28 million

If the total valuation of the reorganized company is to be $20 million, the trustee might establish the following capital structure in step two:

Debentures	**$ 3 million**
Income bonds	**6 million**
Preferred stock	**3 million**
Common stock	**8 million**
	$20 million

Having established the "appropriate" capital structure for the reorganized company, the trustee then must allocate the new securities. In this regard, he may propose that the debenture holders exchange their $9 million in debentures for $3 million in new debentures and $6 million in income bonds; that the subordinated debenture holders exchange their $3 million in securities for preferred stock; and that preferred stockholders exchange their securities for $6 million of common stock in the reorganized company. The common stockholders then would be entitled to $2 million in stock in the reorganized company, or 25 percent of the total common stock of the reorganized company. Before, these stockholders held 100 percent of the stock. It is easy to see why common stockholders would like to see as high a valuation figure as possible. To encourage high valuation, they may attempt to discount the troubles of the company as temporary and argue that the earning potential of the company is favorable.

Thus, each claim is settled in full before a junior claim is settled. The example above represents a relatively "mild" reorganization. In a "harsh" reorganization, debt instruments may be exchanged entirely for common stock in the reorganized company and the old common stock eliminated completely. Had the total valuation figure in the example been $12 million, the trustee might have proposed a new capital structure consisting of $3 million in preferred stock and $9 million in common stock. Only the straight and subordinated debenture holders would receive a settlement in this case. The preferred and the common stockholders of the old company would receive nothing.

These examples serve to show that the common stockholders of a company undergoing reorganization suffer under an absolute priority rule, whereby claims must be settled in the order of their legal priority. From their standpoint, they would much prefer to see claims settled on a *relative priority basis*. Under this rule, new securities are allocated on the basis of the relative market prices of the securities. The common stockholder could never obtain senior securities in a reorganization, but they would be entitled to some common stock if their present stock had value. Because the company is not actually being liquidated, common stockholders argue that a rule of relative priority is really the fairest. However, the absolute priority rule has been upheld by the Supreme Court (*Case* v. *Los Angeles Lumber Products Company*, 1939). Their only recourse is to question whether the reorganization plan is fair and equitable to all security holders and not whether the absolute priority of claims is valid.

CHAPTER XI PROCEDURES

Chapter XI of the Bankruptcy Act permits a failing company to seek an *arrangement*. In essence, an arrangement is a "legal" extension or composition. Only the company itself can initiate an arrangement, by filing a voluntary petition with a federal district court, attesting to the fact that it is unable to pay unsecured creditors and proposing a plan of action. Once the petition is filed, creditors cannot push for collection while an arrangement is being worked out. The court appoints a referee to call a meeting of creditors and discuss the plan proposed by the debtor. In addition, the court may appoint a receiver or trustee if the situation so warrants. The plan proposed by the debtor is subject to amendments by the creditors. Once a plan is approved by the majority of creditors and is judged by the court to be fair, equitable, and feasible, however, it becomes binding on all. In this respect, the arrangement has an advantage over a voluntary extension or composition, wherein creditors do not necessarily have to accept the plan. A large creditor can easily prevent a voluntary settlement from working.

The arrangement applies only to unsecured creditors, however. The claims of secured creditors are left intact; the debtor must pay secured creditors according to the terms of the obligations. An arrangement usually is a cheaper and quicker form of settlement than other types of legal settlements. The method is well suited for the company whose creditors are mostly trade creditors and that has no publicly held fixed-income securities. If a company has publicly held securities and substantial changes in its capital structure are required, these changes usually will be effected under Chapter X, rather than under Chapter XI, of the Bankruptcy Act.

At the time of this writing Congress was considering a major reform of the bankruptcy laws of the United States. Two bills were being considered, one drafted by the Commission of the Bankruptcy Laws (H.R. 31), and the other by the National Conference of Bankruptcy Judges (H.R. 32). It is not clear which of these two bills, if either, will emerge. However, it does seem clear that there will be a major overhaul of the bankruptcy system. Of the two bills, the first calls for the more sweeping changes. Therefore, we will focus our attention on the important changes contained in it. However, major differences between the two bills will be pointed out as we go along. Hopefully, the reader will gain insight into what is likely to come in the way of changes in the Bankruptcy Act.

BANKRUPTCY COURTS

Under each bill, U.S. bankruptcy courts are established with judges appointed for fifteen-year terms. In the Commission bill, the judges are appointed by the president, whereas in the National Conference of Bankruptcy Judges bill, they are appointed by the judicial council for the particular circuit involved. The number and location of bankruptcy courts will be determined by the Judicial Conference of the United States on the basis of a comprehensive survey of case loads. Unlike the present system, the individual courts need not be self-supporting, as expenses will be paid out of appropriations by the federal government. This is the same general revenue support as occurs for other courts.

BANKRUPTCY ADMINISTRATION

In the Commission bill, a separate administrative body is established in the executive branch of the government. Called the U.S. Bankruptcy Administration, its function is to administer the litigated estate. Under the old law, such administration is under the auspices of the court. Frequently, there have been conflicts of interest and inefficiencies under this system. The Commission has therefore recommended the severance of administrative from judicial functions within the bankruptcy system.

The U.S. Bankruptcy Administration would be staffed by permanent employees, and their duties would include many of those now performed by referees, trustees, auctioneers, appraisers, accountants, and attorneys. This would largely replace the appointment of outside administrators by the court, where often there is absence of effective control and where there is little uniformity across the United States. Hopefully, there would also be economies arising from increased efficiency. Headquartered in Washington, the Bankruptcy Administration would have some regional and many local offices.

Under the second bill, H.R. 32, the present system of administration is largely retained and various outside parties are appointed by the court to administer the estate. The most important of these is the trustee. In all cases, the court oversees the administration of the estate. This difference in administration is perhaps the key difference between the two bills.

INVOLUNTARY PETITIONS AND OTHER CHANGES

Under the existing Bankruptcy Act, one of the six acts of bankruptcy must be proven. This frequently results in delays, during which time the debtor's assets are further depleted. Under the first bill, the concept of an act of bankruptcy is abolished and involuntary proceedings can be initiated by a creditor if the business ceases to pay its obligations. To protect the debtor against ill-founded petitions by creditors, however, the court is required to hold immediate hearings after the filing of an involuntary petition. After the filing of the petition and pending determination of the issues involved, the court may order the Bankruptcy Administration to take possession of the property in order to prevent depletion.

In the hearing, the court must determine whether the relief sought in the petition is in the best interests of the debtor and its creditors. After due consideration of the issues of the case, the court either decides that the case is valid and direct relief is in order or dismisses the case.

The bill also provides for a number of changes designed to streamline the administration of a bankrupt estate. Certain red tape involved in the sale of property is eliminated so as to reduce administrative expenses and delays. Changes also are made in the treatment of the recovery of assets transferred before bankruptcy, so as to make it more equitable.

With respect to the distribution of assets, the bill proposes a major simplification of the provisions to make them more equitable among unsecured creditors. Wages to employees and claims for contributions to employee benefit plans are given substantial priority—in preference to all other creditors with the exception of administrative expenses, which come first. Third in priority come taxes accruing within one year prior to bankruptcy. This reduces the government's priority of claim, as the limit now is three years. All other outside claims are lumped together under the heading of general creditors, and the burden of proof of a legally enforceable and allowable claim is made less onerous. However, claims by officers, directors, affiliates, and stockholders are subordinated to those of the general creditors. When the estate is sufficient to pay some but not all of the claimants in a particular priority class, the distribution is made on a pro rata basis.

To eliminate the overlap and confusion involved in Chapters X, XI, and XII of the present Bankruptcy Act, the three chapters are consolidated into one chapter under the first bill, H.R. 31. Under the second bill, H.R. 32, consolidation occurs, but there is a separate chapter for arrangements.

Under the first bill, the court determines whether a trustee is needed on the basis of the circumstances of the case. Where debts exceed $1 million or where there are more than three hundred security holders, however, the presumption is that a trustee will be appointed. The selection itself is by the Bankruptcy Administration, subject to the approval of the court. In reorganizations, the use of a receiver is eliminated.

Rather than have the creditors themselves determine the election of a creditors' committee, the selection is made by the Bankruptcy Administration and the committee will usually be composed of the seven largest creditors. This change is expected to eliminate certain infighting among different creditors and lawyers. Also, the direct involvement of the Securities and Exchange Commission is reduced and its function assumed by the Bankruptcy Administration.

The basic concept of fair and equitable as applied to publicly held securities in a reorganization is retained. However, recognition is given to the fact that the valuation placed on the company is at best an educated guess about the future. An effort is made to expedite the formulation and consummation of a reorganization plan so as to eliminate the unreasonable delays that now occur. The rule of absolute priority is modified to allow equityholders to participate in the plan if they make future contributions that are important to the operation of the reorganized company. The degree of participation in the plan is determined on a basis that will approximate the value of such contributions. This represents a marked departure from the absolute priority rule established in *Case* v. *Los Angeles Lumber Products Company*, 1939.

After all plans for the reorganization of a company are submitted to the Bankruptcy Administration within the allotted time, they are turned over to the court and a date for approval hearings is set. At the hearings, the court evaluates each plan according to its feasibility, the reasonableness of the valuation placed on the company, and the fair and equitable criteria. On the basis of these considerations, the court then approves or disapproves each plan. Approved plans are transmitted to those creditors and equityholders that are entitled to accept or reject a plan. These security holders then accept or reject each of the plans.

The court then sets hearings for the confirmation of any plans that have the requisite majority of acceptances. The court will confirm a plan if it has majority acceptance by each creditor class and majority acceptance by equityholders. If more than one plan has majority acceptance, the court considers the preferences indicated by creditors and equityholders in determining which plan to confirm. Upon confirmation of a plan, it becomes binding on all parties. All rights and interests of equityholders and all claims of creditors other than those contained in the confirmed plan are then terminated.

SUMMARY

Business failure encompasses a wide range of financial difficulty; it occurs whenever a company is unable to meet its current obligations. The remedies applied to a failing company vary in severity with the degree of financial difficulty. Voluntary settlements are informal and must be agreed to by all creditors and the company itself. The difficulty with a voluntary settlement is in obtaining agreement of all parties concerned. Included in voluntary settlements are extensions, compositions, a creditors' committee controlling the operations of the company, and a private liquidation.

Legal settlements are effected, for the most part, under Chapters X and XI of the Bankruptcy Act, as amended by the Chandler Act of 1938. Railroads are reorganized under Section 77 of the Bankruptcy Act. The least "harsh" of the legal procedures is an arrangement under Chapter XI. An arrangement is simply a formal extension or composition. Reorganizations and liquidations occur mostly under Chapter X. In a reorganization, the capital structure of the company is changed so as to reduce the total amount of fixed charges. The reorganized plan has to be fair, equitable, and feasible, as determined by the court and approved by a two-thirds majority of each class of debtholders and a majority of each class of stockholders. If the company cannot be rehabilitated, it will be declared bankrupt by the court and liquidated by a trustee in bankruptcy. Creditors receive liquidating dividends according to the priority of their claims.

In the last section, we described the two bills that at the time of this writing were being considered by Congress to reform the Bankruptcy Act. Depending upon the outcome, the act could be changed in a significant way.

PROBLEMS

1.

Fall Corporation Balance Sheet

Cash	$ 1,000,000	Note payable	$ 1,000,000
Accounts receivable	2,000,000	Accounts payable	4,000,000
Inventories	5,000,000	Accrued wages	3,000,000
Prepaid expenses	1,000,000	Accrued taxes	1,000,000
Total current assets	$ 9,000,000	Total current liabilities	$ 9,000,000
Fixed assets, net	8,000,000	Long-term debt	12,000,000
Goodwill	5,000,000	Equity	1,000,000
Total assets	$22,000,000		$22,000,000

(a) Do you feel that it is likely that the Fall Corporation either is now or will soon be technically insolvent? Why? What steps could management take to correct this situation?

(b) Answer (a) with respect to the bankruptcy concept of insolvency.

(c) Compare and contrast these two concepts of insolvency.

(d) Is it possible that attempts to alleviate one form of insolvency could aggravate the other? How?

(e) Is the balance sheet the best tool for determining technical or fundamental insolvency? Can you suggest better ones?

2. *Research Project*

Compile data on recent bankruptcy cases involving fairly large companies. Learn as much as you can about "stockholder protective committees"; discover how many of these committees there are for each bankruptcy case you study. Finally, compare the amount of money going for legal fees, court costs, etc., as opposed to the amount the creditors finally receive. Do you begin to feel that there might be "self-interest" as well as "friendly" motives behind the creditors' acceptance of a composition? Whom do stockholder protective committees really protect? Can you find any parallels between bankruptcy law and probate law?

3. The Greenwood Corporation is in bankruptcy. The trustee has estimated that the company can earn $1.5 million before interest and taxes (50 percent) in the future. In the new capitalization, he feels that debentures should bear a coupon of 6 percent and have coverage of five times, income bonds (6 percent) should have overall coverage of two times, preferred stock (6.25 percent) should have after-tax coverage of three times, and common stock should be issued on a P/E basis of twelve times. Determine the capital structure that conforms to the trustee's criteria.

4. Assume that the Greenwood Corporation (see problem 3) originally had the following capital structure:

	Book value	Market Value
Senior debentures	$10,000,000	$ 9,000,000
Subordinated debentures	15,000,000	12,000,000
Junior subordinated debentures	5,000,000	2,000,000
Preferred stock (par $100)	5,000,000	1,000,000
Common stock (1,000,000 shares, par value $10)	−10,000,000	1,000,000
	$25,000,000	$25,000,000

Determine which of the new securities each class of old securities holders would get under:

(a) The absolute priority rule

(b) The relative priority rule

5. The Vent Corporation has been liquidated under bankruptcy proceedings. The book and liquidation values are as follows:

	Book	Liquidation
Cash	$ 700,000	$ 700,000
Accounts receivable	2,000,000	1,600,000
Inventory	3,500,000	2,000,000
Office building	5,000,000	3,000,000
Plant	8,000,000	5,000,000
Equipment	7,000,000	3,000,000
Total	$26,200,000	$15,300,000

The liability and equity accounts at the time of liquidation were as follows:

Accounts payable	$ 2,000,000
Accrued federal taxes	500,000
Accrued local taxes	200,000
Notes payable	1,000,000
Accrued wages	500,000
Total current liabilities	$ 4,200,000
Mortgage on office building	$ 3,000,000
First mortgage on plant	3,000,000
Second mortgage on plant	2,000,000
Subordinated debentures	5,000,000
Total long-term debt	$13,000,000
Preferred stock	$ 5,000,000
Common stock	7,000,000
Retained earnings	(3,000,000)
Total	$ 9,000,000
Total	$26,200,000

Expenses of liquidation (lawyers' fees, court costs, etc.) came to 20 percent of the proceeds. The debentures are subordinated only to the two first mortgage bonds. All of the accrued wages are less than three months old and less than $600 per employee. Determine the appropriate distribution of the proceeds of liquidation.

6. *Research Project*
   Read the sections of the Internal Revenue Code that apply to the reorganization of insolvent corporations. What are the tax implications of a transfer of property from an insolvent corporation to another corporation? What conditions must be met? What are the tax implications of the exchange of stocks or securities of an insolvent corporation for those of the corporation to which the property is transferred? What restrictions apply? If you were the financial manager of a solvent corporation negotiating the purchase of assets of an insolvent corporation, how would the information required above be of use to you?

SELECTED REFERENCES

Altman, Edward I., *Corporate Bankruptcy in America.* Lexington, Mass.: Heath Lexington Books, 1971.

_____, "Corporate Bankruptcy Potential, Stockholder Returns and Share Valuation," *Journal of Finance,* 24 (December 1969), 887–900.

_____, "Equity Securities of Bankrupt Firms," *Financial Analysts Journal,* 25 (July–August 1969), 129–33.

_____, "Financial Ratios, Discriminant Analysis and the Prediction of Corporate Bankruptcy," *Journal of Finance,* 23 (September 1968), 589–609.

_____, "Railroad Bankruptcy Propensity," *Journal of Finance,* 26 (May 1971), 333–45.

Beaver, William H., "Financial Ratios as Predictors of Failure," *Empirical Research in Accounting: Selected Studies,* supplement to *Journal of Accounting Research* (1966), pp. 71–111.

_____, "Market Prices, Financial Ratios, and the Prediction of Failure," *Journal of Accounting Research,* 6 (Autumn 1968), 179–92.

Browstein, Gerald W., "Awarding Fair Fees in Bankruptcy: Recent Developments," *Commercial Law Journal,* 76 (March 1971), 64–68.

Collier on Bankruptcy, 14th ed., Vol. 2. New York: Mathew Bender and Company, 1971.

Coogan, Peter F., Richard Broude, and Herman Glatt, "Comments on Some Reorganization Provisions of the Pending Bankruptcy Bills," *Business Lawyer,* 30 (July 1975).

Cyr, Conrad K., "Setting the Record Straight for a Comprehensive Revision of the Bankruptcy Act of 1898," *American Bankruptcy Law Journal,* 49 (Spring 1975).

Deakin, E. B., "A Discriminant Analysis of Predictors of Business Failure," *Journal of Accounting Research,* 10 (Spring 1972), 167–79.

Edmister, Robert O., "An Empirical Test of Financial Ratio Analysis for Small Business Failure Prediction," *Journal of Financial and Quantitative Analysis,* 7 (March 1972), 1477–93.

Gordon, Myron J., "Towards a Theory of Financial Distress," *Journal of Finance,* 26 (May 1971), 347–56.

Krause, Sidney, "Chapters X and XI—A Study in Contrasts," *Business Lawyer,* 19 (January 1964), 511–26.

Lev, Baruch, *Financial Statement Analysis: A New Approach.* Englewood Cliffs, N.J.: Prentice-Hall, 1974.

Murphy, Patrick A., "Restraint and Reimbursement: the Secured Creditor in Reorganization and Arrangement Proceedings," *Business Lawyer,* 30 (November 1974).

Murray, Roger F., "The Penn Central Debacle: Lessons for Financial Analysis," *Journal of Finance,* 26 (May 1971), 327–32.

Report of the Commission on the Bankruptcy Laws of the United States. Committee on the Judiciary, 93rd Cong. 1st sess. Washington, D.C.: Government Printing Office, 1973.

Rutberg, Sidney, *Ten Cents on the Dollar.* New York: Simon & Schuster, 1973.

Stanley, David T., and Marjorie Girth, *Bankruptcy: Problem, Process, Reform.* Washington, D.C.: Brookings Institution, 1971.

Walter, James E., "Determination of Technical Insolvency," *Journal of Business,* 30 (January 1957), 30–43.

Weston, J. Fred, "The Industrial Economics Background of the Penn Central Bankruptcy," *Journal of Finance,* 26 (May 1971), 311–26.

TOOLS of FINANCIAL ANALYSIS and CONTROL

VIII

FINANCIAL RATIO ANALYSIS

In order to make rational decisions in keeping with the objectives of the firm, the financial manager must have at his disposal certain analytical tools. The purpose of this chapter and of the next two is to examine the more important tools of financial analysis. Financial analysis is undertaken by outside suppliers of capital—creditors and investors—and also by the firm itself. The latter's purpose is not only for internal control but also for better understanding what capital suppliers seek in the way of financial condition and performance from it. The type of analysis varies according to the specific interests of the party involved. A trade creditor is interested primarily in the liquidity of a firm. His claim is short-term, and the ability of a firm to pay this claim is best judged by means of a thorough analysis of its liquidity. The claim of a bondholder, on the other hand, is long-term. Accordingly, he would be more interested in the cash-flow ability of the firm to service debt over the long run. The bondholder may evaluate this ability by analyzing the capital structure of the firm, the major sources and uses of funds, its profitability over time, and projections of future profitability.

An investor in a company's common stock is concerned principally with present and expected future earnings and the stability of these earnings about a trend, as well as their covariance with the earnings of other companies. As a result, the investor might concentrate his analysis on the profitability of the firm. He would be concerned with its financial condition insofar as it affects the ability of the firm to pay dividends and to avoid bankruptcy. Finally, in order to bargain more effectively for outside funds, the management of a firm should be interested in all aspects of financial analysis that outside suppliers of capital use in evaluating the firm. In addition, management employs financial analysis for purposes of internal control. In particular, it is concerned with profitability on investment in the various assets of the company and in the efficiency of asset management. Thus, the type of financial analysis undertaken varies according to the particular interests of the analyst. Financial statement analysis is part of a larger information-processing system on which informed decisions can be based.

USE OF FINANCIAL RATIOS

To evaluate the financial condition and performance of a firm, the financial analyst needs certain yardsticks. The yardstick frequently used is a ratio, or index, relating two pieces of financial data to each other. Analysis and interpretation of various ratios should give an experienced and skilled analyst a better understanding of the financial condition and performance of the firm than he would obtain from analysis of the financial data alone.[1]

The analysis of financial ratios involves two types of comparison.

---

[1] For an excellent discussion of the history of ratio analysis, see James O. Horrigan, "A Short History of Financial Ratio Analysis," *Accounting Review*, 43 (April 1968), 284–94.

First, the analyst can compare a present ratio with past and expected future ratios for the same company. For example, the current ratio (the ratio of current assets to current liabilities) for the present year-end could be compared with the current ratio for the preceding year-end. When financial ratios are arrayed on a spread sheet over a period of years, the analyst can study the composition of change and determine whether there has been an improvement or a deterioration in the financial condition and performance of the firm over time. Financial ratios also can be computed for projected, or pro forma, statements and compared with present and past ratios. In the comparisons over time, it is best to compare not only financial ratios but also the raw figures.

The second method of comparison involves comparing the ratios of one firm with those of similar firms or with industry averages at the same point in time. Such a comparison gives insight into the relative financial condition and performance of the firm. Financial ratios for various industries are published by Robert Morris Associates, Dun & Bradstreet, Leo Troy's *Almanac of Business and Industrial Financial Ratios*, and various other credit agencies and trade associations.[2] The analyst should avoid using "rules of thumb" indiscriminately for all industries. For example, the criterion that all companies should have at least a 2-to-1 current ratio is inappropriate. The analysis must be in relation to the type of business in which the firm is engaged and to the firm itself. Many sound companies have current ratios of less than 2 to 1. Only by comparing the financial ratios of one firm with those of similar firms can one make a realistic judgment. In this regard, the analysis of the deviation of the company being analyzed from the overall norm should be based on some knowledge of the distribution of ratios for the companies involved. If the company being studied has a current ratio of 1.4 and the industry norm is 1.8, one would like to know the proportion of companies whose ratios are below 1.4. If it is only 2 percent, we are likely to be much more concerned than if it is 25 percent. Therefore, we need information on the dispersion of the distribution in order to judge the significance of the deviation of a financial ratio for a particular company from the industry norm.[3]

Because reported financial data and the ratios computed from these data are numerical, there is a tendency to regard them as precise portrayals of a firm's true financial status. For some firms, the account-

[2] Robert Morris Associates, an association of bank credit and loan officers, publishes industry averages based upon financial statements supplied to banks by borrowers. Eleven ratios are computed annually for 156 lines of business. In addition, each line of business is broken down according to four size categories. Dun & Bradstreet calculates annually fourteen important ratios for 125 lines of business. Troy, *Almanac of Business and Industrial Financial Ratios* (Englewood Cliffs, N.J.: Prentice-Hall, 1974) shows industry averages for some twenty-two financial ratios. Over 75 industries are reported, and some of the sublistings under each industry are quite extensive. Industry classifications include such things as farms and small retail stores as well as the more usual industries.

[3] For further discussion of this point, see Baruch Lev, *Financial Statement Analysis: A New Approach* (Englewood Cliffs, N.J.: Prentice-Hall, 1974), 62–64.

ing data may closely approximate economic reality. On many occasions, however, it is necessary to go beyond the reported figures in order to analyze properly the financial condition and performance of the firm. Such accounting data as depreciation, reserve for bad debts, and other reserves at best are estimates and may not reflect economic depreciation, bad debts, and other losses.

Moreover, accounting data from different companies should be

Table 25·1   Aldine Manufacturing Company balance sheet

Assets

	March 31, 1977	March 31, 1976
Cash and marketable securities	$ 177,689	$ 175,042
Accounts receivable	678,279	740,705
Inventories, at lower of cost (Fifo) or market	1,328,963	1,234,725
Prepaid expenses	20,756	17,197
Accumulated tax prepayments	35,203	29,165
Current assets	$2,240,890	$2,196,834
Fixed assets at cost	$1,596,886	$1,538,495
Less accumulated depreciation	856,829	791,205
Net fixed assets	$ 740,057	$ 747,290
Investment—long-term	65,376	—
Other assets:		
Goodwill	198,854	198,854
Debenture discount	6,303	6,770
	$3,251,480	$3,149,748

Liabilities and Net Worth

	March 31, 1977	March 31, 1976
Bank loans and notes payable	$ 448,508	$ 356,511
Accounts payable	148,427	136,793
Accrued taxes	36,203	127,455
Other accrued liabilities	190,938	164,285
Current liabilities	$ 824,076	$ 785,044
Long-term debt	630,783	626,460
Stockholders' equity		
Common stock, $1.00 par value	420,828	420,824
Capital surplus	361,158	361,059
Retained earnings	1,014,635	956,361
Total stockholders' equity	$1,796,621	$1,738,244
	$3,251,480	$3,149,748

[handwritten annotations: "Total debt = {" bracketing Current liabilities and Long-term debt; "Net worth" next to Stockholders' equity; "i.e., NET WORTH" next to Total stockholders' equity]

standardized as much as possible. It is important to compare apples with apples and oranges with oranges. Even with standardized figures, however, the analyst should use caution in interpreting the comparisons.

TYPES OF RATIOS

For our purposes, financial ratios can be divided into four types: liquidity, debt, profitability, and coverage ratios. The first two types are ratios computed from the balance sheet; the last two are ratios computed from the income statement and, sometimes, from both the income statement and the balance sheet. It is important to recognize from the outset that no one ratio gives us sufficient information by which to judge the financial condition and performance of the firm. Only when we analyze a group of ratios are we able to make reasonable judgments. In addition, it is very important to take into account any seasonal character in a business. Underlying trends may be assessed only through a comparison of raw figures and ratios at the same time of year. For example, we would not compare a December 31 balance sheet with a May 31 balance sheet but would compare December 31 with December 31.

Although the number of financial ratios that might be computed increases geometrically with the amount of financial data, we concentrate only upon the more important ratios in this chapter. Actually, the ratios needed to assess the financial condition and performance of a company are relatively few in number. To compute unneeded ratios adds both complexity and confusion to the problem. In order to illustrate the ratios discussed in this chapter, we use the balance sheet and income statements of the Aldine Manufacturing Company shown in Tables 25-1 and 25-2.

Table 25·2 Aldine Manufacturing Company statement of earnings

	Year Ended March 31, 1977	Year Ended March 31, 1976
Net sales	$3,992,758	$3,721,241
Cost of goods sold	2,680,298	2,499,965
Selling, general, and administrative expenses	801,395	726,959
Depreciation	111,509	113,989
Interest expense	85,274	69,764
Earnings before taxes	$ 314,282	$ 310,564
Income taxes	163,708	172,446
Earnings after taxes	$ 150,574	$ 138,118
Cash dividends	92,300	88,634
Retained earnings	$ 58,274	$ 49,484

LIQUIDITY RATIOS

Liquidity ratios are used to judge a firm's ability to meet short-term obligations. From them, much insight can be obtained into the present cash solvency of the firm and its ability to remain solvent in the event of adversities. Essentially we wish to compare short-term obligations with the short-term resources available to meet these obligations.

CURRENT RATIO

One of the most general and most frequently used of these ratios is the *current ratio*.

$$\frac{\text{Current assets}}{\text{Current liabilities}}$$

For Aldine, the ratio for the 1977 year-end is

$$\frac{\$2,240,890}{\$824,076} = 2.72$$

The higher the ratio, supposedly, the greater the ability of the firm to pay its bills. However, the ratio must be regarded as a crude measure of liquidity because it does not take into account the liquidity of the individual components of the current assets.[4] A firm having current assets composed principally of cash and current receivables is generally regarded as more liquid than a firm whose current assets consist primarily of inventories.[5] Consequently, we must turn to "finer" tools of analysis if we are to evaluate critically the liquidity of the firm.

ACID-TEST RATIO

A somewhat more accurate guide to liquidity is the *quick,* or *acid-test, ratio:*

$$\frac{\text{Current assets less inventories}}{\text{Current liabilities}}$$

---

[4] For a thorough analysis of the shortcomings of the current ratio, see Kenneth W. Lemke, "The Evaluation of Liquidity: An Analytical Study," *Journal of Accounting Research,* 8 (Spring 1970), 47–77. Lemke shows that changes in the current ratio do not necessarily indicate a change in liquidity, and, therefore, the ratio cannot be interpreted in a consistent manner.

[5] We have defined *liquidity* as the ability to realize value in money—the most liquid of assets. Liquidity has two dimensions: (1) the time required to convert the asset into money, and (2) the certainty of the price realized. To the extent that the price realized on receivables is as predictable as that realized on inventories, receivables would be a more liquid asset than inventories, owing to the shorter time required to convert the asset into money. If the price realized on receivables is more certain than that on inventories, receivables would be regarded as being even more liquid.

For Aldine, this ratio is

$$\frac{\$2,240,890 - \$1,328,963}{\$824,076} = 1.11$$

This ratio is the same as the current ratio, except that it excludes inventories—presumably the least liquid portion of current assets—from the numerator. The ratio concentrates on cash, marketable securities, and receivables in relation to current obligations and thus provides a more penetrating measure of liquidity than does the current ratio.

LIQUIDITY OF RECEIVABLES

To the extent that there are suspected imbalances or problems in various components of the current assets, the financial analyst will want to examine these components separately in his assessment of liquidity. Receivables, for example, may be far from current. To regard all receivables as liquid, when in fact a sizable portion may be past due, overstates the liquidity of the firm being analyzed. Receivables are liquid assets only insofar as they can be collected in a reasonable amount of time. For our analysis of receivables, we have two basic ratios, the first of which is the *average collection period ratio:*

$$\frac{\text{Receivables} \times \text{Days in year}}{\text{Annual credit sales}}$$

or $\dfrac{A/R}{\text{Credit sales/day}}$

For Aldine, this ratio is

$$\frac{\$678,279 \times 365}{\$3,992,758} = 62 \text{ days}$$

$= \dfrac{A/R}{\dfrac{\text{cred. sales}}{365}}$

The average collection period tells us the average number of days receivables are outstanding; that is, the average time it takes to convert them into cash.

The second ratio is the *receivable turnover ratio:*

$$\frac{\text{Annual credit sales}}{\text{Receivables}}$$

For Aldine, this ratio is

$$\frac{\$3,992,758}{\$678,279} = 5.89$$

Actually, these two ratios are inverses of each other. The number of days in the year, 365, divided by the average collection period, 62 days, gives the receivable turnover ratio, 5.89. The number of days in the year divided by the turnover ratio gives the average collection period. Thus, either of these two ratios can be employed.

When credit sales figures for a period are not available, we must resort to the total sales figures. The receivable figure used in the calculation ordinarily represents year-end receivables. However, when sales are seasonal or have grown considerably over the year, using the year-end receivable balance may not be appropriate. With seasonality, an average of the monthly closing balances may be the most appropriate figure to use. With growth, the receivable balance at the end of the year will be deceptively high in relation to sales. In this case, an average of receivables at the beginning and at the end of the year might be appropriate, if the growth in sales was steady throughout the year.

The average collection period ratio or the receivable turnover ratio indicates the slowness of receivables. Either ratio must be analyzed in relation to the billing terms given on the sales. For example, if the average collection period is forty-five days and the terms given are 2/10, net 30,[6] the comparison would indicate that a sizable proportion of the receivables is past due beyond the final due date of thirty days. On the other hand, if the terms are 2/10, net 60, the typical receivable is being collected before the final due date. A comparison of the average collection period and terms given by a specific company with those of other companies in the industry gives us additional insight into the investment in receivables. Too low an average collection period may suggest an excessively restrictive credit policy. The receivables on the books may be of prime quality and yet sales may be curtailed unduly—and profits less than they might be—because of this policy. In this situation, credit standards for an acceptable account should be relaxed somewhat. On the other hand, too high an average collection period may indicate too liberal a credit policy. As a result, a large number of receivables may be past due, with some uncollectible. Here, too, profits may be less than those possible on account of bad-debt losses and the need to finance a large investment in receivables. In this case, credit standards should be raised.

Another means by which we can obtain insight into the liquidity of receivables is through an *aging of accounts*. With this method, we categorize the receivables at a moment in time according to the propor-

---

[6]The notation means that the supplier gives a 2 percent discount if the receivable invoice is paid within ten days and that payment is due within thirty days if the discount is not taken.

tions billed in previous months. For example, we might have the following hypothetical aging of accounts receivable at December 31:

	Proportion of Receivables Billed				
December	November	October	September	August and Before	Total
67%	19%	7%	2%	5%	100%

If the billing terms are 2/10, net 30, this aging tells us that 67 percent of the receivables at December 31 are current, 19 percent are up to one month past due, 7 percent are one to two months past due, and so on. Depending upon the conclusions drawn from our analysis of the aging, we may want to examine more closely the credit and collection policies of the company. In the example above, we might be prompted to investigate the individual receivables that were billed in August and before, in order to determine if any should be charged off. The receivables shown on the books are only as good as the likelihood that they will be collected.

An aging of accounts receivable gives us considerably more information than the calculation of the average collection period, because it pinpoints the trouble spots more specifically. Of particular value is a comparison of different agings over time. With this comparison, we obtain an accurate picture of the investment of a firm in receivables and changes in the basic composition of this investment over time. Comparison of agings for different firms is difficult because most published reports do not include such information.

From a creditor's point of view, it sometimes is desirable to obtain an *aging of accounts payable.* This measure, combined with the less exact turnover of payables (annual purchases divided by payables), allows us to analyze payables in much the same manner as we do receivables. Also, one can compute the average age of a firm's accounts payable. The average age of payables is

$$\frac{\text{Accounts payable} \times 365}{\text{Purchase of raw materials}}$$

where accounts payable is the average balance outstanding for the year, and the denominator is the purchase of raw material during the year. This information is valuable in evaluating the probability that a credit applicant will pay on time. If the average age of payables is forty-eight days, and the terms in the industry are net 30, we know that a portion of the applicant's payables are not being paid on time. A credit check of other suppliers will give insight into the severity of the problem.

LIQUIDITY OF INVENTORIES

We may compute the *inventory turnover ratio* as an indicator of the liquidity of inventory:

$$\frac{\text{Cost of goods sold}}{\text{Average inventory}}$$

For Aldine, the ratio is

$$\frac{\$2,680,298}{\$1,281,844} = 2.09$$

The figure for cost of goods sold used in the numerator is for the period being studied—usually one year; the average inventory figure used in the denominator typically is an average of beginning and ending inventories for the period. As was true with receivables, however, it may be necessary to compute a more sophisticated average when there is a strong seasonal element. The inventory turnover ratio tells us the rapidity with which the inventory is turned over into receivables through sales. This ratio, like other ratios, must be judged in relation to past and expected future ratios of the firm and in relation to ratios of similar firms, the industry average, or both.

Generally, the higher the inventory turnover, the more efficient the inventory management of a firm. However, a relatively high inventory turnover ratio may be the result of too low a level of inventory and frequent stockouts. It might also be the result of too many small orders for inventory replacement. Either of these situations may be more costly to the firm than carrying a larger investment in inventory and having a lower turnover ratio. Again, caution is necessary in interpreting the ratio. When the inventory turnover ratio is relatively low, it indicates slow-moving inventory or obsolescence of some of the stock. Obsolescence may necessitate substantial write-downs, which, in turn, would negate the treatment of inventory as a liquid asset. Because the turnover ratio is a somewhat crude measure, we would want to investigate any perceived inefficiency in inventory management. In this regard, it is helpful to compute the turnover of the major categories of inventory to see if there are imbalances, which may indicate excessive investment in specific components of the inventory. Once we have a hint of a problem, we must investigate it more specifically to determine its cause.

DEBT RATIOS

Extending our analysis to the long-term liquidity of the firm (that is, its ability to meet long-term obligations), several debt ratios may be used. The *debt-to-net-worth* ratio is computed by simply dividing the total debt of the firm (including current liabilities) by its net worth:

$$\frac{\text{Total debt}}{\text{Net worth}}$$

For Aldine, the ratio is

$$\frac{\$1,454,859}{\$1,796,621} = 0.81$$

When intangible assets are significant, they frequently are deducted from net worth to obtain the tangible net worth of the firm. Depending upon the purpose for which the ratio is used, preferred stock sometimes is included as debt rather than as net worth. Preferred stock represents a prior claim from the standpoint of the investor in common stock; consequently, he might include preferred stock as debt when analyzing a firm. The ratio of debt to equity will vary according to the nature of the business and the volatility of cash flows. An electric utility, with very stable cash flows, usually will have a higher debt ratio than will a machine tool company, whose cash flows are far less stable.

A comparison of the debt ratio for a given company with those of similar firms gives us a general indication of the credit-worthiness and financial risk of the firm. The reason that it is a general indication is that the assets and cash flows of the firm provide the wherewithal for payment of debt. To the extent that the asset totals are either overstated or understated with respect to their economic and liquidating values, the measure is faulty. Much more is said about the analysis of financial risk in Chapters 9 and 10.

In addition to the ratio of total debt to equity, we may wish to compute the following ratio, which deals with only the long-term capitalization of the firm:

$$\frac{\text{Long-term debt}}{\text{Total capitalization}}$$

where total capitalization represents all long-term debt and net worth. For Aldine, the ratio is

$$\frac{\$630,783}{\$2,427,404} = 0.26 \quad \leftarrow \text{LT debt + Equity}$$

This measure tells us the relative importance of long-term debt in the capital structure. The ratios computed above have been based upon book value figures; it is sometimes useful to calculate these ratios using market values. The use of debt ratios is considered in Chapter 9, where we take up the problem of capital structure. Again, it is important to compare ratios for the same company over time and also to compare the ratios of one firm with those of similar companies. In summary, debt ratios tell us the relative proportions of capital contributed by creditors and by owners. They represent one means by which to judge the financial risk of the firm, the other being coverage ratios.

COVERAGE RATIOS

Coverage ratios are designed to relate the financial charges of a firm to its ability to service them. Such bond-rating services as Moody's Investors Service and Standard & Poor's make extensive use of these ratios. One of the most traditional of the coverage ratios is the *interest coverage ratio*, simply the ratio of earnings before interest and taxes for a particular reporting period to the amount of interest charges for the period. It is important to differentiate which interest charges should be used in the denominator. The *overall coverage method* stresses the importance of a company's meeting all fixed interest, regardless of the seniority of the claim. Suppose that we have the following financial data for a hypothetical company:

Average earnings before interest and taxes	$2,000,000
Interest on senior 7% bonds	−400,000
	$1,600,000
Interest on junior 8% bonds	160,000

The overall interest coverage would be $2,000,000/$560,000, or 3.57. This method implies that the credit-worthiness of the senior bonds is only as good as the firm's ability to cover all interest charges.

Of the various coverage ratios, the most objectionable is the *prior deductions method*. Using this method, we deduct interest on the senior bonds from average earnings and then divide the residual by the interest on the junior bonds. We find that the coverage on the junior bonds in our example is ten times ($1,600,000/$160,000). Thus, the junior bonds give the illusion of being more secure than the senior obligations. Clearly, this method is inappropriate. The *cumulative deduction method*, perhaps, is the most widely used method of computing interest coverage. Under this method, coverage for the senior bonds would be five times. However, coverage for the junior bonds is determined by adding the interest charges on both bonds and relating the total to average earnings. Thus, the coverage for the junior bonds would be $2,000,000/$560,000 = 3.57 times.

One of the principal shortcomings of an interest coverage ratio is that a firm's ability to service debt is related to both interest and principal payments. Moreover, these payments are not met out of earnings per se, but out of cash. Hence, a more appropriate coverage ratio relates the cash flow of the firm (approximated by earnings before interest and taxes plus depreciation) to the sum of interest and principal payments. The *cash-flow coverage ratio* may be expressed as

$$\frac{\text{Annual cash flow before interest and taxes}}{\text{Interest} + \text{Principal payments } [1/(1-t)]}$$

Net Income + Deprec. + Interest

$1/\frac{1}{2} = 2$

where t is the federal income tax rate. Because principal payments are made after taxes, it is necessary to adjust this figure by $[1/(1-t)]$ so that it corresponds to interest payments, which are made before taxes. If the rate were 50 percent and annual principal payments $100,000, before-tax earnings of $200,000 would be needed to cover these payments.[7]

A broader type of analysis would evaluate the ability of the firm to cover all charges of a fixed nature in relation to its cash flow. In addition to interest and principal payments on debt obligations, we would include preferred stock dividends, lease payments, and possibly even certain essential capital expenditures. As taken up in Chapter 10, an analysis of this type is a far more realistic gauge than is a simple interest coverage ratio in determining whether a firm has the ability to meet its long-term obligations.[8]

In assessing the financial risk of a firm, then, the financial analyst should first compute the debt ratios as a rough measure of financial risk. Depending upon the payment schedule of the debt and the average interest rate, however, debt ratios may or may not give an accurate picture of the ability of the firm to meet its financial obligations. Therefore, he should analyze additionally the cash-flow ability of the firm to service debt. In this way, the financial analyst is able to get an accurate idea of the financial risk of the firm. Neither debt ratios nor coverage ratios are sufficient by themselves.

PROFITABILITY RATIOS

Profitability ratios are of two types: those showing profitability in relation to sales, and those showing profitability in relation to investment. Together these ratios give us indication of the firm's efficiency of operation. We do not take up the calculation of earnings per share or the effect of leverage on earnings per share in this chapter. These topics are considered in Chapter 27.

[7]This statement assumes that earnings before taxes are in excess of $200,000.

[8]Donaldson argues also that the firm's ability to service debt is related to its cash-flow coverage of a number of fixed charges. He develops a probability approach to the problem and proposes that the probability of cash "insolvency" or cash "inadequacy" should be judged in periods of recessions. We examine his approach in more detail in Chapter 10. Gordon Donaldson, "New Framework for Corporate Debt Capacity," *Harvard Business Review*, 40 (March–April 1962), 117–31.

PROFITABILITY IN RELATION TO SALES

The first ratio we consider is the *gross profit margin:*

$$\frac{gross\ profit}{sales} = \frac{\text{Sales less cost of goods sold}}{\text{Sales}}$$

For Aldine, the gross profit margin is

$$\frac{\$1,312,460}{\$3,992,758} = 32.9 \text{ percent}$$

This ratio tells us the profit of the firm relative to sales after we deduct the cost of producing the goods sold. It indicates the efficiency of operations as well as how products are priced. A more specific ratio of profitability is the *net profit margin:*

$$\frac{\text{Net profits after taxes}}{\text{Sales}}$$

For Aldine, this ratio is

$$\frac{\$150,574}{\$3,992,758} = 3.77 \text{ percent}$$

The net profit margin tells us the relative efficiency of the firm after taking into account all expenses and income taxes, but not extraordinary charges.

By considering both ratios jointly, we are able to gain considerable insight into the operations of the firm. For example, if the gross profit margin is essentially unchanged over a period of several years, but the net profit margin has declined over the same period, we know that the cause is either higher expenses relative to sales or a higher tax rate. Therefore, we would analyze these factors more specifically to determine the cause of the problem. On the other hand, if the gross profit margin falls, we know that the cost of producing the goods relative to sales has increased. This occurrence, in turn, may be due to lower prices or to lower operating efficiency in relation to volume. If expenses are constant in relation to sales, we would know that the lower net profit margin is due entirely to the higher cost of producing the goods relative to sales.

There are any number of combinations of changes possible in the gross and net profit margins. Indications of the sort illustrated above tell us where we should investigate further. In our analysis, it is useful to examine over time each of the individual expense items as a percentage of sales. By so doing, we can pick out specific areas of deterioration or improvement.

The second group of profitability ratios relates profits to investments. One of these measures is the *rate of return on common stock equity:*

$$\frac{\text{Net profits after taxes} - \text{Preferred stock dividend}}{\text{Net worth} - \text{Par value of preferred stock}}$$

For Aldine, the rate of return is

$$\frac{\$150,574}{\$1,796,621} = 8.38 \text{ percent}$$

This ratio tells us the earning power on shareholders' book investment and is frequently used in comparing two or more firms in an industry. The figure for net worth used in the ratio may be expressed in terms of market value instead of book value. When we use market value, we obtain the earnings/price ratio of the stock.

A more general ratio used in the analysis of profitability is the *return on assets ratio:*

$$\frac{\text{Net profits after taxes}}{\text{Total tangible assets}}$$

For Aldine, the ratio is[9]

$$\frac{\$150,574}{\$3,046,323} = 4.94 \text{ percent}$$

This ratio is somewhat inappropriate, inasmuch as profits are taken after interest is paid to creditors. Because these creditors provide means by which part of the total assets are supported, there is a fallacy of omission. When financial charges are significant, it is preferable, for comparative purposes, to compute a net operating profit rate of return instead of a return on assets ratio. The *net operating profit rate of return* may be expressed as

$$\frac{\text{Earnings before interest and taxes}}{\text{Total tangible assets}}$$

---

[9] From total assets, we deduct goodwill and the debenture discount and expense to obtain total tangible assets. Because we are interested in profitability of operations, we use net income before extraordinary charges.

Using this ratio, we are able to abstract from differing financial charges (interest and preferred stock dividends). Thus, the relationship studied is independent of the way the firm is financed.[10]

TURNOVER AND EARNING POWER

Frequently, the financial analyst relates total assets to sales to obtain the *turnover ratio:*

$$\frac{\text{Sales}}{\text{Total tangible assets}}$$

Aldine's turnover for the 1977 fiscal year was

$$\frac{\$3,992,758}{\$3,046,323} = 1.31$$

This ratio tells us the relative efficiency with which the firm utilizes its resources in order to generate output. It varies according to the type of company being studied. A food chain has a considerably higher turnover, for example, than does an electric utility. One shortcoming of the turnover ratio is that it places a premium on using old equipment. A firm with equipment that is almost fully depreciated and highly inefficient may show a high turnover but actually lose money. Consequently, the ratio should be used in conjunction with other measures of efficiency.

When we multiply the asset turnover of the firm by the net profit margin, we obtain the return on assets ratio, or *earning power* on total tangible assets.

Asset Turnover Rate × Net Profit Margin

$$\text{Earning Power} = \frac{\text{Sales}}{\text{Total tangible assets}} \times \frac{\text{Net profits after taxes}}{\text{Sales}}$$

$$= \frac{\text{Net profits after taxes}}{\text{Total tangible assets}}$$

For Aldine, we have

$$\frac{\$3,992,758}{\$3,046,323} \times \frac{\$150,574}{\$3,992,758} = 4.94 \text{ percent}$$

Neither the net profit margin nor the turnover ratio by itself provides an adequate measure of operating efficiency. The net profit margin ignores the utilization of assets, whereas the turnover ratio ignores profitability

---

[10] See Eugene M. Lerner and Willard T. Carleton, *A Theory of Financial Analysis* (New York: Harcourt, Brace & Jovanovich, 1966), p. 21.

on sales. The return on assets ratio, or earning power, resolves these shortcomings. An improvement in the earning power of the firm will result if there is an increase in turnover on existing assets, an increase in the net profit margin, or both. Two firms with different asset turnovers and net profit margins may have the same earning power. For example, Firm *A*, with an asset turnover of 4 to 1 and a net profit margin of 3 percent, has the same earning power—12 percent—as Firm *B*, with an asset turnover of $1\frac{1}{2}$ to 1 and a net profit margin of 8 percent.

With all of the profitability ratios, comparisons of a company with similar companies are extremely valuable. Only by comparison are we able to judge whether the profitability of a particular company is good or bad, and why. Absolute figures provide some insight, but it is relative performance that is most important.

PREDICTIVE POWER

In the previous sections, we presented the important ratios used in financial analysis. Which ratios an analyst relies on depends upon his perception of their predictive power relative to the problem at hand—a perception based upon either subjective beliefs or empirical analysis. In helping him predict the future value of a stock, for example, an investor might feel that the return on investment ratio and various profit margin ratios were the most important. Most estimates of the predictive power of financial ratios are based upon the analyst's past experience with them. By their very nature, then, these estimates tend to be subjective and to differ from one analyst to the next.

Several empirical studies have been undertaken that show promise for statistically testing the predictive power of financial ratios. In one, William H. Beaver tested the ability of financial ratios to predict failure.[11] Because this study is described in the preceding chapter, we note here only that many of the thirty ratios studied showed considerable power to detect failure before it actually occurred. Not only did the financial ratios of failed firms differ significantly from those of nonfailed firms, but they deteriorated considerably during the five years prior to failure. Because the ratios were examined individually, with no attempt to test the joint predictive power of various combinations of ratios, it was not possible to select the best group of ratios for predicting failure. However, Beaver found that the best single predictor was the ratio of cash flow to total debt.

[11] "Financial Ratios as Predictors of Failure," *Empirical Research in Accounting: Selected Studies* in *Journal of Accounting Research* (1966), pp. 71–111. For further testing in this regard where capitalized lease data are included, see Rick Elam, "The Effect of Lease Data on the Predictive Ability of Financial Ratios," *Accounting Review*, 50 (January 1975), 25–43. Elam found that the inclusion of these data did not increase the power of financial ratios to predict bankruptcy. For an excellent overall discussion of this type of research, see Lev, *Financial Statement Analysis: A New Approach*, Part II.

In another empirical study, Edward I. Altman employed financial ratios to predict corporate bankruptcy through multiple-discriminant analysis.[12] Because his studies also are described in the preceding chapter, we shall mention only the important results. Out of the twenty-two financial ratios examined, Altman selected the five that did the best combined job in predicting bankruptcy. These ratios were working capital to total assets, retained earnings to total assets, earnings before interest and taxes to total assets, market value of equity to book value of total debt, and sales to total assets. Using these ratios, Altman found the discriminant model to be an accurate predictor of bankruptcy.

Like Altman, Robert O. Edmister employed discriminant analysis successfully to predict failure.[13] However, he analyzed small businesses as opposed to large corporations, lending additional credence to the technique. Edmister used a three-year average of the following financial ratios: funds flow to current liabilities, equity to sales, working capital to sales, current liabilities to equity, inventory to sales, and the trend of the quick ratio relative to the industry average. This study also is described in the preceding chapter.

In a fourth study, James O. Horrigan tested the power of financial ratios to predict corporate bond ratings.[14] With these ratings as the dependent variable, he regressed them against various financial ratios, using a sample of companies. The multiple-regression analysis revealed that working capital to sales, net worth to total debt, sales to net worth, and net operating profit to sales were best for predicting bond ratings. Horrigan concluded that a handful of ratios can be used in combination to predict the long-term credit standing of a firm.

Various models based on financial data have been used to predict good and bad commercial bank loans. Yair E. Orgler used a multiple-regression model to predict which loans would be criticized by bank examiners.[15] The principal financial ratio he used was the ratio of

---

[12]"Financial Ratios, Discriminant Analysis and the Prediction of Corporate Bankruptcy," *Journal of Finance*, 23 (September 1968), 589–609.

[13]"An Empirical Test of Financial Ratio Analysis for Small Business Failure Prediction," *Journal of Financial and Quantitative Analysis*, 7 (March 1972), 1477–93. Other studies dealing with failure prediction include E. B. Deakin, "A Discriminant Analysis of Predictors of Business Failure," *Journal of Accounting Research*, 10 (Spring 1972), 167–79; and Paul A. Meyer and Howard W. Pifer, "Prediction of Bank Failures," *Journal of Finance*, 25 (September 1970), 853–68.

[14]"The Determination of Long-term Credit Standing with Financial Ratios," *Empirical Research in Accounting: Selected Studies*, in *Journal of Accounting Research* (1966), pp. 44–62. Richard R. West, "An Alternative Approach to Predicting Corporate Bond Ratings," *Journal of Accounting Research*, 8 (Spring 1970), 118–25, used a somewhat different model for predicting ratings and found the predictive accuracy to be about the same as Horrigan's. In yet another study, George E. Pinches and Kent A. Mingo, "A Multivariate Analysis of Industrial Bond Ratings," *Journal of Finance*, 28 (March 1973), 1–18, jointly applied factor analysis and M-group multiple-discriminant analysis to predict industrial bond ratings. Testing the 1967–68 period, they found that variables related to earnings stability, size, financial leverage, debt coverage stability, return on investment, and subordination to be the best for predictive purposes.

[15]"A Credit Scoring Model for Commercial Loans," *Journal of Money, Credit, and Banking*, 2 (November 1970), 435–45.

working capital to current assets. The model was only moderately successful in predicting criticized loans. In a study of French commercial loans, Edward I. Altman, Michel Margaine, Michel Schlosser, and Pierre Vernimmen used discriminant analysis in connection with forty-one financial ratios and data on 134 firms.[16] The authors found that their model was relatively effective in predicting loans with repayment problems (14 percent type I errors and 1 percent type II errors).

On the basis of these studies, it appears that financial ratios can be used as predictors of various events. However, the studies described only scratch the surface. As additional tests are undertaken, we shall have a better understanding of which ratios are important in predicting certain types of events.[17] As a result, financial ratio analysis will become more scientific than it is now. No longer will we be dependent upon the subjective experience of the analyst in evaluating which ratios are important. With sufficient testing, meaningful benchmarks can be established which will make financial analysis truly objective in scope.

---

[16] "Financial and Statistical Analysis for Commercial Loan Evaluations: A French Experience," *Journal of Financial and Quantitative Analysis,* 9 (March 1974), 195–211.

[17] See Beaver, "Financial Ratios as Predictors of Failure," p. 72.

SUMMARY

Financial ratios can be divided into four types: liquidity, debt, profitability, and coverage. Each of these types has a special use for the financial analyst. The ratios taken up in this chapter are employed extensively by outside creditors and investors. These ratios are also helpful for managerial control and for providing a better understanding of what outside suppliers of capital expect in the way of financial condition and performance. The usefulness of the ratios depends upon the ingenuity and experience of the financial analyst who employs them. By themselves, financial ratios are fairly meaningless; they must be analyzed on a comparative basis.

A comparison of ratios of the same firm over time is important in evaluating changes and trends in the firm's financial condition and profitability. This comparison may be historical; it may also include an analysis of the future based upon projected financial statements. Ratios may also be judged in comparison with those of similar firms in the same line of business and, when appropriate, with an industry average. Much can be gleaned from a thorough analysis of financial ratios. With empirical testing of the predictive power of ratios, financial ratio analysis is likely to become far more scientific and objective than formerly.

1. High-Low Plumbing Company sells plumbing fixtures on terms of 2/10, net 30. Its financial statements over the last three years follow.

	19__1	19__2	19__3
Cash	$ 30,000	$ 20,000	$ 5,000
Accounts receivable	200,000	260,000	290,000
Inventory	400,000	480,000	600,000
Net fixed assets	800,000	800,000	800,000
	$1,430,000	$1,560,000	$1,695,000
Accounts payable	230,000	300,000	380,000
Accruals	200,000	210,000	225,000
Bank loan—short term	100,000	100,000	140,000
Long-term debt	300,000	300,000	300,000
Common stock	100,000	100,000	100,000
Earned surplus	500,000	550,000	550,000
	$1,430,000	$1,560,000	$1,695,000
Sales	$4,000,000	$4,300,000	$3,800,000
Cost of goods sold	3,200,000	3,600,000	3,300,000
Net profit	300,000	200,000	100,000

Using the ratios taken up in the chapter, analyze the company's financial condition and performance over the last three years. Are there any problems?

2. A company has total annual sales (all credit) of $400,000, and a gross profit margin of 20 percent. Its current assets are $80,000; current liabilities, $60,000; inventories, $30,000; and cash, $10,000.

   (a) How much average inventory should be carried if management wants the inventory turnover to be 4? (Assume a 360-day year for calculations.)

   (b) How rapidly (in how many days) must accounts receivable be collected if management wants to have an average of $50,000 invested in receivables? (Assume a 360-day year.)

3. The data for various companies in the same industry and of about the same size follow.

Company	A	B	C	D	E	F
Sales (in millions)	$ 10	$20	$ 8	$ 5	$ 12	$17
Total assets (in millions)	8	10	6	2.5	4	8
Net income (in millions)	0.7	2	0.8	0.5	1.5	1

   (a) Determine the asset turnover, net profit margin, and earning power for each of the companies.

   (b) Which firms appear to be out of line? What might their problems be? What additional data would you need to confirm your analysis?

4. Using the following information, complete the balance sheet below:

Long-term debt to net worth	.5 to 1
Total asset turnover	2.5 times
Average collection period*	18 days
Inventory turnover	9 times
Gross profit margin	10 percent
Acid-test ratio	1 to 1

Assume a 360-day year, and all sales on credit.

Cash	$ 50,000	Notes and payables	$100,000
Accounts receivable	50,000	Long-term debt	100,000
Inventory	100,000	Common stock	$100,000
Plant and equipment	200,000	Retained earnings	100,000
Total assets	$ 400,000	Total liabilities and worth	$ 400,000

Handwritten margin notes:

$$\frac{A/R \times 360}{Sales} = 18$$

$$\frac{A/R}{sales} = \frac{1}{20}$$

$$Sales = 20(A/R)$$

$$\frac{CGS}{INV} = 9$$

$$\frac{S - CGS}{S} = .10 \quad \text{Gross } \pi \text{ marg}$$

$$\frac{S}{400,000} = 2.5$$

$$S = 1,000,000$$

$$A/R = \frac{1,000,000}{20} = 50,000$$

$$CGS = 900,000$$

$$Gross \pi = 100,000$$

$$\frac{900,000}{INV} = 9$$

$$INV = 100,000$$

$$\left\{ \frac{C.A. - INV}{C.L.} = 1 \right.$$
$$\phantom{\{} 100,000$$

$$CA = Cash + A/R + INV$$

$$CA - INV = 100,000$$

$$(cash + 50,000 + 100,000) - 100,000 = 100,000$$

$$\therefore cash = 50,000$$

$$P + E = 200,000$$

5. The long-term debt section of the balance sheet of the Diters Corporation appears as follows:

$7\frac{1}{4}$% Mortgage bonds of 1995	$2,500,000
$7\frac{5}{8}$% Second-mortgage bonds of 1990	1,500,000
$8\frac{3}{8}$% Debentures of 1988	1,000,000
$9\frac{1}{8}$% Subordinated debentures of 1992	1,000,000
	$6,000,000

(a) If the average earnings before interest and taxes of the Diters Corporation are $1.5 million, what is the overall interest coverage?

(b) Using the cumulative deduction method, determine the coverage for each issue.

6.

U.S. Republic Corporation balance sheet, Dec. 31, 1976

Assets		Liabilities and Stockholders' Equity	
Cash	$ 500,000	Notes payable	$ 2,000,000
Accounts receivable	2,500,000	Accounts payable	1,000,000
Inventory*	3,500,000	Accrued wages	
Fixed assets, net	7,500,000	and taxes	1,000,000
Excess over book value		Long-term debt	6,000,000
of assets acquired	1,000,000	Preferred stock	2,000,000
Total assets	$15,000,000	Common stock	1,000,000
		Retained earnings	2,000,000
		Total liabilities	
		and equity	$15,000,000

* Inventory at 12/31/75 = $1,500,000.

U.S. Republic Corporation statement of income and retained earnings

	Year Ended Dec. 31, 1976	
Net sales:		
Credit		$ 8,000,000
Cash		2,000,000
Total		$10,000,000
Costs and expenses:		
Cost of goods sold	$6,000,000	
Selling, general, and		
administrative expenses	1,000,000	
Depreciation	700,000	
Interest on long-term		
debt	300,000	8,000,000
Net income before taxes		$ 2,000,000
Taxes on income		1,000,000
Net income after taxes		$ 1,000,000
Less: Dividends on preferred stock		120,000
Net income available to common		880,000
Add: Retained earnings at 1/1/76		1,300,000
Subtotal		$ 2,180,000
Less: Dividends paid on common		180,000
Retained earnings at 12/31/76		$ 2,000,000

(a) Fill in the 1976 column.

U.S. Republic Corporation

Ratio	1974	1975	1976	Industry 1976
1. Current ratio	250%	200%		225%
2. Acid-test ratio	100%	90%		110%
3. Receivables turnover	5.0x	4.5x		6.0x
4. Inventory turnover	4.0x	3.0x		4.0x
5. Debt/total capitalization	35%	40%		33%
6. Gross profit margin	39%	41%		40%
7. Net profit margin	17%	15%		15%
8. Rate of return on equity	25%	30%		20%
9. Return on assets	15%	12%		10%
10. NOP rate of return	18.3%	17.5%		17.5%
11. Tangible asset turnover	0.9x	0.8x		1.00x
12. Overall interest coverage	11x	9x		10x

(b) Evaluate the position of the company from the above table. Cite specific ratio levels and trends as evidence.

(c) Indicate which ratios would be of most interest to you and what your decision would be in each of the following situations:

(1) U.S. Republic wants to buy $500,000 worth of raw materials from you, with payment to be due in ninety days.

(2) U.S. Republic wants you, a large insurance company, to pay off its note at the bank and assume it on a ten-year maturity basis at the current coupon of 9 percent.

(3) There are 100,000 shares outstanding and the stock is selling for $80 a share. The company offers you an opportunity to buy 50,000 additional shares at this price.

7. *Research Project*

Altman developed the following final discriminant function:[18]

$$Z = 0.012X_1 + 0.014X_2 + 0.033X_3 + 0.006X_4 + 0.999X_5$$

where X_1 = working capital/total assets
X_2 = retained earnings/total assets
X_3 = earnings before interest and taxes/total assets
X_4 = market value equity/book value of total debt
X_5 = sales/total assets

and where X_1 through X_4 are expressed as whole percents (10 percent = 10) and X_5 is expressed normally (10 percent = .10). Altman concluded from his sample that all firms with a Z score above 2.99 were "nonbankrupt," while all with a Z score below 1.81 were "bankrupt." He further decided that a Z of 2.675 was the cutoff point providing the least misclassifications. *Required:* Obtain the annual reports for several firms in a given industry with asset size between $1 and $25 million (another of Altman's restrictions). Try to separate the strong from the weak on the basis of the above analysis. Then attempt to support your findings with other evidence (declining stock price, rising interest costs, poor earnings trend, and so on).

---

[18] See E. I. Altman, "Financial Ratios, Discriminant Analysis and the Prediction of Corporate Bankruptcy," *Journal of Finance* (September 1968), p. 594.

SELECTED REFERENCES

Altman, Edward I., "Financial Ratios, Discriminant Analysis and the Prediction of Corporate Bankruptcy," *Journal of Finance,* 23 (September 1968), 589–609.

———, "Railroad Bankruptcy Propensity," *Journal of Finance,* 26 (May 1971), 333–45.

Altman, Edward I., Michel Margaine, Michel Schlosser, and Pierre Vernimmen, "Financial and Statistical Analysis for Commercial Loan Evaluation: A French Experience," *Journal of Financial and Quantitative Analysis,* 9 (March 1974), 195–212.

Beaver, William H., "Financial Ratios as Predictors of Failure," *Empirical Research in Accounting: Selected Studies in Journal of Accounting* Research (1966), pp. 71–111.

Benishay, Haskel, "Economic Information on Financial Ratio Analysis," *Accounting and Business Research,* 2 (Spring 1971), 174–79.

Edmister, Robert O., "An Empirical Test of Financial Ratio Analysis for Small Business Failure Predictions," *Journal of Financial and Quantitative Analysis,* 7 (March 1972), 1477–93.

Elam, Rick, "The Effect of Lease Data on the Predictive

Ability of Financial Ratios," *Accounting Review,* 50 (January 1975), 25–43.

Gitman, Lawrence J., "Measuring Overall Corporate Liquidity: A New and Better Ratio," Paper presented at Financial Management Association Meetings, San Diego, October 24–26, 1974.

Helfert, Erich A., *Techniques of Financial Analysis,* Chapter 2. Homewood, Ill.: Richard D. Irwin, 1972.

Horrigan, James C., "The Determination of Long-Term Credit Standing with Financial Ratios," *Empirical Research in Accounting: Selected Studies in Journal of Accounting Research* (1966), pp. 44–62.

————, "A Short History of Financial Ratio Analysis," *Accounting Review,* 43 (April 1968), 284–94.

Jaedicke, Robert K., and Robert T. Sprouse, *Accounting Flows: Income, Funds, and Cash,* Chapter 7. Englewood Cliffs, N.J.: Prentice-Hall, 1965.

Kennedy, N. H., and S. Y. McMullen, *Financial Statements—Form, Analysis and Interpretation,* 5th ed. Homewood, Ill., Richard D. Irwin, 1968.

Lemke, Kenneth W., "The Evaluation of Liquidity: An Analytical Study," *Journal of Accounting Research,* 8 (Spring 1970), 47–77.

Lev, Baruch, *Financial Statement Analysis: A New Approach.* Englewood Cliffs, N.J.: Prentice-Hall, 1974.

O'Connor, Melvin C., "On the Usefulness of Financial Ratios to Investors in Common Stock," *Accounting Review,* 48 (April 1973), 339–52.

Pinches, George E., and Kent A. Mingo, "A Multivariate Analysis of Industrial Bond Ratings," *Journal of Finance,* 28 (March 1973), 1–18.

Troy, Leo, *Almanac of Business and Industrial Financial Ratios.* Englewood Cliffs, N.J.: Prentice-Hall, 1974.

West, Richard R., "An Alternative Approach to Predicting Corporate Bond Ratings," *Journal of Accounting Research,* 8 (Spring 1970), 118–25.

FUNDS-FLOW ANALYSIS and FINANCIAL FORECASTING

The second portion of our examination of the tools of financial analysis and control deals with the analysis of funds flows and financial forecasting. A funds-flow statement is a valuable aid to a financial manager or a creditor in evaluating the uses of funds by a firm and in determining how these uses are financed. In addition to studying past flows, the analyst can evaluate future flows by means of a funds statement based upon forecasts. Such a statement provides an efficient method for the financial manager to assess the growth of the firm and its resulting financial needs and to determine the best way to finance those needs. In particular, funds statements are very useful in planning intermediate- and long-term financing.

Closely related to a projected funds-flow statement are the cash budget and *pro forma* statements. The cash budget is indispensable to the financial manager in determining the short-term cash needs of the firm and, accordingly, in planning its short-term financing. When cash budgeting is extended to include a range of possible outcomes, the financial manager can evaluate the business risk and liquidity of the firm and plan a more realistic margin of safety. This margin of safety might come from adjusting the firm's liquidity cushion, rearranging the maturity structure of its debt, arranging a line of credit with a bank, or a combination of the three. Cash budgets prepared for a range of possible outcomes are valuable also in appraising the ability of the firm to adjust to unexpected changes in cash flows. The preparation of *pro forma* balance sheets and income statements enables the financial manager to analyze the effect of various policy decisions on the future financial condition and performance of the firm. We examine each of these three tools in turn.

SOURCE AND USE OF FUNDS

The flow of funds in a firm may be visualized as a continuous process. For every use of funds, there must be an offsetting source. In a broad sense, the assets of a firm represent the net uses of funds; its liabilities and net worth represent net sources. A funds-flow cycle for a typical manufacturing company is illustrated in Figure 26-1. For the going concern, there is really no starting or stopping point. A finished product is produced with a variety of inputs—namely, raw material, fixed assets, and labor. These inputs ultimately are paid for in cash. The product then is sold either for cash or on credit. A credit sale involves a receivable, which, when collected, becomes cash. If the selling price of the product exceeds all costs (including depreciation on assets) for a period of time, there is a profit for the period; if not, there is a loss. The reservoir of cash, the focal point in the figure, fluctuates over time with the production schedule, sales, collection of receivables, capital expenditures, and financing. On the other hand, reservoirs of raw materials, work in process, finished goods inventory, accounts receivable, and

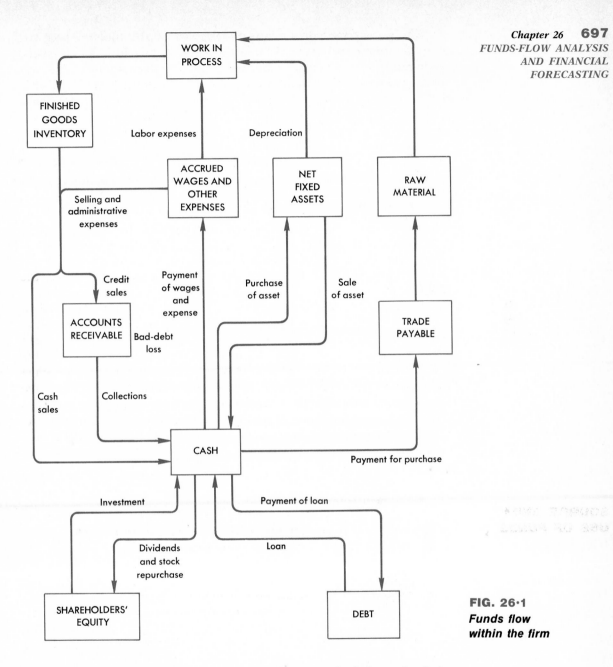

FIG. 26·1
*Funds flow
within the firm*

trade payables fluctuate with sales, the production schedule, and policies with respect to managing receivables, inventories, and trade payables.

The funds statement is a method by which we study the net funds flow between two points in time. These points conform to beginning and ending financial statement dates for whatever period of examination is relevant—a quarter, a year, or five years. It is important to emphasize that the funds statement portrays net rather than gross changes between two comparable financial statements at different dates. For example, gross changes might be thought to include all changes that occur between the two statement dates rather than the sum of these changes—the net change as defined. Although an analysis of the gross funds flow of a firm over time would be much more revealing than an analysis of net funds flow, we are usually constrained by the financial information available—namely, balance sheets and income statements that span particular periods of time. Funds may be defined in several different ways, depending upon the purpose of the analysis. Although they are often defined as cash, many analysts treat funds as working capital—a somewhat broader definition. Other definitions are possible, although the two described are the most common by far. Depending upon the analyst's objective, the definition can be broadened or narrowed. Because a funds-flow analysis on a cash basis serves as a building block for analyses using broader definitions of funds, we begin by defining funds as cash.

FUNDS STATEMENT ON A CASH BASIS

Basically, one prepares a funds statement on a cash basis by (1) classifying net balance sheet changes that occur between two points in time into changes that increase cash and changes that decrease cash; (2) classifying, from the income statement and the surplus statement, the factors that increase cash and the factors that decrease cash; and (3) consolidating this information in a source and use of funds statement form. The first of these steps simply involves placing one balance sheet beside the other and computing the changes in the various accounts.

Sources of funds that increase cash are

1. A net decrease in any asset other than cash or fixed assets
2. A gross decrease in fixed assets (Sale of F A)
3. A net increase in any liability (Incr. debt)
4. Proceeds from the sale of preferred or common stock
5. Funds provided by operations — Net profit + depr.

Funds provided by operations usually are not expressed directly on the income statement. To determine them, one must add back depreciation to net income after taxes. For Aldine Manufacturing Company, our example in the preceding chapter, we have

Net income after taxes	$150,574
Add noncash expenses: depreciation	111,509
Funds provided by operations	$262,083

Thus, the net income of Aldine understates funds provided by operations by $111,509. Depreciation is not a source of funds, for funds are generated only from operations.[1] If operating losses before depreciation are sustained, funds are not provided regardless of the magnitude of depreciation charges.

Uses of funds include

1. A net increase in any asset other than cash or fixed assets
2. A gross increase in fixed assets *(purchase of F.A)*
3. A net decrease in any liability *(lessening of indebtedness)*
4. A retirement or purchase of stock
5. Cash dividends

To avoid double counting, we compute gross changes in fixed assets by adding depreciation for the period to net fixed assets at the ending financial statement date, and subtract from this amount net fixed assets at the beginning financial statement date. The residual represents the gross change in fixed assets for the period. If the residual is positive, as is usually the case, it represents a use of funds; if negative, it represents a source. *(sale)* *(purch)*

Once all sources and uses are computed, they may be arranged in statement form so that we can analyze them better. Table 26-1 shows a source and use of funds statement for the Aldine Manufacturing Company for the fiscal year ended March 31, 1977. The balance sheet and income statement for this corporation, on which the funds statement is

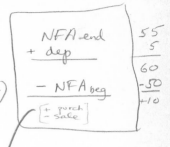

Table 26·1 Aldine Manufacturing Company sources and uses of funds March 31, 1976 to March 31, 1977 (in thousands)

Sources		Uses	
Funds provided by operations:		Dividends	$ 92
Net profit	$150	Additions to fixed assets	104
Depreciation	112	Increase—inventories	94
		Increase—prepaid expenses	4
Decrease—accounts receivable	62	Increase—tax prepayments	6
Increase—bank loans	92	Increase—investments	65
Increase—accounts payable	12	Decrease—accrued taxes	91
Increase—other accruals	27	Increase—cash position	3
Increase—long-term debt	4		
	$459		$459

(Excess of sources over uses)

[1] For an extensive discussion of this concept, see Robert K. Jaedicke and Robert T. Sprouse, *Accounting Flows: Income, Funds, and Cash* (Englewood Cliffs, N.J.: Prentice-Hall, 1965), pp. 80–86.

based, are shown in Tables 25-1 and 25-2 of Chapter 25. When we subtract the total uses of funds in Table 26-1 from the total sources, the difference should equal the actual change in cash between the two statement dates. If it does not, then the analyst must search for the cause of the discrepancy. Frequently, discrepancies will be due to surplus adjustments; and the analyst should be alert to this possibility.[2]

In Table 26-1, we see that the principal uses of funds for the 1977 fiscal year were additions to fixed assets, increases in inventories and in investments, and a sizable decrease in taxes payable. These uses were financed primarily by funds provided by operations in excess of dividends; a decrease in accounts receivable; and by increases in bank loans, payables, and accruals. As sources exceeded slightly the uses of funds, the cash balance rose by $3,000. In a sources and uses of funds analysis, it is useful to place cash dividends opposite net profits and additions to fixed assets opposite depreciation. Doing this allows the analyst to evaluate easily both the amount of dividend payout and the net increase in fixed assets.

FUNDS AS WORKING CAPITAL

Financial analysts frequently prepare a source and use of working capital statement. This statement is very similar to the source and use of funds statement on a cash basis, but it takes into account working capital instead of cash. A source and use of working capital statement for Aldine Manufacturing Company for the year ended March 31, 1977, is shown in Table 26-2.

Table 26·2   Aldine Manufacturing Company sources and uses of working capital March 31, 1976 to March 31, 1977 (in thousands)

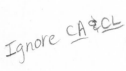

Sources		Uses	
Funds provided by operations:			
Net profit	$150	Dividends	$ 92
Depreciation	112	Additions to fixed assets	104
Increase—long-term debt	4	Increase—investments	65
		Increase—working capital	5
	$266		$266

[2] For a more detailed description of the preparation of a funds-flow statement, see Myron J. Gordon and Gordon Shillinglaw, *Accounting: A Management Approach*, 4th ed. (Homewood, Ill.: Richard D. Irwin, 1969), pp. 497–512.

We see that the only difference between this statement and a funds statement on a cash basis is the omission of changes in the various components of current assets and current liabilities. This statement is analyzed much as the source and use of funds statement is. A source and use of working capital statement is used frequently by bankers, for they often require a borrower to maintain some sort of minimum working capital. It is used also by other lenders and by management for purposes of internal control.

IMPLICATIONS

The analysis of cash and working-capital funds statements gives us a rich insight into the financial operations of a firm—an insight that is especially valuable to the financial manager in analyzing past and future expansion plans of the firm and the impact of these plans on liquidity. He can detect imbalances in the uses of funds and undertake appropriate actions. For example, an analysis spanning the past several years might reveal a growth in inventories out of proportion with the growth of other assets and with sales. Upon analysis, he might find that the problem was due to inefficiencies in inventory management. Thus, a funds statement alerts the financial manager to problems that he can analyze in detail and take proper actions to correct. When a company has a number of divisions, individual funds statements may prove useful. These statements enable top management to appraise the performance of divisions in relation to the funds committed to them.

Another use of funds statements is in the evaluation of the firm's financing. An analysis of the major sources of funds in the past reveals what portion of the firm's growth was financed internally and what portion externally. In evaluating the firm's financing, the analyst will wish to evaluate the ratio of dividends to earnings relative to the firm's total need for funds. Funds statements are useful also in judging whether the firm has expanded at too fast a rate and whether financing is strained. For example, we can determine if trade credit has increased out of proportion to increases in current assets and sales. If trade credit has increased at a significantly faster rate, we would wish to evaluate the consequences of increased slowness in trade payments on the credit standing of the firm and its ability to finance in the future. It is also revealing to analyze the mix of short- and long-term financing in relation to the funds needs of the firm. If these needs are primarily for fixed assets and permanent increases in working capital, we might be disturbed if a significant portion of total financing came from short-term sources.

An analysis of a funds statement for the future is extremely valuable to the financial manager in planning the intermediate- and long-term financing of the firm. It tells him the firm's total prospective need for funds, the expected timing of these needs, and their nature—that is, whether the increased investment is primarily for inventories, fixed assets, and so forth. Given this information, along with the expected changes in trade payables and the various accruals, he can arrange the firm's financing more effectively. In addition, he can determine the expected closing cash position of the firm simply by adjusting the beginning cash balance for the change in cash reflected on the projected source and use statement. In essence, the projected change in cash is a residual. Alternatively, the financial manager can forecast future cash positions of the firm through a cash budget, where direct estimates of future cash flows are made. To this topic we now turn.

CASH BUDGETING

A cash budget involves a projection of future cash receipts and cash disbursements of the firm over various intervals of time. It reveals to the financial manager the timing and amount of expected cash inflows and outflows over the period studied. With this information, he is better able to determine the future cash needs of the firm, plan for the financing of these needs, and exercise control over the cash and liquidity of the firm.

Cash budgets may be for almost any period of time. For near-term forecasts, monthly periods probably are the ones used most frequently, because they take into account seasonal variations in cash flows. When cash flows are extremely volatile but predictable, budgets at more frequent intervals may be necessary for determining peak cash requirements. By the same token, when cash flows are relatively stable, budgeting at quarterly or even longer intervals may be justified. Generally, the further in the future the period for which one is trying to predict cash flows, the more uncertain the forecast. The expense of preparing monthly cash budgets usually is warranted only for predictions concerning the near future.

The cash budget is only as useful as the accuracy of the forecasts that are used in its preparation.[3] The greater the possible dispersion of actual results from those estimated, the more the allowance that must be made for unexpected swings in cash flow. A firm whose cash flows are subject to much uncertainty should provide for either a cash cushion, ready borrowing power, or both to tide it over in periods of adverse cash developments.

---

[3]For an excellent analysis of cost of inaccuracy versus the cost of the forecast itself, see John C. Chambers, Satinder K. Mullick, and Donald D. Smith, "How to Choose the Right Forecasting Technique," *Harvard Business Review*, 49 (July–August 1971), 45–74.

Receipts   The key to the accuracy of most cash budgets is the forecast of sales. This forecast can be based upon an internal analysis, an external one, or both. With an internal approach, salesmen are asked to project sales for the forthcoming period. The product sales managers screen these estimates and consolidate them into sales estimates for product lines. The estimates for the various product lines then are combined into an overall sales estimate for the firm. The basic problem with an internal approach is that it can be too myopic. Often, important trends in the economy and in the industry are overlooked.

For this reason, many companies use an external analysis as well. With an external approach, economic analysts make forecasts of the economy and of industry sales for several years to come. In this regard, regression analysis may be used to estimate the association between industry sales and the economy in general. Given these basic predictions of business conditions and industry sales, the next step is to estimate market share by individual products, prices that are likely to prevail, and the expected reception of new products. Usually, these estimates are made in conjunction with marketing managers. However, the ultimate responsibility should lie with the economic forecasting department. Given this information, an external forecast of sales can be prepared.

When the internal forecast of sales differs from the external one, as it is likely to do, a compromise must be reached. Past experience will show which of the two forecasts is more accurate. In general, the external forecast should serve as the foundation for the final sales forecast. However, it often will need to be modified by the internal forecast. For example, the firm might expect to receive several large orders from customers, and these orders might not show up in the external forecast. By basing the final sales forecast on both internal and external analyses, it usually is more accurate than is either an internal or an external forecast by itself. The final sales forecast should be based upon prospective demand and not be modified initially by internal constraints such as physical capacity. The decision to remove these constraints will depend upon the forecast. The importance of accurate sales forecasts cannot be overestimated, for most of the other forecasts, in some measure, are based upon expected sales.

Given the sales forecast, the next job is to determine the cash receipts from these sales. With cash sales, cash is received at the time of the sale; with credit sales, however, the receipts do not come until later. How much later will depend upon the billing terms given, the type of customer, and the credit and collection policies of the firm. Suppose, for purposes of illustration, that the terms offered by Continental Sheetmetal Company are net 30, meaning that payment is due within thirty

Table 26·3   Schedule of sales receipts (in thousands)

	Nov.	Dec.	Jan.	Feb.	Mar.	Apr.	May	June
Total sales	$300.0	$350.0	$250.0	$200.0	$250.0	$300.0	$350.0	$380.0
Credit sales	270.0	315.0	225.0	180.0	225.0	270.0	315.0	342.0
Collections—								
one month		243.0	283.5	202.5	162.0	202.5	243.0	283.5
Collections—								
two months			27.0	31.5	22.5	18.0	22.5	27.0
Total collections			$310.5	$234.0	$184.5	$220.5	$265.5	$310.5
Cash sales			25.0	20.0	25.0	30.0	35.0	38.0
Total sales receipts			$335.5	$254.0	$209.5	$250.5	$300.5	$348.5

days after the invoice date. Assume also that in the company's experience, 90 percent of receivables are collected, on the average, one month from the date of the sale, and that 10 percent are collected two months from the date of the sale, with no bad-debt losses. Moreover, on the average, 10 percent of total sales are cash sales.

If the sales forecast are those shown in the first line of Table 26-3, we can compute a schedule of the expected sales receipts based upon the above assumptions. This schedule appears in Table 26-3. For January, we see that total sales are estimated to be $250,000, of which $25,000 are cash sales. Of the $225,000 in credit sales, 90 percent, or $202,500, are expected to be collected in February; and 10 percent, or $22,500, are expected to be collected in March. Similarly, sales in other months are broken down according to the same percentages. The firm should be alert to change its assumptions with respect to collections when there is an underlying shift in the payment habits of its customers. For example, if there is a slowdown in the economy, certain customers are likely to become slower in their trade payments. The firm must take account of this change if its cash budget is to be realistic.

From this example, it is easy to see the effect of a variation in sales upon the magnitude and timing of cash receipts, all other things held constant. For most firms, there is a degree of correlation between sales and collection experience. In times of recession and sales decline, the average collection period is likely to lengthen and bad-debt losses increase. Thus, the collection experience of a firm may reinforce a decline in sales, magnifying the downward impact upon total sales receipts.

Cash receipts may arise from the sale of assets, as well as from sales of the product. Suppose, for example, that the firm intends to sell $40,000 in fixed assets in February. Total cash receipts in February, then, would be $294,000. For the most part, the sales of assets is planned in advance and, therefore, is easily predicted for purposes of cash budgeting.

Given the sales forecast, a production schedule may be established. Management may choose either to gear production closely to sales or to produce at a relatively constant rate over time. With the former production strategy, inventory carrying costs generally are lower, but total production costs are higher than with the latter strategy. With steady production, the opposite usually occurs. If sales fluctuate, finished goods inventories build up during certain periods and require storage. Because storage is uneven throughout the year, inventory carrying costs are generally higher than they would be if production were geared to sales. On the other hand, production typically is more efficient. Which alternative is better will depend upon the added cost of carrying inventory when production is geared to sales relative to the savings available if production is steady. The final production schedule embodies decisions with respect to inventory management, a topic taken up in Chapter 16.

Once a production schedule has been established, estimates can be made of the materials that will need to be purchased, the labor that will be required, and any additional fixed assets the firm will need to acquire. As with receivables, there is a lag between the time a purchase is made and the time of actual cash payment. If the average billing terms given by suppliers are net 30, and the firm's policy is to pay its bills at the end of this period, there is approximately a one-month lag between a purchase and the payment. If the production program of Continental Sheetmetal calls for the manufacture of goods in the month preceding forecasted sales, we might have a schedule of expenses like that in Table 26-4. As we see, there is a one-month lag between the time of purchase and the payment for the purchase.

Wages are assumed to increase with the amount of production. Generally, wages are more stable over time than are purchases. When production dips slightly, workers usually are not laid off. When production picks up, labor becomes more efficient with relatively little increase in total wages. Only after a certain point is overtime work required or do new workers have to be hired to meet the increased production schedule. Included in other expenses are general, administrative, and selling

Table 26·4   Schedule of expenses (in thousands)

	Dec.	Jan.	Feb.	Mar.	Apr.	May	June
Purchases	$100	$ 80	$100	$120	$140	$150	$150
Cash payment							
for purchases		100	80	100	120	140	150
Wages paid		80	80	90	90	95	100
Other expenses		50	50	50	50	50	50
Total cash expenses		$230	$210	$240	$260	$285	$300

expenses; property taxes; interest expenses; power, light, and heat expenses; maintenance expenses; and indirect labor and material expenses. These expenses tend to be reasonably predictable over the short run.

In addition to cash expenses, we must take into account capital expenditures, dividends, federal income taxes, and any other cash outflows. Because capital expenditures are planned in advance, they usually are predictable for the short-term cash budget. As the forecast becomes more distant, however, prediction of these expenditures becomes less certain. Dividend payments for most companies are stable and are paid on specific dates. Estimation of federal income taxes must be based upon projected profits for the period under review. Other cash outlays might consist of the repurchase of stock or payment of long-term debt. These outlays are combined with total cash expenses to obtain the schedule of total cash disbursements shown in Table 26-5.

Table 26·5   Schedule of cash disbursements (in thousands)

	Jan.	Feb.	Mar.	Apr.	May	June
Total cash expenses	$230	$210	$240	$260	$285	$300
Capital expenditures		150	50			
Dividend payments			20			20
Income taxes	30			30		
Total cash disbursements	$260	$360	$310	$290	$285	$320

Net cash flow and cash balance

Once we are satisfied that we have taken into account all foreseeable cash inflows and outflows, we combine the cash receipts and cash disbursements schedules to obtain the net cash inflow or outflow for each month. The net cash flow may then be added to beginning cash in January, which is assumed to be $100,000, and the projected cash position computed month by month for the period under review. This final schedule is shown in Table 26-6.

The cash budget shown indicates that the firm is expected to have a cash deficit in April and May. This deficit is caused by a decline in collections through March, capital expenditures totaling $200,000 in February and March, and a cash dividend of $20,000 in March. With the increase in collections in May and June, the cash balance without financing rises to $13,500 in June. The cash budget indicates that peak cash requirements occur in April. If the firm has a policy of maintaining a minimum cash balance of $75,000 and of borrowing from its bank to maintain this minimum, it will need to borrow an additional $66,000 in March. Additional borrowings will peak at $105,500 in April, after which they will decline to $61,500 in June, if all goes according to prediction.

Table 26·6 Net cash flow and cash balance (in thousands)

	Jan.	Feb.	Mar.	Apr.	May	June
Total cash receipts	$335.5	$294.0*	$209.5	$250.5	$300.5	$348.5
Total cash disbursements	260.0	360.0	310.0	290.0	285.0	320.0
Net cash flow	$ 75.5	$(66.0)	$(100.5)	$ (39.5)	$ 15.5	$ 28.5
Beginning cash without financing	100.0	175.5	109.5	9.0	(30.5)	(15.0)
Ending cash without financing	175.5	109.5	9.0	(30.5)	(15.0)	13.5

*Includes sales receipts of $254,000 and cash sale of assets of $40,000.

for min bal 75.0:   Borrow: 66.0   105.5   90.0   61.5

Alternative means of meeting the cash deficit are available. The firm may be able to delay its capital expenditures or its payments for purchases. Indeed, one of the principal purposes of a cash budget is to determine the timing and magnitude of prospective financing needs so that the most appropriate method of financing can be arranged. A decision to obtain long-term financing should be based upon long-range funds requirements and upon considerations apart from a cash forecast. In addition to helping the financial manager plan for short-term financing, the cash budget is valuable to him in managing the firm's cash position. On the basis of a cash budget, he can plan to invest excess funds in marketable securities. The result is an efficient transfer of funds from cash to marketable securities and back.

DEVIATIONS FROM EXPECTED CASH FLOWS

Often, there is a tendency to place considerable faith in the cash budget simply because it is expressed in numbers. It is important to stress again that a cash budget represents merely an *estimate* of future cash flows. Depending upon the care devoted to preparing the budget and the volatility of cash flows resulting from the nature of the business, actual cash flows will deviate more or less widely from those that were expected. In the face of uncertainty, we must provide information about the range of possible outcomes. To analyze cash flows only under one set of assumptions, as is the case with conventional cash budgeting, results in a faulty perspective of the future.

To take into account deviations from expected cash flows, it is desirable to work out additional cash budgets. For example, we might want to base one cash forecast upon the assumption of a maximum probable decline in business, and another upon the assumption of the maximum probable increase in business. By bringing possible events into the open for discussion, management is better able to plan for contingencies. Not only will such discussion sharpen its perspective on the probability of occurrence of a particular event, but it will give management a better understanding of the magnitude of its impact on the firm's cash flows.[4]

Given the preparation of a cash budget based upon expected cash flows, it is often a simple matter to trace through a change in one or a series of figures in order to take into account a large number of possibilities. In determining the spectrum of possible outcomes, simulation techniques can be useful. The computer can be programmed to calculate a cash budget under varying assumptions. With a time-sharing system, the analyst can type in a change in assumptions; and the computer will recompute and print out a new cash budget in a matter of minutes. Examples of a change in assumptions include a decline in sales or an increase in the average collection period. For each set of assumptions and resulting cash budget, a probability of occurrence should be attached. The ease with which reruns can be made with a computer time-sharing system allows extensive analysis of the sensitivity of the firm's expected cash position to changes in assumptions.

The expected cash position plus the probability distribution of possible outcomes gives us a considerable amount of information. We can see the additional funds required or the funds released under various possible outcomes. This information enables us to determine more accurately the minimum cash balance, maturity structure of debt, and borrowing power necessary to give the firm a margin of safety. It enables the financial manager to anticipate sharp changes in the firm's cash position.

We also can analyze the ability of the firm to adjust to deviations from the expected outcomes. For example, if sales should fall off, how flexible are our expenses? What can be cut? By how much? How quickly? How much effort should be devoted to the collection of receivables? In the case of an unexpected increase in business, what additional purchases will be required, and when? Can labor be expanded? Can the present plant handle the additional demand? How much in funds will be needed to finance the buildup? Answers to these questions provide valuable insight into the efficiency and flexibility of the firm under a variety of conditions.[5] In addition, an analysis of this sort helps answer the important question of the costs of various deviations from expected outcomes. Again, simulation is a useful method for evaluating these costs.

From the standpoint of internal planning, it is far better to allow for a range of possible outcomes than to rely solely upon the expected outcome. This allowance is particularly important for firms whose

---

[4] See Gordon Donaldson, "Strategy for Financial Emergencies," *Harvard Business Review,* 47 (November–December 1969), 69.

[5] Donaldson, "Strategy for Financial Emergencies," pp. 71–79, develops a framework for evaluating the resources available to meet adverse financial contingencies.

business is relatively unstable in character. If the plans of the firm are based only upon expected cash flows, the firm is likely to be caught flat-footed in the case of a significant deviation from the expected outcome, and have difficulty making an adjustment. An unforeseen deficit in cash may be difficult to finance on short notice. Therefore, it is extremely important for the firm to be honest with itself and attempt to minimize the costs associated with deviations from expected outcomes by taking the steps necessary to assure accuracy and by preparing additional cash budgets so as to take into account the range of possible outcomes. When significant deviations from expected outcomes occur, the cash budget should be revised in keeping with new information.

In addition to projecting the cash flow of a firm over time, it often is useful to prepare a projected, or *pro forma*, balance sheet and income statement for selected future dates. A cash budget gives us information only as to the prospective future cash positions of the firm, whereas *pro forma* statements embody forecasts of all assets and liabilities as well as of income-statement items. Much of the information that goes into the preparation of the cash budget, however, can be used to derive a *pro forma* statement. As before, the key to accuracy is the sales forecasts.

PRO FORMA STATEMENTS

PRO FORMA BALANCE SHEET

To illustrate the preparation of a *pro forma* balance sheet, suppose that we wish to prepare a *pro forma* statement for Continental Sheet-metal for June 30 and that the company has the following balance sheet at December 31:

Assets (in thousands)		Liabilities (in thousands)	
Cash	$ 100	Bank borrowings	$ 50
Receivables	342	Accounts payable	200
Inventory	350	Accrued wages and expenses	250
		Accrued income taxes	70
Current assets	$ 792	Current liabilities	$ 570
Net fixed assets	800	Net worth	1,022
Total assets	$1,592	Total liabilities and net worth	$1,592

Receivables at June 30 can be estimated by adding to the receivable balance at December 31 the total projected credit sales from January through June, less total projected credit collections for the period. On the basis of the information in the cash budget, receivables at June 30 would be $342,000 + $31,500, or $373,500.

See p. 704
[Table 26.3]

projected
cr. sales - collections
Jan-June.
receivable
bal. in Dec
238.3 + 31.5

If a cash budget is not available, the receivable balance may be estimated on the basis of a turnover ratio. This ratio, which depicts the relationship between credit sales and receivables, should be based upon past experience. To obtain the estimated level of receivables, projected sales simply are divided by the turnover ratio. If the sales forecast and turnover ratio are realistic, the method will produce a reasonable approximation of the receivable balance. The estimated investment in inventories at June 30 may be based upon the production schedule, which, in turn, is based upon the sales forecast. This schedule should show expected purchases, the expected use of inventory in production, and the expected level of finished goods. On the basis of this information, together with the beginning inventory level, a *pro forma* estimate of inventory can be made. Rather than use the production schedule, estimates of future inventory can be based upon a turnover ratio of cost of goods sold to inventory. This ratio is applied in the same manner as for receivables. Suppose that on the basis of a turnover ratio, we estimate inventory to be $420,000 on June 30, a figure that represents a moderate increase over the inventory level of December 31, in keeping with the buildup in sales.

Future net fixed assets are estimated by adding planned expenditures to existing net fixed assets and subtracting from this sum depreciation for the period, plus any sale of fixed assets at book value. From the cash budget, we note that capital expenditures are estimated at $200,000 over the period and that $40,000 in fixed assets will be sold at what we assume to be their depreciated book values. If depreciation for the period is expected to be $110,000, the expected net addition to fixed assets would be $50,000, ($200,000 − $40,000 − $110,000), and projected net fixed assets at June 30 would be $850,000. Because capital expenditures are planned in advance, fixed assets generally are fairly easy to forecast.

Turning now to the liabilities, accounts payable are estimated by adding total projected purchases for January through June, less total projected cash payments for purchases for the period, to the December 31 balance. Our estimate of accounts payable, therefore, is $200,000 + $50,000, or $250,000. The calculation of accrued wages and expenses is based upon the production schedule and the historic relationship between these accruals and production. We assume the estimate of accrued wages and expenses to be $240,000. Accrued income taxes are estimated by adding to the current balance taxes on forecasted income for the six-month period, less the actual payment of taxes. If income taxes for the period are forecast at $60,000, and the firm is scheduled to make $60,000 in actual payments, estimated accrued income taxes at June 30 would be $70,000.

Net worth at June 30 would be the net worth at December 31 plus profits after taxes for the period, less the amount of cash dividends paid. If profits after taxes are estimated at $65,000, net worth at June 30 would be $1,022,000 plus $65,000 minus dividends of $40,000, or $1,047,000. Two items remain: cash and bank loans. We see from the cash budget that estimated cash at June 30 would be $13,500 without additional financing. If the firm has the policy of maintaining a minimum cash balance of $75,000 and borrowing from its bank to maintain this balance, cash at June 30 would be $75,000, and bank borrowings would increase by $61,500 to $111,500. In general, cash and notes payable serve as balancing factors in the preparation of *pro forma* balance sheets, whereby assets and liabilities plus net worth are brought into balance.

Once we have estimated all the components of the *pro forma* balance sheet, they are combined into a balance sheet format. The *pro forma* balance sheet at June 30 is:

Assets (*in thousands*)		Liabilities (*in thousands*)	
Cash	$ 75.0	Bank borrowings	$ 111.5
Receivables	373.5	Accounts payable	250.0
Inventories	420.0	Accrued wages and expenses	240.0
		Accrued income taxes	70.0
Current assets	$ 868.5	Current liabilities	$ 671.5
Net fixed assets	850.0	Net worth	1,047.0
Total assets	$1,718.5	Total liabilities and net worth	$1,718.5

The cash-budget method is but one way to prepare a *pro forma* statement; one also can make direct estimates of all of the items on the balance sheet by projecting financial ratios into the future and then making estimates on the basis of these ratios. Receivables, inventories, accounts payable, and accrued wages and expenses frequently are based upon a historical relationship to sales and production when a cash budget is not available.

PRO FORMA INCOME STATEMENT

The *pro forma* income statement is a projection of income for a period of time in the future. As was true with our other projections, the sales forecast is the key input. Given this forecast, production schedules can be formulated and estimates made of production costs for the product or products. The analyst may wish to evaluate each component of the cost of goods sold. A detailed analysis of purchases, production wages, and overhead costs is likely to produce the most accurate forecasts. Often, however, costs of goods sold are estimated on the basis of past ratios of cost of goods sold to sales.

Selling and administrative expenses are estimated next. Because both of these expenses usually are budgeted in advance, estimates of them are fairly accurate. Typically, these expenses are not overly sensitive to changes in sales in the very short run, particularly to reductions in sales. Next, we estimate other income and expenses as well as interest expenses to obtain net income before taxes. Income taxes are then computed based upon the applicable tax rate and deducted, to arrive at estimated net income after taxes. All of these estimates are then combined into an income statement.

Pro forma statements allow us to study the composition of expected future balance sheets and income statements. Financial ratios may be computed for analysis of the statements; these ratios and the raw figures may be compared with those for present and past balance sheets. Using this information, the financial manager can analyze the direction of change in the financial condition and performance of the firm over the past, the present, and the future. If the firm is accustomed to making accurate estimates, the preparation of a cash budget, *pro forma* statements, or both, literally forces it to plan ahead and to coordinate policy in the various areas of operation. Continual revision of these forecasts keeps the firm alert to changing conditions in its environment and in its internal operations. Again, it is useful to prepare more than one set of *pro forma* statements in order to take into account the range of possible outcomes.

SUMMARY

In this chapter, we continued our examination of the analytical tools of the financial manager; we looked at source and use of funds statements, the cash budget, and *pro forma* statements. The source and use of funds statement gives the financial analyst considerable insight into the uses of funds and how these uses are financed over a specific period of time. Funds-flow analysis is valuable in analyzing the commitment of funds to assets and in planning the firm's intermediate- and long-term financing. The flow of funds studied, however, represents net rather than gross transactions between two points in time.

A cash budget is a forecast of the future cash receipts and cash disbursements of a firm. This forecast is particularly useful to the financial manager in determining the probable cash balances of the firm over the near future and in planning for the financing of prospective cash needs. In addition to analyzing expected cash flows, the financial manager should take into account possible deviations from the expected outcome. An analysis of the range of possible outcomes enables management to better assess the efficiency and flexibility of the firm and to determine the appropriate margin of safety.

Finally, we considered the preparation of *pro forma* balance sheets and income statements. These statements give the financial manager insight into the prospective future financial condition and performance of the firm, giving him yet another tool for financial planning and control.

gross increase in Common + Surplus may indicate NI-div. + Sale of stock

1.

Kohn Corporation comparative balance sheets at Dec. 31 (in millions)

Assets	1971	1972	Liabilities and Net Worth	1971	1972
Cash	$ 5	$ 3	Notes payable	$20	$ 0
Marketable securities	5	7	Accounts payable	5	8
Accounts receivable	10	15	Accrued wages	2	2
Inventories	12	15	Accrued taxes	3	5
Fixed assets, net	50	55	Long-term debt	0	15
Other assets	8	5	Common and surplus	60	70
Total assets	$90	$100	Total liabilities and net worth	$90	$100

4 added to R/E from. N.I.
6 added fr. sale of stock
70-60 = 10

Kohn Corporation statement of income and retained earnings year ended Dec. 31, 19__2

Net sales		$50,000,000
Expenses		
Cost of goods sold	$25,000,000	
Selling, general, and administrative expenses	5,000,000	
Depreciation	5,000,000	
Interest	1,000,000	36,000,000
Net income before taxes		$14,000,000
Less: Taxes		7,000,000
Net income		$ 7,000,000
Add: Retained earnings at 12/31/__1		40,000,000
Subtotal		$47,000,000
Less: Dividends		3,000,000
Retained earnings at 12/31/__2		$44,000,000

7, NI
-3... -Div
4 addition to R/E

Net margin = NIAT / sales

(a) Prepare a source and use of funds statement on a cash basis for 19__2 for the Kohn Corporation.

(b) Prepare a source and use of working capital statement for 19__2 for the Kohn Corporation.

(c) Computing the ratios that you feel to be appropriate, analyze the position of Kohn. Cite specific ratio levels and trends as evidence.

2. Financial statements for the Sennet Corporation follow.

Sennet Corporation balance sheet at Dec. 31 (in millions)

	19__1	19__2		19__1	19__2
Cash	$ 4	$ 5	Accounts payable	$ 8	$10
Accounts receivable	7	10	Notes payable	5	5
Inventory	12	15	Accrued wages	2	3
Total current assets	$23	$30	Accrued taxes	3	2
Net plant	40	40	Total current liabilities	$18	$20
			Long-term debt	20	20
			Common stock	10	10
			Retained earnings	15	20
Total	$63	$70	Total	$63	$70

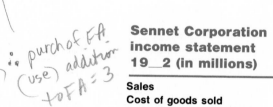

Sennet Corporation income statement 19__2 (in millions)

Sales		$100
Cost of goods sold	$50	
Selling, general, and administrative expenses	15	
Depreciation	3	
Interest	2	70
Net income before taxes		$ 30
Taxes		15
Net income		$ 15

(a) Prepare a source and use of funds statement for Sennet.

(b) Prepare a source and use of working capital statement.

3. Prepare a cash budget for the Ace Manufacturing Company, indicating receipts and disbursements for May, June, and July. The firm wishes to maintain, at all times, a minimum cash balance of $20,000. Determine whether or not borrowing will be necessary during the period and, if it is, when and for how much. As of April 30, the firm had a balance of $20,000 in cash.

Actual Sales		Forecasted Sales	
January	$50,000	May	$ 70,000
February	50,000	June	80,000
March	60,000	July	100,000
April	60,000	August	100,000

Accounts Receivable: 50 percent of total sales are for cash. The remaining 50 percent will be collected equally during the following two months (the firm incurs a negligible bad-debt loss).

Cost of Goods Manufactured: 70 percent of sales. 90 percent of this cost is paid during the first month after incurrence, the remaining 10 percent is paid the following month.

Sales and Administrative Expenses: $10,000 per month plus 10 percent of sales. All of these expenses are paid during the month of incurrence.

Interest payments: A semiannual interest payment on $300,000 of bonds outstanding (6 percent coupon) is paid during July. An annual $50,000 sinking-fund payment is also made.

Dividends: A $10,000 dividend payment will be declared and made in July.

Capital Expenditures: $40,000 will be invested in plant and equipment in June.

Taxes: Income tax payments of $1,000 will be made in July.

4. Given the information that follows, prepare a cash budget for the Central City Department Store for the first six months of 19__2.

(a) All prices and costs remain constant.

(b) Sales are 75 percent for credit and 25 percent for cash.

(c) In terms of credit sales, 60 percent are collected in the month after the sale, 30 percent in the second month, and 10 percent in the third. Bad-debt losses are insignificant.

(d) Sales, actual and estimated, are:

October, 19__1	$300,000	March, 19__2	$200,000
November, 19__1	350,000	April, 19__2	300,000
December, 19__1	400,000	May, 19__2	250,000
January, 19__2	150,000	June, 19__2	200,000
February, 19__2	200,000	July, 19__2	300,000

(e) The store has a gross margin of 20 percent and purchases and pays for each month's anticipated sales in the preceding month.

(f) Wages and salaries are:

January	$30,000	April	$50,000
February	40,000	May	40,000
March	50,000	June	35,000

(g) Rent is $2,000 a month.

(h) Interest on $500,000 of 6 percent bonds is due on the calendar quarter.

(i) A tax prepayment on 19__2 income of $50,000 is due in April.

(j) A capital addition of $30,000 is planned in June.

(k) The company has a cash balance of $100,000 at December 31, 19__1, which is the minimum desired level for cash. Funds can be borrowed in multiples of $5,000 on a monthly basis at 6 percent per annum. Interest is payable on the first of the month following the borrowing and is not accrued.

5. Use the cash budget worked out in problem 4 and with the following additional information prepare a *pro forma* income statement for the first half of 19__2 for the Central City Department Store.

(a) Inventory at 12/31/__1 was $200,000.

(b) Depreciation is taken on a straight-line basis on $250,000 of assets with an average remaining life of ten years and no salvage value.

(c) The tax rate is 50 percent.

SELECTED REFERENCES

Chambers, John C., Satinder K. Mullick, and Donald D. Smith, "How to Choose the Right Forecasting Technique," *Harvard Business Review,* 49 (July–August 1971), 45–74.

Chervany, Norman L., "A Simulation Analysis of Causal Relationship within the Cash Flow Process," *Journal of Financial and Quantitative Analysis,* 5 (December 1970), 445–68.

Helfert, Erich A., *Techniques of Financial Analysis,* 3rd ed., Chapters 1 and 3. Homewood, Ill.: Richard D. Irwin, 1972.

Jaedicke, Robert K., and Robert T. Sprouse, *Accounting Flows: Income, Funds, and Cash,* Chapters 5 and 6. Englewood Cliffs, N.J.: Prentice-Hall, 1965.

Lerner, Eugene M., "Simulating a Cash Budget," *California Management Review,* 11 (Winter 1968), 79–86.

Pappas, James L., and George P. Huber, "Probabilistic Short-Term Financial Planning," *Financial Management,* 3 (Autumn 1973), 36–44.

Parker, George G. C., and Edilberto L. Segura, "How to Get a Better Forecast," *Harvard Business Review,* 49 (March–April 1971), 99–109.

Staubus, G. J., "Alternative Asset Flow Concepts," *Accounting Review,* 41 (July 1966), 397–412.

Trumbull, Wendell, P., "Developing the Funds Statement as the Third Major Financial Statement," *N.A.A. Bulletin,* 45 (April 1963), 21–31.

ANALYSIS
of OPERATING
and FINANCIAL
LEVERAGE

Leverage may be defined as the employment of an asset or funds for which the firm pays a fixed cost or fixed return. The fixed cost or return may be thought of as the fulcrum of a lever. When revenues less variable costs or earnings before interest and taxes exceed the fixed cost or fixed return, positive or favorable leverage results. When they do not, the result is unfavorable leverage. In this chapter, we explore the principles of operating and financial leverage. We should point out that our discussion of financial leverage is only in terms of contractual, or explicit, costs associated with leverage. The "implicit" or "hidden" costs associated with leverage are taken up in Chapters 9 and 10. Thus, the discussion of financial leverage here should not be construed as being complete but as only one component in an overall analysis.

OPERATING LEVERAGE

Operating leverage occurs any time a firm has fixed costs that must be met regardless of volume. In the very long run, of course, all costs are variable. Consequently, our analysis necessarily involves the short run. We employ assets with a fixed cost in the hope that volume will produce revenues more than sufficient to cover all fixed and variable costs. One of the more dramatic examples of operating leverage is in the airline industry, where a large portion of total costs are fixed. Beyond a certain break-even load factor, each additional passenger represents essentially straight profit to the airline. With fixed costs, the percentage change in profits accompanying a change in volume is greater than the percentage change in volume. This occurrence is known as *operating leverage*. Operating leverage may be studied by means of a break-even or cost-volume-profit analysis.

BREAK-EVEN ANALYSIS

To illustrate break-even analysis, consider a firm that produces a quality testing machine that sells for $50 a unit. The company has annual fixed costs of $100,000 and variable costs are $25 a unit regardless of the volume sold. We wish to study the relationship between total costs and total revenues. One means for doing so is with the break-even chart in Figure 27-1, which shows the relationship between profits, fixed costs, variable costs, and volume. By *profits*, we mean operating profits before taxes, excluding interest and other income and expenses.

The intersection of the total cost line with the total revenue line represents the break-even point. The fixed costs that must be recovered from the sales dollar after the deduction of variable costs determines the volume necessary to break even. In Figure 27-1, this break-even point is

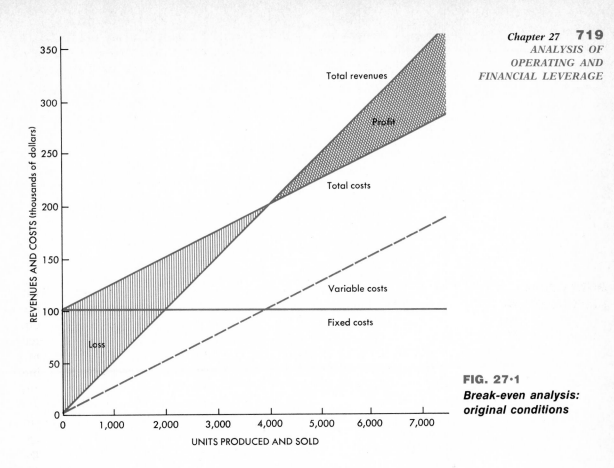

FIG. 27·1
Break-even analysis:
original conditions

4,000 units of output. At the break-even point, variable costs plus fixed costs equal total revenue:

$$F + V(X) = P(X) \qquad (27\text{-}1)$$

where F = fixed costs

V = variable costs per unit

X = volume of output (in units)

P = price per unit

Rearranging Eq. (27-1), the break-even point is

$$\begin{aligned} X &= F/(P - V) \\ &= 100{,}000/(50 - 25) = 4{,}000 \end{aligned} \qquad (27\text{-}2)$$

For each additional increment of volume above the break-even point, there is increasing profit represented by the dotted area in the figure. Likewise, as volume falls below the break-even point, there are increas-

Table 27·1 Relation between profit and volume

Volume (in thousand units)	0	1	2	3	4	5	6	7
Operating profit (in thousands)	−$100	−$75	−$50	−$25	0	$25	$50	$75

ing losses, represented by the lined area. Table 27-1 shows the profit for various levels of volume. We see that the closer the volume to the break-even point, the greater the percentage change in profit in relation to a percentage change in volume.

The degree of operating leverage of a firm at a particular level of output is simply the percentage change in profits over the percentage change in output that causes the change in profits. Thus,

$$\frac{\text{Degree of operating}}{\text{leverage at } X \text{ units}} = \frac{\text{Percentage change in profits}}{\text{Percentage change in output}} \qquad (27\text{-}3)$$

Rather than calculate the percentages involved directly, a simple formula is available for expressing the relationship:

$$\text{DOL at } X \text{ units} = \frac{X(P - V)}{X(P - V) - F} \qquad (27\text{-}4)$$

Suppose that we wished to determine the degree of operating leverage for 5,000 units of output for our hypothetical example firm:

$$\text{DOL at 5,000 units} = \frac{5,000(50 - 25)}{5,000(50 - 25) - 100,000} = 5$$

For 6,000 units of output, we have

$$\text{DOL at 6,000 units} = \frac{6,000(50 - 25)}{6,000(50 - 25) - 100,000} = 3$$

We see, then, that the further the level of output is from the break-even point, the lower the degree of operating leverage.

A break-even chart, like that in Figure 27-1, tells us the relationship between operating profits and volume. The greater the ratio of price to variable costs per unit, the greater the absolute sensitivity of profits to volume and the greater the degree of operating leverage for all levels of output. However, a change in volume is not the only factor that affects profits. Indeed, a change in the selling price, in variable cost per unit, or in fixed costs will affect profits. In the light of Figure 27-1, we examine a favorable change in each of these factors, all other factors held constant.[1]

**Increase
in price**

Figure 27-2 shows the change for an increase in price from $50 to $65 per unit. We see that the break-even point is reduced from 4,000 units to 2,500 units as a result of this price increase; and, of course, profits are $15 per unit greater for each level of volume.

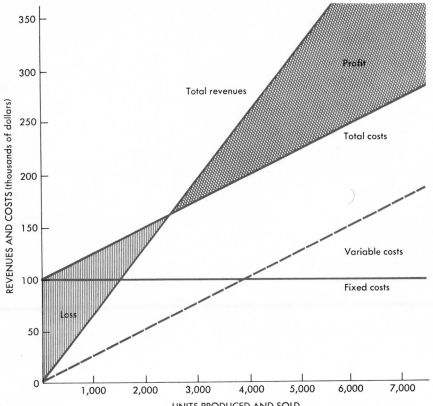

FIG. 27·2
*Break-even analysis:
price increase*

**Decrease
in fixed costs**

For a decrease in fixed costs from $100,000 to $50,000, with the original $50 per unit price, the break-even point is reduced even further. Figure 27-3 illustrates this case. The break-even point now is 2,000 units, and total profits are increased by $50,000 for all levels of volume.

[1] For a mathematical analysis of the effect of changes in these factors on profits, as well as an analysis of the risk associated with such changes, see Thomas A. Morrison and Eugene Kaczka, "A New Application of Calculus and Risk Analysis to Cost-Volume-Profit Changes," *Accounting Review*, 44 (April 1969), 330–43.

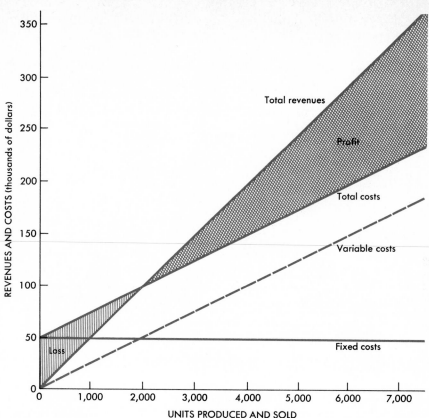

FIG. 27·3
Break-even analysis:
decrease in fixed costs

**Decrease
in variable
costs**

Finally, Figure 27-4 shows the change when variable costs per unit are lowered from $25 to $20. The
break-even point is lowered to 3,333 units, and
profit is $5 greater per unit of output. Table 27-2
summarizes the profits for various levels of volume under the alternatives cited. The last column of the table shows the relationship between
profit and volume if all three of the changes occur simultaneously.

Despite a number of limitations that we shall take up shortly,
break-even analysis gives management a good deal of information about
the operating risk of the company. Given an approximate break-even
point, management can compare fluctuations in expected future volume
with this point to ascertain the stability of profits. Knowledge of this
stability is important to the financial manager in determining the ability
of the firm to service debt, as we shall see shortly.

Such an analysis is important also when planning the acquisition of
assets that will require additional fixed costs. In general, the greater the
fixed costs of a firm, the greater the degree of operating risk. Therefore,
a firm will not wish to undertake an increase in fixed costs unless there
are sufficient benefits to be derived. In this regard, the expected future
trend and stability of volume, together with the ratio of expected price to

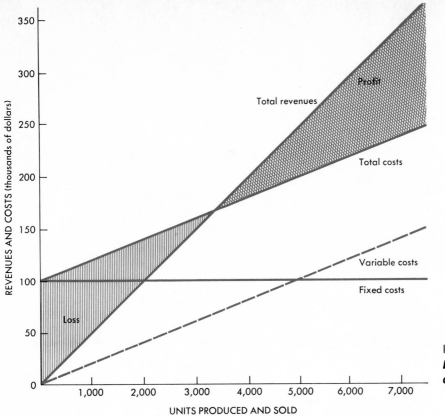

FIG. 27·4
*Break-even analysis:
decrease in variable costs*

expected variable costs per unit, will bear heavily upon the decision to
increase fixed costs. As we saw in the previous discussion, break-even
analysis is useful in determining the change in profits that accompanies
a change in pricing and costs. Depending upon the elasticity of demand
and the ratio of price to variable costs, price cutting to boost volume may
or may not be worthwhile. Break-even analysis provides us with a means
for deciding.

Table 27·2 Relation between profits and volume

Volume (in units)	Profits (in thousands)				
	Original Case	Price ($65)	Fixed Costs ($50,000)	Variable Costs ($20)	All Three
0	−$100	−$100	−$ 50	−$100	−$ 50
2,000	− 50	− 20	0	− 40	40
4,000	0	60	50	20	130
6,000	50	140	100	80	220
8,000	100	220	150	140	310

LIMITATIONS

Although break-even analysis seems simple enough in concept—and this simplicity is one of its virtues—its effectiveness is limited in several ways. These limitations must be recognized and the method modified if it is to provide meaningful results. One assumption of the method is that there is a constant price and variable cost per unit, irrespective of volume. In many cases, the firm's sales volume may influence the market price of a product. For example, increased output may lead to a decline in market price. Moreover, variable costs are likely to increase as the firm approaches full capacity; for example, less efficient labor or costly overtime help may have to be used. These shortcomings of break-even analysis can be remedied by making the relationships between total sales and volume, and total costs and volume, nonlinear, to correspond with economic reality. Figure 27-5 shows an example of some hypothetical curvilinear relationships.

Another difficulty with break-even analysis is the classification of costs as fixed or variable. In practice, many costs defy clear categorization because they are partly fixed and partly variable. These costs are known as semivariable costs. Moreover, we assume that costs classified as fixed remain unchanged over the entire volume range, but this range is limited by the immediate physical capacity of the firm. A steel company may have an idle marginal plant that it can put into operation if it needs additional output, but putting the plant into operation may in-

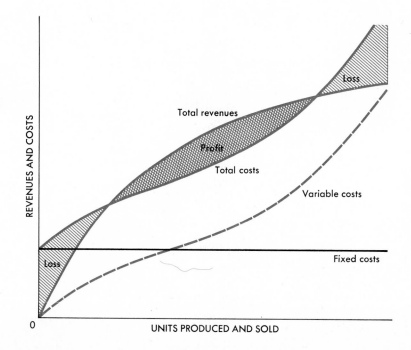

FIG. 27·5
*Break-even analysis:
curvilinear relationship*

crease fixed costs. If the range of volume considered includes this plant, fixed costs would not be constant but would increase in a step function manner at the point in volume at which the plant was to be reopened. For most situations, however, new physical capacity must be constructed if volume is to be increased beyond some critical point. Consequently, a break-even analysis is relevant only for volume up to that point.

Another problem relates to multiple products. Break-even analysis perhaps is best suited for a one-product analysis. When there are multiple products, a single break-even analysis cannot be used unless the product mix remains unchanged. When the product mix does change, it may be necessary to prepare a separate break-even analysis for each product. Here, allocating expenses that are common to all product lines may present a problem.

The information inputs for break-even analysis are usually based upon historical relationships. However, these relationships may not be particularly stable over time. For extreme volume changes, there may be no historical precedent. Moreover, it is not past relationships of costs, volume, and profits that we are trying to judge but, rather, future ones. These estimates are subject to uncertainty and risk—elements that are not taken into account in traditional break-even analysis. In the appendix of this chapter, we present a break-even analysis that takes uncertainty into account.

Finally, we must note that the short-term horizon in break-even analysis is a limitation for longer-range planning. The benefits realized from certain expenditures, such as capital expenditures and research and development outlays, are not likely to be realized during the period of time encompassed by most break-even analyses. A break-even analysis would not justify these expenditures, but they may well be necessary to the continued life of the firm. Despite the many limitations of break-even analysis, however, it can be an important tool to the financial manager if it is employed properly and if it is reasonably appropriate to the situation.[2]

FINANCIAL LEVERAGE

Financial leverage, as defined before, involves the use of funds obtained at a fixed cost in the hope of increasing the return to common stockholders. Favorable or positive leverage is said to occur when the firm earns more on the assets purchased with the funds than the fixed cost of their use. Unfavorable or negative leverage occurs when the firm

[2] For an empirical analysis of operating leverage and risk for samples of electrical utilities, steel companies, and oil companies, see Baruch Lev, "On the Association between Operating Leverage and Risk," *Journal of Financial and Quantitative Analysis*, 9 (September 1974), 627–41.

does not earn as much as the funds cost. The favorability of financial leverage, or "trading on the equity" as it is called, is judged in terms of the effect upon earnings per share to common stockholders. We are interested in determining the relationship between earnings per share and earnings before interest and taxes (EBIT) under various financing alternatives and the indifference points between these alternatives.

CALCULATION OF EARNINGS PER SHARE

To illustrate a break-even analysis of leverage, suppose Cherokee Tire Company with long-term capitalization of $10 million, consisting entirely of common stock, wishes to raise another $5 million for expansion through one of three possible financing plans. The company may finance with (1) all common stock; (2) all debt, at 9 percent interest; or (3) all preferred stock with a 7 percent dividend. Present annual earnings before interest and taxes (EBIT) are $1,400,000, the federal income tax rate is 50 percent, and 200,000 shares of stock are presently outstanding. Common stock can be sold at $50 per share under financing option 1, or 100,000 additional shares of stock.

In order to determine the EBIT break-even, or indifference, points between the various financing alternatives, we begin by calculating earnings per share for some hypothetical level of EBIT. Suppose we wished to know what earnings per share would be under the three financing plans if EBIT were $2 million. The calculations are shown in Table 27-3. We note that interest on debt is deducted before taxes, while preferred stock dividends are deducted after taxes. As a result, earnings available to common stockholders are higher under the debt alternative than they are under the preferred-stock alternative, despite the fact that the interest rate on debt is higher than the preferred-stock dividend rate.

Table 27·3   Calculations of earnings per share under three financing alternatives

	All Common	All Debt	All Preferred
Earnings before interest and taxes (hypothetical)	$2,000,000	$2,000,000	$2,000,000
Interest	—	$ 450,000	—
Earnings before taxes	$2,000,000	$1,550,000	$2,000,000
Income taxes	$1,000,000	$ 775,000	$1,000,000
Earnings after taxes	$1,000,000	$ 775,000	$1,000,000
Prefered stock dividend	—	—	$ 350,000
Earnings available to common stockholders	$1,000,000	$ 775,000	$ 650,000
Number of shares	300,000	200,000	200,000
Earnings per share	$3.33	$3.88	$3.25

Given the information in Table 27-3, we are able to construct a "break-even" or indifference chart similar to what we did for operating leverage. On the horizontal axis we plot earnings before interest and taxes (EBIT) and on the vertical axis, earnings per share (EPS). For each financing alternative, we must draw a straight line to reflect EPS for all possible levels of EBIT. To do so, we need two datum points for each alternative. The first is the EPS calculated for some hypothetical level of EBIT. For $2 million in EBIT, we see in Table 27-3 that earnings per share are $3.33, $3.88, and $3.25 for the common, debt, and preferred-stock financing alternatives. We simply plot these earnings per share at the $2 million mark in EBIT. It is important to recognize that it does not matter which hypothetical level of EBIT we choose for calculating EPS. Assuming good graph paper, one level is as good as the next.

The second datum point is simply the EBIT necessary to cover all fixed financial costs for a particular financing plan, and it is plotted on the horizontal axis. For the common-stock alternative, there are no fixed costs, so the intercept on the horizontal axis is zero. For the debt alternative, we must have EBIT of $450,000 to cover interest charges; so $450,000 becomes the horizontal axis intercept. For the preferred-stock alternative, we must divide total annual dividends by one minus the tax rate in order to obtain the EBIT necessary to cover these dividends. Thus, we need $700,000 in EBIT to cover $350,000 in preferred-stock dividends, assuming a 50 percent tax rate. Again, preferred dividends are deducted after taxes, so it takes more in before-tax earnings to cover them than it does to cover interest. Given the horizontal axis intercepts and earnings per share for some hypothetical level of EBIT, we draw a straight line through the two sets of points. The break-even or indifference chart for Cherokee Tire Company is shown in Figure 27-6.

We see from the figure that the earnings-per-share indifference point between the debt and common-stock financing alternatives is $1,350,000 in EBIT. If EBIT is below that point, the common-stock alternative will provide higher earnings per share; above that point the debt alternative is best. The indifference point between the preferred-stock and the common-stock alternatives is $2,100,000 in EBIT. Above it, the preferred-stock alternative is favored with respect to earnings per share; below it, the common-stock alternative is best. We note that there is no indifference point between the debt and preferred-stock alternatives. The debt alternative dominates for all levels of EBIT and by a constant amount of earnings per share, namely $0.63.

The indifference point between two methods of financing can be determined mathematically by

$$\frac{(\text{EBIT}^* - C_1)(1 - t)}{S_1} = \frac{(\text{EBIT}^* - C_2)(1 - t)}{S_2} \qquad (27\text{-}5)$$

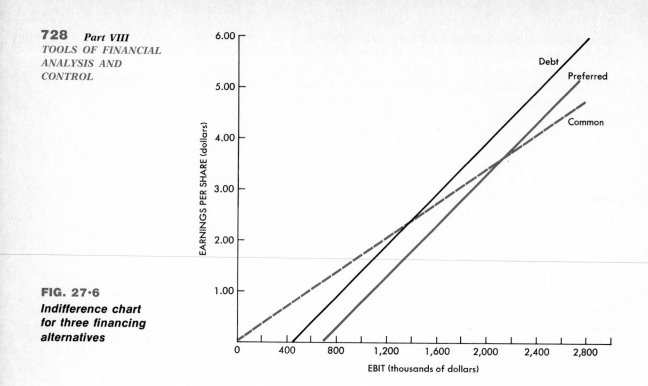

FIG. 27·6

*Indifference chart
for three financing
alternatives*

where EBIT* = the EBIT indifference point between the two methods of
financing for which we solve

C_1, C_2 = annual interest expenses or preferred-stock dividends on a
before-tax basis for financing methods 1 and 2

t = corporate tax rate

S_1, S_2 = number of shares of common stock to be outstanding after
financing for methods 1 and 2

Suppose we wished to determine the indifference point between the
common-stock and the debt-financing alternative in our example. We
would have

$$\frac{(EBIT^* - 0)(0.5)}{300,000} = \frac{(EBIT^* - 450,000)(0.5)}{200,000} \qquad (27\text{-}6)$$

Rearranging, we obtain

$$0.5(EBIT^*)(200,000) = 0.5(EBIT^*)(300,000)$$
$$- 0.5(450,000)(300,000)$$
$$100,000 \ EBIT^* = 135,000,000,000$$
$$EBIT^* = \$1,350,000$$

The indifference point in EBIT, where earnings per share for the two methods of financing are the same, is $1,350,000. This amount can be verified graphically in Figure 27-6. Thus, indifference points for financial leverage can be determined either graphically or mathematically.

The degree of financial leverage at a particular level of EBIT is simply the percentage change in earnings per share in relation to a percentage change in EBIT. To illustrate, suppose EBIT were $2 million in our example. A $1 million increase would raise earnings per share from $3.88 to $6.38, or by approximately 64.4 percent. When this percentage increase is taken over the percentage increase in EBIT, 50 percent, the degree of financial leverage is found to be 1.29. An easier method for determining the degree of financial leverage is

$$\text{Degree of financial leverage at EBIT of } y = \frac{\text{EBIT}}{\text{EBIT} - C} \qquad (27\text{-}7)$$

where C as before is the annual interest expense or preferred-stock dividend on a before-tax basis. For our example, using the debt-financing alternative at $2 million in EBIT, we have

$$\text{DFL at \$2 million} = \frac{2,000,000}{2,000,000 - 450,000} = 1.29$$

For the preferred-stock financing alternative, the degree of financial leverage is

$$\text{DFL at \$2 million} = \frac{2,000,000}{2,000,000 - 700,000} = 1.54$$

Through an EBIT–EPS analysis, we can evaluate various financing plans or degrees of financial leverage with respect to their effect upon earnings per share. The presentation in this chapter has been devoted primarily to the construction of indifference charts as well as to providing other tools for analyzing financial leverage.[3] In Chapter 10, the use of this information is considered in the overall context of determining an appropriate capital structure.

However, certain limitations to the use of these tools of analysis should be pointed out at this time. The type of analysis presented implies that the firm should raise capital by the cheapest means possible—usually debt—as long as the expected return from investment of these funds exceeds their explicit cost. It is important, however, to recognize that this procedure usually is inappropriate if the objective of the firm is to

---

[3] For a mathematical analysis of the relationship between financial leverage and the return on equity, see Sol S. Shalit, "On the Mathematics of Financial Leverage," *Financial Management*, 4 (Spring 1975), 57–66.

maximize shareholder wealth. Implicit costs, represented by a decline in the price/earnings ratio of the common stock because of increased financial risk, are ignored. A decline in the price/earnings ratio may partially or wholly offset the earnings-per-share advantage of using debt. Moreover, there is a tendency in such a static analysis to regard the explicit costs of debt and preferred stock as constant, regardless of the degree of leverage. However, we know that beyond a certain point, lenders require higher and higher rates of interest as leverage increases. In Part III, where we studied both the explicit and the implicit costs of financing, these limitations were analyzed in considerably more detail. We point to the various limitations at this time only so the reader will not be tempted to make a conclusion with respect to financing based solely upon an EBIT–EPS analysis.

COMBINED EFFECT OF TWO TYPES OF LEVERAGE

When financial leverage is combined with operating leverage, the effect of a change in revenues on earnings per share is magnified. The combination of the two increases the dispersion and risk of possible earnings per share. To determine the effect of a change in units of output on earnings per share, we combine the equation for the degree of operating leverage, Eq. (27-4), with that for the degree of financial leverage, Eq. (27-7). Because EBIT is simply $X(P - V) - F$, whereas before X is the units of output, P is price per unit, V is variable cost per unit, and F is fixed costs, Eq. (27-7) can be expressed as

$$\frac{\text{EBIT}}{\text{EBIT} - C} = \frac{X(P - V) - F}{X(P - V) - F - C} \tag{27-8}$$

Combining this equation with that for the degree of operating leverage, Eq. (27-4), we obtain

$$\begin{array}{l} \text{Degree of operating and} \\ \text{financial leverage at } X \text{ units} \end{array} = \frac{X(P - V)}{X(P - V) - F} \cdot \frac{X(P - V) - F}{X(P - V) - F - C}$$

$$= \frac{X(P - V)}{X(P - V) - F - C} \tag{27-9}$$

We see that the amount of fixed financial costs, C, increases the degree of combined leverage over what it would be with operating leverage alone.

Suppose that our hypothetical example firm used to illustrate operating leverage had $200,000 in debt at 8 percent interest. Recall that the selling price was $50 a unit, variable cost $25 a unit, and annual fixed costs were $100,000. Assume that the tax rate is 50 percent, the number of shares of common stock outstanding is 10,000 shares, and that we wish to determine the combined degree of leverage at 8,000 units of output. Therefore,

$$\text{DO \& FL at 8,000 units} = \frac{8,000(50-25)}{8,000(50-25) - 100,000 - 16,000}$$

$$= 2.38$$

Thus, a 10 percent increase in the number of units produced and sold would result in a 23.8 percent increase in earnings per share. Earnings per share at the two levels of output are:

	8,000 units	8,800 units
Sales less total variable costs	$200,000	$220,000
Fixed costs	$100,000	$100,000
EBIT	$100,000	$120,000
Interest	$ 16,000	$ 16,000
Profit before taxes	$ 84,000	$104,000
Taxes	$ 42,000	$ 52,000
Profit after taxes	$ 42,000	$ 52,000
Shares outstanding	10,000	10,000
Earnings per share	$4.20	$5.20

This degree of combined leverage compares with 2.00 for operating leverage alone. We see, then, the relative effect of adding financial leverage on top of operating leverage.

Operating and financial leverage can be combined in a number of different ways to obtain a desirable degree of overall leverage and risk of the firm. High operating risk can be offset with low financial risk and vice versa. The proper overall level of risk involves a tradeoff between total risk (the product of operating and financial risk) and expected return. This tradeoff must be made in keeping with the objective of the firm, and it is discussed in Parts I through III. The discussion here is meant to show how certain tools can be employed to provide information on the two types of leverage and their combined effect.

SUMMARY

Operating leverage may be defined as the employment of an asset with a fixed cost in the hope that sufficient revenue will be generated to cover all fixed and variable costs. We can study the operating leverage of a firm by using a break-even graph. This graph enables us to analyze the relationship between profits, volume, fixed costs, variable costs, and prices. By varying these factors, management may determine the sensitivity of profits and, in so doing, obtain a better understanding of the operating risk of the firm. Whereas break-even analysis is a very useful tool, certain limitations to its effectiveness must be recognized.

Financial leverage is defined as the use of funds with a fixed cost in order to increase earnings per share. By using an indifference chart, we can study the relationship between earnings before interest and taxes (EBIT) and earnings per share under various alternative methods of financing. The degree of sensitivity of earnings per share to EBIT is dependent upon the explicit cost of the method of financing, the number of shares of common stock to be issued, and the nearness to the indifference point. Although an EBIT–EPS chart is useful in analyzing the explicit costs of various methods of financing, it does not take into account any implicit costs inherent in the use of a specific method of financing.

For both operating and financial leverage, we can determine the degree of leverage. In the first case, we relate the change in profits that accompanies a change in output; in the second, the change in earnings per share that accompanies a change in earnings before interest and taxes. By combining the two formulas, we can determine the effect of a change in output upon earnings per share. In this way, we can better depict the relative influence of the two types of leverage.

APPENDIX

PROBABILISTIC CONCEPTS APPLIED TO BREAK-EVEN ANALYSIS

One of the important considerations in the interpretation of a break-even chart is the expected volume. Depending upon this volume, operations for a particular product line will be profitable, break even, or show a loss. Because volume is an estimate, it is subject to uncertainty. Consequently, it is important for management to know the approximate odds for breaking even or showing a loss. This information can be obtained through the incorporation of some relatively simple probability concepts into a break-even analysis. In this appendix, we present a framework for break-even analysis under uncertainty based upon an article by Jaedicke and Robichek.[4]

We shall treat the sales volume for a given period of time as a random variable and assume that the probability distribution of expected outcomes is continuous and normal. In order to apply this concept to a break-even analysis, assume that the selling price and the variable cost per unit of a product are $3,000 and $1,750, respectively, the fixed cost is $5.8 million, and that these values are known with certainty.[5] Using Eq. (27-2), we calculate the break-even point to be

---

[4]See Robert K. Jaedicke and Alexander A. Robichek, "Cost-Volume-Profit Analysis under Conditions of Uncertainty," *Accounting Review*, 39 (October 1964), 917–26.

[5]This example is the same as that used by Jaedicke and Robichek, ibid.

$$X = \frac{\$5.8 \text{ million}}{\$3,000 - \$1,750} = 4,640 \text{ units}$$

Assume further that management estimates that the most likely sales volume is 5,000 units, and that there is approximately a two-thirds probability that actual sales volume will be within 400 units of this amount (between 4,600 and 5,400 units). The distribution is shown in Figure 27-7.

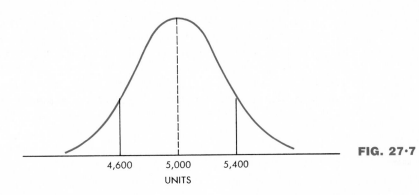

FIG. 27·7

Given a normal distribution with a mean of 5,000 units and a standard deviation of 400 units, it is possible to calculate the probability that volume will be greater or less than a certain amount.[6] The method used is to standardize the distribution in order to determine how many standard deviations a specific volume is from the mean. Suppose we wanted to know the probability that actual volume will be less than the break-even volume of 4,640 units. In standardizing the distribution, we obtain

$$X = \frac{5,000 - 4,640}{400} = \frac{360}{400} = 0.90 \text{ standard deviations}$$

Referring to the normal distribution table found in Appendix B at the end of this book, we find that there is a 0.184 probability that actual volume will be less than the break-even point.

The information in Figure 27-7 can be transformed to give the probability distribution of profits. At 5,000 units of volume, the profit is

$$5,000(3,000) - 5,000(1,750) - \$5.8 \text{ million} = \$450,000$$

The profit for a sales volume of 5,400 units, one standard deviation to the right of the mean, is

[6] For an analysis of this sort when the distribution is assumed to be lognormal, see Jimmy E. Hilliard and Robert A. Leitch, "Cost-Volume-Profit Analysis under Uncertainty: A Log Normal Approach," *Accounting Review,* 50 (January 1975), 69–80.

$$5,400(3,000) - 5,400(1,750) - \$5.8 \text{ million} = \$950,000$$

Thus, the mean of the probability distribution of profits is $450,000, and the standard deviation is ($950,000 − $450,000), or $500,000. The distribution itself is shown in Figure 27-8.

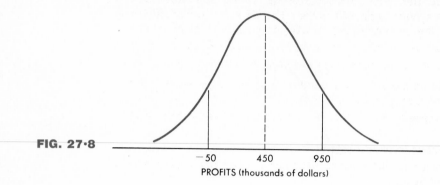

FIG. 27·8

−50   450   950
PROFITS (thousands of dollars)

    With this information, we are able to calculate directly the probability that profits will be greater or less than a certain amount. We know from before that the probability that profits will be less than zero is the probability of not breaking even, or 0.184. Therefore, the probability that profits will be more than zero is 0.816. As the mean profit is $450,000, there is a 50 percent probability that profits will exceed that amount. In a similar manner, the probability that profits will be above or below other amounts can be computed for the entire range of possible outcomes.

    The type of analysis described in this appendix enables management to evaluate operating risk. When a separate analysis is undertaken for each product, management is able to appraise the relative risk associated with each product—that is, the probability that the firm will at least break even or that profits will exceed a certain amount. The method provides a more objective framework for the appraisal of risk than does traditional break-even analysis.

PROBLEMS

1. What effect will a change in a firm's sales volume have on its break-even point, assuming that price remains constant?

2. The Centrex Company is contemplating the purchase of a new machine. The machine will cost $10,000, will be depreciated on a straight-line basis, and will have a life of five years (no salvage). If the firm has a variable cost ratio (variable costs/sales) of .75, how much added annual revenue must the new machine generate so that the firm can maintain the same annual profit (in dollars) as before the purchase?

3. What effect would each of the following have on the degree of operating leverage possessed by a firm?

   (a) The firm becomes more capital-intensive (uses more capital inputs relative to labor inputs).

   (b) The firm has recently initiated a guaranteed annual wage.

4. The Madison Company earns an after-tax profit of $2,400 on sales of $88,000. The average tax rate of the company is 40 percent. The only product of the company sells for $20, of which $15 is variable cost.

   (a) What is the monthly fixed cost of the Madison Company?

   (b) What is its break-even point in units? In dollars?

5. What would be the effect of the following on the break-even point of the Madison Company (problem 4)?

   (a) An increase in price of $5 per unit (assume that volume is constant)

   (b) A decrease in fixed costs of $2,000

   (c) A decrease in variable costs of $1 per unit and an increase in fixed costs of $6,000

6. The Botts Corporation is a new firm that wishes to determine an appropriate capital structure. It can issue 8 percent debt and 6 percent preferred and has a 50 percent tax rate. The total capitalization of the firm will be $5 million, and common will be sold at $20 per share. The possible capital structures are:

Plan	Debt	Preferred	Equity
1	0	0	100%
2	30%	0	70%
3	30%	20%	50%
4	50%	0	50%
5	50%	20%	30%

   (a) Construct an EBIT–EPS chart for the five plans.

   (b) Determine the indifference points.

   (c) Is the maximization of EPS at a given EBIT the sole function of a firm's capital structure? If not, are the points determined in (b) truly "indifference" points?

7. Using Eq. (27-5), compute the indifference point between financial plans #1 and #5 in problem 6. Does it correspond with that plotted on your graph?

8. Several Texas tycoons have decided to organize a new airline that will provide service from Dallas to New York City. All arrangements, including regulatory approval, have been made except the plan of financing. Tycoon A, a conservative type, has suggested that the $10 million needed to organize the corporation should be derived solely from the sale of common stock (1 million shares @ $10). Tycoon B,

who is a bit less conservative, feels that some debt should be included in the capital structure. He argues that half the needed investment should be raised by selling bonds. Currently, such financing can be obtained at a 6 percent coupon rate. Tycoon *C*, who tends toward the speculative side, believes that only 25 percent of the needed investment should be raised from the sale of common stock, the remainder from the sale of bonds. The investment bankers of the new firm have indicated that *C*'s proposal would require at least a 7 percent coupon rate for the bonds.

(a) Assuming the firm earns $200,000 (EBIT), with an average tax rate of 40 percent, what are the earnings per share (EPS) for each proposal? What is the rate of return on total capital (EBIT/Total Capital) for each? What is the rate of return on equity capital (Net Income/Equity Capital) for each? Which alternative provides the highest EPS and the highest return?

(b) Answer the questions outlined in (a), assuming an EBIT of $1 million.

(c) Answer the questions outlined in (a), assuming an EBIT of $2 million.

(d) What arguments might you raise against the use of *B*'s or *C*'s proposal, even if EBIT were anticipated to be high?

(e) Utilizing the three financing methods proposed, construct an EBIT–EPS indifference graph. Determine the approximate indifference points.

9. The Texas tycoons (see problem 8), after talking with their investment bankers, have learned of the existence of preferred stock and convertible debentures. Compute EPS at the $200,000, $1 million, and $2 million EBIT levels for each of the following proposed capitalizations:

(a) $5 million of 7 percent cumulative preferred stock and $5 million of common stock. Compare this result with Tycoon *A*'s proposal in problem 8.

(b) Recompute (a) under the assumption that the preferred stock was convertible at $12.50 per common share and was indeed converted.

(c) $5 million of 5 percent convertible debentures @ $12.50 per share and $5 million of common. Show the EPS before and after conversion for each level of EBIT.

(d) Finally, assume that they use $5 million of the convertible debentures, $3 million of the convertible preferred, and only $2 million of equity. Compute the EPS before and after conversion.

10. The Last Gasp Water Company sells distilled water by the gallon. The price per gallon is 75 cents and variable costs are 40 cents per gallon. Fixed costs involved in production are $1 million. The company has $5 million of 8 percent bonds outstanding.

(a) Compute the degree of operating leverage at 3 million gallons of water produced and sold, at 4 million gallons, at 5 million gallons, at 6 million gallons, and at 7 million gallons.

(b) Compute the degree of financial leverage at the above gallons of water produced and sold. Assume that EBIT is price minus variable cost per gallon times the number of gallons, less the amount of fixed costs.

(c) Compute the degree of combined operating and financial leverage at the above gallons of water produced and sold.

(d) What generalizations can you make?

SELECTED REFERENCES

Haslem, John A., "Leverage Effects on Corporate Earnings," *Arizona Review,* 19 (March 1970), 7–11.

Helfert, Erich A., *Techniques of Financial Analysis,* 3rd ed., Chapter 2. Homewood, Ill.: Richard D. Irwin, 1972.

Hilliard, Jimmy E., and Robert A. Leitch, "Cost-Volume-Profit Analysis under Uncertainty: A Log Normal Approach," *Accounting Review,* 50 (January 1975), 69–80.

Hobbs, J. B., "Volume-Mix-Price Cost Budget Variance Analysis: A Proper Approach," *Accounting Review,* 39 (October 1964), 905–13.

Jaedicke, Robert K., and Alexander A. Robichek, "Cost-Volume-Profit Analysis under Conditions of Uncertainty," *Accounting Review,* 39 (October 1964), 917–26.

Kelvie, William E., and John M. Sinclair, "New Techniques for Breakeven Charts," *Financial Executive,* 36 (June 1968), 31–43.

Lev, Baruch, "On the Association between Operating Leverage and Risk," *Journal of Financial and Quantitative Analysis,* 9 (September 1974), 627–42.

Morrison, Thomas A., and Eugene Kaczka, "A New Application of Calculus and Risk Analysis to Cost-Volume-Profit Changes," *Accounting Review,* 44 (April 1969), 330–43.

Percival, John R., "Operating Leverage and Risk," *Journal of Business Research,* 2 (April 1974), 223–27.

Raun, D. L., "The Limitations of Profit Graphs, Break-even Analysis, and Budgets," *Accounting Review,* 39 (October 1964), 927–45.

Reilly, Frank K., and Roger Bent, "A Specification, Measurement, and Analysis of Operating Leverage," Working Paper, University of Wyoming, 1974.

Reinhardt, U. E., "Break Even Analysis for Lockheed's Tri Star: An Application of Financial Theory," *Journal of Finance,* 28 (September 1973), 821–38.

Shalit, Sol S., "On the Mathematics of Financial Leverage," *Financial Management,* 4 (Spring 1975), 57–66.

APPENDIX A
PRESENT-VALUE TABLES

Table A·1 Present value of one dollar due at the end of n years

N	1%	2%	3%	4%	5%	6%	7%	8%	9%	10%	N
01	0.99010	0.98039	0.97007	0.96154	0.95238	0.94340	0.93458	0.92593	0.91743	0.90909	01
02	.98030	.96117	.94260	.92456	.90703	.89000	.87344	.85734	.84168	.82645	02
03	.97059	.94232	.91514	.88900	.86384	.83962	.81630	.79383	.77218	.75131	03
04	.96098	.92385	.88849	.85480	.82270	.79209	.76290	.73503	.70843	.68301	04
05	.95147	.90573	.86261	.82193	.78353	.74726	.71299	.68058	.64993	.62092	05
06	.94204	.88797	.83748	.79031	.74622	.70496	.66634	.63017	.59627	.56447	06
07	.93272	.87056	.81309	.75992	.71068	.66506	.62275	.58349	.54703	.51316	07
08	.92348	.85349	.78941	.73069	.67684	.62741	.58201	.54027	.50187	.46651	08
09	.91434	.83675	.76642	.70259	.64461	.59190	.54393	.50025	.46043	.42410	09
10	.90529	.82035	.74409	.67556	.61391	.55839	.50835	.46319	.42241	.38554	10
11	.89632	.80426	.72242	.64958	.58468	.52679	.47509	.42888	.38753	.35049	11
12	.88745	.78849	.70138	.62460	.55684	.49697	.44401	.39711	.35553	.31863	12
13	.87866	.77303	.68095	.60057	.53032	.46884	.41496	.36770	.32618	.28966	13
14	.86996	.75787	.66112	.57747	.50507	.44230	.38782	.34046	.29925	.26333	14
15	.86135	.74301	.64186	.55526	.48102	.41726	.36245	.31524	.27454	.23939	15
16	.85282	.72845	.62317	.53391	.45811	.39365	.33873	.29189	.25187	.21763	16
17	.84438	.71416	.60502	.51337	.43630	.37136	.31657	.27027	.23107	.19784	17
18	.83602	.70016	.58739	.49363	.41552	.35034	.29586	.25025	.21199	.17986	18
19	.82774	.68643	.57029	.47464	.39573	.33051	.27651	.23171	.19449	.16351	19
20	.81954	.67297	.55367	.45639	.37689	.31180	.25842	.21455	.17843	.14864	20
21	.81143	.65978	.53755	.43883	.35894	.29415	.24151	.19866	.16370	.13513	21
22	.80340	.64684	.52189	.42195	.34185	.27750	.22571	.18394	.15018	.12285	22
23	.79544	.63416	.50669	.40573	.32557	.26180	.21095	.17031	.13778	.11168	23
24	.78757	.62172	.49193	.39012	.31007	.24698	.19715	.15770	.12640	.10153	24
25	.77977	.60953	.47760	.37512	.29530	.23300	.18425	.14602	.11597	.09230	25

Source: Ezra Solomon, ed., *The Management of Corporate Capital* (New York: Free Press, 1959), pp. 313–16.

Table A·1 Present value of one dollar due at the end of n years (Cont.)

N	11%	12%	13%	14%	15%	16%	17%	18%	19%	20%	N
01	0.90090	0.89286	0.88496	0.87719	0.86957	0.86207	0.85470	0.84746	0.84034	0.83333	01
02	.81162	.79719	.78315	.76947	.75614	.74316	.73051	.71818	.70616	.69444	02
03	.73119	.71178	.69305	.67497	.65752	.64066	.62437	.60863	.59342	.57870	03
04	.65873	.63552	.61332	.59208	.57175	.55229	.53365	.51579	.49867	.48225	04
05	.59345	.56743	.54276	.51937	.49718	.47611	.45611	.43711	.41905	.40188	05
06	.53464	.50663	.48032	.45559	.43233	.41044	.38984	.37043	.35214	.33490	06
07	.48166	.45235	.42506	.39964	.37594	.35383	.33320	.31392	.29592	.27908	07
08	.43393	.40388	.37616	.35056	.32690	.30503	.28478	.26604	.24867	.23257	08
09	.39092	.36061	.33288	.30751	.28426	.26295	.24340	.22546	.20897	.19381	09
10	.35218	.32197	.29459	.26974	.24718	.22668	.20804	.19106	.17560	.16151	10
11	.31728	.28748	.26070	.23662	.21494	.19542	.17781	.16192	.14756	.13459	11
12	.28584	.25667	.23071	.20756	.18691	.16846	.15197	.13722	.12400	.11216	12
13	.25751	.22917	.20416	.18207	.16253	.14523	.12989	.11629	.10420	.09346	13
14	.23199	.20462	.18068	.15971	.14133	.12520	.11102	.09855	.08757	.07789	14
15	.20900	.18270	.15989	.14010	.12289	.10793	.09489	.08352	.07359	.06491	15
16	.18829	.16312	.14150	.12289	.10686	.09304	.08110	.07078	.06184	.05409	16
17	.16963	.14564	.12522	.10780	.09293	.08021	.06932	.05998	.05196	.04507	17
18	.15282	.13004	.11081	.09456	.08080	.06914	.05925	.05083	.04367	.03756	18
19	.13768	.11611	.09806	.08295	.07026	.05961	.05064	.04308	.03669	.03130	19
20	.12403	.10367	.08678	.07276	.06110	.05139	.04328	.03651	.03084	.02608	20
21	.11174	.09256	.07680	.06383	.05313	.04430	.03699	.03094	.02591	.02174	21
22	.10067	.08264	.06796	.05599	.04620	.03819	.03162	.02622	.02178	.01811	22
23	.09069	.07379	.06014	.04911	.04017	.03292	.02702	.02222	.01830	.01509	23
24	.08170	.06588	.05322	.04308	.03493	.02838	.02310	.01883	.01538	.01258	24
25	.07361	.05882	.04710	.03779	.03038	.02447	.01974	.01596	.01292	.01048	25

Table A·1 Present value of one dollar due at the end of n years (*Cont.*)

N	21%	22%	23%	24%	25%	26%	27%	28%	29%	30%	N
01	0.82645	0.81967	0.81301	0.80645	0.80000	0.79365	0.78740	0.78125	0.77519	0.76923	01
02	.68301	.67186	.66098	.65036	.64000	.62988	.62000	.61035	.60093	.59172	02
03	.56447	.55071	.53738	.52449	.51200	.49991	.48819	.47684	.46583	.45517	03
04	.46651	.45140	.43690	.42297	.40960	.39675	.38440	.37253	.36111	.35013	04
05	.38554	.37000	.35520	.34111	.32768	.31488	.30268	.29104	.27993	.26933	05
06	.31863	.30328	.28878	.27509	.26214	.24991	.23833	.22737	.21700	.20718	06
07	.26333	.24859	.23478	.22184	.20972	.19834	.18766	.17764	.16822	.15937	07
08	.21763	.20376	.19088	.17891	.16777	.15741	.14776	.13878	.13040	.12259	08
09	.17986	.16702	.15519	.14428	.13422	.12493	.11635	.10842	.10109	.09430	09
10	.14864	.13690	.12617	.11635	.10737	.09915	.09161	.08470	.07836	.07254	10
11	.12285	.11221	.10258	.09383	.08590	.07869	.07214	.06617	.06075	.05580	11
12	.10153	.09198	.08339	.07567	.06872	.06245	.05680	.05170	.04709	.04292	12
13	.08391	.07539	.06780	.06103	.05498	.04957	.04472	.04039	.03650	.03302	13
14	.06934	.06180	.05512	.04921	.04398	.03934	.03522	.03155	.02830	.02540	14
15	.05731	.05065	.04481	.03969	.03518	.03122	.02773	.02465	.02194	.01954	15
16	.04736	.04152	.03643	.03201	.02815	.02478	.02183	.01926	.01700	.01503	16
17	.03914	.03403	.02962	.02581	.02252	.01967	.01719	.01505	.01318	.01156	17
18	.03235	.02789	.02408	.02082	.01801	.01561	.01354	.01175	.01022	.00889	18
19	.02673	.02286	.01958	.01679	.01441	.01239	.01066	.00918	.00792	.00684	19
20	.02209	.01874	.01592	.01354	.01153	.00983	.00839	.00717	.00614	.00526	20
21	.01826	.01536	.01294	.01092	.00922	.00780	.00661	.00561	.00476	.00405	21
22	.01509	.01259	.01052	.00880	.00738	.00619	.00520	.00438	.00369	.00311	22
23	.01247	.01032	.00855	.00710	.00590	.00491	.00410	.00342	.00286	.00239	23
24	.01031	.00846	.00695	.00573	.00472	.00390	.00323	.00267	.00222	.00184	24
25	.00852	.00693	.00565	.00462	.00378	.00310	.00254	.00209	.00172	.00142	25

Table A·1 Present value of one dollar due at the end of n years (Cont.)

N	31%	32%	33%	34%	35%	36%	37%	38%	39%	40%	N
01	0.76336	0.75758	0.75188	0.74627	0.74074	0.73529	0.72993	0.72464	0.71942	0.71429	01
02	.58272	.57392	.56532	.55692	.54870	.54066	.53279	.52510	.51757	.51020	02
03	.44482	.43479	.42505	.41561	.40644	.39754	.38890	.38051	.37235	.36443	03
04	.33956	.32939	.31959	.31016	.30107	.29231	.28387	.27573	.26788	.26031	04
05	.25920	.24953	.24029	.23146	.22301	.21493	.20720	.19980	.19272	.18593	05
06	.19787	.18904	.18067	.17273	.16520	.15804	.15124	.14479	.13865	.13281	06
07	.15104	.14321	.13584	.12890	.12237	.11621	.11040	.10492	.09975	.09486	07
08	.11530	.10849	.10214	.09620	.09064	.08545	.08058	.07603	.07176	.06776	08
09	.08802	.08219	.07680	.07179	.06714	.06283	.05882	.05509	.05163	.04840	09
10	.06719	.06227	.05774	.05357	.04973	.04620	.04293	.03992	.03714	.03457	10
11	.05129	.04717	.04341	.03998	.03684	.03397	.03134	.02893	.02672	.02469	11
12	.03915	.03574	.03264	.02984	.02729	.02498	.02287	.02096	.01922	.01764	12
13	.02989	.02707	.02454	.02227	.02021	.01837	.01670	.01519	.01383	.01260	13
14	.02281	.02051	.01845	.01662	.01497	.01350	.01219	.01101	.00995	.00900	14
15	.01742	.01554	.01387	.01240	.01109	.00993	.00890	.00798	.00716	.00643	15
16	.01329	.01177	.01043	.00925	.00822	.00730	.00649	.00578	.00515	.00459	16
17	.01015	.00892	.00784	.00691	.00609	.00537	.00474	.00419	.00370	.00328	17
18	.00775	.00676	.00590	.00515	.00451	.00395	.00346	.00304	.00267	.00234	18
19	.00591	.00512	.00443	.00385	.00334	.00290	.00253	.00220	.00192	.00167	19
20	.00451	.00388	.00333	.00287	.00247	.00213	.00184	.00159	.00138	.00120	20
21	.00345	.00294	.00251	.00214	.00183	.00157	.00135	.00115	.00099	.00085	21
22	.00263	.00223	.00188	.00160	.00136	.00115	.00098	.00084	.00071	.00061	22
23	.00201	.00169	.00142	.00119	.00101	.00085	.00072	.00061	.00051	.00044	23
24	.00153	.00128	.00107	.00089	.00074	.00062	.00052	.00044	.00037	.00031	24
25	.00117	.00097	.00080	.00066	.00055	.00046	.00038	.00032	.00027	.00022	25

ANNUITY-

Table A·2   Present value of one dollar per year, n years at r%

Year	1%	2%	3%	4%	5%	6%	7%	8%	9%	10%	Year
1	0.9901	0.9804	0.9709	0.9615	0.9524	0.9434	0.9346	0.9259	0.9174	0.9091	1
2	1.9704	1.9416	1.9135	1.8861	1.8594	1.8334	1.8080	1.7833	1.7591	1.7355	2
3	2.9410	2.8839	2.8286	2.7751	2.7232	2.6730	2.6243	2.5771	2.5313	2.4868	3
4	3.9020	3.8077	3.7171	3.6299	3.5459	3.4651	3.3872	3.3121	3.2397	3.1699	4
5	4.8535	4.7134	4.5797	4.4518	4.3295	4.2123	4.1002	3.9927	3.8896	3.7908	5
6	5.7955	5.6014	5.4172	5.2421	5.0757	4.9173	4.7665	4.6229	4.4859	4.3553	6
7	6.7282	6.4720	6.2302	6.0020	5.7863	5.5824	5.3893	5.2064	5.0329	4.8684	7
8	7.6517	7.3254	7.0196	6.7327	6.4632	6.2098	5.9713	5.7466	5.5348	5.3349	8
9	8.5661	8.1622	7.7861	7.4353	7.1078	6.8017	6.5152	6.2469	5.9852	5.7590	9
10	9.4714	8.9825	8.5302	8.1109	7.7217	7.3601	7.0236	6.7101	6.4176	6.1446	10
11	10.3677	9.7868	9.2526	8.7604	8.3064	7.8868	7.4987	7.1389	6.8052	6.4951	11
12	11.2552	10.5753	9.9539	9.3850	8.8632	8.3838	7.9427	7.5361	7.1607	6.8137	12
13	12.1338	11.3483	10.6349	9.9856	9.3935	8.8527	8.3576	7.9038	7.4869	7.1034	13
14	13.0038	12.1062	11.2960	10.5631	9.8986	9.2950	8.7454	8.2442	7.7861	7.3667	14
15	13.8651	12.8492	11.9379	11.1183	10.3796	9.7122	9.1079	8.5595	8.0607	7.6061	15
16	14.7180	13.5777	12.5610	11.6522	10.8377	10.1059	9.4466	8.8514	8.3125	7.8237	16
17	15.5624	14.2918	13.1660	12.1656	11.2740	10.4772	9.7632	9.1216	8.5436	8.0215	17
18	16.3984	14.9920	13.7534	12.6592	11.6895	10.8276	10.0591	9.3719	8.7556	8.2014	18
19	17.2261	15.6784	14.3237	13.1339	12.0853	11.1581	10.3356	9.6036	8.9501	8.3649	19
20	18.0457	16.3514	14.8774	13.5903	12.4622	11.4699	10.5940	9.8181	9.1285	8.5136	20
21	18.8571	17.0111	15.4149	14.0291	12.8211	11.7640	10.8355	10.0168	9.2922	8.6487	21
22	19.6605	17.6580	15.9368	14.4511	13.1630	12.0416	11.0612	10.2007	9.4424	8.7715	22
23	20.4559	18.2921	16.4435	14.8568	13.4885	12.3033	11.2722	10.3710	9.5802	8.8832	23
24	21.2435	18.9139	16.9355	15.2469	13.7986	12.5503	11.4693	10.5287	9.7066	8.9847	24
25	22.0233	19.5234	17.4131	15.6220	14.0939	12.7833	11.6536	10.6748	9.8226	9.0770	25

Source: Solomon, *Management of Corporate Capital*, pp. 317–20.

Table A·2 Present value of one dollar per year. n years at r% (Cont.)

Year	11%	12%	13%	14%	15%	16%	17%	18%	19%	20%	Year
1	0.9009	0.8929	0.8850	0.8772	0.8696	0.8621	0.8547	0.8475	0.8403	0.8333	1
2	1.7125	1.6901	1.6681	1.6467	1.6257	1.6052	1.5852	1.5656	1.5465	1.5278	2
3	2.4437	2.4018	2.3612	2.3216	2.2832	2.2459	2.2096	2.1743	2.1399	2.1065	3
4	3.1024	3.0373	2.9745	2.9137	2.8550	2.7982	2.7432	2.6901	2.6386	2.5887	4
5	3.6959	3.6048	3.5172	3.4331	3.3522	3.2743	3.1993	3.1272	3.0576	2.9906	5
6	4.2305	4.1114	3.9976	3.8887	3.7845	3.6847	3.5892	3.4976	3.4098	3.3255	6
7	4.7122	4.5638	4.4226	4.2883	4.1604	4.0386	3.9224	3.8115	3.7057	3.6046	7
8	5.1461	4.9676	4.7988	4.6389	4.4873	4.3436	4.2072	4.0776	3.9544	3.8372	8
9	5.5370	5.3282	5.1317	4.9464	4.7716	4.6065	4.4506	4.3030	4.1633	4.0310	9
10	5.8892	5.6502	5.4262	5.2161	5.0188	4.8332	4.6586	4.4941	4.3389	4.1925	10
11	6.2065	5.9377	5.6869	5.4527	5.2337	5.0286	4.8364	4.6560	4.4865	4.3271	11
12	6.4924	6.1944	5.9176	5.6603	5.4206	5.1971	4.9884	4.7932	4.6105	4.4392	12
13	6.7499	6.4235	6.1218	5.8424	5.5831	5.3423	5.1183	4.9095	4.7147	4.5327	13
14	6.9819	6.6282	6.3025	6.0021	5.7245	5.4675	5.2293	5.0081	4.8023	4.6106	14
15	7.1909	6.8109	6.4624	6.1422	5.8474	5.5755	5.3242	5.0916	4.8759	4.6755	15
16	7.3792	6.9740	6.6039	6.2651	5.9542	5.6685	5.4053	5.1624	4.9377	4.7296	16
17	7.5488	7.1196	6.7291	6.3729	6.0472	5.7487	5.4746	5.2223	4.9897	4.7746	17
18	7.7016	7.2497	6.8399	6.4674	6.1280	5.8178	5.5339	5.2732	5.0333	4.8122	18
19	7.8393	7.3658	6.9380	6.5504	6.1982	5.8775	5.5845	5.3162	5.0700	4.8435	19
20	7.9633	7.4694	7.0248	6.6231	6.2593	5.9288	5.6278	5.3527	5.1009	4.8696	20
21	8.0751	7.5620	7.1016	6.6870	6.3125	5.9731	5.6648	5.3837	5.1268	4.8913	21
22	8.1757	7.6446	7.1695	6.7429	6.3587	6.0113	5.6964	5.4099	5.1486	4.9094	22
23	8.2664	7.7184	7.2297	6.7921	6.3988	6.0442	5.7234	5.4321	5.1668	4.9245	23
24	8.3481	7.7843	7.2829	6.8351	6.4338	6.0726	5.7465	5.4509	5.1822	4.9371	24
25	8.4217	7.8431	7.3300	6.8729	6.4641	6.0971	5.7662	5.4669	5.1951	4.9476	25

— ANNUITY —

Table A·2   Present value of one dollar per year. n years at r% (Cont.)

Year	21%	22%	23%	24%	25%	26%	27%	28%	29%	30%	Year
1	0.8264	0.8197	0.8130	0.8065	0.8000	0.7937	0.7874	0.7813	0.7752	0.7692	1
2	1.5095	1.4915	1.4740	1.4568	1.4400	1.4235	1.4074	1.3916	1.3761	1.3609	2
3	2.0739	2.0422	2.0114	1.9813	1.9520	1.9234	1.8956	1.8684	1.8420	1.8161	3
4	2.5404	2.4936	2.4483	2.4043	2.3616	2.3202	2.2800	2.2410	2.2031	2.1662	4
5	2.9260	2.8636	2.8035	2.7454	2.6893	2.6351	2.5827	2.5320	2.4830	2.4356	5
6	3.2446	3.1669	3.0923	3.0205	2.9514	2.8850	2.8210	2.7594	2.7000	2.6427	6
7	3.5079	3.4155	3.3270	3.2423	3.1611	3.0833	3.0087	2.9370	2.8682	2.8021	7
8	3.7256	3.6193	3.5179	3.4212	3.3289	3.2407	3.1564	3.0758	2.9986	2.9247	8
9	3.9054	3.7863	3.6731	3.5655	3.4631	3.3657	3.2728	3.1842	3.0997	3.0190	9
10	4.0541	3.9232	3.7993	3.6819	3.5705	3.4648	3.3644	3.2689	3.1781	3.0915	10
11	4.1769	4.0354	3.9018	3.7757	3.6564	3.5435	3.4365	3.3351	3.2388	3.1473	11
12	4.2785	4.1274	3.9852	3.8514	3.7251	3.6060	3.4933	3.3868	3.2859	3.1903	12
13	4.3624	4.2028	4.0530	3.9124	3.7801	3.6555	3.6381	3.4272	3.3224	3.2233	13
14	4.4317	4.2646	4.1082	3.9616	3.8241	3.6949	3.5733	3.4587	3.3507	3.2487	14
15	4.4890	4.3152	4.1530	4.0013	3.8593	3.7261	3.6010	3.4834	3.3726	3.2682	15
16	4.5364	4.3567	4.1894	4.0333	3.8874	3.7509	3.6228	3.5026	3.3896	3.2832	16
17	4.5755	4.3908	4.2190	4.0591	3.9099	3.7705	3.6400	3.5177	3.4028	3.2948	17
18	4.6079	4.4187	4.2431	4.0799	3.9279	3.7861	3.6536	3.5294	3.4130	3.3037	18
19	4.6346	4.4415	4.2627	4.0967	3.9424	3.7985	3.6642	3.5386	3.4210	3.3105	19
20	4.6567	4.4603	4.2786	4.1103	3.9539	3.8083	3.6726	3.5458	3.4271	3.3158	20
21	4.6750	4.4756	4.2916	4.1212	3.9631	3.8161	3.6792	3.5514	3.4319	3.3198	21
22	4.6900	4.4882	4.3021	4.1300	3.9705	3.8223	3.6844	3.5558	3.4356	3.3230	22
23	4.7025	4.4985	4.3106	4.1371	3.9764	3.8273	3.6885	3.5592	3.4384	3.3254	23
24	4.7128	4.5070	4.3176	4.1428	3.9811	3.8312	3.6918	3.5619	3.4406	3.3272	24
25	4.7213	4.5139	4.3232	4.1474	3.9849	3.8342	3.6943	3.5640	3.4423	3.3286	25

Table A·2 Present value of one dollar per year. n years at r% (Cont.)

Year	31%	32%	33%	34%	35%	36%	37%	38%	39%	40%	Year
1	0.7634	0.7576	0.7519	0.7463	0.7407	0.7353	0.7299	0.7246	0.7194	0.7143	1
2	1.3461	1.3315	1.3172	1.3032	1.2894	1.2760	1.2627	1.2497	1.2370	1.2245	2
3	1.7909	1.7663	1.7423	1.7188	1.6959	1.6735	1.6516	1.6302	1.6093	1.5889	3
4	2.1305	2.0957	2.0618	2.0290	1.9969	1.9658	1.9355	1.9060	1.8772	1.8492	4
5	2.3897	2.3452	2.3021	2.2604	2.2200	2.1807	2.1427	2.1058	2.0699	2.0352	5
6	2.5875	2.5342	2.4828	2.4331	2.3852	2.3388	2.2939	2.2506	2.2086	2.1680	6
7	2.7386	2.6775	2.6187	2.5620	2.5075	2.4550	2.4043	2.3555	2.3083	2.2628	7
8	2.8539	2.7860	2.7208	2.6582	2.5982	2.5404	2.4849	2.4315	2.3801	2.3306	8
9	2.9419	2.8681	2.7976	2.7300	2.6653	2.6033	2.5437	2.4866	2.4317	2.3790	9
10	3.0091	2.9304	2.8553	2.7836	2.7150	2.6495	2.5867	2.5265	2.4689	2.4136	10
11	3.0604	2.9776	2.8987	2.8236	2.7519	2.6834	2.6180	2.5555	2.4956	2.4383	11
12	3.0995	3.0133	2.9314	2.8534	2.7792	2.7084	2.6409	2.5764	2.5148	2.4559	12
13	3.1294	3.0404	2.9559	2.8757	2.7994	2.7268	2.6576	2.5916	2.5286	2.4685	13
14	3.1522	3.0609	2.9744	2.8923	2.8144	2.7403	2.6698	2.6026	2.5386	2.4775	14
15	3.1696	3.0764	2.9883	2.9047	2.8255	2.7502	2.6787	2.6106	2.5457	2.4839	15
16	3.1829	3.0882	2.9987	2.9140	2.8337	2.7575	2.6852	2.6164	2.5509	2.4885	16
17	3.1931	3.0971	3.0065	2.9209	2.8398	2.7629	2.6899	2.6206	2.5546	2.4918	17
18	3.2008	3.1039	3.0124	2.9260	2.8443	2.7668	2.6934	2.6236	2.5573	2.4941	18
19	3.2067	3.1090	3.0169	2.9299	2.8476	2.7697	2.6959	2.6258	2.5592	2.4958	19
20	3.2112	3.1129	3.0202	2.9327	2.8501	2.7718	2.6977	2.6274	2.5606	2.4970	20
21	3.2147	3.1158	3.0227	2.9349	2.8519	2.7734	2.6991	2.6285	2.5616	2.4979	21
22	3.2173	3.1180	3.0246	2.9365	2.8533	2.7746	2.7000	2.6294	2.5623	2.4985	22
23	3.2193	3.1197	3.0260	2.9377	2.8543	2.7754	2.7008	2.6300	2.5628	2.4989	23
24	3.2209	3.1210	3.0271	2.9386	2.8550	2.7760	2.7013	2.6304	2.5632	2.4992	24
25	3.2220	3.1220	3.0279	2.9392	2.8556	2.7765	2.7017	2.6307	2.5634	2.4994	25

Table B·1 Area of normal distribution that is X standard deviations to the left or right of the mean

Number of Standard Deviations from Mean (X)	Area to the Left or Right (One tail)	Number of Standard Deviations from Mean (X)	Area to the Left or Right (One tail)
0.00	.5000	1.55	.0606
0.05	.4801	1.60	.0548
0.10	.4602	1.65	.0495
0.15	.4404	1.70	.0446
0.20	.4207	1.75	.0401
0.25	.4013	1.80	.0359
0.30	.3821	1.85	.0322
0.35	.3632	1.90	.0287
0.40	.3446	1.95	.0256
0.45	.3264	2.00	.0228
0.50	.3085	2.05	.0202
0.55	.2912	2.10	.0179
0.60	.2743	2.15	.0158
0.65	.2578	2.20	.0139
0.70	.2420	2.25	.0122
0.75	.2264	2.30	.0107
0.80	.2119	2.35	.0094
0.85	.1977	2.40	.0082
0.90	.1841	2.45	.0071
0.95	.1711	2.50	.0062
1.00	.1577	2.55	.0054
1.05	.1469	2.60	.0047
1.10	.1357	2.65	.0040
1.15	.1251	2.70	.0035
1.20	.1151	2.75	.0030
1.25	.1056	2.80	.0026
1.30	.0968	2.85	.0022
1.35	.0885	2.90	.0019
1.40	.0808	2.95	.0016
1.45	.0735	3.00	.0013
1.50	.0668		

755

(handwritten notes)

PV - P. 16
IRR - P. 17, 18
Bond yields - P. 36
Funds flow P.698 ★

Problems:
1) Trade credit - bank loan - factor DECISION p.488
2) Annual percentage interest cost - discounts foregone p.455 ← discounts vs. commercial paper vs bank loans
3) Compound interest - nominal vs effective int. rate p.452

NFA end + dep
- NFA beg
if + ? then there was a purch. (use)
if - ? then there was a sale (source)